PRINCIPLES OF

BUSINESS INFORMATION SYSTEMS

PRINCIPLES OF
BUSINESS
INFORMATION
SYSTEMS

Ralph Stair, George Reynolds and Thomas Chesney

COURSE TECHNOLOGY
CENGAGE Learning

Australia · Brazil · Japan · Korea · Mexico · Singapore · Spain · United Kingdom · United States

COURSE TECHNOLOGY
CENGAGE Learning

Principles of Business Information Systems
Ralph Stair, George Reynolds and Thomas Chesney

Publisher: Tom Rennie

Development Editor: Charlotte Loveridge

Content Project Editor: Lucy Mills

Manufacturing Manager: Helen Mason

Production Controller: Maeve Healy

Marketing Manager: Rosella Proscia

Typesetter: ICC Macmillan Inc.

Cover design: Adam Renvoize

Text design: Design Deluxe Ltd, Bath, UK

For product information and technology assistance, contact
emea.info@cengage.com.
For permission to use material from this text or product,
and for permission queries, email
clsuk.permissions@cengage.com

Products and services that are referred to in this book may be either trademarks and/or registered trademarks of their respective owners. The publishers and author/s make no claim to these trademarks.

British Library Cataloguing-in-Publication Data
A catalogue record for this book is available from the British Library.

ISBN: 978-1-84480-779-6

Cengage Learning EMEA
Cheriton House, North Way, Andover, Hampshire, SP10 5BE,
United Kingdom

Cengage Learning products are represented in Canada by Nelson Education Ltd.

For your lifelong learning solutions, visit **www.cengage.co.uk**
Purchase e-books or e-chapters at: **http://estore.bized.co.uk**

Printed by Seng Lee Press, Singapore
2 3 4 5 6 7 8 9 10 – 11 10 09

For Tahseena

Brief Contents

Contents

1 Overview 1

2 Information Technology Concepts 67

3 Business Information Systems 231

4 Systems Development 385

5 Information
   Systems in
   Business and
   Society 475

Preface

As organizations continue to operate in an increasingly competitive and global marketplace, workers in all areas of business including accounting, finance, human resources, marketing, operations management, and production must be well prepared to make the significant contributions required for success. Regardless of your future role, you will need to understand what information systems can and cannot do and be able to use them to help you accomplish your work. You will be expected to discover opportunities to use information systems and to participate in the design of solutions to business problems employing information systems. You will be challenged to identify and evaluate information systems options. To be successful, you must be able to view information systems from the perspective of business and organizational needs. For your solutions to be accepted, you must recognise and address their impact on fellow workers, customers, suppliers, and other key business partners. For these reasons, a course in information systems is essential for students in today's high-tech world.

The primary objective of *Principles of Business Information Systems* is to provide the best information systems text and accompanying materials for the first information technology course required of all business students. We want you to learn to use information technology to ensure your personal success in your current or future job and to improve the success of your organization. Principles of Business Information Systems stands proudly at the beginning of the IS curriculum and remains unchallenged in its position as the only IS principles text offering the basic IS concepts that every business student must learn to be successful.

This text has been written specifically for the introductory course in the IS curriculum. *Principles of Business Information Systems* treats the appropriate computer and IS concepts together with a strong managerial emphasis on meeting business and organizational needs.

Approach of the Text

Principles of Business Information Systems offers the traditional coverage of computer concepts, but it places the material within the context of meeting business and organizational needs. Placing IS concepts in this context and taking a general management perspective sets the text apart from general computer books thus making it appealing not only to those studying for IS degrees but also to students from other fields of study. The text isn't overly technical, but rather deals with the role that information systems play in an organization and the key principles a manager needs to grasp to be successful. These principles of IS are brought together and presented in a way that is both understandable and relevant. In addition, this book offers an overview of the entire IS discipline, while giving students a solid foundation for further study in advanced IS courses as programming, systems analysis and design, project management, database management, data communications, website and systems development, electronic commerce and mobile commerce applications, and decision support. As such, it serves the needs of both general business students and those who will become IS professionals.

IS Principles First, Where They Belong

Exposing students to fundamental IS principles is an advantage for students who do not later return to the discipline for advanced courses. Since most functional areas in business rely on information systems, an understanding of IS principles helps students in other course work. In addition, introducing students to the principles of information systems helps future business function managers employ information systems successfully and avoid mishaps that often result in unfortunate consequences. Furthermore, presenting IS concepts at the introductory level creates interest among general business students who may later choose information systems as a field of concentration.

Goals of this Text

Principles of Business Information Systems has four main goals:

1 To provide a core of IS principles with which every business student should be familiar
2 To offer a survey of the IS discipline that will enable all business students to understand the relationship of IS courses to their curriculum as a whole
3 To present the changing role of the IS professional
4 To show the value of the discipline as an attractive field of specialisation

By achieving these goals, *Principles of Business Information Systems* will enable students to understand and use fundamental information systems principles so that they can function more efficiently and effectively as workers, managers, decision makers, and organizational leaders.

IS Principles

Principles of Business Information Systems, although comprehensive, cannot cover every aspect of the rapidly changing IS discipline. The authors, having recognised this, provide students an essential core of guiding IS principles to use as they face career challenges ahead. Think of principles as basic truths, rules, or assumptions that remain constant regardless of the situation. As such, they provide strong guidance in the face of tough decisions. A set of IS principles is highlighted at the beginning of each chapter. The ultimate goal of *Principles of Business Information Systems* is to develop effective, thinking, action-oriented employees by instilling them with principles to help guide their decision making and actions.

Survey of the IS Discipline

This text not only offers the traditional coverage of computer concepts but also provides a broad framework to impart students with a solid grounding in the business uses of technology. In addition to serving general business students, this book offers an overview of the entire IS discipline and solidly prepares future IS professionals for advanced IS courses and their careers in the rapidly changing IS discipline.

Changing Role of the IS Professional

As business and the IS discipline have changed, so too has the role of the IS professional. Once considered a technical specialist, today the IS professional operates as an internal consultant to all functional areas of the organization, being knowledgeable about their needs and competent in bringing the power of information systems to bear throughout the organization. The IS

professional views issues through a global perspective that encompasses the entire organization and the broader industry and business environment in which it operates.

The scope of responsibilities of an IS professional today is not confined to just his or her
employer but encompasses the entire interconnected network of employees, suppliers, customers,
competitors, regulatory agencies, and other entities, no matter where they are located. This
broad scope of responsibilities creates a new challenge: how to help an organization survive in
a highly interconnected, highly competitive global environment. In accepting that challenge, the
IS professional plays a pivotal role in shaping the business itself and ensuring its success. To
survive, businesses must now strive for the highest level of customer satisfaction and loyalty
through competitive prices and ever-improving product and service quality. The IS professional
assumes the critical responsibility of determining the organization's approach to both overall
cost and quality performance and therefore plays an important role in the ongoing survival of the
organization. This new duality in the role of the IS employee – a professional who exercises a
specialist's skills with a generalist's perspective – is reflected throughout the book.

IS as a Field for Further Study

Employment of computer and information systems managers is expected to grow much faster
than the average for all occupations. Technological advancements will boost the employment of
computer-related workers; in turn, this will boost the demand for managers to direct these workers. In addition, job openings will result from the need to replace managers who retire or move
into other occupations.

A career in IS can be exciting, challenging, and rewarding! It is important to show the value of
the discipline as an appealing field of study and that the IS graduate is no longer a technical
recluse. Today, perhaps more than ever before, the IS professional must be able to align IS and
organizational goals and to ensure that IS investments are justified from a business perspective.
The need to draw bright and interested students into the IS discipline is part of our ongoing responsibility. Upon graduation, IS graduates at many schools are among the highest paid of all
business graduates. Throughout this text, the many challenges and opportunities available to IS
professionals are highlighted and emphasised.

Changes to the International Edition

Principles of Business Information Systems is an adaptation of the popular U.S. text-book *Principles of Information Systems,* now in its eight edition. With a more international outlook, this book is suitable for students in the U.K., Europe and South Africa on introductory BIS or MIS courses. The new title reflects the fact that this book has boosted its business emphasis but retained its technology focus.

Continuing to present IS concepts with a managerial emphasis, this edition retains the overall vision, framework, and pedagogy that made the previous U.S. editions so popular:

- *Principles of Business Information Systems* keeps the same five part structure, is packed with real world examples and business cases, and highlights ethical issues throughout.
- It is still an IS text aimed at those studying business and management.

However, in order to increase its international relevance, we have made a number of changes. The main improvements are:

- Cases are now more international in flavour and have a broader sector spread, reflecting a wider variety of business types (including SMEs).
- The book has been brought completely up to date in terms of innovations in IT.
- Legal and ethical issues in IT have been made more international.
- Chapter 5 now has expanded sections on data modelling, data warehousing and data mining with examples.
- A new simpler, cleaner design.
- Instead of a separate e-commerce chapter, e-commerce is now treated alongside other operational systems, where it should be – it has become another essential that businesses must have.
- A new chapter on pervasive computing, reflecting the move of the computer away from the desktop to enter almost every aspect of our lives.

Structure of the Text

Principles of Business Information Systems is organized into five parts – an overview of information systems, an introduction to information technology concepts, an examination of different classes of business information systems, a study of systems development and a focus on information systems in business and the wider society.

The content of each chapter is as follows:

Chapter 1, An Introduction to Information Systems

Chapter 1 creates a framework for the entire book. Major sections in this chapter become entire chapters in the text. This chapter describes the components of an information system and introduces major classes of business information systems. It offers an overview of systems development and outlines some major challenges that IS professionals face.

Chapter 2, Information Systems in Organizations

Chapter 2 gives an overview of business organizations and presents a foundation for the effective and efficient use of IS in a business environment. We have stressed that the traditional mission of IS is to deliver the right information to the right person at the right time. In the section on virtual organizational structure, we discuss that virtual organizational structures allow work to be separated from location and time. Work can be done anywhere, anytime. The concept of business process reengineering (BPR) is introduced and competitive advantage is examined – higher quality products, better customer service, and lower costs.

Chapter 3, Hardware: Input, Processing, and Output Devices

This chapter concentrates on the hardware component of a computer-based information system (CBIS) and reflects the latest equipment and computer capabilities – computer memory is explained and a variety of hardware platforms are discussed including mobile technology.

Chapter 4, Software: Systems and Application Software

You cannot come into contact with a computer, without coming into contact with software. This chapter examines a wide range of software and related issues including operating systems and application software, open source and proprietary software, software for mobile devices and copyrights and licenses.

Chapter 5 Organizing and Storing Data

Databases are the heart of almost all IS. A huge amount of data is entered into computer systems every day. Chapter 5 examines database management systems and how they can help businesses. The chapter includes a brief overview of how to organize data in a database, a look at database administration and discusses how data can used competitively by examining both data mining and business intelligence.

Chapter 6 Computer Networks

The power of information technology greatly increases when devices are linked, or networked, which is the subject of this chapter. Today's decision makers need to access data wherever it resides. They must be able to establish fast, reliable connections to exchange messages, upload and download data and software, route business transactions to processors, connect to databases and network services, and send output to printers. This chapter examines the hardware involved and examines the world's biggest computer network, the Internet.

Chapter 7 Operational Systems

Operation systems, such as transaction processing systems allow firms to buy and sell. Without systems to perform these functions, the firm could not operate. Organizations today are moving from a collection of non-integrated transaction processing systems to highly integrated enterprise resource planning systems to perform routine business processes and maintain records about them. These systems support a wide range of business activities associated with supply chain management and customer relationship management. This chapter examines transaction processing systems and enterprise resource planning systems.

Chapter 8 Management Information and Decision Support Systems

This chapter begins with a discussion of decision making and examines the decision making process. Both management information systems and decision support systems are examined in detail. Their ability to help managers make better decisions is emphasized.

Chapter 9 Knowledge Management and Specialized Information Systems

A discussion of knowledge management leads onto a discussion of some of the special-purpose systems discussed in the chapter, including expert and knowledge-based systems. The other topics discussed include robotics, vision systems, virtual reality, and a variety of other special-purpose systems. We discuss embedded artificial intelligence, where artificial intelligence capabilities and applications are placed inside products and services.

Chapter 10 Pervasive Computing

The move of information systems to leave the office desktop and enter every aspect of our lives is well underway. Many businesses are exploiting this to their advantage, as are their customers. This chapter examines some of the technologies that are enabling all of this to happen. New ones are being introduced almost every month. It is important that businesses understand the potential benefits they can bring.

Chapter 11 Systems Analysis

This chapter and the next examine where information systems come from. Systems investigation and systems analysis, the first two steps of the systems development, are discussed. This chapter provides specific examples of how new or modified systems are initiated and analyzed in a number of industries. This chapter emphasizes how a project can be planned, aligned with corporate goals and rapidly developed.

Chapter 12 Systems Design and Implementation

This chapter looks at how the analysis discussed in Chapter 11 can be used to design and build IT solutions. The chapter mainly looks at developing a new system but also examines solving a problem by buying an existing IS that has already been developed.

Chapter 13 Security, Privacy, and Ethical Issues in Information Systems

This last chapter looks at security, privacy, and ethical issues, something that is in the background throughout the text. A wide range of non-technical issues associated with the use of information systems provide both opportunities and threats to modern organizations. The issues span the full spectrum – from preventing computer waste and mistakes, to avoiding violations of privacy, to complying with laws on collecting data about customers, to monitoring employees.

About the Authors

Ralph Stair received a B.S. in Chemical Engineering from Purdue University, an M.B.A. from Tulane University, and a Ph.D. from the University of Oregon. He has taught information systems at many universities. He has published numerous articles and books, including *Succeeding With Technology, Programming in BASIC,* and many more.

George Reynolds is an assistant professor in the Information Systems department of the College of Business at the University of Cincinnati. He received a B.S. in Aerospace Engineering from the University of Cincinnati and an M.S. in Systems Engineering from West Coast University. He taught part-time at Xavier University, the University of Cincinnati, Miami University, and the College of Mount Saint Joseph while working full-time in the information systems industry, including positions at the Manned Spacecraft Center in Houston, Texas; the Jet Propulsion Lab in Pasadena, California; and Procter and Gamble in Cincinnati, Ohio.

Thomas Chesney is lecturer in information systems at Nottingham University Business School. Thomas has a Ph.D. in Information Systems from Brunel University an M.Sc. in Informatics from Edinburgh University where his specialism was knowledge management and engineering and a B.Sc. in Information Management from the Queen's University of Belfast. He is a fellow of the Higher Education Academy and a member of the Association for Information Systems.

Acknowledgements

We are indebted to the following reviewers for their perceptive feedback and expert insight on early drafts of this text:

- Stephen Batty, Bristol Business School, University of the West of England
- Jason F. Cohen, University of the Witwatersrand, Johannesburg
- Elad Harison, Faculty of Economics and Business, University of Groningen and the United Nations University-MERIT
- Hanifa Abdullah, School of Computing, University of South Africa
- Malcolm Berry, University of Reading Business School
- Professor Said Selim, College of Information Technology, University of Dubai
- Dr. Joseph Akomode, College of Information Technology, University of Dubai
- Dr. Igal Karin, Sapir Academic College, Israel

Supplements

There is a companion CD-Rom in the back of this book and an accompanying website. This book and its accompanying materials are not a substitute for your lectures, but they should give you a solid basis on which to build your understanding of Business Information Systems.

MIS Companion CD-Rom

Course Technology's MIS Companion CD-Rom, which is comprised of training lessons in:

- Microsoft Excel
- Access
- MIS concepts

The Companion CD is integrated throughout the book. Wherever you see the CD icon in the chapter margins, there is additional related material on the CD.

ExamView Testbank and Test Generator

ExamView® is a powerful objective-based test generator that enables instructors to create paper, LAN- or Web-based tests from testbanks designed specifically for this textbook.

This CD-based product is only available from your Cengage Learning sales representative.

Companion Website

Visit the supporting website at www.cengage.co.uk/stair_principles to find further teaching and learning material, including:

For students:

Multiple-choice questions
This bank of questions allows you access to 20 multiple choice questions for each chapter where you can test yourself, submit your answers and monitor your progress. Special testing software randomly selects 20 questions from a database of 50 per chapter, so you can quiz yourself multiple times on any given chapter.

Links to useful websites
This resource takes you to interesting and useful websites, and all the urls referenced throughout the text.

Glossary of key terms
The glossary of key terms from the text is also available online for reference.

Activities
These hands-on activities test your comprehension of IS topics and enhance your skills using Microsoft Office. Using these links, you can access three critical thinking exercises per chapter; each activity asks you to work with an Office tool or do some research on the Internet.

Online readings
This feature allows you access to a computer database which contains articles relating to hot topics in Information Systems.

For lecturers:

Power Point slides
A set of Power Point slides is available for each chapter to serve as a teaching aid for lecture presentations and help students focus on the main topics of each chapter.

Sample syllabus
A sample syllabus with sample course outlines is provided to make planning your course easier.

Solutions
Solutions to all end of chapter material are provided in a separate document.

Figure files
Electronic copies of all the figures used in the edition are available for lecturers to create their own presentations.

Classic cases
A set of over 85 cases from earlier editions of the textbook are included here, spanning a broad range of companies and industries.

Walkthrough Tour

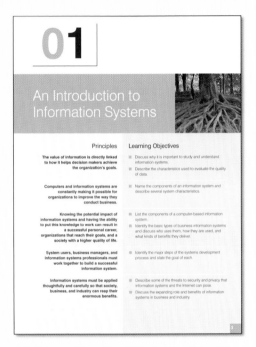

Principles and Learning Objectives are listed at the start of each chapter and reflect what you should be able to accomplish after completing each chapter.

Information Systems @ Work is an extra case in each chapter which relates how information systems are used in a variety of business career areas.

Why Learn About sets the stage by briefly describing the significance of the chapter's content.

Ethical and Societal Issues is another case study, concentrating on ethical challenges and societal impact of information systems from the real world.

CD-Rom icons draw attention to relevant material on the Companion CD-Rom.

Key Terms are explained in the margin and explained in full in a Glossary at the end of the book, enabling you to find explanations of key terms quickly.

Summary at the end of chapter provides a thorough re-cap of the issues in each chapter, helping you to assess your understanding and revise key content.

Self-Assessment Tests allow you to review and test your understanding of key chapter concepts. The answers are provided at the back of the book.

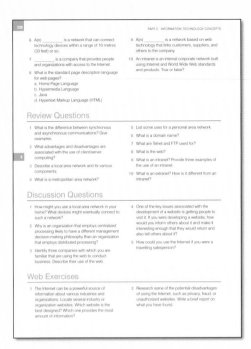

Review Questions help reinforce and test your knowledge and understanding, and provide a basis for group discussions and activities.

Web Exercises encourage you to apply your knowledge to the Internet.

Case Studies at the end of each chapter provide a wealth of practical information. Each case explores a chapter concept or problem that a real-world company or organization has faced.

Discussion Questions ask more challenging, in-depth questions, suitable for more advanced learning and postgraduate students.

Notes allow you to explore the subject further, and act as a starting point for projects and assignments.

PART 1

Overview

01

An Introduction to Information Systems

Principles	Learning Objectives
The value of information is directly linked to how it helps decision makers achieve organizational goals.	▪ Discuss why it is important to study and understand information systems.
	▪ Describe the characteristics used to evaluate the quality of data.
Computers and information systems are constantly making it possible for organizations to improve the way they conduct business.	▪ Name the components of an information system and describe several system characteristics.
Knowing the potential impact of information systems and having the ability to put this knowledge to work can result in a successful personal career, organizations that reach their goals, and a society with a higher quality of life.	▪ Identify the basic types of business information systems and discuss who uses them, how they are used, and what kinds of benefits they deliver.
System users, business managers, and information systems professionals must work together to build a successful information system.	▪ Identify the major steps of the systems development process and state the goal of each.
Information systems must be applied thoughtfully and carefully so that society, business, and industry can reap their enormous benefits.	▪ Describe some of the threats to security and privacy that information systems and the Internet can pose.
	▪ Discuss the expanding role and benefits of information systems in business and industry.

Information systems are used in almost every imaginable profession. Sales representatives use information systems to advertise products, communicate with customers, and analyze sales trends. Managers use them to make major decisions, such as whether to build a manufacturing plant or research a cancer drug. From a small music store to huge multinational companies, businesses of all sizes could not survive without information systems to perform accounting and finance operations. Regardless of your chosen career, you will use information systems to help you achieve goals.

This chapter presents an overview of information systems. The sections on hardware, software, databases, telecommunications, e-commerce and m-commerce, transaction processing and enterprise resource planning, information and decision support, special purpose systems, systems development, and ethical and societal issues are expanded to full chapters in the rest of the book. We will start by exploring the basics of information systems.

1.1 What is an Information System?

People and organizations use information every day. Many retail chains, for example, collect data from their shops to help them stock what customers want and to reduce costs. Businesses use information systems to increase revenues and reduce costs. We use automated teller machines outside banks and access information over the Internet. Information systems usually involve computers, and together, they are constantly changing the way organizations conduct business. Today we live in an information economy. Information itself has value, and commerce often involves the exchange of information rather than tangible goods. Systems based on computers are increasingly being used to create, store, and transfer information. Using information systems, investors make multimillion-euro decisions, financial institutions transfer billions of euros around the world electronically, and manufacturers order supplies and distribute goods faster than ever before. Computers and information systems will continue to change businesses and the way we live. To define an information system, we will start by examining what a system is.

1.1.1 What is a System?

A central concept of this book is that of a **system**. A system is a set of elements or components that interact to accomplish goals. The elements themselves and the relationships among them determine how the system works. Systems have inputs, processing mechanisms, outputs, and feedback (see Figure 1.1). A system processes the input to create the output. For example, consider an automatic car wash. Tangible inputs for the process are a dirty car, water, and various cleaning ingredients. Time, energy, skill, and knowledge also serve as inputs to the system because they are needed to operate it.

system A set of elements or components that interact to accomplish goals.

Figure 1.1 Components of a System *A system's four components consists of input, processing, output, and feedback.*

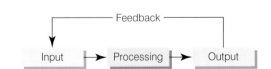

The processing mechanisms consist of first selecting which cleaning option you want (wash only, wash with wax, wash with wax and hand dry, etc.) and communicating that to the operator of the car wash. A feedback mechanism is your assessment of how clean the car is. Liquid sprayers shoot clear water, liquid soap, or car wax depending on where your car is in the process and which options you selected. The output is a clean car. As in all systems, independent elements or components (the liquid sprayer, foaming brush, and air dryer) interact to create a clean car.

System performance can be measured in various ways. **Efficiency** is a measure of what is produced divided by what is consumed. For example, the efficiency of a motor is the energy produced (in terms of work done) divided by the energy consumed (in terms of electricity or fuel). Some motors have an efficiency of 50 percent or less because of the energy lost to friction and heat generation.

efficiency A measure of what is produced divided by what is consumed.

Effectiveness is a measure of the extent to which a system achieves its goals. It can be computed by dividing the goals actually achieved by the total of the stated goals. For example, a company might want to achieve a net profit of €100 million for the year with a new information system. Actual profits, however, might only be €85 million for the year. In this case, the effectiveness is 85 percent (85/100 = 85 percent).

effectiveness A measure of the extent to which a system achieves its goals; it can be computed by dividing the goals actually achieved by the total of the stated goals.

Evaluating system performance also calls for using performance standards. A **system performance standard** is a specific objective of the system. For example, a system performance standard for a marketing campaign might be to have each sales representative sell €100 000 of a certain type of product each year (see Figure 1.2a). A system performance standard for a manufacturing process might be to provide no more than 1 percent defective parts (see Figure 1.2b). After

system performance standard A specific objective of the system.

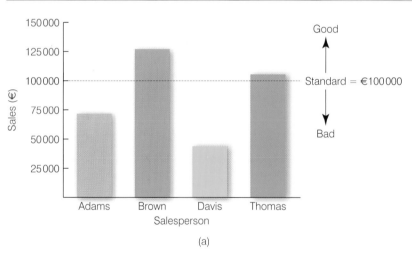

(a)

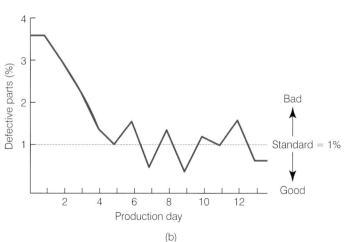

(b)

Figure 1.2 System Performance Standards
(a) Sales broken down by sales person
(b) Percentage of defective parts

standards are established, system performance is measured and compared with the standard. Variances from the standard are determinants of system performance.

1.1.2 What is Information?

Information is a collection of facts. Information can take many forms – text, numbers, images, audio clips, and video clips are all examples. A closely related term is 'data'. The traditional view is that the input into an information system is data. The information system then processes that data, and outputs information. So the difference between data and information is to do with how much processing the collection of facts have undergone. Unfortunately, this distinction is of little practical use, and the two terms can be used interchangeably. As we will see, the output of one information system is the input to another information system, and trying to distinguish between data and information in this situation just leads to confusion – under the traditional view, the 'information' which is output from the first system would turn into 'data' just before it is input into the second system!

1.1.3 What is an Information System?

Now that we have defined the terms 'system' and 'information', we can define an information system: an **information system (IS)** is a set of interrelated components that collect, manipulate, store, and disseminate information and provide a feedback mechanism to meet an objective. It is the feedback mechanism that helps organizations achieve their goals, such as increasing profits or improving customer service.

information system (IS) A set of interrelated components that collect, manipulate, store, and disseminate information and provide a feedback mechanism to meet an objective.

input The activity of gathering and capturing data.

In information systems, **input** is the activity of gathering and capturing data. In producing paycheques, for example, the number of hours every employee works must be collected before the cheques can be calculated or printed. In a university grading system, instructors must submit student grades before a summary of grades for the semester can be compiled and sent to the students.

processing Converting or transforming input into useful outputs.

Processing means converting or transforming this input into useful outputs. Processing can involve making calculations, comparing data and taking alternative actions, and storing data for future use. In a payroll application, the number of hours each employee worked must be converted into net, or take-home, pay. Other inputs often include employee ID number and department. The required processing can first involve multiplying the number of hours worked by the employee's hourly pay rate to get gross pay. If weekly hours worked exceed 35 hours, overtime pay might also be included. Then tax must be deducted along with contributions to health and life insurance or savings plans to get net pay.

After these calculations and comparisons are performed, the results are typically stored. Storage involves keeping data and information available for future use, including output.

output Production of useful information, often in the form of documents and reports.

Output involves producing useful information, usually in the form of documents and reports. Outputs can include paycheques for employees, reports for managers, and information supplied to stockholders, banks, government agencies, and other groups. As we have already said, output from one system can become input for another. For example, output from a system that processes sales orders can be used as input to a customer billing system. Computers typically produce output on printers and display screens. Output can also be handwritten or manually produced reports, although this is not common.

feedback Output that is used to make changes to input or processing activities.

Lastly, **feedback** is information from the system that is used to make changes to input or processing activities. For example, errors or problems might make it necessary to correct input data or change a process. Consider a payroll example. Perhaps the number of hours an employee worked was entered as 400 instead of 40 hours. Fortunately, most information systems check to make sure that data falls within certain ranges. For number of hours worked, the range might be from 0 to 100 hours because it is unlikely that an employee would work more than 100 hours in a week. The information system would determine that 400 hours is out of range and provide feedback. The feedback is used to check and correct the input on the number of hours worked to 40.

Feedback is also important for managers and decision makers. For example, a furniture maker could use a computerized feedback system to link its suppliers and plants. The output from an information system might indicate that inventory levels for mahogany and oak are getting low – a potential problem. A manager could use this feedback to decide to order more wood from a supplier. These new inventory orders then become input to the system. In addition to this reactive approach, a computer system can also be proactive – predicting future events to avoid problems. This concept, often called **forecasting**, can be used to estimate future sales and order more inventory before a shortage occurs. Forecasting is also used to predict the strength of hurricanes and possible landing sites, future stock-market values, and who will win a political election.

forecasting Predicting future events.

1.1.4 The Characteristics of Valuable Information

To be valuable to managers and decision makers, information should have some and possibly all of the characteristics described in Table 1.1. Many shipping companies, for example, can determine the exact location of inventory items and packages in their systems, and this information makes them responsive to their customers. In contrast, if an organization's information is not accurate or complete, people can make poor decisions costing thousands, or even millions, of euros. Many claim, for example, that the collapse and bankruptcy of some companies, such as drug companies and energy-trading firms, was a result of inaccurate accounting and reporting

Table 1.1 Characteristics of Valuable Information

Characteristics	Definitions
Accessible	Information should be easily accessible by authorized users so they can obtain it in the right format and at the right time to meet their needs
Accurate	Accurate information is error free. In some cases, inaccurate information is generated because inaccurate data is fed into the transformation process
Complete	Complete information contains all the important facts, but not more facts than are necessary (see the Simple characteristic below)
Economical	Information should also be relatively economical to produce. Decision makers must always balance the value of information with the cost of producing it
Flexible	Flexible information can be used for a variety of purposes. For example, information on how much inventory is on hand for a particular part can be used by a sales representative in closing a sale, by a production manager to determine whether more inventory is needed, and by a financial executive to determine the total value the company has invested in inventory
Relevant	Relevant information is important to the decision maker
Reliable	Reliable information can be depended on. In many cases, the reliability of the information depends on the reliability of the data-collection method. In other instances, reliability depends on the source of the information. A rumor from an unknown source that oil prices might go up might not be reliable (even though it might be useful)

(*continued*)

Table 1.1 *Continued*

Characteristics	Definitions
Secure	Information should be secure from access by unauthorized users
Simple	Information should be simple, not overly complex. Sophisticated and detailed information might not be needed. In fact, too much information can cause information overload, whereby a decision maker has too much information and is unable to determine what is really important
Timely	Timely information is delivered when it is needed. Knowing last week's weather conditions will not help when trying to decide what coat to wear today
Verifiable	Information should be verifiable. This means that you can check it to make sure it is correct, perhaps by checking many sources for the same information

information, which led investors and employees alike to misjudge the actual state of the company's finances and suffer huge personal losses. As another example, if an inaccurate forecast of future demand indicates that sales will be very high when the opposite is true, an organization can invest millions of euros in a new plant that is not needed. Furthermore, if information is not relevant, not delivered to decision makers in a timely fashion, or too complex to understand, it can be of little value to the organization.

The value of information is directly linked to how it helps decision makers achieve their organization's goals. For example, the value of information might be measured in the time required to make a decision or in increased profits to the company. Consider a market forecast that predicts a high demand for a new product. If you use this information to develop the new product and your company makes an additional profit of €10 000, the value of this information to the company is €10 000 minus the cost of the information.

1.1.5 Manual and Computerized Information Systems

An information system can be manual or computerized. For example, some investment analysts manually draw charts and trend lines to assist them in making investment decisions. Tracking data on stock prices (input) over the last few months or years, these analysts develop patterns on graph paper (processing) that help them determine what stock prices are likely to do in the next few days or weeks (output). Some investors have made millions of euros using manual stock analysis information systems. Of course, today many excellent computerized information systems follow stock indexes and markets and suggest when large blocks of stocks should be purchased or sold to take advantage of market discrepancies.

computer-based information system (CBIS) A single set of hardware, software, databases, telecommunications, people, and procedures that are configured to collect, manipulate, store, and process data into information.

A **computer-based information system (CBIS)** is a single set of hardware, software, databases, telecommunications, people, and procedures that are configured to collect, manipulate, store, and process data into information. For example, a company's payroll, order entry, or inventory-control system is an example of a CBIS. CBISs can also be embedded into products. Some new cars and home appliances include computer hardware, software, databases, and even telecommunications to control their operations and make them more useful. This is often called 'embedded', 'pervasive', or 'ubiquitous' computing. CBISs have evolved into sophisticated analysis tools.

technology infrastructure All the hardware, software, databases, telecommunications, people, and procedures that are configured to collect, manipulate, store, and process data into information.

The components of a CBIS are illustrated in Figure 1.3. Information technology (IT) refers to hardware, software, databases, and telecommunications. A business's **technology infrastructure** includes all the hardware, software, databases, telecommunications, people, and procedures that are configured

Figure 1.3 The Components of a Computer-Based Information System

Hardware

People

Software

Procedures

Telecommunications

Databases

to collect, manipulate, store, and process data into information. The technology infrastructure is a set of shared IS resources that form the foundation of each computer-based information system.

Hardware

Hardware consists of computer equipment used to perform input, processing, and output activities. Input devices include keyboards, mice and other pointing devices, automatic scanning devices, and equipment that can read magnetic ink characters. Investment firms often use voice-response technology to allow customers to access their balances and other information with spoken commands. Processing devices include computer chips that contain the central processing unit and main memory. One processor chip, called the 'Bunny Chip' by some, mimics living organisms and can be used by the drug industry to test drugs instead of using animals, such as rats or bunnies.[1] The experimental chip could save millions of euros and months of time in drug research costs. Processor speed is also important. A large IBM computer used by U.S. Livermore National Laboratories to analyze nuclear explosions is possibly the fastest in the world (up to 300 teraflops – 300 trillion operations per second).[2] The super fast computer, called Blue Gene, costs about €29 million.

> **hardware** Any machinery (most of which uses digital circuits) that assists in the input, processing, storage, and output activities of an information system.

The many types of output devices include printers and computer screens. Bond traders, for example, often use an array of six or more computer screens to monitor bond prices and make split-second trades throughout each day. Another type of output device is a printer to print photos from a digital camera. Such printers accept the memory card direct from the camera. There are also many special-purpose hardware devices. Computerized event data recorders (EDRs) are now being placed into vehicles (Figure 1.4). Like an airplane's black box, EDRs record a vehicle's speed, possible engine problems, a driver's performance, and more. The technology is being used to monitor vehicle operation, determine the cause of accidents, and investigate whether truck drivers are taking required breaks.

Figure 1.4
Computerized Dashboard
Computerized event data recorders record a vehicle's speed, possible engine problems, driver's performance, and more.

SOURCE: Istock.

Software

Software consists of the computer programs that govern the operation of the computer. These programs allow a computer to process payroll, send bills to customers, and provide managers with information to increase profits, reduce costs, and provide better cus-

software The computer programs that govern the operation of the computer.

tomer service. With software, people can work anytime at any place. Software, along with manufacturing tools, for example, can be used to fabricate parts almost anywhere in the world.[3] Software called 'Fab Lab', controls tools, such as cutters, milling machines, and other devices. A Fab Lab system, which costs about €15 000, has been used to make radio frequency tags to track animals in Norway, engine parts to allow tractors to run on processed castor beans in India, and many other fabrication applications.

The two types of software are system software, such as Microsoft Windows XP, which controls basic computer operations, including start-up and printing; and applications software, such as Microsoft Office, which allows you to accomplish specific tasks, including word processing and drawing charts. Sophisticated application software, such as Adobe Creative Suite, can be used to design, develop, print, and place professional-quality advertising, brochures, posters, prints, and videos on the Internet.

Databases

A **database** is an organized collection of facts and information, typically consisting of two or more related data files. An organization's database can contain information on customers, employees, inventory, competitors' sales, online purchases, and much more.

database An organized collection of information.

Most managers and executives consider a database to be one of the most valuable parts of a computer-based information system. One California real estate development company uses databases to search for homes that are undervalued and purchase them at bargain prices.[4] It uses the database to analyze crime statistics, prices, local weather reports, school districts, and more to find homes whose values are likely to increase. The database has helped the company realize an average 50 percent return on investment. Increasingly, organizations are placing important databases on the Internet, which makes them accessible to many, including unauthorized users.

Telecommunications, Networks, and the Internet

Telecommunication is the electronic transmission of signals for communications, which enables organizations to carry out their processes and tasks through computer networks. Large restaurant chains, for example, can use telecommunications systems and satellites to link hundreds of restaurants to plants and headquarters to speed credit card authorization and report sales and payroll data. **Networks** connect computers and equipment in a building, around the country, or around the world to enable electronic communication. Investment firms can use wireless networks to connect thousands of investors with brokers or traders. Many hotels use wireless telecommunications to allow guests to connect to the Internet, retrieve voice messages, and exchange e-mail without plugging their computers or mobile devices into a phone socket. Wireless transmission also allows drones, such as Boeing's Scan Eagle, to fly using a remote control system and monitor buildings and other areas.

> **telecommunications** The electronic transmission of signals for communications; enables organizations to carry out their processes and tasks through effective computer networks.

> **network** Computers and equipment that are connected in a building, around the country, or around the world to enable electronic communications.

The **Internet** is the world's largest computer network, actually consisting of thousands of interconnected networks, all freely exchanging information. Research firms, colleges, universities, schools, and businesses are just a few examples of organizations using the Internet. People use the Internet to research information, buy and sell products and services, make travel arrangements, conduct banking, and download music and videos, among other activities. After downloading music, you can use audio software to change a song's tempo, create mixes of your favourite tunes, and modify sound tracks to suit your personal taste. You can even mix two or more songs simultaneously, which is called 'mashing'. You can also use many of today's mobile phones to connect to the Internet from around the world and at high speeds.[5] This not only speeds communications, but allows you to conduct business electronically. Some airline companies are providing Internet service on their flights so that travellers can send and receive e-mail, check investments, and browse the Internet. Internet users can create blogs (weblogs) to store and share their thoughts and ideas with others around the world.[6] You can also record and store TV programs on computers or special viewing devices and watch them later.[7] Often called 'place shifting', this technology allows you to record TV programs at home and watch them at a different place when it's convenient.

> **Internet** The world's largest computer network, actually consisting of thousands of interconnected networks, all freely exchanging information.

The World Wide Web (WWW), or the Web, is a network of links on the Internet to documents containing text, graphics, video, and sound. Information about the documents and access to them are controlled and provided by tens of thousands of special computers called 'web servers'. The Web is one of many services available over the Internet and provides access to many hundreds of millions of documents.

The technology used to create the Internet is also being applied within companies and organizations to create **intranets**, which allow people within an organization to exchange information and work on projects. One company, for example, uses an intranet to connect its 200 global operating companies and 20 000 employees. An **extranet** is a network based on web technologies that allows selected outsiders, such as business partners and customers, to access authorized resources of a company's intranet. Companies can move all or most of their business activities to an extranet site for corporate customers. Many people use extranets every day without realizing it – to track shipped goods, order products from their suppliers, or access customer assistance from other companies. If you log on to the FedEx site (www.fedex.com) to check the status of a package, for example, you are using an extranet.

> **intranet** An internal company network built using Internet and World Wide Web standards and products that allows people within an organization to exchange information and work on projects.

> **extranet** A network based on web technologies that allows selected outsiders, such as business partners, suppliers, or customers, to access authorized resources of a company's intranet.

People

People are the most important element in most computer-based information systems. The people involved include users of the system and information systems personnel, including all the people who manage, run, program, and maintain the system.

Procedures

Procedures include the strategies, policies, methods, and rules for using the CBIS, including the operation, maintenance, and security of the computer. For example, some procedures describe when each program should be run. Others describe who can access facts in the database, or what to do if a disaster, such as a fire, earthquake, or hurricane, renders the CBIS unusable. Good procedures can help companies take advantage of new opportunities and avoid potential disasters. Poorly developed and inadequately implemented procedures, however, can cause people to waste their time on useless rules or result in inadequate responses to disasters, such as hurricanes or tornadoes.

procedures The strategies, policies, methods, and rules for using a CBIS.

1.2 Business Information Systems

The most common types of information systems used in business organizations are those designed for electronic and mobile commerce, transaction processing, management information, and decision support. In addition, some organizations employ special-purpose systems, such as virtual reality, that not every organization uses. Together, these systems help employees in organizations accomplish routine and special tasks – from recording sales, processing

Information Systems @ Work

Speeding Up Insurance Claims with New Information Systems

Insurance companies employ claims adjusters to visit property damaged by disaster, analyze the damage, and estimate the value required to repair the property. Each estimate can take considerable time and effort. Adjusters might visit four or five properties in the morning and afternoon, then return to the office where they review notes taken at each property, consult reference charts to calculate repair costs, fill out paper forms, and enter data into the corporate information system. A cheque is then issued from the insurance company to the victim of the disaster. Multiply the complexity of this process by the thousands of claims that an insurance company processes each year, and the result is a lot of paperwork, wasted time, and mistakes.

The executives at Gore Mutual Insurance of Cambridge, Ontario, Canada, wanted to streamline the claims adjustment process, making it more effective and efficient by applying new information systems. They partnered with a start-up software company named Symbility to create a state-of-the-

art solution. The goal of the new system was to process claims onsite during the damage inspection. Gore Mutual wanted to eliminate paper notes that adjusters carried back to the office for processing. Even processing on a notebook PC in a van onsite wasn't efficient enough. Symbility turned to tablet and handheld PCs with handwriting recognition to provide the ideal solution. Tablet and handheld PCs allow users to enter data by writing on the touch screen with a stylus.

Symbility designed pen-based software to run on Windows tablet PCs and handheld PCs. Adjusters can now take notes, sketch floor plans and diagrams, even transfer digital photos from mobile phones. All forms and reference charts are accessible and easy to manipulate. The adjuster's PC is connected over a wireless network to a special information service provided by Symbility that supports all the calculations, data manipulation, and processing required to adjust claims. For a claims adjuster, it's like holding the power of the corporate server in their hand.

Gore Mutual found that the tablet PC solution let adjusters spend more time meeting with customers in the field. Estimates were calculated quickly and accurately. Symbility estimates that the system results in claims being settled up to six times faster and more accurately.

The pen-based solution was such a hit that Symbility now supports claim processing for many insurance companies at around $20 per claim. In this way, Symbility plays the role of an application service provider (ASP). ASPs design and maintain software and systems and lease the use of the software to businesses. This benefits businesses in a number of ways. The business can focus on its primary goals rather than worrying about developing and maintaining the technology components of an information system. Because the ASP's primary purpose is to develop the best systems possible, the quality of the service is typically higher than if the business developed its own system.

As with most good information systems, the end result of the Symbility solution was a huge reduction of tedious procedures for claims adjusters and fewer opportunities for human error. More importantly, the system frees claim adjusters to do what they do best: evaluate damage and help people continue with their lives.

Considering recent devastation by hurricanes, mudslides, forest fires, and other natural disasters, the speed with which claims are processed affects more than an insurance company's bottom line. In catastrophic events, insurance companies are hard pressed to process claims efficiently. Imagine a technology that allows a company to process 6000 claims in the amount of time that it typically processes 1000. Such a system could mean the difference between life and death for homeless survivors. Symbility's pen-based claims processing system does just that.

Questions

1 Explain how the information system components hardware, software, databases, telecommunications, people, and procedures combine to provide a solution for insurance claims adjusters.

2 What benefits did Gore Mutual enjoy by working with Symbility rather than going it on their own?

3 What technologies used in this system are more readily available today than they were five years ago? How long might it be before this system becomes outdated?

4 What other professions would benefit from a pen-based wireless system like Symbility's?

SOURCES: John Cox, 'Insurance adjusters use pen-based GUI and wireless', *Network World,* October 5, 2005, www.techworld.com. 'Symbility Solutions to Demonstrate the Power of "Insurance Mobility"', *PRNewswire,* January 17, 2006, http://biz.yahoo.com/prnews/060117/nytu128.html?.v=41. Symbility website, accessed February 22, 2006, www.symbilitysolutions.com.

payrolls, and supporting decisions in various departments, to examining alternatives for large-scale projects and opportunities. Although these systems are discussed in separate sections in this chapter and explained in more detail later, they are often integrated in one product and delivered by the same software package. For example, some enterprise resource planning packages process transactions, deliver information, and support decisions (see Figure 1.5).

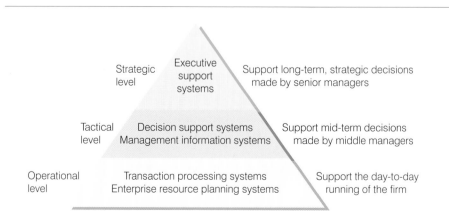

Figure 1.5 Business Information Systems

1.2.1 Electronic and Mobile Commerce

E-commerce involves any business transaction executed electronically between companies (business-to-business, 'B2B'), companies and consumers (business-to-consumer, 'B2C'), consumers and other consumers (consumer-to-consumer, 'C2C'), business and the public sector, and consumers and the public sector. You might assume that e-commerce is reserved mainly for consumers visiting websites for online shopping, but web shopping is only a small part of the e-commerce picture; the major volume of e-commerce – and its fastest growing segment – is business-to-business (B2B) transactions that make purchasing easier for corporations. This growth is being stimulated by increased Internet access, growing user confidence, better payment systems, and rapidly improving Internet and web security. E-commerce also offers opportunities for small businesses to market and sell at a low cost worldwide, allowing them to enter the global market. **Mobile commerce (m-commerce)** refers to transactions conducted anywhere, anytime. M-commerce relies on wireless communications that managers and corporations use to place orders and conduct business with handheld computers, portable phones, laptop computers connected to a network, and other mobile devices.

e-commerce Any business transaction executed electronically between companies (business-to-business), companies and consumers (business-to-consumer), consumers and other consumers (consumer-to-consumer), business and the public sector, and consumers and the public sector.

mobile commerce (m-commerce) Conducting business transactions electronically using mobile devices such as smartphones.

E-commerce offers many advantages for streamlining work activities. Figure 1.6 provides a brief example of how e-commerce can simplify the process of purchasing new office furniture

Figure 1.6
E-Commerce Greatly
Simplifies Purchasing

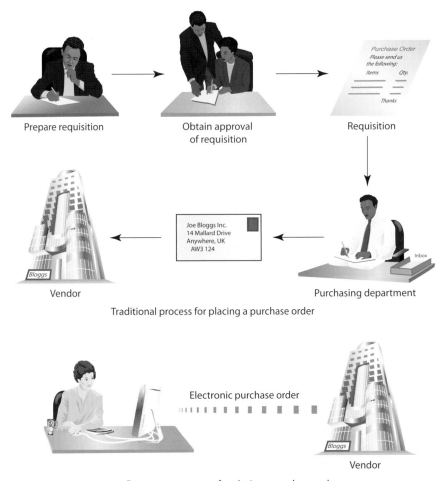

Prepare requisition

Obtain approval
of requisition

Requisition

Joe Bloggs Inc.
14 Mallard Drive
Anywhere, UK
AW3 124

Inbox

Vendor

Purchasing department

Traditional process for placing a purchase order

Electronic purchase order

Vendor

E-commerce process for placing a purchase order

from an office-supply company. In the manual system, a corporate office worker must get approval for a purchase that exceeds a certain amount. That request goes to the purchasing department, which generates a formal purchase order to procure the goods from the approved vendor. Business-to-business e-commerce automates the entire process. Employees go directly to the supplier's website, find the item in a catalogue, and order what they need at a price set by their company. If approval is required, the approver is notified automatically. As the use of e-commerce systems grows, companies are phasing out their traditional systems. The resulting growth of e-commerce is creating many new business opportunities.

E-commerce can enhance a company's stock prices and market value. Today, several e-commerce firms have teamed up with more traditional brick-and-mortar businesses to draw from each other's strengths. For example, e-commerce customers can order products on a website and pick them up at a nearby store.

In addition to e-commerce, business information systems use telecommunications and the Internet to perform many related tasks. Electronic procurement (e-procurement), for example, involves using information systems and the Internet to acquire parts and supplies. **Electronic business (e-business)** goes beyond e-commerce and e-procurement by using information systems and the Internet to perform all business-related tasks and functions, such as accounting, finance, marketing, manufacturing, and human resource activities. E-business also includes working with customers, suppliers, strategic partners, and stakeholders. Compared with traditional business strategy, e-business strategy is flexible and adaptable.

electronic business (e-business) Using information systems and the Internet to perform all business-related tasks and functions.

1.2.2 Enterprise Systems: Transaction Processing Systems and Enterprise Resource Planning

Transaction Processing Systems

Since the 1950s, computers have been used to perform common business applications. Many of these early systems were designed to reduce costs by automating routine, labour-intensive business transactions. A **transaction** is any business-related exchange, such as payments to employees, sales to customers, or payments to suppliers. Thus, processing business transactions was the first computer application developed for most organizations. A **transaction processing system (TPS)** is an organized collection of people, procedures, software, databases, and devices used to record completed business transactions. If you understand a transaction processing system, you understand basic business operations and functions.

transaction Any business-related exchange, such as payments to employees, sales to customers, and payments to suppliers.

transaction processing system (TPS) An organized collection of people, procedures, software, databases, and devices used to record completed business transactions.

Enterprise systems help organizations perform and integrate important tasks, such as paying employees and suppliers, controlling inventory, sending out invoices, and ordering supplies. In the past, companies accomplished these tasks using traditional transaction processing systems. Today, they are increasingly being performed by enterprise resource planning systems. For example, Whirlpool Corporation, the large appliance maker, used enterprise resource planning to reduce inventory levels by 20 percent and cut about 5 percent from its freight and warehousing costs by providing managers with information about inventory levels and costs.[8] The new system may have also helped the company increase its revenues by about €0.7 billion.

One of the first business systems to be computerized was the payroll system. The primary inputs for a payroll TPS are the number of employee hours worked during the week and the pay rate. The primary output consists of paycheques. Early payroll systems produced employee paycheques and related reports required by tax authorities. Other routine applications include sales ordering, customer billing and customer relationship management, and inventory control. Some car companies, for example, use their TPSs to buy billions of euros of needed parts each year through websites. Because these systems handle and process daily business exchanges, or transactions, they are all classified as TPSs.

Enterprise Resource Planning

An **enterprise resource planning (ERP) system** is a set of integrated programs that manages the vital business operations for an entire multi-site, global organization. An ERP system can replace many applications with one unified set of programs, making the system easier to use and more effective.

enterprise resource planning (ERP) system A set of integrated programs capable of managing a company's vital business operations for an entire multi-site, global organization.

Although the scope of an ERP system might vary from company to company, most ERP systems provide integrated software to support manufacturing and finance. In such an environment, a forecast is prepared that estimates customer demand for several weeks. The ERP system checks what is already available in finished product inventory to meet the projected demand. Manufacturing must then produce inventory to eliminate any shortfalls. In developing the production schedule, the ERP system checks the raw materials and packing-materials inventories and determines what needs to be ordered to meet the schedule. Most ERP systems also have a purchasing subsystem that orders the needed items. In addition to these core business processes, some ERP systems can support functions such as human resources, sales, and distribution. The primary benefits of implementing an ERP system include easing adoption of improved work processes and increasing access to timely data for decision making (see Figure 1.7).

1.2.3 Information and Decision Support Systems

The benefits provided by an effective TPS are tangible and justify their associated costs in computing equipment, computer programs, and specialized personnel and supplies. A TPS can speed business activities and reduce clerical costs. Although early accounting and financial TPSs were already valuable, companies soon realized that they could use the data stored in these systems to help managers make better decisions, whether in human resource management, marketing, or administration. Satisfying the needs of managers and decision makers continues to be a major factor in developing information systems.

Figure 1.7 SAP *SAP AG, a German software company, is one of the leading suppliers of ERP software. The company employs more than 34 000 people in more than 50 countries.*

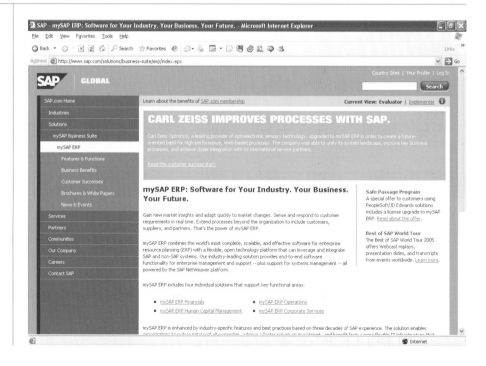

Management Information Systems

A **management information system (MIS)** is an organized collection of people, procedures, software, databases, and devices that provides routine information to managers and decision makers. An MIS focuses on operational efficiency. Marketing, production, finance, and other functional areas are supported by MISs and linked through a common database. MISs typically provide standard reports generated with data and information from the TPS, meaning the output of a TPS is the input to a MIS. Producing a report that describes inventory that should be ordered is an example of an MIS.

management information system (MIS) An organized collection of people, procedures, software, databases, and devices that provides routine information to managers and decision makers.

MISs were first developed in the 1960s and typically use information systems to produce managerial reports. In many cases, these early reports were produced periodically – daily, weekly, monthly, or yearly. Because of their value to managers, MISs have proliferated throughout the management ranks. For instance, the total payroll summary report produced initially for an accounting manager might also be useful to a production manager to help monitor and control labour and job costs.

Decision Support Systems

By the 1980s, dramatic improvements in technology resulted in information systems that were less expensive but more powerful than earlier systems. People at all levels of organizations began using personal computers to do a variety of tasks; they were no longer solely dependent on the IS department for all their information needs. People quickly recognized that computer systems could support additional decision-making activities. A **decision support system (DSS)** is an organized collection of people, procedures, software, databases, and devices that support problem-specific decision making (see Figure 1.8). The focus of a DSS is on making

decision support system (DSS) An organized collection of people, procedures, software, databases, and devices used to support problem-specific decision making.

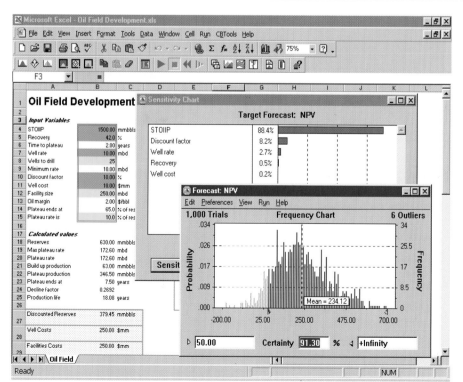

Figure 1.8 DSS
Decisioneering provides decision support software called Crystal Ball, which helps business people of all types assess risks and make forecasts. Shown here is the Standard Edition being used for oil field development.

SOURCE: Crystal Ball screenshot courtesy of Decisioneering, Inc.

effective decisions. Whereas an MIS helps an organization 'do things right', a DSS helps a manager 'do the right thing'.

In addition to assisting in all aspects of problem-specific decision making, a DSS can support customers by rapidly responding to their phone and e-mail enquiries. A DSS goes beyond a traditional MIS by providing immediate assistance in solving problems. Many of these problems are unique and complex, and information is often difficult to obtain. For instance, an car manufacturer might try to determine the layout for its new manufacturing facility. Traditional MISs are seldom used to solve these types of problems; a DSS can help by suggesting alternatives and assisting in final decision making.

Decision support systems are used when the problem is complex and the information needed to make the best decision is difficult to obtain and use. So a DSS also involves managerial judgment and perspective. Managers often play an active role in developing and implementing the DSS. A DSS recognizes that different managerial styles and decision types require different systems. For example, two production managers in the same position trying to solve the same problem might require different information and support. The overall emphasis is to support, rather than replace, managerial decision making.

The essential elements of a DSS include a collection of models used to support a decision maker or user (model base), a collection of facts and information to assist in decision making (database), and systems and procedures (dialogue manager or user interface) that help decision makers and other users interact with the DSS. Software is often used to manage the database – the database management system (DBMS) – and the model base – the model management system (MMS).

In addition to DSSs for managers, group decision support systems and executive support systems use the same approach to support groups and executives.[9] A group decision support system, also called a group support system, includes the DSS elements just described and software, called groupware, to help groups make effective decisions. An executive support system, also called an executive information system, helps top-level managers, including a firm's president, vice presidents, and members of the board of directors, make better decisions. An executive support system can assist with strategic planning, top-level organizing and staffing, strategic control, and crisis management.

1.2.4 Knowledge Management, Artificial Intelligence, Expert Systems, and Virtual Reality

In addition to TPSs, MISs, and DSSs, organizations often rely on specialized systems. Many use knowledge management systems (KMSs), an organized collection of people, procedures, software, databases, and devices to create, store, share, and use the organization's knowledge and experience. According to a survey of CEOs, firms that use KMSs are more likely to innovate and perform better.[10]

In addition to knowledge management, companies use other types of specialized systems. The Nissan Motor Company, for example, has developed a specialized system for their vehicles called 'Lane Departure Prevention' that nudges a car back into the correct lane if it veers off course.[11] The system uses cameras and computers to adjust braking to get the vehicle back on course. The system switches off when the driver uses turn signals to change lanes. Other specialized systems are based on the notion of **artificial intelligence (AI)**, in which the computer system takes on the characteristics of human intelligence. The field of artificial intelligence includes several subfields (see Figure 1.9). Some people predict that in the future, we will have nanobots, small molecular-sized robots, travelling throughout our bodies and in our bloodstream, keeping us healthy.[12] Other nanobots will be embedded in products and services, making our lives easier and creating new business opportunities.

artificial intelligence (AI) The ability of computer systems to mimic or duplicate the functions or characteristics of the human brain or intelligence.

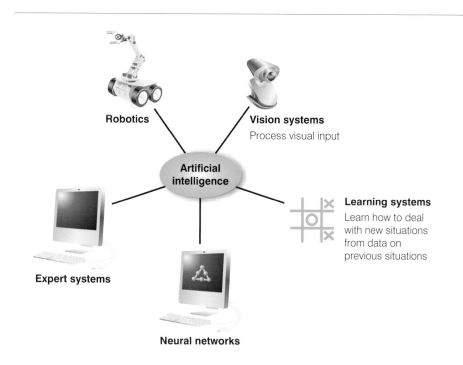

Figure 1.9 The Major Elements of Artificial Intelligence

Artificial Intelligence

Robotics is an area of artificial intelligence in which machines take over complex, dangerous, routine, or boring tasks, such as welding car frames or assembling computer systems and components. Vision systems allow robots and other devices to 'see', store, and process visual images. Natural language processing involves computers understanding and acting on verbal or written commands in English, Spanish, or other human languages. Learning systems allow computers to learn from past mistakes or experiences, such as playing games or making business decisions, and neural networks is a branch of AI that allows computers to recognize and act on patterns or trends. Some successful stock, options, and futures traders use neural networks to spot trends and make them more profitable with their investments.

Expert Systems

Expert systems give the computer the ability to make suggestions and act like an expert in a particular field. It can help the novice user perform at the level of an expert. The unique value of expert systems is that they allow organizations to capture and use the wisdom of experts and specialists. Therefore, years of experience and specific skills are not completely lost when a human expert dies, retires, or leaves for another job. Expert systems can be applied to almost any field or discipline. They have been used to monitor nuclear reactors, perform medical diagnoses, locate possible repair problems, design and configure IS components, perform credit evaluations, and develop marketing plans for a new product or new investment strategy. The collection of data, rules, procedures, and relationships that must be followed to achieve value or the proper outcome is contained in the expert system's **knowledge base**.

expert system A system that gives a computer the ability to make suggestions and act like an expert in a particular field.

knowledge base A component of an expert system that stores all relevant information, data, rules, cases, and relationships used by the expert system.

Virtual Reality

Virtual reality is the simulation of a real or imagined environment that can be experienced visually in three dimensions. Originally, virtual reality referred to immersive virtual reality, which means the user becomes fully immersed in an

virtual reality The simulation of a real or imagined environment that can be experienced visually in three dimensions.

artificial, computer-generated 3D world. The virtual world is presented in full scale and relates properly to the human size. It can represent any 3D setting, real or abstract, such as a building, an archaeological excavation site, the human anatomy, a sculpture, or a crime scene reconstruction. Virtual worlds can be animated, interactive, and shared. Through immersion, the user can gain a deeper understanding of the virtual world's behaviour and functionality. Virtual reality can also refer to applications that are not fully immersive, such as mouse-controlled navigation through a 3D environment on a graphics monitor, stereo viewing from the monitor via stereo glasses, stereo projection systems, and others.

A variety of input devices, such as head-mounted displays (see Figure 1.10), data gloves, joysticks, and handheld wands, allow the user to navigate through a virtual environment and to interact with virtual objects. Directional sound, tactile and force feedback devices, voice recognition, and other technologies enrich the immersive experience. Because several people can share and interact in the same environment, virtual reality can be a powerful medium for communication, entertainment, and learning.

Figure 1.10 A Head-Mounted Display *The head-mounted display (HMD) was the first device to provide the wearer with an immersive experience. A typical HMD houses two miniature display screens and an optical system that channels the images from the screens to the eyes, thereby presenting a stereo view of a virtual world. A motion tracker continuously measures the position and orientation of the user's head and allows the image-generating computer to adjust the scene representation to the current view. As a result, the viewer can look around and walk through the surrounding virtual environment.*

SOURCE: Frank Chmura/Alamy.

It is difficult to predict where information systems and technology will be in 10 to 20 years. It seems, however, that we are just beginning to discover the full range of their usefulness. Technology has been improving and expanding at an increasing rate; dramatic growth and change are expected for years to come. Without question, a knowledge of the effective use of information systems will be critical for managers both now and in the long term. But how are these information systems created?

1.3 Systems Development

Systems development is the activity of creating or modifying business systems. Systems development projects can range from small to very large in fields as diverse as stock analysis and video game development. People inside a company can develop systems, or companies can use outsourcing, hiring an outside company to perform some or all of a systems development project. Outsourcing allows a company to focus on what it does best and delegate other functions to companies with expertise in systems development. Outsourcing, however, is not the best alternative for all companies.

systems development The activity of creating or modifying existing business systems.

Developing information systems to meet business needs is highly complex and difficult – so much so that it is common for IS projects to overrun budgets and exceed scheduled completion dates. Her Majesty's Revenue and Customs (HMRC), which collects taxes in the UK, settled out of court with an outsourcing company to recover funds lost due to a tax-related mistake caused by a failed systems development project.[13] The failed project overpaid about €2.5 billion to some families with children or taxpayers in a low-income tax bracket. One strategy for improving the results of a systems development project is to divide it into several steps, each with a well-defined goal and set of tasks to accomplish (see Figure 1.11). These steps are summarized next.

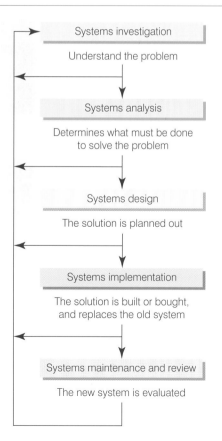

Figure 1.11 An Overview of Systems Development

1.3.1 Systems Investigation and Analysis

The first two steps of systems development are systems investigation and analysis. The goal of the systems investigation is to gain a clear understanding of the problem to be solved or opportunity to be addressed. A cruise line company, for example, might launch a systems investigation to determine whether a development project is feasible to automate purchasing at ports around the world. After an organization understands the problem, the next question is, 'Is the problem worth solving?'. Given that organizations have limited resources – people and money – this question deserves careful consideration. If the decision is to continue with the solution, the next step, systems analysis, defines the problems and opportunities of the existing system. During systems investigation and analysis, as well as design maintenance and review, discussed next, the project must have the complete support of top-level managers and focus on developing systems that achieve business goals.[14]

1.3.2 Systems Design, Implementation, and Maintenance and Review

Systems design determines how the new system will work to meet the business needs defined during systems analysis. Systems implementation involves creating or acquiring the various system components (hardware, software, databases, etc.) defined in the design step, assembling them, and putting the new system into operation. The purpose of systems maintenance and review is to check and modify the system so that it continues to meet changing business needs.

1.4 Information Systems in Society, Business, and Industry

Information systems have been developed to meet the needs of all types of organizations and people, and their use is spreading throughout the world to improve the lives and business activities of many citizens. To provide their enormous benefits, however, information systems must be implemented with thought and care. The speed and widespread use of information systems opens users to a variety of threats from unethical people.

Ethical and Societal Issues

Snipermail Executive Serves Hard Time

When you picture a criminal 'hacker', you probably think of a young, socially isolated deviant in a dark room tapping away at the keyboard in the middle of the night. You probably wouldn't picture a 46-year-old Boca Raton, Florida, executive hacking systems in his office in the middle of the afternoon. It's time to shatter that stereotype.

The ex-principle owner of Snipermail, Inc. is that executive. This chief executive officer (CEO) is not exactly what some would consider a reputable businessman, even when he's not hacking private networks. Snipermail is a spam company; it develops e-mail marketing strategies for businesses and matches its clients with e-mail lists of spam targets.

Snipermail contracted with a client that used Acxiom Corporation's services. Acxiom, with head-quarters in Little Rock, Arkansas, manages personal information on consumers, along with financial and corporate data for a variety of companies, including Fortune 500 firms. To work with its client, Snipermail was provided with an Acxiom network account that allowed it to access certain limited database records at Acxiom.

Seizing the opportunity, associates at Snipermail used their limited access to the Acxiom system and sophisticated decryption software to illegally obtain passwords to access the entire Acxiom database. Over time, those associates downloaded more than one billion private data records from Acxiom containing names, e-mail addresses, and phone numbers of clients. The CEO planned to merge the data with the Snipermail database of spam targets and sell it to clients.

It isn't easy to download 8.2 GB of private valuable data without being noticed. Acxiom discovered the theft and it wasn't long before investigators traced the digital footprints to Snipermail.

On July 22, 2004, the CEO of Snipermail was charged with the largest computer crime indictment in U.S. history. On February 22, 2006 he was sentenced to eight years in prison for 120 counts of unauthorized access of a protected computer, two counts of access device fraud, and one count of obstruction of justice. The CEO's six associates and accomplices were of little help to him. They all struck deals with the Department of Justice and implicated the CEO in exchange for their own freedom.

The law enforcement agencies involved had strong words for anyone who might think stealing information over the Internet is harmless. 'This sentence reflects the seriousness of these crimes,' said U.S. Attorney Bud Cummins of the Eastern District of Arkansas. 'At first blush, downloading computer files in the privacy of your office may not seem so terribly serious. But, if you are stealing propriety information worth tens of millions of dollars from a well-established and reputable company, you can expect to be punished accordingly.'

'Neither the Internet nor cyberspace will ever be a safe haven for individuals who attempt this type of cyber crime. The Secret Service, along with our law enforcement partners, will hunt you down, key-stroke by keystroke, until you face a jury of your peers,' said Brian Marr, Special Agent in Charge of the Little Rock office of the U.S. Secret Service. 'The investigation of cyber crime, particularly as it relates to computer intrusion, is one of the FBI's top priorities,' said William C. Temple, Special Agent in Charge of the Little Rock office of the Federal Bureau of Investigation. 'The success of this investigation should send a strong message to those who might consider becoming involved in similar criminal activity.'

Questions

1 Explain carefully who you think the victims are in the Snipermail case.

2 Do you think eight years is an appropriate sentence for this CEO? Why or why not?

3 What actions could Acxiom have taken to prevent its customers and their associates from accessing sensitive information?

4 In what ways could this incident negatively affect Acxiom?

SOURCES: Grant Gross, 'IT Exec Sentenced to Eight Years for Data Theft', *IDG News Service*, February 23, 2006, www.idg.com. 'Scott Levine Gets 8 Years in Data Theft Case', *4Law* website, accessed February 23, 2006, www.4law.co.il/arkan1.htm.

1.4.1 Security, Privacy, and Ethical Issues in Information Systems and the Internet

Although information systems can provide enormous benefits, they do have some drawbacks.[15] Figure 1.12 reveals the annual cost of losses of about 250 organizations that responded to a survey. Computer-related mistakes are also a concern. In Japan, a financial services firm had trading losses of ¥245 million due to a typing mistake in entering a trade.

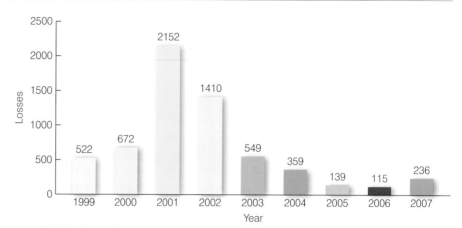

Figure 1.12 The Cost of Computer Attacks: Average Losses per Organization (in Thousands of Euros)

SOURCE: CSI 2007 Computer Crime and Security (Computer Security Institute).

Increasingly, the ethical use of systems has been highlighted in the news. Ethical issues concern what is generally considered right or wrong. Some IS professionals believe that computers may create new opportunities for unethical behaviour. For example, a faculty member of a medical school falsified computerized research results to get a promotion – and a higher salary. In another case, a company was charged with using a human resource information system to time employee layoffs and firings to avoid paying pensions. More and more, the Internet is also associated with unethical behaviour. Unethical investors have placed false rumours or incorrect information about a company on the Internet and tried to influence its stock price to make money. Information theft, such as stealing credit card numbers and other personal information, is another issue.

To protect against these threats, you can install security and control measures. For example, many software products can detect and remove viruses and spam, or unwanted e-mail, from computer systems. Information systems can help reduce other types of crime as well. In a New Zealand city, a free computer centre has cut vandalism by keeping young people off the street and giving residents a sense of pride. When a pair of headphones disappeared from the centre, the community rallied to make sure that they were promptly returned.

You can install firewalls (software and hardware that protect a computer system or network from outside attacks) to avoid viruses and prevent unauthorized people from gaining access to your computer system. You can also use identification numbers and passwords. Some security experts propose installing web cameras and hiring 'citizen spotters' to monitor them. Use of information systems also raises work concerns, including job loss through increased efficiency and some potential health problems from making repetitive motions. Ergonomics, the study of designing and positioning workplace equipment, can help you avoid health-related problems of using computer systems.

1.4.2 Computer and Information Systems Literacy

In the twenty-first century, business survival and prosperity has continued to become more difficult. For example, increased mergers among former competitors to create global conglomerates, continued downsizing of corporations to focus on their core businesses and to improve efficiencies, efforts to reduce trade barriers, and the globalization of capital all point to the increased internationalization of business organizations and markets. In addition, business issues and decisions are becoming more complex and must be made faster. Whatever career path you take, understanding information systems will help you cope, adapt, and prosper in this challenging environment.

A knowledge of information systems will help you make a significant contribution on the job. It will also help you advance in your chosen career or field. Managers are expected to identify opportunities to implement information systems to improve their business. They are also expected to lead IS projects in their areas of expertise. To meet these personal and organizational goals, you must acquire both computer literacy and information systems literacy. **Computer literacy** is a knowledge of computer systems and equipment and the ways they function. It stresses equipment and devices (hardware), programs and instructions (software), databases, and telecommunications.

Information systems literacy goes beyond knowing the fundamentals of computer systems and equipment. **Information systems literacy** is the knowledge of how data and information are used by individuals, groups, and organizations. It includes knowledge of computer technology and the broader range of information systems. Most important, however, it encompasses how and why this technology is applied in business. Knowing about various types of hardware and software is an example of computer literacy. Knowing how to use hardware and software to increase profits, cut costs, improve productivity, and increase customer satisfaction is an example of information systems literacy. Information systems literacy can involve recognizing how and why people (managers, employees, stockholders, and others) use information systems; being familiar with organizations, decision-making approaches, management levels, and information needs; and understanding how organizations can use computers and information systems to achieve their goals. Knowing how to deploy transaction processing, management information, decision support, and expert systems to help an organization achieve its goals is a key aspect of information systems literacy.

> **computer literacy** Knowledge of computer systems and equipment and the ways they function; it stresses equipment and devices (hardware), programs and instructions (software), databases, and telecommunications.
>
> **information systems literacy** Knowledge of how data and information are used by individuals, groups, and organizations.

1.4.3 Information Systems in the Functional Areas of Business

Information systems are used in all functional areas and operating divisions of business. In finance and accounting, information systems forecast revenues and business activity, determine the best sources and uses of funds, manage cash and other financial resources, analyze investments, and perform audits to make sure that the organization is financially sound and that all financial reports and documents are accurate. Sales and marketing use information systems to develop new goods and services (product analysis), select the best location for production and distribution facilities (place or site analysis), determine the best advertising and sales approaches (promotion analysis), and set product prices to get the highest total revenues (price analysis).

In manufacturing, information systems process customer orders, develop production schedules, control inventory levels, and monitor product quality. In addition, information systems help to design products (computer-assisted design, or CAD), manufacture items (computer-assisted manufacturing, or CAM), and integrate machines or pieces of equipment (computer-integrated manufacturing, or CIM). Human resource management uses information systems to screen applicants, administer performance tests to employees, monitor employee productivity, and more. Legal information systems analyze product liability and warranties and help to develop important legal documents and reports.

1.4.4 Information Systems in Industry

In addition to being used in every department in a company, information systems are used in almost every industry or field in business. The airline industry develops Internet auction sites to offer discount fares and increase revenue. Investment firms use information systems to analyze stocks, bonds, options, the futures market, and other financial instruments, and provide improved services to their customers. Banks use information systems to help make sound loans and good investments, as well as to provide online check payment for account holders. The transportation industry uses information systems to schedule trucks and trains to deliver goods and services at the lowest cost. Publishing companies use information systems to analyze markets and to develop and publish newspapers, magazines, and books. Healthcare organizations use information systems to diagnose illnesses, plan medical treatment, track patient records, and bill patients. Retail companies are using the web to take orders and provide customer service support. Retail companies also use information systems to help market products and services, manage inventory levels, control the supply chain, and forecast demand. Power management and utility companies use information systems to monitor and control power generation and usage. Professional services firms employ information systems to improve the speed and quality of services they provide to customers. Management consulting firms use intranets and extranets to offer information on products, services, skill levels, and past engagements to their consultants. These industries are discussed in more detail as we continue through the book.

1.5 Global Challenges in Information Systems

Changes in society as a result of increased international trade and cultural exchange, often called globalization, have always had a big impact on organizations and their information systems. In his book *The World Is Flat,* Thomas Friedman describes three eras of globalization (see Table 1.2).[16] According to Friedman, we have progressed from the globalization of countries to the globalization of multinational corporations and individuals. Today, people in remote areas can use the Internet to compete with, and contribute to, other people, the largest corporations, and entire countries. These workers are empowered by high-speed Internet access, making the world seem smaller and effectively levelling the global playing field. In the Globalization 3 era, designing a new airplane or computer can be separated into smaller subtasks and then completed by a person or small group that can do the best job. These workers can be located in India, China, Russia, Europe, and other areas of the world. The subtasks can then be combined or reassembled into the complete design. This approach can be used to prepare tax returns, diagnose a patient's medical condition, fix a broken computer, and many other tasks.

Today's information systems have led to greater globalization. High-speed Internet access and networks that can connect individuals and organizations around the world create more international opportunities. Global markets have expanded. People and companies can get products and services from around the world, instead of around the corner or across town. These opportunities, however, introduce numerous obstacles and issues, including challenges involving culture, language, and many others.

Table 1.2 Eras of Globalization

Era	Dates	Characterized by
Globalization 1	Late 1400–1800	Countries with the power to explore and influence the world
Globalization 2	1800–2000	Multinational corporations that have plants, warehouses, and offices around the world
Globalization 3	2000–today	Individuals from around the world who can compete and influence other people, corporations, and countries by using the Internet and powerful technology tools

■ *Cultural challenges:* Countries and regional areas have their own cultures and customs that can significantly affect individuals and organizations involved in global trade.

■ *Language challenges:* Language differences can make it difficult to translate exact meanings from one language to another.

■ *Time and distance challenges:* Time and distance issues can be difficult to overcome for individuals and organizations involved with global trade in remote locations. Large time differences make it difficult to talk to people on the other side of the world. With long distance, it can take days to get a product, a critical part, or a piece of equipment from one location to another location.

■ *Infrastructure challenges:* High-quality electricity and water might not be available in certain parts of the world. Telephone services, Internet connections, and skilled employees might be expensive or not readily available.

■ *Currency challenges:* The value of different currencies can vary significantly over time, making international trade more difficult and complex.

■ *Product and service challenges:* Traditional products that are physical or tangible, such as a car or bicycle, can be difficult to deliver to the global market. However, electronic products (e-products) and electronic services (e-services) can be delivered to customers electronically, over the phone, networks, through the Internet, or other electronic means. Software, music, books, manuals, and help and advice can all be delivered over the Internet.

■ *Technology transfer issues:* Most governments don't allow certain military-related equipment and systems to be sold to some countries. Even so, some believe that foreign companies are stealing the intellectual property, trade secrets, copyrighted materials, and counterfeiting products and services.[17]

■ *National laws:* Every country have a set of laws that must be obeyed by citizens and organizations operating in the country. These laws can deal with a variety of issues, including trade secrets, patents, copyrights, protection of personal or financial data, privacy, and much more. Laws restricting how data enters or exits a country are often called 'trans-border data-flow laws'. Keeping track of these laws and incorporating them into the procedures and computer systems of multinational and trans-national organizations can be very difficult and time consuming, requiring expert legal advice.

■ *Trade agreements:* Countries often enter into trade agreements with each other. The EU has trade agreements among its members.[18] The North American Free Trade Agreement (NAFTA) and the Central American Free Trade Agreement (CAFTA) are other examples.[19] Others include the Australia–United States Free Trade Agreement and agreements between Bolivia and Mexico, Canada and Costa Rica, Canada and Israel, Chile and Korea, Mexico and Japan, the U.S. and Jordan, and many others.[20]

Summary

The value of information is directly linked to how it helps decision makers achieve the organizational goals. Information systems are used in almost every imaginable career area. Regardless of your chosen career, you will find that information systems are indispensable tools to help you achieve your goals. Learning about information systems can help you get your first job, earn promotions, and advance your career.

Information is a collection of facts. To be valuable, information must have several characteristics: It should be accurate, complete, economical to produce, flexible, reliable, relevant, simple to understand, timely, verifiable, accessible, and secure. The value of information is directly linked to how it helps people achieve their organization's goals.

Computers and information systems are constantly making it possible for organizations to improve the way they conduct business. A system is a set of elements that interact to accomplish a goal or set of objectives. The components of a system include inputs, processing mechanisms, and outputs. A system uses feedback to monitor and control its operation to make sure that it continues to meet its goals and objectives.

System performance is measured by its efficiency and effectiveness. Efficiency is a measure of what is produced divided by what is consumed; effectiveness measures the extent to which a system achieves its goals. A systems performance standard is a specific objective.

Knowing the potential impact of information systems and having the ability to put this knowledge to work can result in a successful personal career, organizations that reach their goals, and a society with a higher quality of life. Information systems are sets of interrelated elements that collect (input), manipulate and store (process), and disseminate (output) data and information. Input is the activity of capturing and gathering new data, processing involves converting or transforming data into useful outputs, and output involves producing useful information. Feedback is the output that is used to make adjustments or changes to input or processing activities.

The components of a computer-based information system (CBIS) include hardware, software, databases, telecommunications and the Internet, people, and procedures. The types of CBISs that organizations use can be classified into: (1) e-commerce and m-commerce, TPS and ERP systems, (2) MIS and DSS, and (3) specialized business information systems. The key to understanding these types of systems begins with learning their fundamentals.

E-commerce involves any business transaction executed electronically between parties such as companies (business to business), companies and consumers (business to consumer), business and the public sector, and consumers and the public sector. The major volume of e-commerce and its fastest-growing segment is business-to-business

transactions that make purchasing easier for big corporations. E-commerce also offers opportunities for small businesses to market and sell at a low cost worldwide, thus allowing them to enter the global market right from start-up. M-commerce involves 'anytime, anywhere' computing that relies on wireless networks and systems.

The most fundamental system is the transaction processing system (TPS). A transaction is any business-related exchange. The TPS handles the large volume of business transactions that occur daily within an organization. An enterprise resource planning (ERP) system is a set of integrated programs that can manage the vital business operations for an entire multi-site, global organization. A management information system (MIS) uses the information from a TPS to generate information useful for management decision making.

A decision support system (DSS) is an organized collection of people, procedures, databases, and devices that help make problem-specific decisions. A DSS differs from an MIS in the support given to users, the emphasis on decisions, the development and approach, and the system components, speed, and output.

Specialized business information systems include knowledge management, artificial intelligence, expert, and virtual reality systems. Knowledge management systems are organized collections of people, procedures, software, databases, and devices used to create, store, share, and use the organization's knowledge and experience. Artificial intelligence (AI) includes a wide range of systems in which the computer takes on the characteristics of human intelligence. Robotics is an area of artificial intelligence in which machines perform complex, dangerous, routine, or boring tasks, such as welding car frames or assembling computer systems and components. Vision systems allow robots and other devices to have 'sight' and to store and process visual images. Natural language processing involves computers interpreting and acting on verbal or written commands in English, Spanish, or other human languages. Learning systems let computers learn from past mistakes or experiences, such as playing games or making business decisions, while neural networks is a branch of artificial intelligence that allows computers to recognize and act on patterns or trends. An expert system (ES) is designed to act as an expert consultant to a user who is seeking advice about a specific situation. Originally, the term 'virtual reality' referred to immersive virtual reality, in which the user becomes fully immersed in an artificial, computer-generated 3D world. Virtual reality can also refer to applications that are not fully immersive, such as mouse-controlled navigation through a 3D environment on a graphics monitor, stereo viewing from the monitor via stereo glasses, stereo projection systems, and others.

System users, business managers, and information systems professionals must work together to build a successful information system. Systems development involves creating or modifying existing business systems. The major steps of this process and their goals include systems investigation (gain a clear understanding of what the problem is), systems analysis (define what the system must do to solve the problem), systems design (determine exactly how the system will work to meet the business needs), systems implementation (create or acquire the various system components defined in the design step), and systems maintenance and review (maintain and then modify the system so that it continues to meet changing business needs).

Information systems must be applied thoughtfully and carefully so that society, business, and industry can reap their enormous benefits. Information systems play a fundamental and ever-expanding role in society, business, and industry. But their use can also raise serious security, privacy, and ethical issues. Effective information systems can have a major impact on corporate strategy and organizational success. Businesses around the globe are enjoying better safety and service, greater efficiency and effectiveness, reduced expenses, and improved decision making and control because of information systems. Individuals who can help their businesses realize these benefits will be in demand well into the future.

Computer and information systems literacy are prerequisites for numerous job opportunities, and not only in the IS field. Computer literacy is knowledge of computer systems and equipment, and information systems literacy is knowledge of how data and information are used by individuals, groups, and organizations. Today, information systems are used in all the functional areas of business, including accounting, finance, sales, marketing, manufacturing, human resource management, and legal information systems. Information systems are also used in every industry, such as airlines, investment firms, banks, transportation companies, publishing companies, healthcare, retail, power management, professional services, and more.

Self-Assessment Test

1 A(n) _____ is a set of interrelated components that collect, manipulate, and disseminate data and information and provide a feedback mechanism to meet an objective.

2 A(n) _____ is a set of elements or components that interact to accomplish a goal.

3 What is a measure of what is produced divided by what is consumed?

   a. efficiency
   b. effectiveness
   c. performance
   d. productivity

4 Graphs, charts, and figures are examples of physical models. True or False?

5 A(n) _____ consists of hardware, software, databases, telecommunications, people, and procedures.

6 Computer programs that govern the operation of a computer system are called _____.

   a. feedback
   b. feedforward
   c. software
   d. transaction processing systems

7 What is an organized collection of people, procedures, software, databases, and devices used to create, store, share, and use the organization's experience and knowledge?

   a. TPS (transaction processing system)
   b. MIS (management information system)
   c. DSS (decision support system)
   d. KMS (knowledge management system)

8 _____ involves anytime, anywhere commerce that uses wireless communications.

9 What determines how a new system will work to meet the business needs defined during systems investigation?

a. systems implementation
b. systems review
c. systems development
d. systems design

10 _____ literacy is a knowledge of how data and information are used by individuals, groups, and organizations.

Review Questions

1 What is an information system? Explain some of the ways in which information systems are changing our lives.

2 Define the term 'system'. Give several examples.

3 What are the components of any information system?

4 What is feedback? What are possible consequences of inadequate feedback?

5 What is a computer-based information system? What are its components?

6 Identify three functions of a transaction processing system.

7 What is the difference between an intranet and an extranet?

8 What is m-commerce? Describe how it can be used.

9 Identify three elements of artificial intelligence.

10 Identify the steps in the systems development process and state the goal of each.

Discussion Questions

1 Describe how information systems are used in your college or university.

2 Explain using examples the difference between e-commerce and m-commerce.

3 What is the difference between an MIS and a DSS?

4 Discuss the potential use of virtual reality to enhance the learning experience for new automobile drivers. How might such a system operate? What are the benefits and potential disadvantages of such a system?

5 Discuss how information systems are linked to the business objectives of an organization.

Web Exercises

1 Throughout this book, you will see how the Internet provides a vast amount of information to individuals and organizations. We will stress the World Wide Web, or simply the Web, which is an important part of the Internet. Most large universities and organizations have an address on the Internet, called a website or home page. The address of the website for this publisher is www.cengage.co.uk/stair. You can gain access to the Internet through a browser, such as Microsoft Internet Explorer or Safari. Using an Internet browser, go to the Cengage Learning website. Try to obtain information on this book. You might be asked to develop a report or send an e-mail message to your instructor about what you found.

2 Go to an Internet search engine, such as www.google.co.uk, and search for information about knowledge management. Write a brief report that summarizes what you found and the companies that provide knowledge management products.

3 Using the Internet, search for information on the use of information systems in a company or organization that interests you. How does the organization use technology to help accomplish its goals?

Case One

Shroff International Travel Care Opens Door to Philippines

In many markets, large superstores are seriously threatening the livelihood of small local business owners. This is true online as well. How can a local travel agency compete with Travelocity, Expedia, and Priceline? One answer lies in finding your unique niche.

Shroff International Travel Care, Incorporated (SITCI) found its niche. SITCI is a small travel agency with two offices in and near Manila in the Philippines. SITCI prides itself on its extensive knowledge of travel in the region, and its high level of customer satisfaction. SITCI believes that it can provide customers with better deals, more effective service, and more options than the big online travel companies.

SITCI recently decided to automate their reservations system through a web-based service. 'If you take a look at the reservations process in the travel industry, most of them are excellent candidates for automation,' states Arjun Shroff, CEO and managing director of the company. Taking the business online provides several advantages: (1) Shroff can present travel options to customers in a more organized manner to be viewed anytime, (2) the website provides self-service for customers to book their own flights, hotels, and ground transportation, and (3) the website transforms the business from a local entity to a global entity.

The website (www.airlinecenter.info) provides deals and information on tour packages, resorts and hotels, visa applications, airline reservations, embassy listings, and limousine services. Airline reservations are provided through the Amadeus global travel distribution system. Amadeus is a global provider of IT applications designed for the travel and tourism industry. Amadeus also provides the transaction processing system that allows customers to pay for flights and accommodations through SITCI's website.

The new system has freed up time for SITCI travel agents to work on the more complicated reservations and ticketing work. 'Information technology allows our agency to enhance our product and service offerings, provide better and modern service to our existing customers, and even reach out to new customers. You simply cannot do without IT today,' Shroff said.

Mr. Shroff takes his national responsibilities seriously and believes that taking his business online will help move the country forward. 'We have to be very creative and innovative in attracting tourists to the Philippines; sincerity in dealings, continuous presence in all local and international travel trade-related shows will keep the country on the go,' Mr. Shroff said. Arjun Shroff trained with the International Air Transport Associations and Universal Federation of Travel Agents Association (IATA/UFTA) in Switzerland and has spent 29 years in the travel industry in various countries.

Questions

1 Tour the www.airlinecenter.info website. Who do you think this website is primarily designed to assist – local customers or global customers? Do you think SITCI have the right customer in mind? Explain your answer.

2 How does www.airlinecenter.info empower SITCI travel agents to provide better personal service to customers?

3 How might SITCI further develop its website to provide unique services to the global market that could not be provided by the big online companies?

4 If you were planning a trip to tour the Philippines, who would you rather work with, Expedia.co.uk or SITCI? Explain your answer.

SOURCES: Jenalyn Rubio, 'Local travel company invests in online reservation system', *Computerworld Philippines*, February 23, 2006, www.itnetcentral.com/computerworld/default.asp. Shroff International Travel Care Incorporated (SITCI) website, February 23, 2006, www.airlinecenter.info.

Case Two

Nissan's 180-Degree Turn with Parts Distribution

In the early 1990s, Nissan Motor Company, Ltd. was highly respected as Japan's number two automotive company. In the mid-1990s, Nissan suffered an unfortunate series of events that overwhelmed the company with debt and nearly put it out of business. The company was revived thanks to a buy-in from Renault Motors and a new CEO named Carlos Ghosen. At the turn of the millennium, Nissan was working hard to reverse their downward spiral with a recovery program called 'Nissan 180', the code name for the 180-degree turn that was required of the business.

One key to turning around Nissan's decline was the complete re-engineering of its North American parts distribution system – the pipeline that supplied parts to its 1300 North American dealers. This information system was extremely complex, tracking 1.75 billion parts in transit at any point in time – approaching one trillion parts per year. Nissan knew that their distribution system was fraught with inefficiencies that detracted from their customer satisfaction ratings.

Nissan's 'fill rate', its ability to fulfil their dealers' inventory needs, was measured at 95 percent while its key competitor's fill rate was at 99 percent. Although this might not seem a big difference, it indicates that 5 percent of Nissan customers who dropped off their vehicles for repair had to rent a car and wait several days for the repair to be completed due to the unavailability of parts.

To fix the system, Nissan reduced the number of parts suppliers it used from 700 to 350. Then it worked to improve the flow of parts from those suppliers. The focus was on delivering the right parts to the right dealers at the right time. This area of business is called 'supply chain management'. Information systems are highly valued for their ability to streamline supply chain management. Nissan searched for the right information system to help with

its supply chain. It ended up choosing a solution provided by two companies: IBM and Viewlocity Inc.

Viewlocity provided its Control Tower software, a popular supply chain visibility and event management system. IBM worked to integrate the software solution into Nissan's current information systems and into those of Nissan suppliers. The Control Tower software let Nissan watch inventories more closely, order from suppliers earlier, and plan ahead. The results for Nissan have been significant: It has reduced procurement costs by 22 percent; increased on-time deliveries; improved communication between supplier, carrier, and dealer; and improved customer satisfaction. It now projects a return on investment of up to 68 percent in three years.

Nissan's investment in solving one small problem in its business processes provides insight into the complexity of evaluating and developing information systems in today's businesses. The smooth flow of information in an organization has a dramatic effect on a business's ability to compete.

Questions

1 What was the problem Nissan was trying to solve? Explain how information systems helped solve this problem.

2 Identify the input and output for this system, and the processing that the system does. What would be appropriate feedback for this system?

3 Using the categories described in the section of this chapter on business information systems, what sort of information system did Nissan use?

4 List some other industries that might benefit from a similar system.

SOURCES: 'Nissan North America scores impressive gains in getting parts to dealers', *IBM Success Stories,* October 7, 2005, www.ibm.com/us/. Nissan Corporate Information, February 19, 2006, www.nissan-global.com/EN/COMPANY, *Viewlocity* on the Web, February 19, 2006, www.viewlocity.com.

Case Three

Discovery Communications Digs Out of Mountains of Documents

Discovery Communications, Inc. (DCI) is the leading global real-world media and entertainment company. DCI presents real-world content through documentaries and television programs over the Discovery Channel and many other network brands in 160 countries and 35 languages. DCI's unique brand of programming has been combining education with entertainment since 1985.

Like all global corporations, DCI works hard to distribute mission-critical information and materials to its 5000-person global workforce. Unknown to most television viewers, each program produced involves a significant amount of legal and strategic paperwork; on average, this amounts to a six-inch stack of production documents for every program. The paperwork assists DCI in maintaining production lifecycles and articulating the legal rights of ownership. Creating and accessing these documents was a cumbersome and tedious chore for DCI personnel. The documents were stored at various locations, which made searches for documents time consuming. Once located, it was difficult to tell if the document was current and up to date. DCI needed a system that would allow employees at any location to access up-to-date production documents for its programs without any time delay.

This type of business problem falls under the information system heading of 'knowledge management'. Knowledge management, or KM, is a term used to identify systems that collect, transfer, secure, and manage knowledge in terms of resources, documents, and people skills within an organization. Successful knowledge management systems help an organization make the best use of that knowledge. DCI required a special type of KM system that focused on document management. Fortunately for them, KM is popular in industry today and many companies were eager to provide a solution for DCI's problem.

DCI worked with Carefree Technologies (an IBM partner company acquired by Integro, Inc.) for their document management system. Carefree Technologies turned to IBM's Lotus Domino Document Manager system, a document management solution that would centralize and streamline the process of document creation, filing, management, and retrieval.

Carefree Technologies and DCI agreed on IBM's WebSphere Portal as the primary user interface for the document management system. As the name implies, WebSphere would act as a web-based interface to the database of documents and allow Carefree Technology's development team to customize the system for DCI's needs. A portal is an application that provides access to a commonly used information system and communication tools from one central interface, typically a web page.

Carefree Technology's developers found it easy to merge the document management system with other portal services such as news, information, and communications tools. The final product goes beyond the original hopes and expectations for the system. The portal helps employees track and manage the television production process and easily find the documents they need. In addition, employees can use links to external websites and a news service from LexisNexis to keep abreast of the latest trends in the television industry. Through the integration and customization of IBM's systems, Carefree Technologies and DCI's IT staff have enhanced its portal by integrating it with other business tools, instant messaging, and web conferencing to further enhance productivity levels.

Questions

1 What companies were involved in developing DCI's new system? What role did each company play in the development process?

2 What is the purpose of a corporate portal? What convenience does DCI's new portal provide for its employees?

3 Why do you think knowledge management is so popular today? What advantages can it provide a company?

4 What were the most important steps in organizing the millions of documents in DCI's systems? Why?

SOURCES: 'Discovery Communications Unifies Working Environment with IBM Portal and Enterprise Document Management Solution', *IBM Success Stories*, August 24, 2005, www.ibm.com. 'Volantis Chosen by Discovery to Deliver Global Mobile Portal', *M2 Presswire*, March 1, 2005, www.lexis-nexis.com. Discovery Communications, Inc. corporate home page, accessed February 23, 2006, http://corporate.discovery.com/.

Notes

1 Schupak, Amanda, 'The Bunny Chip', *Forbes,* August 15, 2005, p. 53.

2 Brennan, Peter, 'IBM Claims Fastest Computer', *Rocky Mountain News,* June 14, 2005, p. 6B.

3 Port, Otis, 'Desktop Factories', *Business Week,* May 2, 2005, p. 22.

4 Barron, Kelly, 'Hidden Value', *Fortune,* June 27, 2005, p. 184[B].

5 Yun, Samean, 'New 3G Cell Phones Aim to Be Fast', *Rocky Mountain News,* August 1, 2005, p. 1B.

6 Tynan, Dan, 'Singing the Blog Electric', *PC World,* August 2005, p. 120.

7 Mossberg, Walter, 'Device Lets You Watch Shows on a Home TV, TiVo from Elsewhere', *Wall Street Journal,* June 30, 2005, p. B1.

8 Anthes, Gary, 'Supply Chain Whirl', *Computerworld,* June 8, 2005, p. 27.

9 Majchrzak, Ann, et al., 'Perceived Individual Collaboration Know-How Development', *Information Systems Research,* March 2005, p. 9.

10 Darroch, Jenny, 'Knowledge Management, Innovation, and Firm Performance', *Journal of Knowledge Management,* Vol. 9, No. 3, March 2005, p. 101.

11 Staff, 'Nissan Developing Smart Cars', *CNN Online,* March 1, 2005.

12 Kurzweil, Ray, 'Long Live AI', *Forbes,* August 15, 2005, p. 30.

13 Staff, 'Tax Credit Fiasco Costs EDS £71m', bbc.co.uk, November 22, 2005.

14 Hess, H.M., 'Aligning Technology and Business', *IBM Systems Journal,* Vol. 44, No. 1, 2005, p. 25.

15 Cavusoglu, Huseyin, et al., 'The Value of Intrusion Detection Systems in Information Technology Security Architecture', *Information Systems Research,* March 2005, p. 28.

16 Friedman, Thomas, 'The World Is Flat', *Farrar, Straus and Giroux,* 2005, p. 488.

17 Balfour, Frederik, 'Invasion of the Brain Snatchers', *Business Week,* May 9, 2005, p. 24.

18 Europa – The European Union On-Line (website), www.europa.eu.int, January 15, 2006.

19 Smith, Geri, et al., 'Central America Is Holding Its Breath', *Business Week,* June 20, 2005, p. 52.

20 SICE – Foreign Trade Information System (website), www.sice.oas.org/tradee.asp, January 15, 2006.

02

Information Systems in Organizations

Principles

The use of information systems to add value to the organization is strongly influenced by organizational structure, and the organization's attitude and ability to change.

Because information systems are so important, businesses need to be sure that improvements to existing systems, or completely new systems help lower costs, increase profits, improve service, or achieve a competitive advantage.

Cooperation between business managers and IS personnel is the key to unlocking the potential of any new or modified system.

Learning Objectives

- Identify the value-adding processes in the supply chain and describe the role of information systems within them.
- Provide a clear definition of 'organizational structure' and 'organizational change' and discuss how these affect the implementation of information systems.

- Identify some of the strategies employed to lower costs or improve service.
- Define the term 'competitive advantage' and discuss how organizations are using information systems to achieve such an advantage.
- Discuss how organizations justify the need for information systems.

- Define the types of roles, functions, and careers available in information systems.

Why Learn About Information Systems in Organizations?

The impact that computers have had in organizations cannot be overstated. Office work has been transformed almost beyond all recognition, and many workers could not operate without their computer. All of this happened before the rise in popularity of the Internet as a channel for sharing information. When that happened, the Internet changed everything all over again! No matter what path your career takes, you will almost certainly come into contact with information systems every day. Marketing departments, accounts departments, order processing, shipping and logistics all rely on information systems. Researchers, medical doctors, mechanics – it is difficult to think of a profession where the computer does not play a central role. Even musicians use information systems to get the sound they want. In this chapter, you will see how the use of information systems in every part of organizations can help produce higher-quality products and increase their returns on investment.

2.1 An Introduction to Organizations

An **organization** is a formal collection of people and other resources established to accomplish a set of goals. The primary goal of a for-profit organization is to maximize shareholder value, often measured by the price of the company stock. Non-profit organizations include social groups, religious groups, universities, charities and other organizations that do not have profit as their goal.

organization A formal collection of people and other resources established to accomplish a set of goals.

An organization is a system, which, as you will recall from Chapter 1, means that it has inputs, processing mechanisms, outputs, and feedback. Resources such as materials, people, and money serve as inputs to the organizational system from the environment, go through a transformation mechanism, and then are produced as outputs to the environment. The outputs from the transformation mechanism are usually goods or services, which are of higher relative value than the inputs alone. Through adding value or worth, organizations attempt to achieve their goals.

How does the organizational system increase the value of resources? In the transformation mechanism, subsystems contain processes that help turn inputs into goods or services of increasing value. These processes increase the relative worth of the combined inputs on their way to becoming final outputs. Consider a car maker. Its inputs are the staff it has hired, the assembly equipment it has bought, raw materials such as metal and plastic and pre-assembled components such car radios. The processing that it does is turning the materials into finished vehicles, which are the output. The finished product is worth more than the cost of the components. This amount is the value that has been added.

value chain A series (chain) of activities that includes inbound logistics, warehouse and storage, production, finished product storage, outbound logistics, marketing and sales, and customer service.

The **value chain**, popularized by Michael Porter in his book, *Competitive Strategy*,[1] is a useful tool for analyzing where and how this value gets added. The value chain is a series (chain) of activities that includes inbound logistics, warehouse and storage, production, finished product storage, outbound logistics, marketing and sales, and customer service. The value chain of a manufacturing company is shown in Figure 2.1.

Analyzing value chains when developing information systems often results in efficient transaction processing systems (explained fully in a later chapter), an expanding market, and the sharing of information.[2] The value chain is used to examine what happens to raw material to add value to them before the finished product is sold to customers. Information systems can be focused on those activities that add the most value. The value chain can also reveal linkages between different activites (say marketing and production) which can be exploited using IS (to increase communication between the two for instance).

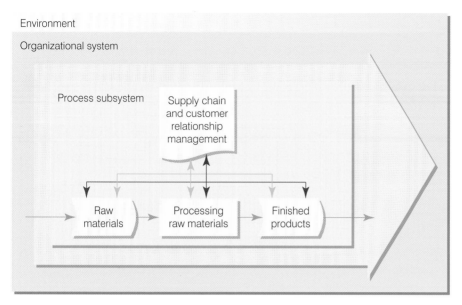

Figure 2.1 The Value Chain of a Manufacturing Company *Managing raw materials, inbound logistics, and warehouse and storage facilities is called 'upstream management', and managing finished product storage, outbound logistics, marketing and sales, and customer service is called 'downstream management'.*

■ Material and physical flow ■ Decision flow □ Value flow ■ Data flow □ Information system(s)

The value chain is just as important (although it can be a little more difficult to apply to) to companies that don't manufacture products, but provide services, such as tax preparers and legal firms. By adding a significant amount of value to their products and services, companies ensure success.

Supply chain management (SCM) and customer relationship management (CRM) are two key parts of managing the value chain. SCM helps determine what supplies are required for the value chain, what quantities are needed to meet customer demand, how the supplies should be processed (manufactured) into finished goods and services, and how the shipment of supplies and products to customers should be scheduled, monitored, and controlled.[3] For example, in the car manufacturing company mentioned on page 36, SCM can identify key suppliers and parts, negotiate with vendors for the best prices and support, make sure that all supplies and parts are available to manufacture cars, and send finished products to dealerships around the country when they are needed. Increasingly, SCM is accomplished using the Internet and electronic marketplaces (e-marketplaces).[4] When an organization has many suppliers, it can use business-to-business exchanges such as eBay Business (http://business.ebay.co.uk) to negotiate good prices and service.

CRM programs help a company manage all aspects of customer encounters, including marketing and advertising, sales, customer service after the sale, and help retain loyal customers. CRM can assist a company with collecting data on customers, contacting customers, informing them about new products, and actively selling products to existing and new customers. Often, CRM software uses a variety of information sources, including sales from retail stores, surveys, e-mail, and Internet browsing habits, to compile comprehensive customer profiles. CRM systems can also collect customer feedback which can be used to design new products and services. Tesco, the UK's largest retail operation, encourages its customers to use its Clubcard, which allows it to collect information on customer transactions. It uses this information to provide outstanding customer service and deliver loyalty rewards and perks to valued customers[5] (see Figure 2.2). In return customers are rewarded with discounts on Tesco products, holidays, and other deals.

Figure 2.2 Tesco
Website *Tesco uses its
website to help with
customer relationship
management.*

What role does an information system play in these processes? A traditional view of information systems holds that organizations use them to control and monitor processes and ensure effectiveness and efficiency. Under this view, the output from a company's information systems is used to make changes to company processes. These changes could involve using different raw materials (inputs), designing new assembly-line procedures (product transformation), or developing new products and services (outputs). Here, the information system is external to the process and serves to monitor or control it.

A more contemporary view however, holds that information systems are often so intimately involved that they are part of the process itself. From this perspective, the information system plays an integral role in the process, whether providing input, aiding product transformation, or producing output. Consider a phone directory business that creates phone books for international businesses. A customer requests a phone directory listing all steel suppliers in Western Europe. Using its information system, the directory business can sort files to find the suppliers' names and phone numbers and organize them into an alphabetical list. The information system itself is an a inseparable part of this process. It does not just monitor the process externally but works as part of the process to transform raw data into a product. In this example, the information system turns input (names and phone numbers) into a sellable output (a phone directory). The same system might also provide the input (the files storing the data) and output (printed pages for the directory).

This latter view provides a new perspective on how and why businesses can use information systems. Rather than attempting to understand information systems independently of the organization, we must consider the potential role of information systems within the process itself, often leading to the discovery of new and better ways to accomplish the process.

2.1.1 Organizational Structures

'Organizational structure' refers to organizational subunits and the way they relate to each other. An organization's structure depends on its approach to management, and can affect how it views and uses information systems. The types of organizational structures typically include traditional, project, team, and virtual.

organizational structure
Organizational subunits and the way they relate to the overall organization.

Traditional Organizational Structure

A **traditional organizational structure**, also called a hierarchical structure, is like a managerial pyramid where the hierarchy of decision making and authority flows from the strategic management at the top, down to operational management and non-management employees. Compared to lower levels, the strategic level, including the managing director of the company and directors, has a higher degree of decision authority, more impact on business goals, and more unique problems to solve (see Figure 2.3).

traditional organizational structure An organizational structure similar to a managerial pyramid, where the hierarchy of decision making and authority flows from strategic management at the top down to operational management and non-management employees. Also called a hierarchical structure.

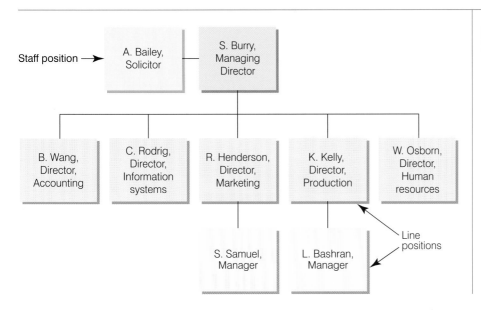

Figure 2.3 A Traditional Organizational Structure

In most cases, department heads report to a managing director or top-level manager. The departments are usually divided according to function and can include marketing, production, information systems, finance and accounting, research and development, and so on. The positions or departments that are directly associated with making, packing, or shipping goods are called line positions. A production manager who reports to a director of production is an example of a line position. Other positions might not be directly involved with the formal chain of command but instead assist a department or area. These are staff positions, such as a solicitor reporting to the managing director.

Today, the trend is to reduce the number of management levels, or layers, in the traditional organizational structure. This type of structure, often called a **flat organizational structure**, empowers employees at lower levels to make decisions and solve problems without needing permission from mid-level managers. **Empowerment** gives employees and their managers more responsibility and authority to make decisions, take action, and have more control over their jobs. For example, an empowered shop assistant can respond to customer requests and problems without needing permission

flat organizational structure An organizational structure with a reduced number of management layers.

empowerment Giving employees and their managers more responsibility and authority to make decisions, take certain actions, and have more control over their jobs.

2

from a manager. In a factory, empowerment might mean that an assembly-line worker can stop production to correct a problem before the product is passed to the next station.

Information systems can be a key element in empowering employees because they provide the information employees need to make decisions. The employees might also be empowered to develop or use their own personal information systems, such as a simple forecasting model or spreadsheet.

Project and Team Organizational Structures

A **project organizational structure** is centred on major products or services. For example, in a manufacturing firm that produces baby food and other baby products, each line is produced by a separate unit. Traditional functions such as marketing, finance, and production are positioned within these major units (see Figure 2.4). Many project teams are temporary – when the project is complete, the members go on to new teams formed for another project.

project organizational structure
A structure centred on major products or services.

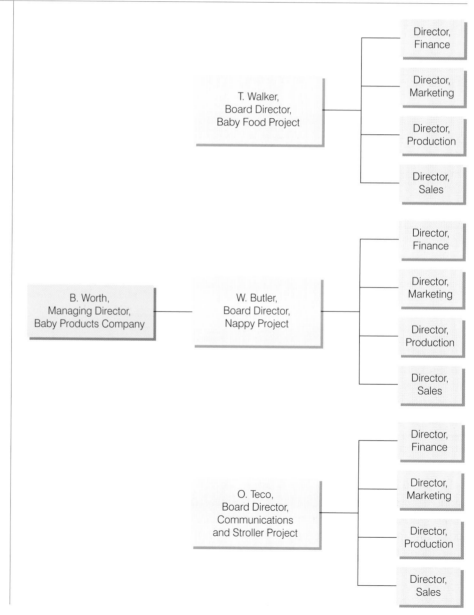

Figure 2.4 A Project Organizational Structure

The **team organizational structure** is centred on work teams or groups. In some cases, these teams are small; in others, they are very large. Typically, each team has a leader who reports to an upper-level manager. Depending on its tasks, the team can be temporary or permanent. A healthcare company, for example, can form small teams to organize its administrators, physicians, and others to work with individual patients.

team organizational structure A structure centred on work teams or groups.

Virtual Organizational Structure

A **virtual organizational structure** is made up of individuals, teams, or complete business units that work with other individuals, teams, or complete business units in different geographic locations. This almost always requires the use of the Internet (or other telecommunications) and the teams can exist for a few weeks or years. The people involved might be in different countries and operating in different time zones. In other words, virtual organizational structures allow people who work together to be separated by location and time.

virtual organizational structure A structure that employs individuals, groups, or complete business units in geographically dispersed areas that can last for a few weeks or years, often requiring telecommunications or the Internet.

The people might never meet physically, which explains the use of the word 'virtual'. In Chapter 10, we will examine some of the technologies that make this form of collaborative work possible. Despite their physical separation, members of a virtual organization can collaborate on any aspect of a project, such as supplying raw materials, producing goods and services, and delivering goods and services to the marketplace.

A company can use a virtual organizational structure with its own dispersed workers who have distinct skills and abilities to reduce costs. PriceWaterhouseCoopers, a global accounting giant, uses virtual teams of 5 to 50 people in the learning and education department.[6] According to Peter Nicolas, the company's Learning Solutions manager, 'Virtual teaming is the norm for us'. The company takes advantage of software and technology, including Microsoft Live Meeting, Centra Software's Virtual-Classroom Application, and Lotus Notes from IBM, to help the teams work from distant locations.

In addition to reducing costs or increasing revenues, a virtual organizational structure can provide an extra level of security. For instance, dispersing employees and using a virtual structure can provide an ability to deal with a disaster at the primary location. If this happened, the company would still have sufficient employees at other locations to keep the business running. Today's workers are performing company work at home, at a customer's location, in coffee shops, on pleasure boats, and at convenient work centres in suburbia. People can work at any time. Using the Internet and e-mail, workers can put the finishing touches on a new business proposal in Europe or Asia, while co-workers in North America are sleeping.

Successful virtual organizational structures share key characteristics. One strategy is to have in-house employees concentrate on the firm's core businesses and use virtual employees, groups, or businesses to do everything else. Using information systems to manage the activities of a virtual structure is essential, often requiring specialized software to coordinate joint work. Even with sophisticated IS tools though, teams may still need face-to-face meetings, especially at the beginning of new projects.

2.1.2 Organizational Change

Most organizations are constantly undergoing change, both minor and major. The need for **organizational change** can be caused by internal factors, such as those initiated by employees at all levels, or external factors, such as activities wrought by competitors, stockholders, new laws, community regulations, natural occurrences (such as hurricanes), and general economic conditions. In the 1990s, the Internet caused massive changes in the way millions of organizations did business.

organizational change The responses that are necessary so that for-profit and non-profit organizations can plan for, implement, and handle change.

2

Change can be sustaining or disruptive. Sustaining change such as new or cheaper production equipment can help an organization improve its operation. For example, many factories are now able to use robots because prices for robots are falling and their useful lifetime is increasing, leading to a big market in second-hand robots.[7]

Disruptive change, on the other hand, often harms an organization's performance or even puts it out of business. In general, disruptive technologies might not originally have good performance, low cost, or even strong demand. Over time, however, they often replace existing technologies. They can cause good, stable companies to fail when they don't change or adopt the new technology. VoIP telephone technology is currently disrupting the business models of established companies such as BT (http://www.bt.com) who, in response, are moving toward providing broadband Internet connections as their main product.

Overcoming resistance to change, especially disruptive change, can be the hardest part of bringing information systems into a business. Occasionally, employees even attempt to sabotage a new information system because they do not want to learn the new procedures and commands. The best way to avoid this resistance is to involve the employees in the decision to implement the change, and consult them on the development or purchase of the information system.

When a company introduces a new information system, a few members of the organization must become agents of change – champions of the new system and its benefits. Understanding the dynamics of change can help them confront and overcome resistance so that the new system can be used to maximum efficiency and effectiveness.

A significant portion of an organization's expenses are used to hire, train, and compensate talented staff. So organizations try to control costs by determining the number of employees they need to maintain high-quality goods and services. Strategies to contain costs are outsourcing, on-demand computing, and downsizing.

outsourcing Contracting with outside professional services to meet specific business needs.

Outsourcing involves contracting with outside professional services to meet specific business needs. Often, companies outsource a specific business process, such as recruiting and hiring employees, developing advertising materials, promoting product sales, or setting up a global telecommunications network. Organizations often outsource a process to focus more closely on their core business – and target limited resources to meet strategic goals. Everton Football Club, for example, has recently outsourced all processing of credit and debit card payments from its stadium shop, online store and call centres because it had become a complex operation that was not part of its core operation. They were able to save time and money by not having to train their staff to do this.[8]

Other reasons for outsourcing are to trim expenses or benefit from the expertise of a service provider. A growing number of organizations, however, are finding that outsourcing does not necessarily lead to reduced costs. One of the primary reasons for cost increases is poorly written contracts that tack on charges from the outsourcing vendor for each additional task. Other potential drawbacks of outsourcing include loss of control and flexibility, overlooked opportunities to strengthen core competency, and low employee morale.

on-demand computing Contracting for computer resources to rapidly respond to an organization's varying workflow. Also called 'on-demand business' and 'utility computing'.

On-demand computing is an extension of the outsourcing approach, and many companies offer on-demand computing to business clients and customers. On-demand computing, also called on-demand business and utility computing, involves rapidly responding to the organization's flow of work as the need for computer resources varies. It is often called 'utility computing' because the organization pays for computing resources from a computer or consulting company just as it pays for electricity from a utility company. This approach treats the information system – including hardware, software, databases, telecommunications, personnel, and other components – more as a service than as separate products. In other words, instead of purchasing hardware, software, and database systems, the organization only pays a fee for the systems it needs at peak times. The approach can save money because the organization does not pay for systems that it doesn't routinely need. It also allows the organization's IS staff to concentrate on more strategic issues.

Downsizing involves reducing the number of employees to cut costs. The term 'rightsizing' is also used. Rather than pick a specific business process to downsize, companies usually look to downsize across the entire company. Downsizing clearly reduces total payroll costs, though employee morale can suffer.

downsizing Reducing the number of employees to cut costs.

Employers need to be open to alternatives for reducing the number of employees and use layoffs as the last resort. It's simpler to encourage people to leave voluntarily through early retirement or other incentives. Voluntary downsizing programs often include a buyout package offered to certain classes of employees (for example, those over 50 years old). The buyout package offers employees certain benefits and cash incentives if they voluntarily retire from the company. Other options are job sharing and transfers.

Organizational learning is closely related to organizational change. According to the concept of organizational learning, organizations adapt to new conditions or alter their practices over time. Assembly-line workers, secretaries, shop assistants, managers, and executives all learn better ways of doing business and incorporate them into their day-to-day activities. Collectively, these adjustments based on experience and ideas are called 'organizational learning'. In some cases, the adjustments can be a radical redesign of business processes, often called 'reengineering'. In other cases, these adjustments can be more incremental, a concept called 'continuous improvement'. Both adjustments reflect an organization's strategy, the long-term plan of action for achieving their goals.

organizational learning The adaptations to new conditions or alterations of organizational practices over time.

Ethical and Societal Issues

Royal Mail Collects Vehicle Telemetry

Royal Mail collects and delivers letters and packages throughout the U.K. Every working day it collects items from 113000 post boxes, 14300 Post Office branches and from some 87000 businesses. These pass through 70 mail centres, 8 regional distribution centres and 3000 delivery offices. A fleet of around 30000 vans and lorries (and 33000 bicycles) are used to deliver them to their final destination, six days a week.

This fleet is costly to maintain and Royal Mail is keen to determine if it can reduce the number of vehicles required. A decision was taken to pilot a scheme to try to improve vehicle usage, reduce costs, and improve quality of service. The pilot was performed with a few hundred vans and involved installing a system in each to record vehicle telemetry. The system consisted of sensors inside each vehicle along with an aerial for data transmission, and analysis tools to examine the data collected.

This data included vehicle location recorded every five minutes, when engines were started and stopped, fuel consumption, amount of acceleration and deceleration, and driver operating hours. The pilot study ran for 14 weeks.

The data was analyzed to minimize vehicle downtime, maximize vehicle usage, manage fuel consumption, manage accidents, and, interestingly, effect a cultural change in the way that vehicle assets were treated.

Prior to the pilot, Royal Mail carefully agreed a set of terms of reference with the Communication Workers Union (CWU), the body that represents postal workers. The CWU were understandably concerned that the data collected should not be used for purposes other than those stated in the agreed terms. Workers may have been worried about having to answer for taking an unusual route one day, perhaps because an accident blocked a

(continued)

road. The system records the new route, but is unable to record the accident that caused the change. Perhaps by the time the data is analyzed the driver will have forgotten the reason for going a different way. Royal Mail will have to overcome concerns such as these if it is to roll the system out to all of its vehicles. In fact, a pilot scheme is a very good way of identifying such concerns.

Questions

1 How much say should employees have in the data that their employer collects about them? Should Royal Mail drivers be worried about downsizing? If the aim of this system was to rightsize the Royal Mail fleet, should employees be told this?

2 Suggest some ways in which the data collected could be analyzed to achieve an increase in the quality of service Royal Mail provides.

3 Even if no workers union existed, why would it still be a good idea for managers to consult employees about the planned introduction of a system such as this?

4 In response to suggestions about installing tracking devices on vehicles (or even people) many respond by saying 'Big Brother is watching you'. What do you think they mean by this, and how would you allay their fears? Maybe you agree with them – explain why.

SOURCES: Royal Mail (website), http://www.royalmail.com/; Communication Workers Union (website), http://www.cwu.org; Vehicle Telemetry Project Terms and Conditions, working document 09-09-05 (website), http://www.cwu.org/uploads/documents/outdoor%20Vehicle%20Telemetry%20TOR.doc.

2.1.3 Reengineering and Continuous Improvement

To stay competitive, organizations must occasionally make fundamental changes in the way they do business. In other words, they must change the activities, tasks, or processes they use to achieve their goals. **Reengineering**, also called 'process redesign' and 'business process reengineering' (BPR), involves the radical redesign of business processes, organizational structures, information systems, and values of the organization to achieve a breakthrough in business results. Reengineering can reduce delivery times, increase product and service quality, enhance customer satisfaction, and increase revenues and profitability. When Mittal Steel South Africa's Vanderbijlpark Plant reengineered its steelmaking operations, introducing new automated systems, it was able to reduce the amount of raw materials used in its processes and increase its output of steel, which was of a higher quality than before. They were also able to reduce processing time and improve plant availability.[9]

reengineering Also known as 'process redesign' and 'business process reengineering' (BPR). The radical redesign of business processes, organizational structures, information systems, and values of the organization to achieve a breakthrough in business results.

In contrast to simply automating the existing work process, reengineering challenges the fundamental assumptions governing their design. It requires finding and vigorously challenging old rules blocking major business process changes. These rules are like anchors weighing down a firm and keeping it from competing effectively. Table 2.1 provides some examples of such rules.

The Northern Ireland Civil Service is introducing a electronic and document records management system (EDRM) to improve its efficiency. Processes have been reengineered so that instead of records being held in different departments and in different formats (on paper, in databases and even in e-mail), a centralized system will provide access to up-to-date and secure information. It is hoped the system will also reduce the amount of paper the service uses.[10]

continuous improvement Constantly seeking ways to improve business processes to add value to products and services.

In contrast to reengineering, the idea of **continuous improvement** is to constantly seek ways to improve business processes and add value to products and services. This continual change will increase customer satisfaction and loyalty and ensure long-term profitability. Manufacturing companies make continual product changes and improvements. Service organizations regularly find ways to provide faster and more effective assistance to customers. By doing so, these companies increase customer loyalty, minimize the chance of customer dissatisfaction, and diminish the opportunity for competitive inroads. Table 2.2 compares these two strategies.

2.1.4 User Satisfaction and Technology Acceptance

To be effective, reengineering and continuous improvement efforts must result in satisfied users and be accepted and used throughout the organization. You can determine the actual usage of an information system by the amount of technology diffusion and infusion.

Technology diffusion is a measure of how widely technology is spread throughout an organization. An organization in which computers and information systems are located in most departments and areas has a high level of technology diffusion. Some online merchants, such as BT (http://www.bt.com), have a high diffusion and use computer systems to perform most of their business functions, including marketing, purchasing, and billing.

technology diffusion A measure of how widely technology is spread throughout the organization.

Technology infusion, on the other hand, is the extent to which technology permeates an area or department. In other words, it is a measure of how deeply embedded technology is in an area of the organization. Some architectural firms, for example, use computers in all aspects of designing a building from drafting

technology infusion The extent to which technology is deeply integrated into an area or department.

Table 2.1 Selected Business Rules that Affect Business Processes

Rule	Original Rationale	Potential Problem
Hold small orders until full lorry load shipments can be assembled	Reduce delivery costs	Customer delivery is slow
Do not accept an order until customer credit is approved	Reduce potential for bad debt	Customer service is poor
Let headquarters make all merchandising decisions	Reduce number of items carried in inventory	Customers perceive organization has limited product selection

Table 2.2 Comparing Business Process Reengineering and Continuous Improvement

Business Process Reengineering	Continuous Improvement
Strong action taken to solve serious problem	Routine action taken to make minor improvements
Top-down change driven by senior executives	Bottom-up change driven by workers
Broad in scope; cuts across departments	Narrow in scope; focus is on tasks in a given area
Goal is to achieve a major breakthrough	Goal is continuous, gradual improvements
Often led by outsiders	Usually led by workers close to the business
Information system integral to the solution	Information systems provide data to guide the improvement team

to final blueprints. The design area, thus, has a high level of infusion. Of course, a firm can have a high level of infusion in one part of its operations and a low level of diffusion overall. The architectural firm might use computers in all aspects of design (high infusion in the design area), but not to perform other business functions, including billing, purchasing, and marketing (low diffusion). Diffusion and infusion often depend on the technology available now and in the future, the size and type of the organization, and the environmental factors that include the competition, government regulations, suppliers, and so on. This is often called the 'technology, organization, and environment' (TOE) framework.[11]

An active research area in IS involves identifying why people accept and use one system, but dislike and therefore don't use, another. One early model, the Technology Acceptance Model (TAM), shows that people will use a system is it is easy to use and useful to them. This in itself is unhelpful to IS developers, however TAM has been the basis for an large body of research that is ongoing, and which hopes to produce more practical results.

Although an organization might have a high level of diffusion and infusion, with computers throughout the organization, this does not necessarily mean that information systems are being used to their full potential.

Information Systems @ Work

Wimbledon on the Web

The All England Lawn Tennis and Croquet Club is responsible for staging the most famous tennis tournament in the world – the Lawn Tennis Championships at Wimbledon. The first competition in 1877 was seen by just a few hundred spectators. Today, nearly 500 000 descend on London each July to try to catch a game between players from over 60 nations. Many millions more keep up with progress on television, radio, and the Internet.

Keeping the Web content up to date during the tournament is a challenge. Fans want up-to-the-minute reports, photographs, video, and commentary. The number of editorial staff increases in the lead up to July and few of them have a background in IT. Therefore, the organizers needed some way to easily and quickly let writers publish material on the website.

Their adopted solution was IBM's Workplace Web Content Management system. This system allows journalists and other writers to enter their articles in rich text format via their Internet browser. The software is designed to have the look and feel of a word processor, something that is familiar to writers. Standard templates are included so that all the articles are formatted the same. Once the writer submits an article, the HTML code (the language most web content is written in) is generated and is passed to the senior editors. They receive the articles and approve them, sending them on to the person who is responsible for uploading them to the Web. This process ensures a consistent, professional look to the entire site, properly ordered content to allow for easy searching by fans, and allows for the removal of many bottlenecks, such as the web master not having the text in the right format.

Crucially, the system separates content and presentation. That is the overriding principle. Writers can create their articles in any way they want without having to concern themselves with technical details such as hyperlinks, HTML, uploading files, etc. On the other hand, the web master can change the templates and have all new articles submitted in the new style. They can edit layouts and have these applied across the entire site easily and quickly while the writers watch the games.

One key benefit of the system was that it is run through a web browser. This means that there was no need to install new software on the writers' laptops, which reduced the complexity of the implementation. In additional benefit, the new publishing environment was run with few servers involved, giving an additional cost saving.

Questions

1 Why were users saisfied with the new system? Would it have been easier just to teach the writers about HTML and let them upload their own files to the Internet? What would be wrong with this approach?

2 What benefits do you think the new system has delivered?

3 Do you think fans really care whether the website has a consistent look? Do you think visitors to any website care if one page on the site has the same look and feel as the other pages? List some of the factors that you think people care about when 'accepting' a website.

4 Could the separation of technical knowledge and domain knowledge be applied in other areas of other organizations?

SOURCES: Wimbledon (website), http://www.wimbledon.org/en_GB/about/index.html, March 12, 2007. IBM Workplace Web Content Management (website), http://www-142.ibm.com/software/workplace/products/product5.nsf/wdocs/homepage, March 12, 2007.

Staff, 'IBM Helps Wimbledon Create a Rich Web Site for Fans Worldwide', http://www-306.ibm.com/software/success/cssdb.nsf/CS/JFTD-6QXKN8?OpenDocument&Site=linuxatibm&cty=en_us, June 20, 2006.

2.1.5 The Applications Portfolio

In Chapter 1, we looked at how information systems can be classified by the management level of the user. The **applications portfolio** is perhaps a more useful classification scheme. It sorts information systems according the contribution they make to the business. According to the applications portfolio, there are four types of system:

1 Support: **Support applications** are nice to have, but not essential. They include things that are convenient but without them, the organization can still conduct business. Typical support applications include electronic diaries and instant messaging software, used to let employees in an office communicate with each other.

2 Key operational: **Key operational applications** are essential. Without them, the organization would not be able to do business. Transaction processing systems, mentioned in Chapter 1 and discussed fully in Chapter 8, are an example. If the checkout system at a Tesco shop malfunctions, Tesco would be unable to sell goods until it was repaired. The website of every e-commerce business is key operational.

3 Strategic: A **strategic application** is an information system that gives a business an advantage over some or all of its competitors. Some ideas for what this advantage might be are discussed later in this chapter in the section on Competitive Advantage (page 48). The term 'strategic' should not be confused with the same term used to describe senior management in a business. A strategic system could appear anywhere in the company hierarchy.

4 Future strategic: A **future strategic application** (also known as a 'potential strategic' or 'high potential' application) is an idea for, or a prototype of, an information system which, if developed, might one day become a strategic system. A company may have ten future strategic systems and decide to only invest in one. This decision is often a judgment call made by senior management. It may be that the technology to develop a future strategic system is currently too expensive and the company is waiting for prices to fall.

applications portfolio A scheme for classifying information systems according to the contribution they make to the organization.

support application Support applications make work more convenient but are not essential.

key operational application Key operational applications are essential. Without them the organization could not conduct business.

strategic application A strategic application gives a firm a competitive advantage.

future strategic application Future strategic applications are ideas for systems which, if fully developed and deployed, might one day become strategic applications.

There is an endless cycle at work with systems starting life in one part of the portfolio, and finishing in another. Typically an innovative, leading company will come up with an idea for a potential strategic system. If they invest it in and, if it is successful, it becomes a strategic system. Their competitors see that they have an advantage and so create their own versions of the system.

Eventually, the system will become industry standard and now be key operational. In the meantime, the innovative company will have had more ideas for future strategic systems, and so the cycle starts again. Companies that see themselves as industry followers rather than industry leaders will not have strategic or future strategic systems in their portfolio.

2.1.6 Success Factors

Many writers have suggested reasons why some information systems are implemented successfully and why others are not. It is of vital importance that a company's information systems are aligned with the company's goals. Misalignment is a frequently cited reason for information systems failure. The main way of achieving **alignment** is for senior managers to consider the business processes they have in place to achieve company goals, and ask what information systems are needed to support these business processes. Less frequently a business, typically a small business or even a single entrepreneur, will consider what technology is available to them and ask what business goals can be achieved with it. In this case, information technology is dictating business strategy instead of business strategy dictating what information technology is used. Both are valid paths to alignment.

alignment When the output from an information system is exactly what is needed to help a company achieve its strategic goals, the two are said to be in alignment.

Other common success factors are:

- Senior management must be committed to the development or purchase of the information system and support it fully.

- End users of the system should be involved as early, and as much as possible, in the development or purchase or the system.

requirements engineering Also known as 'requirements analysis' and 'requirements capture'. Identifying what an information systems is needed (required) to do. Once the requirements have been identified, a solution can then be designed.

- Time must be taken to carefully determine what the system must do, something known as **requirements engineering**. Requirements must be clearly stated and understood and accepted by everyone involved.

- Strong project management in the development or purchase of the information system.

Later on in this text we will examine Joint Application Development, a method for creating IS which places users at the centre of the development.

2.2 Competitive Advantage

A **competitive advantage** is the ability of a firm to outperform its industry, that is, to earn a higher rate of profit than the industry norm[12] and can result from higher-quality products, better customer service, and lower costs. Establishing and maintaining a competitive advantage is complex. An organization often uses its information system to help it do this. Ultimately, it is not how much a company spends on information systems but how it makes and manages investments in technology. Companies can spend less and get more value.

competitive advantage The ability of a firm to outperform its industry, that is, to earn a higher rate of profit than the industry norm.

five-forces model A widely accepted model that identifies five key factors that can lead to attainment of competitive advantage, including (1) the rivalry among existing competitors, (2) the threat of new entrants, (3) the threat of substitute products and services, (4) the bargaining power of buyers, and (5) the bargaining power of suppliers.

2.2.1 Factors that Lead Firms to Seek Competitive Advantage

A number of factors can lead a company to seek to attain a competitive advantage. Michael Porter, a prominent management theorist, suggested a simple but widely accepted model of the competitive forces in an industry, also called the **five-forces model**. A strong force can put a business at a disadvantage and lead it to invest in technology that can weaken it. The five forces are: (1) the rivalry among existing competitors, (2) the threat of new entrants, (3) the threat of substitute products and services, (4) the bargaining power of buyers, and (5) the bargaining power of suppliers. The more these forces combine in any instance, the more likely firms will seek competitive advantage and the more dramatic the results of such an advantage will be.

Given the five market forces just mentioned, Porter and others have proposed a number of strategies to attain competitive advantage, including cost leadership, differentiation, niche strategy, altering the industry structure, creating new products and services, and improving existing product lines and services.[13] In some cases, one of these strategies becomes dominant. For example, with a cost leadership strategy, cost can be the key consideration, at the expense of other factors if need be.

Cost Leadership

The intent of a cost leadership strategy is to deliver the lowest possible products and services. In the U.K., supermarket Asda has used this strategy for years. Cost leadership is often achieved by reducing the costs of raw materials through aggressive negotiations with suppliers, becoming more efficient with production and manufacturing processes, and reducing warehousing and shipping costs. Some companies use outsourcing to cut costs when making products or completing services.

Differentiation

The intent of differentiation as a strategy is to deliver different products and services. This strategy can involve producing a variety of products, giving customers more choices, or delivering higher-quality products and services. Many car companies make different models that use the same basic parts and components, giving customers more options. Other car companies attempt to increase perceived quality and safety to differentiate their products. Some consumers are willing to pay higher prices for vehicles that differentiate on higher quality or better safety.

Niche Strategy

A niche strategy will deliver to only a small, niche market. Porsche, for example, doesn't produce inexpensive estate cars or saloons. It makes high-performance sports cars and four-wheel drives. Rolex only makes high-quality, expensive watches. It doesn't make inexpensive, plastic watches that can be purchased for €20 or less.

Altering the Industry Structure

Changing the industry to become more favourable to the company or organization is another strategy companies use. The introduction of low-fare airline carriers, such as EasyJet, has forever changed the airline industry, making it difficult for traditional airlines to make high profit margins. To fight back, airlines such as British Airways cut their flight prices and started to emphasize their strengths over low-cost airlines in their advertising. These include landing in central airports rather than airports many miles out of the city they supposedly serve, and extra staff and resources to cope if there is a fault with an aircraft, or adverse weather grounds all planes. Creating **strategic alliances** can also alter the industry structure. A strategic alliance, also called a 'strategic partnership', is an agreement between two or more companies that involves the joint production and distribution of goods and services.

strategic alliance (strategic partnership) An agreement between two or more companies that involves the joint production and distribution of goods and services.

Creating New Products and Services

Some companies introduce new products and services periodically or frequently as part of their strategy. This strategy can help a firm gain a competitive advantage, especially in the computer industry and other high-tech businesses. If an organization does not introduce new products and services every few months, the company can quickly stagnate, lose market share, and decline. Companies that stay on top are constantly developing new products and services.

Improving Existing Product Lines and Service

Making real or perceived improvements to existing product lines and services is another strategy. Manufacturers of household products are always advertising 'new and improved' products. In some cases, the improvements are more perceived than real refinements; usually, only minor changes are made to the existing product, such as reducing the amount of sugar in a breakfast cereal. Some mail order companies are improving their service by using Radio Frequency Identification (RFID) tags to identify and track the location of their products as they are shipped from one location to another. Customers and managers can instantly locate products as they are shipped from suppliers to the company, to warehouses, and finally to customers.

Other potentially successful strategies include being the first to market, offering customized products and services, and hiring talented staff, the assumption being that the best people will determine the best products and services to deliver to the market and the best approach to deliver these products and services. Companies can also combine one or more of these strategies.

2.3 Evaluating IS

Once an information system has been implemented, management will want to assess how successful it has been in achieving its goals. Often this is a difficult thing to do, and many businesses do not attempt to take anything more than an informal approach to evaluation.[14] Business can use measurements of productivity, return on investment (ROI), net present value, and other measures of performance to evaluate the contributions their information systems make to their businesses.

2.3.1 Productivity

Developing information systems that measure and control productivity is a key element for most organizations. **Productivity** is a measure of the output achieved divided by the input required. A higher level of output for a given level of input means greater productivity; a lower level of output for a given level of input means lower productivity. The numbers assigned to productivity levels are not always based on labour hours – productivity can be based on factors such as the amount of raw materials used, resulting quality, or time to produce the goods or service. The value of the productivity number is not as significant as how it compares with other time periods, settings, and organizations.

productivity A measure of the output achieved divided by the input required. Productivity = (Output / Input) × 100%.

After a basic level of productivity is measured, an information system can monitor and compare it over time to see whether productivity is increasing. Then a company can take corrective action if productivity drops below certain levels. In addition to measuring productivity, an information system can be used within a process to significantly increase productivity. Thus, improved productivity can result in faster customer response, lower costs, and increased customer satisfaction.

In the late 1980s and early 1990s, overall productivity did not seem to improve as a company increased its investments in information systems. Often called the productivity paradox, this situation troubled many economists who were expecting to see dramatic productivity gains. In the early 2000s, however, productivity again seemed on the rise.

return on investment (ROI) One measure of IS value that investigates the additional profits or benefits that are generated as a percentage of the investment in IS technology.

2.3.2 Return on Investment and the Value of Information Systems

One measure of IS value is **return on investment (ROI)**. This measure investigates the additional profits or benefits that are generated as a percentage of the investment in IS technology. A small business that generates an additional profit of €20 000 for the year as a result of an investment of €100 000 for additional computer equipment and software would have a return on investment of 20 percent (€20 000/€100 000). In many cases, however, it can be difficult to accurately measure ROI.[15]

Earnings Growth

Another measure of IS value is the increase in profit, or earnings growth, it brings. For instance, a mail-order company might install an order-processing system that generates a 7 percent earnings growth compared with the previous year.

Market Share

Market share is the percentage of sales that a product or service has in relation to the total market. If installing a new online catalogue increases sales, it might help a company increase its market share by 20 percent.

Customer Awareness and Satisfaction

Although customer satisfaction can be difficult to quantify, about half of today's best global companies measure the performance of their information systems based on feedback from internal and external users. Some companies use surveys and questionnaires to determine whether the IS investment has increased customer awareness and satisfaction.

Total Cost of Ownership

Another way to measure the value of information systems was developed by the Gartner Group and is called the **total cost of ownership (TCO)**. This approach breaks total costs into areas such as the cost to acquire the technology, technical support, administrative costs, and end-user operations. Other costs in TCO include retooling and training costs. TCO can help to develop a more accurate estimate of the total costs for systems that range from desktop computers to large mainframe systems. Market research groups often use TCO to compare products and services.

total cost of ownership (TCO)
The measurement of the total cost of owning computer equipment, including desktop computers, networks, and large computers.

Return on investment, earnings growth, market share, customer satisfaction, and TCO are only a few measures that companies use to plan for and maximize the value of their IS investments. Regardless of the difficulties, organizations must attempt to evaluate the contributions that information systems make to assess their progress and plan for the future. Information technology and personnel are too important to leave to chance.

Risk

In addition to the return-on-investment measures of a new or modified information system, managers should also consider the risks of designing, developing, and implementing these systems. Information systems can sometimes be costly failures. Some companies, for example, have attempted to implement ERP systems and failed, costing them millions of dollars. In other cases, e-commerce applications have been implemented with little success. The costs of development and implementation can be greater than the returns from the new system.

2.4 Careers in Information Systems

Realizing the benefits of any information system requires competent and motivated IS personnel, and many companies offer excellent job opportunities. Professionals with careers in information systems typically work in an IS department as web developers, computer programmers, systems analysts, database developers and administrators, computer operators, technical support or in other positions. In addition to technical skills, they need skills in written and verbal communication, an understanding of organizations and the way they operate, and the ability to work with people and in groups. Today, many good information, business, and computer science schools require these business and communications skills of their graduates.

In general, IS professionals are charged with maintaining the broadest perspective on organizational goals. Most medium to large organizations manage information resources through an IS department. In smaller businesses, one or more people might manage information resources, with support from outsourced services. As shown in Figure 2.5, the IS department has three primary responsibilities: operations, systems development, and support.

Figure 2.5 The IS Department

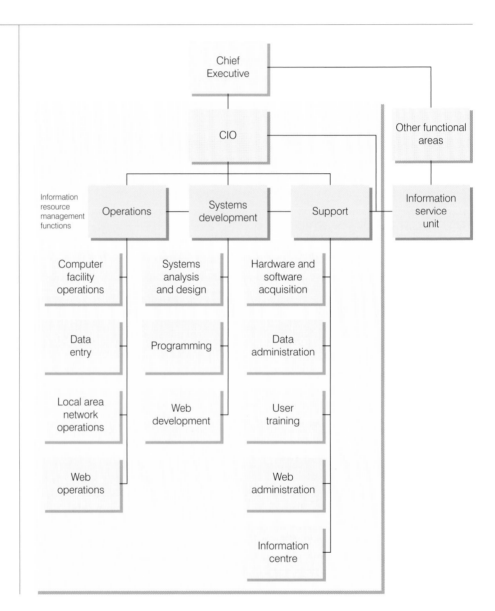

2.4.1 Operations

People in the operations component of a typical IS department work with information systems in corporate or business unit computer facilities. They tend to focus more on the efficiency of IS functions rather than their effectiveness.

System operators primarily run and maintain IS equipment, and are typically trained at technical schools or through on-the-job experience. They are responsible for starting, stopping, and correctly operating mainframe systems, networks, back-up drives, disk devices, printers, and so on. Other operations include scheduling, hardware maintenance, and preparing input and output. Data-entry operators convert data into a form the computer system can use. They can use terminals or other devices to enter business transactions, such as sales orders and payroll data. Increasingly, data entry is being automated – captured at the source of the transaction rather than entered later. In addition, companies might have local area network (LAN) and web operators who run the local network and any websites the company has.

2.4.2 Systems Development

The systems development component of a typical IS department focuses on specific development projects and ongoing maintenance and review. Systems analysts and programmers, for example, address these concerns to achieve and maintain IS effectiveness. The role of a systems analyst is multifaceted. Systems analysts help users determine what outputs they need from the system and construct plans for developing the necessary programs that produce these outputs. Systems analysts then work with one or more programmers to make sure that the appropriate programs are purchased, modified from existing programs, or developed. A computer programmer uses the plans the systems analyst created to develop or adapt one or more computer programs that produce the desired outputs.

With the dramatic increase in the use of the Internet, intranets, and extranets, many companies have web or Internet developers who create effective and attractive websites for customers, internal personnel, suppliers, stockholders, and others who have a business relationship with the company.

2.4.3 Support

The support component of a typical IS department provides user assistance in hardware and software acquisition and use, data administration, user training and assistance, and web administration. In many cases, support is delivered through an information centre.

Because IS hardware and software are costly, a specialized support group often manages computer hardware and software acquisitions. This group sets guidelines and standards for the rest of the organization to follow in making purchases. It must gain and maintain an understanding of available technology and develop good relationships with vendors.

A database administrator focuses on planning, policies, and procedures regarding the use of corporate data and information. For example, database administrators develop and disseminate information about the organization's databases for developers of IS applications. In addition, the database administrator monitors and controls database use.

User training is a key to get the most from any information system, and the support area ensures that appropriate training is available. Training can be provided by internal staff or from external sources. For example, internal support staff can train managers and employees in the best way to enter sales orders, to receive computerized inventory reports, and to submit expense reports electronically. Companies also hire outside firms to help train users in other areas, including the use of word processing, spreadsheets, and database programs.

Web administration is another key area for support staff. With the increased use of the Internet, web administrators are sometimes asked to regulate and monitor Internet use by employees and managers to make sure that it is authorized and appropriate. Web administrators also maintain the organization's website to keep it accurate and current, which can require substantial resources.

The support component typically operates the helpdesk. A helpdesk provides users with assistance, training, application development, documentation, equipment selection and setup, standards, technical assistance, and troubleshooting.

2.4.4 Information Service Units

An information service unit is basically a miniature IS department attached and directly reporting to a functional area in a large organization. Notice the information service unit shown in Figure 2.5. Even though this unit is usually staffed by IS professionals, the project assignments and the resources necessary to accomplish these projects are provided by the functional area to which it reports. Depending on the policies of the organization, the salaries of IS professionals staffing the information service unit might be budgeted to either the IS department or the functional area.

2.4.5 Typical IS Titles and Functions

The organizational chart shown in Figure 2.5 is a simplified model of an IS department in a typical medium or large organization. Many organizations have even larger departments, with increasingly specialized positions such as librarian or quality assurance manager. Smaller firms often combine the roles shown in Figure 2.5 into fewer formal positions.

The Chief Information Officer

The role of the chief information officer (CIO) is to employ an IS department's equipment and personnel to help the organization attain its goals. The CIO is a senior manager concerned with the overall needs of the organization, and sets organization-wide policies, and plans, manages, and acquires information systems. Some of the CIO's top concerns include integrating IS operations with business strategies, keeping up with the rapid pace of technology, and defining and assessing the value of systems development projects. The high level of the CIO position reflects that information is one of the organization's most important resources. A CIO works with other high-level officers of an organization, including the finance director and the executive officer, in managing and controlling total corporate resources. CIOs must also work closely with advisory committees, stressing effectiveness and teamwork and viewing information systems as an integral part of the organization's business processes – not an adjunct to the organization. Thus, CIOs need both technical and business skills.

LAN Administrator

local area network (LAN) A computer network that connects computer systems and devices within a small area, such as an office, home, or several floors in a building.

Local area network (LAN) administrators set up and manage the network hardware, software, and security processes. They manage the addition of new users, software, and devices to the network. They also isolate and fix operations problems. LAN administrators are in high demand and often solve both technical and non-technical problems.

Internet Careers

These careers are in the areas of web operations, web development, and web administration. As with other areas in IS, many top-level administrative jobs are related to the Internet. These career opportunities are found in both traditional companies and those that specialise in the Internet.

Internet jobs within a traditional company include Internet strategists and administrators, Internet systems developers, Internet programmers, and Internet or website operators.

Systems Developers

Systems developers design and write software. Typically developers will be graduates with degrees in technical subjects such as computer science, mathematics or engineering. However, many big employers have graduate recruitment schemes where degree subject is less important than an ability to learn. On such schemes, graduates are taught the skills they need. The skills needed by developers include the ability to design solutions to problems and communicate these solutions to other developers and to users, and the technical skill to create these solutions. Software development can be extremely challenging and exciting.

Often, systems developers are employed to create software to support business goals, such as develop the organization's transaction processing system. Alternatively, systems developers may work in a software house, where the software they write is the product the organization sells. One of the fastest growing areas of software development is the games industry, with many universities now offering degrees in games development.

Other IS Careers

Other IS career opportunities include technical writing (creating technical manuals and user guides), and user interface design.

Often, the people filling IS roles have completed some form of certification. **Certification** is a process for testing skills and knowledge resulting in an endorsement by the certifying authority that an individual is capable of performing a particular job. Certification frequently involves specific, vendor-provided or vendor-endorsed coursework. Popular certification programs include Microsoft Certified Systems Engineer, Certified Information Systems Security Professional (CISSP), Oracle Certified Professional, and many others.

> **certification** A process for testing skills and knowledge, which results in a statement by the certifying authority that states an individual is capable of performing a particular kind of job.

Summary

The use of information systems to add value to the organization is strongly influenced by organizational structure, and the organization's attitude and ability to change. An organization is a formal collection of people and other resources established to accomplish a set of goals. The primary goal of a for-profit organization is to maximize shareholder value. Non-profit organizations include social groups, religious groups, universities, and other organizations that do not have profit as the primary goal.

Organizations are systems with inputs, transformation mechanisms, and outputs. Value-added processes increase the relative worth of the combined inputs on their way to becoming final outputs of the organization. The value chain is a series (chain) of activities that includes (1) inbound logistics, (2) warehouse and storage, (3) production, (4) finished product storage, (5) outbound logistics, (6) marketing and sales, and (7) customer service.

Organizational structure refers to how organizational subunits relate to the overall organization. Several basic organizational structures include traditional, project, team, and virtual. A virtual organizational structure employs individuals, groups, or complete business units in geographically dispersed areas.

These can involve people in different countries operating in different time zones and different cultures. Organizational change deals with how profit and non-profit organizations plan for, implement, and handle change. Change can be caused by internal or external factors. According to the concept of organizational learning, organizations adapt to new conditions or alter practices over time.

Because information systems are so important, businesses need to be sure that improvements to existing systems, or completely new systems help lower costs, increase profits, improve service, or achieve a competitive advantage. Business process reengineering involves the radical redesign of business processes, organizational structures, information systems, and values of the organization, to achieve a breakthrough in results. Continuous improvement to business processes can add value to products and services.

The extent to which technology is used throughout an organization can be a function of technology diffusion, infusion, and acceptance. Technology diffusion is a measure of how widely technology is in place throughout an organization. Technology infusion is the extent to which technology permeates an area or department. User satisfaction with a computer system and the information it generates depends on the quality of the system and the resulting information.

Outsourcing involves contracting with outside professional services to meet specific business needs. This approach allows the company to focus more closely on its core business and to target its limited resources to meet strategic goals. Downsizing involves reducing the number of employees to reduce payroll costs; however, it can lead to unwanted side effects.

Competitive advantage is usually embodied in either a product or service that has the most added value to consumers and that is unavailable from the competition or in an internal system that delivers benefits to a firm not enjoyed by its competition. The five-forces model explains factors that lead firms to seek competitive advantage: The rivalry among existing competitors, the threat of new market entrants, the threat of substitute products and services, the bargaining power of buyers, and the bargaining power of suppliers. Strategies to address these factors and to attain competitive advantage include cost leadership, differentiation, niche strategy, altering the industry structure, creating new products and services, improving existing product lines and services, and other strategies.

Cooperation between business managers and IS personnel is the key to unlocking the potential of any new or modified system. Information systems personnel typically work in an IS department. The chief information officer (CIO) employs an IS department's equipment and personnel to help the organization attain its goals. Systems analysts help users determine what outputs they need from the system and construct the plans needed to develop the necessary programs that produce these outputs. Systems analysts then work with one or more system developers to make sure that the appropriate programs are purchased, modified from existing programs, or developed. The major responsibility of a computer programmer is to use the plans developed by the systems analyst to build or adapt one or more computer programs that produce the desired outputs.

Computer operators are responsible for starting, stopping, and correctly operating mainframe systems, networks, tape drives, disk devices, printers, and so on. LAN administrators set up and manage the network hardware, software, and security processes. Trained personnel are also needed to set up and manage a company's Internet site, including Internet strategists, Internet systems developers, Internet programmers, and website operators. Information systems personnel can also support other functional departments or areas.

In addition to technical skills, IS personnel need skills in written and verbal communication, an understanding of organizations and the way they operate, and the ability to work with people (users). In general, IS personnel are charged with maintaining the broadest enterprise-wide perspective.

Self-Assessment Test

1 The value chain is a series of activities that includes inbound logistics, warehouse and storage, production, finished product storage, outbound logistics, marketing and sales, and customer service. True or False?

2 A(n) _____ is a formal collection of people and other resources established to accomplish a set of goals.

3 User satisfaction with a computer system and the information it generates often depends on the quality of the system and the resulting information. True or False?

4 The concept in which organizations adapt to new conditions or alter their practices over time is called _____.
a. organizational learning
b. organizational change
c. continuous improvement
d. reengineering

5 _____ involves contracting with outside professional services to meet specific business needs.

6 Technology infusion is a measure of how widely technology is spread throughout an organization. True or False?

7 Reengineering is also called _____.

8 What is a measure of the output achieved divided by the input required?
   a. efficiency
   b. effectiveness
   c. productivity
   d. return on investment

9 _____ is a measure of the additional profits or benefits generated as a percentage of the investment in IS technology.

10 Who is involved in helping users determine what outputs they need and constructing the plans needed to produce these outputs?
   a. CIO
   b. applications programmer
   c. systems programmer
   d. systems analyst

11 The systems development component of a typical IS department focuses on specific development projects and ongoing maintenance and review. True or false?

12 The _____ is typically in charge of the IS department or area in a company.

Review Questions

1 What is the value chain?

2 What is the difference between a virtual organizational structure and a traditional organizational structure?

3 What is reengineering? What are the potential benefits of performing a process redesign?

4 What is the difference between technology infusion and technology diffusion?

5 List and define the basic organizational structures.

6 What is downsizing? How is it different from outsourcing?

7 What are some general strategies employed by organizations to achieve competitive advantage?

8 What are several common justifications for implementing an information system?

9 What is on-demand computing? What two advantages does it offer to a company?

10 What is the role of a systems developer? What is the role of a programmer? Are they different, and if so, how?

Discussion Questions

1 You have decided to open an Internet site to buy and sell used music CDs to other students. Describe the value chain for your new business.

2 What are the advantages of using a virtual organizational structure? What are the disadvantages?

3 How might you measure user satisfaction with a registration program at a college or university? What are the important features that would make students and faculty satisfied with the system?

4 There are many ways to evaluate the effectiveness of an information system. Discuss two methods and describe when one method would be preferred over another method.

5 A company has a prototype that it classes in the applications portfolio as potential strategic. If they develop it and it turns out to be strategic, is there any way they can sustain the advantage it brought? Or will it be destined to be copied by competitors which will errode its advantage?

Web Exercises

1 This book emphasizes the importance of information. You can get information from the Internet by going to a specific address, such as www.ibm.com, the home page of the IBM corporation, or a search engine such as www.google.co.uk.

Using Google, search for information about a company or topic discussed in Chapters 1 or 2. You might be asked to develop a report or send an e-mail message to your instructor about what you find.

2 Use the Internet to search for information about user satisfaction. You can use a search engine or a database at your college or university. Write a brief report describing what you find.

Case One

Hitwise and Web Data

Founded in 1997 and now operating in the U.S., U.K., Australia, New Zealand, Hong Kong, and Singapore, Hitwise describes itself as an 'online competitive intelligence service'. This means that for its customers, Hitwise supplies information about how many people are visiting their website, their age, sex, and geographic location, which sites they visit before going to the website, and which they visit next (so-called 'clickstream data'), reports on the search terms used to find the website, how visitors interact with the website, including which pages they look at and for how long, and reports on websites of competitors. The company was set up in response to the relatively rich data that was being collected by the big Internet players such as Yahoo! and Amazon, when data was unavailable about other major companies whose web presence was less established.

Hitwise produce their reports from a variety of data sources, the main one being internet service providers (ISPs). An ISP is a company that provides Internet access to its customers. The ISPs, representing a wide range of geographic regions in cities and rural areas, sell Hitwise their usage logs, which contain metrics on page requests, page visits and average visit length. This is complemented by demographic data collected from other sources to build up a picture of transactional behaviour across thousands of websites every day.

The data provided by Hitwise is incredible useful, allowing a company to benchmark itself against competitors, tailor the website to the people who actually visit it, target these people in their promotions, and look for strategic alliances. Hitwise customers include a range of companies both big and small.

Hitwise is careful not to extract personal information on web surfers in accordance with local and international privacy guidelines. Its method is audited each year by PriceWaterhouseCoopers.

Questions

1 How might a company use information about which website a web surfer has been to immediately before they come to theirs? How could this be used to continuously improve its website?

2 How might a company use information about which website a web surfer goes to immediately after they visit theirs? How could this be used to continuously improve its website?

3 Wouldn't it be useful for Hitwise's customers to know personal details on visitors to their website? Why do Hitwise not collect this information?

4 Should web surfers be concerned that companies can collect their clickstream data? Should the surfer be paid for the use of their clickstream data?

SOURCE: Hitwise Data (website), http://www.hitwise.co.uk.

Case Two

Innocent Drinks Stays in Touch

In the summer of 1998, three Cambridge University graduates spent about £500 on fruit, used it to make smoothie drinks, and sold them from a stall at a small music festival in London. Customers were given the option of putting their empty bottles in one of two rubbish bins. Beside both was a sign that said 'Do you think we should give up our jobs to make these smoothies?' and on one of the bins was printed 'Yes', and on the other 'No'. At the end of the day, the 'Yes' bin was full. The three promptly resigned their jobs and formed Innocent Drinks, manufacturing pure fruit smoothies. Their business attitude is based on five ethics:

1 Making 100 percent natural products that are good for people.

2 Buying all ingredients ethically.

3 Using ecologically sound packaging materials.

4 Reducing carbon emissions across the entire business system.

5 Giving 10 percent of profits each year to charities in the countries where its fruit comes from.

One of the founders, Richard Reed, said 'right from the outset we have always been looking at how we can use technology to help the human, not to replace the human; to engage with consumers, to get feedback from retailers to make sure that ordering goes seamlessly behind the scenes, that we can communicate office to office. There are a million different ways that technology can support and enhance the human, and that is where we try to use technology to further our business internationally.' He suggests that executive sponsorship from the very top is key: 'you can give all this technology to people, but if you give them a decision-making tool on their desktop, do not assume they are going to make better decisions if you have not told them what to do with that information', and sees technology as a communication tool to communicate with fruit growers, agents and customers throughout the world. Innocents Drinks have a 'family': anyone can join by e-mailing them. The 'family' is Innocent's way of staying in touch with the people who drink their products. Each week they e-mail 'family members' with news and competitions. If you join, according to their website, they will also 'invite you to nice events like Fruitstock (our free festival) and maybe send you the odd present if you're lucky. Finally, we'll very occasionally ask you what you reckon we should do next, as we sometimes get confused.'

Questions

1 How might Innocent use technology to help maintain its five ethics?

2 Explain some ways technology could help Innocent stay in touch with fruit growers.

3 Why do you think executive support so important in technology development? Could a project go ahead without it? What would such a project look like?

4 Do you think the 'Innocent Family' is a good idea? Explain your answer.

SOURCES: Innocent Drinks (website), http://www.innocentdrinks.co.uk; Glick, B., 'Keep the Customer Satisfied', a Computing web seminar that looked at how small firms can attract and build custom, *Computing*, March 15, 2007.

Case Three

2

Itochu Kenzai Uses IS to Reduce Organizational Waste

An environmental management system (EMS) is a set of cohesive elements that an organization can use to minimize its impact on the environment. The International Organization for Standardization (ISO) is the world's largest developer of standards. ISO standards contribute to making the development, manufacturing, and supply of products and services more efficient, safer, and cleaner. The ISO 14001 is an internationally accepted standard for an EMS, and is a sought distinction.

Itochu Kenzai Corporation, a building materials company in Tokyo, Japan, was certified ISO 14001-compliant, but only under the condition that it would take steps to reduce its environmental waste. One way in which it was to do so was to dramatically reduce its use of paper. This, of course, required the use of electronic documents and information systems that supported their management.

'We started out with the desire to eliminate paperwork for large quantities of forms that had a low frequency of use among the various forms generated', relates Mr. Yoshihiro Sakamoto, team manager of systems operations at Itochu Kenzai. Before the introduction of an electronic document management system, 'the output of accounting-related legal forms alone was responsible for about 80 000 pages per month, and on the fourth and fifth of each month, printers were operating night and day for monthly processing. Employees had to attend to the printers to keep them from running out of paper. Because 30 000 items of building materials are necessary to build one house, building materials extend to a wide variety of areas, and the number of items handled reached as high as 700 000 per month. All those items require documentation'.

Itochu Kenzai chose IBM DB2 Content Manager OnDemand as the electronic document solution and the IBM eServer iSeries system as the server. The IBM iSeries system was installed at the head office, collected accounting data, and performed electronic data interchange (EDI) with several dozen suppliers. The company also installed servers at 25 of its business centres throughout Japan to run business systems for the issuance of delivery slips, invoices, and other forms of content. After four years of effort, the company is entirely

operating with digitally converted business-related documents, and retrieving data and storage on compact discs.

The company has eliminated the printing of approximately 190 000 pages (equivalent to 100 boxes of paper) per month of legal documents and business-related documents. Itochu Kenzai is storing all these documents in electronic form. If these documents were stored for ten years, the savings obtained would be equivalent to about 12 000 boxes of paper. Not only is the company saving in paper, there is also substantial savings in personnel costs and warehouse storage expenses. The savings amounted to more than ¥700 000 (€4500) per month, or about ¥8 million (€52 000) per year. In addition, staff have been freed up to concentrate on core operations. The solution has become an extremely important part of the company system.

Before adopting the IBM content management solution, printed documents were archived in cardboard boxes stored in warehouses and typically never used. With DB2 Content Management OnDemand, that information is now easily retrieved and utilized. Itochu Kenzai management is discovering that the information that used to be discarded to warehouses has value.

Questions

1 How has Itochu Kenzai's move to become ISO 14001-compliant helped the environment?

2 How has Itochu Kenzai's move to become ISO 14001-compliant helped Itochu Kenzai?

3 Who is ultimately responsible for the pressure placed on companies to become environmentally friendly? Businesses? Governments? Citizens?

4 Often, refitting a company with new environmentally friendly technologies ends up saving the company money in the long run. What reasons might a company have for resisting such change?

SOURCES: ISO14001 'Itochu Kenzai Reduces Printing by 190,000 Pages per Month with Electronic Storage Solution from IBM', *IBM Case Studies*, November 21, 2005, www.ibm.com. ISO (website), www.iso14000.com, March 8, 2006. Itochu Kenzai (website), www.ick.co.jp/english/default.htm, March 8, 2006.

Notes

1 Porter, M.E., 1980, *Competitive Strategy*, Free Press, New York.

2 Zhu, K., Kraemer, K., 'Post-Adoption Variations in Usage and Value of E-Business by Organizations', *Information Systems Research*, March 2005, p. 61.

3 McDougall, Paul, 'Tools to Tune Supply Chains', *Information Week*, January 9, 2006, p. 62.

4 Grey, W., et al., 'The Role of E-Marketplaces in Relationship-based Supply Chains', *IBM Systems Journal*, Vol. 44, No. 1, 2005, p. 109.

5 Rowley, Jennifer, 'Customer Relationship Management Through the Tesco Clubcard Loyalty Scheme', *International Journal of Retail & Distribution Management*, March 1, 2005, p. 194.

6 Gordon, Jack, 'Do Your Virtual Teams Deliver Only Virtual Performance?', *Training Magazine*, June 1, 2005.

7 Robotwork (website), http://www.robots.com/, October 31, 2007.

8 Dav Friedlos, 'Everton Kicks Off Outsourced Contract', *Computing*, January 16, 2007.

9 See Siemens VAI (website), http://www.industry.siemens.com/metals-mining/en/index.htm/, October 31, 2007.

10 Kelly, Lisa, 'Northern Ireland Civil Service Goes Electronic', *Computing*, January 16, 2007.

11 Tornatzky, L., Fleischer, M., 'The Process of Technological Innovation', *Lexington Books* (Lexington, MA, 1990), and Zhu, K., Kraemer, K., 'Post-Adoption Variations in Usage and Value of E-Business by Organizations', *Information Systems Research*, March 2005, p. 61.

12 Besanko, D., Dranove, D.; Shanley, M.; Schaefer, S., *Economics of Strategy*, 4th ed., (New Jersey: Wiley, 2007).

13 Porter, M.E., Millar, V., 'How Information Systems Give You Competitive Advantage', *Journal of Business Strategy*, Winter 1985. See also Porter, M.E., *Competitive Advantage* (New York: Free Press, 1985).

14 Irani, Z., Love, P.E.D., 'Evaluating the Impact of IT on the Organization' in Galliers, R.; Leidner, D. (eds), *Strategic Information Management*, 3rd ed (Burlington, MA: Butterworth-Heinemann, 2003).

15 Huber, Nick, 'Return on Investment: Analysts to Offer Tips on Measuring the Value of IT,' *Computer Weekly*, April 26, 2005, p. 20.

World Views Case

High Performance Computing in South Africa: Computing in Support of African Development

Alan Hogarth
Glasgow Caledonian University

South Africa is currently in the process of expanding its scientific research and innovation base with a direct link to social and economic development. Part of this process was the recognition that an Information and Communications Technology (ICT) strategy was needed. Two major enabling domains were highlighted and these were Computational Science and High Performance Computing. Major examples in this regard are Biotechnology, particularly with reference to research into the major infectious diseases such as HIV/AIDS and tuberculosis, advanced manufacturing technology, technologies to utilise and protect our natural resources and ensure food security (e.g., climate systems analysis and disaster forecasting), and technology for poverty reduction (e.g., behavioural modelling in social research; financial management; HPC in SMEs). Funding for three years (2006–2008) has been secured for the high performance computing initiative. In addition, parallel investment in a South African National Research Network (SANReN), intended to provide high bandwidth connectivity for South African researchers, has been planned.

In his 2002 State of the Nation address, President Thabo Mbeki of South Africa singled out Information and Communication Technology (ICT) as *'a critical and pervasive element in economic development,'* and recommended the establishment of an *'ICT University.'* This led to the establishment of the Meraka Institute of which The Centre for High Performance Computing (CHPC) is a component.

These developments within South Africa are aligned with initiatives to stimulate research, development and technology across the African continent. A 'Plan for Collective Action' was adopted by

African Ministers of Science and Technology in Dakar in November 2005, in a meeting organized jointly by New Partnership for Africa's Development (Nepad) and the African Union (AU). It highlights initiatives and projects that are crucial to enabling Africa to mobilize and strengthen its capacities to engage effectively in scientific and technological development.

The three conceptual pillars of the 'Plan for Collective Action' are capacity building, knowledge production, and technological innovation. The Plan has twelve sub-programmes based on specific content areas, one of which is Information and Communications Technology. The ICT sub-programme will aim at establishing a continental research network on ICTs. It will bring together leading universities and research centres to design and implement projects that generate software to use with African content. Its specific goals will be to:

■ stimulate technical change and innovation in ICTs

■ build skills in local software research and development; and

■ build knowledge of Open Source Software and promote its application in education, health and conduct of science.

However, one drawback at the moment is the exorbitant price of bandwidth on the African continent.

Funding, at this stage largely from the government, has been secured for the establishment of the central physical facility together with the appointment of scientific and technical staff by mid-2006. Cooperation with similar facilities in developing countries such as Brazil and India are seen as essential to the success of the South African project, given this country's largely developing economy. Currently discussions have been held with colleagues in India with a view to establishing a relationship similar to that envisaged with those colleagues in Brazil.

A key objective will be that of identifying projects that will be supported through the CHPC. These projects will be identified and selected on the basis of national importance and also those which are deemed to be appropriate for location in the CHPC. In the future we will see the use of computers become critical to problems as diverse as drug design to combat diseases malaria and HIV/AIDS through the development of models for predicting drought and preventing crop failures. High performance computing is now being positioned at the centre of innovative technologies. The impact of design through scientific computing on economies driven by innovation will be significant.

The creation of a national Centre for High Performance Computing will permit South African scientists and engineers to be active at the cutting edge of their respective research disciplines within a vibrant intellectual atmosphere. The benefits of the linkage between research and innovation that is enabled through the CHPC will be felt not only in university laboratories but throughout the wider South African economy. The building of a critical mass in state-of-the-art high-performance computing equipment as well as high-level scientific computing expertise in an intellectual common space will be central to achieving the goal of making the African Renaissance a reality.

Questions

1 How important is a national ICT strategy for South Africa? Justify your answer.

2 What benefits could be accrued by the South African population by implementing such a strategy?

3 As a Programme Director of the CHPC in charge of research and development what general criteria would you apply when selecting a proposed project?

4 Given the recognised need for the ICT strategy what areas do you think require the most immediate funding in order that the strategy becomes successful?

SOURCE: Adam, R., de la Rey, C., Naidoo, K., Reddy, D. "High Performance Computing in South Africa: Computing in Support of African Development," *CTWatch Quarterly,* Volume 2, Number 1, Feb 2006

World Views Case

The Importance of Collaboration and Trust in Virtual Organizations

Alan Hogarth
Glasgow Caledonian University

In the current age of the global and digital economy and virtual teams there has been an increasing interest in trust. Consequently there has been an acknowledgement of the importance of trust in both business organizations and in academic literature. Trust is seen as essential in business dealings in virtual organizations as Mr C. Handy says, *'Virtuality requires trust to make it work: Technology on its own is not enough'*. J. Lipnack and J. Stamps agree with him when they argue that, *'in the networks and virtual teams of the Information Age, trust is a 'need to have' quality in productive relationships'*. Furthermore, according to L. Platt *'trust is essential to any virtual team as these teams do not have everyday interaction'* and as such the possibility of losing trust is much higher. While trust has been identified as a key feature for the success of interactions in virtual organizations, empirical research in this area has remained limited. However one major research project by Jarvenpaa and Leidner, involving the study of seventy-five teams of university students, highlighted significant differences in the behaviours and strategies between the teams. Although this study was a useful academic research exercise it does have some limitations when attempting to apply its findings in a business context. For example tasks and projects may not be as well-articulated in this context, and external factors (e.g. clients' specifications) may require changes in the direction of an already assigned project, unlikely in a student project. However in a business based setting of a virtual team project, managed by a virtual organization and involving a group of geographically dispersed employees, the content, both formal and informal, of communication, helps in building and maintaining an interactive social situation and can act as the frame for reference for constructing the trust relationship.

For example, Mr. R. Tucker and Ms. N. Panteli of the University of Bath, pursued a study of eighteen global virtual teams within a global IT organization. The study involved interviews with individuals

Georg Winkens/Istock

employed at the specific organization and who were part of culturally diverse, geographically dispersed and technology-enabled global virtual teams. One major finding of the study was the influence and importance of 'power' on trust in virtual teams. Power, defined as the capability of one party to exert an influence on another to act in a prescribed manner, is often a function of both dependence and the use of that dependence as leverage. In considering power within virtual teams there is an increasing recognition in the literature that knowledge is indeed power and that within these teams, the team member with power at any given time is the one with the most relevant knowledge at that time. Several interviewees described the power within their team as originating from knowledge and noted that at any given point in time the most powerful was the individual with the most relevant information. In these situations significant emphasis was placed upon collaboration and the use of persuasive power. *'Power tended to move based on whatever activities were going on at that time. I guess it followed those that were most knowledgeable at any point in time. This is not surprising as the reason we selected the external design company was because of their knowledge.'*

Shared goals are also recognised as a key characteristic of virtual teams. They should provide a means to developing a common sense of identity for team members which can be of particular benefit to those global virtual teams which meet infrequently or perhaps not at all. However, even though shared goals are important for the success of virtual teams, these should not be taken for granted. Importantly, the construction of shared goals is often by no means a one-off activity, but rather a process that requires the participation of all parties involved. Though this could be a time-consuming, iterative and difficult process it is far better to invest in it as early in the project as possible as opposed to resolving the issues that can result from team members with conflicting goals and poor levels of trust. Facilitators are also important in global virtual teams as they can have an enabling role in constructing shared goals. The role of a facilitator is to help with team-building techniques at the early stage of the virtual team project. The following examples from a case study show that the use of shared goals features prominently.

'We had a very definite vision of how we wanted the relationships to work. We were keen to engage and excite the other companies. We gave them an overview of our business and worked hard to try and give them the full picture to create a vision if you like.'

'At the very start of the project the project managers from each company got together and put together a comprehensive contract . . . It was developed jointly and was very comprehensive. We went through a lot of iterative discussions to make sure that the document was extremely well thought out.'

Further to the issues of shared goals and power, the importance of face-to-face interaction cannot be underestimated. However, the opportunities to meet face-to-face are not always possible and are often curtailed due to economic pressures or restrictive deadlines. Despite these problems well organized and efficient virtual teams will arrange regular meetings via other media such as videoconferencing systems. Team members generally agree that this mode of group communication offers more feedback and therefore facilitates understanding more effectively than voicemail and email. Furthermore teams that work well together also tend to include a social and fun element in their interactions that can aid in creating a stronger shared social context. The importance of trust in virtual teams then cannot be underestimated. Also, collaboration in constructing team goals between virtual team members is essential as it can provide the 'glue' to hold team members together long enough to make possible the development of mutual trust. However, the construction of shared goals is not often a one-off activity and frequently requires the involvement of all parties involved. Therefore it is far better to invest in building trust as early in the project as possible in order that the virtual team bonds as a productive unit.

Questions

1 Explain why you think 'trust' is vital in virtual teams?
2 Discuss the relevance of 'power' in virtual team interactions?

3 As a member of a virtual team what benefits can you envisage from conducting a team meeting using a videoconferencing system?

4 What differences, in regard to issues of 'trust' and 'power,' would you expect to find between a virtual team comprised of students in an academic setting and employees in a virtual project team in a business setting? Consequently, how would each team's goal setting activities be affected by your answer?

SOURCE: 'Trust in Global Teams', Panteli.N. ARIADNE, Issue 43, April 2005

PART 2

Information Technology Concepts

03

Hardware: Input, Processing, and Output Devices

Principles

Assembling an effective, efficient set of computer hardware devices requires understanding their role in supporting the underlying information systems and the needs of the organization. The computer hardware objectives are subordinate to, but supportive of, the information systems and the needs of the organization.

When selecting computer hardware, you must consider the current and future needs of the information systems and the organization. Your choice of a hardware device should always allow for later improvements to meet evolving organizational needs.

Learning Objectives

- Describe how to select and organize computer hardware components to support information system (IS) objectives and business needs.

- Describe the power, speed, and capacity of central processing and memory devices.
- Describe the access methods, capacity, and portability of secondary storage devices.
- Discuss the speed, functionality, and importance of input and output devices.
- Identify popular classes of computer systems and discuss the role of each.

Why Learn About Hardware?

Organizations invest in computer hardware to improve employee productivity, reduce costs, expand business opportunities, increase flexibility and provide better customer service. Those that don't might be stuck with outdated hardware that often fails and cannot take advantage of the latest software advances. As a result, obsolete hardware can place an organization at a competitive disadvantage. Managers, no matter what their career field and educational background, are expected to know enough about hardware to help define the business needs that the hardware must support. In addition, managers must be able to ask good questions and evaluate options when considering hardware investments for their area of the business. Managers in marketing, sales, and human resources often help IS specialists assess opportunities to apply computer hardware and evaluate the options and features specified for the hardware. Managers in finance and accounting especially must keep an eye on the bottom line, guarding against overspending, yet be willing to invest in computer hardware when and where business conditions warrant it. This chapter concentrates on the hardware component of a computer-based information system (CBIS).

3.1 Hardware

Hardware consists of any machinery (most of which uses digital circuits) that assists in the input, processing, storage, and output activities of an information system. When making hardware decisions, the overriding consideration of a business should be how hardware can support the objectives of the information system and the goals of the organization. To assemble an effective and efficient system, you should select and organize components while understanding the trade-offs between overall system performance and cost, control, and complexity. For instance, in building a car, manufacturers try to match the intended use of the vehicle to its components. Race cars, for example, require special types of engines, transmissions, and tyres. Selecting a transmission for a race car requires balancing how much engine power can be delivered to the wheels (efficiency and effectiveness) with how expensive the transmission is (cost), how reliable it is (control), and how many gears it has (complexity). Similarly, organizations assemble computer systems so that they are effective, efficient, and well suited to the tasks that need to be performed.

People involved in selecting their organization's computer hardware must clearly understand current and future business requirements so they can make informed acquisition decisions.

Consider the following examples of applying business knowledge to reach critical hardware decisions.

- Zürcher Kantonalbank (ZKB) provides banking services for both individuals and businesses in Switzerland. Companies in Switzerland are often interdependent on many others, and it was important for ZKB to understand how one can affect the others, for example, whether small firms would be able to survive the bankruptcy of a larger firm. The need to find an IT solution capable of running complex financial models at high speed was critical for the business. After much testing, they implemented a grid computing solution, described later on in this chapter. This approach is extremely scalable – ZKB can easily add more processors to the grid. Even with this solution, a single calculation can take up to 100 hours.[1]

- Freelance animator and digital filmmaker Angie Taylor, based in the U.K., works in a variety of locations. She needed the ability to use plug-in hardware components such as digital cameras, to render graphics in near real-time, and to access the Internet, from anywhere she was working. The solution she chose, the Dell Precision M60 Mobile

Workstation, supports up to two gigabytes of RAM and was designed to meet the specific high-end computing needs of graphic artists and professionals needing top-specification computing power. This hardware allows Taylor to take work anywhere which saves her time, and lets her remain in close contact with clients.[2]

■ CERN, the European Organization for Nuclear Research, is the world's largest particle physics laboratory, situated on the border between France and Switzerland. Its main function is to run high energy particle accelerators for physics research, in which elementary particles are collided at extremely high speeds. The accelerators generate vast quantities of data, which is sent over the Internet to laboratories around the world for distributed processing. To achieve this, CERN is setting up a data centre of 6000 computers and using Hewlett-Packard networking technology.[3]

As these examples show, choosing the right computer hardware requires understanding its relationship to the information system and the needs of the organization. Furthermore, hardware objectives are subordinate to, but supportive of, the information system and the current and future needs of the organization.

3.1.1 Hardware Components

Computer system hardware components include devices that perform input, processing, data storage, and output (see Figure 3.1). Recall that any system must be able to process (organize and manipulate) data, and a computer system does so through an interplay between one or more central processing units and primary storage. Each **central processing unit (CPU)** consists of three associated elements: the arithmetic/logic unit, the control unit, and the register areas. The **arithmetic/logic unit (ALU)** performs mathematical calculations and makes logical comparisons. The **control unit** sequentially accesses program instructions, decodes them, and coordinates the flow of data in and out of the ALU, registers, primary and secondary storage, and

central processing unit (CPU) The part of the computer that consists of three associated elements: the arithmetic/logic unit, the control unit, and the register areas.

arithmetic/logic unit (ALU) The part of the CPU that performs mathematical calculations and makes logical comparisons.

control unit The part of the CPU that sequentially accesses program instructions, decodes them, and coordinates the flow of data in and out of the ALU, registers, primary storage, and even secondary storage and various output devices.

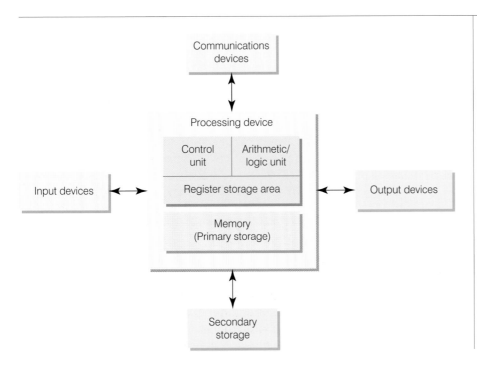

Figure 3.1 Hardware Components *These components include the input devices, output devices, communications devices, primary and secondary storage devices, and the central processing unit (CPU). The control unit, the arithmetic/logic unit (ALU), and the register storage areas constitute the CPU.*

register A high-speed storage area in the CPU used to temporarily hold small units of program instructions and data immediately before, during, and after execution by the CPU.

various output devices. **Registers** are high-speed storage areas used to temporarily hold small units of program instructions and data immediately before, during, and after execution by the CPU.

Executing any machine-level instruction involves two phases: instruction and execution. During the instruction phase, a computer performs the following steps:

■ **Step 1:** Fetch instruction. The computer reads the next program instruction to be executed and any necessary data into the processor.

■ **Step 2:** Decode instruction. The instruction is decoded and passed to the appropriate processor execution unit. Each execution unit plays a different role: The arithmetic/logic unit performs all integer arithmetic operations, the floating-point unit deals with non-integer operations, the load/store unit manages the instructions that read or write to memory, the branch processing unit predicts the outcome of a branch instruction in an attempt to reduce disruptions in the flow of instructions and data into the processor, the memory-management unit translates an application's addresses into physical memory addresses, and the vector-processing unit handles vector-based instructions that accelerate graphics operations.

instruction time (I-time) The time it takes to perform the fetch-instruction and decode-instruction steps of the instruction phase.

The time it takes to perform the instruction phase (Steps 1 and 2) is called the **instruction time (I-time)**.

The second phase is execution. During the execution phase, a computer performs the following steps:

■ **Step 3:** Execute instruction. The hardware element, now freshly fed with an instruction and data, carries out the instruction. This could involve making an arithmetic computation, logical comparison, bit shift, or vector operation.

■ **Step 4:** Store results. The results are stored in registers or memory.

execution time (e-time) The time it takes to execute an instruction and store the results.

machine cycle The instruction phase followed by the execution phase.

The time it takes to complete the execution phase (Steps 3 and 4) is called the **execution time (E-time)**.

After both phases have been completed for one instruction, they are performed again for the second instruction, and so on. Completing the instruction phase followed by the execution phase is called a **machine cycle** (see Figure 3.2). Some processing units can speed processing by using

Figure 3.2 Execution of an Instruction *In the instruction phase, a program's instructions and any necessary data are read into the processor (1). Then the instruction is decoded so the central processor can understand what to do (2). In the execution phase, the ALU does what it is instructed to do, making either an arithmetic computation or a logical comparison (3). Then the results are stored in the registers or in memory (4). The instruction and execution phases together make up one machine cycle.*

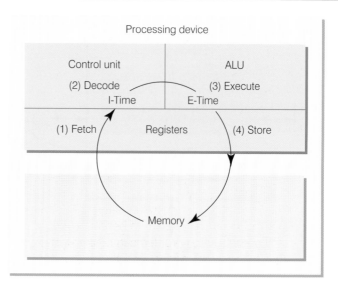

pipelining, whereby the processing unit gets one instruction, decodes another, and executes a third at the same time. The Pentium 4 processor, for example, uses two execution unit pipelines. This means the processing unit can execute two instructions in a single machine cycle.

pipelining A form of CPU operation in which multiple execution phases are performed in a single machine cycle.

3.2 Processing and Memory Devices: Power, Speed, and Capacity

The components responsible for processing – the CPU and memory – are housed together in the same box or cabinet, called the system unit. All other computer system devices, such as the monitor, secondary storage, and keyboard, are linked directly or indirectly into the system unit housing. In the next two sections, we investigate the characteristics of these important devices.

3.2.1 Processing Characteristics and Functions

Because organizations want efficient processing and timely output, they use a variety of measures to gauge processing speed. These measures include the time it takes to complete a machine cycle and clock speed.

Machine Cycle Time

As you've seen, a computer executes an instruction during a machine cycle. The time in which a machine cycle occurs is measured in nanoseconds (one-billionth of one second) and picoseconds (one-trillionth of one second). Machine cycle time also can be measured by how many instructions are executed in one second. This measure, called **MIPS**, stands for millions of instructions per second. MIPS is another measure of speed for computer systems of all sizes.

MIPS Millions of instructions per second.

Clock Speed

Each CPU produces a series of electronic pulses at a predetermined rate, called the **clock speed**, which affects machine cycle time. The control unit in the CPU manages the stages of the machine cycle by following predetermined internal instructions, known as **microcode**. You can think of microcode as predefined, elementary circuits and logical operations that the processor performs when it executes an instruction. The control unit executes the microcode in accordance with the electronic cycle, or pulses of the CPU 'clock'. Each microcode instruction takes at least the same amount of time as the interval between pulses. The shorter the interval between pulses, the faster each microcode instruction can be executed.

clock speed A series of electronic pulses produced at a predetermined rate that affects machine cycle time.

microcode Predefined, elementary circuits and logical operations that the processor performs when it executes an instruction.

Because the number of microcode instructions needed to execute a single program instruction – such as performing a calculation or printing results – can vary, the clock speed is not directly related to the true processing speed of the computer.

Clock speed is often measured in **megahertz** (MHz, millions of cycles per second) or **gigahertz** (GHz, billions of cycles per second). Unfortunately, as the clock speed of the CPU increases, additional heat is generated that can corrupt the data and instructions the computer is trying to process. Because this can lead to errors that cause a program to behave erratically, chip and computer manufacturers must be wary of potential heat problems in their new designs.

megahertz (MHz) Millions of cycles per second.

gigahertz (GHz) Billions of cycles per second.

In past years, organizations typically bought the fastest chips with no concern for the chip's power requirements. Now the chip's power requirement has become an important consideration.

3

For example, IT services provider Fiducia AG processes some 20 million transactions per day for 900 German banks. The firm plans to upgrade to more powerful and more energy-efficient UltraSPARC T1-microprocessor-based servers from Sun Microsystems that will replace four old servers with one server and cut power costs by nearly €750 000 per year.[4]

Physical Characteristics of the CPU

Most CPUs are collections of digital circuits imprinted on silicon wafers, or chips, each no bigger than the tip of a pencil eraser. To turn a digital circuit on or off within the CPU, electrical current must flow through a medium (usually silicon) from point A to point B. The speed the current travels between points can be increased by either reducing the distance between the points or reducing the resistance of the medium to the electrical current.

Reducing the distance between points has resulted in ever-smaller chips, with the circuits packed closer together. In the 1960s, shortly after patenting the integrated circuit, Gordon Moore, former chairman of the board of Intel (the largest microprocessor chip maker), hypothesized that progress in chip manufacturing ought to make it possible to double the number of transistors (the microscopic on/off switches) on a chip roughly every 18 months. When actual results bore out his idea, the doubling of transistor densities on a single chip every 18 months became known as **Moore's Law**, and this rule of thumb has become a goal that chip manufacturers have met for over four decades. As shown in Figure 3.3, the number of transistors on a chip continues to climb.

Moore's Law A hypothesis that states that transistor densities on a single chip double every 18 months.

The minimum width of basic circuit features of a chip today is 90 nanometres (one billionth of a metre). Intel has already announced its Pentium Extreme Edition 955 desktop processor based on a chip with 65-nanometer processing technology.[5] Intel is also constructing an advanced semiconductor manufacturing facility in Israel capable of high-volume production of 45-nanometer chips.[6] In addition to increased processing speeds, Moore's Law means decreasing costs. As silicon-based components and computers gain in performance, they become cheaper to produce, and therefore more plentiful, more powerful, and more a part of our everyday lives.

Figure 3.3 Moore's **Law** *Transistor densities on a single chip double every 18 months.*

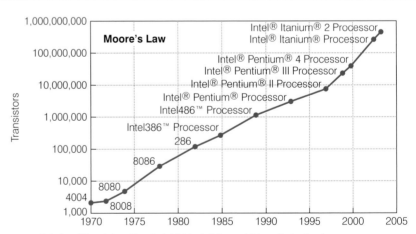

SOURCE: Data from 'Moore's Law: Overview', Intel (website), www.intel.com/technology/silicon/mooreslaw/index.htm, January 21, 2006.

Researchers are taking many approaches to continue to improve the performance of computers:

■ Chips built from superconductive metals such as carbon that allow current to flow with minimal electrical resistance.

- Optical processors that use light waves instead of electrical current to represent bits.
- Strained silicon, a technique that boosts performance and lowers power consumption by stretching silicon molecules farther apart, thus allowing electrons to meet less resistance and flow faster.
- Forming the tiny circuits for a computer from tiny carbon nanotubes only one to three nanometres in diameter.
- Extreme miniaturisation using radio waves to manipulate atoms into executing a simple computer program.

When selecting a CPU, organizations must balance the benefits of speed with cost. CPUs with faster clock speeds and machine cycle times are usually more expensive than slower ones. This expense, however, is a necessary part of the overall computer system cost, for the CPU is typically the single largest determinant of the price of many computer systems.

3.2.2 Main Memory Characteristics and Functions

Primary storage, main memory, or simply 'memory', is located physically close to the CPU, but not on the CPU chip itself. It provides the CPU with a working storage area for program instructions and data. The chief feature of memory is that it rapidly provides the data and instructions to the CPU.

primary storage (main memory; memory) The part of the computer that holds program instructions and data. Primary storage, also called main memory or memory, is closely associated with the CPU. Memory holds program instructions and data immediately before or after the registers.

Storage Capacity

Like the CPU, memory devices contain thousands of circuits imprinted on a silicon chip. Each circuit is either conducting electrical current (on) or not (off). Data is stored in memory as a combination of on or off circuit states. Usually eight bits are used to represent a character, such as the letter 'T'. Eight bits together form a **byte (B)**. In most cases, storage capacity is measured in bytes, with one byte equivalent to one character of data. The contents of the U.S. Library of Congress, with over 126 million items and over 850 km of bookshelves, would require about 20 petabytes of digital storage. Table 3.1 lists units for measuring computer storage.

byte (B) Eight bits that together represent a single character of data.

Table 3.1 Computer Storage Units

Name	Abbreviation	Number of Bytes
Byte	B	1
Kilobyte	KB	2^{10}
Megabyte	MB	2^{20}
Gigabyte	GB	2^{30}
Terabyte	TB	2^{40}
Petabyte	PB	2^{50}
Exabyte	EB	2^{60}

Types of Memory

There are several forms of memory, as shown in Figure 3.4. Instructions or data can be temporarily stored in and read from **random access memory (RAM)**. With the current design of RAM chips, they are volatile storage devices, meaning they lose their contents if the current is turned off or disrupted (as in a power surge, blackout, or electrical noise generated by lightning or nearby machines). RAM chips are mounted directly on the computer's main circuit board or in other chips mounted on peripheral cards that plug into the computer's main circuit board. These RAM chips consist of millions of switches that are sensitive to changes in electric current.

random access memory (RAM) A form of memory in which instructions or data can be temporarily stored.

3

Figure 3.4 Basic Types of Memory Chips

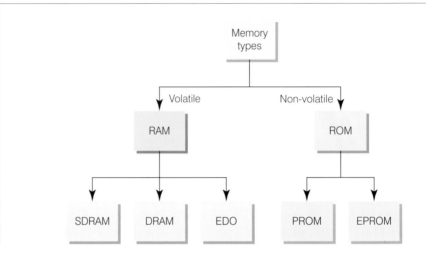

RAM comes in many varieties. The mainstream type of RAM is Extended Data Out, or EDO RAM, which is faster than older types of RAM. Another kind is called Dynamic RAM (DRAM) and is based on single-transistor memory cells. SDRAM, or Synchronous DRAM, employs a minimum of four transistors per memory cell and needs high or low voltages at regular intervals – every two milliseconds (two one-thousands of a second) – to retain its information. Compared with EDO RAM, SDRAM provides a faster transfer speed between the microprocessor and the memory.

read-only memory (ROM) A non-volatile form of memory.

Read-only memory (ROM), another type of memory, is non-volatile. In ROM, the combination of circuit states is fixed, and therefore its contents are not lost if the power is removed. ROM provides permanent storage for data and instructions that do not change, such as programs and data from the computer manufacturer, including the instructions that tell the computer how to start up when power is turned on.

There are other types of non-volatile memory as well. In programmable read-only memory (PROM), the desired data and instructions – and hence the desired circuit state combination – must first be programmed into the memory chip. Thereafter, PROM behaves like ROM. A common use of PROM chips is for storing the instructions to popular video games, such as those for GameBoy and Xbox. Game instructions are programmed onto the PROM chips by the game manufacturer. Instructions and data can be programmed onto a PROM chip only once.

Erasable programmable read-only memory (EPROM) is similar to PROM except, as the name implies, the memory chip can be erased and reprogrammed. A form of EPROM memory is used to store information on RFID chips (discussed later in this chapter) that identify and track the items to which they are attached. The contents of EPROM can be changed each time the item is moved throughout the supply chain.

Although microprocessor speed has doubled every 18 months over the past decade, memory performance has not kept pace. In effect, memory has become the principal bottleneck to system performance. The use of **cache memory**, a type of high-speed memory that a processor can access more rapidly than main memory, helps to ease this bottleneck. Frequently used data is stored in easily accessible cache memory instead of slower memory such as RAM. Because cache memory holds less data, the CPU can access the desired data and instructions more quickly than selecting from the larger set in main memory. Thus, the CPU can execute instructions faster, improving the overall performance of the computer system. There are three types of cache memory. The Level 1 (L1) cache is on the CPU chip. The Level 2 (L2) cache memory can be accessed by the CPU over a high-speed dedicated interface. The latest processors go a step further and place the L2 cache directly on the CPU chip itself and provide high-speed support for a tertiary Level 3 (L3) external cache. Deerfield, the low-power version of Intel's 64-bit servers called the Itanium 2 chip, was introduced with 1.5 MB of Level 3 cache.

> **cache memory** A type of high-speed memory that a processor can access more rapidly than main memory.

When the processor needs to execute an instruction, the instruction's operation code indicates whether the data will be in a register or in memory. If the operation code specifies a register as the source, it is taken from there. Otherwise, the processor looks for the data in the L1 cache, then the L2 cache, and then the L3 cache. If the data is not in any cache, the CPU requests the data from main memory. If the data is not stored in main memory, the system has to retrieve the data from secondary storage. It can take from one to three clock cycles to fetch information from the L1 cache, while the CPU waits and does nothing. It takes 6 to 12 cycles to get data from an L2 cache on the processor chip. It can take dozens of cycles to fetch data from an L3 cache and hundreds of cycles to fetch data from secondary storage. Because this hierarchical arrangement of memory helps the CPU find data faster, it bridges a widening gap between processor speeds, which are increasing at roughly 50 percent per year, and DRAM access rates, which are climbing at only 5 percent per year.

Costs for memory capacity continue to decline. However, when considered on a megabyte-to-megabyte basis, memory is still considerably more expensive than most forms of secondary storage.

Memory capacity contributes to the effectiveness of a CBIS. The specific applications of a CBIS determine the amount of memory required for a computer system. For example, complex processing problems, such as computer-assisted product design, require more memory than simpler tasks such as word processing. Also, because computer systems have different types of memory, they might need other programs to control how memory is accessed and used. In other cases, the computer system can be configured to maximize memory usage. Before purchasing additional memory, an organization should address all these considerations.

3.2.3 Multiprocessing

Generally, **multiprocessing** involves the simultaneous execution of two or more instructions at the same time. One form of multiprocessing uses coprocessors. A **coprocessor** speeds processing by executing specific types of instructions while the CPU works on another processing activity. Coprocessors can be internal or external to the CPU and can have different clock speeds than the CPU. Each type of coprocessor performs a specific function. For example, a math coprocessor chip speeds mathematical calculations, and a graphics coprocessor chip decreases the time it takes to manipulate graphics.

A **multicore microprocessor** combines two or more independent processors into a single computer so that they can share the workload and boost processing capacity. In addition, a dual-core processor enables people

> **multiprocessing** The simultaneous execution of two or more instructions at the same time.
>
> **coprocessor** The part of the computer that speeds processing by executing specific types of instructions while the CPU works on another processing activity.
>
> **multicore microprocessor** A microprocessor that combines two or more independent processors into a single computer so they can share the workload and deliver a big boost in processing capacity.

to perform multiple tasks simultaneously such as playing a game and burning a CD. AMD and Intel are battling for leadership in the multicore processor marketplace. In late 2005, Intel announced that it would replace a planned multicore Xeon processor (Whitefield) with a new chip (Tigerton) designed to reduce the current performance gap between Intel's server multicore chips and AMD Opteron processors.[7]

An example of processes that require a multicore microprocessor include a medical CAT scan, which generates a three-dimensional image of the internals of an object based on many two-dimensional x-ray images taken around the same axis of rotation. In a similar process, Chevron uses seismic waves (rather than x-rays) that travel through rock in search of energy reserves. The prodigious amount of data generated is processed by over 700 dual-core processor servers from Advanced Micro Devices to yield a three-dimensional image of the Earth's subsurface. The increased memory capabilities and processing speed of the systems yield an improved image resolution and in less time than was previously required.[8]

3.2.4 Parallel Computing

parallel computing The simultaneous execution of the same task on multiple processors to obtain results faster.

massively parallel processing systems A form of multiprocessing that speeds processing by linking hundreds or thousands of processors to operate at the same time, or in parallel, with each processor having its own bus, memory, disks, copy of the operating system, and applications.

single instruction/multiple data (SIMD) A form of parallel computing in which the processors all execute the same instruction on many data values simultaneously.

multiple instruction/multiple data (MIMD) A form of parallel computing in which the processors all execute different instructions.

grid computing The use of a collection of computers, often owned by multiple individuals or organizations, to work in a coordinated manner to solve a common problem.

Parallel computing is the simultaneous execution of the same task on multiple processors to obtain results faster. Systems with thousands of such processors are known as **massively parallel processing systems**. There are different approaches to achieving parallel computing. **Single instruction/multiple data (SIMD)** parallel processors all execute the same instruction on many data values simultaneously. **Multiple instruction/multiple data (MIMD)** parallel processors all execute different instructions. The processors might communicate with one another to coordinate when executing a computer program or they might run independently of one another but under the direction of another processor that distributes the work to the other processors and collects their processing results. The dual-core processors mentioned earlier are a simple form of parallel computing.

Grid computing is the use of a collection of computers, often owned by multiple individuals or organizations, to work in a coordinated manner to solve a common problem. Grid computing is a low-cost approach to parallel computing. The grid can include dozens, hundreds, or even thousands of computers that run collectively to solve extremely large processing problems. Key to the success of grid computing is a central server that acts as the grid leader and traffic monitor. This controlling server divides the computing task into subtasks and assigns the work to computers on the grid that have (at least temporarily) surplus processing power. The central server also monitors the processing, and if a member of the grid fails to complete a subtask, it restarts or reassigns the task. When all the subtasks are completed, the controlling server combines the results and advances to the next task until the whole job is completed.

Through the World Community Grid, more than 100 000 people donate unused time from about 170 000 computers. The grid invites volunteers to download software, which runs when their computer is on, but they're not using it, and enables computers on the grid to solve scientific problems and create public databases for scientific research. A project must hold potential for contributing to the greater good to be eligible for support. For example, the World Community Grid is currently using its massive computational powers to test thousands of human immunodeficiency virus (HIV) mutations against tens of thousands of chemical compounds. The goal is to help scientists design effective therapies to stop potential drug-resistant viral strains from causing AIDS.[9]

The most frequent business uses for parallel computing include modelling, simulating, and analyzing large amounts of data. In today's challenging marketplace, consumers are demanding increased product features and a whole array of new services. These consumer demands have forced companies to find more effective and insightful ways of gathering and analyzing information about existing and potential customers. Collecting and organizing this enormous amount of data is difficult.

3.3 Secondary Storage

3

Driven by such factors as needing to retain more data longer to meet government regulatory concerns, store new forms of digital data such as audio and video, and keep systems running under the onslaught of ever-increasing volumes of e-mail, the amount of data that companies store digitally is increasing at a rate of close to 100 percent per year! Organizations need a way to store large amounts of data and instructions more permanently than main memory allows. **Secondary storage**, also called permanent storage, serves this purpose.

secondary storage (permanent storage) Devices that store larger amounts of data, instructions, and information more permanently than allowed with main memory.

Compared with memory, secondary storage offers the advantages of non-volatility, greater capacity, and greater economy. On a cost-per-megabyte basis, most forms of secondary storage are considerably less expensive than primary memory (see Table 3.2). The selection of secondary storage media and devices requires understanding their primary characteristics – access method, capacity, and portability.

As with other computer system components, the access methods, storage capacities, and portability required of secondary storage media are determined by the information system's

Table 3.2 Comparative Cost of Secondary Storage Media

Description	Storage Capacity (GB)	Cost per GB
Office Depot CD-R spindle	0.7	€0.05
3½-inch bulk diskette, IBM format, DS/HD	0.14	€0.07
HP DDS-3 tape cartridge	24.0	€0.17
Maxell data tape, 4MM	24.0	€0.22
HP AIT-2 data cartridge	100.0	€0.58
Maxell CD-RW disks with jewel cases	0.7	€1.40
Office Depot DVD-RW rewriteable media spindle	4.7	€4.00
HP 9.1 GB rewriteable optical disk	9.1	€7.90
Office Depot DVD-R recordable media spindle	4.7	€9.60
SanDisk compact flash memory card	1.0	€75.00
SanDisk memory stick flash memory card	0.256	€103.00
PNY optima DDR SDRAM memory upgrade	0.512	€104.00

SOURCE: Office Depot (website), www.officedepot.com, February 5, 2006.

objectives. An objective of a credit card company's information system, for example, might be to rapidly retrieve stored customer data to approve customer purchases. In this case, a fast access method is critical. In other cases, such as equipping a sales force with laptop computers, portability and storage capacity might be major considerations in selecting and using secondary storage media and devices.

Storage media that allow faster access are generally more expensive than slower media. The cost of additional storage capacity and portability vary widely, but they are also factors to consider. In addition to cost and portability, organizations must address security issues to allow only authorized people to access sensitive data and critical programs. Because the data and programs kept in secondary storage devices are so critical to most organizations, all of these issues merit careful consideration.

3.3.1 Access Methods

Data and information access can be either sequential or direct. **Sequential access** means that data must be accessed in the order in which it is stored. For example, inventory data might be stored sequentially by part number, such as 100, 101, 102, and so on. If you want to retrieve information on part number 125, you must read and discard all the data relating to parts 001 through 124.

sequential access A retrieval method in which data must be accessed in the order in which it is stored.

direct access A retrieval method in which data can be retrieved without the need to read and discard other data.

direct access storage device (DASD). A device used for direct access of secondary storage data.

Direct access means that data can be retrieved directly, without the need to pass by other data in sequence. With direct access, it is possible to go directly to and access the needed data – for example, part number 125 – without having to read through parts 001 through 124. For this reason, direct access is usually faster than sequential access. The devices used only to access secondary storage data sequentially are simply called sequential access storage devices (SASDs); those used for direct access are called **direct access storage devices (DASDs).**

3.3.2 Devices

The most common forms of secondary storage include magnetic tapes, magnetic disks, virtual tapes, and optical disks. Some of these media (magnetic tape) allow only sequential access, while others (magnetic disks and optical disks) provide direct and sequential access.

Magnetic Tape

Magnetic tape is a type of sequential secondary storage medium, now used primarily for storing backups of databases. Similar to the tape found in audio and videocassettes, magnetic tape is a Mylar film coated with iron oxide. Portions of the tape are magnetized to represent bits. If the computer needs to read data from the middle of a reel of tape, it must first pass all the tape before the desired piece of data – one disadvantage of magnetic tape. When information is needed, it can take time to retrieve the proper tape and mount it on the tape reader to get the relevant data into the computer. Despite the falling prices of hard drives, tape storage is still a popular choice for low-cost data backup for off-site storage in the event of a disaster. The main disadvantage with tape is that it is sequential. However this does not matter when recovering from a disaster (if the hard drive fails for instance), as the goal is to read the entire tape onto a new hard drive.

magnetic tape A secondary storage medium; Mylar film coated with iron oxide with portions of the tape magnetized to represent bits.

Technology is improving to provide tape storage devices with greater capacities and faster transfer speeds. In addition, the bulky tape drives used to read and write on large reels of tapes in the early days of computing have been replaced with much smaller tape cartridge devices measuring a few millimetres in diameter that take up much less floor space and allow hundreds of tape cartridges to be stored in a small area.

Magnetic Disks

Magnetic disks are also coated with iron oxide; they can be thin metallic platters (hard disks) or Mylar film (diskettes) (see Figure 3.5). As with magnetic tape, magnetic disks represent bits using small magnetized areas. When reading from or writing data onto a disk, the disk's read/write head can go directly to the desired piece of data. Thus, the disk is a direct-access storage medium. Because direct access allows fast data retrieval, this type of storage is ideal for companies that need to respond quickly to customer requests, such as airlines and credit card firms. For example, if a manager needs information on the credit history of a customer or the seat availability on a particular flight, the information can be obtained in seconds if the data is stored on a direct access storage device.

magnetic disk A common secondary storage medium, with bits represented by magnetized areas.

Figure 3.5 Hard Disks and Diskettes

SOURCE: Istock.

Magnetic disk storage varies widely in capacity and portability. Removable magnetic disks, such as diskettes or Zip disks, are nearly obsolete. Hard disks, though more costly and less portable, are more popular because of their greater storage capacity and quicker access time.

Raid

One concern with the most critical mechanical components inside a disk storage device, the disk drives, the fans, and other input/output devices, is that, like most things that move, they can break. Organizations now require that their data-storage devices be 'fault tolerant', that is, they can continue with little or no loss of performance if one or more key components fails. A **redundant array of independent/inexpensive disks (RAID)** is a method of storing data that generates extra bits of data from existing data, allowing the system to create a 'reconstruction map' so that if a hard drive fails, it can rebuild lost data. With this approach, data is split and stored on different physical disk drives using a technique called striping, to evenly distribute the data. RAID technology has been applied to storage systems to improve system performance and reliability.

redundant array of independent/inexpensive disks (RAID) A method of storing data that generates extra bits of data from existing data, allowing the system to create a 'reconstruction map' so that if a hard drive fails, the system can rebuild lost data.

disk mirroring A process of storing data that provides an exact copy that protects users fully in the event of data loss.

RAID can be implemented in several ways. In the simplest form, RAID subsystems duplicate data on drives. This process, called **disk mirroring**, provides an exact copy that protects users fully in the event of data loss. However, to keep complete duplicates of current backups, organizations need to double the amount of their storage capacity. Thus, disk mirroring is expensive. Other RAID methods are less expensive because they only partly duplicate the data, allowing storage managers to minimize the amount of extra disk space (or overhead) they must purchase to protect data. RAID is important for any business that is reliant on data such as insurance companies, banks and many Internet businesses such as Google and Amazon.

Virtual Tape

Virtual tape is a storage technology that manages less frequently needed data so that it appears to be stored entirely on tape cartridges, although some parts might actually be located on faster hard disks. The software associated with a virtual tape system is sometimes called a virtual tape server. Virtual tape can be used with a sophisticated storage-management system that moves data to slower but less costly forms of storage media as people use the data less often. Virtual tape technology can decrease data access time, lower the total cost of ownership, and reduce the amount of floor space consumed by tape operations. IBM and Storage Technology are well-established vendors of virtual tape systems.

virtual tape A storage device that manages less frequently needed data so that it appears to be stored entirely on tape cartridges, although some parts of it might actually be located on faster hard disks.

Optical Disks

Another type of secondary storage medium is the **optical disk**. An optical disk is a rigid disk of plastic onto which data is recorded by special lasers that physically burn pits in the disk. Areas between pits are known as 'lands'. Data is directly accessed from the disk by an optical disk device which uses a low-power laser that measures the difference in reflected light caused by a pit or a land on the disk.

optical disk A rigid disk of plastic onto which data is recorded by special lasers that physically burn pits in the disk.

compact disk read-only memory (CD-ROM) A common form of optical disk on which data, once it has been recorded, cannot be modified.

A common optical disk is the **compact disk read-only memory (CD-ROM)** with a storage capacity of about 700 MB of data. After data is recorded on a CD-ROM, it cannot be modified – the disk is 'read-only'. A CD burner, the informal name for a CD recorder, is a device that can record data to a compact disk. CD-recordable (CD-R) and CD-rewritable (CD-RW) are the two most common types of drives that can write CDs, either once (in the case of CD-R) or repeatedly (in the case of CD-RW). CD-rewritable (CD-RW) technology allows computer users to back up data on CDs. It should be noted that CD-R and CD-RW are not as reliable as software CDs bought in shops such as PC World. The reason is that the pits in the bought CD are actually burnt into the disk (i.e. there is a physical bump) whereas with CD-R and CD-RW the pits are simulated by changing the disk's reflectivity so that, when read, the laser is reflected as if by a real pit.

Digital Versatile Disk

A **digital versatile disk (DVD)** looks like a CD but can store about 135 minutes of digital video or several gigabytes of data. Software, video games, and movies are often stored or distributed on DVDs. At a data transfer rate of 1.352 MB/second, the access speed of a DVD drive is faster than that of the typical CD-ROM drive.

digital versatile disk (DVD) A storage medium used to store digital video or computer data.

DVDs have replaced recordable and rewritable CD disks (CD-R and CD-RW) as the preferred format for sharing movies and photos. Whereas a CD can hold about 700 MB of data, a single-sided DVD can hold around 4.5 GB, with double-sided DVDs having a capacity of about 9 GB. Unfortunately, DVD manufacturers haven't agreed on a recording standard, so there are several types of recorders and disks. Recordings can be made on record-once disks (DVD-R and DVD+R) or on rewritable disks (DVD-RW, DVD+RW, and DVD-RAM). Not all types of rewritable DVDs are compatible with other types. Dell and Hewlett-Packard use DVD+RW; Apple, Gateway, and IBM offer DVD-R. Dell and other manufacturers use DVD+/-RW.

The two types of competing high-definition video-disk formats are called HD-DVD and Blu-ray Disk. Both formats were originally based on blue-laser technology that stores at least three times as much data as a DVD now holds.[10] Traditional magneto-optical (MO), CD, and DVD formats all use red lasers. Because the wavelength of blue light is shorter than that of red light, the beam from a blue laser makes a much smaller spot on the recording layer of a disk. A smaller spot means less space is needed to record one bit of data, so more data can be stored on a disk. The primary use for these new formats is in home entertainment equipment to store high definition video, though these formats can also store computer data.

Holographic Disk

Holographic versatile disk (HVD) is an advanced optical disk technology still in the research stage that would store more data than even the Blu-ray and HD DVD optical disk systems. One approach to HVD records data through the depth of the storage media in three dimensions by splitting a laser beam in two – the signal beam carries the data, and the reference beam positions where the data is written and reads it. This approach can record and read one billion bits of data with each flash of light. A holographic disk is expected to hold about 200 GB of data – 50 times as much as a DVD. HVD will also write data as much as ten times faster.[11]

Memory Cards

A group of computer manufacturers formed the Personal Computer Memory Card International Association (PCMCIA) to create standards for a peripheral device known as a PC memory card. These PC memory cards come is a range of sizes, from stamp size to credit card size, and can be installed in an adapter or slot in many personal computers. To the rest of the system, the PC memory card functions as a hard disk drive. Memory cards are often used in mobile devices such as digital cameras, MP3 players, **smartphones** and laptops. Although the cost per megabyte of storage is greater than for traditional hard disk storage, these cards are less prone to fail than hard disks, are portable, and are relatively easy to use. Software manufacturers often store program instructions on a memory card for use with laptop computers. Memory cards use flash memory.

smartphone A phone that combines the functionality of a mobile phone, camera, web browser, e-mail tool, and other devices into a single handheld device.

Flash memory is a silicon computer chip that, unlike RAM, is non-volatile and keeps its memory when the power is shut off. It gets its name from the fact that the microchip is organized so that a section of memory cells (called a block) is erased or reprogrammed in a single action, or 'flash'. Solid-state

flash memory A silicon computer chip that, unlike RAM, is non-volatile and keeps its memory when the power is shut off.

disks (SSDs) that use flash memory are supplementing or replacing traditional hard drives that employ power-hungry spinning platters with mobile read/write heads near data surfaces.[12] The result is longer laptop battery life and more protection for data. Another advantage is that a flash memory system reboots faster than hard disks.[13] Digital music players and cameras use flash memory to hold music and photos. Compared with other types of secondary storage, flash memory can be accessed more quickly and consumes less power and storage space. The primary disadvantage is cost. Flash memory chips cost much more per megabyte than a traditional hard disk. Figure 3.6 shows one application of flash memory technology.

Figure 3.6 Flash
Disk/USB Key *Flash*
memory is used to
conveniently carry
electronic documents
and other files.

SOURCE: Istock.

Ethical and Societal Issues

Backup Storage Media and Identity Theft

After two weeks of internal investigations, Marriott International reported that backup computer tapes had gone missing from its time-share division offices. The tapes contained credit card account information and other personal information on about 206 000 time-share owners and Marriott customers and employees. Company officials stated that it was not clear whether the tapes were stolen or lost. All involved parties were notified in case identity thieves gained access to the information.

Identity theft is the crime in which an impostor uses stolen personal identification information to obtain credit, merchandise, or services in the name of the victim. Companies assume the responsibility of keeping such information secure. So far, no direct correlation has been proven between data breaches such as that at Marriott and cases of identity theft. However, there are about 10 million cases of identity theft each year. The sources of the stolen data are often unknown. It is assumed that much of the information is stolen from businesses.

Besides the danger to personal privacy, the companies responsible also suffer. The public embarrassment resulting from data theft detracts from a company's reputation and ability to win customers. Substantial costs are also involved in notifying victims of the possible theft. Companies could avoid this trouble and expense by using inexpensive methods of protecting data.

Most companies employ courier services to transport backup tapes to and from storage. However, the backups are not always safely delivered to the storage facility. In addition, accounting and inventory of backup tapes in storage can be lacking. When tapes are lost, the courier or storage facility is usually to blame, leading to suspicions of theft.

To better protect the data stored for back up, it can be encrypted so that if stolen it remains unreadable. Encryption is a technique that converts data into a secret code. In-line appliances can encrypt backup data prior to being written to tape with little effect on performance. Because the data is encrypted prior to transport, it is secure in transit and in storage.

Some feel that for businesses to take this problem seriously, government needs to apply pressure through additional legislation. Others argue that data reported as lost typically cannot be used on its own by thieves and is deactivated or changed when the theft is realized anyway, reducing the need for legislation. Improvements in networking and storage technologies will eventually solve this dilemma for those concerned about privacy. Until then, thousands of database records will likely be accessed without authorization due to the loss or theft of corporate storage media.

Questions

1 How can the theft of a credit card number or bank account number be a danger to the victim?

2 Why is tape the most common medium used for backing up data?

3 To what extent should laws hold companies responsible for the security of the data they keep? Should encryption be required?

4 If you were responsible for the safety of Marriott's backup data, what security measures would you take?

SOURCES: Rosenwald, Michael S., 'Marriott Discloses Missing Data Files', *Washington Post,* December 28, 2005, www.washingtonpost.com; Damoulakis, Jim, 'Do We Really Care About Storage Security?', *Computerworld,* February 7, 2006, www.computerworld.com; Lawson; Stephen, 'Bank Tape Lost with Data on 90,000 Customers', *Computerworld,* January 11, 2006, www.computerworld.com.

3.3.3 Enterprise Storage Options

Businesses increasingly need to store large amounts of data created throughout the organization. Such large secondary storage is called enterprise storage, and comes in three forms: attached storage, network-attached storage (NAS), and storage area networks (SANs).

Attached Storage

Attached storage methods include the tape, hard disks, and optical devices discussed previously, which are connected directly to a single computer. Attached storage methods, though simple and cost effective for single users and small groups, do not allow systems to share storage, and they make it difficult to back up data.

Because of the limitations of attached storage, firms are turning to network-attached storage (NAS) and storage area networks (SANs). These alternative forms of enterprise data storage enable an organization to share data-storage resources among a much larger number of computers and users, resulting in improved storage efficiency and greater cost-effectiveness. In addition, they simplify data backup and reduce the risk of downtime. Nearly one-third of system downtime is a direct result of data-storage failures, so eliminating storage problems as a cause of downtime is a major advantage.

Network-Attached Storage

Network-attached storage (NAS) employs storage devices that attach to a network instead of to a single computer. NAS includes software to manage

network-attached storage (NAS) Storage devices that attach to a network instead of to a single computer.

storage access and file management and relieve the users' computers of those tasks. The result is that both application software and files can be served faster because they are not competing for the same processor resources. Computer users can share and access the same information, even if they are using different types of computers. Common applications for NAS include consolidated storage, Internet and e-commerce applications, and digital media.

Storage Area Network

A **storage area network (SAN)** is a special-purpose, high-speed network that provides direct connections between data-storage devices and computers across the enterprise (see Figure 3.7). A SAN also integrates different types of storage subsystems, such as multiple RAID storage devices and magnetic tape backup systems, into a single storage system. Use of a SAN off-loads the network traffic associated with storage onto a separate network. The data can then be copied to a remote location, making it easier for companies to create backups and implement disaster recovery policies.

storage area network (SAN) The technology that provides high-speed connections between data-storage devices and computers over a network.

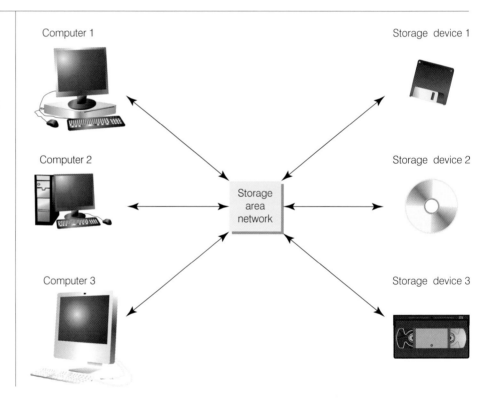

Figure 3.7 Storage Area Network *A SAN provides high-speed connections between data-storage devices and computers over a network.*

Computer 1

Computer 2

Computer 3

Storage area network

Storage device 1

Storage device 2

Storage device 3

Using a SAN, an organization can centralize the people, policies, procedures, and practices for managing storage, and a data-storage manager can apply the data consistently across an enterprise. This centralization eliminates inconsistent treatment of data by different system administrators and users, providing efficient and cost-effective data-storage practices.

A fundamental difference between NAS and SAN is that NAS uses file input/output, which defines data as complete containers of information, while SAN deals with block input/output, which is based on subsets of data smaller than a file. SAN manufacturers include EMC, Hitachi Data Systems Corporation, Xiotech, and IBM.

As organizations set up large-scale SANs, they use more computers and network connections, which become difficult to manage. In response, software tools designed to automate storage using previously defined policies are finding a place in the enterprise. Known as **policy-based storage management**, the software products from industry leaders such as Veritas Software Corporation, Legato Systems, Inc., EMC, and IBM automatically allocate storage space to users, balance the loads on servers and disks, and reroute networks when systems go down – all based on policies set up by system administrators.

policy-based storage management Automation of storage using previously defined policies.

The trend in secondary storage is toward higher capacity, increased portability, and automated storage management. Organizations should select a type of storage based on their needs and resources. In general, storing large amounts of data and information and letting users access it quickly makes an organization more efficient. Businesses can also choose pay-per-use services, where they rent space on massive storage devices housed either at a service provider (e.g., Hewlett-Packard or IBM) or on the customer's premises, paying only for the amount of storage they use. This approach is sensible for organizations with wildly fluctuating storage needs, such as those involved in the testing of new drugs or developing software.

3.4   Input and Output Devices

Input and output devices are part of a computer's user interface, which includes other hardware devices and software that allow you to interact with a computer system. These are the parts that are seen by the user and are therefore often of more concern to the user than memory and processing speeds. They are used to provide data and instructions to the computer and receive results from it. As with other computer system components, an organization should keep its business goals in mind when selecting input and output devices. For example, many restaurant chains use handheld, mobile input devices that let waiters delivery orders to the kitchen efficiently and accurately. These systems have also cut costs by helping to track inventory and market to customers.

3.4.1   Characteristics and Functionality

In general, businesses want input devices that let them rapidly enter data into a computer system, and they want output devices that let them produce useful results. When selecting input and output devices, businesses need to consider the form of the output they want, the nature of the data required to generate this output, and the speed and accuracy they need for both. Some organizations have very specific needs for output and input, requiring devices that perform specific functions. The more specialized the application, the more specialized the associated system input and output devices.

The speed and functions of input and output devices should be balanced with their cost, control, and complexity. More specialized devices might make it easier to enter data or output information, but they are generally more costly, less flexible, and more susceptible to malfunction.

The Nature of Data

Getting data into the computer – input – often requires transferring human-readable data, such as a sales order, into the computer system. 'Human-readable' means data that people can read and understand. A sheet of paper containing inventory figures is an example of human-readable data. In contrast, machine-readable data can be understood and read by computer devices (e.g., the universal bar code that scanners read in supermarkets) and is typically stored as bits or bytes. Some data can be read by both people and machines, such as the magnetic ink (explained later in this chapter) on bank cheques. Usually, people begin the input process by organizing human-readable data and transforming it into machine-readable data. Every keystroke on a keyboard, for example, turns a human language character into a digital code that the machine can understand.

Data Entry and Input

data entry Converting human-readable data into a machine-readable form.

data input Transferring machine-readable data into the system.

Getting data into the computer system is a two-stage process. First, the human-readable data is converted into a machine-readable form through **data entry**. The second stage involves transferring the machine-readable data into the system. This is **data input**.

Today, many companies are using online data entry and input – they communicate and transfer data to computer devices directly connected to the computer system. Online data entry and input places data into the computer system in a matter of seconds. Organizations in many industries require the instantaneous updating offered by this approach. For example, when airline personnel need to enter a last-minute reservation, they can use online data entry and input to record the reservation as soon as it is made. Reservation agents at other terminals can then access this data to make a seating check before they make another reservation. Many entrepreneurs have started e-businesses cheaply by having customers do their own data entry. When you buy a DVD at Canadian company DVDBoxOffice.com, you type your own address directly into their database, which means they don't have to employ someone to do this. The address label is printed out and stuck on your parcel, giving DVDBoxOffice (and you) low cost and efficient operation.

Source Data Automation

Regardless of how data gets into the computer, it should be captured and edited at its source. **Source data automation** involves capturing and editing data where the data is originally created and in a form that can be directly input to a computer, thus ensuring accuracy and timeliness. For example, using source data automation, salespeople enter sales orders into the computer at the time and place they take the order. Any errors can be detected and corrected immediately. If any item is temporarily out of stock, the salesperson can discuss options with the customer. Prior to source data automation, orders were written on paper and entered into the computer later (usually by a administrator, not the person who took the order).

source data automation Capturing and editing data where the data is initially created and in a form that can be directly input to a computer, thus ensuring accuracy and timeliness.

Sometimes the handwritten information wasn't legible or, worse yet, got lost. If problems occurred during data entry, the administrator had to contact the salesperson or the customer to 'recapture' the data needed for order entry, leading to further delays and customer dissatisfaction.

3.4.2 Input Devices

You can use hundreds of devices for data entry and input. They range from special-purpose devices that capture specific types of data to more general-purpose input devices. Some of the special-purpose data entry and input devices are discussed later in this chapter. First, we focus on devices used to enter and input general types of data, including text, audio, images, and video for personal computers.

Keyboard and Mouse

A keyboard and a computer mouse are the most common devices used for entry and input of data such as characters, text, and basic commands. Some companies are developing keyboards that are more comfortable, more easily adjusted, and faster to use than standard keyboards. These ergonomic keyboards, such as the split keyboard by Microsoft and others, are designed to avoid wrist and hand injuries caused by hours of typing. Other keyboards include touchpads that let you enter sketches on the touchpad and text using the keys. Another innovation is the wireless mouse and keyboard, which keep a physical desktop free from clutter.

You use a computer mouse to point to and click symbols, icons, menus, and commands on the screen. The computer takes a number of actions in response, such as placing data into the computer system. Some of these devices are shown in Figure 3.8.

Figure 3.8 Mouse and Keyboard

Speech-Recognition Technology

Speech-recognition technology enables a computer equipped with a source of audio input such as a microphone to interpret human speech as an means of providing data or instructions to the computer. The most basic systems require you to train the system to recognize your speech patterns or are limited to a small vocabulary of words. More advanced systems can recognize continuous speech without requiring you to break up your speech into discrete words. Very advanced systems used by the government and military can interpret a new voice and understand a rich vocabulary.

speech-recognition technology Input devices that recognize human speech.

Companies that must constantly interact with customers are eager to reduce their customer support costs while improving the quality of their service. In the U.S., Pacific Gas and Electric (PG&E) serves five million electric customers and four million natural gas customers. The firm implemented speech-recognition technology to automate the account identification process and to provide other customer self-service functions. Some 38 percent of customer service calls are satisfied using the system without speaking directly to a customer service representative. This yields a savings of nearly $2 million per year based on the average cost of $5 for a PG&E customer service representative to handle a call.[14]

Digital Cameras

Digital cameras record and store images or video in digital form (see Figure 3.9). When you take pictures, the images are electronically stored in the camera. You can download the images to a computer either directly or by using a flash memory card. After you store the images on the computer's hard disk, you can edit them, send them to another location, paste them into another application, or print them. For example, you can download a photo of your project team captured by a digital camera and then post it on a website or paste it into a project status report. Digital cameras have eclipsed film cameras used by professional photographers for photo quality and features such as zoom, flash, exposure controls, special effects, and even video-capture capabilities.

digital camera An input device used with a PC to record and store images and video in digital form.

A reasonable quality digital camera now costs around €300. The primary advantage of digital cameras is saving time and money by eliminating the need to process film. In fact, digital cameras that can easily transfer images to CDs have made the consumer film business of Kodak and Fujitsu nearly obsolete. Until film-camera users switch to digital cameras, Kodak is

Figure 3.9 A Digital
Camera

SOURCE: Istock.

allowing photographers to have it both ways. When you want to develop print film, Kodak offers the option of placing pictures on a CD in addition to the traditional prints. After the photos are stored on the CD, they can be edited, placed on a website, or sent electronically to business associates or friends around the world. Organizations are now using digital cameras for security and other business purposes. Many estate agents for instance, take photos of the houses they sell when they evaluate them. Traffic wardens take pictures of the cars they ticket, to prove they have been parked illegally.

Terminals

Inexpensive and easy to use, terminals are input and display devices that perform data entry and input at the same time. A terminal is connected to a complete computer system, including a processor, memory, and secondary storage. These functions could be part of the terminal itself, as would be the case if a PC was being used as a terminal, or they could be provided by a server. After you enter general commands, text, and other data via a keyboard or mouse, it is converted into machine-readable form and transferred to the processing portion of the computer system. Terminals, normally connected directly to the computer system by telephone lines or cables, can be placed in offices, in warehouses, and on the factory floor.

Scanning Devices

You can input image and character data using a scanning device. A page scanner is like a copy machine. You typically insert a page you want to input into the scanner or place it face down on the glass plate of the scanner, cover it, and then scan it. With a handheld scanner, you manually move or roll the scanning device over the image you want to scan. Both page and handheld scanners can convert monochrome or colour pictures, forms, text, and other images into machine-readable digits. Many companies are looking to scanning devices to help them manage their documents and reduce the high cost of using and processing paper.

Optical Data Readers

You can also use a special scanning device called an 'optical data reader' to scan documents. The two categories of optical data readers are for optical mark recognition (OMR) and optical character recognition (OCR). You use OMR readers for test scoring and other purposes when test takers use pencils to fill in boxes on OMR paper, which is also called a 'mark sense form'. OMR systems are used in multiple-choice tests. In comparison, most OCR readers use reflected light to recognize and scan various characters. With special software, OCR readers can convert handwritten or typed documents into digital data. After being entered, this data can be shared, modified, and distributed over computer networks to hundreds or thousands of people.

Magnetic Ink Character Recognition (MICR) Devices

In the 1950s, the banking industry became swamped with paper cheques, loan applications, bank statements, and so on. Magnetic ink character recognition (MICR), a system for reading banking data quickly, was introduced to solve this problem. With MICR, data is placed on the bottom of a check or other form using a special magnetic ink. Using a special character set, data printed with this ink is readable by people and computers (see Figure 3.10).

Figure 3.10 MICR Device *Magnetic ink character recognition technology codes data on the bottom of a cheque or other form using special magnetic ink, which is readable by people and computers. For an example, look at the bottom of a bank cheque.*

SOURCE: Profimedia International s.r.o./Alamy.

Magnetic Stripe Card

A **magnetic stripe card** stores limited amounts of data by modifying the magnetism of tiny iron-based particles contained in a band on the card. The magnetic stripe is read by physically swiping the card past a reading head. Magnetic stripe cards are commonly used in credit cards, transportation tickets, and driving licenses.

magnetic stripe card A type of card that stores limited amounts of data by modifying the magnetism of tiny iron-based particles contained in a band on the card.

Point-of-Sale Devices

Point-of-sale (POS) devices are terminals used in retail operations to enter sales information into the computer system. The POS device then computes the

point-of-sale (POS) device A terminal used in retail operations to enter sales information into the computer system.

Figure 3.11 A POS in a supermarket

SOURCE: David Hancock/Alamy.

total charges. Many POS devices also use other types of input and output devices, such as keyboards, bar-code readers, printers, and screens. A POS is shown in Figure 3.11.

Automated Teller Machine (ATM) Devices

Another type of special-purpose input/output device, the automated teller machine (ATM) is a terminal that bank customers use to perform withdrawals and other transactions with their bank accounts. The ATM, however, is no longer used only for cash and bank receipts. Companies use various ATM devices, sometimes called kiosks, to support their business processes. Some can dispense tickets, such as for airlines, concerts, and soccer games. Some colleges and universities use them to produce transcripts. For this reason, the input and output capabilities of ATMs are varied. Like POS devices, ATMs can work with other types of input and output devices. Unisys, for example, has developed an ATM kiosk that allows bank customers to make cash withdrawals, pay bills, and receive advice on investments and retirement planning.

Pen Input Devices

With special hardware and software, data can be input by touching a screen with a pen input device. This can be used to activate a command or cause the computer to perform a task, enter handwritten notes, and draw objects and figures. Handwriting recognition software can convert handwriting on the screen into text. The Tablet PC from Microsoft and its hardware partners can transform handwriting into typed text and store the 'digital ink' just the way a person writes it. Users can use a pen to write and send e-mail, add comments to Word documents, mark up PowerPoint presentations, and even hand-draw charts in a document. That data can then be moved, highlighted, searched, and converted into text. If perfected, this interface is likely to become widely used. Pen input is especially attractive if you are uncomfortable using a keyboard. The success of pen input depends on how accurately handwriting can be read and translated into digital form and at what cost.

Pestproof, a pest control company in Northern England, is using pen-based, digital reporting technology to speed up the creation of its customers' assessment reports. In the past, reports were completed on paper, which then had to be taken to head office to be typed up. Pestproof technicians, who are home based, only come into the main office sporadically. This created bottlenecks and meant head office did not have up-to-date information. Now, using digital pens and digital paper, technicians fill in the forms in the same way as they did when using traditional pen and paper. The data is transmitted immediately to head office via a Bluetooth connection with the technician's mobile phone. The data is then collated and integrated directly into Microsoft Excel for analysis and the creation of the report. Customers can access their reports online to receive instant advice about the type of pesticide used, the work carried out and action to take in case of an emergency.[15]

Many delivery firms use pen input devices to collect a signature from customers at their door.

Touch-Sensitive Screens

Advances in screen technology allow display screens to function as input as well as output devices. By touching certain parts of a touch-sensitive screen, you can start a program or trigger other types of action. Touch-sensitive screens are popular input devices for some small computers because they do not require a keyboard, which conserves space and increases portability. Touch screens are frequently used on photocopy machines to enable users to select various options and at fast-food restaurants for personnel to enter customer choices.

Microsoft has recently released 'Surface', a touch-sensitive computer in the shape of a coffee table. Designed to operate without a mouse and keyboard, Surface lets users interact with it by touching the screen using more than one finger at a time. This is another approach by Microsoft to ultimately bring the computer into living rooms, just like the television, and become an integral part of daily life.

Bar-Code Scanners

A bar-code scanner employs a laser scanner to read a bar-coded label. This form of input is used widely in grocery shop checkouts and in warehouse inventory control. Often, bar-code technology is combined with other forms of technology to create innovative ways for capturing data.

Radio Frequency Identification

The purpose of a **radio frequency identification (RFID)** system is to process data sent by a mobile device, called a tag, to an RFID reader, according to the needs of an IS program. One popular application of RFID is to place a microchip on retail items and install in-store readers that track the inventory on the shelves to determine when shelves should be restocked. The RFID tag chip includes a special form of EPROM memory that holds data about the item to which the tag is attached. A radio frequency signal can update this memory as the status of the item changes. The data transmitted by the tag might provide identification, location information, or details about the product tagged, such as date manufactured, retail price, colour, or date of purchase.

radio frequency identification (RFID) A technology that employs a microchip with an antenna that broadcasts its unique identifier and location to receivers.

The two basic types of RFID tags are passive and active. Passive tags have no internal power source. An incoming radio frequency signal from the reader triggers a tiny electrical current in the antenna of the RFID tag, which powers the integrated circuit in the tag and transmits a response communicating the information it has been programmed to deliver. Passive RFID tags are small, do not require batteries, have an unlimited life span, and send signals that can be heard from a distance of a few yards. Active RFID tags have an internal power source, which powers the tag so that it can generate an outgoing signal. Active tags can be heard over a longer distance and have more memory than passive tags. Currently, the smallest active tags are about the size of a coin. Because passive tags are less expensive to manufacture and require no battery, most RFID tags today are passive. The popularity of RFID tags continues to grow. Toyota was one of the first automobile manufacturers to employ a smart key with an active RFID tag that allows a car to acknowledge the key's presence within approximately three feet of the sensor. The driver can open the doors and start the car while the key remains in a purse or pocket. London's Oyster card (see Figure 3.12) uses RFID technology to let public transport passengers pay their fare. Passengers top up their card with funds and a reader in the station takes payment off the built-in chip. This same technology is used in similar applications all over the world.

Figure 3.12 The Oyster Card

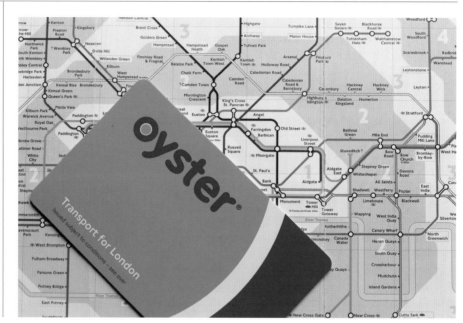

SOURCE: Ashley Cooper/Alamy

3.4.3 Output Devices

Computer systems provide output to decision makers at all levels of an organization so they can solve a business problem or capitalize on a competitive opportunity. In addition, output from one computer system can provide input into another computer system. The desired form of this output might be visual, audio, or even digital. Whatever the output's content or form, output devices are designed to provide the right information to the right person in the right format at the right time.

Display Monitors

The display monitor is a device similar to a TV screen that displays output from the computer. Because some monitors use a cathode-ray tube to display images, they are sometimes called CRTs. The cathode-ray tube in such a monitor generates one or more electron beams. As the beams strike a phosphorescent compound (phosphor) coated on the inside of the screen, a dot on the screen called a pixel lights up. A **pixel** is a dot of colour on a photo image or a point of light on a display screen. It appears in one of two modes: on or off. The electron beam sweeps across the screen so that as the phosphor starts to fade, it is struck and lights up again.

pixel A dot of colour on a photo image or a point of light on a display screen.

With today's wide selection of monitors, price and overall quality can vary tremendously. The quality of a screen image is often measured by the number of horizontal and vertical pixels used to create it. The more pixels per square centimetre, the higher the resolution, or clarity and sharpness, of the image. For example, a screen with a 1024 × 768 resolution (786 432 pixels) has a higher sharpness than one with a resolution of 800 × 600 (480 000 pixels). Another way to measure image quality is the distance between one pixel on the screen and the next nearest pixel, which is known as dot pitch. The common range of dot pitch is from 0.25 mm to 0.31 mm. The smaller the dot pitch, the better the picture. A dot pitch of 0.28 mm or smaller is considered good. Greater pixel densities and smaller dot pitches yield sharper images of higher resolution.

The characteristics of screen colour depend on the quality of the monitor, the amount of RAM in the computer system, and the monitor's graphics adapter card. The Colour/Graphics Adapter (CGA) was one of the first technologies to display colour images on the screen. Today, Super Video Graphics Array (SVGA) displays are standard, providing vivid colours and high resolution. Digital Video Interface (DVI) is designed to maximize the visual quality of digital display devices such as flat-panel LCD computer displays.

Liquid Crystal Displays (LCDs)

LCD displays are flat displays that use liquid crystals – organic, oil-like material placed between two polarizers – to form characters and graphic images on a backlit screen. These displays are easier on your eyes than CRTs because they are flicker-free, brighter, and don't emit the type of radiation that worries some CRT users. In addition, LCD monitors take up less space and use less than half of the electricity required to operate a comparably sized CRT monitor. Thin-film transistor (TFT) LCDs are a type of liquid crystal display that assigns a transistor to control each pixel, resulting in higher resolution and quicker response to changes on the screen. TFT LCD monitors are rapidly displacing competing CRT technology, and are commonly available in sizes from 12 to 30 inches.

LCD display Flat display that uses liquid crystals – organic, oil-like material placed between two polarizers – to form characters and graphic images on a backlit screen.

Organic Light-Emitting Diodes

Organic light-emitting diode (OLED) technology is based on research by Eastman Kodak Company and is appearing on the market in small electronic devices. OLEDs use the same base technology as LCDs, with one key difference: Whereas LCD screens contain a fluorescent backlight and the LCD acts as a shutter to selectively block that light, OLEDs directly emit light. OLEDs can provide sharper and brighter colours than LCDs and CRTs, and because they don't require a backlight, the displays can be half as thick as LCDs and can be used in flexible displays. Another big advantage is that OLEDs don't break when dropped. OLEDs are currently limited to use in mobile phones, car radios, and digital cameras, but might be used in computer displays – if the average display lifetime can be extended.[16]

Printers and Plotters

One of the most useful and popular forms of output is called 'hard copy', which is simply paper output from a printer. The two main types of printers are laser printers and inkjet printers, and they are available with different speeds, features, and capabilities. Some can be set up to accommodate paper forms, such as blank cheque forms and invoice forms. Newer printers allow businesses to create customized printed output for each customer from standard paper and data input using full colour. Ticket-receipt printers such as those used in restaurants, ATMs, and point-of-sale systems are in wide-scale use.

The speed of the printer is typically measured by the number of pages printed per minute (ppm). Like a display screen, the quality, or resolution, of a printer's output depends on the number of dots printed per inch (dpi). A 600-dpi printer prints more clearly than a 300-dpi printer. A recurring cost of using a printer is the inkjet or laser cartridge that must be replaced periodically – every few thousand pages for laser printers and every 500 to 900 pages for inkjet

Figure 3.13 Laser **Printer** *Laser printers, available in a wide variety of speeds and price ranges, have many features, including colour capabilities. They are a popular solution for printing hard copies of information.*

SOURCE: Istock.

printers. Figure 3.13 shows a laser printer. A later section discusses considerations for selecting a printer.

Laser printers are generally faster than inkjet printers and can handle more volume than inkjet printers. Laser printers print 15 to 50 pages per minute (ppm) for black and white and 4 to 20 ppm for colour. Inkjet printers print 10 to 30 ppm for black and white and 2 to 10 ppm for colour.

For colour printing, inkjet printers print vivid hues and with an initial cost much less than colour laser printers. Inkjet printers can produce high-quality banners, graphics, greeting cards, letters, text, and prints of photos.

Plotters are a type of hard-copy output device used for general design work. Businesses typically use plotters to generate paper or acetate blueprints, schematics, and drawings of buildings or new products.

Digital Audio Player

A **digital audio player** is a device that can store, organize, and play digital music files. **MP3** (MPEG-1 Audio Layer-3) is a popular format for compressing a sound sequence into a very small file while preserving the original level of sound quality when it is played. By compressing the sound file, it requires less time to download the file and less storage space on a hard drive.

digital audio player A device that can store, organize, and play digital music files.

MP3 A standard format for compressing a sound sequence into a small file.

You can use many different music devices smaller than a pack of cards to download music from the Internet and other sources. These devices have no moving parts and can store hours of music. Apple expanded into the digital music market with its iPod and the iTunes Music Store, which allows you to find music online, preview it, and download it in a way that is safe, legal, and affordable. In October 2005, Apple unveiled a new iPod with a 2.5-inch screen that can play video, including selected TV

Figure 3.14 iPod
Apple's iPod, a digital music player for Mac and Windows, has a 2.5-inch screen and can play video.

SOURCE: D. Hurst/Alamy.

shows you can download from the iTunes Music Store (see Figure 3.14).[17] There are dozens of MP3 manufacturers, including Dell, Sony, Samsung, Iomega, and Motorola, whose Rokr product is the first iTunes-compatible phone.

The use of audio players has not yet taken off in businesses. Recording and reviewing voice data is one application (for example, recording meetings) but people are often not comfortable with this. A 'killer application' for this technology is business may be on the way, but for now, this is mainly used for entertainment.

Special-Purpose Input and Output Devices

Many additional input and output devices are used for specialized or unique applications. Some examples of such devices are discussed in the following sections.

Computer-Based Navigation Systems

Computer-based navigation systems are global positioning systems (GPSs), satellite-based radio navigation systems that can guide you to specified destinations. These systems come in all shapes and sizes and with varying capabilities – from PC-based systems factory-installed in cars for guiding you across the country to handheld units you carry while hiking through the forest. All systems need a GPS antenna to receive satellite signals pinpointing your location. High-end systems for cars include a gyroscope and a connection to the car's speed sensor to enable accurate positioning even if the GPS signal is blocked by tunnels or tall buildings. Your location is superimposed on a map stored on CDs or a DVD. The latter allows for more detailed maps and eliminates the need to shuffle CDs. Some systems are voice activated so you don't have to take your eyes off the road to enter a destination. Portable systems can be moved from one car to another or carried in your rucksack. Some systems come with dynamic rerouting capability where the path recommended depends on weather and road conditions continually transmitted to a receiver in your car connected to a satellite radio system. These systems are useful for all sorts of employees including a mobile sales force and drivers making deliveries.

Multiple Function Printers

A number of manufacturers offer multiple-function printers that can copy, print (in colour or black and white), fax, and scan. Such multifunctional devices are often used when people need to do a relatively low volume of copying, printing, faxing, and scanning. The typical price of multifunction printers ranges from €100 to €400, depending on features and capabilities. Because these devices take the place of one or more pieces of equipment, they are less expensive to acquire and maintain than a stand-alone fax, plus a stand-alone printer, plus a stand-alone copier, and so on. Also, eliminating equipment that was once located on a countertop or desktop clears a significant amount of workspace for other work-related activities. As a result, such devices are popular in homes and small businesses.

Eyebud Screens

Eyebud screens are portable media devices that display video in front of one eye (see Figure 3.15). They employ optical technology that provides very high resolution and 'enlarges' the video or images. With the proximity of the screen to the eye and the magnifying effect of the optical technology, using an eyebud screen is like watching a 275 cm display from 3.5 m away. Such devices enable users of portable media devices to capture the big-screen, movie-screen, or home-theatre experience, wherever they are. Eyebud screens are unlikley to be used in businesses any time soon, but again, a 'killer application' may be in development.

Figure 3.15 The Eyebud *The eyebud screen displays 'enlarged' and high-resolution video.*

SOURCE: Reprinted with permission of eMagin Corporation.

3D Printers

Three-dimensional printers create objects out of wax, resin, plaster or polymer and are often used in the manufacturing industry. A designer can turn the product design on their computer into a physical object very quickly using a 3D printer (see Figure 3.16).

Figure 3.16 A 3D printer

SOURCE: Courtesy of Laser Lines Ltd.

Information Systems @ Work

Wireless Communication at House of Fraser

Founded in 1877, Beatties sells clothing, cosmetics, and housewares in outlets throughout the U.K. It was bought by House of Fraser in 2005 and is currently being rebranded by them. In addition, House of Fraser are using the Beatties stores to experiment with new communication technologies.

House of Fraser are keen to free staff from their desks so they can spend more time on the shop floor dealing with customers and focusing on the retail side of the business. However, staff also need to be 'contactable'. The new system is a wireless mobility system that allows staff to 'walk and talk'. This replaces an existing PA system, which is used

by many retailers to make a store-wide announcement such as 'will a member of cosmetics please come to the aisle four'. The new system connects to the existing telephone system, which simplifies and lowers the cost of installation. Staff will carry handsets around with them, which means they can be contacted at any time. The handset can be used to make calls and send/receive texts. It has a hands-free mode which includes an auto answer feature. This, when used with a headset, automatically answers the phone so that the staff member can carry on using both hands to do whatever it was they were doing. House of Fraser expects the new

(continued)

system to provide reliable communications, improve the contactability of staff, increase productivity and the service supplied to customers, and deliver big cost savings because there is one maintenance contract for all its stores.

Questions

1 Are House of Fraser's expectations realistic? Can a wireless phone system deliver all that it says it will? How?

2 Are there any downsides to staff being constantly contactable?

3 Think of your past experiences at a large retail store. How might they change if the store had a system such as this?

4 What else could House of Fraser do to improve the service it supplies to customer?

SOURCES: Multitone (website), http://www.multitone.co.uk; Friedlos, D., 'House of Fraser Goes Wireless: Communications Systems to Provide a Common Network', *Computing*, January 26, 2007; House of Fraser (website), http://www.houseoffraser.co.uk/.

3.5 Types of Computer Systems, Selection, and Upgrading

3.5.1 Types of Computer Systems

Computer systems can range from small handheld computers to massive supercomputers that fill an entire room. We start first with the smallest computers.

Handheld Computers

Handheld computers are single-user computers that provide ease of portability because of their small size – some are as small as a credit card. These systems often include a variety of software and communications capabilities. Most are compatible with and can communicate with desktop computers over wireless networks. Some even add a built-in GPS receiver with software that can integrate the location data into the application. For example, if you click an entry in an electronic address book, the device displays a map and directions from your current location. Such a computer can also be mounted in your car and serve as a navigation system. One of the shortcomings of handheld computers is that they require lots of power relative to their size.

handheld computer A single-user computer that provides ease of portability because of its small size.

A smartphone combines the functionality of a mobile phone, camera, web browser, e-mail tool, MP3 player, and other devices into a single handheld device. Smartphones will continue to evolve as new applications are defined and installed on the device. The applications might be developed by the manufacturer of the handheld device, by the operator of the communications network on which it operates, or by any other third-party software developer.

Portable Computers

Many computer manufacturers offer a variety of **portable computers**, those that can be carried easily – from laptops, to notebooks, to subnotebooks, to tablet computers. A laptop computer is a small, lightweight PC about the size of a three-ring notebook. The even smaller and lighter notebook and subnotebook computers offer similar computing power. Some notebook and subnotebook computers fit into docking stations of desktop computers to provide additional storage and processing capabilities.

portable computer A computer small enough to be carried easily.

Tablet PCs (introduced earlier) are portable, lightweight computers that allow you to roam the office, home, or factory floor carrying the device like a clipboard. Recall that you can enter text with a writing stylus directly on the screen thanks to built-in handwriting recognition software. Other input methods might include an on-screen (virtual) keyboard, speech recognition, or a physical keyboard. Tablet PCs that only support input via a writing stylus are called 'slates'. The convertible tablet PC comes with a swivel screen and can be used as a traditional notebook or as a pen-based tablet PC.

Thin Client

A **thin client** is a low-cost, centrally managed computer with no extra drives, such as a CD or DVD drive, or expansion slots. These computers have limited capabilities and perform only essential applications, so they remain 'thin' in terms of the client applications they include. These stripped-down versions of desktop computers do not have the storage capacity or computing power of typical desktop computers, nor do they need it for the role they play. With no hard disk, they never pick up viruses or suffer a hard disk crash. Unlike personal computers, thin clients download software from a network when needed, making support, distribution, and updating of software applications much easier and less expensive. Some organizations find it difficult to have users accept thin clients, preferring the features of a full-fledged computer.

thin client A low-cost, centrally managed computer with essential but limited capabilities and no extra drives, such as a CD or DVD drive, or expansion slots.

Desktop Computers

Desktop computers are relatively small, inexpensive single-user computer systems that are highly versatile. Named for their size – the parts are small enough to fit on or beside an office desk – desktop computers can provide sufficient memory and storage for most business computing tasks.

desktop computer A relatively small, inexpensive, single-user computer that is highly versatile.

Workstations

Workstations are more powerful than desktop computers but still small enough to fit on a desktop. They are used to support engineering and technical users who perform heavy mathematical computing, computer-aided design (CAD), and other applications requiring a high-end processor. Such users need very powerful CPUs, large amounts of main memory, and extremely high-resolution graphic displays.

workstation A more powerful personal computer that is used for technical computing, such as engineering, but still fits on a desktop.

Servers

A **server** is a computer used by many users to perform a specific task, such as running network or for Internet applications. Servers typically have large memory and storage capacities, along with fast and efficient communications abilities. A web server handles Internet traffic and communications. An Internet caching server stores websites that a company uses frequently. An enterprise server stores and provides access to programs that meet the needs of an entire organization. A file server stores and coordinates program and data files. A transaction server processes business transactions. Server systems consist of multiuser computers, including supercomputers, mainframes, and other servers. Often an organization will house a large number of servers in the same room, where the access to the machines can be controlled and authorized support personnel can more easily manage and maintain them from this single location. Such a facility is called a 'server farm'.

server A computer designed for a specific task, such as network or Internet applications.

Servers offer great **scalability**, the ability to increase the processing capability of a computer system so that it can handle more users, more data, or more transactions in a given period. Scalability is increased by adding more, or more powerful, processors. Scaling up adds more powerful processors, and scaling out adds many more equal (or even less powerful) processors to increase the total data-processing capacity.

scalability The ability to increase the capability of a computer system to process more transactions in a given period by adding more, or more powerful, processors.

blade server A server that houses many individual computer motherboards that include one or more processors, computer memory, computer storage, and computer network connections.

A **blade server** houses many computer motherboards that include one or more processors, computer memory, computer storage, and computer network connections. These all share a common power supply and air-cooling source within a single chassis. By placing many blades into a single chassis, and then mounting multiple chassis in a single rack, the blade server is more powerful, but less expensive than traditional systems based on mainframes or server farms of individual computers. In addition, the blade server approach takes much less physical space than traditional server farms.[18]

Mainframe Computers

A **mainframe** computer is a large, powerful computer shared by dozens or even hundreds of concurrent users connected to the machine over a network (see Figure 3.17). The mainframe computer must reside in a data centre with special heating, ventilating, and air-conditioning (HVAC) equipment to control temperature, humidity, and dust levels. In addition, most mainframes are kept in a secure data centre with limited access to the room. The construction and maintenance of a controlled-access room with HVAC can add hundreds of thousands of dollars to the cost of owning and operating a mainframe computer.

mainframe computer A large, powerful computer often shared by hundreds of concurrent users connected to the machine via terminals.

Figure 3.17
A Mainframe Computer
Mainframe computers have been the workhorses of corporate computing for more than 50 years. They can support hundreds of users simultaneously and handle all of the core functions of a corporation.

SOURCE: Ace Stock Limited/Alamy.

The role of the mainframe is undergoing some remarkable changes as lower-cost, single-user computers become increasingly powerful. Many computer jobs that used to run on mainframe computers have migrated onto these smaller, less-expensive computers. This information-processing migration is called 'computer downsizing'. One company that is using computer downsizing to its advantage is Starwood Hotels and Resorts Worldwide, which owns the Sheraton,

Westin, W, Le Meredien, St. Regis, and Four Points hotel chains. Starwood is downsizing its reservation system from an aging mainframe to a number of servers. The firm can now improve the performance of the reservation system and add new features as necessary.[19]

The new role of the mainframe is as a large information-processing and data-storage utility for an organization – running jobs too large for other computers, storing files and databases too large to be stored elsewhere, and storing backups of files and databases created elsewhere. The mainframe can handle the millions of daily transactions associated with airline and hotel reservation systems. Its massive storage and input/output capabilities enable it to play the role of a video computer, providing full-motion video to multiple, concurrent users.

Supercomputers

Supercomputers are the most powerful computers with the fastest processing speed and highest performance (see Figure 3.18). They are special-purpose machines designed for applications that require extensive and rapid computational capabilities. Originally, supercomputers were used primarily by government agencies to perform the high-speed number crunching needed in weather forecasting and military applications. With recent reductions in the cost of these machines, they are now used more broadly for commercial purposes. For example, golf club maker Ping, Inc., uses a Cray supercomputer to run simulations of golf club designs and reduce the development time from weeks to days.[20]

supercomputers The most powerful computer systems with the fastest processing speeds.

Figure 3.18 IBM's **Blue Gene/L System at the Lawrence Livermore National Laboratory**
This is the fastest supercomputer in the world and can perform 136.8 trillion floating-point operations per second.

SOURCE: Lawrence Livermore National Library.

3.5.2 Selecting and Upgrading Computer Systems

Computer systems are often upgraded by installing additional memory, faster processors, more hard disk storage, or various input and output devices to support new or changing business needs. Organizations only need to replace or upgrade their technology when it no longer meets their needs. Given typical failure rates, most organizations can safely plan to keep a desktop computer four or more years. However, if the system fails after the standard three-year warranty period, it might be more cost effective to replace it with an upgraded model rather than fixing it. Companies plan to replace notebooks, which face rougher handling by users, every three or four years. As they replace workstations and notebooks, organizations should consider rolling over the most capable, but older personal computers to less-demanding users. Companies are sometimes forced to upgrade otherwise usable machines because of the memory and CPU requirements of newer versions of resource-intensive software.

Many large corporations set their own internal computer standards by selecting specific computer configurations from a small set of manufacturers. The goal is to reduce hardware support costs and increase the organization's flexibility. Business units that adopt different hardware complicate future corporate IS projects. For example, installing software is much easier if similar equipment from the same manufacturer is involved, rather than new and different systems at each installation site.

When upgrading to new computer hardware, whether it be for a single individual or for a large, multinational corporation, you must dispose of the old equipment properly. The National Recycling Coalition estimates nearly 500 million personal computers will have become obsolete in the period from 1997 to 2007. A typical CRT monitor contains three to nine pounds of lead. Printed circuit boards contain beryllium, cadmium, flame retardants, and other compounds that can contaminate the air and groundwater, exposing people to carcinogens and other toxins. Unfortunately, some people and organizations do not realize the potential for harm from improper disposal of their computer hardware, nor have they budgeted for the costs associated with proper disposal. Three major computer hardware vendors – Dell, IBM, and Hewlett-Packard – offer disposal programs for any computer hardware, regardless of brand. They follow environment-friendly recycling practices and do not export the waste. Some reputable vendors offer e-waste disposal and recycling services. If the computer hardware still has a useful life, it can be donated to schools or charitable organizations.

Hard Drive Considerations

The optimal hard drive for a computer depends on several considerations. Because its main role is to provide long-term data storage, capacity, speed, and media capabilities are key features. Today's business software and large video, audio, and graphics files require lots of storage, so a hard drive capacity of at least 100 GB is recommended. Other considerations are access speed (look for 10 milliseconds or less) and hard drive cache size. Many single-user computers employ fans to help cool the internal components. These fans can cause the case to resonate and make the system seem loud. It is wise to select a system with fans, hard drive, and power supply that are classified as 'quiet'.

Main Memory Considerations

Main memory stores software code, while the processor reads and executes the code. Having more RAM means you can run software faster. Systems with 1 GB of RAM are well suited to take advantage of today's advanced personal productivity software (word processing, spreadsheet, graphics, and database) and multimedia programs.

As discussed earlier, your system's processor, main memory, and cache memory depend heavily on each other to achieve optimal system functionality. The original manufacturer of your computer considers this interdependency when designing and choosing the parts for the system. If you plan to upgrade your system's main memory beyond 512 MB, you should consult your supplier to understand the trade-off between the amount of main memory, the size of cache memory, and system performance.

Printer Considerations

As mentioned earlier, laser printers and inkjet printers are the two primary types of printers, and the differences between the two are diminishing. Although most inkjet printers are colour and laser printers are monochrome, there are also colour laser printers. All produce sharp images, with resolutions of 600 × 600 dots per inch (dpi) to 1800 × 1800 dpi now common. The major differences are in price, colour, and speed.

You should consider two cost factors when purchasing a printer. The first is the cost of the printer. Prices for laser printers range from €150 to over €1500, while prices for inkjet printers range from €40 to €300. Also consider operating cost. Laser printers can handle larger volumes of printing with a longer life for the ink/toner products, giving them a much lower operating cost than inkjet printers. Laser printers typically have operating costs from less than €0.01 to €0.03 per page for black-and-white pages and €0.06 to €0.13 for colour pages. Inkjet printers can have operating costs from €0.02 to €0.06 per page for black-and-white pages and €0.07 to €0.14 for colour pages. The cost for printing photos on special paper can exceed €0.4 per page for either type of printer because of the high cost of the photo-quality paper.

Summary

Assembling an effective, efficient set of computer hardware devices requires understanding their role in supporting the underlying information systems and the needs of the organization. The computer hardware objectives are subordinate to, but supportive of, the information systems and the needs of the organization. Hardware includes any machinery (often using digital circuitry) that assists with the input, processing, and output activities of a computer-based information system (CBIS). A computer system is an integrated assembly of physical devices with at least one central processing mechanism; it inputs, processes, stores, and outputs data and information.

You should select and organize hardware to effectively and efficiently attain computer system objectives. These objectives should, in turn, support IS objectives and organizational goals. Balancing specific computer system objectives in terms of cost, control, and complexity should guide selection.

Processing is performed by cooperation between the central processing unit (CPU) and memory. The CPU has three main components: the arithmetic/logic unit (ALU), the control unit, and the register areas. The ALU performs calculations and logical comparisons. The control unit accesses and decodes instructions and coordinates data flow. The registers are temporary holding areas for instructions to be executed by the CPU.

When selecting computer hardware, you must consider the current and future needs of the information systems and the organization. Your choice of a hardware device should always allow for later improvements to meet evolving organi-zational needs. Computer system processing speed is also affected by clock speed, which is measured in megahertz (MHz). As the clock speed of the CPU increases, heat is generated that can corrupt the data and instructions the computer is trying to process.

Processing speed is also limited by physical constraints, such as the distance between circuitry points and circuitry materials. Advances in superconductive metals, optical processors, strained silicon, carbon nanotubes, and extreme miniaturization will result in faster CPUs.

Primary storage, or memory, provides working storage for program instructions and data to be processed and provides them to the CPU. Storage capacity is measured in bytes. A common form of memory is random access memory (RAM). RAM is volatile – loss of power to the computer erases its contents and comes in many different varieties, including EDO, dynamic RAM (DRAM), and synchronous DRAM (SDRAM).

Read-only memory (ROM) is non-volatile and contains permanent program instructions for execution by the CPU. Other non-volatile memory types include programmable read-only memory (PROM) and erasable programmable read-only memory (EPROM). Cache memory is a type of high-speed memory that CPUs can access more rapidly than RAM.

Processing that uses several processing units is called 'multiprocessing', of which there are many forms. A coprocessor executes one type of instruction while the CPU works on others. A multicore microprocessor is one that combines two or more independent processors into a single computer so they can share the workload. Parallel computing is the simultaneous execution of the same task on multiple processors to obtain results faster. Massively parallel processing involves linking many processors to work together to solve complex problems. Grid computing is the use of a collection of computers, often owned by multiple individuals or organizations, to work in a coordinated manner to solve a common problem.

Computer systems can store larger amounts of data and instructions in secondary storage, which is less volatile and has greater capacity than memory. The primary characteristics of secondary storage media and devices include access method, capacity, portability, and cost. Storage media can implement either sequential access or direct access. Sequential access requires data to be read or written in sequence. Direct access means that data can be located and retrieved directly from any location on the media.

Common forms of secondary storage include magnetic tape, magnetic disk, virtual tape, optical disk, digital video disk (DVD), holographic versatile disk (HVD), memory cards, and flash memory. Redundant array of independent/inexpensive disks (RAID) is a method of storing data that generates extra bits of data from existing data, allowing the system to more easily recover data in the event of a hardware failure. Network-attached storage (NAS) and storage area networks (SAN) are alternative forms of data storage that enable an organization to share data resources among a much larger number of computers and users for improved storage efficiency and greater cost-effectiveness.

Input and output devices allow users to provide data and instructions to the computer for processing and allow subsequent storage and output. These devices are part of a user interface through which human beings interact with computer systems. Input and output devices vary widely, but they share common characteristics of speed and functionality.

Computer input devices include a keyboard, a mouse, speech recognition, digital cameras, terminals, scanners, optical data readers, magnetic ink character recognition devices, magnetic stripe cards, point-of-sale devices, automated teller machines, pen input devices, touch-sensitive screens, bar-code scanners, and radio frequency identification tags.

Output devices provide information in different forms, from hard copy to sound to digital format. Display monitors are standard output devices; monitor quality is determined by size, colour, and resolution. Liquid crystal display and organic light-emitting diode technology is enabling improvements in the resolution and size of computer monitors. Other output devices include printers and plotters. Printers are popular hard-copy output devices whose quality is measured by speed and resolution. Plotters output hard copy for general design work. MP3 is a standard format for compressing the amount of data it takes to accurately represent sound. Numerous music devices based on the compressed music are available.

Computer systems are generally divided into two categories: single user and multiple users. Single-user systems include handheld, portable, thin client, desktop, and workstation computers. Handheld computers provide ease of portability because of their small size. They include palmtop computers and smartphones. A variety of portable computers are available, including the laptop, notebook, subnotebook, and tablet computer. The thin client is a diskless, inexpensive computer used for accessing server-based applications and the Internet. Desktop computers are relatively small, inexpensive computer systems that are highly versatile. Workstations are advanced PCs with greater memory, processing, and graphics abilities.

Multiuser systems include servers, blade servers, mainframes, and supercomputers. A computer server is a computer designed for a specific task, such as network or Internet applications. Servers typically have large memory and storage capacities, along with fast and efficient communications abilities. A blade server houses a number of individual computer motherboards that include one or more processors, computer memory, computer storage, and computer network connections. These all share a common power supply and air-cooling source within a single chassis. Mainframe computers have greater processing capabilities, while supercomputers are extremely fast computers used to solve the most intensive computing problems.

Computer systems can be upgraded by changing hard drives, memory, printers, DVD burners, and other devices. Care must be taken in the disposal of obsolete systems because computer hardware contains many potentially harmful metals and chemicals.

Self-Assessment Test

1 Organizations that don't invest in computer hardware might find they are at a competitive disadvantage. True or false?

2 The overriding consideration for a business making hardware decisions should be how the hardware can support the objectives of the information system and _____.

3   Which represents a larger amount of data – a terabyte or a gigabyte?

4   Which of the following components performs mathematical calculations and makes logical comparisons?

   a. control unit   c. ALU

   b. register   d. main memory

5   Executing an instruction by the CPU involves two phases: the instruction phase and the _____ phase.

6   _____ involves capturing and editing data when the data is originally created and in a form that can be directly input to a computer, thus ensuring accuracy and timeliness.

7   A form of parallel processing in which a number of computers, often owned by multiple individuals or organizations, work in a coordinated manner to solve a common problem is _____.

   a. massively parallel processing

   b. multicore processing

   c. grid computing

   d. coprocessing

8   Three fundamental strategies for providing data storage are _____.

   a. expandable, non-expandable, and static

   b. attached storage, network-attached storage, and storage area networks

   c. sequential, direct, indirect

   d. hard drive, CD-ROM, DVD

9   As the clock speed of the CPU increases, what problem occurs?

10   Which of the following technologies employs a microchip to broadcast its unique identifier and location to receivers?

   a. radio frequency identification

   b. bar-code scanning

   c. biometrics

   d. GPS

Review Questions

1   When determining the appropriate hardware components of a new information system, what role must the user play?

2   What is a blade server? What advantages does it offer over an ordinary server?

3   Identify three basic characteristics of RAM and ROM.

4   What is RFID technology? Identify three practical uses for this technology.

5   Identify at least two ways businesses can take advantage of digital photography technology.

6   Give three practical examples of using speech-recognition devices.

7   What is the difference between SIMD and MIMD parallel processing?

8   Why are the components of all information systems described as interdependent?

9   What is the difference between sequential and direct access of data?

10   Identify several types of secondary storage media in terms of access method, capacity, portability, and cost per GB of storage.

Discussion Questions

1   Briefly describe how RFID technology works.

2   Briefly outline some issues and associated solutions for discarding old computer hardware.

3   Imagine that you are the business manager for your university. What type of computer would you recommend for broad deployment in the university's computer labs – a standard desktop personal computer or a thin client? Why?

4 Assuming that cost was no object, identify and briefly describe the features of your ideal computer monitor. Explain your selection.

5 Briefly discuss several data-storage issues that face the modern organization.

Web Exercises

1 Do research on the web to document the current state of computer hardware disposal. What are some of the issues? What solutions are there to this problem? Write a brief report summarizing your findings.

2 Do research on the web to identify the current status of the use of radio frequency identification chips in the pharmaceutical industry. Write a brief report summarizing your findings.

Case One

British Airways Donates Old PCs

Non-profit company Maxitech refurbishes and recycles unwanted PCs. Their service includes collecting old PCs (and other equipment), wiping their hard disks clean, then either selling them or giving them to charity. According to Maxitech, around two million working, reasonably high specification PCs are dumped in the U.K. every year. Similar statistics are seen throughout the world. These add to an existing environmental problem, when they could have been used for many years to come.

British Airways (BA) is one of their suppliers. Based at Heathrow, BA is keen to contribute to its surrounding community. It donates its unwanted PCs via Maxitech to the charity Help the Aged, who plan to use them in their centres in West London (where Heathrow is situated). Older Internet users (often known as 'silver surfers') use the Internet to communicate with friends and relatives, develop new interests, and have access to health advice, although their use is often more diverse than this.

Under the scheme, BA benefit by being seen as community spirited; old computers are re-used rather than dumped; and citizens benefit from the use of perfectly acceptable machines.

Similar companies operate throughout the world. In South Africa, for example, there are strict laws that govern the disposal of electronic goods. Old PCs cannot simply be dumped, and charities such as Maxitech in the U.K., or Reworx Africa in South Africa are a perfect solution.

Questions

1 Why do Maxitech take great care to wipe old hard disks? How can they guarantee they have done this?

2 Why are more companies not doing something similar to BA?

3 Why do computers go out of date quicker than the working lifetime of their parts?

4 What benefit does BA get out of being seen as 'community spirited'?

SOURCES: Maxitech (website), http://maxitech.biz; Young, T., 'BA Gives Computers to Charity in New Initiative', *Computing,* January 25, 2007; Fujitsu-Siemens Computers, 'Recycling in Africa', http://www.fujitsu-siemens.com/aboutus/company_information/business_excellence/environmental_care/popup_south_africa.html, September 6, 2007.

Case Two

Printing and Paper Waste

According to a report by OKI printing solutions and CEBR (The Centre for Economic Business Research), 'Outsourced Printing – A Waste of Paper', more than one billion pounds could be saved in the U.K. through more efficient printing. The report claims that £16.7 billion is spent on printing each year in the U.K. alone, with £5 billion of this going to external printers, the remainder going on in house printing. Some economists believe this expenditure is hampering business growth. OKI claim that 20 percent of the outsourced printing is never even used but eventually discarded. Savings can be made by public sectors simply by printing a higher percentage of work in-house and more fully utilizing office printers.

The education sector is among the worst offenders. It, along with the public administration sector, lose around £140 million a year through excessive outsourcing and poor internal print management. The education sector along could save £80 million a year with a more efficient approach to printing.

'Improving the organization of printing – currently regarded as a relatively small area of business management – could yield productivity benefits of as much as £1 billion a year,' said chief executive at CEBR Douglas McWilliams. 'This amounts to some 0.1 percent of national income: enough to have a real knock-on effect for the whole U.K. economy, as well as individual businesses'.

The education sector is identified as the largest potential beneficiary of bringing more printing in-house and better internal printing practices with scope for savings of around £80 million a year.

Given the technologies currently available, we might question why the education sector prints so much. Consider lecture notes – many students own laptops and PCs, yet insist on printing out notes rather than reading them on screen. Why is paper still so popular? Some suggestions are that paper is convenient to hold while reading (unlike a laptop computer), notes can easily be made in the margins (while notes can be made electronically, the technology for drawing diagram doodles and linking passages with annotated arrows, etc. is not yet as good as a ball-point pen), and there is no fear of a systems crash the night before an exam destroying the ability to read paper notes.

Questions

1 How would you convince your fellow students to use your school's printers less?

2 What other reasons can you think of to explain why reading on paper is still more popular than reading from a computer screen?

3 How could a company ensure that all of its outsourced printing is used and not discarded?

4 Think of an office – are there any other inefficiencies that technology could do away with?

SOURCES: OKI Printing Solutions, '£1 Billion a Year Savings on Print Could Boost the Economy', http://www.oki.co.uk/?pid=37&nid=6178&cid=125&chid=10, October 31, 2007; Young, T., UK Wastes £1bn on Printing', *Computing*, January 30, 2007.

Case Three

Oyster Card Eases Commute

Transport for London's Oyster Card is a contactless smartcard that is used to pay for journeys on the London Underground, London Buses and on limited train journeys out of the city. Travellers pre-pay or top up their card periodically at Underground stations or online. To use the card they must then hold it close to a reader located at the entrance to the platform or on the bus. (By using RFID technology, the card does not have to touch the reader, hence the name 'contactless'.) This is repeated at the end of the journal and the system calculates the cost of the journal and debits the amount from the traveller's account. This information is stored in a chip in the card, then later a central database is updated. The system is advertised as being:

1 A time saver, meaning travellers do not have to queue to purchase tickets.

2 Efficient for users, with the system automatically calculating the cheapest amount the journey could have cost and debiting that figure.

3 Easy to use.

London mayor Ken Livingstone is keen to see the system extended and has offered to pay for the installation of readers for rail operators so that more commuters from outside the city can benefit from it. Train operating companies have been accused of delaying a decision to accept this offer as, while they can see the benefit for customers, they cannot see the benefit for themselves because the mayor will not pay for ongoing operating and maintenance costs.

Questions

1 An Oyster card represents a concept known as e-money. Explain what you think this means and how the system could be extended outside of public transport. What would some of the barriers to adoption be? Why would people choose or not choose to carry this card?

2 Why do you think Livingstone is keen to see the system extended?

3 Are rail operators' concerns justified? If you were mayor, how would you respond?

4 Consider the other technologies discussed in this chapter. Can you suggest any ways in which some of them could be used to improve public transport?

SOURCES: Transport for London (website), http://www.tfl.gov.uk/tfl; Staff, 'Train Operators Urged to Adopt Oyster', *Computing,* January 29, 2007.

Notes

[1] 'Zürcher Kantonalbank Accelerates Risk Assessment with an IBM Grid', http://www-306.ibm.com/software/success/cssdb.nsf/cs/STRD-6XDHZV?OpenDocument&Site=default&cty=en_us, January 16, 2007.

[2] 'Dell Precision M60 Mobile Workstation Provides Accomplished Animator and Digital Filmmaker with the Power, Flexibility, and Speed Needed to Work From Any Location', http://www.dell.com/downloads/global/casestudies/2004_angie.pdf, January 17, 2007.

[3] 'ProCurve Networking Partners with CERN to Unlock the Secrets of the Universe', http://h71028.www7.hp.com/ERC/downloads/4AA0-7311EEW.pdf, January 18, 2007.

[4] Thibodeau, Patrick, 'Cool Chips Offer Some Help to Data Centers', *Computerworld,* December 12, 2005.

[5] Krazit, Tom, 'Intel Readying New Extreme Edition Processor', *Computerworld,* November 17, 2005.

[6] Kirk, Jeremy, 'Intel to Build $3.5B Chip Plant in Israel', *Computerworld,* December 1, 2005.

[7] Krazit, Tom, 'Intel Alters Server Processor Road Map', *Computerworld,* October 25, 2005.

[8] Thibodeau, Patrick, 'Chevron Adopts Opteron for High Performance Computing', *Computerworld,* December 13, 2005, www.computerworld.com.

[9] Jones, K.C., 'Supercomputer Fights AIDS', *InformationWeek*, November 21, 2005.

[10] Williams, Martyn, 'Analysis: Fuzzy HD Picture to Come into Focus at CES', *Computerworld,* January 3, 2006.

[11] Mearian, Lucas, 'Japanese Holographic Storage Firm to Ship 200GB Drives in '06', *Computerworld,* October 24, 2005.

[12] Krazit, Tom, 'Intel's Latest Flash Chip Runs Faster with More Storage', *Computerworld,* November 17, 2005.

[13] Jacobi, Jon L., 'Flash Memory to Speed Up Hard Drives', *PCWorld Magazine,* September 2005, www.pcmagazine.com.

[14] Hoffman, Thomas, 'Speech Recognition Powers Utility's Customer Service', *Computerworld,* September 12, 2005.

[15] Kelly, Lisa, 'Digital Pens Spell Problems for Pests', *Computing,* January 9, 2007.

[16] Nystedt, Dan, 'Top LCD Maker Bets Research on LCD Backlights', *Computerworld,* September 21, 2005.

[17] Krazit, Tom, 'Apple Unveils Video iPod, Strikes Deal with ABC', *Computerworld,* October 12, 2005.

[18] Mearian, Lucas, 'Japanese Bank Expects Server Consolidation to Save It Millions', *Computerworld,* October 10, 2005.

[19] Lai, Eric, 'Starwood Checks in with Object Database for Reservations', *Computerworld,* January 16, 2006.

[20] Thibodeau, Patrick, 'Smaller Companies Eye Supercomputing', *Computerworld,* August 2, 2006.

3

04

Software: Systems and Application Software

```
else
    htmlFrame.styleSheets(1).disabled = false;

viewMode = 1; // WYSIWYG
htmlFrame.onkeyup = null;
document.getElementById('iView').contentWindow.document.onkeyd
document.getElementById('iView').contentWindow.document.ormouse
document.getElementById('iView').contentWindow.document.onconte

iText = htmlFrame.body.innerText;
htmlFrame.body.innerHTML = iText;

DrawBarFocus();

// Show all controls
document.all.iView.style.height = document.body.clientHeight-(y
ddoitris.style.display = 'inline';
ddoitris.style.display = 'inline';
document.getElementById('selhead').style.display = 'block';
document.getElementById('selhead2').style.display = 'block';
iView.focus();
```

Principles

Systems and application software are critical in helping individuals and organizations achieve their goals.

Do not develop proprietary application software unless doing so will meet a compelling business need that can provide a competitive advantage.

Choose a programming language whose functional characteristics are appropriate for the task at hand, considering the skills and experience of the programming staff.

The software industry continues to undergo constant change; users need to be aware of recent trends and issues to be effective in their business and personal life.

Learning Objectives

- Identify and briefly describe the functions of the two basic kinds of software.

- Outline the role of the operating system and identify the features of several popular operating systems.

- Discuss how application software can support personal, workgroup, and enterprise business objectives.

- Outline the overall evolution and importance of programming languages and clearly differentiate among the generations of programming languages.

- Identify several key software issues and trends that have an impact on organizations and individuals.

Why Learn About Software?

In this chapter, you will learn about systems and application software. You cannot come into contact with a computer without coming into contact with software. Software gives the computer the ability to accept input, process calculations and other operations, and produce output. Regardless of your job you will almost certainly use software at some point, most likely every hour of every day, whether to check e-mail, surf the web, process orders, analyze sales figures, create music or an animated film. Today, most organizations could not function without accounting software to print payroll cheques, enter sales orders, and send out bills. You can also use software to help you prepare your personal income taxes, keep a budget, and play amazing games. Software can truly advance your career and enrich your life. Since the 1950s, businesses have greatly increased their expenditures on software compared with hardware.

4

An Overview of Software

Software consists of computer programs that control the workings of computer hardware. A **computer program** is a sequence of instructions for the computer. **Documentation** describes the program functions to help the user operate the computer system. The program displays some documentation on screen, while other forms appear in external resources, such as printed manuals. People using commercially available software are usually asked to read and agree to end-user license agreements (EULAs). After reading the EULA, you normally have to click an 'I agree' button before you can use the software, which can be one of two basic types: systems software and application software.

computer program A sequence of instructions for the computer.

documentation The text that describes the program functions to help the user operate the computer system.

Systems software is the set of programs that coordinates the activities and functions of the hardware and other programs throughout the computer system. Each type of systems software is designed for a specific CPU and class of hardware. The combination of a hardware configuration and systems software is known as a 'computer system platform'.

Application software consists of programs that run on the systems software to help users complete a task. Common examples include word processors and spreadsheets. Before a person, group, or enterprise decides on the best approach for acquiring application software, they should analyze their goals and needs carefully.

4.1 Systems Software

Controlling the operations of computer hardware is one of the most critical functions of systems software. Systems software also allow users to run application software, or 'applications'. Types of systems software include operating systems, utility programs, and middleware.

4.1.1 Operating Systems

An **operating system (OS)** is a set of programs that controls the computer hardware and acts as an interface with applications. Operating systems can control one or more computers, or they can allow multiple users to interact with one computer. The various combinations of OS, computers, and users include the following:

operating system (OS) A set of computer programs that controls the computer hardware and acts as an interface with application programs

■ *Single computer with a single user:* This system is commonly used in a personal computer or a handheld computer that allows one user at a time.

- *Single computer with multiple users:* This system is typical of larger, mainframe computers that can accommodate hundreds or thousands of people, all using the computer at the same time.

- *Multiple computers:* This system is typical of a network of computers, such as a home network with several computers attached or a large computer network with hundreds of computers attached around the world.

- *Special-purpose computers:* This system is typical of a number of special-purpose computers, such as those that control sophisticated military aircraft, the space shuttle, and some home appliances.

The OS, which plays a central role in the functioning of the complete computer system, is usually stored on disk. After you start, or 'boot up', a computer system, portions of the OS are transferred to memory as they are needed. You can also boot a computer from a CD, DVD, or even a keychain or thumb drive that plugs into a USB port.[1] A storage device that contains some or all of the OS is often called a 'rescue disk' because you can use it to start the computer if you have problems with the primary hard disk. Some OS for small computers use an 'Instant On' feature that significantly reduces the time needed to boot a computer.

Most business people don't really care about operating systems: as long as the system is easy to use and useful, they are happy. However, it still is useful for managers to know a little about what system software does, so they can make an informed choice when choosing the OS the business should use. Ease of use, cost, and security are just some of the things managers should be concerned with.

The collection of programs that make up the OS performs a variety of activities, including the following:

- Performing common computer hardware functions.
- Providing a user interface and input/output management.
- Providing a degree of hardware independence.
- Managing system memory.
- Managing processing tasks.
- Providing networking capability.
- Controlling access to system resources.
- Managing files.

The **kernel**, as its name suggests, is the heart of the OS and controls the most critical processes. The kernel ties all of the OS components together and regulates other programs. Each of these activities is now discussed.

kernel The heart of the operating system, which controls the most critical processes.

Common Hardware Functions

All applications need the OS to perform certain tasks, such as the following:

- Get input from the keyboard or another input device.
- Retrieve data from disks.
- Store data on disks.
- Display information on a monitor or printer.

Each of these tasks requires a detailed set of instructions. The OS converts a basic request into the set of detailed instructions that the hardware requires. In effect, the OS acts as an intermediary between the application and the hardware. The typical OS performs hundreds of such tasks, translating each into one or more instructions for the hardware. The OS notifies the user if input or output devices need attention, if an error has occurred, and if anything abnormal happens in the system.

User Interface and Input/Output Management

One of the most important functions of any OS is providing a user interface. A **user interface** allows people to access and command the computer system. The first user interfaces for mainframe and personal computer systems were command based. A **command-based user interface** requires you to give text commands to the computer to perform basic activities. For example, the command ERASE TAXRTN07 would cause the computer to erase a file called TAXRTN07. RENAME and COPY are other examples of commands used to rename files and copy files from one location to another. Many operating systems that use a graphical user interface, discussed next, also have powerful command-based features.[2]

A **graphical user interface (GUI)** uses pictures (called icons) and menus displayed on screen to send commands to the computer system. Many people find that GUIs are easier to use than command-based interfaces because they intuitively grasp the functions. Today, the most widely used graphical user interface is Microsoft Windows. As the name suggests, Windows is based on the concept of a window, or a portion of the display screen, dedicated to a specific application. The screen can display several windows at once. GUIs have contributed greatly to the increased use of computers (see Figure 4.1).

user interface The element of the operating system that allows you to access and command the computer system.

command-based user interface A user interface that requires you to give text commands to the computer to perform basic activities.

graphical user interface (GUI) An interface that allows users to manipulate icons and menus displayed on screen to send commands to the computer system.

Figure 4.1 Graphical **User Interfaces** *Windows XP, Red Hat Linux 8.0, and Mac OS X are examples of graphical user interfaces.*

Windows XP

Red Hat Linux

Mac OS X

Hardware Independence

application program interface (API) An interface that allows applications to make use of the operating system.

To run, applications request services from the OS through a defined **application program interface (API)**, as shown in Figure 4.2. Programmers can use APIs to create application software without having to understand the inner workings of the OS.

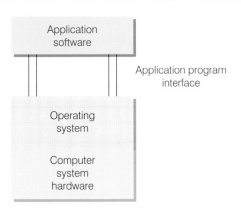

Figure 4.2 Application Program Interface Links Application Software to the Operating System

Suppose that a computer manufacturer designs new hardware that can operate much faster than before. If the same OS for which an application was developed can run on the new hardware, minimal (or no) changes are needed to the application to enable it to run on the new hardware. If APIs did not exist, the application developers might have to completely rewrite the application to take advantage of the new, faster hardware. Most businesses don't know about APIs, but without them, upgrading hardware to ensure the company software still works would become a major problem.

Memory Management

Another OS task is to control how memory is accessed and to maximize available memory and storage. Newer OS typically manage memory better than older OS. The memory-management feature of many OS allows the computer to execute program instructions effectively and speed processing. One way to increase the performance of an old computer is to upgrade to a newer OS and increase the amount of memory.

Most OS support virtual memory, which allocates space on the hard disk to supplement the immediate, functional memory capacity of RAM. Virtual memory works by swapping programs or parts of programs between memory and one or more disk devices – a concept called paging. This reduces CPU idle time and increases the number of jobs that can run in a given time span.

Processing Tasks

The task-management features of today's OS manage all processing activities. Task management allocates computer resources to make the best use of each system's assets. Task-management software can permit one user to run several programs or tasks at the same time (multitasking) and allow several users to use the same computer at the same time (time-sharing).

An OS with multitasking capabilities allows a user to run more than one application at the same time. Without having to exit a program, you can work in one application, easily pop into another, and then jump back to the first program, picking up where you left off. Better still, while you're working in the foreground in one program, one or more other applications can be churning away, unseen, in the background, sorting a database, printing a document, or performing other lengthy operations that otherwise would monopolize your computer and leave you staring at the screen unable to perform other work. Multitasking can save users a considerable amount of time and effort.

Time-sharing allows more than one person to use a computer system at the same time. For example, 15 customer service representatives might be entering sales data into a computer system for a mail-order company at the same time. In another case, thousands of people might be simultaneously using an online computer service to get stock quotes and valuable business news.

The ability of the computer to handle an increasing number of concurrent users smoothly is called 'scalability'. This feature is critical for systems expected to handle a large number of users, such as a mainframe computer or a web server. Because personal computer OSs usually are oriented towards single users, they do not need to manage multiple-user tasks often.

Networking Capability

The OS can provide features and capabilities that aid users in connecting to a computer network. For example, Apple computer users have built-in network access, and the various current versions of Microsoft Windows let users link to other devices and the Internet.

Access to System Resources and Security

Because computers often handle sensitive data that can be accessed over networks, the OS needs to provide a high level of security against unauthorized access to the users' data and programs. Typically, the OS establishes a login procedure that requires users to enter an identification code and a matching password. If the identification code is invalid or if the password does not match the identification code, the user cannot gain access to the computer. The OS also requires that user passwords change frequently – such as every 20 to 40 days. If the user is successful in logging on to the system, the OS records who is using the system and for how long. The OS also reports any attempted breaches of security.

File Management

The OS manages files to ensure that files in secondary storage are available when needed and that they are protected from access by unauthorized users. Many computers support multiple users who store files on centrally located disks or tape drives. The OS keeps track of where each file is stored and who can access them. The OS must determine what to do if more than one user requests access to the same file at the same time. Even on stand-alone personal computers with only one user, file management is needed to track where files are located, what size they are, when they were created, and who created them.

4.1.2 Current Operating Systems

Early OSs were very basic. Recently, however, more advanced OSs have been developed, incorporating some features previously available only with mainframe OS.[3] The choice of operating system depends on many factors – the software that it has to run, the number of users, the level of security required, cost, level of support available, and memory and other hardware requirements of the OS.

Microsoft Windows

Around 90 percent of all PCs run Microsoft operating software, the various versions and editions of Windows. The most recent of these is Vista, which is the first that can be downloaded from Microsoft's website.[4] New features include an updated graphical user interface which uses a three-dimensional style, improved search facilities, and new tools for creating multimedia such as Windows DVD Maker (see Figure 4.3). Vista also includes tools for developers to make it easier for them to write high quality applications that run on it. The main selling point of Vista is its increased security, as many of its predecessors were vulnerable to computer viruses. However, given the memory requirements of Vista, many users have to upgrade their hardware to be able to use it.

Apple Computer Operating Systems

Apple computers, using Apple's Mac OS, are popular, especially in the fields of publishing, education, graphic arts, music, movies, and media. Software developed for the Macintosh often

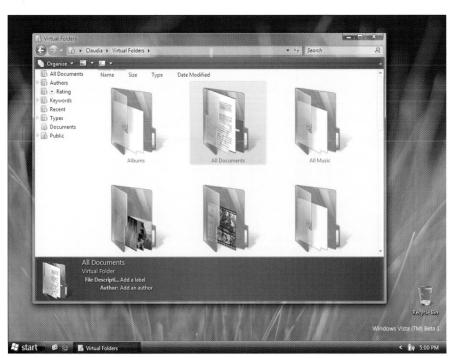

Figure 4.3 Microsoft Vista Operating System

SOURCE: Courtesy of Microsoft Corporation.

provides cutting-edge options for creative people. GarageBand, for example, is Macintosh software that allows you to create your own music the way a professional does, and it can sound like a small orchestra. Pro Tools is another software program used to edit digital music. Apple often provide features not available from Microsoft. Starting in July 2001, the Mac OS X was installed on all new Macs. It included an entirely new user interface that provided a new visual appearance for users – including luminous, semitransparent, and three-dimensional elements, such as buttons, scroll bars, windows, and fluid animation to enhance the user's experience. Since then, OS X has been upgraded with additional releases, with many new features, including support for 64-bit computing, display tools so that programs such as calculators, dictionaries, and calendars can be accessed easily, and search tools that allow you to locate documents, music, images, e-mails, contacts, and other information on your computer by searching the contents of your files.[5] The Mac OS is shown in Figure 4.4.

Linux

Linux is an OS developed by Finish student Linus Torvalds in 1991. This OS is distributed under the GNU General Public License, and its source code is freely available to everyone. It is, therefore, called an open-source operating system. This doesn't mean however, that Linux and its assorted distributions are free – companies and developers can charge money for a distribution as long as the source code remains available. Linux is actually only the kernel of an OS, the part that controls hardware, manages files, separates processes, and so forth. Several combinations of Linux are available, with various sets of capabilities and applications to form a complete OS. Each of these combinations is called a distribution of Linux. Several large computer vendors, including IBM, Hewlett-Packard, and Intel, now support the Linux operating system.[6] For example, IBM has more than 500 programmers working with Linux, primarily because of its security features. Many CIOs are considering switching to Linux and open-source software because of security and cost concerns with Microsoft software.

Figure 4.4 Mac OS

4.1.3 Workgroup Operating Systems

To keep pace with user demands, the technology of the future must support a world in which network usage, data-storage requirements, and data-processing speeds increase at a dramatic rate. This rapid increase in communications and data-processing capabilities pushes the boundaries of computer science and physics. Powerful and sophisticated OS are needed to run the servers that meet these business needs for workgroups. Small businesses, for example, often use workgroup OSs to run networks and perform critical business tasks.

Windows Server

Microsoft designed Windows Server to perform a host of tasks that are vital for websites and corporate web applications. For example, Microsoft Windows Server can be used to coordinate large data centres. The OS also works with other Microsoft products. It can be used to prevent unauthorized disclosure of information by blocking text and e-mails from being copied, printed, or forwarded to other people.

Microsoft Windows Advanced Server, Limited Edition was the first 64-bit version of the Windows Server family. It was designed to run on the 64-bit Itanium processor from Intel (also known as the IA64). This OS enables Microsoft to begin competing with rival Linux vendors (Red Hat, Caldera, SuSE, and TurboLinux), which already have 64-bit Itanium versions of their Linux distributions. In addition, Sun Microsystems and IBM have had 64-bit UNIX OSs for years.

UNIX

UNIX is a powerful OS originally developed by AT&T for minicomputers. UNIX can be used on many computer system types and platforms, from personal computers to mainframe systems. UNIX also makes it much easier to move programs and data among computers or to connect mainframes and personal computers to share resources. There are many variants of UNIX – including HP/UX from Hewlett-Packard, AIX from IBM, UNIX SystemV from UNIX Systems Lab,

Solaris from Sun Microsystems, and SCO from Santa Cruz Operations. Sun Microsystems hopes that its open-source Solaris will attract developers to make the software even better.[7]

NetWare

NetWare is a network OS sold by Novell that can support users on Windows, Macintosh, and UNIX platforms. NetWare provides directory software to track computers, programs, and people on a network, helping large companies to manage complex networks. NetWare users can log on from any computer on the network and use their own familiar desktop with all their applications, data, and preferences.

Red Hat Linux

Red Hat Software offers a Linux network OS that taps into the talents of tens of thousands of volunteer programmers who generate a steady stream of improvements for the Linux OS. The Red Hat Linux network OS is very efficient at serving web pages and can manage a cluster of up to eight servers. The film *Lord of the Rings* used Linux and hundreds of servers to deliver many of the special effects shown in the finished film. Linux environments typically have fewer virus and security problems than other OSs. Distributions such as SuSE and Red Hat have proven Linux to be a very stable and efficient OS.

Mac OS X Server

The Mac OS X Server is the first modern server OS from Apple Computer. It provides UNIX-style process management. Protected memory puts each service in its own well-guarded chunk of dynamically allocated memory, preventing a single process from going awry and bringing down the system or other services. Under pre-emptive multitasking, a computer OS uses some criteria to decide how long to allocate to any one task before giving another task a turn to use the OS. Pre-empting is the act of taking control of the OS from one task and giving it to another. A common criterion for pre-empting is elapsed time. In more sophisticated OSs, certain applications can be given higher priority than other applications, giving the higher-priority programs longer processing times. Pre-emptive multitasking ensures that each process gets the right amount of CPU time and the system resources it needs for optimal efficiency and responsiveness.

4.1.4   Enterprise Operating Systems

New mainframe computers provide the computing and storage capacity to meet massive data-processing requirements and offer many users high performance and excellent system availability, strong security, and scalability. In addition, a wide range of application software has been developed to run in the mainframe environment, making it possible to purchase software to address almost any business problem. As a result, mainframe computers remain the computing platform of choice for mission-critical business applications for many companies. z/OS from IBM, MPE/iX from Hewlett-Packard, and Linux are three examples of mainframe OSs.

z/OS

The z/OS is IBM's first 64-bit enterprise OS. It supports IBM's z900 and z800 lines of mainframes that can come with up to sixteen 64-bit processors. (The 'z' stands for 'zero downtime'.) The OS provides several new capabilities to make it easier and less expensive for users to run large mainframe computers. The OS has improved workload management and advanced e-commerce security. The IBM zSeries mainframe, like previous generations of IBM mainframes, lets users subdivide a single computer into multiple smaller servers, each of which can run a different application. In recognition of the widespread popularity of a competing OS, z/OS allows partitions to run a version of the Linux OS. This means that a company can upgrade to a mainframe that runs the Linux OS.

MPE/iX, HP-UX, and Linux

Multiprogramming Executive with integrated POSIX (MPE/iX) is the Internet-enabled OS for the Hewlett-Packard e3000 family of computers. MPE/iX is a robust OS designed to handle a variety of business tasks, including online transaction processing and web applications. It runs on a broad range of HP e3000 servers – from entry-level to workgroup and enterprise servers within the data centres of large organizations. HP-UX is a mainframe OS from Hewlett-Packard, and is designed to support Internet, database, and a variety of business applications. It can work with Java programs and Linux applications. The OS comes in four versions: foundation, enterprise, mission critical, and technical. HP-UX supports Hewlett-Packard's computers and those designed to run Intel's Itanium processors. Red Hat Linux for IBM mainframe computers is another example of an enterprise operating system.

4.1.5 Mobile Operating Systems

New OS and other software are changing the way we interact with personal digital assistants (PDAs), mobile phones, digital cameras, TVs, and other appliances. These OS are also called 'embedded operating systems' because they are typically embedded within a device, such as an automobile, TV recorder, or other device. Some of these OS allow you to synchronize hand-held devices with PCs using cradles, cables, and wireless connections. Mobile phones also use embedded OS (see Figure 4.5). In addition, some OS have been developed for special-purpose devices, such as TV set-top boxes, computers on the space shuttle, computers in military weapons, and computers in some home appliances. In Chapter 10, we will examine more applications of these devices. The following are some of the more popular OS for such devices.

Figure 4.5 Mobile Phones Have Embedded Operating Systems *Many mobile phones have an embedded OS, which is blurring the distraction between mobile phone and smartphone.*

SOURCE: Istock.

Palm OS

PalmSource makes the Palm operating system that is used in over 30 million handheld computers and smartphones manufactured by Palm, Inc., and other companies. Palm also develops and supports applications, including business, multimedia, games, productivity, reference and education, hobbies and entertainment, travel, sports, utilities, and wireless applications. Today, Palm has about half of the market for PDA or handheld OS. Microsoft has about 30 percent of the market; Linux and other companies account for the rest of the PDA market.

Windows Embedded

Windows Embedded, or Windows CE, is a family of Microsoft OS included with or embedded into small computer devices such as handheld computers, TV set-top boxes, and automated industrial machines. Windows Embedded represents a key step in taking Microsoft closer to its vision of anywhere, anytime access to web-based content and services. It is an embedded OS for use in mobile devices, such as smartphones and PDAs, and other devices, such as digital cameras, thin clients, and automotive computers. PDAs with Windows CE try to bring as much of the functionality of a desktop PC as possible to a handheld device. Such a PDA is a programmable computer that performs most of the tasks of a dedicated device.

Information Systems @ Work

Gas Natural: Improving Customer Service with Mobile Software

Gas Natural is Spain's largest natural gas distributor, with 4.5 million domestic customers. While once the only option for natural gas in Spain, Gas Natural suddenly found itself threatened by strong competition due to recently deregulated markets. These competitive forces drove Gas Natural to emphasize customer service to retain customers. They focused on managing and fulfilling its customers' service requirements, responding to problems quickly, and getting the job done right the first time.

Gas Natural uses a decentralized approach to field service; that is, it contracts its field service to a broad network of independent franchises to install, repair, and maintain gas service at the customer's location. The system Gas Natural used to communicate with field service workers was archaic and slow. Paper work orders were mailed to the service franchises, who dispatched them to field engineers. Upon completion of the service call, the engineer logged the status of the order on paper forms and mailed them back to Gas Natural where administrators would enter the information into the database system. This lack of real-time communication

between service engineers and dispatchers at Gas Natural led to frustration for all, especially customers.

The sales force at Gas Natural was equally hampered. Like the field service workers, it lacked real-time access to corporate information while away from the office and so was unable to leverage the information needed to close deals. Gas Natural required software that would eliminate the need for paper service requests and forms and put their field engineers and sales force in touch with headquarters.

Gas Natural found a solution to their problems with Workforce Management software from the Swedish software company isMobile (www.ismobile.com). The isMobile company works with its clients to help them become real-time enterprises with short lead times and high productivity at the lowest possible cost, which is just what Gas Natural needed.

Within three months, isMobile had replaced the clipboards that Gas Natural engineers and sales representatives carried with state-of-the-art PDAs running custom isMobile software connected to

(continued)

back-end systems at Gas Natural. Using the new system, service requests are passed from customer to Gas Natural to service franchise to engineer in moments. The system makes better use of the engineer's time and decreases response time to jobs. Engineers can now finish the job in one visit because they can access useful information through the software running on their mobile PCs.

Gas Natural sales representatives are now armed with real-time information from the company's customer resource management (CRM) systems and mobile sales software tools, empowering them to target new and existing customers with custom-designed service bundles.

By empowering field engineers and sales representatives with the information they need when they need it, Gas Natural has become a customer-centred, responsive business. The new software solution has provided the company with a higher level of market security.

Questions

1 How does a deregulated market positively affect customers and challenge businesses?

2 What role did software play in empowering Gas Natural to better serve its customers and gain new customers?

3 Besides increasing customer satisfaction, what benefits do you think Gas Natural's new system provided for the franchise businesses that provide its service engineers?

4 What other businesses can you think of that have increased customer satisfaction through the use of innovative software to gain a competitive advantage? How?

SOURCES: 'Gas Natural Energizes Its Field Force Operations by Enabling Everyplace Access to Realtime Data', *IBM Success Story*, November 2, 2005, www-306.ibm.com/software/success/cssdb.nsf/CS/ JSTS-6HKRPY?OpenDocument&Site=wsappserv; 'Madrid Backs Gas Natural Takeover,' *BBC News*, February 5, 2006, http://news.bbc.co.uk/ 2/hi/business/4677696.stm; isMobile (website), www.ismobile.com, March 4, 2006.

Windows Mobile

Windows Mobile is a family of Microsoft OS for mobile or portable devices. Windows Mobile includes Pocket PC, Pocket PC Phone Edition, and SmartPhone. These OS offer features such as handwriting recognition, instant messaging technology, support for more secure Internet connections, and the ability to beam information to devices running the Pocket PC or Palm OS. They also have advanced telecommunications capabilities, discussed in more detail in Chapter 6. Motorola, Samsung, Dell, Hewlett-Packard, and Toshiba have products that run Windows Mobile. Wireless services are often available with devices that use Windows Mobile.

4.1.6 Utility Programs

Utility programs help to perform maintenance or correct problems with a computer system. For example, some utility programs merge and sort sets of data, keep track of computer jobs being run, compress files of data before they are stored or transmitted over a network (thus saving space and time), and perform other important tasks. Another type of utility program allows people and organizations to tap into unused computer power over a network. Often called 'grid computing', the approach can be very efficient and less expensive than purchasing additional hardware or computer equipment. In the future, grid computing could become a common feature of OS and provide inexpensive, on-demand access to computer power and resources.

utility programs Programs that help to perform maintenance or correct problems with a computer system.

Utility programs often come installed on computer systems, but you can also purchase utility programs separately (see Figure 4.6). The following sections examine some common types of utilities.

Hardware Utilities

Some hardware utilities are available from companies such as Symantec, which produces Norton Utilities. Hardware utilities can check the status of all parts of the PC, including hard

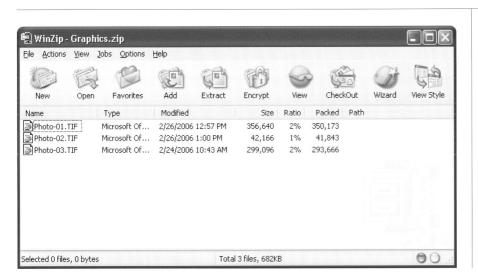

Figure 4.6 WinZip, a File Compression Utility

disks, memory, modems, speakers, and printers. Disk utilities check the hard disk's boot sector, file allocation tables, and directories, and analyze them to ensure that the hard disk is not damaged. Disk utilities can also optimize the placement of files on a crowded disk.

Virus-Detection and Recovery Utilities

Computer viruses from the Internet and other sources can be a nuisance – and sometimes can completely disable a computer. Virus-detection and recovery software can be installed to constantly monitor and protect the computer. If a virus is found, the software can eliminate the virus, or 'clean' the computer system. To keep the virus-detection and recovery software current and make sure that the software checks for the latest viruses, it can be easily updated automatically through the Internet. Symantec and McAfee are two companies that make virus-detection and recovery software.

File-Compression Utilities

File-compression programs can reduce the amount of disk space required to store a file or reduce the time it takes to transfer a file over the Internet. A popular program on Windows PCs is WinZip (www.winzip.com), which generates zip files, which are collections of one or more compressed files. A zip file has a .zip extension, and its contents can be easily un-zipped to their original size. MP3 (Motion Pictures Experts Group-Layer 3) is a popular file-compression format used to store, transfer, and play music and audio files, such as podcasts – audio programs that can be downloaded from the Internet. MP3 can compress files ten times smaller than the original file with near-CD-quality sound. Software, such as iTunes from Apple, can be used to store, organize, and play MP3 music files.

Spam and Pop-Up Blocker Utilities

Getting unwanted e-mail (spam) and having annoying and unwanted ads pop up on your screen while you are on the web can be frustrating and a big waste of time. A number of utility programs can be installed to help block unwanted e-mail spam and pop-up ads, including Cloudmark SpamNet, IhateSpam, Spamnix, McAfee SpamKiller, and Ad-aware.

Network and Internet Utilities

A broad range of network and systems management utility software is available to monitor hardware and network performance and trigger an alert when a web server is crashing or a network problem occurs. Although these general management features are helpful, what is needed is a way to pinpoint the cause of the problem. Topaz from Mercury Interactive is an example of software called an 'advanced web-performance monitoring utility'. It is designed to sound an alarm when it detects problems and let network administrators isolate the most likely causes of the problems. Its Auto RCA (root-cause analysis) module uses statistical analysis with built-in rules to measure system and web performance. Actual performance data is compared with the rules, and the results can help pinpoint where trouble originated – in the application software, database, server, network, or the security features.

Server and Mainframe Utilities

Some utilities enhance the performance of servers and mainframe computers. IBM has created systems-management software that allows a support person to monitor the growing number of desktop computers in a business attached to a server or mainframe computer. With this software, the support people can sit at their personal computers and check or diagnose problems, such as a hard disk failure on a network computer. The support people can even repair individual systems anywhere on the organization's network, often without having to leave their desks. The direct benefit is to the system manager, but the business gains from having a smoothly functioning information system. Utility programs can meet the needs of a single user, workgroup, or enterprise, as listed in Table 4.1. These programs perform useful tasks – from tracking jobs to monitoring system integrity.

Virtualization software can make computers act like or simulate other computers.[8] The result is often called a 'virtual machine'. Virtual PC for Mac, for example, allows you to run software written for Windows on an Apple Macintosh computer. Using virtualization software, servers and mainframe computers can run software applications written for different operating systems. For example, you can use a server or mainframe to test and run a number of PC applications, such as spreadsheets, word processors, and databases, at the same time. A virtual machine can also run older programs that cannot run on current operating systems. WMWare Workstation, for example, allows today's Windows computers to run applications written for older operating systems, such as Windows 3.1.[9]

Other Utilities

Utility programs are available for almost every conceivable task or function.[10] For example, you can use Microsoft Windows Rights Management Services with Microsoft Office programs to manage and protect important corporate documents. ValueIT is a utility that can help a company

Table 4.1 Examples of Utility Programs

Personal	Workgroup	Enterprise
Software to compress data so that it takes less hard disk space	Software to provide detailed reports of work-group computer activity and status of user accounts	Software to archive contents of a database by copying data from disk to tape
Screen saver	Software that manages an uninterruptible power supply to do a controlled shutdown of the workgroup computer in the event of a loss of power	Software that compares the content of one file with another and identifies any differences
Virus-detection software	Software that reports unsuccessful user logon attempts	Software that reports the status of a particular computer job

verify the value of investments in information systems and technology. Widgit Software has developed an important software utility that helps people with visual disabilities use the Internet. The software converts icons and symbols into plain text that can be easily seen. Another software utility allows a manager to see every keystroke a worker makes on a computer system. Monitoring software can catalogue the Internet sites that employees visit and the time that employees are working at their computer.

In addition, you can use many search tools to find important files and documents.[11] Most of these desktop search tools are free and available from a number of popular Internet sites.[12] Yahoo! Desktop Search, Ask Jeeves Desktop Search, Google Desktop, and MSN Deskbar are examples (see Figure 4.7).

Figure 4.7 Desktop Search Tool *With a desktop search tool, such as Google Desktop, you can search through files on your computer.*

4.2 Middleware

Middleware is software that allows different systems to communicate and exchange data. Middleware can also be used as an interface between the Internet and older legacy systems. (Legacy software is a previous, major version that continues to be used.) For example, middleware can be used to transfer a request for information from a corporate customer on the corporate website to a traditional database on a mainframe computer and return the results to the customer on the Internet.

middleware Software that allows different systems to communicate and exchange data.

4.3 Application Software

The primary function of application software is to apply the power of the computer to give people, workgroups, and the entire enterprise the ability to solve problems and perform specific tasks. When you need the computer to do something, you use one or more application programs. As such, users are more concerned about application software than system software. The application programs interact with systems software, and the systems software then directs the computer hardware to perform the necessary tasks. Applications help you perform common tasks, such as create and format text documents, perform calculations, or manage information, though some applications are more specialized. Pfizer, for example, has developed application software to detect the early signs of Parkinson's disease.[13] The new software detects slight trembling in speech patterns not detectable by the human ear that predicts the disease.

The functions performed by application software are diverse, and range from personal productivity to business analysis. Application software, for example, can be used to help sales managers track sales of a new item in a test market. Another example of innovative applications in business is voice stress software, which is being developed to help detect fraud in the insurance industry. Pilot programs have been very successful in detecting scam insurance companies or people who try to make false claims. In general, applications can complete sales orders, control inventory, pay bills, write paycheques to employees, and provide financial and marketing information to managers and executives. Most of the computerized business jobs and activities discussed in this book involve the use of application software. We begin by investigating the types and functions of application software.

4.3.1　Overview of Application Software

Proprietary software and off-the-shelf software are important types of application software (see Figure 4.8). A company can develop a one-of-a-kind program for a specific application (called proprietary software). Proprietary software is not in the public domain, that is, you can't walk into a shop an buy it. A company can also purchase or acquire an existing software program (sometimes called off-the-shelf software because it can literally be purchased 'off the shelf' in a shop). The relative advantages and disadvantages of proprietary software and off-the-shelf software are summarized in Table 4.2. Many companies use off-the-shelf software. Key questions for selecting off-the-shelf software include the following:

1　Will the software run on the OS and hardware you have selected?
2　Does the software meet the essential business requirements that have been defined?
3　Is the software manufacturer financially solvent and reliable?
4　Does the total cost of purchasing, installing, and maintaining the software compare favourably to the expected business benefits?

Some off-the-shelf programs can be modified, in effect blending the off-the-shelf and customized approaches.

Figure 4.8 Types of Application Software

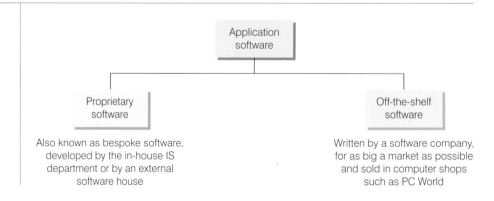

Designed properly – and with provisions for minor tailoring for each user – the same software package can be sold to many users. As a result, software vendors often provide a wide range of services, including installing their standard software, modifying the software as the customer requires, training users, and providing other consulting services.

Another approach to obtaining a customized software package is to use an application service provider. An **application service provider (ASP)** is a company that can provide the software, support, and computer hardware on which to run the software from the user's facilities. An ASP can also simplify a complex corporate software package so that it is easier for the users to set up and manage. ASPs provide contract customization of off-the-shelf software, and they speed deployment of new applications while helping IS managers avoid implementation headaches, reducing the need for many skilled IS staff members and decreasing project start-up expenses. Such an approach allows companies to devote more time and resources to more important tasks. Using an ASP makes the most sense for relatively small, fast-growing companies with limited IS resources. It is also a good strategy for companies that want to deploy a single, functionally focused application quickly, such as setting up an e-commerce website or supporting expense reporting. Contracting with an ASP might make less sense, however, for larger companies with major systems that have their technical infrastructure already in place.

> **application service provider (ASP)** A company that provides software, support, and the computer hardware on which to run the software from the user's facilities.

Table 4.2 A Comparison of Proprietary and Off-the-Shelf Software

Proprietary Software		Off-the-Shelf Software	
Advantages	**Disadvantages**	**Advantages**	**Disadvantages**
You can get exactly what you need in terms of features, reports, and so on	It can take a long time and significant resources to develop required features	The initial cost is lower because the software firm can spread the development costs over many customers	An organization might have to pay for features that are not required and never used
Being involved in the development offers control over the results	In-house system development staff may become hard pressed to provide the required level of ongoing support and maintenance because of pressure to move on to other new projects	The software is likely to meet the basic business needs – you can analyze existing features and the performance of the package	The software might lack important features, thus requiring future modification or customization. This can be very expensive because users must adopt future releases of the software as well
You can modify features that you might need to counteract an initiative by competitors or to meet new supplier or customer demands. A merger with or acquisition of another firm also requires software changes to meet new business needs	There is more risk concerning the features and performance of the software that has yet to be developed	The package is likely to be of high quality because many customer firms have tested the software and helped identify its bugs	The software might not match current work processes and data standards

Using an ASP involves some risks – sensitive information could be compromized in a number of ways, including unauthorized access by employees or computer hackers; the ASP might not be able to keep its computers and network up and running as consistently as necessary; or a disaster could disable the ASP's data centre, temporarily putting an organization out of business. These are legitimate concerns that an ASP must address. Some popular applications are now discussed.

4.3.2 Personal Application Software

Hundreds of computer applications can help people at work, home and university. The features of some personal application software are summarized in Table 4.3. In addition to these general-purpose programs, thousands of other personal computer applications perform specialized tasks: to help you do your taxes, create videos, write songs, lose weight, prepare a will, get medical advice, repair your computer, fix your car, etc. This type of software, often called user software or personal productivity software, includes the general-purpose tools and programs that support individual needs.

Word Processing

Word processing applications are installed on most PCs today. These applications come with a vast array of features, including those for checking spelling, creating tables, inserting formulas, creating graphics, and much more (see Figure 4.9). This book (and most like it) was entered into a word processing application using a personal computer.

Spreadsheet Analysis

Spreadsheets are powerful tools for individuals and organizations. Features of spreadsheets include graphics, limited database capabilities, statistical analysis, built-in business functions,

---

Figure 4.9 Word **Processing Program** *Word processing applications can be used to write and collaborate on documents such as letters, professional documents, work reports, and term papers. This one is Google Docs which is accessed through an Internet browser. Using Google Docs, your documents are available to you from any computer connected to the Internet.*

Table 4.3 Examples of Personal Application Software

Type of Software	Explanation	Example	Vendor
Word processing	Create, edit, and print text documents	Word Pages	Microsoft (Office) Apple (iWork)
Spreadsheet	Provide a wide range of built-in functions for statistical, financial, logical, database, graphics, and date and time calculations	Excel Numbers Lotus 1-2-3	Microsoft (Office) Apple (iwork) Lotus/IBM
Database	Store, manipulate, and retrieve data	Access Approach FileMaker dBASE	Microsoft (Office) Lotus/IBM FileMaker Databased Intelligence Inc.
Online information services	Obtain a broad range of information from commercial services	Google MSN	Google Microsoft
Graphics	Develop graphs, illustrations, and drawings	Illustrator FreeHand	Adobe Macromedia
Project management	Plan, schedule, allocate, and control people and resources (money, time, and technology) needed to complete a project according to schedule	Project for Windows Project Schedule	Microsoft Scitor
Financial management	Provide income and expense tracking and reporting to monitor and plan budgets (some programs have investment portfolio management features)	Money Managing Your Money Quicken	Microsoft Meca Software Intuit
Desktop publishing (DTP)	Use with personal computers and high-resolution printers to create high-quality printed output, including text and graphics; various styles of pages can be laid out; art and text files from other programs can also be integrated into 'published' pages	QuarkXPress Publisher InDesign	Quark Microsoft Adobe
Presentation	Animated/Slide-show type business presentations	PowerPoint Keynote	Microsoft (Office) Apple (iWork)

4

and much more (see Figure 4.10). The business functions include calculation of depreciation, present value, internal rate of return, and the monthly payment on a loan, to name a few. Optimization is another powerful feature of many spreadsheet programs. Optimization allows the spreadsheet to maximize or minimize a quantity subject to certain constraints. For example, a small furniture manufacturer that produces chairs and tables might want to maximise its profits. The constraints could be a limited supply of lumber, a limited number of workers who can assemble the chairs and tables, or a limited amount of various hardware fasteners that might be required. Using an optimization feature, such as Solver in Microsoft Excel, the spreadsheet can determine what number of chairs and tables to produce with labour and material constraints to maximize profits.

Figure 4.10 A
Spreadsheet Program.
Another application from
Google.

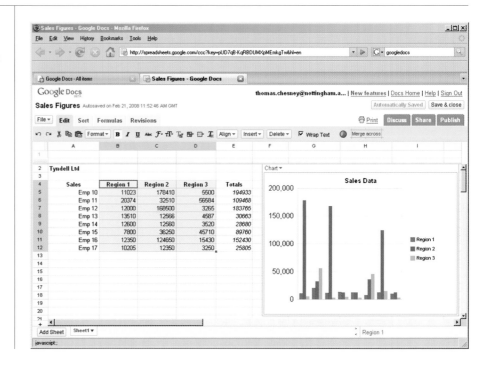

Database Applications

Database applications are ideal for storing, manipulating, and retrieving data, and are central to most information systems. These applications are particularly useful when you need to manipulate a large amount of data and produce reports and documents. Database manipulations include merging, editing, and sorting data. The uses of a database application are varied. You can keep track of a CD collection, the items in your flat, tax records, and expenses. A student club can use a database to store names, addresses, phone numbers, and dues paid. In business, a database application can help process sales orders, control inventory, order new supplies, send letters to customers, and pay employees. Databases can be used to help create dynamic websites that are easily maintained. Database management systems can be used to track orders, analyze weather data to make forecasts for the next several days, and summarize medical research results. A database can also be a front end to another application. For example, you can use a database application to enter and store income tax information, then export the stored results to other applications, such as a spreadsheet or tax-preparation application (see Figure 4.11). After being entered into a database application, information can be manipulated and used to produce reports and documents. Because of the importance of databases, the entire next chapter deals exclusively with them.

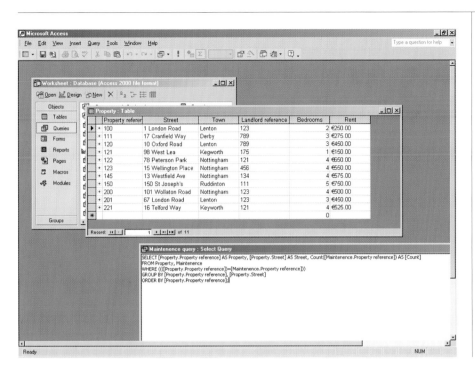

Figure 4.11 Database
Program

Graphics Program

It is often said that a picture is worth a thousand words. With today's graphics programs, it is easy to develop attractive graphs, illustrations, and drawings (see Figure 4.12). Graphics programs can be used to develop advertising brochures, announcements, and full-colour presentations, and to organize and edit photographic images. If you need to make a presentation at work or for an assignment, you can use a special type of graphics program called a presentation application to develop slides and then display them while you are delivering your presentation. Because of their popularity, many colleges and departments require students to become

Figure 4.12 Graphics
Program *Graphics
programs can help you
make a presentation at
school or work. They can
also be used to develop
attractive brochures,
illustrations, drawings, and
maps, and to organize and
edit photographic images.*

proficient at using presentation graphics programs. Many presentation applications, such as PowerPoint by Microsoft, consist of a series of slides. Each slide can be displayed on a computer screen, printed as a handout, or (more commonly) projected onto a large viewing screen for audiences. Powerful built-in features allow you to develop attractive slides and complete presentations.

Software Suites and Integrated Software Packages

A **software suite** is a collection of single application programs packaged in a bundle. As such, softwrae suites represent an economical way for small businesses to get powerful applications.

software suite A collection of single application programs packaged in a bundle.

Software suites can include word processors, spreadsheets, database management systems, graphics programs, communications tools, web development tools and more. Software suites offer many advantages. The software programs have been designed to work similarly, so after you learn the basics for one application, the other applications are easy to learn and use. Buying software in a bundled suite is cost effective; the programs usually sell for a fraction of what they would cost individually.

Microsoft Office, Apple iWork, Sun Microsystems's StarOffice, and the Open Source OpenOffice are examples of popular general-purpose software suites for personal computer users (see Figure 4.13). Microsoft Office has the largest market share. The Free Software Foundation offers software similar to Sun Microsystems's StarOffice that includes word processing, spreadsheet, database, presentation graphics, and e-mail applications for the Linux OS. OpenOffice is another Office suite for Linux.[14] Each of these software suites includes a spreadsheet program, word processor, database program, and graphics package with the ability to move documents, data, and diagrams among them (see Table 4.4). Thus, a user can create a spreadsheet and then cut and paste that spreadsheet into a document created using the word processing application.

Figure 4.13 Software Suite *A software suite, such as Microsoft Office, offers a collection of powerful programs, including word processing, spreadsheet, database, graphics, and other programs. The programs in a software suite are designed to be used together. In addition, the commands, icons, and procedures are the same for all programs in the suite.*

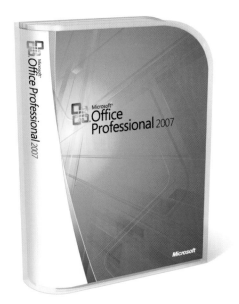

SOURCE: Microsoft® Software.

Microsoft Office (along with other software suites) goes beyond its role as a mainstream package of ready-to-run applications with the extensive custom development facilities of Visual Basic for Applications (VBA) – a built-in facility that is part of every Office application. Using VBA, users can enhance off-the-shelf applications to tailor the programs for special tasks.

Other Personal Application Software

In addition to the software already discussed, people can use many other interesting and powerful application software tools. Web browsers such as Mozilla Firefox are used to access information over the Internet, and packages such as Outlook are used to read e-mail. In some cases, the features and capabilities of more specialized applications can more than justify the cost of an entire computer system. TurboTax, for example, is a popular tax-preparation program. Other exciting software packages have been developed for training and distance learning. Using this type of software, some universities offer complete degree programs over the Internet. Engineers, architects, and designers often use computer-aided design (CAD) software to design and develop buildings, electrical systems, plumbing systems, and more. Autosketch, CorelCAD, and AutoCad are examples of CAD software. Other programs perform a wide array of statistical tests. Two popular statistical applications in the social sciences are SPSS and SAS.

4.4 Programming Languages

Both OS and application software are written in coding schemes called 'programming languages'. The primary function of a **programming language** is to provide instructions to the computer system so that it can perform a processing activity. IS professionals work with programming languages, which are sets of keywords, symbols, and rules for constructing statements by which people can communicate instructions to be executed by a computer. Programming involves translating what a user wants to accomplish into a code that the computer can understand and execute. Program code is the set of instructions that signal the CPU to perform circuit-switching operations. In the simplest coding schemes, a line of code typically contains a single instruction such as, 'Retrieve the data in memory address X'. As discussed in Chapter 3, the instruction is then decoded during the instruction phase of the machine cycle. Like writing a report or a paper in English, writing a computer program in a programming language requires the programmer to follow a set of rules. Each programming language uses symbols that have special meaning. Each language also has its own set of rules, called the **syntax** of the language. The language syntax dictates how the symbols should be combined into statements capable of conveying meaningful instructions to the CPU. A rule that 'variable names must start with a letter' is an example. A variable is a quantity that can take on different values. Program variable names such as SALES, PAYRATE, and TOTAL follow the rule because they start with a letter, whereas variables such as %INTEREST, $TOTAL, and #POUNDS do not.

programming language Sets of keywords, symbols, and a system of rules for constructing statements by which humans can communicate instructions to be executed by a computer.

syntax A set of rules associated with a programming language.

Table 4.4 Major Components of Leading Software Suites

Personal Productivity Function	Microsoft Office	Sun Microsystems StarOffice/ OpenOffice	Apple iWork
Word Processing	Word	Writer	Pages
Spreadsheet	Excel	Calc	Numbers
Presentation Graphics	PowerPoint	Impress	Keynote
Database	Access	Base	

The only time most managers come into contact with programming languages is when working with software developers to create proprietary software. At such times, it is useful to know some basics.

4.4.1 The Evolution of Programming Languages

The desire to use the power of information processing efficiently in problem solving has pushed the development of newer programming languages. The evolution of programming languages is typically discussed in terms of generations of languages (see Table 4.5).

First-generation languages required the programmer to use binary digits (zeros and ones) in blocks of eight to build up programs. These blocks represented basic instructions such as 'add' or 'read the contents of a memory address'. This address would itself be represented in binary. Programs written in machine language were long and difficult for a human reader to understand.

Second-generation languages, or assembly languages, replaced each machine language instruction with a one word mnemonic such as 'ADD'. This mnemonic told the CPU to add together a series of values which would appear in the code immediately after the mnemonic. The use of mnemonics made programs more readable, although they were just as long as when written in machine language.

The development of third-generation languages, such as C and BASIC, allowed tasks to be acomplished using much less code, at least from the programmer's point of view. Here, a number of machine language instructions that together achieved a common, useful task, were grouped and given a single name, so that programmers could use them in their programs just by including that name. An example is 'PRINT'. Rather than need to know the machine language instructions to print something on the screen, a programmer could simple type 'PRINT HELLO' and the word 'HELLO' would appear on the screen. These groups of instructions are known as 'macros'. Programs were much more readable, hence easier to understand by humans and as such, more people got interested in computer programming.

Fourth-generation languages (4GLs) are more specialized and often have a main application or strength, such as constructing and querying a database (SQL) or building a graphical user interface (Visual Basic). Fourth-generation languages allowed certain tasks to be achieved more quickly than with general purpose third-generation languages.

Programming languages used to create artificial intelligence or expert systems applications are often called fifth-generation languages (5GLs). FLEXPERT, for example, is an expert system

Table 4.5 The Evolution of Programming Languages

Generation	Language	Approximate Development Date	Sample Statement or Action
First	Machine language	1940s	00010101
Second	Assembly language	1950s	MVC
Third	High-level language	1960s	READ SALES
Fourth	Query and database languages	1970s	PRINT EMPLOYEE NUMBER IF GROSS PAY > 1000
Beyond Fourth	Natural and intelligent languages	1980s	IF gross pay is greater than 40, THEN pay the employee overtime pay.

used to perform plant layout and helps companies determine the best placement for equipment and manufacturing facilities. Fifth-generation languages are sometimes called 'natural languages' because they use even more English-like syntax than 4GLs. They allow programmers to communicate with the computer by using normal sentences. For example, computers programmed in fifth-generation languages can understand queries such as 'How many athletic shoes did our company sell last month?'.

Often languages are classed as being 'procedural' or 'object oriented'. Procedural languages separate data elements from the procedures or actions that will be performed on them; object oriented programming languages tie them together into units called 'objects'. An 'object' consists of data and the actions that can be performed on the data. For example, an object could be data about an employee and all the operations (such as payroll calculations) that might be performed on the data. Building programs and applications using object-oriented programming languages is like constructing a building using prefabricated modules or parts. The object containing the data, instructions, and procedures is a programming building block. The same objects (modules or parts) can be used repeatedly. One of the primary advantages of an object is that it contains reusable code. In other words, the instruction code within that object can be reused in different programs for a variety of applications, just as the same basic prefabricated door can be used in two different houses. An object can relate to data on a product, an input routine, or an order-processing routine. An object can even direct a computer to execute other programs or to retrieve and manipulate data. So, a sorting routine developed for a payroll application could be used in both a billing program and an inventory control program. By reusing program code, programmers can write programs for specific application problems more quickly (see Figure 4.14). By combining existing program objects with new ones, programmers can easily and efficiently develop new object-oriented programs to accomplish organizational goals.

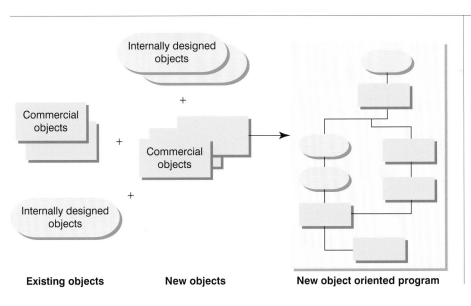

Existing objects   **New objects**   **New object oriented program**

Figure 4.14 Reusable Code in Object-Oriented Programming

Programmers often start writing object oriented programs by developing one or more user interfaces, usually in a Windows or web environment. You can create programs to run in a Windows or web environment by using forms to design and develop the type of interface you want. You can select and drag text boxes to add descriptions, buttons that can be clicked and executed, a list box that contains several choices that can be selected, and other input/output features. After creating the Windows interface, you can write programming code to convert tasks a user selects in the interface into actions the computer performs. By combining existing program objects with new ones, programmers can easily and efficiently develop new object-oriented programs to accomplish organizational goals.

compiler A special software program that converts the programmer's source code into the machine-language instructions consisting of binary digits.

With third-generation and higher-level programming languages, each statement in the language translates into several instructions in machine language. A special software program called a **compiler** converts the programmer's source code into the machine-language instructions consisting of binary digits, as shown in Figure 4.15. A compiler creates a two-stage process for program execution. First, the compiler translates the program into a machine language; second, the CPU executes that program. Another approach is to use an interpreter, which is a language translator that carries out the operations called for by the source code. An interpreter does not produce a complete machine-language program. After the statement executes, the machine-language statement is discarded, the process continues for the next statement, and so on.

4

Figure 4.15 How a Compiler Works *A compiler translates a complete program into a complete set of binary instructions (Stage 1). After this is done, the CPU can execute the converted program in its entirety (Stage 2).*

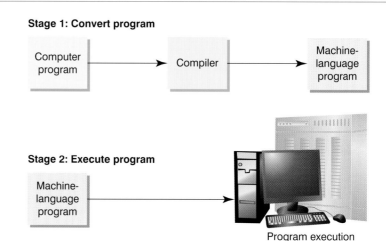

4.5 Software Issues and Trends

Because software is such an important part of computer systems, issues such as software bugs, licencing, upgrades, and global software support have received increased attention and are of great relevance to businesses. We highlight several of these in this section.

4.5.1 Software Bugs

A software bug is a defect in a computer program that keeps it from performing as it is designed to perform. Some software bugs are obvious and cause the program to terminate unexpectedly. Other bugs are subtler and allow errors to creep into your work. Computer and software vendors say that as long as people design and program hardware and software, bugs are inevitable. The following list summarizes tips for reducing the impact of software bugs.

- Register all software so that you receive bug alerts, fixes, and patches.
- Check the manual or online sources for work-arounds.
- Access the support area of the manufacturer's website for patches.
- Install the latest software updates.
- Before reporting a bug, make sure that you can re-create the circumstances under which it occurs.

- After you can re-create the bug, call the manufacturer's technical support line.
- Avoid buying the latest release of software for several months or a year until the software bugs have been discovered and removed.

4.5.2 Copyrights and Licences

Most software products are protected by law using copyright or licencing provisions. Those provisions can vary, however. In some cases, you are given unlimited use of software on one or two computers. This is typical with many applications developed for personal computers. In other cases, you pay for your usage – if you use the software more, you pay more. This approach is becoming popular with software placed on networks or larger computers. Most of these protections prevent you from copying software and giving it to others without restrictions. Some software now requires that you register or activate it before it can be fully used. Registration and activation sometimes put software on your hard disk that monitors activities and changes your computer system.

4.5.3 Open-Source Software

Open-source software is freely available to anyone in a form that can be easily modified. The Open Source Initiative (OSI) is a non-profit corporation dedicated to the development and promotion of open-source software (see the OSI website at www.opensource.org for more information on the group's efforts). Users can download the source code and build the software themselves, or the software developers can make executable versions available along with the source. Open-source software development is a collaborative process – developers around the world use the Internet to keep in close contact via e-mail and to download and submit new software. Major software changes can occur in days rather than weeks or months. Many open-source software packages are widely used, including the Linux OS; Apache, a popular web server; Sendmail, a program that delivers e-mail for most systems on the Internet; and Perl, a programming language used to develop Internet application software.

Why would an organization run its business using software that's free? Can something that's given away over the Internet be stable or reliable or sufficiently supported to place at the core of a company's day-to-day operations? The answer is surprising – open-source software is often more reliable and secure than commercial software.[15] How can this be? First, by making a program's source code readily available, users can fix any problems they discover. A fix is often available within hours of the problem's discovery. Second, with the source code for a program accessible to thousands of people, the chances of a bug being discovered and fixed before it does any damage are much greater than with traditional software packages. Some software companies are also starting to reveal their source code. IBM recently made about €750 000 worth of software patents available to open-source software developers at no charge.[16]

There are, however, disadvantages of using open-source software. Although open-source systems can be obtained for next to nothing, the up-front costs are only a small piece of the total cost of ownership that accrues over the years that the system is in place.[17] Some claim that open-source systems contain many hidden costs, particularly for user support or solving problems with the software. Licenced software comes with guarantees and support services that open-source software does not. Still, many businesses appreciate the additional freedom that open-source software provides. The question of software support is the biggest stumbling block to the acceptance of open-source software at the corporate level. Getting support for traditional software packages is easy – you call a company's support number or access its website; but how do you get help if an open-source package doesn't work as expected? Because the open-source community is very active on the Internet, you look there for help. Through use of Internet discussion areas, you can communicate with others who use the same software, and you might

Ethical and Societal Issues

Weighing the Benefits of Open-Source

In 2004, the city of Munich's administration decided to switch its 14 000 computers used by local government employees from the Microsoft Windows OS to a Linux distribution, a free open-source OS. The OS was customized to meet the needs of users. The reason for the move was given as a matter of principle: Munich wanted to control their own technological destiny and not place the functioning of government in the hands of a commercial vendor who has proprietary standards and who is accountable to shareholders rather than to citizens.

Others had already made this decision and more are following suit. The state owned Industrial and Commercial Bank of China (ICBC) is rolling out Linux in all of its 20000 retail branches as the basis for its web server and new terminal platform. Vienna's local government is migrating its desktop PCs to Linux. The U.K. government consider open-source software alongside proprietary ones in all IT Procurements, awarding contracts on a value for money basis. They actively try to avoid becoming locked in to closed standards. The French parliament is adopting Linux on its 1100 PCs.

Why all this fuss over software? It isn't just a matter of price. The reason governments like open-source software is its accessibility. Open-source software can be tweaked, edited, and dissected whenever needed; it also has no secrets. Traditional, proprietary, licenced software is just the opposite – it is one big secret. Using software packages such as Microsoft Windows is similar to owning a car with no bonnet to access the engine. You are provided with a slick user interface – a dashboard, steering wheel, and pedals – but if you are curious about how it works or need to repair it, you are out of luck.

Supporters of open-source software development have a simple philosophy: When programmers can read, redistribute, and modify the source code, the software evolves for everyone's benefit. People improve it, people adapt it, and people fix bugs. Development can happen at a speed that, compared with the slow pace of conventional software development, seems astonishing.

Opponents of the open-source movement, such as Microsoft, have sought to discredit the software. They have suggested that the very openness of the software makes it vulnerable to hackers and terrorists. Microsoft has also funded studies that have found that Windows has a lower cost of ownership than Linux.

While working to discredit Linux, Microsoft has made moves to open up some of its code under an initiative called 'shared source'. The shared source effort allows certain approved governments and large corporate clients to access most of the Windows software source code. Microsoft has also made available portions of the source code for Windows CE, the Microsoft OS for handheld PCs and mobile phones, so others can more easily develop applications for it.

The one major drawback of open-source software – and the major challenge for the Linux OS – is the lack of application programs for personal computing. Since Microsoft holds a monopoly in the desktop PC OS market, the vast majority of software is written for Microsoft Windows. The software developed for Linux is much smaller in quantity, variety, and some may argue in quality. While an inexpensive alternative to Microsoft Office called Star Office was written to run on Linux, and a Windows-like interface, called Lindows for Linux is available, most users are more comfortable with the familiar Microsoft software. Since a solid business model for open-source development is still in the blueprint stages, developers have little incentive to create software that will be given away for free. Companies such as IBM, however, are finding success in distributing Linux to their customers, and profiting from the design, training, and support aspects of Linux-based information systems.

Questions

1 What are some of the difficulties faced by local authorities when migrating to Linux?

2 How can software companies like Microsoft compete against the trend towards open-source software?

3 How could a government calculate the cost of changing to an alternative platform such as Linux against the cost of the typical Windows/Office upgrade?

4 How would the costs of changing platforms differ over the next five years and multiple upgrades of Windows and Office?

SOURCES: 'Microsoft at the Power Point', *Economist.com*, www.economist.com, September 11, 2003; Open Source Initiative (website), www.opensource.org/, February 8, 2004; Sun Microsystems Star Office (website), wwws.sun.com/software/star/staroffice/6.0/, February 8, 2004; Marson, I., 'Munich picks its Linux distro', ZDNet UK; Trombly, M., 'Microsoft Fights Piracy In China, Linux Wins'. *Information Week*, September 6, 2005; Marson, I., 'Vienna to Softly Embrace Linux', *ZDNet UK*, January 25, 2005; Open Source Software version 2, http://www.govtalk.gov.uk/documents/oss_policy_version2.pdf; Sanders, T., 'French Parliament Switches to Linux', vnunet.com, March 13, 2007.

even reach someone who helped develop it. Users of popular open-source packages can get correct answers to their technical questions within a few hours of asking for help on the appropriate Internet forum. Another approach is to contact one of the many companies emerging to support and service such software – for example, Red Hat for Linux, C2Net for Apache, and Sendmail, Inc., for Sendmail. These companies offer high-quality, for-pay technical assistance.

4.5.4 Shareware, Freeware, and Public Domain Software

Many software users are doing what they can to minimize software costs. Some are turning to **shareware and freeware** – software that is very inexpensive or free, usually for use in personal computers, but whose source code cannot be modified. Freeware can be used to perform a variety of tasks. Spybot Search and Destroy is a freeware program to detect and eliminate spyware. Perio Personal Firewall can protect a computer from viruses and intruders. OpenOffice is an office suite that contains a word processor, a spreadsheet, and a presentation program. PhotoPlus 6 is a photo-editing program, and Picasa is a photo-editing and managing program. The website www.SourceForge.net is a resource for programmers to freely exchange programs and program code. It allows programmers to create, participate, and evaluate program code. Over 80 000 programs are at various stages of completion.

shareware and freeware Software that is very inexpensive or free, but whose source code cannot be modified.

Shareware might not be as powerful as commercial software, but provides what some people need at a good price. In some cases, you can try the software before sending a nominal fee to the software developer. Some shareware and freeware is in the public domain, often called public domain software. This software is not protected by copyright laws and can be freely copied and used. Although shareware and freeware can be free or inexpensive to acquire, it can be more expensive to use and maintain over time compared with software that is purchased. If the software is hard to use and doesn't perform all the required functions, the cost of wasted time and lost productivity can be far greater than the cost of purchasing better software. Shareware, freeware, and public domain software is often not open-source – that is, the source code is not available and cannot be modified.

4.5.5 Software Upgrades

Software companies revise their programs and sell new versions periodically. In some cases, the revised software offers new and valuable enhancements. In other cases, the software uses complex program code that offers little in terms of additional capabilities. In addition, revised software can contain bugs or errors. When software companies stop supporting older software versions or releases, some customers feel forced to upgrade to the newer software. Deciding whether to purchase the newest software can be a problem for organizations and people with a large investment in software. Should the newest version be purchased when it is released? Some users do not always get the most current software upgrades or versions, unless they include significant improvements or capabilities. Instead, they might upgrade to newer software only when it offers vital new features. Software upgrades usually cost much less than the original purchase price.

4.5.6 Global Software Support

Large global companies have little trouble persuading vendors to sell them software licences for even the most far-flung outposts of their company. But can those same vendors provide adequate support for their software customers in all locations? Supporting local operations is one of the biggest challenges IS teams face when putting together standardized, company-wide systems. Slower technology growth markets, such as Eastern Europe and Latin America, might not have any official vendor presence. Instead, large vendors such as Sybase, IBM, and Hewlett-Packard typically contract with local providers to support their software.

One approach that has been gaining acceptance is to outsource global support to one or more third-party distributors. The user company can still negotiate its licence with the software vendor directly, but then the vendor hands the global support contract to a third-party supplier. The supplier acts as a middleman between software vendor and user, often providing distribution, support, and invoicing.

In today's computer systems, software is an increasingly critical component. Whatever approach people and organizations take to acquire software, everyone must be aware of the current trends in the industry. Informed users are wiser consumers, and they can make better decisions.

Summary

Systems and application software are critical in helping individuals and organizations achieve their goals. Software consists of programs that control the workings of the computer hardware. The two main categories of software are systems software and application software. Systems software is a collection of programs that interacts between hardware and application software, and includes operating systems, utility programs, and middleware. Application software can be proprietary or off the shelf, and enables people to solve problems and perform specific tasks.

An operating system (OS) is a set of computer programs that controls the computer hardware to support users' computing needs. An OS converts an instruction from an application into a set of instructions needed by the hardware. This intermediary role allows hardware independence. An OS also manages memory, which involves controlling storage access and use by converting logical requests into physical locations and by placing data in the best storage space, perhaps virtual memory.

An OS manages tasks to allocate computer resources through multitasking and time-sharing. With multitasking, users can run more than one application at a time. Time-sharing allows more than one person to use a computer system at the same time.

The ability of a computer to handle an increasing number of concurrent users smoothly is called 'scalability', a feature critical for systems expected to handle a large number of users.

An OS also provides a user interface, which allows users to access and command the computer. A command-based user interface requires text commands to send instructions; a graphical user interface (GUI), such as Windows, uses icons and menus.

Software applications use the OS by requesting services through a defined application program interface (API). Programmers can use APIs to create application software without having to understand the inner workings of the OS. APIs also provide a degree of hardware independence so that the underlying hardware can change without necessarily requiring a rewrite of the software applications.

Over the years, several popular OSs have been developed. These include several proprietary OSs used primarily on mainframes. MS-DOS is an early OS for IBM-compatibles. Older Windows OSs are GUIs used with DOS. Newer versions, such as Windows Vista and XP, are fully functional OSs that do not need DOS. Apple computers use proprietary OSs such as Mac OS and Mac OS X. UNIX is a powerful OS that can be used on many computer system types and platforms, from personal computers to mainframe systems. UNIX makes it easy to move programs and data among computers or to connect mainframes and personal computers to share resources. Linux is the kernel of an OS whose source code is freely available to everyone. Several variations of Linux are available, with sets of capabilities and applications to form a complete OSs, for example, Red Hat Linux. z/OS and MPE iX are OSs for mainframe computers. Some OSs have been developed to support consumer appliances such as Palm OS, Windows CE .Net, Windows XP Embedded, Pocket PC, and variations of Linux.

Utility programs can perform many useful tasks and often come installed on computers along with the OS. This software is used to merge and sort sets of data, keep track of computer jobs being run, compress files of data, protect against harmful computer viruses, and monitor hardware and network performance. Middleware is software that allows different systems to communicate and transfer data back and forth.

Do not develop proprietary application software unless doing so will meet a compelling business need that can provide a competitive advantage. Application software applies the power of the computer to solve problems and perform specific tasks. User software, or personal productivity software, includes general-purpose programs that enable users to improve their personal effectiveness, increasing the quality and amount of work that can be done. Software that helps groups work together is often called 'work-group application software', and includes group scheduling software, e-mail, and other software that enables people to share ideas. Enterprise software that benefits the entire organization can also be developed or purchased. Many organizations are turning to enterprise resource planning software, a set of integrated programs that manage a company's vital business operations for an entire multi-site, global organization.

Building proprietary software (in-house or on contract) has the following advantages: The organization will get software that more closely matches its needs; by being involved with the development, the organization has further control over the results; and the organization has more flexibility in making changes. The disadvantages include the following: It is likely to take longer and cost more to develop, the in-house staff will be hard pressed to provide ongoing support and maintenance, and there is a greater risk that the software features will not work as expected or that other performance problems will occur.

Purchasing off-the-shelf software has many advantages. The initial cost is lower, there is a lower risk that the software will fail to work as expected, and the software is likely to be of higher quality than proprietary software. Some disadvantages are that the organization might pay for features it does not need, the software might lack important features requiring expensive customization, and the system might require process reengineering.

Some organizations have taken a third approach – customizing software packages. This approach usually involves a mixture of the preceding advantages and disadvantages and must be carefully managed.

An application service provider (ASP) is a company that can provide the software, support, and computer hardware on which to run the software from the user's facilities. ASPs provide contract customization of off-the-shelf software, and they speed deployment of new applications while helping IS managers avoid implementation headaches. Use of ASPs reduces the need for many skilled IS staff members and also lowers a project's start-up expenses.

Although hundreds of computer applications can help people at school, home, and work, the primary applications are word processing, spreadsheet analysis, database, graphics, and online services. A software suite, such as SmartSuite, WordPerfect, StarOffice, or Microsoft Office, offers a collection of powerful programs.

Choose a programming language whose functional characteristics are appropriate for the task

at hand, considering the skills and experience of the programming staff. All software programs are written in coding schemes called programming languages, which provide instructions to a computer to perform some processing activity. The several classes of programming languages include machine, assembly, high-level, query and database, object-oriented, and visual programming languages.

Programming languages have changed since their initial development in the early 1950s. In the first generation, computers were programmed in machine language, and the second generation of languages used assembly languages. The third generation consisted of many high-level programming languages that used English-like statements and commands. They were converted to machine language by special software called a compiler, and included BASIC, COBOL, FORTRAN, and others. Fourth-generation languages include database and query languages such as SQL.

Fifth-generation programming languages combine rules-based code generation, component management, visual programming techniques, reuse management, and other advances. Visual and object-oriented programming languages – such as Smalltalk, C++, and Java – use groups of related data, instructions, and procedures called 'objects', which serve as reusable modules in various programs. These languages can reduce program development and testing time. Java can be used to develop applications on the Internet.

The software industry continues to undergo constant change; users need to be aware of recent trends and issues to be effective in their business and personal life. Software bugs, software licencing and copyrighting, open-source software, shareware and freeware, multiorganizational software development, software upgrades, and global software support are all important software issues and trends.

A software bug is a defect in a computer program that keeps it from performing in the manner intended. Software bugs are common, even in key pieces of business software.

Open-source software is software that is freely available to anyone in a form that can be easily modified. Open-source software development and maintenance is a collaborative process with developers around the world using the Internet to keep in close contact via e-mail and to download and submit new software. Shareware and freeware can reduce the cost of software, but sometimes they might not be as powerful as commercial software. Also, their source code usually cannot be modified.

Multiorganizational software development is the process of extending software development beyond a single organization by finding others who share the same business problem and involving them in a common development effort.

Software upgrades are an important source of increased revenue for software manufacturers and can provide useful new functionality and improved quality for software users.

Global software support is an important consideration for large, global companies putting together standardized, company-wide systems. A common solution is outsourcing global support to one or more third-party software distributors.

Self-Assessment Test

1 _____ is the process of swapping programs or parts of programs between memory and disk.

2 The file manager component of the OS controls how memory is accessed and maximizes available memory and storage. True or False?

3 The primary function of application software is to apply the power of the computer to give people, workgroups, and the entire enterprise the ability to solve problems and perform specific tasks. True or False?

4 Software that enables users to improve their personal effectiveness, increasing the amount of work they can do and its quality is called

_____.

a. personal productivity software
b. operating system software
c. utility software
d. graphics software

5 Software used to solve a unique or specific problem that is usually built in house, but can also be purchased from an outside company is called _____.

6   A program to detect and eliminate viruses is an example of what type of software?

   a. personal productivity software
   b. operating system software
   c. utility software
   d. applications software

7   A part of every Microsoft Office application that provides a means of enhancing off-the-shelf applications to allow users to tailor the programs is called _____.

   a. Visual Basic for Applications
   b. SmallTalk
   c. Norton Utilities
   d. Java

8   A class of application software that helps groups work together and collaborate is called

   _____.

9   Each programming language has its own set of rules, called the _____ of the language.

10   A special software program called 'middleware' performs the conversion from the programmer's source code into the machine-language instructions consisting of binary digits and results in a machine-language program. True or False?

Review Questions

1   What is the difference between systems and application software? Give four examples of personal productivity software.

2   How do software bugs arise?

3   What is a software suite? Give several examples.

4   Name four operating systems that support the personal, workgroup, and enterprise spheres of influence.

5   What is middleware?

6   Define the term 'utility software' and give two examples.

7   Identify the two primary sources for acquiring application software.

8   What is open-source software? What is the biggest stumbling block with the use of open-source software?

9   Briefly discuss the advantages and disadvantages of frequent software upgrades.

10   List some main functions of spreadsheet software.

Discussion Questions

1   Assume that you must take a computer programming course next term. What language do you think would be best for you to study? Why? Do you think that a professional programmer needs to know more than one programming language? Why or why not?

2   You are going to buy a personal computer. What operating system features are important to you? What operating system would you select?

3   How can application software improve the effectiveness of a large enterprise? What are some of the benefits associated with implementation of an enterprise resource planning system? What are some of the issues that could keep the use of enterprise resource planning software from being successful?

4   Describe three personal productivity software packages you are likely to use the most. What personal productivity software packages would you select for your use?

5   If you were the IT manager for a large manufacturing company, what issues might you have with the use of open-source software? What advantages might there be for use of such software?

Web Exercises

1 Use the Internet to search for three popular freeware utilities that you would find useful. Write a report that describes the features of these three utility programs.

2 Do research on the Web to develop a two-page report summarizing any open-source software project. What does the software hope to achieve? Why do you think expert software developers are developing it and giving it away?

Case One

4

Open-Source in South Africa

A South African government council has recommended that official government policy promotes the use of open-source software, by expressing a preference for open-source when there is no compelling reason to adopt a proprietary alternative. The document recommends that the selection criteria for all software be based on efficiency, effectiveness, and economy of service. It also recommends that the government should use open-source software to promote access to information by citizens. South Africa finds it has little influence with proprietary software, most of which is created with other markets in mind. It is acknowledged that this is the same with most open-source projects, but that open-source gives users the ability to change and adapt the code. This is something that some groups in South Africa, for instance, the Council for Scientific and Industrial Research, are keen to do.

Others have seen the potential for open-source in South Africa. The Go Open Source campaign ran for two years, trying to raise awareness generally and plan for a transition to open-source within the South African government. Recently the organization providing computing resources to South African schools, SchoolNet Namibia, rejected Microsoft's offer to put its Windows operating in schools, preferring to keep the Linux OS. The department of agriculture is planning to migrate its infrastructure to one based on open standards.

One of the concerns for moving to open-source is the need for skilled developers to do the work. According to Kugan Soobramani, senior manager and government it officer, 'when they talk about open-source, everybody says, it's free, it's free, it's free, but it's not free to develop applications – that's where the costs come in'.

Unsurprisingly, Microsoft has lobbied against policies favouring or mandating the use of open-source software, claiming that decisions should be made according to what is best in the given situation, not going with open-source by default. The wording of the council's document allows for this position.

Questions

1 What are some of the challenges faced by the South African government when purchasing software?

2 How might open-source software benefit the South African government?

3 How might open-source software hinder the South African government?

4 What could Soobramani do to reduce development costs?

SOURCES: Go Open Source in South Africa (website), http://www.go-opensource.org/; Festa, P., 'South Africa Considers Open Source', *CNET News.com*, February 5, 2003; Khan, B., Open source gives South African farmers a leg-up, *Tectonic,* November 22, 2005.

Case Two

Select Comfort Finds Comfort in ERP

Select Comfort is the bed company that invented the "sleep number" system, which provides a range of mattress firmness settings to accommodate sleeping preferences. Founded in 1987, the Minneapolis, Minnesota-based company delivered net sales of $691 million in 2005. The company has 32 U.S.-issued or pending patents and was ranked by Furniture/Today as the top bedding retailer in the nation for the sixth consecutive year.

Needless to say, a company of this size depends on enterprise-wide software systems to provide access to valuable information throughout the organization. A few years ago, Select Comfort began moving away from its hard-to-maintain legacy systems to integrated enterprise resource planning (ERP) software. The e-Business Suite from Oracle provides ERP services through a convenient Web-based interface. The suite helps Select Comfort coordinate its sophisticated made-to-order manufacturing operations in South Carolina and Utah, and keep mattress orders flowing smoothly from the store to the factory to the customer's home. Select Comfort adopted several e-Business Suite modules to assist in varying parts of its business: an order management module to fulfill the hundreds of mattress orders it receives daily, a customer relationship management (CRM) module for keeping track of customer interaction, and modules that handle typical business needs such as assets management, general ledger, payables, purchasing, and receivables. The ERP system ensures that all these modules and services are synchronized and centralized so they can provide up-to-date information.

Seeking to make use of the latest technologies, Select Comfort adopted business intelligence (BI) software from Siebel Systems, Inc. BI software allows a business to combine its databases and extract useful information to apply to business strategies. The BI software from Siebel caught the interest of Select Comfort because of its power and ease of use. Select Comfort plans to deploy Siebel Business Analytics to 2,500 users company-wide by 2008. The software will deliver alerts and dashboard capabilities to show how the company's 400 stores are performing in real time.

Select Comfort had concerns about using enterprise-wide software from two vendors, Oracle and Siebel. When companies adopt new software, the software must be able to integrate with existing systems. Select Comfort resigned itself to the fact that it would have to work with Siebel on integration issues.

Shortly after Select Comfort purchased the Siebel software, Oracle announced that it was purchasing Siebel. The partnership means that the Siebel BI software will eventually be integrated with Oracle's database and ERP software. David Dobrin, an analyst at B2B Analysts, Inc., in Cambridge, Massachusetts, said Select Comfort will likely have to wait for a strong link between the products. Integration "will take years and years, and probably Oracle will have to do a major revision to data systems," he said.

Questions

1 What benefits does Select Comfort's ERP system provide that individual software solutions from a variety of vendors could not?

2 What risk did Select Comfort assume when it chose software from a different vendor?

3 How might standards assist companies who prefer to use the services of different software vendors?

4 Why do you think most large enterprises outsource their ERP systems to software companies like Oracle, Siebel, and IBM rather than developing their own?

SOURCES: Songini, Marc, "Retailer Hopes for Oracle-Siebel Integration," *Computerworld*, January 16, 2006, *www.computerworld.com*. Oracle Enterprise Management Web site, accessed March 4, 2006, *www.oracle.com/enterprise_manager/index.html*. Select Comfort Web site, accessed March 4, 2006, *www.selectcomfort.com*.

Case Three

DreamWorks SKJ Goes Completely Open-Source

Steven Spielberg, Jeffrey Katzenberg, and David Geffen launched DreamWorks SKG in October 1994. They have subsequently produced motion picture hits such as *Antz, Shrek, Madagascar, A.I., Galaxy Quest, Saving Private Ryan*, and *Wallace and Gromit – The Curse of the Were-Rabbit*.

DreamWorks was originally set up with expensive servers from Sun Microsystems and workstations from SGI running the UNIX operating system, high-end graphics software, and other specialized systems. Around the turn of the millennium, DreamWorks started experimenting with Intel-based servers running Linux, the open-source operating system. Using Intel/Linux servers, DreamWorks produced *Shrek* in 2001 on a system that cost half as much and was four times as powerful as the SGI/UNIX system used to produce *Antz* in 1998. DreamWorks had caught the open-source fever.

Since then, DreamWorks has steadily transformed itself into a complete user of open-source software. The biggest challenge has been finding the specialty software required for motion picture animation and production to run on the Linux platform. With little Linux software commercially available, DreamWorks has been writing its own. Working with third-party software partners and HP, DreamWorks has been translating, or porting, its software from its old SGI/UNIX system to Linux. This is no small task considering that its in-house animation software includes millions of lines of code.

After DreamWorks ported its production software to Linux, it focused on its business applications. Recently, DreamWorks replaced a dozen of its core legacy applications with custom-designed software using a service-oriented architecture. A service-oriented architecture, commonly known as 'SOA', defines the use of software services to support the requirements of software users. In an SOA environment, nodes on a network make resources available to network users as independent services that the participants access in a standardized way.

The systems that DreamWorks updated using SOA include tasks such as tracking copyright, accessing human resources data, and pulling information from back-end ERP systems. Linux provides the API and tools to make SOA easy to develop. Developers also used the jBoss Enterprise Middleware Suite for software development. JBoss is a global leader in open-source middleware software and provides the industry's leading services and tools to transform businesses to SOA. DreamWorks used these tools to develop a new service that authenticates employee roles and responsibilities against company directories to provide access to applications. It also built a new services-based copyright application that provides authorization and authentication for incoming feature film scripts.

'Having a Linux operating environment and HP Linux servers in racks saves critical data centre space,' said Abe Wong, DreamWorks' head of IT. 'In the animation world, data centre space is extremely valuable. We've freed up space for the animation technology group to put in full racks of render-farms space to focus on films as opposed to running servers.' Not only has the move to open-source freed space, but it's provided a more transparent and modular system architecture that is easy to build on and maintain.

Questions

1 What benefits has DreamWorks enjoyed since migrating to open-source systems?

2 What price did DreamWorks have to pay for adopting systems that were not standard to the motion picture animation industry?

3 Why do you think the SGI special-purpose systems that DreamWorks formerly used were so much more expensive than the Intel/Linux systems it uses now?

4 How has open-source SOA systems provided DreamWorks with a unique edge over its competition?

SOURCES: Havenstein, Heather, 'DreamWorks Animation Aims for Open-Source with SOA Project', *Computerworld*, www.computerworld.com, February 28, 2006; jBoss (website), http://jboss.com, March 4, 2006; DreamWorks (website), www.dreamworks.com, March 4, 2006.

Notes

1 Staff, 'Make Your Thumb Drive Bootable', *PC Magazine,* September 6, 2005, p. 88.

2 Dunn, Scott, 'Windows' Command Line Puts You in Control', *PC World,* September 2005, p. 146.

3 Dahl, Eric, 'The Truth About Windows Alternatives', *PC World,* September 2005, p. 75.

4 Ricadela, Aaron, 'Microsoft Plans Downloadable Versions of Windows Vista, Office', *InformationWeek,* January 18, 2007.

5 Staff, 'Spotlight: Find Anything Fast', www.apple.com/macosx/features/spotlight, September 16, 2005.

6 Hamm, Steve, 'Linux, Inc.', *Business Week,* January 31, 2005, p. 60.

7 Thibodeau, Patrick, 'Sun Begins Its Release of Open-Source Solaris Code,' *Computerworld,* January 31, 2005, p. 6.

8 Babcock, Charles, 'Virtual's New Reality', *Information Week,* July 4, 2005, p. 28.

9 Duntemann, Jeff, 'Inside the Virtual Machine', *PC Magazine,* September 20, 2005, p. 66.

10 Mossberg, Walter, 'Software to Help You Download from iPods', *Wall Street Journal,* January 12, 2006, p. B1.

11 Dunn, Scott, 'Deep File Divers', *PC World,* October 2005, p. 89.

12 Rubenking, Neil, 'Yahoo! Enters Desktop Search Fray', *PC Magazine,* February 22, 2005, p. 31.

13 Hensley, Scott, 'New Test May Detect Parkinson's Early', *Wall Street Journal,* January 7, 2005, p. B1.

14 Mendelson, Edward, 'Office Software on the Cheap', *PC Magazine,* September 6, 2005, p. 64.

15 Boulanger, Alan, 'Open-Source Versus Proprietary Software: Is One More Reliable and Secure than the Other?' *IBM Systems Journal,* Vol. 44, No. 2, 2005, p. 239.

16 Hamm, Steve, 'One Way to Hammer at Windows', *Business Week,* January 24, 2005, p. 36.

17 Joch, Alan, 'The Real Cost of Open Source', *FCW.com,* www.fcw.com, May 3, 2005.

4

05

Organizing and Storing Data

Principles

Data management and modelling are key aspects of organizing data and information.

A well-designed and well-managed database is central to almost all information systems and is an extremely valuable tool in supporting decision making.

The number and type of database applications will continue to evolve and yield real business benefits.

Learning Objectives

- Define general data management concepts and terms, highlighting the advantages of the database approach to data management.

- Describe the relational database model and outline its basic features.

- Identify the common functions performed by all database management systems and identify popular user database management systems.

- Identify and briefly discuss current database applications.

Why Learn About Organizing Data?

Having had an overview of IS in organizations, and examined different types of hardware and software, we now turn to look at using that hardware and software to store and process data. Databases are the heart of almost all IS. A huge amount of data is entered into computer systems every day. In this chapter, you will learn about database management systems and how they can help you. If you become a marketing manager, you can access a vast store of data on existing and potential customers from surveys, their web habits, and their past purchases. This information can help you sell products and services. If you work in business law, you will have access to past cases and legal opinions from sophisticated legal databases. This information can help you win cases and protect your organization legally. If you become a human resource (HR) manager, you will be able to use databases to analyze the impact of raises, employee insurance benefits, and retirement contributions on long-term costs to your company. Using database management systems will likely be a critical part of your job. In this chapter, you will see how you can use data mining to extract valuable information to help you succeed. This chapter starts by introducing basic concepts of database management systems. Additional practial instruction on how to use Microsoft Access to set up a database is given on this book's accompanying CD.

5.1 Data Management and Data Modelling

At the centre of almost every information system is a database, used to store data so that it can be processed to provide useful information. A database is used by almost every firm to record a history of that firm's transactions. This historical data can be hugely useful in uncovering patterns and relationships the firm had never even considered before, a practice known as 'data mining', something that is explained later in this chapter. The most common type of database is a relational database, so-named because the basic structure for storing data is a table, and the word relation is another name for a table. A **relational database** is defined as a series of related tables, stored together with a minimum of duplication to achieve consistent and controlled pool of data.

relational database A series of related tables, stored together with a minimum of duplication to achieve consistent and controlled pool of data.

So a relational database is made up of a number of tables. In loose terms, each table stores the data about someone or something of interest to the firm. This someone or something is known as an **entity**. (We will see later that sometimes the data about one entity is stored in two or more tables, and sometimes the data about two or more entities are stored in one table.) For example, a small business selling office furniture might have a customer table to store all the data about their customers, a supplier table to store information about suppliers, and an order table that records all the orders that are placed by its customers. In this example there are three entities – customer, order, and supplier.

entity A person, place or thing about whom or about which an organization wants to store data.

The rows in a table collect together all the data about one specific entity. For example, in the customer table, each row stores all the data about one particular customer – Jane Smith for instance, or Desmond Paton. These rows are known as **records**. The columns in a table are the specific items of data that get stored, for example, first name, surname or telephone number. These columns are known as **fields** or attributes.

record A row in a table; all the data pertaining to one instance of an entity

field A characteristic or attribute of an entity that is stored in the database

So a database is made up of tables, which are made up of records, which are made up of fields. This is illustrated in Figure 5.1 using the customer table example. Notice that in the figure, each customer has been given a unique customer number. This is because, as can be seen, there are two customers called Jane Wilson. Both work for the same company and therefore have the same address and phone number. The database needs some way of differentiating

Customer_Number	First_Name	Surname	Address1	Address2
10	Jane	Wilson	London Road	Oxford
11	John	Smith	Quai d'Orsay	Paris
12	Jane	Wilson	London Road	Oxford
13	Desmond	Paton	Marshall Street	Johannesburg
14	Susan	Haynes	Baker Street	London

Figure 5.1 The Customer Table for a Fictitious Office Furniture Seller

between them, and that is the job of the customer number, which is the **primary key**. Every table should have a primary key field used to identify individual records, and also to create relationships between tables, something we will examine next.

The advantages and disadvantages of using a relational database to store data are listed in Table 5.1.

primary key A field in a table that is unique – each record in that table has a different value in the primary key field. The primary key is used to uniquely identify each record, and to create relationships between tables.

Table 5.1 Advantages and Disadvantages of the Database Approach

Advantages	Explanation
Improved strategic use of corporate data	Accurate, complete, up-to-date data can be made available to decision makers where, when, and in the form they need it. The database approach can also give greater visibility to the organization's data resource
Reduced data redundancy	Data is organized by the DBMS and stored in only one location. This results in more efficient use of system storage space
Improved data integrity	With the traditional approach, some changes to data were not reflected in all copies of the data kept in separate files. This is prevented with the database approach because no separate files contain copies of the same piece of data
Easier modification and updating	The DBMS coordinates updates and data modifications. Programmers and users do not have to know where the data is physically stored. Data is stored and modified once. Modification and updating is also easier because the data is stored in only one location in most cases
Data and program independence	The DBMS organizes the data independently of the application program, so the application program is not affected by the location or type of data. Introduction of new data types not relevant to a particular application does not require rewriting that application to maintain compatibility with the data file
Better access to data and information	Most DBMS have software that makes it easy to access and retrieve data from a database. In most cases, users give simple commands to get important information. Relationships between records can be more easily investigated and exploited, and applications can be more easily combined
Standardization of data access	A standardized, uniform approach to database access means that all application programs use the same overall procedures to retrieve data and information

(*continued*)

Table 5.1 *Continued*

Advantages	Explanation
A framework for program development	Standardized database access procedures can mean more standardization of program development. Because programs go through the DBMS to gain access to data in the database, standardized database access can provide a consistent framework for program development. In addition, each application program need address only the DBMS, not the actual data files, reducing application development time
Better overall protection of the data	Accessing and using centrally located data is easier to monitor and control. Security codes and passwords can ensure that only authorized people have access to particular data and information in the database, thus ensuring privacy
Shared data and information resources	The cost of hardware, software, and personnel can be spread over many applications and users. This is a primary feature of a DBMS

Disadvantages	Explanation
More complexity	DBMS can be difficult to set up and operate. Many decisions must be made correctly for the DBMS to work effectively. In addition, users have to learn new procedures to take full advantage of a DBMS
More difficult to recover from a failure	With the traditional approach to file management, a failure of a file affects only a single program. With a DBMS, a failure can shut down the entire database
More expensive	DBMS can be more expensive to purchase and operate. The expense includes the cost of the database and specialized personnel, such as a database administrator, who is needed to design and operate the database. Additional hardware might also be required

5.1.1 Relationships Between Tables

Consider the customer table (Figure 5.1) and the order table (Figure 5.2) in the office furniture seller's database. It should be obvious that there is a relationship between these two – the firm needs to know which orders have been placed by which customer, otherwise they wouldn't know where to ship the goods, or who to charge for them. How this relationship is created in a database is shown in Figure 5.2, which shows the order table. The fourth record in the table is an order for a computer desk. The first field in the table, order number, is the order table's primary

Figure 5.2 The Order Table for a Fictitious Office Furniture Seller

Order_Number	Description	Price	Colour	Customer_Number
100	Swivel chair	€89	Black	10
101	Coat rack	€15	Silver	10
102	White board	€23	White	11
103	Computer desk	€150	Brown	13
104	Filing cabinet	€50	Gray	10

key. Then there are details of what the order is, description, price and colour. The last field on the right hand side is the customer number. This creates the relationship between order and customer – customer 13 has ordered the computer desk. To find out who customer 13 is, look back at Figure 5.1, find 13 in the customer number field, and we see it is Desmond Paton. We also find the delivery address – the desk is being shipped to South Africa. The customer number, in the order table, is known as a **foreign key**.

> **foreign key** When a primary key is posted into another table to create a relationship between the two, it is known as a foreign key.

This is an extremely convenient and useful way of organizing data (refer back to Table 5.1). It means, in this case, that the delivery address doesn't have to be stored twice – once with the order and again with the customer details. Storing the same information twice is very bad practice and leads to all sorts of problems. If a customer moves and one address is updated but the other is not, then the firm has useless data – they don't know which address is the correct one. A large part of organizing data involves deciding which fields are going to be primary keys and identifying where the foreign keys should be. A process for making that decision is described next.

5.1.2 Designing Relational Databases

This section describes an approach to designing a relational database. A database design is also known as a data model or a database schema. It is a list of all the tables in the database, along with all the fields, with any primary and foreign keys identified. The approach has four stages:

1 Identify all entities.
2 Identify all relationships between entities.
3 Identify all attributes.
4 Resolve all relationships.

If you are trying this approach out for yourself, you are unlikely to get the perfect data model first time. The approach is iterative, that is, once you do all four stages once, examine the resulting schema. If it doesn't work perfectly, go back to stage one and adjust your list of entities, then go through the rest of the stages again. Do this over and over again until, eventually, a good data model emerges.

Identify Entities

The first step is to identify all the entities you want to store data about. This is usually done by interviewing the firm's managers and staff. If there are too many of them to interview, sometimes database designers will use a questionnaire to get opinions from as many people as possible. If you are designing a database for a student project, you will probably think that this first step is the easy bit, but in fact getting the right list of entities is vital if your data model is to be useful, and it is often not a trivial task, specifically because you have to interview different people and each might give you a different list! (This problem is examined more closely in a later chapter on system development.)

Identify Relationships

You next need to identify any relationships that exist between entities. The sort of relationships that you have to identify are relationships that the firm wants to store information about. For example, there might be a relationship between customers and suppliers – some of them might play golf together. However, this is unlikely to be the sort of thing the firm will want to store. The relationship between customers and orders is definitely something that the firm will want to store, so that they can see which customers have placed which orders. Like identifying entities, identifying relationships between them is not trivial and may take several attempts to get right.

Once you identify a relationship, there are three things you need to document about it: its degree, cardinality, and optionality.

degree The number of entities involved in a relationship.

The **degree** of a relationship is simply how many entities are involved, and this figure is often two. When the degree is two, it is known as a 'binary relationship'.

cardinality In a relationship, cardinality is the number of one entity that can be related to another entity.

The **cardinality** of a relationship is whether each entity in the relationship is related to one or more than one of the other entities. For example, going back to the customer-order relationship, each order is placed by just one customer, but each customer can place many orders. Hence the cardinality in this case is one to many (1 : M). Cardinality for a binary relationship can be one to one (1 : 1), one to many (1 : M) or many to many (M : M).

optionality If a binary relationship is optional for an entity, that entity doesn't have to be related to the other.

Lastly, the **optionality** documents whether the relationship must exist for each entity, or whether it is optional. For instance, an order must be placed by a customer – there is no option. An order can't exist unless a customer has placed it! However, a customer can be in the database even though they have no current orders, so the relationship is optional for the customer.

All of the above is documented in an entity-relationship diagram, shown in Figure 5.3.

Figure 5.3 Entity Relationship Diagram (E-RD) with Notation Explained

The crow's foot notation means 'many', so a supplier supplies many products, but each product is supplied by only one supplier.

The 0 and | represent optionality – a 0 means the relationship is optional so a customer doesn't have to have an order. A | means not-optional (or 'obligatory') so an order has to have one (and only one) customer.

It is important to note that the database designer doesn't get to make up the degree, cardinality and optionality herself. These are dictated to her by what are known as the **enterprise rules**, which the designer must uncover by, usually, interviewing staff. An example of the enterprise rules describing the customer-order relationship is as follows:

enterprise rules The rules governing relationships between entities.

- Each order must be placed by one and only one customer.
- Each customer can place many orders, but some won't have placed any orders.

Enterprise rules are specific to the firm. For example, consider the relationship between employee and car, which a firm wants to store so it can manage its parking spaces. One employee can own as many cars as he can afford, so does that mean this relationship is one to many? Not necessarily. If the firm has decided that it is only going to store information on one car for each of its employees then the relationship is one to one, regardless of how many cars each actually owns. The relationship will probably be optional on one side because not every employee will own a car, but every car in the database will be owned by an employee.

Identify Attributes

The third stage is to identify all the attributes that are going to be stored for each entity. An attribute should be the smallest sensible piece of data that is to be stored. For example, customer name is probably a bad attribute – customer first name and surname would be better (some databases also include title and initial as separate attributes). Why is this? It is so that first name and surname can be accessed separately. For example if you wanted to start a letter to a customer, 'Dear John', you would be unable to do this if you had stored the name as 'John Smith'. In this case, the letter would have to read 'Dear John Smith'. As before, attributes can be identified by interviewing staff.

Resolve Relationships

The customer-order relationship was implemented by taking the primary key of customer and posting it as a foreign key in the order table. This is essentially what resolving a relationship means – deciding how to implement it. Sometimes a relationship between two entities will result in three tables being implemented, sometimes one, most often two. There are a series of rules to decide what tables to implement and which primary keys to use as a foreign key.

First, let us examine the customer-order relationship more closely to see why we implemented it the way we did.

If we had taken the order table primary key (order number) and posted it as a foreign key in the customer table, we would have had two problems, both illustrated in Figure 5.4. First, we have a repeating group – that means we would be trying to squeeze more than one piece of information into one cell in the database, in this case the fact that customer 10 has three orders. We also have a null (blank space) because customers 12 and 14 haven't placed any orders. Posting the customer number into the order table (look back at Figure 5.2) solves both those problems. Basically, the null isn't too big a problem, but a relational database cannot cope with a repeating group. Trying to implement the relationship by posting order number into the customer table simply won't work.

Customer_ Number	First_Name	Surname	Address1	Address2	Order_ Number
10	Jane	Wilson	London Road	Oxford	100,101,104
11	John	Smith	Quai d'Orsay	Paris	102
12	Jane	Wilson	London Road	Oxford	
13	Desmond	Paton	Marshall Street	Johannesburg	103
14	Susan	Haynes	Baker Street	London	

Figure 5.4 Posting Order Number into Customer for a Fictitious Office Furniture Seller

A full discussion of resolving relationships is beyond the scope of this book. However, there only are six types of binary relationship. Figure 5.5 gives one example of each and explains how to implement it. Note that the figure illustrates the most 'elegant' way to resolve each relationship, not necessarily the most efficient in terms of access time. A company with a lot of data would implement their database for speed rather than elegance. (What this means in practice is that their database would have some nulls in the foreign keys.)

What you should end up with after you resolve each relationship is a list of tables along with all primary and foreign keys identified, such as that shown in Figure 5.6. This could then be implemented using a database management system.

Figure 5.5 The Six Types of Binary Relationship

1. One-to-one relationship, obligatory on both sides.

    Employee – Passport

    Each employee must have one and only one passport, each passport must have one and only one employee.

    To resolve this relationship, combine both entities into one table.

2. One-to-one relationship, optional on one side.

    Employee – Company car

    Each employee might have one and only one company car, each company car is owned by one and only one employee.

    To resolve this relationship, take the primary key from employee and post it as a foreign key in company car.

3. One-to-one relationship, optional on both sides.

    Employee – Laptop

    Each employee might have one laptop, each laptop might belong to one employee (but some are for general use and therefore won't belong to anyone).

    To resolve this relationship, implement three tables – an employee table, a latop table and a new table that we will call 'owns'. The owns table only has two fields – employee number and laptop number. The primary key of owns is a 'composite key' i.e. it is the employee number and laptop number combined, and each combination of the two is unique.

4. One-to-many relationship, many side obligatory to one side.

    Customer – Order

    A customer can place many orders, but might have placed no orders, each order must be placed by one and only one employee.

    Resolve this relationship by taking the primary key from customer and posting it as a foreign key in order.

5. One-to-many relationship, many side optional to one side.

    Student – Elective module

    A student might take one elective module, each module is taken by many students (i.e. the students don't have to take an elective module).

    Most companies would implement this in the same way as for Relationship 4 above. However, the way to avoid nulls in the foreign key is to implement three tables – one for student, one for elective module, and one that we'll call 'studies' (as a student studies a module). The studies table just have two fields – student number and module number. The primary key of the studies table is student number (or you could implement a composite key).

6. Many-to-many relationship.

    Student – Tutor

    Each tutor teaches many students, each student is taught by many tutors.

    To resolve this relationship, implement three tables – one for student, one for tutor, and a third we'll call teaches. The teaches table has two fields – student number and tutor number, and its primary key is a composite key, i.e. a combination of student number and tutor number.

Figure 5.6 A Database Design (Also Known as a Data Model or a Database Schema)
Primary keys are identified with a # symbol, foreign keys are underlined.

Customer{Customer_Number#, FirstName, Surname, Telephone}

Order{Order_Number#, Description, Price Colour, <u>Customer_Number</u>}

Supplier{Supplier_Number#, Company_Name, Contact_FirstName, Contact_Surname, Telephone}

5.2 Database Management Systems

How do we actually create, implement, use, and update a database? The answer is found in the database management system. A DBMS is a group of programs used as an interface between a database and application programs or between a database and the user. The capabilities and types of database systems, however, vary, but generally they provide the following.

5.2.1 Creating and Modifying the Database

Schemas or designs are entered into the DBMS (usually by database personnel) via a data definition language. A **data definition language (DDL)** is a collection of instructions and commands used to define and describe data and relationships in a specific database. A DDL allows the database's creator to describe the data and relationships. Structured Query Language (SQL) is a DDL. Figure 5.7 shows four SQL statements to create a database called Lettings, a table called Landlords and insert a record about John Smith.

data definition language (DDL) A collection of instructions and commands used to define and describe data and relationships in a specific database.

```
CREATE DATABASE Lettings;

USE Lettings;

CREATE TABLE landlords(
Firstname CHAR(10),
Surname CHAR(10),
Telephone CHAR(10));

INSERT INTO landlords(
'John', 'Smith', '123456');
```

Figure 5.7 SQL as a DDL

Another important step in creating a database is to establish a **data dictionary**, a detailed description of all data used in the database. The data dictionary describes all the fields in the database, their range of accepted values, the type of data (such as alphanumeric or numeric), the amount of storage space needed for each, and a note of who can access each and who updates each. Figure 5.8 shows a typical data dictionary entry.

data dictionary A detailed description of all the data used in the database.

Attribute	Data Type	Primary Key?	Required?
Customer_Number	Text	Y	Y
First_Name	Text	N	Y
Surname	Text	N	Y
Date_of_Birth	Date	N	N

Figure 5.8 A Typical Data Dictionary Entry for the Customer Table for a Fictitious Office Furniture Seller

A data dictionary helps achieve the advantages of the database approach in these ways:

■ *Reduced data redundancy:* By providing standard definitions of all data, it is less likely that the same data item will be stored in different places under different names.

For example, a data dictionary reduces the likelihood that the same part number would be stored as two different items, such as PT_NO and PARTNO.

- *Increased data reliability:* A data dictionary and the database approach reduce the chance that data will be destroyed or lost. In addition, it is more difficult for unauthorized people to gain access to sensitive data and information.

- *Assists program development:* With a data dictionary, programmers know what data is stored and what data type each field is. This information is valuable when writing programs that make use of the data.

- *Easier modification of data and information:* The data dictionary and the database approach make modifications to data easier because users do not need to know where the data is stored. The person making the change indicates the new value of the variable or item, such as part number, that is to be changed. The database system locates the data and makes the necessary change.

5.2.2 Storing and Retrieving Data

One function of a DBMS is to be an interface between an application program and the database. When an application program needs data, it requests that data through the DBMS. Suppose that to calculate the total price of a new car, a car dealer pricing program needs price data on the engine option – six cylinders instead of the standard four cylinders. The application program thus requests this data from the DBMS. In doing so, the application program follows a logical access path. Next, the DBMS, working with various system programs, accesses a storage device, such as disk drives, where the data is stored. When the DBMS goes to this storage device to retrieve the data, it follows a path to the physical location (physical access path) where the price of this option is stored. In the pricing example, the DBMS might go to a disk drive to retrieve the price data for six-cylinder engines. This relationship is shown in Figure 5.9.

Figure 5.9 Logical and Physical Access Paths

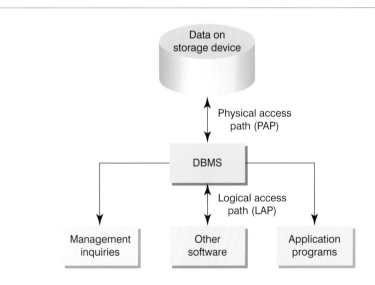

This same process is used if a user wants to get information from the database. First, the user requests the data from the DBMS. For example, a user might give a command, such as LIST ALL OPTIONS FOR WHICH PRICE IS GREATER THAN 200 DOLLARS. This is the logical access path (LAP). Then, the DBMS might go to the options price section of a disk to get the information for the user. This is the physical access path (PAP).

Two or more people or programs attempting to access the same record in the same database at the same time can cause a problem. For example, an inventory control program might attempt to reduce the inventory level for a product by ten units because ten units were just shipped to a customer. At the same time, a purchasing program might attempt to increase the inventory level for the same product by 200 units because more inventory was just received. Without proper database control, one of the inventory updates might not be correctly made, resulting in an inaccurate inventory level for the product. **Concurrency control** can be used to avoid this potential problem. One approach is to lock out all other application programs from access to a record if the record is being updated or used by another program.

> **concurrency control** A method of dealing with a situation in which two or more people need to access the same record in a database at the same time.

5.2.3 Manipulating Data and Generating Reports

After a DBMS has been installed, employees, managers, and consumers can use it to review reports and obtain important information. Some databases use Query-by-Example (QBE), which is a visual approach to developing database queries or requests (see Figure 5.10).

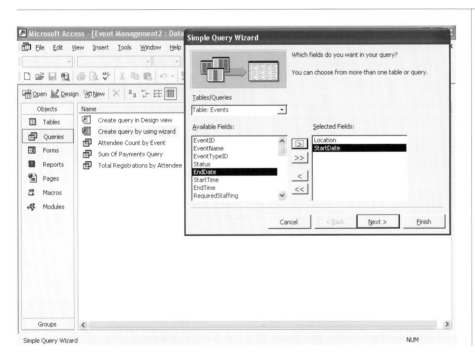

Figure 5.10 Query by Example *Some databases use Query by Example (QBE) to generate reports and information.*

Alternatively, SQL can be used to query the database. For example, SELECT * FROM EMPLOYEE WHERE JOB_CLASSIFICATION = "C2".

This will output all employees who have a job classification of 'C2'. The '*' tells the DBMS to include all columns from the EMPLOYEE table in the results. In general, the commands that are used to manipulate the database are part of the **data manipulation language (DML)**, of which SQL is an example. (So SQL is both a DDL and DML.) SQL commands can be used in a computer program, to query a database, which is convenient for programmers.

> **data manipulation language (DML)** The commands that are used to manipulate the data in a database.

SQL, which is pronounced like the word 'sequel', was developed in the 1970s at the IBM Research Laboratory in San Jose, California. In 1986, the American National Standards Institute

(ANSI) adopted SQL as the standard query language for relational databases. Since ANSI's acceptance of SQL, interest in making SQL an integral part of relational databases on both mainframe and personal computers has increased. SQL has many built-in functions, such as average (AVG), find the largest value (MAX), find the smallest value (MIN), and others. Table 5.2 contains examples of SQL commands.

SQL lets programmers learn one powerful query language and use it on systems ranging from PCs to the largest mainframe computers (see Figure 5.11). Programmers and database users also find SQL valuable because SQL statements can be embedded into many programming languages (discussed in Chapter 4), such as C++, Visual Basic and COBOL. Because SQL uses standardized and simplified procedures for retrieving, storing, and manipulating data in a database system, the popular database query language can be easy to understand and use.

Figure 5.11 Structured
Query Language
*Structured Query Language
(SQL) has become an
integral part of most
relational databases, as
shown by this screen from
Microsoft Access 2003.*

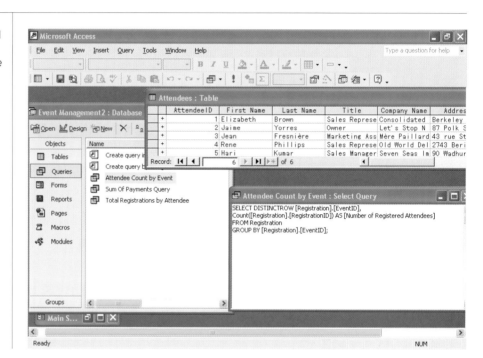

Table 5.2 Examples of SQL Commands

SQL Command	Description
SELECT ClientName, Debt FROM Client WHERE Debt > 1000	This query displays all clients (ClientName) and the amount they owe the company (Debt) from a database table called Client for clients who owe the company more than €1000 (WHERE Debt > 1000)
SELECT ClientName, ClientNum, OrderNum FROM Client, Order WHERE Client.ClientNum=Order.ClientNum	This command is an example of a join command that combines data from two tables: the client table and the order table (FROM Client, Order). The command creates a new table with the client name, client number, and order number (SELECT ClientName, ClientNum, OrderNum). Both tables include the client number, which allows them to be joined. This is indicated in the WHERE clause, which states that the client number in the client table is the same as (equal to) the client number in the order table (WHERE Client.ClientNum=Order.ClientNum)
GRANT INSERT ON Client to Guthrie	This command is an example of a security command. It allows Bob Guthrie to insert new values or rows into the Client table

After a database has been set up and loaded with data, it can produce any desired reports, documents, and other outputs, as shown in Figure 5.12. These outputs usually appear in screen displays or hard-copy printouts. The output-control features of a database program allow you to select the records and fields to appear in reports. You can also make calculations specifically for the report by manipulating database fields. Formatting controls and organization options (such as report headings) help you to customize reports and create flexible, convenient, and powerful information-handling tools.

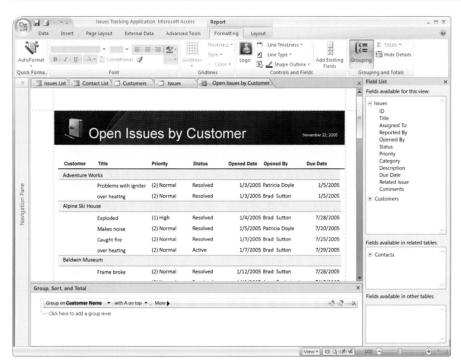

Figure 5.12 Database Output *A database application offers sophisticated formatting and organization options to produce the right information in the right format.*

SOURCE: Courtesy of Microsoft Corporation.

A DBMS can produce a wide variety of documents, reports, and other outputs that can help organizations achieve their goals. The most common reports select and organize data to present summary information about some aspect of company operations. For example, accounting reports often summarize financial data such as current and past-due accounts. Many companies base their routine operating decisions on regular status reports that show the progress of specific orders toward completion and delivery. Polygon, for example, has developed the Color-Net database to help traders of rare gemstones perform routine processing activities, including the buying and selling of precious gemstones.[1]

Databases can also provide support to help executives and other people make better decisions. A database by Intellifit, for example, can be used to help shoppers make better decisions and get clothes that fit when shopping online.[2] The database contains true sizes of apparel from various clothing companies that do business on the web. The process starts when a customer's body is scanned into a database at one of the company's locations, typically in a shopping mall. About 200 000 measurements are taken to construct a 3-D image of the person's body shape. The database then compares the actual body dimensions with sizes given by web-based clothing stores to get an excellent fit. According to one company executive, 'We're 90 percent (accurate) about the sizes and the styles and the brands that will fit you best.'

A database is central to every business selling over the Internet. Amazon, for example, has a huge amount of data that other books sellers must envy, on customers' past purchases, which it uses to make personal recommendations and generate more sales. Each time a returning customer comes back to the website, a report is produced (which becomes part of the webpage itself, something described later in this chapter and again in Case One, page 178) of their recommendations.

5.2.4 Database Administration

Database systems require a skilled **database administrator (DBA)**. A DBA is expected to have a clear understanding of the fundamental business of the organization, be proficient in the use of selected database management systems, and stay abreast of emerging technologies and new design approaches. The role of the DBA is to plan, design, create, operate, secure, monitor, and maintain databases. Typically, a DBA has a degree in computer science or management information systems and some on-the-job training with a particular database product or more extensive experience with a range of database products.

database administrator (DBA) The role of the database administrator is to plan, design, create, operate, secure, monitor, and maintain databases.

The DBA works with users to decide the content of the database – to determine exactly what entities are of interest and what attributes are to be recorded about those entities. Thus, personnel outside of IS must have some idea of what the DBA does and why this function is important. The DBA can play a crucial role in the development of effective information systems to benefit the organization, employees, and managers.

The DBA also works with programmers as they build applications to ensure that their programs comply with database management system standards and conventions. After the database is built and operating, the DBA monitors operations logs for security violations. Database performance is also monitored to ensure that the system's response time meets users' needs and that it operates efficiently. If there is a problem, the DBA attempts to correct it before it becomes serious.

data administrator A non-technical position responsible for defining and implementing consistent principles for a variety of data issues.

Some organizations have also created a position called the **data administrator**, a non-technical, but important role that ensures that data is managed as an important organizational resource. The data administrator is responsible for defining and implementing consistent principles for a variety of data issues, including setting data standards and data definitions that apply across all the databases in an organization. For example, the data administrator would ensure that a term such as 'customer' is defined and treated consistently in all corporate databases. This person also works with business managers to identify who should have read or update access to certain databases and to selected attributes within those databases. This information is then communicated to the database administrator for implementation. The data administrator can be a high-level position reporting to top-level managers.

5.2.5 Selecting a Database Management System

The database administrator often selects the database management system for an organization. The process begins by analyzing database needs and characteristics. The information needs of the organization affect the type of data that is collected and the type of database management system that is used. Important characteristics of databases include the following:

- *Database size:* The number of records or files in the database.
- *Database cost:* The purchase or lease costs of the database.
- *Concurrent users:* The number of people who need to use the database at the same time (the number of concurrent users).

■ *Performance:* How fast the database is able to update records.

■ *Integration:* The ability to be integrated with other applications and databases.

■ *Vendor:* The reputation and financial stability of the database vendor.

For many organizations, database size doubles about every year or two.[3] Wal-Mart, for example, adds billions of rows of data to its databases every day. Its database of sales and marketing information is approximately 500 terabytes large. According to Dan Phillips, Wal-Mart's vice president of information systems, 'Our database grows because we capture data on every item, for every customer, for every store, every day.' Wal-Mart deletes data after two years and doesn't track individual customer purchases. Scientific databases are likely the largest in the world. The U.K.'s forensic DNA database is vast and NASA's Stanford Linear Accelerator Centre stores about 1000 terabytes of data.[4]

5.2.6 Using Databases with Other Software

Database management systems are often used with other software packages or the Internet. A DBMS can act as a front-end application or a back-end application. A front-end application is one that directly interacts with people or users. Marketing researchers often use a database as a front end to a statistical analysis program. The researchers enter the results of market questionnaires or surveys into a database. The data is then transferred to a statistical analysis program to determine the potential for a new product or the effectiveness of an advertising campaign. A back-end application interacts with other programs or applications; it only indirectly interacts with people or users. When people request information from a website, the website can interact with a database (the back end) that supplies the desired information. For example, you can connect to a university website to find out whether the university's library has a book you want to read. The website then interacts with a database that contains a catalogue of library books and articles to determine whether the book you want is available.

5.3 Database Applications

Database applications manipulate the content of a database to produce useful information. David Frayne, for example, uses database analysis tools to find undervalued property in California.[5] Frayne, a former database programmer, has seen a 50 percent return on many of the houses and real estate he has fixed up and sold. His database application, called Scraper, searches through thousands of potential properties to find the best values.

Common manipulations are searching, filtering, synthesizing, and assimilating the data contained in a database using a number of database applications. These applications allow users to link the company databases to the Internet, set up data warehouses, use databases for strategic business intelligence, place data at different locations, use online processing and open connectivity standards for increased productivity, and search for and use unstructured data, such as graphics, audio, and video.[6]

5.3.1 Linking Databases to the Internet

Linking databases to the Internet is an incredibly useful application for organizations and individuals. Every e-commerce website uses database technology to dynamically create its webpages, saving vast amounts of efforts. Every time you visit Amazon, for instance, or the South African fashion retailer Edgars, or one of thousands of other Internet businesses, the pages you see are created at that time from a database of product and customer information. This simplifies the maintenance of the website – to add new stock, all that needs to be done is enter a new record in the product table.

Yahoo! and several educational partners are scanning books and articles into large web-based databases.[7] Called the Open-Content Alliance, they plan to offer free access to material that is no longer under copyright agreements. General Electric and Intermountain Health Care are developing a comprehensive web database on medical treatments and clinical protocols for doctors.[8] The database is expected to cost about €74 million to develop and should help physicians more accurately diagnose patient illnesses. Some banner ads on websites are linked directly with sophisticated databases that contain information on products and services.[9] This allows people to get product and service information without leaving their current website. LetsGoDigital, a company that sells cameras and other digital products over the Internet, based in the Netherlands, uses this approach.

Developing a seamless integration of traditional databases with the Internet is often called a 'semantic web'. A semantic web allows people to access and manipulate a number of traditional databases at the same time through the Internet. Many software vendors – including IBM, Oracle, Microsoft, Macromedia, Inline Internet Systems, and Netscape Communications – are incorporating the capability of the Internet into their products. Such databases allow companies to create an Internet-accessible catalogue, which is nothing more than a database of items, descriptions, and prices.

In addition to the Internet, organizations are gaining access to databases through networks to get good prices and reliable service. Connecting databases to corporate websites and networks can lead to potential problems, however. One database expert believes that up to 40 percent of websites that connect to corporate databases are susceptible to hackers taking complete control of the database. By typing certain characters in a form on some websites, a hacker can issue SQL commands to control the corporate database.

5.3.2   Data Warehouses and Data Mining

The data necessary to make sound business decisions is stored in a variety of locations and formats. This data is initially captured, stored, and managed by transaction processing systems that are designed to support the day-to-day operations of the organization. For decades, organizations have collected operational, sales, and financial data with their transaction processing systems (explained fully in Chapter 7). The data can be used to support decision making using data warehouses and data mining.

Data Warehouses

A **data warehouse** is a database or a collection of databases that holds business information from many sources in the enterprise, covering all aspects of the company's processes, products, and customers. The data warehouse provides business users with a multidimensional view of the data they need to analyze business conditions. A data warehouse stores historical data that has been extracted from transaction processing systems, as well as data from external sources (see Figure 5.13). This operational and external data is 'cleaned' to remove inconsistencies and integrated to create a new information database that is more suitable for business analysis.

data warehouse A database or collection of databases that collects business information from many sources in the enterprise, covering all aspects of the company's processes, products, and customers.

Data warehouses typically start out as very large databases, containing millions and even hundreds of millions of data records. As this data is collected from various sources, one data warehouse is built that business analysts can use. To keep it accurate, the data warehouse receives regular updates. Old data that is no longer needed is purged. It is common for a data warehouse to contain from three to ten years of current and historical data. Data-cleaning tools can merge data from many sources to make the warehouse, automate data collection and verification, delete unwanted data, and maintain the data. Data warehouses can also get data from unique sources. Oracle's Warehouse Management software, for example, can accept information from radio frequency identification (RFID) technology, which is being used to tag products

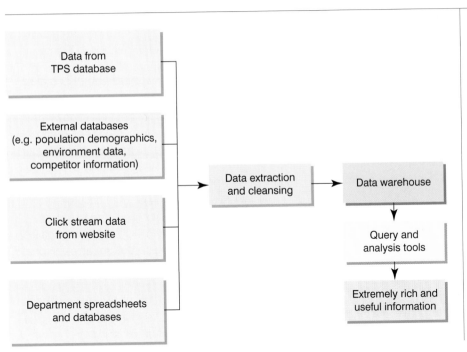

Figure 5.13 Elements of a Data Warehouse

Ethical and Societal Issues

Google: Protecting User Data from the Government

The practice of data warehousing raises huge privacy issues. All sorts of information about individuals can be mined from sources that were never intended to generate this information. Throughout Europe, laws protect individuals from this behaviour – the Data Protection Act in the U.K. for instance, explained in Chapter 13. In the U.S., one law goes in the other diection. The United States Patriot Act provides the U.S. government with wide-reaching authority to request information from businesses regarding the activities of suspected terrorists. Privacy advocates are working to limit that reach. In 2006, the Web search company Google found itself stuck between cooperation with U.S. government requests for information and its commitment to pre-serving its users' privacy. Its refusal to release database records to the federal government landed Google in court.

Google maintains huge databases filled with information on billions of websites. When you search the Web using a keyword in the Google website, you aren't really searching the Web, but rather Google's database that represents the current state of the Web. Google also maintains databases of search statistics that can be mined to learn about user interests and general search trends. Google and the other search companies also maintain private detailed information that includes the specific searches made by specific IP addresses. IP addresses can be connected to actual users through information provided by Internet service providers. Most search engine companies and Internet service providers keep this information confidential.

The U.S. government requested information from web search businesses as part of its efforts to obtain data on Internet activity to achieve its law

(continued)

5

enforcement goals, from national security to the prosecution of online crime. Although Google's three biggest competitors complied with U.S. Department of Justice (DOJ) requests for data, Google refused the subpoena. In addition to wanting records of a week of search queries, which could amount to billions of search terms, the Google subpoena requested a random list of a million web addresses in its index. Google complained that the request was unnecessary, overly broad, would be onerous to comply with, would jeopardize its trade secrets, and could expose identifying information about its users. The DOJ asked a federal judge to compel Google to turn over records on millions of its users' search queries.

Philip B. Stark, a statistics professor at the University of California, Berkeley, was hired by the DOJ to analyze search engine data in the case, and said in legal documents that search engine data provides crucial insight into information on the Internet. 'Google is one of the most popular search engines', he wrote in a court document related to the case. Thus, he said, Google's databases of web addresses and user searches 'are directly relevant'.

Google, whose corporate slogan is 'Don't Be Evil', complained that providing such information to the government would be detrimental to the trust that users place in the company. 'Google's acceding to the request would suggest that it is willing to reveal information about those who use its services', Google said in an October letter to the DOJ. 'This is not a perception Google can accept. And one can envision scenarios where queries alone could reveal identifying information about a specific Google user, which is another outcome that Google cannot accept'.

Customer trust is a valuable commodity to a company like Google who has recently become more personal with its customers through its desktop search software. A new feature in the software allows users to 'Search across Computers' to find information stored on multiple networked computers. This capability is made possible by having Google index personal files in its own database. The digital-rights advocacy organization Electronic Frontier Foundation (EFF) warns users away from the service, stating that it makes it possible for law enforcement officials to examine personal documents from your hard drive without your knowledge. For Google to comply with government requests would mean a serious undermining of customer trust for the company and the possibility of failure of some of its products.

The federal judge in the Google case ruled that Google was required to give the government addresses of 50 000 randomly selected websites indexed by its search engine but not any personal information on Google users. The ruling was considered to be a significant victory for Google and privacy rights advocates. 'We will always be subject to government subpoenas, but the fact that the judge sent a clear message about privacy is reassuring', Google lawyer Nicole Wong wrote on the company's website. 'What his ruling means is that neither the government nor anyone else has carte blanche when demanding data from Internet companies'.

Questions

1 Did Google's stance provide the company with an advantage over its competition?

2 What risk did Google take in not initially complying with government requests?

3 Do you feel Google was supporting or obstructing justice in its refusal to give up private information to its government? Why?

4 Should a government have the right to force a legitimate business to take an action that might damage its relationship with its customers?

SOURCES: Hong, Jae C., 'Google Resists U.S. Subpoena of Search Data', *New York Times*, www.nytimes.com, January 20, 2006. Liedtke, Michael, 'Google Avoids Surrendering Search Requests to Government', *Mercury News*, www.mercurynews.com, March 17, 2006. Tweney, Dylan, 'Google's Private Lives', *Technology Review*, www.technologyreview.com, February 17, 2006.

as they are shipped or moved from one location to another.[10] A data warehouse can be extremely difficult to establish, with the typical cost exceeding €2 million.

Data Mining

Data mining is the process of analyzing data to try to discover patterns and relationships within the data. Typically, a data warehouse is mined. Like gold mining, data mining sifts through mountains of data to find a few nuggets of valuable information. There are a number of data mining tools and techniques. Association rules algorithms are used to find associations between items in the data. A question that an association rule algorithm might be used to answer is, if someone buys eggs, how likely is it that they will also buy cheese? This information could be used in a super market to layout the goods in the best configuration. SPSS Clementine (Figure 5.14) is an easy to use yet extremely powerful data mining application.

data mining The process of analyzing data to try to discover patterns and relationships within the data

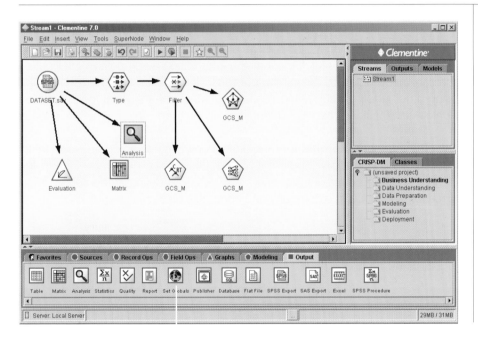

Figure 5.14

SPSS Clementine

Data mining is used extensively in marketing to improve customer retention; identify cross-selling opportunities; manage marketing campaigns; market, channel, and pricing analysis; and customer segmentation analysis (especially one-to-one marketing). Data-mining tools help users find answers to questions they haven't thought to ask.

E-commerce presents another major opportunity for effective use of data mining. Attracting customers to websites is tough; keeping them can be tougher. For example, when retail websites launch deep-discount sales, they cannot easily determine how many first-time customers are likely to come back and buy again. Nor do they have a way of understanding which customers acquired during the sale are price sensitive and more likely to jump on future sales. As a result, companies are gathering data on user traffic through their websites and storing that data in databases. This data is then analyzed using data-mining techniques to personalize and customize website, and develop sales promotions targeted at specific customers.

Traditional DBMS vendors are well aware of the great potential of data mining. Thus, companies such as Oracle, Sybase, Tandem, and Red Brick Systems are all incorporating data-mining functionality into their products. Table 5.3 summarizes a few of the most frequent applications for data mining. See Case Two on page 179 for an explanation of one data mining algorithm.

Business Intelligence

Closely linked to the concept of data mining is the use of databases for business-intelligence purposes. **Business intelligence (BI)** involves gathering enough of the right information in a timely manner and usable form and analyzing it so that it can be used to have a positive effect on business strategy, tactics, or operations.[11] 'Right now, we are using our BI tools to generate on-demand statistics and process-control reports,' said Steve Snodgrass, CIO of Granite Rock Company.[12] The company uses Business Objects to produce graphic displays of construction supplies, including concrete and asphalt. Business intelligence turns data into useful information that is then distributed throughout an enterprise.

business intelligence The process of gathering enough of the right information in a timely manner and usable form and analyzing it to have a positive impact on business strategy, tactics, or operations.

competitive intelligence One aspect of business intelligence limited to information about competitors and the ways that knowledge affects strategy, tactics, and operations.

Competitive intelligence is one aspect of business intelligence and is limited to information about competitors and the ways that knowledge affects strategy, tactics, and operations. Competitive intelligence is a critical part of a company's ability to see and respond quickly and appropriately to the changing marketplace. Competitive intelligence is not espionage, the use of illegal means to gather information. In fact, almost all the information a competitive-intelligence professional needs can be collected by examining published information sources, conducting interviews, and using other legal, ethical methods. Using a variety of analytical tools, a skilled competitive-intelligence professional can by deduction fill the gaps in information already gathered.

counterintelligence The steps an organization takes to protect information sought by 'hostile' intelligence gatherers.

The term '**counterintelligence**' describes the steps an organization takes to protect information sought by 'hostile' intelligence gatherers. One of the most effective counterintelligence measures is to define 'trade secret' information relevant to the company and control its dissemination.

Table 5.3 Common Data-Mining Applications

Application	Description
Branding and positioning of products and services	Enable the strategist to visualize the different positions of competitors in a given market using performance (or other) data on dozens of key features of the product and then to condense all that data into a perceptual map of only two or three dimensions
Customer churn	Predict current customers who are likely to switch to a competitor
Direct marketing	Identify prospects most likely to respond to a direct marketing campaign (such as a direct mailing)
Fraud detection	Highlight transactions most likely to be deceptive or illegal
Market basket analysis	Identify products and services that are most commonly purchased at the same time (e.g., nail polish and lipstick)
Market segmentation	Group customers based on who they are or on what they prefer
Trend analysis	Analyze how key variables (e.g., sales, spending, promotions) vary over time

Information Systems @ Work

Combating Spam E-mails

Spam e-mails are a problem for just about every Internet user. Spam e-mails are unsolicited messages sent to a large number of recipients. The word spam is taken from a Monty Python sketch where the dialogue and action were obscured by people repeatedly shouting 'Spam! Spam! Spam!'. This represents the problem of spam to many people – wanted messages are getting drowned out by the volume of unwanted messages.

So what can be done?

You might be able to program spam filter software to search the text of each incoming email for certain keywords, for example 'Sale', 'Discount', or 'Viagra'. Messages with more than, say, three of these words could be flagged as spam or even deleted and not delivered. This would be an unsophisticated approach that the spammers (who will change their behaviour as soon as someone does something to block spam) could easily get around by, for example changing the word 'Discount' to 'D1sc0unt'. In addition, this approach might block many legitimate messages.

This approach is known as a 'bag of words', where the system is scanning for words that are in the message, or in the 'bag'. More sophisticated systems will not only look for occurrences of the words but also their proximity to other occurances. For instance one rule might be, 'if the word "Sale" is found within ten words of "Discount", that message is flagged as spam'. But where do the bag of words and the rules come from?

Computer scientists have used large databases of e-mail messages to attempt to data mine rules to help identify spam. Just about every approach you could think of has been tried, but as an example the following might be a small part of a table in such a database. The numbers show the number of occurrences of each word in the database.

As you can guess, this database would have to be huge to accommodate even a small fraction of the words used in all the e-mails. This database could be run through a data mining algorithm to find the most useful words for the 'bag'.

Other approaches people have used to stop spam include having every sender sign up as a 'friend' on a webpage, and only let messages from friends though. If someone who isn't on the list tries to send a message they will get a simple reply asking them to sign up to the friend list. This approach requires a database to store lists of friends. The opposite of this approach is 'blacklisting', where the recipient creates a list of people who in the past have sent spam. These names are then blocked.

'Munging' is the technique of not letting spammers get hold of your e-mail address in the first place. Many spammers use automatic software agents, known as 'bots', to trawl the web and collection any phrase with an @ symbol in it, as these are likely to be e-mail addresses. Mungers might publicize their e-mail address on their webpage as 'myname |at| mydomain.com', to stop this.

The anti-spam company Habeas have come up with another approach. They give users a poem to include in the header of the e-mail (the header contains information sent but not seen by the recipient, on how the computer should handle the data being transmitted). E-mails with the poem in the header are allowed through, those that don't, aren't. The interesting point here is that if spammers include the poem in their own messages they are breaking copyright law and will be prosecuted by Habeas. This should make it more difficult for spammers to come up with a 'workaround'.

Message	'Sale'	'Discount'	'Winner'	'Success'	Spam?
E-mail 1	0	1	0	0	N
E-mail 2	0	0	3	0	Y
E-mail 3	2	3	0	2	Y
E-mail 4	1	0	1	1	N
E-mail 5	0	0	3	4	Y

(continued)

Questions?

1 Why is spam a problem?

2 How does spam impact on an organization?

3 Explain how data mining could be used to identify spam. What would the data mining algorithm have to do to find the 'bag of words'?

4 What would a spammer's response to this be, if they want to keep sending out spam?

SOURCES: O'Brien, Cormac, Vogel, Carl, 'Spam Filters: Bayes vs. Chi-Squared; Letters vs. Words', ACM International Conference Proceeding Series, vol. 49.

5.3.3 Distributed Databases

Distributed processing involves placing processing units at different locations and linking them via telecommunications equipment. A **distributed database** – a database in which the data is spread across several smaller databases connected through telecommunications devices – works on much the same principle. A user in the London branch of a clothing manufacturer, for example, might make a request for data that is physically located at corporate headquarters in Milan, Italy. The user does not have to know where the data is physically stored (see Figure 5.15).

distributed database A database in which the data is spread across several smaller databases connected via telecommunications devices.

Figure 5.15 The Use of a Distributed Database

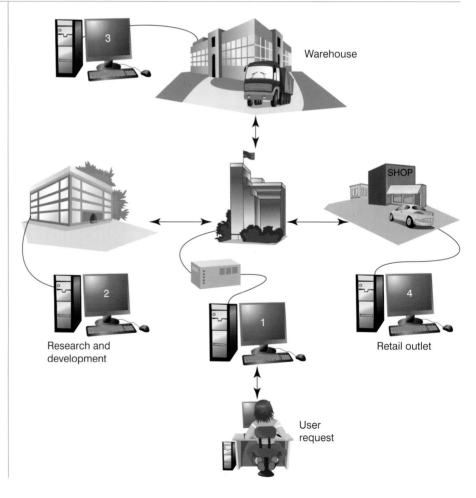

Warehouse

Research and development

Retail outlet

User request

For the clothing manufacturer, computers might be located at the headquarters, in the research and development centre, in the warehouse, and in a company-owned retail store. Telecommunications systems link the computers so that users at all locations can access the same distributed database no matter where the data is actually stored.

Distributed databases give organizations more flexibility in how databases are organized and used. Local offices can create, manage, and use their own databases, and people at other offices can access and share the data in the local databases. Giving local sites more direct access to frequently used data can improve organizational effectiveness and efficiency significantly. The New York City Police Department, for example, has about 35 000 officers searching for information located in over 70 offices around the city.[13] According to one database programmer, 'They had a lot of information available in a lot of different database systems and wanted fingertip access to the information in a very user-friendly front-end.' Dimension Data helped the police department by developing an US$11(€8) million system to tie their databases together. 'Now, we can send them critical details before they even arrive at the scene,' said police commissioner Raymond Kelly. The new distributed database is also easier for police officers to use.

Despite its advantages, distributed processing creates additional challenges in integrating different databases (information integration), maintaining data security, accuracy, timeliness, and conformance to standards.[14] Distributed databases allow more users direct access at different sites; thus, controlling who accesses and changes data is sometimes difficult.[15] Also, because distributed databases rely on telecommunications lines to transport data, access to data can be slower.

To reduce telecommunications costs, some organizations build a **replicated database**. A replicated database holds a duplicate set of frequently used data. The company sends a copy of important data to each distributed processing location when needed or at predetermined times. Each site sends the changed data back to update the main database on an update cycle. This process, often called data synchronization, is used to make sure that replicated databases are accurate, up to date, and consistent with each other. A railway, for example, can use a replicated database to increase punctuality, safety, and reliability. The primary database can hold data on fares, routings, and other essential information. The data can be continually replicated and downloaded from the master database to hundreds of remote servers across the country. The remote locations can send back the latest figures on ticket sales and reservations to the main database.

> **replicated database** A database that holds a duplicate set of frequently used data.

5.3.4 Online Analytical Processing (OLAP)

For nearly two decades, databases and their display systems have provided flashy sales presentations and trade show demonstrations. All you have to do is ask where a certain product is selling well, for example, and a colourful table showing sales performance by region, product type, and time frame appears on the screen. Called **online analytical processing (OLAP)**, these programs are now being used to store and deliver data warehouse information efficiently. The leading OLAP software vendors include Cognos, Comshare, Hyperion Solutions, Oracle, MineShare, WhiteLight, and Microsoft. (Note that, in this context, the word 'online' does not refer to the Internet – it simply means that a query is made and answered immediately, as opposed to a user submitting a query and the processing taking place at some other time, for instance at night when the servers are used less.)

> **online analytical processing (OLAP)** Software that allows users to explore data from a number of perspectives.

The value of data ultimately lies in the decisions it enables. Powerful information-analysis tools in areas such as OLAP and data mining, when incorporated into a data warehousing architecture, bring market conditions into sharper focus and help organizations deliver greater competitive value. OLAP provides top-down, query-driven data analysis; data mining provides bottom-up, discovery-driven analysis. OLAP requires repetitive testing of user-originated theories; data mining requires no assumptions and instead identifies facts and conclusions based on patterns discovered. OLAP, or multidimensional analysis, requires a great deal of human ingenuity and interaction with the database to find information in the database. A user of a data-mining tool does not need to figure out what questions to ask; instead, the approach is, 'here's the data, tell me what interesting patterns emerge'. For example, a data-mining tool in a credit card company's customer database can construct a profile of fraudulent activity from historical information. Then, this profile can be applied to all incoming transaction data to identify and stop fraudulent behaviour, which might otherwise go undetected. Table 5.4 compares the OLAP and data-mining approaches to data analysis.

5.3.5 Visual, Audio, and Other Database Systems

Organizations are increasingly finding a need to store large amounts of visual and audio signals in an organized fashion. Credit card companies, for example, enter pictures of charge slips into an image database using a scanner. The images can be stored in the database and later sorted by customer name, printed, and sent to customers along with their monthly statements. Image databases are also used by physicians to store x-rays and transmit them to clinics away from the main hospital. Financial services, insurance companies, and government branches are using image databases to store vital records and replace paper documents. Drug companies often need to analyze many visual images from laboratories. The PetroView database and analysis tool allows petroleum engineers to analyze geographic information to help them determine where to drill for oil and gas. Recently, a visual-fingerprint database was used to solve a 40-year-old murder case in California. Visual databases can be stored in some object-relational databases or special-purpose database systems. Many relational databases can also store graphic content.

Combining and analyzing data from different databases is an increasingly important challenge. Global businesses, for example, sometimes need to analyze sales and accounting data stored around the world in different database systems. Companies such as IBM are developing virtual database systems to allow different databases to work together as a unified database system. DiscoveryLink, one of IBM's projects, can integrate biomedical data from different sources. The Centre for Disease Control (CDC) also has the problem of integrating more than 100 databases on various diseases.

In addition to visual, audio, and virtual databases, there are a number of other special-purpose database systems. Spatial data technology involves using a database to store and access data according to the locations it describes and to permit spatial queries and analysis. MapExtreme is spatial technology software from MapInfo that extends a user's database so that it can store, manage, and manipulate location-based data. Police departments, for example,

Table 5.4 Comparison of OLAP and Data Mining

Characteristic	OLAP	Data Mining
Purpose	Supports data analysis and decision making	Supports data analysis and decision making
Type of analysis supported	Top-down, query-driven data analysis	Bottom-up, discovery-driven data analysis
Skills required of user	Must be very knowledgeable of the data and its business context	Must trust in data mining tools to uncover valid and worthwhile hypotheses

can use this type of software to bring together crime data and map it visually so that patterns are easier to analyze. Police officers can select and work with spatial data at a specified location, within a rectangle, a given radius, or a polygon such as their area of jurisdiction. For example, a police officer can request a list of all alcohol shops within a two-mile radius of the police station. Builders and insurance companies use spatial data to make decisions related to natural hazards. Spatial data can even be used to improve financial risk management with information stored by investment type, currency type, interest rates, and time.

5.3.6 Object-Oriented and Object-Relational Database Management Systems

An **object-oriented database** uses the same overall approach of object-oriented programming that was first discussed in Chapter 4. With this approach, both the data and the processing instructions are stored in the database. For example, an object-oriented database could store monthly expenses and the instructions needed to compute a monthly budget from those expenses. A traditional DBMS might only store the monthly expenses. In an object-oriented database, a method is a procedure or action. A sales tax method, for example, could be the procedure to compute the appropriate sales tax on an order. A message is a request to execute or run a method. Many object-oriented databases have their own query language, called object query language (OQL), which is similar to SQL, discussed earlier.

object-oriented database A database that stores both data and its processing instructions.

An object-oriented database uses an **object-oriented database management system (OODBMS)** to provide a user interface and connections to other programs. A number of computer vendors sell or lease OODBMS, including eXcelon, Versant, Poet, and Objectivity. Object-oriented databases are used by a number of organizations. Versant's OODBMS, for example, is being used by companies in the telecommunications, financial services, transportation, and defence industries. The Object Data Standard is a design standard by the Object Database Management Group (www.odmg.org) for developing object-oriented database systems.

object-oriented database management system (OODBMS) A group of programs that manipulate an object-oriented database and provide a user interface and connections to other application programs.

An **object-relational database management system (ORDBMS)** provides a complete set of relational database capabilities plus the ability for third parties to add new data types and operations to the database. These new data types can be audio, images, unstructured text, spatial, or time series data that require new indexing, optimization, and retrieval features. Each of the vendors offering ORDBMS facilities provides a set of application programming interfaces to allow users to attach external data definitions and methods associated with those definitions to the database system. They are essentially offering a standard socket into which users can plug special instructions. DataBlades, Cartridges, and Extenders are the names applied by Oracle and IBM to describe the plug-ins to their respective products. Other plug-ins serve as interfaces to web servers.

object-relational database management system (ORDBMS) A DBMS capable of manipulating audio, video, and graphical data.

Summary

Data management and modelling are key aspects of organizing data and information. Data is one of the most valuable resources that a firm possesses. The most common way to organize data is in a relational database. A relational database is made up of tables, each table is made up of records and each record is made up of fields. Loosely, each table stores information about an entity. An entity is someone or something that the firm wants to store information about. The fields are the characteristics or attributes about the entity that are stored. A record collects together all the fields of a particular instance of an entity. A primary key uniquely identifies each record.

Designing a database involves identifying entities and the relationships between them, as well as the attributes of each entity. There are rules to follow to convert related entities into a data model, a list of all tables to be implemented in the database, with primary and foreign key identified. Basic data manipulations include selecting, projecting, and joining.

A well-designed and well-managed database is central to almost all information systems and is an extremely valuable tool in supporting decision making. A DBMS is a group of programs used as an interface between a database and its users and other application programs. When an application program requests data from the database, it follows a logical access path. The actual retrieval of the data follows a physical access path. Records can be considered in the same way: A logical record is what the record contains; a physical record is where the record is stored on storage devices. Schemas are used to describe the entire database, its record types, and their relationships to the DBMS. Schemas are entered into the computer via a data definition language, which describes the data and relationships in a specific database. Another tool used in database management is the data dictionary, which contains detailed descriptions of all data in the database.

After a DBMS has been installed, the database can be accessed, modified, and queried via a data manipulation language. A specialised data manipulation language is Structured Query Language (SQL). SQL is used in several popular database packages today and can be installed on PCs and mainframes.

Popular single-user DBMS include Corel Paradox and Microsoft Access. IBM, Oracle, and Microsoft are the leading DBMS vendors.

Selecting a DBMS begins by analyzing the information needs of the organization. Important characteristics of databases include the size of the database, the number of concurrent users, its performance, the ability of the DBMS to be integrated with other systems, the features of the DBMS, the vendor considerations, and the cost of the database management system.

The number and types of database applications will continue to evolve and yield real business benefits. Organizations are building data warehouses, which are relational database management systems specifically designed to support management decision making. Data mining, which is the automated discovery of patterns and relationships in a data warehouse, is emerging as a practical approach to generating hypotheses about the patterns and anomalies in the data that can be used to predict future behaviour.

Predictive analysis is a form of data mining that combines historical data with assumptions about future conditions to forecast outcomes of events such as future product sales or the probability that a customer will default on a loan.

Business intelligence is the process of getting enough of the right information in a timely manner and usable form and analyzing it so that it can have a positive effect on business strategy, tactics, or operations. Competitive intelligence is one aspect of business intelligence limited to information about competitors and the ways that information affects strategy, tactics, and operations. Competitive intelligence is not espionage – the use of illegal means to gather information. Counterintelligence describes the steps an organization takes to protect information sought by 'hostile' intelligence gatherers.

With the increased use of telecommunications and networks, distributed databases, which allow multiple users and different sites access to data that may be stored in different physical locations, are gaining in popularity. To reduce telecommunications costs, some organizations build replicated databases, which hold a duplicate set of frequently used data.

Online analytical processing (OLAP) programs are being used to store data and allow users to explore the data from a number of different perspectives.

An object-oriented database uses the same overall approach of object-oriented programming, first discussed in Chapter 4. With this approach, both the data and the processing instructions are stored in the database. An object-relational database management system (ORDBMS) provides a complete set of relational database capabilities, plus the ability for third parties to add new data types and operations to the database. These new data types can be audio, video, and graphical data that require new indexing, optimization, and retrieval features.

In addition to raw data, organizations are increasingly finding a need to store large amounts of visual and audio signals in an organized fashion. There are also a number of special-purpose database systems.

Self-Assessment Test

1 A relational database is made up of
   a. worksheets
   b. documents
   c. tables
   d. files

2 A _____ is a person, place or thing about whom or about which a firm wants to store information.

3 _____ dictate the type of relationships that exist between entities.

4 A _____ uniquely identifies a record.

5 When identifying relationships between entities, you must identify the degree, _____, and optionality.

6 The commands used to access and report information from the database are part of the _____.
   a. data definition language
   b. data manipulation language
   c. data normalization language
   d. schema

7 Access is a popular DBMS for _____.
   a. personal computers
   b. graphics workstations
   c. mainframe computers
   d. supercomputers

8 A(n) _____ holds business information from many sources in the enterprise, covering all aspects of the company's processes, products, and customers.

9 An information-analysis tool that involves the automated discovery of patterns and relationships in a data warehouse is called _____.
   a. a relational database
   b. data mining
   c. predictive analysis
   d. business intelligence

10 _____ allows users to explore corporate data from a number of perspectives.

Review Questions

1 What is an attribute? How is it related to an entity?

2 Define the term 'database'. How is it different from a database management system?

3 What are the advantages of the database approach?

4 What is a database schema, and what is its purpose?

5 What is the difference between a data definition language (DDL) and a data manipulation language (DML)?

6 How do you resolve a many-to-many relationship?

7 What is a distributed database system?

8 What is data mining? What is OLAP? How are they different?

9 What is an ORDBMS? What kind of data can it handle?

10 What is business intelligence? How is it used?

Discussion Questions

1 You have been selected to represent the student body on a project to develop a new database for a student club you belong to. What actions might you take to fulfill this responsibility to ensure that the project meets the needs of students and is successful?

2 Your company wants to increase revenues from its existing customers. How can data mining be used to accomplish this objective?

3 Make a list of the databases in which data about you exists. How is the data in each database captured? Who updates each database and how often? Is it possible for you to request a printout of the contents of your data record from each database? What data privacy concerns do you have?

4 You are the vice president of information technology for a large, multinational consumer packaged goods company (such as Procter and Gamble, Unilever, or Gillette). You must make a presentation to persuade the board of directors to invest €5 million to establish a competitive-intelligence group – including people, data-gathering services, and software tools. What key points do you need to make in favour of this investment? What arguments can you anticipate that others might make?

5 Identity theft, where people steal your personal information, continues to be a threat. Assume that you are the database administrator for a corporation with a large database. What steps would you implement to help you prevent people from stealing personal information from the corporate database?

Web Exercises

1 Use a search engine to find information on specific products for one of the following topics: business intelligence, object-oriented databases, or audio databases. Write a brief report describing what you found, including a description of the database products and the companies that developed them.

2 Use a search engine to find three companies in an industry that interests you, that use a database management system. Describe how databases are used in each company. Could the companies survive without the use of a database management system? Why?

Case One

Databases and Web pages

One of the most important uses of database technology in recent years has been in the creation of dynamic web pages. Static web pages, as the name suggest, do not change – everyone who views a static page sees the same thing. Dynamic web pages, however, can change, which means that, for instance, each customer to an e-commerce site can be shown a different welcome page. You may have seen this sort of thing when you visit a web page for the second time, and there is a

message saying 'Welcome Back' followed by your name.

This is just one use of dynamic web pages.

One approach to creating dynamic web pages involves something known as 'server side processing'. Here, a user requests a web page from a web server. That server, based on parameters supplied by the user or from elsewhere, searches a database to gather the relevant information, assembles that information into an HTML page, and sends the page along with any addition files (such as audio files or images) back to the user, who views it as a normal web page.

Consider when you go onto Amazon to search for something, say a Harry Potter book. You type your search term 'Harry Potter' into the relevant text box and click on 'Search'. At that point, the Amazon server searches its database to find anything related to your search term, then takes what the database outputs and creates a web page in HTML to display that output, which it then delivers to your computer.

This is an amazingly useful technology. Consider this – if a new Harry Potter product becomes available (a new edition for example), to add it to their web page, all that Amazon have to do is add it as a new record in their product table – they don't have to edit any HTML at all! The same goes for a discontinued product – delete it from the database and it's gone from the web page. This makes it extremely easy to keep the web page up to date. It also simplifies things when the website is redesigned. In addition, this technology lets Amazon give a service that no high street book shop could ever easily replicate – personal recommendations. Using data mining techniques, Amazon can search its database for patterns in sales and make suggestions to returning customers such as 'you might be interested in this . . .', or 'customers who bought this, also bought . . .'.

Questions

1 List all the benefits you can think that dynamic web pages can supply. Look at the Amazon website. Would it be possible to create it using static web pages? Explain your answer.

2 Explain using sample database tables how Amazon can make purchase suggestions to returning customers.

3 How else might Amazon use the data it collects?

4 How could this technology be useful to an entrepreneur wanting to start his or her own business?

Case Two

HandWriting Recognition with Nearest Neighbour

Handwriting recognition is an important application – many touch screen mobile devices allow input in this way, with the user writing each character on the screen with a stylus. Some of these systems require a learning period, where the device asks the user to write several words, so it can 'learn' to recognize its owner's handwriting. What the system is actually doing is building up a database of examples of the user's writing, which it can expand every time the user writes something new. This database then becomes the 'training data', which the system uses to recognize new writing. Each character that is written gets stored as a record in the database, with the fields being a tiny square of the screen, perhaps with the value 1 representing if the square is black (blue in the diagram), a 0 if it is blank (green), and values in-between for shades of gray (where the stylus has lightly touched the screen) – like the letter T shown in the right column.

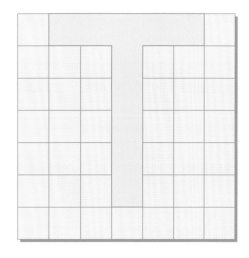

A portion of the record in the character table in the database for this T would look like this:

Letter	1,7	2,7	3,7	4,7	5,7	6,7	7,7	1,6	2,6
T	0	1	1	1	1	1	0	0	0

and so on. (The field names are the coordinates of the grid – 1,7 is the top left hand corner, 2,7 is the square beside it which is the first cell of the horizontal line of the T.)

To see how this might be used to identify a letter T from a letter L, consider the nearest neighbour data mining algorithm. The nearest neighbour can be visualized very easily if there are only two or three fields. Any more fields and it becomes impossible for us to illustrate it. So let's consider the above table, pretending that it only contains three fields – Letter, 1,7 and 2,7. If we had five examples of T and five of L, we could plot out the data on a two dimensional grid as follows:

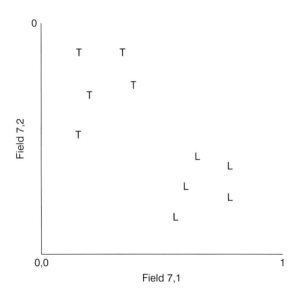

In the figure there are two clear clusters, one for Ts and one for Ls (although in practice such as clear cut between the two would rarely, if ever, happen). When the user types a new letter, if it is closest (or 'nearest', hence the name) to the T cluster then the computer recognizes that letter as a 'T'. If it is closest to the L cluster, it recognizes it as an 'L'.

Humans can see instantly which datapoint is closest to another, but how does a computer 'see' this? Well, the computer can easily calculate the distance between two datapoints using Pythagoras' Theorem, something you will have studied in school.

The nearest neighbour approach is simple to implement but is extremely calculation costly – if there are 1000 examples of letters in the database, then it must perform the Pythagoras calculation 1000 times to find the nearest datapoint. And in the above example there would be only 50 (7 × 7 plus letter) fields in the table. On a real touch screen, there would be many more, although using sophisticated algorithms not all of them would be stored.

Questions

1 Why would the nearest neighbour approach not be suitable for handwriting recognition on a real mobile device?

2 Do you think handwriting is a good way to input data in the first place? Explain your answer.

3 Using the web if you have to, remind yourself of Pythagoras' Theorem and the calculation that the computer must do.

4 Why can the makers of mobile devices not simply include their own database of handwriting in the system? Why do they need users create their own?

Case Three

Blackboard and WebCT

Blackboard and WebCT are two virtual learning environments used by tutors to deliver material to students and facilitate interaction between the tutors and the students, and among the students themselves. The two companies merged in 2006 and the two products became one. The Blackboard Learning System allows documents such as course notes to be posted so that students can access them through a web browser, and lets tutors create and manage discussion boards, e-mail, blogs, and live chat. Links can be created between the material and external web pages to enhance the student experience. At the centre of the Blackboard Learning System is a database that contains information about all students enrolled on a course, all course materials, and stores all interactions (for instance discussion board posts) that have happened. When a student logs into the system they see the latest material on a secure web page, created dynamically from the material in the database. This makes maintenance of the system

very easy – to upload a new document all the tutor has to do is save it in the database (again via a web interface) rather than having to edit HTML code.

Systems like the Blackboard Learning System are expensive. Critics say that this expense is wasted and that the system gives nothing that cannot be obtained for free elsewhere. Consider a tutor who wants to use email, a discussion forum, live chat and a blog – each of these things is available for free from Yahoo, Google, MSN and Blogger respectively. The tutor could upload videos to YouTube or photos/images to MySpace for free, and record his or her own audio files using Media Player. Webspace is available for free from many hosting services. Open source (i.e. free) HTML editors are easy to use to create webpages and more open source software can be used to upload those pages to the free webspace. (In any case, most universities will provide webspace for tutors' webpages and an email system, so there is no need to register for free versions of these technologies.)

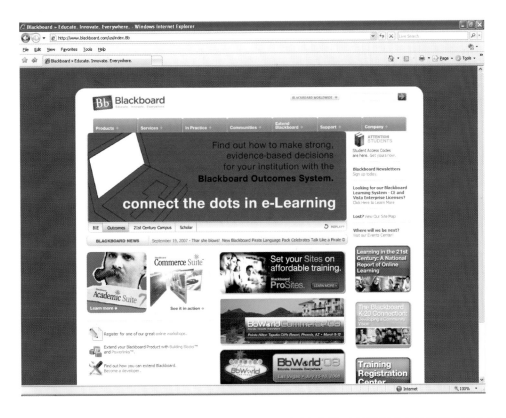

Questions

1 What is the advantage of using the Blackboard Learning System over the free software that does the same thing? What are the disadvantages?

2 Create a data model for a system such as Blackboard using the approach shown in this chapter.

3 What additional functionality could Blackboard give that would be difficult for a tutor to get elsewhere? (Consider the data mining section of this chapter.)

4 Universities often choose a learning environment centrally – individual tutors may not have much say in the matter, and students even less. If you had the chance to tell university decision makers, what functionality would you want to see in a learning environment and what existing functionality (assuming your tutor uses an online learning environment) is not used by you?

Notes

1 Novellino, Teresa, 'Polygon Launches Colored Gemstone Database', *Business Media,* February 24, 2005.

2 Schuman, Evan, 'Company Offers a High Tech Way to Get Clothes to Fit', *CIO Insight,* March 18, 2005.

3 Staff, 'Data, Data, Everywhere', *Information Week,* January 9, 2006, p. 49.

4 Staff, 'Biggest Brother: DNA Evidence', *The Economist,* January 5, 2006.

5 Barron, Kelly, 'Hidden Value', *Fortune,* June 27, 2005, p. 184.

6 Gray, Jim; Compton, Mark, 'Long Anticipated, the Arrival of Radically Restructured Database Architectures Is Now Finally at Hand', *ACM Queue,* vol. 3, no. 3, April 2005.

7 Delaney, Kevin, 'Yahoo, Partners Plan Web Database', *Wall Street Journal,* October 3, 2005, p. B6.

8 Kranhold, Kathryn, 'High-Tech Tool Planned for Physicians', *Wall Street Journal,* February 17, 2005, p. D3.

9 Staff, 'In-Ad Search', *New Media Age,* January 13, 2006, p. 28.

10 Hall, Mark, 'Databases Can't Handle RFID', *Computerworld,* February 7, 2005, p. 8.

11 Johnson, Avery, 'Hotels Take 'Know Your Customers' to a New Level', *Wall Street Journal,* February 7, 2006, p. D1.

12 McAdams, Jennifer, 'Business Intelligence: Power to the People', *Computerworld,* January 2, 2006, p. 24.

13 Murphy, David, 'Fighting Crime in Real Time', *PC Magazine,* September 28, 2005, p. 70.

14 Kay, Russell, 'Enterprise Information Integration', *Computerworld,* September 19, 2005, p. 64.

15 Babcock, Charles, 'Protection Gets Granular', *InformationWeek,* September 23, 2005, p. 58.

06

Computer Networks

Principles

Effective communications are essential to organizational success.

Communications technology lets more people send and receive all forms of information over great distances.

The Internet is like many other technologies – it provides a wide range of services, some of which are effective and practical for use today, others are still evolving, and still others will fade away from lack of use.

Because the Internet and the World Wide Web are becoming more universally used and accepted for business use, management, service and speed, privacy, and security issues must continually be addressed and resolved.

Learning Objectives

- Define the terms 'communications' and 'telecommunications' and describe the components of a telecommunications system.

- Identify several communications hardware devices and discuss their function.
- Describe many of the benefits associated with a telecommunications network.
- Define the term 'communications protocols' and identify several common ones.

- Briefly describe how the Internet works, including alternatives for connecting to it and the role of Internet service providers.
- Describe the World Wide Web and the way it works.
- Explain the use of web browsers, search engines, and other web tools.
- Outline a process for creating web content.

- Define the terms 'intranet' and 'extranet' and discuss how organizations are using them.

<table>
<tr><td>Why Learn About Computer Networks?</td><td>We have examined hardware and software, and paid special attention to how data is organized for storage. The power of information technology greatly increases when devices are linked, or networked, which is the subject of this chapter. Today's decision</td></tr>
</table>

makers need to access data wherever it resides. They must be able to establish fast, reliable connections to exchange messages, upload and download data and software, route business transactions to processors, connect to databases and network services, and send output to printers. Regardless of your chosen career field, you will need the communications capabilities provided by computer networks. The world's largest network is the Internet. To say that the Internet has had a big impact on organizations of all types and sizes would be a huge understatement. Since the early 1990s when the Internet was first used for commercial purposes, it has affected all aspects of business. Businesses use the Internet to sell and advertise their products and services, reaching out to new and existing customers. People working in every field and at every level use the Internet in their jobs. Whatever your career, you will probably use the Internet daily.

6.1 Telecommunications

Telecommunications refers to the electronic transmission of signals for communications, by such means as telephone, radio, and television. Telecommunications impacts businesses greatly because it lessens the barriers of time and distance. Telecommunications is not only changing the way businesses operate, but the nature of commerce itself. As networks are connected with one another and transmit information more freely, a competitive marketplace demands excellent quality and service from all organizations.

telecommunications The electronic transmission of signals for communications; enables organizations to carry out their processes and tasks through effective computer networks.

Figure 6.1 shows a general model of telecommunications. The model starts with a sending unit (1), such as a person, a computer system, a terminal, or another device, that originates the message. The sending unit transmits a signal (2) to a telecommunications device (3). The telecommunications device – a hardware component that facilitates electronic communication – performs many tasks, which can include converting the signal into a different form or from one type to another. The telecommunications device then sends the signal through a medium (4). A telecommunications medium is any material substance that carries an electronic signal to support communications between a sending and receiving device. Another telecommunications device (5) connected to the receiving computer (6) receives the signal. The process can be reversed, and the receiving unit (6) can send another message to the original

Figure 6.1 Elements of a Telecommunications System
Telecommunications devices relay signals between computer systems and transmission media.

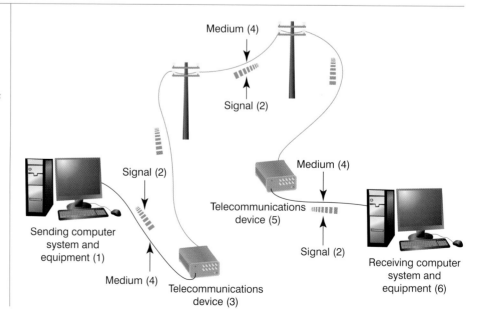

sending unit (1). An important characteristic of telecommunications is the speed at which information is transmitted, which is measured in bits per second (bps). Common speeds are in the range of thousands of bits per second (Kbps) to millions of bits per second (Mbps) and even billions of bits per second (Gbps).

Advances in telecommunications technology allow us to communicate rapidly with clients and co-workers almost anywhere in the world. Communication between two people can occur synchronously or asynchronously. With synchronous communication, the receiver gets the message almost instantaneously, when it is sent. Phone communication is an example of synchronous communication. With asynchronous communication, there is a measurable delay between the sending and receiving of the message, sometimes hours or even days. Sending a letter through the post office or by e-mail are examples of asynchronous communications. Both types of communications are important in business. However, to use telecommunications effectively, you must carefully analyze telecommunications media and devices.

6.1.1 Channel Bandwidth

Telecommunications **channel bandwidth** refers to the rate at which data is exchanged, usually measured in bits per second (bps) – the broader the bandwidth, the more information can be exchanged at one time. **Broadband communications** can exchange data very quickly, as opposed to **narrowband communications**, which supports a much lower rate of data exchange. Telecommunications professionals consider the capacity of the channel when they recommend transmission media for a business. In general, today's organizations need more bandwidth for increased transmission speed to carry out their daily functions. To increase bandwidth, first consider the different types of telecommunications media you can use.

channel bandwidth The rate at which data is exchanged over a communications channel, usually measured in bits per second (bps).

broadband communications A telecommunications system in which a very high rate of data exchange is possible.

narrowband communications A telecommunications system that supports a much lower rate of data exchange than broadband.

6.1.2 Guided Transmission Media Types

Transmission media can be divided into two broad categories: guided transmission media, in which communications signals are guided along a solid medium; and wireless, in which the communications signal is broadcast over airwaves as a form of electromagnetic radiation.

There are many different guided transmission media types. Table 6.1 summarizes the guided media types by physical media type. Several guided transmission media types are discussed in the sections following the table.

Table 6.1 Guided Transmission Media Types

Guided Media Types			
Media Type	**Description**	**Advantages**	**Disadvantages**
Twisted-pair wire	Twisted pairs of copper wire, shielded or unshielded	Used for telephone service; widely available	Transmission speed and distance limitations
Coaxial cable	Inner conductor wire surrounded by insulation	Cleaner and faster data transmission than twisted-pair wire	More expensive than twisted-pair wire
Fibre-optic cable	Many extremely thin strands of glass bound together in a sheathing; uses light beams to transmit signals	Diameter of cable is much smaller than coaxial; less distortion of signal; capable of high transmission rates	Expensive to purchase and install
Broadband over power lines	Data is transmitted over standard high-voltage power lines	Can provide Internet service to rural areas where cable and phone service may be non-existent	Can be expensive and may interfere with ham radios and police and fire communications

Twisted-Pair Wire

Twisted-pair wire contains two or more twisted pairs of wire, usually copper (see Figure 6.2a). Proper twisting of the wire keeps the signal from 'bleeding' into the next pair and creating electrical interference. Because the twisted-pair wires are insulated, they can be placed close together and packaged in one group. Hundreds of wire pairs can be grouped into one large wire cable.

Twisted-pair wires are classified by category, depending on the frequency of data transmission. The lower categories are used primarily in homes. Higher categories are sometimes used in smaller networks. Ten gigabit ethernet (IEEE 802.3an) is an emerging standard for transmitting data at the speed of 10 billion bits per second for limited distances over shielded twisted-pair wires. It will be used for the high-speed links that connect groups of computers or to move data stored in large databases on large computers to stand-alone storage devices.[1]

Coaxial Cable

Figure 6.2b shows a typical coaxial cable. Coaxial cable falls in the middle of the guided transmission media in terms of cost and performance. The cable itself is more expensive than twisted-pair wire but less so than fibre-optic cable (discussed next). However, the cost of installation and other necessary communications equipment makes it difficult to compare the total costs of each media. Coaxial cable offers cleaner and crisper data transmission (less noise)

Figure 6.2 **Types of Guided Transmission Media** *(a)* *Twisted-pair wire* *(b)* *Coaxial cable* *(c)* *Fibre-optic cable*

6

(a)

(b)

(continued)

Figure 6.2 *Continued*

(c)

SOURCES: (a) Istock; (b) Helene Rogers/Alamy (c) K-PHOTOS/Alamy.

than twisted-pair wire. It also offers a higher data transmission rate. Companies such as Virgin Media are aggressively courting customers for telephone service, enticing them away from the phone companies such as BT by bundling Internet and phone services along with TV.

Fibre-Optic Cable

Fibre-optic cable, consisting of many extremely thin strands of glass or plastic bound together in a sheathing (a jacket), transmits signals with light beams (see Figure 6.2c). These high-intensity light beams are generated by lasers and are conducted along the transparent fibres. These fibres have a thin coating, called cladding, which effectively works like a mirror, preventing the light from leaking out of the fibre. The much smaller diameter of fibre-optic cable makes it ideal when there is not room for bulky copper wires – for example, in crowded conduits, which can be pipes or spaces carrying both electrical and communications wires. In such tight spaces, the smaller fibre-optic telecommunications cable is very effective. Because fibre-optic cables are immune to electrical interference, they can transmit signals over longer distances with fewer expensive repeaters to amplify or rebroadcast the data. Fibre-optic cable and associated telecommunications devices are more expensive to purchase and install than their twisted-pair wire counterparts, although the cost is decreasing.

Laying thousands of miles of fibre-optic cable across its vast expanses is credited for helping propel India into the high-tech world. With the capability that this infrastructure provided, Indian workers were able to collaborate closely with their Western counterparts even though they were thousands of miles away.[2] As a result, India has emerged as a key business partner to many firms that have outsourced part of their business operations or that use Indian firms for information systems projects.

Broadband Over Power Lines

Many utilities, cities, and organizations are experimenting with providing network connections over standard high-voltage power lines. Manassas, Virginia, became the first city in the U.S. to offer this service to all its citizens. To access the Internet, broadband over power lines (BPL) users connect their computer to a special hardware device that plugs into any electrical wall socket. A potential issue with BPL is that transmitting data over unshielded power lines can interfere with both ham radio broadcasts, and police and fire radios. However, BPL can provide Internet service in rural areas where broadband access is unavailable because electricity is prevalent in homes, even more than telephone lines.[3]

6.1.3 Wireless Transmission Media Types

Many technologies are used to transmit communications wirelessly. The major technologies include microwave, satellite, radio, and infrared. Their key distinguishing feature is the frequency at which signals are transmitted. These are summarized in Table 6.2 and discussed next.

Microwave Transmission

Microwave is a high-frequency (300 MHz–300 GHz) signal sent through the air (see Figure 6.3). Terrestrial (Earth-bound) microwaves are transmitted by line-of-sight devices, so that the line of

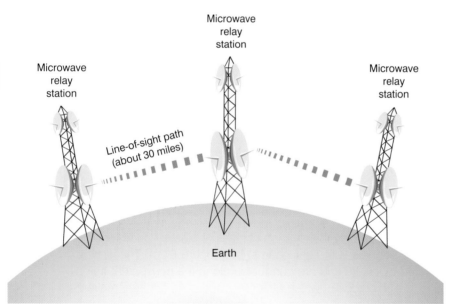

Figure 6.3 Microwave **Communications** *Because they are line-of-sight transmission devices, microwave dishes are frequently placed in relatively high locations, such as atop mountains, towers, or tall buildings.*

Microwave relay station

Microwave relay station

Microwave relay station

Line-of-sight path (about 30 miles)

Earth

Table 6.2 Wireless Technologies

Technology	Description	Advantages	Disadvantages
Microwave – terrestrial and satellite	High-frequency radio signal (300 MHz–300 GHz) sent through atmosphere and space (often involves communications satellites)	Avoids cost and effort to lay cable or wires; capable of high-speed transmission	Must have unobstructed line of sight between sender and receiver; signal highly susceptible to interception
Radio	Operates in the 30–300 MHz range	Supports mobile users; costs are dropping	Signal highly susceptible to interception
Infrared	Signals sent through air as light waves	Lets you move, remove, and install devices without expensive wiring	Must have unobstructed line of sight between sender and receiver; transmission effective only for short distances

sight between the transmitter and receiver must be unobstructed. Typically, microwave stations are placed in a series – one station receives a signal, amplifies it, and retransmits it to the next microwave transmission tower. Such stations can be located roughly 30 miles apart before the curvature of the Earth makes it impossible for the towers to 'see one another'. Microwave signals can carry thousands of channels at the same time.

A communications satellite also operates in the microwave frequency range (see Figure 6.4). The satellite receives the signal from the Earth station, amplifies the relatively weak signal, and then rebroadcasts it at a different frequency. The advantage of satellite communications is that it can receive and broadcast over large geographic regions. Such problems as the curvature of the Earth, mountains, and other structures that block the line-of-sight microwave transmission make satellites an attractive alternative. Geostationary, low earth orbit, and small mobile satellite stations are the most common forms of satellite communications.

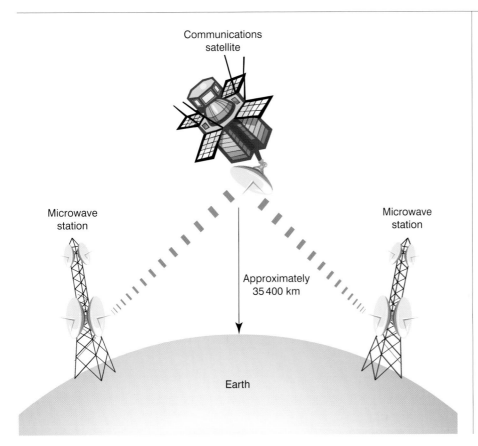

Figure 6.4 Satellite **Transmission** *Communications satellites are relay stations that receive signals from one Earth station and rebroadcast them to another.*

A geostationary satellite orbits the Earth directly over the equator, approximately 35 400 km (22 000 miles) above the Earth so that it appears stationary. Three such satellites, spaced at equal intervals (120 angular degrees apart), can cover the entire world. A geostationary satellite can be accessed using a dish antenna aimed at the spot in the sky where the satellite hovers.

A low earth orbit (LEO) satellite system employs many satellites, each in a circular orbit at an altitude of a few hundred kilometres. The satellites are spaced so that, from any point on the Earth at any time, at least one satellite is on a line of sight.

A very small aperture terminal (VSAT) is a two-way satellite ground station with a dish antenna smaller than three meters in diameter. Many retail chains employ this technology to support point-of-sale transactions, including credit cards. News organizations employ VSAT dishes that run on battery power to transmit news stories from remote locations. VSAT technology is being used to rebuild the telecommunications infrastructure in Afghanistan and Iraq.

Radio Transmission

Radio transmission operates in the 30 Hz–300 MHz range. At this frequency, radio waves can travel through many obstructions such as walls. Whereas radio transmission usually provides a means to listen to music and talk shows, this form of transmission can also be used to send and receive data. In fact, many of the exciting, new wireless technologies such as RFID chips, Bluetooth and Wi-Fi wireless networks (discussed in a later chapter) are based on radio transmission. Mobile phones also operate using radio waves to provide two-way communications. With cellular transmission, a local area, such as a city, is divided into cells. As a car or vehicle with a cellular device, such as a mobile phone, moves from one cell to another, the cellular system passes the phone connection from one cell to another (see Figure 6.5). The signals from the cells are transmitted to a receiver and integrated into the regular phone system. Mobile phone users can thus connect to anyone who has access to regular phone service, such as a child at home or a business associate in London. They can also contact other mobile phone users. Because cellular transmission uses radio waves, people with special receivers can listen to mobile phone conversations, therefore they are not secure.

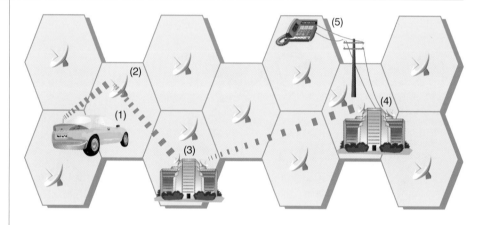

Figure 6.5 A Typical Mobile Transmission Scenario *Using a car phone, the caller dials the number (1). The signal is sent from the car's antenna to the low-powered mobile antenna located in that cell (2). The signal is sent to the regional mobile phone switching office, also called the mobile telephone subscriber office (MTSO) (3). The signal is switched to the local telephone company switching station located nearest the call destination (4). Now integrated into the regular phone system, the call is switched to the number originally dialled (5), all without the need for operator assistance.*

Ford Motor and its service provider Sprint are pioneers in the conversion of employees from using land lines to mobile phone service. In 2005, Ford converted over 8000 employees. The initial deployment covered Ford's product development department, which is a user group that is very collaborative and highly mobile.[4]

Infrared Transmission

Another mode of transmission, called infrared transmission, sends signals through the air via light waves at a frequency of 300 GHz and above. Infrared transmission requires line-of-sight transmission and short distances – under a few hundred metres. Infrared transmission can be used to connect a display screen, a printer, and a mouse to a computer, meaning there are no wires to clutter up the desk. Some special-purpose phones can also use infrared transmission. You can use infrared to establish a wireless network, with the advantage that devices can be moved, removed, and installed without expensive wiring and network connections.

The Apple remote (see Figure 6.6) is a remote control made for use with Apple products with infrared capabilities. It has just six buttons: Menu, Play/Pause, Volume Up, Volume Down,

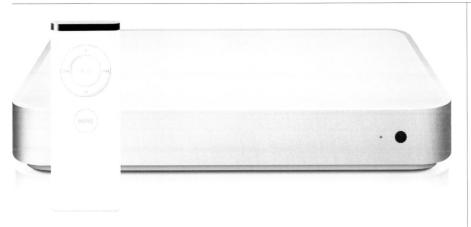

Figure 6.6 The Apple Remote

SOURCE: Courtesy of Apple.

Previous/Rewind, and Next/Fast-forward. The Mac Mini features an infrared port designed to work with the Apple remote and support Front Row, a multimedia application that allows users to access shared iTunes and iPhoto libraries and video throughout their home.[5]

6.1.4 Telecommunications Hardware

Telecommunications hardware devices include modems, multiplexers, and front-end processors.

Modems

At different stages in the communication process, telecommunications often uses transmission media of different types and capacities. If you use an analogue telephone line to transfer data, it can only accommodate an **analogue signal** (a variable signal continuous in both time and amplitude so that any small fluctuations in the signal are meaningful). Because a computer generates a **digital signal** representing bits, you need a special device to convert the digital signal to an analogue signal, and vice versa (see Figure 6.7). Translating data from digital to analogue is called 'modulation', and translating data from analogue to digital is called 'demodulation'. Thus, these devices are modulation/demodulation devices, or **modems**.

analogue signal A variable signal continuous in both time and amplitude so that any small fluctuations in the signal are meaningful.

digital signal A signal that represents bits.

modem A telecommunications hardware device that converts (modulates and demodulates) communications signals so they can be transmitted over the communication media.

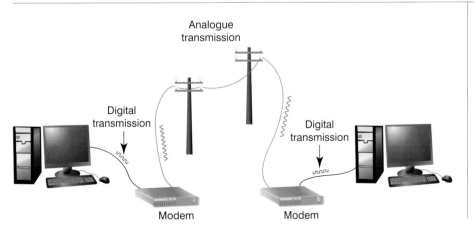

Figure 6.7 How a Modem Works *Digital signals are modulated into analogue signals, which can be carried over existing phone lines. The analogue signals are then demodulated back into digital signals by the receiving modem.*

Modems can dial telephone numbers, originate message sending, and answer incoming calls and messages. Cellular modems in laptop computers allow people on the go to communicate with other computer systems and devices.

multiplexer A device that encodes data from two or more data sources onto a single communications channel, thus reducing the number of communications channels needed and therefore, lowering telecommunications costs.

Multiplexers

A **multiplexer** is a device that encodes data from two or more data sources onto a single communications channel, thus reducing the number of communications channels needed and therefore, lowering telecommunications costs (see Figure 6.8).

Figure 6.8 Use of a Multiplexer to Consolidate Data Communications Onto a Single Communications Link

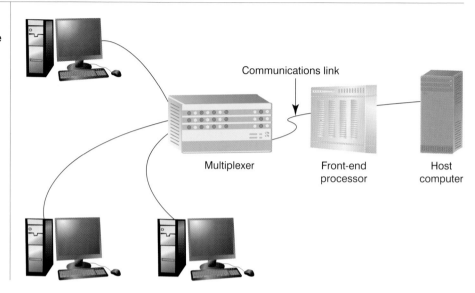

Communications link

Multiplexer

Front-end processor

Host computer

Front-End Processors

front-end processor A special-purpose computer that manages communications to and from a computer system serving hundreds or even thousands of users.

Front-end processors are special-purpose computers that manage communications to and from a computer system serving hundreds or even thousands of users. They poll user devices to see if they have messages to send and facilitate efficient, error-free communications. By performing this work, the front-end processor relieves the primary computer system of much of the overhead processing associated with telecommunications.

6.2 Networks and Distributed Processing

A **computer network** consists of communications media, devices, and software needed to connect two or more computer systems or devices. The computers and devices on the networks are called 'network nodes'. After they are connected, the nodes can share data, information, and processing jobs. Increasingly, businesses are linking computers in networks to streamline work processes and allow employees to collaborate on projects. If a company uses networks effectively, it can grow into an agile, powerful, and creative organization. Organizations can use networks to share hardware, programs, and databases. Networks can transmit and receive information to improve organizational effectiveness and efficiency. They enable geographically separated workgroups to share information, which fosters teamwork, innovative ideas, and new business strategies.

computer network The communications media, devices, and software needed to connect two or more computer systems and/or devices.

6.2.1 Network Types

Depending on the physical distance between nodes on a network and the communications and services it provides, networks can be classified as personal area, local area, metropolitan area, or wide area.

Personal Area Networks

A **personal area network (PAN)** is a wireless network that connects information technology devices within a range of three metres or so. One device serves as the controller during wireless PAN initialization, and this controller device mediates communication within the PAN. The controller broadcasts a beacon that synchronizes all devices and allocates time slots for the devices. With a PAN, you can connect a laptop, digital camera, and portable printer without physical cables. You could download digital image data from the camera to the laptop and then print it on a high-quality printer – all wirelessly. The Bluetooth communication protocol is the industry standard for PAN communications.

personal area network (PAN) A network that supports the interconnection of information technology within a range of three metres or so.

Metro AG is a major German retailer that owns and operates about 2400 wholesale stores, supermarkets, hypermarkets, department stores, and specialty retailers (such as home improvement and consumer electronics). The firm is testing a new voice-operated, smart tag system equipped with Bluetooth communications to help warehouse personnel quickly and accurately fill merchandise orders. Item pickers wear a headset to receive instructions on which items to pick. They also wear a high-tech glove that gathers product information from the RFID chip on each item that they pick from the shelves. The glove and RFID chip communicate using Bluetooth technology. If workers accidentally pick the wrong product, they receive a message requesting them to repeat the process. The main benefits of the voice-operated RFID picking system are that work sequences aren't interrupted by employees having to manually compare product identification data on the item to the description on a written list.[6]

Local Area Networks

A network that connects computer systems and devices within a small area, such as an office, home, or several floors in a building is a local area network (LAN). Typically, LANs are wired into office buildings and factories (see Figure 6.9). Although LANs often use unshielded twisted-pair wire, other media – including fibre-optic cable – is also popular. Increasingly, LANs are using some form of wireless communications.

An example of a sophisticated LAN is the one that DigitalGlobe uses. DigitalGlobe is the company responsible for the detailed satellite images accessed by millions of Google Earth users. The firm uses a high-speed LAN (10 GB/sec) to connect workers to its huge file storage system (200 TB) so that new images can be quickly captured and added to its rapidly growing repository of Earth photos.[7]

A basic type of LAN is a simple peer-to-peer network that a small business might use to share files and hardware devices such as printers. In a peer-to-peer network, you set up each computer as an independent computer, but let other computers access specific files on its hard drive or share its printer. These types of networks have no server. Instead, each computer is connected to the next machine. Examples of peer-to-peer networks include Windows for Workgroups, Windows NT, and AppleShare. Performance of the computers on a peer-to-peer network is usually slower because one computer is actually sharing the resources of another computer. However, these networks provide a good foundation from which small businesses can grow. The software cost is minimal, and businesses can use the network cards if they decide to enlarge the system. In addition, peer-to-peer networks are becoming cheaper, faster, and easier to use for home-based businesses.

With more people working at home, connecting home computing devices and equipment into a unified network is on the rise. Small businesses are also connecting their systems and equipment. A home or small business can connect network, computers, printers, scanners, and other devices. A person working on one computer, for example, can use data and programs stored on another computer's hard disk. In addition, several computers on the network can share a single printer. To make home and small business networking a reality, many companies are offering standards, devices, and procedures.

Figure 6.9 A Typical **LAN** *All network users within an office building can connect to each other's devices for rapid communication. For instance, a user in research and development could send a document from her computer to be printed at a printer located in the desktop publishing centre.*

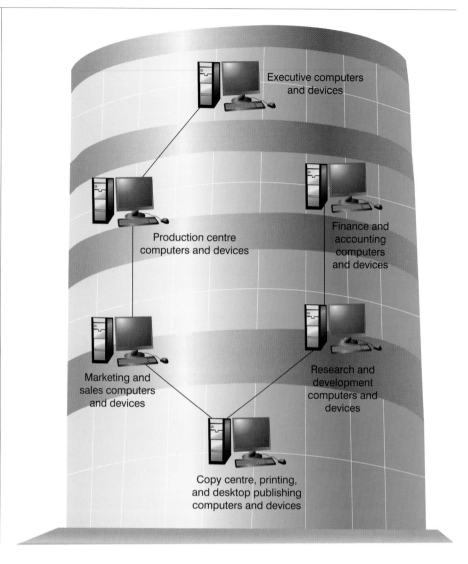

Executive computers and devices

Production centre computers and devices

Finance and accounting computers and devices

Marketing and sales computers and devices

Research and development computers and devices

Copy centre, printing, and desktop publishing computers and devices

6

Ethical and Societal Issues

Sharing Workstations at Sisters of Mercy Health System

Thanks to telecommunications and networking technologies, users no longer need to gather at one location to access their data and information. Using a typical local area network (LAN), an employee can access business records from any workstation on the premises and often from any Internet-connected computer in the world.

Doctors, nurses, and others in the medical profession find this particularly useful as they access patient records from a patient's bedside, nursing station, radiology department, or business office. In a hospital, dozens of clinicians might share a workstation every day. In this setting, users are mostly on their feet and on the move and cannot sit at a computer for any length of time. As doctors and nurses move to a new patient, they stop at the nearest workstation to view the related patient information.

In addition, doctors and staff rarely have time to log on and log off, especially in the emergency room. 'Authentication has become a major pain-point for us,' says Mick Murphy, chief technology officer at Sisters of Mercy Health System, a five-state, 18-hospital healthcare system in the U.S. 'Logging onto each of these systems and searching for the records of a specific individual every time a clinician moves to a new patient is completely untenable,' says Murphy. 'Our users would revolt.'

Leaving the workstations logged on using a shared account is not an option. Systems use logs and username and password-based security to restrict access to medical records. Even in a secure environment, where only accredited clinicians can enter, everyone accessing the information must log on each time they need to see a patient record and log out when they are finished.

Murphy set out to improve the network in several ways. First, he wanted to automate the process of logging on and off. To avoid leaving sensitive information viewable to unauthorized people, he wanted the screen to black out when the clinician using it moved away a certain distance. Murphy also wanted to organize the account-generation system so that all users were classified as having a particular role, such as surgical nurse. Each role would be associated with access restrictions to protect private information from those who did not need it. Murphy also wanted to easily dissolve accounts throughout the systems when clinicians left the organization. In other words, the employee's accounts on all interconnected systems would be deleted when the employee was removed from the payroll.

Mick Murphy found a solution to all of these challenges in Sentillion's Vergence communications software. Vergence integrates role-based provisioning, advanced biometric and proximity-based security, single sign-on, and front-end integration of diverse back-end systems based on a common identifier, such as the patient's name. In addition, the software maintains a fully auditable electronic record of each access to sensitive data showing who accessed it, when, from what terminal, and what tasks that person performed.

The new system uses biometrics – a fingerprint scan – and a password for authentication. Clinicians also wear proximity badges that communicate with

the workstation to identify who is approaching and when the clinician leaves. The first time they use a workstation, clinicians log on using a password and fingerprint scan. When a clinician walks away from the terminal, the screen goes blank to preserve privacy, but the background applications continue running. When the clinician returns, if no one else has used that terminal, the system recognizes the clinician from the proximity badge and reactivates the screen. If someone else has used the terminal in the interim, the clinician must use the fingerprint scanner to log on; however, because the applications continue running, access takes only a few seconds rather than several minutes.

After they log on, clinicians use the patient name to access all related records. Patient records are stored on different proprietary systems. By using middleware, clinicians can select records from these disparate systems and merge them together into a single record. As a result, clinicians are unaware of the background systems, reducing the complexity and time needed to access patient information, allowing medical personnel to concentrate on patient care.

Questions

1 How do network requirements and use differ for hospital clinicians compared with other typical businesses?

2 Why did Murphy want to organize users into particular roles?

3 Do you think the solution Murphy chose protects patient privacy as securely as possible? Why or why not?

4 An alternative solution might supply all clinicians with portable wireless tablet PCs. How might this alternative solution compare with the one used in this case study both negatively and positively?

SOURCES: Latamore, Bert, 'When the Doctor Walks Up, the Computer all but Says Hello', *Computerworld,* www.computerworld.com, March 22, 2006; Sintillion (website), www.sentillion.com, April 9, 2006; Microsoft Windows Tablet PC Healthcare (website), www.microsoft.com/windowsxp/tabletpc/evaluation/bymarket/healthcare, April 9, 2006.

Metropolitan Area Networks

A **metropolitan area network (MAN)** is a telecommunications network that connects users and their computers in a geographical area that spans a campus or city. Most MANs have a range of roughly up to 100 kilometres. For example, a MAN might redefine the many networks within a city into a single larger network or connect several LANs into a single campus LAN. EasyStreet

metropolitan area network (MAN) A telecommunications network that connects users and their devices in a geographical area that spans a campus or city.

(an Internet service provider) and OnFibre (a metro network solutions provider) designed a MAN for the city of Portland, Oregon, to provide local businesses fast (more than 1 Gps), low-cost Internet connections.[8]

Wide Area Networks

A **wide area network (WAN)** is a telecommunications network that connects large geographic regions. A WAN might be privately owned or rented and includes public (shared users) networks. When you make a long-distance phone call or access the Internet, you are using a WAN. WANs usually consist of computer equipment owned by the user, together with data communications equipment and telecommunications links provided by various carriers and service providers (see Figure 6.10).

wide area network (WAN) A telecommunications network that ties together large geographic regions.

Figure 6.10 A Wide Area Network *WANs are the basic long-distance networks used around the world. The actual connections between sites, or nodes (shown by dashed lines), might be any combination of satellites, microwave, or cabling. When you make a long-distance telephone call or access the Internet, you are using a WAN.*

International Networks

Networks that link systems among countries are called **international networks**. However, international telecommunications involves special problems. In addition to requiring sophisticated equipment and software, international networks must meet specific national and international laws regulating the electronic flow of data across international boundaries, often called transborder data flow. Some countries have strict laws limiting the use of telecommunications and databases, making normal business transactions such as payroll costly, slow, or even impossible. Other countries have few laws concerning telecommunications and database use. These countries, sometimes called

international network A network that links users and systems in more than one country.

data havens, allow other governments and companies to process data within their boundaries. International networks in developing countries can have inadequate equipment and infrastructure that can cause problems and limit the usefulness of the network.

Marks & Spencer PLC has a substantial international presence with 550 stores worldwide operating in 30 countries. It depends on an international network to link all its stores to capture daily sales and track results. It also deals with roughly 2000 direct suppliers of finished products located in places such as Bangalore, Bangladesh, Delhi, Hong Kong, Istanbul, and Sri Lanka. Reliable international communications are also required for it to work quickly and effectively with its supply base so that it can acquire goods more efficiently while still meeting the firm's strict trading standards. The firm is working with Cable & Wireless PLC to implement an Internet protocol virtual private network to provide Voice over Internet Protocol (VoIP) at its 400 U.K. stores and a converged voice/data IP international network for all its operations.[9] The stores involved in the first phase of the development have experienced a great improvement in the response times of customer-facing systems, such as payment processing and customer ordering, as well as stock ticketing, e-mail, and personnel management systems.[10]

Mesh Networking

Mesh networking is a way to route communications among network nodes (computers or other device) by allowing for continuous connections and reconfiguration around blocked paths by 'hopping' from node to node until a connection can be established. In the full mesh topology, each node (workstation or other device) is connected directly to each of the other nodes. In the partial mesh topology, some nodes might be connected to all the others, and other nodes are connected only to nodes with which they frequently exchange communications (see Figure 6.11). Mesh networks are very robust: If one node fails, all the other nodes can still communicate with each other, directly or through one or more intermediate nodes. Mesh networks are being set up to blanket large areas to provide Internet access, secure connections to corporate networks, and VoIP calls. Many cities throughout Europe are setting up mesh networks to give residents, sometimes free, Internet access.

mesh networking A way to route communications between network nodes (computers or other device) by allowing for continuous connections and reconfiguration around blocked paths by 'hopping' from node to node until a connection can be established.

6

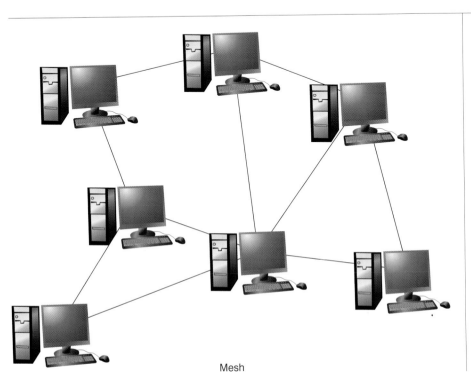

Figure 6.11 Partial Mesh Network

Mesh

6.2.2 Distributed Processing

When an organization needs to use two or more computer systems, it can use one of three basic processing alternatives: centralized, decentralized, or distributed. With **centralized processing**, all processing occurs in a single location or facility. This approach offers the highest degree of control because a single centrally managed computer performs all data processing.

centralized processing
Processing alternative in which all processing occurs at a single location or facility.

decentralized processing
Processing alternative in which processing devices are placed at various remote locations.

With **decentralized processing**, processing devices are placed at various remote locations. Each computer system is isolated and does not communicate with another system. Decentralized systems are suitable for companies that have independent operating divisions.

With distributed processing, computers are placed at remote locations but connected to each other via telecommunications devices. One benefit of distributed processing is that managers can allocate data to the locations that can process it most efficiently.

The September 11, 2001, terrorist attacks on the World Trade Center in New York and the current relatively high level of natural disasters such as hurricane Katrina in the Gulf of Mexico in the southern U.S. in 2005 sparked many companies to distribute their workers, operations, and systems much more widely, a reversal of the recent trend towards centralization. The goal is to minimize the consequences of a catastrophic event at one location while ensuring uninterrupted systems availability.

6.2.3 Client/Server Systems

Users can share data through file server computing, which allows authorized users to download entire files from certain computers designated as file servers. After downloading data to a local computer, a user can analyze, manipulate, format, and display data from the file (see Figure 6.12).

Figure 6.12 File Server Connection *The file server sends the user the entire file that contains the data requested. The user can then analyze, manipulate, format, and display the downloaded data with a program that runs on the user's personal computer.*

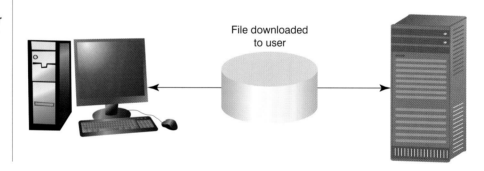

File downloaded to user

client/server An architecture in which multiple computer platforms are dedicated to special functions such as database management, printing, communications, and program execution.

In **client/server** architecture, multiple computer platforms are dedicated to special functions such as database management, printing, communications, and program execution. These platforms are called servers. Each server is accessible by all computers on the network. Servers can be computers of all sizes; they store both application programs and data files and are equipped with operating system software to manage the activities of the network. The server distributes programs and data to the other computers (clients) on the network as they request them. An application server holds the programs and data files for a particular application, such as an inventory database. The client or the server can do the processing. An e-mail server sends and receives e-mails. A web server sends out web pages.

A client is any computer (often a user's personal computer) that sends messages requesting services from the servers on the network. A client can converse with many servers concurrently (see Figure 6.13). Table 6.3 lists the advantages and disadvantages of client/server architecture.

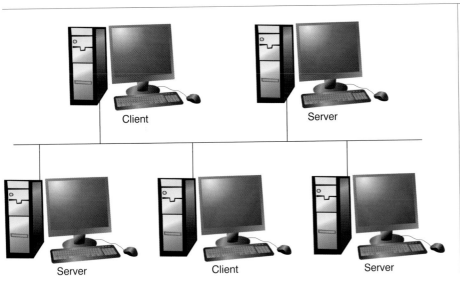

Figure 6.13
Client/Server Connection
Multiple computer platforms, called servers, are dedicated to special functions. Each server is accessible by all computers on the network. The client requests services from the servers, provides a user interface, and presents results to the user.

6.2.4 Communications Protocols and Hardware

A **communications protocol** is a set of rules that governs the exchange of information over a communications channel. The goal is to ensure fast, efficient, error-free communications over an imperfect communication channel. Protocols govern several levels of a telecommunications network. For example, some protocols determine data interchange at the hardware device level, and other protocols determine data interchange at the application program level. Many communications protocols govern the international, national, or industry level. With the spread of wireless network technology to support devices such as PDAs, mobile computers, and mobile phones, the telecommunications industry needed new protocols to connect these devices. Wireless communications protocols are still evolving as the industry matures. The Institute for Electrical and Electronics Engineers (IEEE) has been instrumental in defining numerous telecommunications standards. Wi-Fi has evolved and improved over time in terms of its ability to transmit data at higher speeds and over increasing distances. Wi-Fi has proven so popular that 'hot spots' are popping up in places such as airports, coffee shops, college campuses, libraries, and restaurants. Dozens of cities and many business organizations are using Wi-Fi technology to connect to people on the go.

> **communications protocol** A set of rules that governs the exchange of information over a communications channel.

Table 6.3 Advantages and Disadvantages of Client/Server Architecture

Advantages	Disadvantages
Moving applications from mainframe computers and terminal-to-host architecture to client/server architecture can yield significant savings in hardware and software support costs	Moving to client/server architecture is a major two- to five-year conversion process
Minimizes traffic on the network because only the data needed to satisfy a user query is moved from the database to the client device	Controlling the client/server environment to prevent unauthorized use, invasion of privacy, and viruses is difficult
Security mechanisms can be implemented directly on the database server through the use of stored procedures	Using client/server architecture leads to a multivendor environment with problems that are difficult to identify and isolate to the appropriate vendor

Wi-Fi versus WiMAX

WiMAX offers faster data speeds and broader coverage than Wi-Fi. It can support mobile users who are within a range of approximately 50 kilometres from the WiMAX serving antenna at a transmission rate of up to 70 Mbps. It also offers a higher quality of service that can support applications such as digital life-size videoconferencing where Wi-Fi cannot. Currently, Wi-Fi speeds are less than half those of WiMAX and users must be within a few hundred metres of a hot spot. However, the WiMAX standard for mobile users is still being defined and hardware and software to support it are not yet broadly available at competitive prices. When they are, Wi-Fi adopters will have to decide if the additional benefits of WiMAX can justify the cost of conversion to WiMAX.

Smart Antenna Technology

Conventional wireless communications employs a single antenna at the source and another single antenna at the destination. However, a signal (an electromagnetic field) can suffer from multipath effects when it encounters obstructions (e.g., buildings, hills), which cause the wave fronts to scatter so that they take different paths to reach the destination. The result can be fading, cutout, and intermittent reception leading to a reduction in the effective data speed and an increase in the number of errors. Using two or more antennas or MIMO (multiple input, multiple output), along with the transmission of multiple signals (one for each antenna) at the source and the destination, eliminates these multipath problems. MIMO technology is being used with digital television (DTV), wireless local area networks, MANs, and mobile communications. MISO (multiple input, single output) and SIMO (single input, multiple output) are other approaches to solving these problems.

Ultra Wideband (UWB)

Ultra wideband (UWB) transmissions consist of a stream of pulses only picoseconds (one trillionth or 10–12 of a second) wide. These extremely short impulses result in high frequencies spread over a wide band, which is why this technology is called 'ultra wideband'. UWB could potentially dominate the short range wireless market as it offers the desirable characteristics of very high bandwidth and low power consumption.

3G Wireless Communication

The International Telecommunications Union (ITU) established a single standard for mobile networks in 1999. The goal was to standardize future digital wireless communications and allow global roaming with a single handset. Called IMT-2000, now referred to as 3G, this standard provides for faster transmission speeds in the range of 2–4 Mbps that will enable applications such as VoIP, video telephony, mobile multimedia, and interactive gaming. Originally, 3G was supposed to be a single, unified, worldwide standard, but the 3G standards effort split into several different standards. One standard is the Universal Mobile Telephone System (UMTS) that is the preferred solution for European countries that use Global System for Mobile communications (GSM). GSM is the de facto wireless telephone standard in Europe with more than 120 million users worldwide in 120 countries. Another 3G-based standard is Code-Division Multiple Access (CDMA) that is used in Australia, Canada, China, India, Israel, Mexico, South Korea, the U.S., and Venezuela. The wide variety of 3G cellular communications protocols can support many business applications. The challenge is to enable these protocols to intercommunicate and support fast, reliable, global wireless communications.

4G Wireless Communications

4G stands for fourth-generation broadband mobile wireless. 4G is expected to deliver more advanced versions of enhanced multimedia, smooth streaming video, universal access, portability across all types of devices, and hopefully, worldwide roaming capability. 4G will also provide increased data transmission rates in the 20–40 Mbps range. (This is roughly 10 to 20 times faster than the current rates of the ADSL service used in many homes.)

Switches, Bridges, Routers, and Gateways

In addition to communications protocols, certain hardware devices switch messages from one network to another at high speeds. A **switch** uses the physical device address in each incoming message on the network to determine to which output port it should forward the message to reach another device on the same network. A **bridge** connects one LAN to another LAN that uses the same telecommunications protocol. A **router** forwards data packets across two or more distinct networks toward their destinations through a process known as 'routing'. A **gateway** is a network device that serves as an entrance to another network.

6.2.5 Communications Software

In Chapter 4, you learned that all computers have operating systems that control many functions. When an application program requires data from a disk drive, it goes through the operating system. Now consider a computer attached to a network that connects large disk drives, printers, and other equipment and devices. How does an application program request data from a disk drive on the network? The answer is through the network operating system.

A **network operating system (NOS)** is systems software that controls the computer systems and devices on a network and allows them to communicate with each other. The NOS performs the same types of functions for the network as operating system software does for a computer, such as memory and task management and coordination of hardware. When network equipment (such as printers, plotters, and disk drives) is required, the NOS makes sure that these resources are used correctly. In most cases, companies that produce and sell networks provide the NOS. For example, NetWare is the NOS from Novell, a popular network environment for personal computer systems and equipment.

Software tools and utilities are available for managing networks. With **network-management software**, a manager on a networked personal computer can monitor the use of individual computers and shared hardware (such as printers), scan for viruses, and ensure compliance with software licenses. Network-management software also simplifies the process of updating files and programs on computers on the network – a manager can make changes through a communications server instead of on individual computers. In addition, network-management software protects software from being copied, modified, or downloaded illegally and performs error control to locate telecommunications errors and potential network problems. Some of the many benefits of network-management software include fewer hours spent on routine tasks (such as installing new software), faster response to problems, and greater overall network control.

Network management is one of the most important tasks of IS managers. In fact, poor management of the network can cause a whole company to suffer. Because companies use networks to communicate with customers and business partners, network outages or slow performance can even mean a loss of business. Network management includes a wide range of technologies and processes that monitor the infrastructure and help IS staff identify and address problems before they affect customers, business partners, or employees.

Fault detection and performance management are the two types of network-management products. Both employ the Simple Network Management Protocol (SNMP) to obtain key information from individual network components. SNMP allows anything on the network, including switches, routers, firewalls, and even operating systems and server products and utilities, to communicate with

switch A telecommunications device that uses the physical device address in each incoming message on the network to determine to which output port it should forward the message to reach another device on the same network.

bridge A telecommunications device that connects one LAN to another LAN that uses the same telecommunications protocol.

router A telecommunications device that forwards data packets across two or more distinct networks towards their destinations, through a process known as routing.

gateway A telecommunications device that serves as an entrance to another network.

network operating system (NOS) Systems software that controls the computer systems and devices on a network and allows them to communicate with each other.

network-management software Software that enables a manager on a networked desktop to monitor the use of individual computers and shared hardware (such as printers), scan for viruses, and ensure compliance with software licences.

management software about its current operations and state of health. SNMP can also control these devices and products, telling them to redirect traffic, change traffic priorities, or even to shut down.

Fault management software alerts IS staff in real time when a device is failing. Equipment vendors place traps (code in a software program for handling unexpected or unallowable conditions) on their hardware to identify problems. In addition, the IS staff can place agents – automated pieces of software – on networks to monitor functions. When a device exceeds a given performance threshold, the agent sends an alarm to the company's IS fault management program. For example, if a CPU registers that it is more than 80 percent busy, the agent might trigger an alarm.

Performance management software sends messages to the various devices (i.e., polls them) to sample their performance and to determine whether they are operating within acceptable levels. The devices reply to the management system with performance data that the system stores in a database. This real-time data is correlated to historical trends and displayed graphically so that the IS staff can identify any unusual variations.

Today, most IS organizations use a combination of fault management and performance management to ensure that their network remains up and running and that every network component and application is performing acceptably. With the two technologies, the IS staff can identify and resolve fault and performance issues before they affect customers and service. The latest network-management technology even incorporates automatic fixes – the network-management system identifies a problem, notifies the IS manager, and automatically corrects the problem before anyone outside the IS department notices it.

Sierra Pacific is a wood products provider in the U.S. that, prior to installing network-management software, learned about network problems in the worst way – from users calling the network operations centre to complain. The company has operations in about 50 distributed server locations, including deep in the woods where users are connected through routers to a high-speed network. Sierra Pacific installed Systems Intrusion Analysis and Reporting Environment open-source software on all servers to collect network and performance data around the clock and forward it to a central network server. Now, Sierra Pacific has the data it needs to identify bottlenecks and failed components before users are affected.[11]

6.3 The Internet

The Internet is the world's largest computer network. Actually, the Internet is a collection of interconnected networks, all freely exchanging information. Nobody knows exactly how big the Internet is because it is a collection of separately run, smaller computer networks. There is no single place where all the connections are registered. Figure 6.14 shows the staggering growth of the Internet, as measured by the number of Internet host sites or domain names. Domain names are discussed later in the chapter.

The Internet is truly international in scope, with users on every continent – including Antarctica. China has spent many billions in its telecommunications infrastructure in the last few years. In 2005, almost 100 million Chinese people were connected to the Internet. China, however, restricts the use of the Internet.[12] In 2005, for example, China implemented new Internet rules. According to the Xinhua News Agency of China, '[Only] healthy and civilized news and information that is beneficial to the improvement of the quality of the nation, beneficial to its economic development and conductive to social progress will be allowed. The sites are prohibited from spreading news and information that goes against state security and public interest'. The penalties for sharing unauthorized information are severe, with more than one Internet user being imprisoned for things they have published online.

The ancestor of the Internet was the **ARPANET**, a project started by the U.S. Department of Defense (DoD) in 1969. The ARPANET was both an experiment in reliable networking and a means to link DoD and military research

ARPANET A project started by the U.S. Department of Defense (DoD) in 1969 as both an experiment in reliable networking and a means to link DoD and military research contractors, including many universities doing military-funded research.

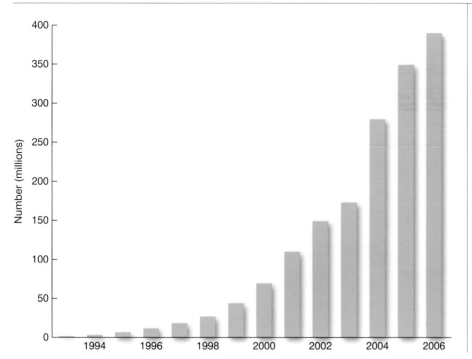

Figure 6.14 Internet Growth: Number of Internet Domain Names

SOURCE: Data from 'The Internet Domain Survey', www.isc.org.

6

contractors, including many universities doing military-funded research. (ARPA stands for the Advanced Research Projects Agency, the branch of the DoD in charge of awarding grant money. The agency is now known as DARPA – the added D is for Defense.) The ARPANET was highly successful, and every university in the country wanted to use it. This wildfire growth made it difficult to manage the ARPANET, particularly its large and rapidly growing number of university sites. So, the ARPANET was broken into two networks: MILNET, which included all military sites, and a new, smaller ARPANET, which included all the non-military sites. The two networks remained connected, however, through use of the **Internet Protocol (IP)**, which enables traffic to be routed from one network to another as needed. Katie Hafner's book, *Where Wizards Stay Up Late: The Origins of the Internet,* gives a detailed description of the history of the Internet.[13]

> **Internet Protocol (IP)** A communication standard that enables traffic to be routed from one network to another as needed.

Today, people, universities, and companies are attempting to make the Internet faster and easier to use. Robert Kahn, who managed the early development of the ARPANET, wants to take the Internet to the next level. He is president of the non-profit organization National Research Initiatives, which provides guidance and funding for the development of a national information infrastructure. The organization is looking into using 'digital objects', which allow all types of computer systems to use and share programs and data. To speed Internet access, a group of corporations and universities called the University Corporation for Advanced Internet Development (UCAID) is working on a faster, new Internet. Called Internet2 (I2), Next Generation Internet (NGI) or Abilene (depending on the universities or corporations involved) the new Internet offers the potential of faster Internet speeds, up to 2 Gbps per second or more.[14] Some I2 connections can transmit data at 100 Mbps per second, which is about 200 times faster than dial-up connections. This speed would allow you to transfer the contents of a DVD in less than a minute.

6.3.1 How the Internet Works

The Internet transmits data from one computer (called a host) to another (see Figure 6.15). If the receiving computer is on a network to which the first computer is directly connected, it can send

Figure 6.15 Routing Messages Over the Internet

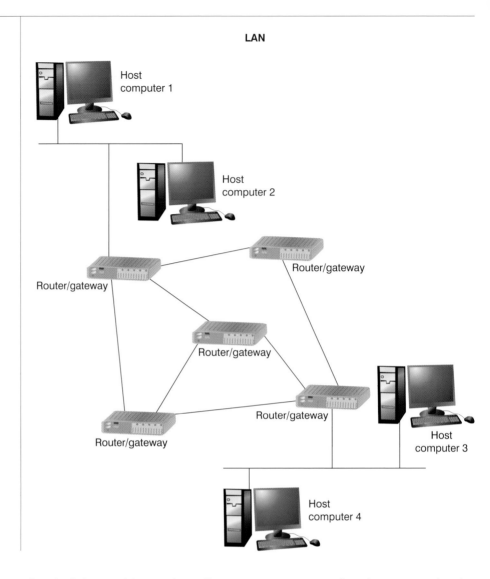

LAN

Host computer 1

Host computer 2

Router/gateway

Router/gateway

Router/gateway

Router/gateway

Router/gateway

Host computer 3

Host computer 4

the message directly. If the receiving and sending computers are not directly connected to the same network, the sending computer relays the message to another computer which forwards it on. The message might be sent through a router to reach the forwarding computer. The forwarding host, which needs to be attached to at least one other network, delivers the message directly if it can or passes it to another forwarding host. A message can pass through a dozen or more forwarders on its way from one part of the Internet to another.

The various networks that are linked to form the Internet work much the same way – they pass data around in chunks called packets, each of which carries the addresses of its sender and its receiver. The set of conventions used to pass packets from one host to another is known as the Internet Protocol (IP). Many other protocols are used in connection with IP. The best known is the **Transmission Control Protocol (TCP)**, which operates at the transport layer. Many people use TCP/IP as an abbreviation for the combination of TCP and IP used by most Internet applications. After a network following these standards links to a **backbone** – one of the Internet's high-speed, long-distance communications links – it becomes part of the worldwide Internet community.

Each computer on the Internet has an assigned address called its **uniform resource locator (URL)**, to identify it to other hosts. The URL gives

Transmission Control Protocol (TCP) The widely used transport-layer protocol that most Internet applications use with IP.

backbone One of the Internet's high-speed, long-distance communications links.

uniform resource locator (URL) An assigned address on the Internet for each computer.

those who provide information over the Internet a standard way to designate where Internet elements such as servers, documents, and newsgroups can be found. Consider the URL for Cengage Learning, http://www.cengage.co.uk.

The 'http' specifies the access method and tells your software to access a file using the Hypertext Transport Protocol. This is the primary method for interacting with the Internet. In many cases, you don't need to include http:// in a URL because it is the default protocol. Thus, http://www.cengage.co.uk can be abbreviated to www.cengage.co.uk.

The 'www' part of the address signifies that the files associated with this website reside on the World Wide Web server of 'cengage.co.uk'. The 'cengage.co.uk' itself is the domain name that identifies the Internet host site. Domain names must adhere to strict rules. They always have at least two parts, with each part separated by a dot (full stop). For some Internet addresses, the far right part of the domain name is the country code (such as uk for the United Kingdom, au for Australia, ca for Canada, dk for Denmark, fr for France, and jp for Japan). Many Internet addresses have a code denoting affiliation categories. (Table 6.4 contains a few popular categories.) The far left part of the domain name identifies the host network or host provider, which might be the name of a university or business.

Originally, Herndon, Virginia-based Network Solutions, Inc. (NSI), was the sole company in the world with the direct power to register addresses using .com, .net, or .org domain names. However its government contract ended in October 1998, as part of the U.S. government's move to turn management of the web's address system over to the private sector. Today, other companies, called registrars, can register domain names, and additional companies are seeking accreditation to register domain names from the Internet Corporation for Assigned Names and Numbers (ICANN). Some registrars are concentrating on large corporations, where the profit margins might be higher, compared with small businesses or individuals.

An **Internet service provider (ISP)** is any company that provides people and organizations with access to the Internet. Thousands of organizations serve as Internet service providers, ranging from universities to major communications giants such as BT and AT&T. To use this type of connection, you must have an account with the service provider and software that allows a direct link via TCP/IP. In most cases, ISPs charge a monthly fee of around €20 for unlimited Internet connection through a standard modem. Some ISPs are experimenting with low-fee or no-fee Internet access, though strings are attached to the no-fee offers in most cases, typically that the user must subscribe to telephone services as well.

Internet service provider (ISP)
Any company that provides people or organizations with access to the Internet.

6.4 Internet Applications

Many people believe the terms 'Internet' and 'World Wide Web' are synonymous. However the Web, which is examined next, is just one application of the Internet. Others also discussed in this section are e-mail, telnet and FTP. More applications are given in Chapter 10.

Table 6.4 Some Top-Level Domain Affiliations

Affiliation ID	Affiliation
com	Commercial organizations
edu	Educational sites (mostly based in the U.S.)
gov	Government sites (mostly based in the U.S.)
net	Networking organizations
org	Organizations

6.4.1 The World Wide Web

The **World Wide Web** was developed by Tim Berners-Lee at CERN, the European Organization for Nuclear Research in Geneva. He originally conceived of it as an internal document-management system. From this modest beginning, the World Wide Web (web, WWW, or W3) has grown to a collection of tens of thousands of independently owned computers that work together as one in an Internet service. These computers, called web servers, are scattered all over the world and contain every imaginable type of data. Thanks to the high-speed Internet circuits connecting them and some clever cross-indexing software, users can jump from one web computer to another effortlessly, creating the illusion of using one big computer. Because of its ability to handle multimedia objects, including linking multimedia objects distributed on web servers around the world, the Web has become the most popular means of information access on the Internet today.

World Wide Web (WWW or W3) A collection of tens of thousands of independently owned computers that work together as one in an Internet service.

The Web is a menu-based system that uses the client/server model. It organizes Internet resources throughout the world into a series of menu pages, or screens, that appear on your computer. Each web server maintains pointers, or links, to data on the Internet and can retrieve that data. However, you need the right hardware and telecommunications connections, or the Web can be painfully slow.

Data can exist on the Web as ASCII characters, word processing files, audio files, graphic and video images, or any other sort of data that can be stored in a computer file. A website is like a magazine, with a cover page called a **home page** which includs links to the rest of its material. The words on a website are typically written in hypertext. **Hypertext** allows the linking of certain words to other web pages, so users can click on them to access related material. This feature gives the Web its name, as all information is linked together like a spider's web.

home page A cover page for a website that has graphics, titles, and text.

hyptertext Text used to connect web pages, allowing users to access information in whatever order they wish.

Hypertext Markup Language (HTML) The standard page description language for web pages.

HTML tags Codes that let the web browser know how to format text – as a heading, as a list, or as body text – and whether images, sound, or other elements should be inserted.

Hypertext Markup Language (HTML) is the standard page description language for web pages. One way to think about HTML is as a set of highlighter pens that you use to mark up plain text to make it a web page – one colour for the headings, another for bold, and so on. The **HTML tags** let the browser know how to format the text: as a heading, as a list, or as main text, for example. HTML also tells whether pictures, videos, and other elements should be inserted, and where they should go. Users mark up a page by placing HTML tags before and after a word or words. For example, to turn a sentence into a heading, you place the <h1> tag at the start of the sentence. At the end of the sentence, you place the closing tag </h1>. When you view this page in your browser, the sentence will be displayed as a heading. So, an HTML file is made up of two things: text and tags. The text is your message, and the tags are codes that mark the way words will be displayed. All HTML tags are enclosed in a set of angle brackets (< and >), such as <h2>. The closing tag has a forward slash in it, such as </b> for closing bold. Consider the following text and tags:

<h1 align="center">Principles of Business Information Systems</h1>

This HTML code centres Principles of Information Systems as a major, or level 1, heading. The 'h1' in the HTML code indicates a first-level heading. On some web browsers (discussed next), the heading might be 14-point type size with a Times Roman font. On other browsers, it might be a larger 18-point size in a different font. There is a standard, but not all browsers stick to it. Figure 6.16 shows a simple document and its corresponding HTML tags. Notice the <html> tag at the top indicating the beginning of the HTML code. The <title> indicates the beginning of the title: 'Cengage Learning – Shaping the Future of Global Learning' The </title> tag indicates the end of the title.

Figure 6.16 Sample Hypertext Markup Language *Shown at the left on the screen is a document, and at the right are the corresponding HTML tags.*

SOURCE: www.course.com

Some newer web standards are gaining in popularity, including Extensible Markup Language (XML), Extensible Hypertext Markup Language (XHTML), Cascading Style Sheets (CSS), Dynamic HTML (DHTML), and Wireless Markup Language (WML). WML can display web pages on small screens, such as smartphones and PDAs. XHTML is a combination of XML and HTML that has been approved by the World Wide Web Consortium (W3C).

Extensible Markup Language (XML) is a markup language for web documents containing structured information, including words and pictures. XML does not have a predefined tag set. With HTML, for example, the <h1> tag always means a first-level heading. The content and formatting are contained in the same HTML document. With XML, web documents contain the content of a web page. The formatting of the content is contained in a separate style sheet. A few typical instructions in XML follow:

Extensible Markup Language (XML) The markup language for web documents containing structured information, including words, pictures, and other elements.

<chapter>Hardware
<topic>Input Devices
<topic>Processing and Storage Devices
<topic>Output Devices

How the preceding content is formatted and displayed on a web page is contained in the corresponding style sheet, such as the following cascading style sheet (CSS). Note that the chapter title 'Hardware' is displayed on the web page in a large font (18 points). 'Hardware' will appear in bold blue text. 'Input Devices' and the other titles will appear in a smaller font (12 points) in italic red text.

chapter: (font-size: 18pt; color: blue; font-weight: bold; display: block; font-family: Arial;margin-top: 10pt; margin-left: 5pt)
topic: (font-size: 12pt; color: red; font-style: italic; display: block; font-family: Arial;margin-left: 12pt)

XML includes the capabilities to define and share document information over the web. A company can use XML to exchange ordering and invoicing information with its customers. CSS improves web page presentation, and DHTML provides dynamic presentation of web content. These standards move more of the processing for animation and dynamic content to the web browser, discussed next, and provide quicker access and displays.

Web Browsers

A **web browser** translates HTML so you can read it. It provides a graphical interface to the Web. The menu consists of graphics, titles, and text with hypertext links. **Hypermedia** links you to Internet resources, including text documents, graphics, sound files, and newsgroup servers. As you choose an item or resource, or move from one document to another, you might be accessing various computers on the Internet without knowing it, while the Web handles all the connections. The beauty of web browsers and the Web is that they make surfing the Internet fun. Clicking with a mouse on a highlighted word or graphic whisks you effortlessly to computers halfway around the world. Most browsers offer basic features such as support for backgrounds and tables, displaying a web page's HTML source code, and a way to create hot lists of your favourite sites. Web browsers enable net surfers to view more complex graphics and 3D models, as well as audio and video material, and to run small programs embedded in web pages called **applets**. A web browser plug-in is an external program that is executed by a web browser when it is needed. For example, if you are working with a web page and encounter an Adobe pdf file, the web browser will typically run the external Adobe pdf reader program or plug-in to allow you to open the file. Microsoft Internet Explorer and Netscape Navigator are examples of web browsers for PCs. Safari is a popular web browser from Apple for their Macintosh computer, and Mozilla Firefox is a web browser available in numerous languages that can be used on PCs, computers with the Linux operating system, and Apple Mac computers (see Figure 6.17).

web browser Software that creates a unique, hypermedia-based menu on a computer screen, providing a graphical interface to the Web.

hypermedia An extension of hypertext where the data, including text, images, video and other media, on web pages is connected allowing users to access information in whatever order they wish.

applet A small program embedded in web pages.

6

Figure 6.17 Mozilla Firefox

SOURCE: Courtesy of Mozilla Foundation.

Information Systems @ Work

E-Petitions and the U.K. Government

In November 2006, the British government launched e-petitions, a web-based system that allowed any citizen to create a public petition which could be signed by other visitors to the website. The system is essentially a more convenient form of the traditional paper petitions which have been delivered by hand or by post to the Prime Minister at Downing Street, London for many years. To create en e-petition, you must first search the database to make sure no one else has already launched one which is the same, then it's just a matter of providing some basic personal information and completing the following sentence – 'We the undersigned petition the Prime Minister to...'. Each petition has an expiry date and the creator has an option of writing a brief background to the petition. To sign a petition, you will need to give your name, address and e-mail. Once you have done this, you will receive an e-mail asking you to confirm that you wish to add your name to the petition by clicking a link. Citizens, charities and campaign groups have not been slow to make use of the system. At the time of writing there are over 7000 current petitions. These can be viewed on the website by their popularity (how many people have signed up to them) or by start or end date. The most popular can gain well over 70 000 electronic signatures. The government, and even the prime minister personally, can and does respond to the petitions it receives, sometimes before the dealine for signing up passes, perhaps to clarify the government's stance on certain issues. For instance, one popular petition asked the prime minister to continue funding The Red Arrows, a Royal Air Force aerobatics team. Then Prime Minister

Tony Blair responded personally assuring that the future of this team was safe.

Every person who signs such a petition will receive an e-mail detailing the government's response to the issues raised. The reason for implementing e-petitions is to enable as many people as possible to make their views known to the government. The service is also intended to enable smaller groups who may not have the funds to set up a website to still collect signatures online. The software behind the site is open source and thus available to anyone who wants to use it.

Questions

1 Do you think the Web really empowers citizens and brings them closer to their government?

2 Not all of the petitions are serious. One stated 'we the undersigned petition the Prime Minister to stand on his head and juggle ice cream'. Should this petition ever have appeared on the site? Why or why not?

3 Technology use is becoming so common and affordable that governments, if they wanted to, could soon be able to determine public opinion from all its citizens on any subject very quickly. Describe how such a system might work from the government's perspective and the perspective of the citizens.

4 Do you think such a system would be a good thing? Explain your answer.

SOURCES: E-petitions (website), http://petitions.pm.gov.uk/; Staff, 'Downing Street Launches E-petitions' (website), http://www.pm.gov.uk/output/Page10411.asp, November 13, 2006.

Search Engines and Web Research

Looking for information on the Web is like browsing in a library – without the alphabetic listing of books in the card catalogue, it is difficult to find information. Web search tools – called **search engines** – take the place of the card catalogue. Most search engines, such as Google (Figure 6.18), are free. They make money by, among other things, **search engine** A web search tool.
charging advertisers to put ad banners in their search engine results. Companies often pay a search engine for a sponsored link, which is usually displayed at the top of the list of links for an Internet search. Google has almost 60 percent of search volume.[15]

Figure 6.18 Google Is a Popular Search Engine on the Web

Search engines that use keyword indexes produce an index of all the text on the sites they examine. Typically, the engine reads at least the first few hundred words on a page, including the title and any keywords or descriptions that the author has built into the page structure. The engine throws out common words such as 'and', 'the', 'by', and 'for'. The engine assumes remaining words are valid page content; it then alphabetizes these words (with their associated sites) and places them in an index where they can be searched and retrieved. Some companies include a meta tag in the HTML header for search engine robots from sites such as Google to find and use. Meta tags are not shown on the web page when it is displayed; they only help search engines discover and display a website. To place the search results in the most relevant order, Google counts the number of links that are made to each from other websites, and puts the one with the most at the top.

Today's search engines do more than look for words, phrases, or sentences on the web. For example, you can use Google to search for images and video.[16] You can even search for geographic locations to get a view from the skies using satellites.[17] Google, for example, offers Google Maps and Google Earth to provide aerial views. After downloading and installing Google Earth, you can type an address and Google will show you the neighbourhood or even a house in some cases. Microsoft Virtual Earth and Local Search also give aerial views and close-ups of some locations, including retail stores in some cases.[18] You can also use news organizations' websites, such as the BBC's (http://news.bbc.co.uk/), to access current information on a variety of topics. Some websites maintain versions in different languages, especially for research purposes. In addition, many ordinary web users are publishing lists of their favourite web pages along with explanations of what they are, to classify web content and to make it easier for them (and others) to retrieve information. Such lists are known as 'folksonomies' although this word has been voted one of the most annoying Internet terms.

Web Programming Languages

Java An object-oriented programming language from Sun Microsystems based on C++ that allows small programs (applets) to be embedded within an HTML document.

There are a number of important web programming languages. **Java**, for example, is an object-oriented programming language from Sun Microsystems based on the C++ programming language, which allows small programs – the applets mentioned earlier – to be embedded within an HTML document. When the user clicks the appropriate part of an HTML page to retrieve an applet from a web server, the applet is downloaded onto the client workstation, where it begins executing. Unlike other programs, Java software can run on any type of computer. Programmers use Java to make web pages come alive, adding splashy graphics, animation, and real-time updates.

The relationship among Java applets, a Java-enabled browser, and the Web is shown in Figure 6.19. To develop a Java applet, the author writes the code for the client computer and installs that on the web server. The user accesses the web page on a personal computer, which serves as a client. The web page contains an additional HTML tag called APP, which refers to the Java applet. A rectangle on the page is occupied by the Java applet. If the user clicks the rectangle to execute the Java applet, the client computer checks to see whether a copy of the applet is already stored locally on its hard drive. If it is not, the computer accesses the web server and requests that the applet be downloaded. The applet can be located anywhere on the Web. If the user has a Java-enabled browser (such as Sun HotJava or Netscape Navigator), the applet is downloaded to the user's computer and is executed in the browser.

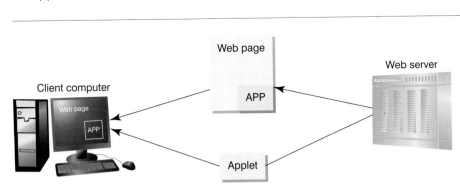

Figure 6.19
Downloading an Applet from a Web Server

The user accesses the web page from a web server. If the user clicks the APP rectangle to execute the Java applications, the client's computer checks for a copy on its local hard drive. If it does not find the applet, the client requests the web server to download the applet.

The web server that delivers the Java applet to the web client cannot determine what kind of hardware or software environment the client is running, and the developer who creates the Java applet does not have to worry about whether it will work correctly on Windows, UNIX, and Mac OS. Java is thus often described as a 'cross-platform' programming language.

In addition to Java, companies use a variety of other programming languages and tools to develop websites. JavaScript, VBScript, and ActiveX (used with Internet Explorer) are Internet languages used to develop web pages and perform important functions, such as accepting user input. Hypertext Preprocessor, or PHP, is an open-source programming language. PHP code or instructions can be embedded directly into HTML code. Unlike some other Internet languages, PHP can run on a web server, with the results being transferred to a client computer. PHP can be used on a variety of operating systems. It can also be used with a variety of database management systems, such as DB2, Oracle, Informix, MySQL, and many others. These characteristics – running on different operating systems and database management systems, and being an open source language – make PHP popular with many web developers.

Developing Web Content

The art of web design involves working within the technical limitations of the Web and using a set of tools to make appealing designs. A study at Glamorgan University Business School in Wales, for example, concluded that women prefer web pages with more colour in the background and informal pictures and images.[19] Men prefer darker colours and like 3D, moving images. You can create a web page using one of the following approaches: (a) write your copy with a word processor, and then use an HTML converter to convert the page into HTML format; (b) use an HTML editor to write text (it will add HTML tags at the same time); (c) edit an existing HTML template (with all the tags ready to use) to meet your needs; (d) use an ordinary text editor such as Notepad and type the start and end tags for each item.

After you develop web content, your next step is to place, or publish, the content on a web server, so others can access it. Popular publishing options include using ISPs, free sites, and web hosting. Some ISPs also provide limited web space, typically 1 to 6 MB, as part of their monthly fee. If more disk space is needed, there are additional charges. Free sites offer limited space for a website. In return, free sites often require the user to view advertising or agree to other terms and conditions. Web hosting services provide space on their websites for people and businesses that don't have the financial resources, time, or skills to host their own website. A web host charges a monthly fee, depending on services offered. Some web hosting sites include domain name registration, web authoring software, and activity reporting and monitoring of the website. Often, FTP (described later in this chapter) is used to copy files from the developer's computer to the web server.

Some web developers are creating programs and procedures to combine two or more websites into one website, called a 'mash-up'.[20] A mash-up is named for the process of mixing two or more (often hip-hop) songs into one song. A website containing crime information, for example, can be mashed up with a mapping website to produce a website with crime information placed on top of a map of a metropolitan area. People are becoming very creative in how they mash up several websites into new ones. Mashing up websites is becoming popular, but not everyone is happy with the practice. Some companies are trying to block the mash-up of the content on their website without permission.

After a website has been constructed, a content management system (CMS) can keep the website running smoothly. CMS consists of both software and support. Companies that provide CMS can charge from €11 000 to more than €400 000 annually, depending on the complexity of the website being maintained and the services being performed. Leading CMS vendors include BroadVision, Focumentum, EBT, FileNet, Open Market, and Vignette.

Many products make it easy to develop web content and interconnect web services, discussed in the next section. Microsoft, for example, has introduced a development and web services platform called .NET. The .NET platform allows developers to use different programming languages to create and run programs, including those for the web. The .NET platform also includes a rich library of programming code to help build XML web applications.

Web Services

Web services consist of standards and tools that streamline and simplify communication among websites, promising to revolutionize the way we develop and use the Web for business and personal purposes. Internet companies, including Amazon, eBay, and Google, are now using web services. Amazon, for example, has developed Amazon Web Services (AWS) to make the contents of its huge online catalogue available by other websites or software applications.

web services Standards and tools that streamline and simplify communication among websites for business and personal purposes.

The key to web services is XML. Just as HTML was developed as a standard for formatting web content into web pages, XML is used within a web page to describe and transfer data between web service applications. XML is easy to read and has wide industry support. Besides XML, three other components are used in web service applications:

1 SOAP (Simple Object Access Protocol) is a specification that defines the XML format for messages. SOAP allows businesses, their suppliers, and their customers to communicate with each other. It provides a set of rules that makes it easier to move information and data over the Internet.

2 WSDL (Web Services Description Language) provides a way for a web service application to describe its interfaces in enough detail to allow a user to build a client application to talk to it. In other words, it allows one software component to connect to and work with another software component on the Internet.

3 UDDI (Universal Discovery Description and Integration) is used to register web service applications with an Internet directory so that potential users can easily find them and carry out transactions over the Web.

6.4.2 E-mail

E-mail or electronic mail is a method of sending communications over computer networks. It is no longer limited to simple text messages. Depending on your hardware and software, and the hardware and software of your recipient, you can embed sound and images in your message and attach files that contain text documents, spreadsheets, graphics, or executable programs. E-mail travels through the systems and networks that make up the Internet. Gateways can receive e-mail messages from the Internet and deliver them to users on other networks. Thus, you can send e-mail messages to anyone in the world if you know that person's e-mail address and you have access to the Internet or another system that can send e-mail. For large organizations whose operations span a country or the world, e-mail allows people to work around the time zone changes. Some users of e-mail claim that they eliminate two hours of verbal communications for every hour of e-mail use.

Some companies use bulk e-mail to send legitimate and important information to sales representatives, customers, and suppliers around the world. With its popularity and ease of use, however, some people feel they are drowning in too much e-mail. Many e-mails are copies sent to a large list of corporate users. Users are taking a number of steps to cope with and reduce their mountain of e-mail. For instance, some users only look at their in-boxes once each day. Many companies have software scan incoming messages for possible junk or bulk e-mail, called spam, and delete it or place it in a separate file. Some have banned the use of copying others in on e-mails unless it is critical.

6.4.3 Telnet and FTP

Telnet is a terminal emulation protocol that enables you to log on to other computers on the Internet to gain access to their publicly available files. Telnet is particularly useful for perusing library holdings and large databases. It is also called 'remote logon'.

File Transfer Protocol (FTP) is a protocol that describes a file transfer process between a host and a remote computer. Using FTP, users can copy files from one computer to another. Companies, for example, use it to transfer vast amounts of business transactional data to the computers of its customers and suppliers. You can also use FTP to gain access to a wealth of free software on the Internet. FTP can be used to upload or download content to a website.

Telnet A terminal emulation protocol that enables users to log on to other computers on the Internet to gain access to public files.

File Transfer Protocol (FTP) A protocol that describes a file transfer process between a host and a remote computer and allows users to copy files from one computer to another.

6.5 Intranets and Extranets

An intranet is an internal company network built using Internet and World Wide Web standards and products. Employees of an organization use it to gain access to company information. After getting their feet wet with public websites that promote company products and services, corporations are seizing the Web as a swift way to streamline – even transform – their organizations. A big advantage of using an intranet is that many people are already familiar with Internet technology, so they need little training to make effective use of their corporate intranet.

An intranet is an inexpensive yet powerful alternative to other forms of internal communication, including conventional computer setups. One of an intranet's most obvious virtues is its ability to reduce the need for paper. Because web browsers run on any type of computer, the same electronic information can be viewed by any employee. That means that all sorts of documents (such as internal phone books, procedure manuals, training manuals, and requisition forms) can be inexpensively converted to electronic form on the Web and be constantly updated. An intranet provides employees with an easy and intuitive approach to accessing information that was previously difficult to obtain. For example, it is an ideal solution to providing information to a mobile sales force that needs access to rapidly changing information. An example is shown in Figure 6.20.

Figure 6.20 An Intranet
An intranet is an internal corporate network used by employees to gain access to company information.

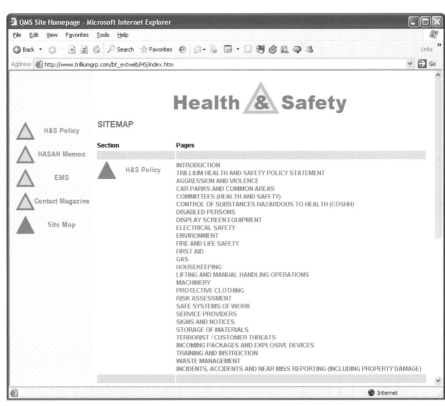

SOURCE: Trillium sample intranet, www.trilliumgrp.com.

A rapidly growing number of companies offer limited access to their intranet to selected customers and suppliers. Such networks are referred to as extranets, and connect people who are external to the company. An extranet is a network that links selected resources of the intranet of a company with its customers, suppliers, or other business partners. Again, an extranet is built around web technologies. Eikos Risk Applications in South Africa, for example, use an extranet to provide tailored content to its clients. The firm is an insurance broker and their extranet gives clients access to policy information, information about claims and facility management reports. Clients log in to the extranet on a secure web page.

Security and performance concerns are different for an extranet than for a website or network-based intranet. User authentication and privacy are critical on an extranet so that information is protected. Obviously, performance must be good to provide quick response to customers and suppliers. Table 6.5 summarizes the differences between users of the Internet, intranets, and extranets.

Table 6.5 Summary of Internet, Intranet, and Extranet Users

Type	Users	Need User ID and Password?
Internet	Anyone	No
Intranet	Employees and managers	Yes
Extranet	Employees, managers and business partners	Yes

Secure intranet and extranet access applications usually require the use of a **virtual private network (VPN)**. A virtual private network (VPN) is a secure connection between two points on the Internet. VPNs transfer information by encapsulating traffic in IP packets and sending the packets over the Internet, a practice called **tunneling**. Most VPNs are built and run by ISPs. Companies that use a VPN from an ISP have essentially outsourced their networks to save money on wide area network equipment and personnel.

virtual private network (VPN) A secure connection between two points on the Internet.

tunnelling The process by which VPNs transfer information by encapsulating traffic in IP packets over the Internet.

Summary

Effective communications are essential to organizational success. Telecommunications refers to the electronic transmission of signals for communications, including telephone, radio, and television. Telecommunications is creating profound changes in business because it removes the barriers of time and distance.

The elements of a telecommunications system include a sending unit, such as a person, a computer system, a terminal, or another device, that originates the message. The sending unit transmits a signal to a telecommunications device, which performs a number of functions such as converting the signal into a different form or from one type to another. A telecommunications device is a hardware component that facilitates electronic communication. The telecommunications device then sends the signal through a medium, which is anything that carries an electronic signal and serves as an interface between a sending device and a receiving device. The signal is received by another telecommunications device that is connected to the receiving computer. The process can then be reversed, and another message can pass from the receiving unit to the original sending unit. With synchronous communications, the receiver gets the message instantaneously, when it is sent. Voice and phone communications are examples. With asynchronous communications, there is a delay between sending and receiving the message. A communications channel is the transmission medium that carries a message from the source to its receivers.

Communications technology lets more people send and receive all forms of information over greater distances. The telecommunications media that physically connect data communications devices can be divided into two broad categories: Guided transmission media, in which communications signals are guided along a solid medium, and wireless media, in which the communications signal is sent over airwaves. Guided transmission media include twisted-pair wire cable, coaxial cable, fibre-optic cable, and broadband over power lines. Wireless media types include microwave, cellular, and infrared.

A modem is a telecommunications hardware device that converts (modulates and demodulates) communications signals so they can be transmitted over the communication media.

A multiplexer is a device that encodes data from two or more data sources onto a single communications channel, thus reducing the number of communications channels needed and therefore, lowering telecommunications costs.

A front-end processor is a special-purpose computer that manages communications to and from a computer system serving hundreds or even thousands of users.

Telecommunications carriers offer a wide array of phone and dialling services, including digital subscriber line (DSL) and wireless telecommunications.

The effective use of networks can turn a company into an agile, powerful, and creative organization, giving it a long-term competitive advantage. Networks let users share hardware, programs, and databases across the organization. They can transmit and receive information to improve organizational effectiveness and efficiency. They enable geographically separated workgroups to share documents and opinions, which fosters teamwork, innovative ideas, and new business strategies.

The physical distance between nodes on the network and the communications and services provided by the network determines whether it is called a personal area network (PAN), local area network (LAN), metropolitan area network (MAN), or wide area network (WAN). A PAN connects information technology devices within a range of about ten metres. The major components in a LAN are a network interface card, a file server, and a bridge or gateway. A MAN connects users and their computers in a geographical area larger than a LAN but smaller than a WAN. WANs link large geographic regions, including communications between countries, linking systems from around the world. The electronic flow of data across international and global boundaries is often called transborder data flow.

A mesh network is a way to route communications between network nodes (computers or other device) by allowing for continuous connections and reconfiguration around blocked paths by 'hopping' from node to node until a connection can be established.

A client/server system is a network that connects a user's computer (a client) to one or more host computers (servers). A client is often a PC that requests services from the server, shares processing tasks with the server, and displays the results. Many companies have reduced their use of mainframe computers in favour of client/server systems using midrange or personal computers to achieve cost savings, provide more control over the desktop, increase flexibility, and become more responsive to business changes. The start-up costs of these systems can be high, and the systems are more complex than a centralized mainframe computer.

When people on one network want to communicate with people or devices in a different organization on another network, they need a common communications protocol and various network devices to do so. A communications protocol is a set of rules that govern the exchange of information over a communications channel. There are a myriad of communications protocols, including international, national, and industry standards.

In addition to communications protocols, telecommunications uses various devices. A switch uses the physical device address in each incoming message on the network to determine which output port to forward the message to in order to reach another device on the same network. A bridge is a device that connects one LAN to another LAN that uses the same telecommunications protocol. A router forwards data packets across two or more distinct networks towards their destinations, through a process known as routing. A gateway is a network device that serves as an entrance to another network.

When an organization needs to use two or more computer systems, it can follow one of three basic data-processing strategies: centralized, decentralized, or distributed. With centralized processing, all processing occurs in a single location or facility. This approach offers the highest degree of control. With decentralized processing, processing devices are placed at various remote locations. The individual computer systems are isolated and do not communicate with each other. With distributed processing, computers are placed at remote locations but are connected to each other via telecommunications devices. This approach helps minimize the consequences of a catastrophic event at one location while ensuring uninterrupted systems availability.

Communications software performs important functions, such as error checking and message formatting. A network operating system controls the computer systems and devices on a network, allowing them to communicate with one another. Network-management software enables a manager to monitor the use of individual computers and shared hardware, scan for viruses, and ensure compliance with software licenses.

The Internet is like many other technologies – it provides a wide range of services, some of which are effective and practical for use today, others are still evolving, and still others will fade away from lack of use. The Internet started with ARPANET, a project sponsored by the U.S. Department of Defense (DoD). Today, the Internet is the world's largest computer network. Actually, it is a collection of interconnected networks, all freely exchanging information. The Internet transmits data from one computer (called a host) to another. The set of conventions used to pass packets from one host to another is known as the Internet Protocol (IP). Many other protocols are used with IP. The best known is the Transmission Control Protocol (TCP). TCP is so widely used that many people refer to the Internet protocol as TCP/IP, the combination of TCP and IP used by most Internet applications. Each computer on the Internet has an assigned address to identify it from other hosts, called its uniform resource locator (URL). There are several ways to connect to the Internet: Via a LAN whose server is an Internet host or via an online service that provides Internet access.

An Internet service provider is any company that provides access to the Internet. To use this type of connection, you must have an account with the service provider and software that allows a direct link via

TCP/IP. Among the value-added services ISPs provide are electronic commerce, intranets, and extranets, website hosting, web transaction processing, network security and administration, and integration services.

Because the Internet and the World Wide Web are becoming more universally used and accepted for business use, management, service and speed, privacy, and security issues must continually be addressed and resolved. A rapidly growing number of companies are doing business on the Web and enabling shoppers to search for and buy products online. For many people, it is easier to shop on the Web than search through catalogues or trek to the high street.

The steps to creating a web page include organizing storage space on a web server; writing your copy with a word processor, using an HTML editor, editing an existing HTML document, or using an ordinary text editor to create your page; opening the page using a browser, viewing the result on a web browser, and correcting any tags; adding links to your home page to take viewers to another home page; adding pictures and sound; uploading the HTML file to your website; reviewing the web page to make sure that all links are working correctly; and advertising your web page. After a website has been constructed, a content management system (CMS) can be used to keep the website running smoothly. Web services are also used to develop web content. Web services consist of a collection of standards and tools that streamline and simplify communication among websites, which could revolutionize the way people develop and use the Web for business and personal purposes.

An intranet is an internal corporate network built using Internet and World Wide Web standards and products. It is used by the employees of an organization to gain access to corporate information. Computers using web server software store and manage documents built on the Web's HTML format. With a web browser on your PC, you can call up any web document – no matter what kind of computer it is on. Because web browsers run on any type of computer, the same electronic information can be viewed by any employee. That means that all sorts of documents can be converted to electronic form on the Web and constantly be updated.

An extranet is a network that links selected resources of the intranet of a company with its customers, suppliers, or other business partners. It is also built around web technologies. Security and performance concerns are different for an extranet than for a website or network-based intranet. User authentication and privacy are critical on an extranet. Obviously, performance must be good to provide quick response to customers and suppliers.

Management issues and service and speed affect all networks. No centralized governing body controls the Internet. Also, because the amount of Internet traffic is so large, service bottlenecks often occur. Privacy, fraud, and security issues must continually be addressed and resolved.

Self-Assessment Test

1 Voice and phone communications are examples of asynchronous communications. True or false?

2 Two broad categories of transmission media are _____.
   a. guided and wireless
   b. shielded and unshielded
   c. twisted and untwisted
   d. infrared and microwave

3 Some utilities, cities, and organizations are experimenting with the use of _____ to provide network connections over standard high-voltage power lines.

4 Which of the following is a telecommunications service that delivers high-speed Internet access to homes and small businesses over existing phone lines?
   a. BPL
   b. DSL
   c. Wi-Fi
   d. Ethernet

5 A device that encodes data from two or more devices onto a single communications channel is called a(n) _____.

6 A(n) _____ is a network that can connect technology devices within a range of 10 metres (33 feet) or so.

7 _____ is a company that provides people and organizations with access to the Internet.

8 What is the standard page description language for web pages?
   a. Home Page Language
   b. Hypermedia Language
   c. Java
   d. Hypertext Markup Language (HTML)

9 A(n) _____ is a network based on web technology that links customers, suppliers, and others to the company.

10 An intranet is an internal corporate network built using Internet and World Wide Web standards and products. True or false?

Review Questions

1 What is the difference between synchronous and asynchronous communications? Give examples.

2 What advantages and disadvantages are associated with the use of client/server computing?

3 Describe a local area network and its various components.

4 What is a metropolitan area network?

5 List some uses for a personal area network.

6 What is a domain name?

7 What are Telnet and FTP used for?

8 What is the Web?

9 What is an intranet? Provide three examples of the use of an intranet.

10 What is an extranet? How is it different from an intranet?

Discussion Questions

1 How might you use a local area network in your home? What devices might eventually connect to such a network?

2 Why is an organization that employs centralized processing likely to have a different management decision-making philosophy than an organization that employs distributed processing?

3 Identify three companies with which you are familiar that are using the Web to conduct business. Describe their use of the Web.

4 One of the key issues associated with the development of a website is getting people to visit it. If you were developing a website, how would you inform others about it and make it interesting enough that they would return and also tell others about it?

5 How could you use the Internet if you were a travelling salesperson?

Web Exercises

1 The Internet can be a powerful source of information about various industries and organizations. Locate several industry or organization websites. Which website is the best designed? Which one provides the most amount of information?

2 Research some of the potential disadvantages of using the Internet, such as privacy, fraud, or unauthorized websites. Write a brief report on what you have found.

Case One

Delivering People

Scott Boyes has worked in the Canadian transportation industry for years. The company he worked for previously shuttled railway crew members to train locations where they were needed. Scott found that this company was slow to adopt new telecommunications technologies. The van drivers who shuttled the railway workers could not communicate with the dispatcher while en route. At each stop, the drivers would have to call the dispatcher to find out where to go next. This problem frustrated all involved, especially the railways that paid for the shuttle service. 'With an eye to controlling their margins and cutting costs, railways want more accurate ETAs from their crew transportation providers and the flexibility to accept new trip orders and reroute quickly,' Boyes said. He added, 'This is something the current providers can't give them.'

Boyes recognized that the business was in a quagmire and not about to change. He identified an opportunity for a new tech-savvy business to enter the market and provide the level of service that the railways wanted. Boyes felt that he was the person that could deliver that service. In May 2005, he founded Toronto-based RailCrewXpress and hired some of his former co-workers to help build the company. From day one, Scott Boyes and his associates saw telecommunications technology and information systems as the key to set the company apart from the competition.

'The whole premise of our pitch to our investors and the railways was the technology platform on which we intended to serve the railways,' said Boyes. He worked with a mobile computing hardware company, Mississauga, and a mobile wireless software provider, MobileDataforce, to create a unique wireless telecommunications system that connects drivers with dispatchers and the company information systems. The system tracks drivers from home base and provides dispatchers with the power to manage routing dynamically while vehicles are en route.

Not only does the system allow for dynamic routing changes, but it also collects information and develops a history that includes routes and driving times. It can then analyze this data to optimize the efficiency of dispatches and routing. The system also automates the tasks of billing customers and paying drivers.

The biggest challenge in building the system was using the most economical networking technologies based on the location of the van. The system is designed to automatically switch between satellite and general packet radio service (GPRS) data transmission, depending on the van's location. The less costly GPRS is used in populated areas where coverage is available, and expensive satellite service is used outside of GPRS coverage areas. The system can intelligently decide how much information to send and when so that it does not lose information when switching between technologies. Their next project involves using magnetic-strip readers or RFID scanners in vans to scan passenger ID badges, and track their locations much the way UPS and other shipping companies track the movement of packages.

Questions

1 What advantages does RailCrewXpress have over its competition, Scott's former employer?

2 How does the concept of real-time monitoring relate to RailCrewXpress? In general, what is the benefit of real-time monitoring?

3 What mistakes did Boyes' previous employer make? How could they have prevented Boyes from leaving and creating formidable competition?

4 How do you think Boyes' previous employer will react to the new competition? What is RailCrewXpress doing to ensure its dominance in the market?

SOURCES: Jedras, Jeff, 'A Tech Team Effort Keeps the Trains Running on Time', *Computer World Canada,* www.itworldcanada.com, February 17, 2006; Press release, 'RailCrewXpress Selects MobileDataForce as Part of Team Delivering Mobile Computing Solution for Transport Fleet', www.prweb.com/releases/2006/1/prweb334473.htm, January 18, 2006.

Case Two

Firwood Paints on the Web

Firwood Paints in Bolton, England, manufactures specialty paints and surface coatings for industrial applications. Established in 1925, the company operates from three U.K. sites servicing over 2000 global customers. Firwood employs 50 people who research, develop, test, and manufacture high-performance products to precise British standards.

Until recently, customers relied on telephone and fax communications to place orders with Firwood. As the company grew, the cost of processing orders became a concern to Firwood management. Most disturbing was that the cost of processing small orders was as high as for large orders. Firwood wanted to implement a system that would increase its customer base, while decreasing the amount it was spending on transaction processing. Martin Wallen, managing director at Firwood, explains: 'The market was getting increasingly competitive as volumes and margins shrank, and we needed a strategy that would reverse this trend, help us reach new markets, improve customer service to retain existing accounts, and cut the costs of doing business on smaller accounts.'

Firwood engaged Stratagem, an information systems consulting firm, which recommended a web solution. An interactive website would allow Firwood to offer better service and information to all of its customers and provide self-service sales for smaller orders, freeing its sales force to focus on big accounts.

Firwood had recently installed new enterprise resource planning (ERP) systems to improve the company's efficiency. The challenge was to develop a web-based system for its customers that would seamlessly connect to its current information infrastructure. Because its ERP systems and servers were designed by IBM, Firwood looked to IBM solutions for its new web-based system. Martin Wallen explains the new system: 'when customers place orders online, the integrated solution generates all the necessary internal documentation, avoiding human error, saving time, and giving us a clearer audit trail and analysis tool than we have ever had before.'

The introduction of web-based ordering and account management is expected to lead to a

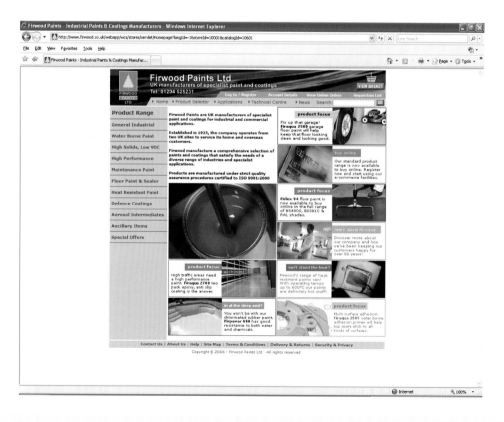

dramatic reduction in administrative workload for Firwood, saving time and money. Small customers can order single and lower-value items at low transaction costs to the company thanks to the automated sales data-entry system. The website also provides enhanced customer service with online account information served directly from the internal ERP system.

Internet and web technologies have provided valuable communications links between people, businesses, and organizations. Data, voice, and video are streaming over the Internet backbone as people and automated systems communicate, access information, and conduct business. Like Firwood, most businesses are doing away with older, less efficient, and more expensive methods of communication and turning to new Internet technologies.

Questions

1 Why is it important that the new web system connects to Firwood's current information infrastructure

2 What would be the difference between the old and new system, from the customer's point of view?

3 What do you think is the Internet's primary advantage for a small business such as Firwood?

4 Can you think of any disadvantages the new system might have?

SOURCES: Staff, 'Firwood Paints Brightens Up Sales with Web Innovation', *IBM Success Story*, www.ibm.com, January 19, 2005; Firwood Paints (website), www.firwood.co.uk, April 21, 2006.

Case Three

6

FUJI Market Switches to Web-Based Ordering System

FUJI Market is the largest supermarket chain by sales and size in Shikoku, one of Japan's four main islands. FUJI has nearly 90 stores and 10 000 employees and is growing rapidly. Many companies are making use of networking technologies, databases, and information systems to centralize business operations. Although centralization provides a unified view of business activities, some business functions are best left decentralized. As businesses grow, it takes more time to route all transactions through a central authority. When FUJI made this discovery, it decided to allow individual stores to make their own operating decisions and to replace old ways of doing business with more efficient processes.

'After we grew beyond 80 stores, it became almost impossible for us to continue making operational and marketing decisions centrally from our headquarters,' says Toshihiko Yamanaka, manager of M2 Systems Co., Ltd., a subsidiary of FUJI Company Ltd. that provides IT services to the supermarket chain. For example, FUJI's order placement system for perishable goods was inefficient and wasteful. FUJI headquarters ordered perishable goods for all 80 stores. 'We had to call or fax written requests to our suppliers by noon. Employees estimated how much of each item they thought their store would need, even though it was still too early to accurately predict what the inventory level would be later in the day', explains Yamanaka.

FUJI's inflexible mainframe-based system made it difficult for employees at the individual stores to order their own stock. To do so would require installing 1000 terminals, each requiring proprietary client software and dedicated lines for data communications in the stores and at the vendor locations. FUJI searched for a more practical alternative.

FUJI restructured its store operations with new systems that use Internet and Java technology-based web applications. Web-based inventory and merchandise applications were installed based on IBM WebSphere software. New application and database servers were installed to support the system, named the SEISEN ordering system. The SEISEN ordering system allows employees at each store to order produce, deli items, dairy, and meat via the Web. It provides employees with an electronic order book to confirm sales results to determine how much merchandise to order. Employees can review estimated customer visits, budgets, and losses resulting from discarded items to assist them in placing orders.

'Having a web-based application helps employees interact quickly and easily with our suppliers and place orders later in the day when they can better estimate the stock they need,' explains Yamanaka. The system has provided multiple benefits. By avoiding the installation of specialized terminals and software at each store, the company has saved ¥71 million and avoids the associated ongoing maintenance costs. With one vendor for all its hardware and software components, FUJI can keep system management simple, speed application development, and ensure that it can easily integrate new components as its infrastructure grows. Resource costs are expected to decline because the new web-based applications are easier to use and do not require additional specialized training or knowledge.

With its new SEISEN ordering system in place, FUJI is now looking to restructure other store operations such as its supply chain management (SCM) system and, eventually, customer relationship management (CRM) system. It is planning to use Internet and web technologies for all of its information systems to minimize operational waste, enable decentralized decision making at each store, and lower IT costs.

Questions

1 Why was the Internet and web a better alternative to a private network for FUJI's order processing system?

2 Why do you think FUJI decided to use a system based on Java technology and web applications?

3 What concerns might FUJI executives have about sending private business transactions over a public network? What precautions can they apply to address those concerns?

4 How do you think the vendors that supply FUJI's perishable goods have been affected by this new system?

SOURCES: IBM Success Stories, 'FUJI Company Rings Up Operational Savings with IBM Web-based Solutions', www.ibm.com, February 28, 2006; FUJI Co. (website), 'Fuji Co., Ltd.: Company Snapshot', www.corporateinformation.com/snapshot.asp?Cusip=C39236560, May 2, 2006.

© Jeremy Sutton-Hibbert/Alamy

Notes

[1] Webster, John S., 'Ethernet Over Copper', *Computerworld,* March 27, 2006.

[2] Di Stefano, Theodore F., 'India's Hi-Tech Dominance: How Did IT Happen?, *E-Commerce Times,* April 14, 2006.

[3] Orzech, Dan, 'Surfing Through the Power Grid', *Wired News,* October 20, 2005.

[4] Pappalardo, Denise, 'Ford Not Quite in Cruise Control', www.networkworld.com, *Network World,* February 27, 2006.

[5] Honan, Mathew, 'Apple Unveils Intel-Powered Mac Minis', *Computerworld,* February 28, 2006.

[6] Blau, John, 'Metro Shows Voice-Operated RFID Device at CeBIT', *Computerworld,* March 8, 2006.

[7] Mearian, Lucas, 'Google Earth's Photographer Builds Out Infrastructure', *Computerworld,* March 1, 2006.

[8] Staff, 'EasyStreet and OnFibre Bring State-of-the-Art Network to Portland', Press Releases, OnFibre (website), www.onfibre.com, January 20, 2005.

[9] Betts, Mitch, 'Global Dispatches: Hitachi Replacing PCs with Thin Clients to Boost Security', *Computerworld,* May 30, 2005.

[10] About Us – Strategic Relationships – Marks & Spencer – Cable & Wireless (website), www.cw.com/US/about_us/strategic_relationships/cisco/cisco_customers_ms.html.

[11] Dubie, Denise, 'Sierra Pacific Taps Open Source Management Tools', *Network World,* December 12, 2005.

[12] Staff, 'China Tightens Web-Content Rules', *Wall Street Journal,* September 26, 2005, B3.

[13] Hafner, Katie, 'Where Wizards Stay Up Late: The Origins of the Internet', Touchstone, Rockefeller Center, New York, New York, 1996.

[14] Internet2 (website), November 29, 2005, www.internet2.edu.

[15] Miller, Michael, 'Web Portals Make a Comeback', *PC Magazine,* October 4, 2005, p. 7.

[16] Pike, Sarah, 'The Expert's Guide to Google, Yahoo!, MSN, and AOL', *PC Magazine,* October 4, 2005, p. 112.

[17] Guth, Robert, et al., 'Sky-High Search Wars', *Wall Street Journal,* May 24, 2005, p. B1.

[18] Staff, 'Microsoft Looks for a Place Among Competitors with MSN Local Search', *Rocky Mountain News,* June 21, 2005, p. 6B.

[19] Staff, 'Study: Web Site's Appearance Matters', *CNN Online,* August 11, 2005.

[20] Hof, Robert, 'Mix, Match, and Mutate', *Business Week,* July 25, 2005, p. 72.

6

World Views Case

Australian Film Studio Benefits from Broadband Networks . . . and Location

Sigi Goode
The Australian National University

It's been a hectic 24 hours at Fire Is a Liquid Films, a small Australian film-production studio. The firm's 18 staff members have just finished rendering scenes from three feature films, pitched ideas for two TV commercials, and delivered two milestone (progress) updates to production clients. Thanks to the power of broadband networking, the employees have accomplished most of this work without leaving their small studio. Of her company's tight deadlines and advanced technology, Toni Brasting, managing director, explains, 'We play to our strengths in terms of location and technology.

'Our work ranges from cleaning up footage to improve color or contrast, up to full-blown CGI modeling and rendering. We work with TV commercials right up to feature film houses, and from one or two frames up to entire scenes. We can capitalize on our geographic location. With most feature films being shot in the U.S. or Europe, [clients] can send us their digital footage before they go to bed, and we can work on the scene during our daytime. By the time they wake up, the processed footage is ready and waiting for them. We rely heavily on our broadband network infrastructure to move digital data around. Depending on the quality and duration of the footage, the upload process can take anywhere from a few minutes for a brief scene to a few hours for an entire feature at DVD quality. Most of our clients prefer to deal with individual scenes in this way because it allows them to shuffle their work flow priorities around.

'Most films and commercials used to be shot on 35 mm analogue film, which can take time to process. The trend is moving more and more towards digital video because it can be easily edited and manipulated. With 35mm, if you wanted to bid on work with a film studio, it helped if you were fairly close by so [that] you could have access to the film reels for digitizing purposes. With the advent of digital video and broadband networking, we can bid on projects anywhere in the world, from the *Matrix* to *28 Days Later*. The actors can get a better feel for each scene, and the director can place each scene in greater context: Their vision comes to life quicker.

Mark Evans/Istock

Michael Kurtz/Istock

'For editing, we mostly use Final Cut Pro on our Macintosh systems – the Macs are easy to use, and they look good, too (which impresses clients when they tour the studio). They run Mac OS X, which was originally based on BSD UNIX. Occasionally, we need to develop a new technique for a project, so it's useful to have access to software source code. Mac OS X gives us good support for our own open-source Linux tools.

'Another technique we use is laptop imaging. Clients like the feeling that we're taking care of them and that they are our focus. When one of our teams goes to meet a client for a pitch or a milestone up-date, they can pull a laptop off the shelf and build a customized hard-drive image right from their desk-top with Norton Ghost or one of our home-brewed imaging applications. The image software 'bakes' a hard-drive image on the fly, which includes the OS, editing software, and relevant film footage. If nec-essary, we can also include correspondence and storyboards – we can have that client's entire rela-tionship history right there in the meeting. We're also about to start phasing in tablet PCs with scribe pens so that we can work on potential storyboards during the meeting itself.

'The other important part of our processing platform is our render farm. It's basically a room full of identical Linux-based PCs, which work on a problem in parallel. We use commodity PC hardware and high-speed networking to allow each machine to work on the problem at once. It means we can get supercomputer performance at a fraction of the cost. We use our desktop machines to edit in draft res-olution (which is of inferior quality but much faster to render or preview). When we're happy with the cut, we 'rush it' to the render farm to process the final piece of footage. We also offer render farm leasing services, so other film companies can send us their raw model files, use the render farm over the net-work, and then download their completed footage. We then invoice them for processing time – they never have to leave their offices'.

Questions

1 How might open-source software benefit a small business? What problems might a small business encounter when using open-source software?

2 The studio profiled in this case processes tasks during a client firm's downtime. What other tasks could be accomplished more inexpensively or more efficiently by using providers in other geographic locations?

3 What other types of firms could also benefit from a render farm? What firms do you know of that actively make use of this technology?

4 Are modern firms too reliant on electronic networking? If so, what can be done about this drawback? What paper-based systems could the firm use if its electronic systems fail?

5 How might wireless networking improve the operation of systems such as this firm's render farm?

Note: All names have been changed at the request of the interviewee.

World Views Case

Virtual Learning Environment Provides Instruction Flexibility

Vida Bayley and Kathy Courtney
Coventry University, United Kingdom

One of the major components of Coventry University's teaching and learning strategy has been the introduction and use of a Virtual Learning Environment (VLE) using the WebCT (Web Course Tools) product platform. The Joint Information Systems Committee (JISC) in the U.K. has set out a definition of a Virtual Learning Environment and states that it refers to the components that support online interactions of various kinds taking place between learners and tutors.

A central aim of the university was to enhance face-to-face teaching and to offer greater flexibility to both teaching staff and students. It created a central support unit – CHED (Centre for Higher Education Development) – to introduce and develop new initiatives in teaching and learning across the university. In addition, a task force of academic staff was established to lead and facilitate these initiatives in collaboration with CHED. Through these developments and with the support of the university's Computing Services unit, WebCT was implemented as a core instrument in achieving the university's educational vision. The WebCT application allows course material and resources to be placed on the Web and provides staff and students with a set of tools that can be customized to course and module requirements. In brief, it also contains the following functions, which JISC considers to be essential features of a VLE:

Controlled access to curriculum with mapping to elements that can be individually assessed and recorded
Tracking mechanisms for student activities and performance
Support of online learning through content development
Communication and feedback mechanisms between various participants in the learning process
Incorporation of links to other internal/external systems

In line with the aims and goals of the VLE strategy, Coventry Business School has been active for a number of years in the development of curricula and modules to create innovative learning communities and to engage students in the learning process. One of the most successful programs the Business School developed was the B.A. in Business Enterprise (B.A.B.E) degree. The Business Enterprise course was a learning program designed to develop graduates who would be able to proactively manage business-related tasks, solve business problems, and influence the business environment in which they work. A central element of the program was that it would enable students to lay the foundation for lifelong learning, in which students take responsibility for continual learning and personal development through a variety of media. The incorporation of WebCT into the B.A.B.E program marked a significant departure from established methods of teaching, learning, and assessment in the Business School.

Although the school had previously used a variety of computer-based activities within the learning environment, their use was limited to individual modules and in many cases even restricted. In accounting and information technology courses, software products such as EQL tutorials (EQL International Ltd. is a developer of e-learning and computer-based assessment solutions) were used as supplementary teaching material and for online assessment or self-test exercises. The WinEcon package (PC-based introductory economics software) had been developed with Bristol University through a consortium of eight U.K. economics departments and was used by the Economics subject group in course teaching. In other subject areas, the teaching staff provided students with web URLs related to particular reading or assessment topics, which could be easily accessed via the Internet.

Chris Schmidt/Istock

In contrast, the Business Enterprise program was designed for delivery via the World Wide Web, so module delivery, program management, and staff/student communication were all built around WebCT.

This program was the first to be offered by the university via the World Wide Web. And it was significant because it was not designed solely for distance learning but rather to make use of the range of tools offered by the WebCT platform for teaching and learning both within a classroom setting and off campus via the Internet. WebCT tools were used to structure and to provide web-based access to course and module materials, and communications facilities were adapted to dovetail with existing classroom-based teaching and learning. Of particular importance was the consideration by the teaching team of how the Web software features could add value to the traditional teaching/learning modes and methods that they would be supporting or replacing. This evaluation in turn spurred individual lecturers to examine their teaching practice, stimulated ideas about the applicability of web-based teaching, and encouraged staff to develop their knowledge of and skills related to the university's intranet and the Internet. After these opportunities were identified and placed within the context of the module and course objectives, lecturers then customized the WebCT features and integrated them within the overall teaching and learning framework. The benefit to students is flexibility: Course and module content is accessible from outside the university and outside of teaching hours. Course materials either can be placed within WebCT as HTML documents (so they can be edited directly online) or can be uploaded as individual applications, such as PowerPoint slides, Word documents, and Excel spreadsheets.

Effective communication and feedback are important aspects of a successful learning environment. One way of facilitating peer group communication and communication between students and staff was to use the discussion forum/bulletin board facilities provided by the software. The B.A.B.E program used this feature as the primary mode of delivering information to the student community. All course- and module-related announcements, such as class rescheduling, changes to assessment deadlines, and meeting arrangements, for example, were made via the main bulletin board. The flexibility that the software provides for creating discussion areas allowed lecturers to construct arenas for students to work individually on specific projects yet be involved as group members in discussions centred on common themes. Being asynchronous, these discussion groups allowed students to become involved in an ongoing exchange of ideas, reflect on their own and others' contributions, and thereby facilitate their own learning. In addition to the discussion forum, WebCT incorporates a chat facility that can enable a small group of students to participate in online, real-time conversations. An additional advantage of this type of synchronous communication is that both students and lecturers could develop group management and e-moderation skills. In addition, the Business School linked the Web e-mail facilities available in WebCT to the e-mail provided to all students by Coventry University, allowing messages to be transmitted within modules. This meant that messages were module specific and did not get lost in the larger system – especially in modules with large numbers of students.

The student presentation area of WebCT was used to allow students to create their own web pages, which could be displayed and shared, thus providing them with an opportunity to gain new skills and an understanding of an important part of the processes involved in managing a business enterprise.

The Business School also uses STile, a portal that was developed to provide students with a range of resources that are available on the university's intranet. The portal contains an easy-to-use link to WebCT.

In the course of the development of the B.A.B.E program, it became apparent that for the success of new IT innovations, such as web-based teaching, the project staff must identify and involve key stakeholders, particularly when a radical restructuring of teaching and learning methods is needed. These stakeholders include administrative personnel, teaching professionals, and also those who are at the very centre of learning activity – the student body. The university benefited greatly by actively involving students and staff in the design, use, and evaluation of their educational environment. The experience of the B.A.B.E venture highlighted the fact that in order to transform the students' learning experience, all the stakeholders needed to understand how to construct a fit between the needs and expectations of the learner, the skills and pedagogical tools of the practitioners, and the tools available within the VLE. The rewards have been great. The establishment of a VLE, with WebCT as its centre, has generated a new excitement in the approach to university teaching, stimulating reflection, reinvention, and transformation and creating a 'journey of learning' for both students and teaching staff.

Although the B.A.B.E degree program has now been modified under the current course structure, many of its innovative features have been transferred and embedded into teaching and learning processes across the whole of the undergraduate business program.

In addition, WebCT has enabled the Business School to introduce and develop with business partners new, forward-looking projects, such as the development and delivery of the Post Graduate Certificate, Post Graduate Diploma, and MA in Communications Management via the Cable and Wireless Virtual Academy. It has also played a significant role in the establishment of learning communities and development of work-based learning projects with public-sector organizations such as the National Health Service, local authorities, and private-sector enterprises.

Questions

1 Why do you think that a discussion forum would motivate you to use the Internet to access learning resources?

2 What do you think the use of e-mail facilities would contribute to your learning?

3 Discuss the advantages that a VLE with Internet access could offer students in developing their learning. Are there any disadvantages?

4 Identify and discuss the different types of contributions that various stakeholders could make to a student's learning process.

PART 3

Business Information Systems

07

Operational Systems

Principles

An organization must have information systems that support the routine, day-to-day activities that occur in the normal course of business and help a company add value to its products and services.

Traditional transaction processing systems support the various business functions of organizations that have not yet implemented enterprise resource planning systems.

Electronic and mobile commerce allow transactions to be made by the customer, with less need for sales staff, and open up new opportunities for conducting business.

A company that implements an enterprise resource planning system is creating a highly integrated set of systems, which can lead to many business benefits.

Learning Objectives

- Identify the basic activities and business objectives common to all transaction processing systems.
- Identify key control and management issues associated with transaction processing systems.

- Describe the inputs, processing, and outputs for the transaction processing systems associated with the order processing, purchasing, and accounting business functions.

- Define e- and m-commerce and describe various forms of e-commerce.

- Identify the challenges multinational corporations must face in planning, building, and operating their transaction processing systems.
- Discuss the advantages and disadvantages associated with the implementation of an enterprise resource planning system.

You might recall from Chapter 2 that operational systems support the day-to-day running of a firm. Operational systems, such as transaction processing systems (TPS), allow firms to buy and sell. Without systems to perform these functions, the firm could not operate. Organizations today are moving from a collection of non-integrated transaction processing systems to highly integrated enterprise resource planning systems to perform routine business processes and maintain records about them. These systems support a wide range of business activities associated with supply chain management and customer relationship management (as mentioned in Chapter 1). Although they were initially thought to be cost-effective only for very large companies, even small and mid-sized companies are now implementing these systems to reduce costs and improve service.

Employees who work directly with customers – whether in sales, customer service, or marketing – require high-quality transaction processing systems and their associated information to provide good customer service. Companies selling online need electronic- and mobile-commerce software to allow customer to perform transactions. No matter what your role, it is very likely that you will provide input to or use the output from your organization's systems. Your effective use of these systems will be essential to raise the productivity of your firm, improve customer service, and enable better decision making. Thus, it is important that you understand how these systems work and what their capabilities and limitations are. This chapter begins by discussing the various TPS of a typical organization and also covers the use of systems to provide a set of integrated and coordinated systems to meet the needs of the firm.

7.1 Transaction Processing Systems

Every organization has many transaction processing systems (TPS). These systems include order processing, inventory control, payroll, accounts payable, accounts receivable, and the general ledger, to name just a few. The input to these systems includes basic business transactions, such as a customer placing an order, an employee purchasing supplies, a customer payment, an employee signing on and off at the start and end of a day. The processing activities include data collection, data editing, data correction, data manipulation, data storage, and document production. The result of processing business transactions is that the organization's records are updated to reflect the status of the operation at the time of the last processed transaction.

A TPS also has a second important function – it collects data which is input to other essential information systems – management information systems, decision support systems, and other special-purpose information systems (all discussed in the following chapters). A transaction processing system serves as the foundation for these other systems. These higher-level systems require the basic business transaction data captured by the TPS (see Figure 7.1).

Transaction processing systems support routine operations in the business. The amount of support for decision making that a TPS directly provides managers and workers is low.

Because TPS often perform activities related to customer contacts – such as order processing and invoicing – these information systems play a critical role in providing value to the customer. For example, by capturing and tracking the movement of each package, shippers such as FedEx can provide timely and accurate data on the exact location of a package. Shippers and receivers can access an online database and, by providing the air bill number of a package, find the package's current location. If the package has been delivered, they can see who signed for it (a service that is especially useful in large companies where packages can become 'lost' in internal distribution systems and mailrooms). Such a system provides the basis for added value through improved customer service (Figure 7.2).

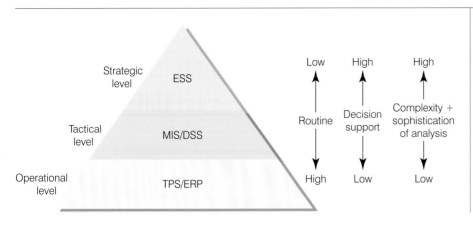

Figure 7.1 TPS, ERP and MIS/DSS in Perspective

Figure 7.2 *FedEx adds value to its service by providing timely and accurate data online on the exact location of a package.*

7.1.1 Traditional Transaction Processing Methods and Objectives

With **batch processing systems**, business transactions are accumulated over a period of time and prepared for processing as a single unit or batch (see Figure 7.3a). Transactions are accumulated for the appropriate length of time needed to meet the needs of the users of that system. For example, it might be important to process invoices and customer payments for the accounts receivable system daily. On the other hand, the payroll system might receive process data weekly to create cheques, update employee earnings records, and distribute labour costs. The essential characteristic of a batch processing system is that there is some delay between an event and the eventual processing of the related transaction to update the organization's records.

With **online transaction processing (OLTP)**, each transaction is processed immediately, without the delay of accumulating transactions into a batch (see Figure 7.3b). Consequently, at any time, the data in an online system reflects the

batch processing system A form of data processing where business transactions are accumulated over a period of time and prepared for processing as a single unit or batch.

online transaction processing (OLTP) A form of data processing where each transaction is processed immediately, without the delay of accumulating transactions into a batch.

Figure 7.3 Batch
Versus Online
Transaction Processing
*(a) Batch processing inputs
and processes data in
groups. (b) In online
processing, transactions
are completed as they
occur.*

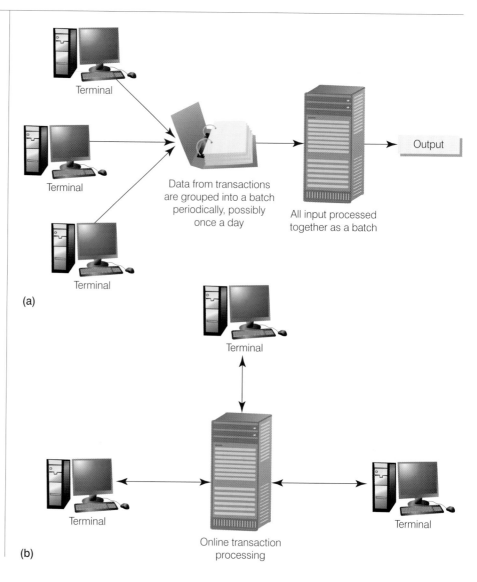

current status. This type of processing is essential for businesses that require access to current data such as airlines, ticket agencies, and stock investment firms. Many companies find that OLTP helps them provide faster, more efficient service, one way to add value to their activities in the eyes of the customer. Increasingly, companies are using the Internet to capture and process transaction data such as customer orders and shipping information from e-commerce applications.

Although the technology is advanced enough, TPS applications do not always run using on-line processing. For many applications, batch processing is more appropriate and cost effective. Payroll transactions and billing are typically done via batch processing. Specific goals of the organization define the method of transaction processing best suited for the various applications of the company.

Because of the importance of transaction processing, organizations expect their TPS to accomplish a number of specific objectives, some of which are listed next. Depending on the specific nature and goals of the organization, any of these objectives might be more important than others.

■ *Process data generated by and about transactions.* The primary objective of any TPS is to capture, process, and update databases of business data required to support routine business activities. Utilities, telecommunications companies, and financial-services organizations especially are under pressure to process ever-larger volumes of online transactions.

■ *Maintain a high degree of accuracy and integrity.* Ensuring that the data is processed accurately and completely is critical because reports generated by the TPS are used to execute key operational activities such as filling customer orders and scheduling shipments to various customer locations.

■ *Avoid processing fraudulent transactions.* Related to data integrity is the need to avoid processing fraudulent transactions. Standard Chartered, a London-based international bank, recently implemented anti-money-laundering software to monitor banking trans-actions against terrorist watch lists, and flags transactions between individuals, organiza-tions, or countries deemed high risk.[1]

■ *Produce timely user responses and reports.* The ability to conduct business transactions quickly can be essential for an organization's bottom line. For instance, if bills (invoices) are sent to customers a few days later than planned, payment is delayed, possibly forc-ing the firm to seek costly short-term borrowing to avoid cash flow problems. As a result, firms employ monitoring systems to measure and ensure system performance.

■ *Increase labour efficiency.* Before businesses used computers, manual processes often required rooms full of administrators and office equipment to process the necessary busi-ness transactions. Today, TPS substantially reduce these and other labour requirements.

■ *Help improve customer service.* Another objective of a TPS is to assist an organization in providing fast, efficient service.

■ *Help build and maintain customer loyalty.* A firm's TPS are often the means for customers to communicate. Customer interaction with these systems must, therefore, keep cus-tomers satisfied and returning. A recent web study by Allulent, Inc., found that 55 percent of consumers surveyed said that a frustrating online shopping experience diminishes their overall opinion of that retailer. Surprisingly, nearly 33 percent said they might stop shopping at the retailer's brick-and-mortar store as well.[2]

■ *Achieve competitive advantage.* A goal common to almost all organizations is to gain and maintain a competitive advantage (discussed in Chapter 2). When a TPS is devel-oped or modified, the personnel involved should carefully consider the significant and long-term benefits the new or modified system might provide. Table 7.1 summarizes some of the ways that companies can use transaction processing systems to achieve competitive advantage.

Table 7.1 Examples of Transaction Processing Systems for Competitive Advantage

Competitive Advantage	Example
Customer loyalty increased	Customer interaction system to monitor and track each customer interaction with the company
Superior service provided to customers	Tracking systems that customers can access to determine shipping status
Better relationship with suppliers	Internet marketplace to allow the company to purchase products from suppliers at discounted prices
Superior information gathering	Order configuration system to ensure that products ordered will meet customers' objectives
Costs dramatically reduced	Warehouse management system employing RFID technology to reduce labour hours and improve inventory accuracy
Inventory levels reduced	Collaborative planning, forecasting, and replenishment to ensure the right amount of inventory is in stores

7.1.2 Transaction Processing Activities

TPS capture and process data of fundamental business transactions. This data is used to update databases and to produce a variety of reports people both within and outside the enterprise use. The business data goes through a **transaction processing cycle** that includes data collection, data editing, data correction, data manipulation, data storage, and document production (see Figure 7.4).

transaction processing cycle The process of data collection, data editing, data correction, data manipulation, data storage, and document production.

Figure 7.4 Data-Processing Activities Common to Transaction Processing Systems

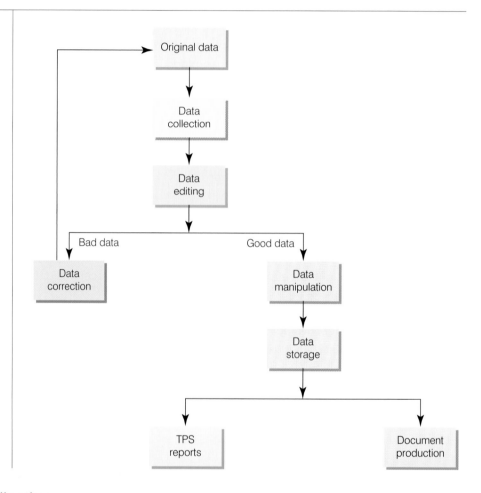

Data Collection

Capturing and gathering all data necessary to complete the processing of transactions is called **data collection**. In some cases, it can be done manually, such as by collecting handwritten sales orders or a customer typing in their credit card details on a web page. In other cases, data collection is automated via special input devices such as barcode scanners and RFID readers.

data collection Capturing and gathering all data necessary to complete the processing of transactions.

Data collection begins with a transaction (e.g., taking a customer order) and results in data that serves as input to the TPS. Data should be captured at its source and recorded accurately in a timely fashion, with minimal manual effort, and in an electronic or digital form that can be directly entered into the computer. This approach is called 'source data automation'. An example of source data automation is a barcode reader at a supermarket which speeds the checkout process. Using barcodes is quicker and more accurate than having a shop assistant enter codes manually at the cash register. The product ID for each item is determined automatically, and its price is retrieved from the item database. This TPS uses the price data to determine the customer's bill. It also updates the shop's inventory database and its database of purchases. This data is then used by the shop's management information systems to generate reports (discussed in the next chapter).

Data Editing and Correction

An important step in processing transaction data is to perform **data editing** for validity and completeness to detect any problems. For example, quantity and cost data must be numeric and names must be alphabetic; otherwise, the data is not valid. Often, the codes associated with an individual transaction are edited against a database containing valid codes. If any code entered (or scanned) is not present in the database, the transaction is rejected. For example, when you are buying something online, the system will usually check whether you have entered a correctly formatted e-mail address, and will not allow the transaction to proceed if you have not. A **data correction** involves re-entering data that was not typed or scanned properly. It is not enough simply to reject invalid data. The system should also provide error messages that alert those responsible for editing the data. Error messages must specify the problem so proper corrections can be made. For example, a scanned barcode must match a code in a master table of valid codes. If the code is misread or does not exist in the table, the shop assistant should be given an instruction to rescan the item or type the information manually.

data editing The process of checking data for validity and completeness.

data correction The process of re-entering data that was not typed or scanned properly.

Data Manipulation

Another major activity of a TPS is **data manipulation**, the process of performing calculations and other data transformations related to business transactions. Data manipulation can include classifying data, sorting data into categories, performing calculations, summarizing results, and storing data in the organization's database for further processing. In a payroll TPS, for example, data manipulation includes multiplying an employee's hours worked by the hourly pay rate. Overtime pay and tax deductions are also calculated.

data manipulation The process of performing calculations and other data transformations related to business transactions.

Data Storage

Data storage involves updating one or more databases with new transactions. As has already been emphasized several times in this chapter, this data can be further processed and manipulated by other systems so that it is available for management reporting and decision making. Thus, although transaction databases can be considered a by-product of transaction processing, they have a pronounced effect on nearly all other information systems and decision-making processes in an organization.

data storage The process of updating one or more databases with new transactions.

Document Production and Reports

Document production involves generating output records, documents, and reports. These can be hard-copy paper reports or displays on computer screens (sometimes referred to as 'soft copy'). Printed paycheques, for example, are hard-copy documents produced by a payroll TPS, whereas an outstanding balance report for invoices might be a soft-copy report displayed by an accounts receivable TPS.

document production The process of generating output records and reports.

In addition to major documents such as cheques and invoices, most TPS provide other useful management information and decision support, such as printed or on-screen reports that help managers and employees perform various activities. A report showing current inventory is one example; another might be a document listing items ordered from a supplier to help an administrator check the order for completeness when it arrives. A TPS can also produce reports required by law, such as tax statements.

Information Systems @ Work

Retailers Turn to Smart Carts

The retail industry is going through an extraordinary metamorphosis as transactions are increasingly supported by a wide variety of digital technologies. The previous chapter provided many examples of businesses expanding to the Web to reach more customers. New forms of transaction data collection are also evident in bricks-and-mortar stores. For example, consider the rapidly expanding number of self-service checkout systems in popular grocery stores, department stores, super discount stores, home warehouse stores, and even fast food restaurants.

Fujitsu calls it the 'pervasive retailing environment': the use of digital technologies to integrate wired and wireless network devices to facilitate transactions in retail stores. Self-serve checkouts are only the tip of the iceberg. Soon customers will have access to product information from any location in the store through devices like Fujitsu's U-Scan Shopper. Mounted on a shopping trolley, the U-Scan Shopper is a rugged wireless computer with an integral bar code scanner. The device provides services to shoppers as well as retailers.

The device reduces checkout time by allowing customers to scan and bag items themselves as they pick them off the shelves. Shoppers can view the running total to see exactly how much is being spent as they shop: no more surprises at the checkout counter. If an item is missing a price, the device can be used as a price-checker. Consumers can also use the U-Scan Shopper to place orders with departments in the store for pickup. For example, you can place a deli or prescription order when you arrive at the store and pick it up at the deli counter or pharmacy. The U-Scan Shopper also provides a store directory so you can easily find the department or goods you want.

U-Scan devices are integrated into the store network and Internet. This means customers can upload a shopping list to the store's website before leaving home, and then download the list to the shopping cart upon arriving at the store. When shopping is completed, the U-Scan device uploads information to the self-serve checkout and the shopper is out the door after a quick swipe of a debit or credit card.

For retailers, the U-Scan device offers what Fujitsu calls 'true 1:1 marketing' that enables personalized in-store advertisement campaigns that are relevant both to shoppers' preferences and to their location in the store. Location is determined by shelf-mounted, battery-powered infrared transmitters that track the movement of U-Scan devices through the store. As a shopper passes the condiments aisle, for example, the shopping cart display might post a message stating, 'It has been over a month since you purchased mustard. If you want to pick some up today, turn down this aisle.' A retailer can offer special deals to each consumer. For example, as a shopper passes the condiments aisle, a message on the U-Scan device might state, 'You have just won an electronic coupon for 89 pence off mustard. Turn now to take advantage of this special deal!'. The 89 pence would be deducted as the item is scanned on the U-Scan device.

Discussion Questions

1 What transaction processing services does the U-Scan Shopper provide for consumers?

2 How does U-Scan technology provide retailers with a competitive advantage? Why might you choose a U-Scan store over one without U-Scan devices?

3 What security concerns might be raised by retailers who adopt U-Scan technology? How do they compare with other TPS? How might they be addressed?

4 What other types of services might be provided for customers and retailers through U-Scan devices?

SOURCES: Wallace, Brice, 'U-Scan Could Be Your New Shopping Pal,' *Deseret Morning News,* http://deseretnews.com/dn/view/0,1249,605154892,00.html, September 18, 2005; staff, 'Wireless Shopping Cart Runs Windows CE', *Windows for Devices.com,* www.windowsfordevices.com, February 18, 2005; Fujitsu Transaction Solutions Inc. (website), www.fujitsu.com/us/services/retailing, accessed, May 4, 2006.

7

7.2 Traditional Transaction Processing Applications

This section presents an overview of several common transaction processing systems that support the order processing, purchasing, and accounting business functions (see Table 7.2).

Table 7.2 Systems that Support Order Processing, Purchasing, and Accounting Functions

Order Processing	Purchasing	Accounting
Order processing	Inventory control (raw materials, packing materials, spare parts, and supplies)	Budget
Sales configuration		Accounts receivable
Shipment planning		Payroll
Shipment execution	Purchase order processing	Asset management
Inventory control (finished product)	Receiving	General ledger
Accounts receivable	Accounts payable	

7.2.1 Order Processing Systems

The traditional TPS for order processing include order entry, sales configuration, shipment planning, shipment execution, inventory control, and accounts receivable. Running these systems efficiently and reliably is critical to an enterprise. Figure 7.5 is a system-level flowchart that shows the various systems and the information that flows among them. Table 7.3 summarizes the input, processing, and output (IPO) of the essential systems that include the traditional order processing systems.

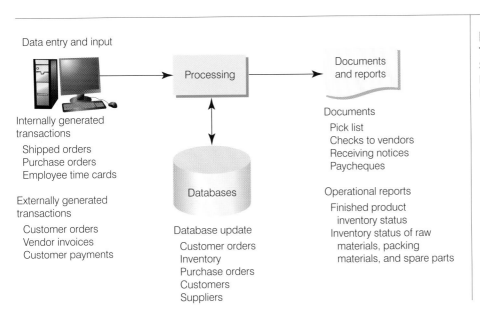

Figure 7.5 Traditional TPS Systems that Support the Order Processing Business Function

Data entry and input

Processing

Documents and reports

Internally generated transactions
Shipped orders
Purchase orders
Employee time cards

Externally generated transactions
Customer orders
Vendor invoices
Customer payments

Databases

Database update
Customer orders
Inventory
Purchase orders
Customers
Suppliers

Documents
Pick list
Checks to vendors
Receiving notices
Paycheques

Operational reports
Finished product inventory status
Inventory status of raw materials, packing materials, and spare parts

Beaulieu Group LLC is the third-largest carpet manufacturer in the world. Its major customers include U.S. home improvement chains The Home Depot and Lowe's Companies. Its most popular brands are Beaulieu, Coronet, Hollytex, and Laura Ashley Home. In an effort to stream-line its traditional order processing process, the firm equipped 250 of its commercial accounts sales staff with an order entry application that runs on a Pocket PC. With the new system, sales-people enter customer orders, access the company's pricing databases, and make changes to orders over a wireless network. If a wireless connection cannot be made at the customer's site, the salesperson can enter orders on the Pocket PC and then transmit the data later when com-munications can be established. The new process has improved the way salespeople interact with customers and reduced the time they spend filling out paperwork. Previously, orders had to be written out at a customer's site and then sent to the company's central office, where clerical workers keyed them into an order processing system. As a result, the salespeople spent too much time on administrative work entering and correcting orders and not enough time selling.

Table 7.3 IPO of the Traditional TPS Systems that Support Order Processing

System	Input	Processing	Output
Order entry	Customer order information via a variety of means: data entry by sales rep, customer input, mail, phone, e-commerce, or computer to computer via EDI or XML formats	Order is checked for completeness and accuracy. On-hand inventory is checked to ensure each item can be shipped in the quantity ordered or a substitute item is suggested	An open order record
Sales configuration	Customer order information including model and options desired	Review customer order information and ensure the configuration will meet the customer's needs; suggest additional options and features when appropriate	Revised customer order
Shipment planning	Open orders, i.e., orders received but not yet shipped	Determine which open orders will be filled when and from which location each order will be shipped to minimize delivery costs and meet customer desired delivery dates	Pick list for each order to be filled from each shipping location showing the items and quantities needed to fill the order
Shipment execution	Pick list and data entered by warehouse operations personnel as they fill the order	Data entered by warehouse operations personnel captured and used to update record of what was shipped to the customer	A shipped order record specifying exactly what was shipped to the customer – this can be different than what was ordered
Inventory control (finished product)	Record of each item picked to fill a customer order	Inventory records are updated to reflect current quantity of each item	Updated inventory database and various management reports
Accounts receivable	Shipped order records received from shipment execution that show precisely what was shipped on each order; payments from customers	Determine amount owed by each customer for each order placed	Invoice statement containing details of each order and its associated costs; customers' accounts receivable data is updated

7.2.2 Purchasing Systems

The traditional TPS that support the purchasing business function include inventory control, purchase order processing, receiving, and accounts payable (see Figure 7.6). Table 7.4 shows the input, processing, and output associated with this collection of systems. Figure 7.7 shows how RFID technology is helping inventory control.

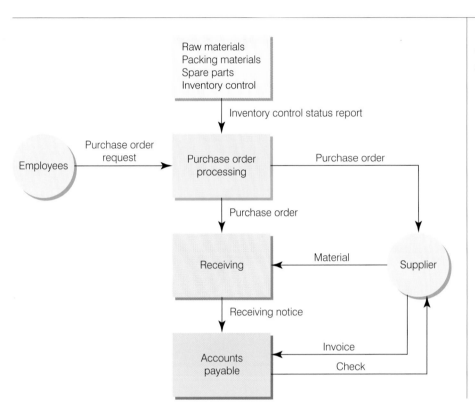

Figure 7.6 Traditional TPS Systems that Support the Purchasing Business Function

Table 7.4 IPO for the Traditional TPS Systems that Support Purchasing

System	Input	Processing	Output
Inventory control	Records reflecting any increase or decrease in the inventory of specific items of raw materials, packing materials, or spare parts	Withdrawals are subtracted from inventory counts of specific items; additions are added to the inventory count	The inventory record of each item is updated to reflect its current count
Purchase order processing	Inventory records, employee-prepared purchase order requests, information on preferred suppliers	Items that need to be ordered are identified, quantities to be ordered are determined, qualified supplier with whom to place the order is identified	Purchase orders are placed with preferred suppliers for items
Receiving	Information on the quantity and quality of items received	Receipt is matched to purchase order, input data is edited for accuracy and completeness	Receiving report is created, inventory records are updated to reflect new receipts
Accounts payable	Purchase orders placed, information on receipts, supplier invoices	Supplier invoice matched to original purchase order and receiving report	Payment generated to supplier

Figure 7.7 *Many companies use RFID tags to shorten order processing time and improve inventory accuracy*

SOURCE: Courtesy of Intermec Technologies.

7.2.3 Accounting Systems

accounting systems Systems that include budget, accounts receivable, payroll, asset management, and general ledger.

The primary **accounting systems** include the budget, accounts receivable, payroll, asset management, and general ledger (see Figure 7.8). Table 7.5 shows the input, processing, and output associated with these systems.

7.3 Electronic and Mobile Commerce

7.3.1 Electronic Commerce

electronic commerce Conducting business transactions (e.g., distribution, buying, selling, and servicing) electronically over computer networks such as the Internet, extranets, and corporate networks.

Electronic commerce is conducting a business transaction (e.g., distribution, buying, selling, and servicing) electronically over computer networks, primarily the Internet but also extranets, and corporate networks. Business activities that are strong candidates for conversion to e-commerce are paper based, time-consuming, and inconvenient for customers. Thus, some of the first business processes that companies converted to an e-commerce model were those related to buying and selling. Integrated e-commerce systems directly link a firm's website, which allows customers to place orders, with its order processing system. This is the traditional **business-to-consumer (B2C) e-commerce** model.

business-to-consumer (B2C) e-commerce A form of e-commerce in which customers deal directly with an organization and avoid intermediaries.

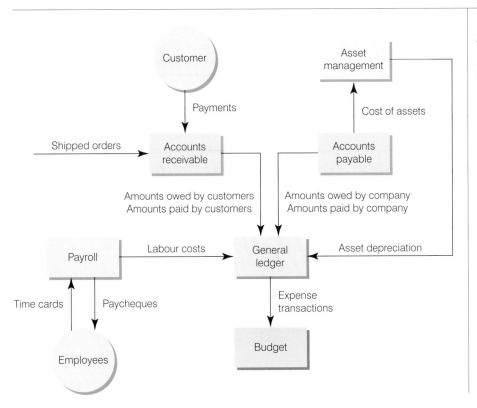

Figure 7.8 Traditional TPS Systems that Support the Accounting and Finance Business Function

Table 7.5 IPO for the Traditional TPS Systems that Support Accounting

System	Input	Processing	Output
Budget	Amounts budgeted for various categories of expense	Accumulates amount spent in each budget category	Budget status report showing amount under/over budget
Accounts receivable	Shipment records specifying exactly what was shipped to a customer	Determines amount to be paid by customer including delivery costs and taxes	Customer bills and monthly statements, management reports summarizing customer payments
Payroll	Number of hours worked by each employee, employee pay rate, employee tax and withholding information	Calculates employee gross pay and net pay and amount to be withheld for various taxing agencies and employee benefit programs	Payroll cheque and stub, payroll register (a summary report of all payroll transactions),W-2 forms
Asset management	Data regarding the purchase of capital assets	Calculates depreciation and net value of all corporate assets	Listing of all assets showing purchase price and current value after depreciation
General ledger	All transactions affecting the financial standing of the firm	Posts financial transactions to appropriate accounts specified in the firms chart of accounts	Financial reports such as the profit and loss statement, balance sheet

Early business-to-consumer (B2C) e-commerce pioneers competed with the traditional 'bricks-and-mortar' retailers. For example, in 1995, Amazon.com challenged well-established U.S. book-sellers Waldenbooks and Barnes and Noble. Although Amazon did not become profitable until 2003, the firm has grown from selling only books on a U.S. website, to selling a wide variety of products (including clothes, CDs, DVDs, home and garden supplies, and consumer electronic devices) on international websites in Canada, China, France, Germany, Japan, and the U.K.[3] The reasons people shop online rather than go to high street shops include convenience, because there is often a wider product range available online, and because costs are often less online. In addition, many sellers personalize their web pages for each individual customer, something high street shops cannot do (see Figure 7.9). This personalization is sometimes called **B2Me e-commerce**. By using B2C e-commerce to sell directly to consumers, producers or providers of consumer products can eliminate the middlemen, or intermediaries, between them and the consumer. In many cases, this squeezes costs and inefficiencies out of the supply chain and can lead to higher profits and lower prices for consumers.[4] The elimination of intermediate organizations between the producer and the consumer is called 'disintermediation'.

B2Me A form of e-commerce where the business treats each customer as a separate market segment. Typical B2Me features include customizing a website for each customer, perhaps based on their previous purchases and personalized (electronic) marketing literature.

Figure 7.9 A
Screenshot from Amazon.co.uk with a Personal Shopper's Tab and Product Recommendations

Dell is an example of a manufacturer that has successfully embraced this model to achieve a strong competitive advantage. People can specify their own unique computer online and Dell assembles the components and ships the computer directly to the consumer within five days. Dell does not inventory computers and does not sell through intermediate resellers or distributors. The savings are used to increase Dell's profits and reduce consumer prices.

Business-to-business (B2B) e-commerce is a subset of e-commerce where all the participants are organizations. B2B e-commerce is a useful tool for connecting business partners in a virtual supply chain to cut re-supply times and reduce costs. Many travel agents specialize in organizing business travel. Business Travel Direct in the U.K. provide flight and hotel bookings, tailoring their service for business customers. The sort of things B2B travel agents must deal with that high street agents may not are, for example, that the person who purchases the flight tickets may not be the person who will be travelling, and the decision on whether to travel may be made by a group rather than an individual.

business-to-business (B2B) e-commerce A subset of e-commerce where all the participants are organizations.

Consumer-to-consumer (C2C) e-commerce is another subset of e-commerce that involves consumers selling directly to other consumers. eBay is an example of a C2C e-commerce site; customers buy and sell items directly to each other through the site. Founded in 1995, eBay has become one of the most popular websites in the world where 181 million users buy and sell items valued at many billions of euros.[5] Other popular online auction websites include Craigslist, uBid, Yahoo! Auctions, Onsale, WeBidz, and many others. The growth of C2C is responsible for reducing the use of the classified pages of a newspaper to advertise and sell personal items.

consumer-to-consumer (C2C) e-commerce A subset of e-commerce that involves consumers selling directly to other consumers.

e-government is the use of information and communications technology to simplify the sharing of information, speed formerly paper-based processes, and improve the relationship between citizen and government. Government-to-consumer (G2C), government-to-business (G2B), and government-to-government (G2G) are all forms of e-government, each with different applications. For example, citizens can use G2C applications to submit their tax returns online, apply for planning permission, and submit e-petitions. G2B applications support the purchase of materials and services from private industry by government procurement offices, enable firms to bid on government contracts, and help businesses receive current government regulations related to their operations. G2G applications are designed to improve communications among the various levels of government.

e-government The use of information and communications technology to simplify the sharing of information, speed formerly paper-based processes, and improve the relationship between citizen and government.

7.3.2 Mobile Commerce

Mobile commerce (m-commerce) relies on the use of wireless devices, such as personal digital assistants, mobile phones, and smartphones, to transact. Handset manufacturers such as HTC, Plan and Sony Ericsson are working with communications carriers such as Orange to develop wireless devices, related technology, and services. In addition, content providers and mobile service providers are working together more closely than ever. Content providers recognize that customers want access to their content whenever and wherever they go, and mobile service providers seek out new forms of content to send over their networks.

According to the GSM Association, there are 1.8 billion mobile phone users in the world but only 12 to 14 percent of them have ever accessed the Web from their phones. (GSM stands for Global System for Mobile communication, which is a European digital standard for mobile telephony.) The Internet Corporation for Assigned Names and Numbers (ICANN) created a .mobi domain in late 2005 to help attract mobile users to the Web.[6] mTID Top Level Domain Ltd. of Dublin, Ireland, is responsible for administration of this domain and helping to ensure that the .mobi destinations work fast, efficiently, and effectively with user handsets.[7] In most Western European countries, communicating via wireless devices is common, and consumers are much more willing to use m-commerce. Japanese consumers are generally enthusiastic about new technology and are much more likely to use mobile technologies for making purchases.

For m-commerce to work effectively, the interface between the wireless device and its user needs to improve to the point that it is nearly as easy to purchase an item on a wireless device as it is to purchase it on a home computer. In addition, network speed must improve so that users do not become frustrated. Security is also a major concern, particularly in two areas: the security of the transmission itself and the trust that the transaction is being made with the intended party. Encryption can provide secure transmission. Digital certificates can ensure that transactions are made between the intended parties.

The handheld devices used for m-commerce have several limitations that complicate their use. Their screens are small, perhaps no more than a few square centimetres, and might be able to display only a few lines of text. Their input capabilities are limited to a few buttons, so entering data can be tedious and error prone. They have less processing power and less bandwidth than desktop computers, which are usually hardwired to a high-speed LAN. They also operate on

Ethical and Societal Issues

Mobile Banking in South Africa

The mobile phone is increasingly being considered as a remote control to the digital world. Banks, marketing agencies, those in the entertainment industry, and a host of other businesses are focused on creating useful m-commerce applications that will increase revenues. The ability to carry out transactions from any location any time using a mobile phone is revolutionizing the manner in which some people conduct our day-to-day activities. For instance, take the case of Wizzit.

About 16 million South Africans, over half of the adult population, have no bank account. However, 30 percent of these people do have mobile phones. With mobile banking, they could use their mobile phones to send money to relatives, pay for goods and services, check balances and pay bills. Wizzit, is trying to get them to do just that. With over 2000 so called 'Wizzkids' to 'spread the word' and drum up business, now eight out of ten Wizzit customers previously had no bank account and had never used an ATM. Wizzit, a division of the South African Bank of Athens, describes itself as a virtual bank and, as such, it has no branches. Since it started at the end of 2004, it now has over 50 000 customers.

This means that many South Africans now no longer have to carry cash around, which can be risky. In addition, many relatives who have left the country can send money home securely, quickly,

and cheaply. This is making a big difference to poorer people who rely on their families abroad. Money sent home from ex-patriots is a key part of South Africa's economy. Even for those who already have a bank account, mobile banking will mean they no longer have to travel to (often distant), bank branches, something that takes on average 30 minutes and costs around 15 rand for bus fare. According to Consultative Group to Assist the Poor (CGAP) a Wizzit account can be one-third cheaper than an equivalent account at one of South Africa's big retail banks. A CGAP survey found customers use Wizzit because it is cheap, safe, convenient, and fast.

Questions

1   Why is a Wizzit account considered 'safe'?

2   What concerns would you have about using your mobile phone in this way?

3   How could Wizzit overcome these fears?

4   Which activities that you currently perform on a PC could be transferred to a mobile phone and which could not? Why?

SOURCES: *The Economist*, 'Phoney finance', http://www.economist.com/finance/displaystory.cfm?story_id=8089667, October 26, 2006, accessed June 14, 2007; Consultative Group to Assist the Poor, 'Mobile Phone Banking and Low-Income Customers, Evidence from South Africa', http://www.cgap.org/publications/mobilephonebanking.pdf, accessed June 14, 2007.

limited-life batteries. For these reasons, it is currently impossible to directly access many websites with a handheld device. Web developers must rewrite web applications so that users with handheld devices can access them.

7.4 Enterprise Resource Planning, Supply Chain Management, and Customer Relationship Management

As defined in Chapter 4, enterprise resource planning (ERP) is a set of integrated programs that manage a company's vital business operations for an entire multisite, global organization. Recall that a business process is a set of coordinated and related activities that takes one or more kinds of input and creates an output of value to the customer of that process. The customer might be a traditional external customer who buys goods or services from the firm. An example of such a process is capturing a sales order, which takes customer input and generates an order. The customer of a business process might also be an internal customer, such as a worker in another department of the firm. For example, the shipment process creates the necessary internal documents needed by workers in the warehouse and shipping functions to pick, pack, and ship orders. At the core of the ERP system is a database which is shared by all users so that all business functions have access to current and consistent data for operational decision making and planning, as shown in Figure 7.10.

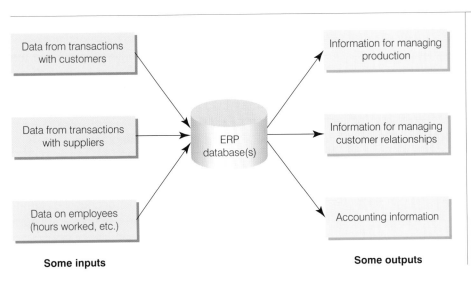

Figure 7.10 Enterprise Resource Planning System *An ERP integrates business processes and the ERP database.*

ERP systems (see Figure 7.11) evolved from materials requirement planning systems (MRP) developed in the 1970s. These systems tied together the production planning, inventory control, and purchasing business functions for manufacturing organizations. During the late 1980s and early 1990s, many organizations recognized that their legacy transaction processing systems lacked the integration needed to coordinate activities and share valuable information across all the business functions of the firm. As a result, costs were higher and customer service poorer

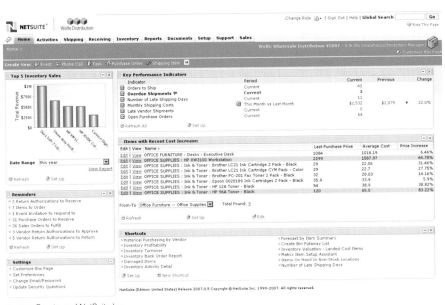

Figure 7.11 NetERP Software *NetERP software from NetSuite provides tightly integrated, comprehensive ERP solutions for businesses, giving them access to real-time business intelligence and thus enabling better decision making.*

SOURCE: Courtesy of NetSuite Inc.

than desired. The impending year 2000 (Y2K) problem that people expected to cause date-related processing to operate incorrectly after January 1, 2000, provided further impetus for organizations all over the world to review, modify, and upgrade their computer systems. Many firms used the Y2K issue to justify scrapping large parts of their existing information systems and converting to new ERP systems. Large organizations were the first to take on the challenge of implementing ERP. As they did, they uncovered many advantages as well as some disadvantages, summarized in the following sections.

7.4.1 Advantages of ERP

Increased global competition, new needs of executives for control over the total cost and product flow through their enterprises, and ever-more-numerous customer interactions drive the demand for enterprise-wide access to real-time information. ERP offers integrated software from a single vendor to help meet those needs. The primary benefits of implementing ERP include improved access to data for operational decision making, elimination of inefficient or outdated systems, improvement of work processes, and technology standardization. ERP vendors have also developed specialized systems for specific applications and market segments.

Improved Access to Data for Operational Decision Making

ERP systems operate via an integrated database, using one set of data to support all business functions. The systems can support decisions on optimal sourcing or cost accounting, for instance, for the entire enterprise or business units from the start, rather than gathering data from multiple business functions and then trying to coordinate that information manually or reconciling data with another application. The result is an organization that looks seamless, not only to the outside world but also to the decision makers who are deploying resources within the organization. The data is integrated to facilitate operational decision making and allows companies to provide greater customer service and support, strengthen customer and supplier relationships, and generate new business opportunities.

For example, success in the retail industry is determined by a retailer's ability to have the right products on shop shelves and priced correctly when customers come to buy. As a result, retailers need accurate, current, point-of-sale data and inventory data to match the merchandise assortment in their shops to the needs of their local markets.

Elimination of Costly, Inflexible Legacy Systems

Adoption of an ERP system enables an organization to eliminate dozens or even hundreds of separate systems and replace them with a single, integrated set of applications for the entire enterprise. In many cases, these systems are decades old, the original developers are long gone, and the systems are poorly documented. As a result, the systems are extremely difficult to fix when they break, and adapting them to meet new business needs takes too long. They become an anchor around the organization that keeps it from moving ahead and remaining competitive. An ERP system helps match the capabilities of an organization's information systems to its business needs – even as these needs evolve.

Improvement of Work Processes

Competition requires companies to structure their business processes to be as effective and customer oriented as possible. ERP vendors do considerable research to define the best business processes. They gather requirements of leading companies within the same industry and combine them with research findings from research institutions and consultants. The individual application modules included in the ERP system are then designed to support these **best practices**, the most efficient and effective ways to complete a business process. Thus, implementation of an ERP system ensures good work processes based on best practices. For example, for managing customer

best practices The most efficient and effective ways to complete a business process.

payments, the ERP system's finance module can be configured to reflect the most efficient practices of leading companies in an industry. This increased efficiency ensures that everyday business operations follow the optimal chain of activities, with all users supplied with the information and tools they need to complete each step.

Upgrade of Technology Infrastructure

In an ERP system, an organization can upgrade and simplify the information technology it employs. When implementing ERP, a company must determine which hardware, operating systems, and databases it wants to use. While centralizing and formalizing these decisions, the organization can eliminate the hodgepodge of multiple hardware platforms, operating systems, and databases it is currently using – most likely from a variety of vendors. Standardizing on fewer technologies and vendors reduces ongoing maintenance and support costs as well as the training load for those who must support the infrastructure.

7.4.2 Disadvantages of ERP Systems

Unfortunately, implementing ERP systems can be difficult and error-prone. Some of the major disadvantages of ERP systems are the expense and time required for implementation, the difficulty in implementing the many business process changes that accompany the ERP system, the problems with integrating the ERP system with other systems, the risks associated with making a major commitment to a single vendor, and the risk of implementation failure.

Expense and Time in Implementation

Getting the full benefits of ERP takes time and money. Although ERP offers many strategic advantages by streamlining a company's TPS, large firms typically need three to five years and spend tens of millions of euros to implement a successful ERP system.

Difficulty Implementing Change

In some cases, a company has to radically change how it operates to conform to the ERP's work processes – its best practices. These changes can be so drastic to long-time employees that they retire or quit rather than go through the change. This exodus can leave a firm short of experienced workers. Sometimes, the best practices simply are not appropriate for the firm and cause great work disruptions.

Difficulty Integrating with Other Systems

Most companies have other systems that must be integrated with the ERP system, such as financial analysis programs, e-commerce operations, and other applications. Many companies have experienced difficulties making these other systems operate with their ERP system. Other companies need additional software to create these links.

Risks in Using One Vendor

The high cost to switch to another vendor's ERP system makes it extremely unlikely that a firm will do so. After a company has adopted an ERP system, the vendor has less incentive to listen and respond to customer concerns. The high cost to switch also increases risk – in the event the ERP vendor allows its product to become outdated or goes out of business. Selecting an ERP system involves not only choosing the best software product but also the right long-term business partner.

Risk of Implementation Failure

Implementing an ERP system is extremely challenging and requires tremendous amounts of resources, the best IS and businesspeople, and plenty of management support. Unfortunately, ERP installations occasionally fail, and problems with an ERP implementation can require expensive solutions.

The following list provides tips for avoiding many common causes for failed ERP implementations:

■ Assign a full-time executive to manage the project.

■ Appoint an experienced, independent resource to provide project oversight and to verify and validate system performance.

■ Allow sufficient time for transition from the old way of doing things to the new system and new processes.

■ Plan to spend a lot of time and money training people; many project managers recommend that €7000–€15,000 per employee be budgeted for training of personnel.

■ Define metrics to assess project progress and to identify project-related risks.

■ Keep the scope of the project well defined and contained to essential business processes.

■ Be wary of modifying the ERP software to conform to your firm's business practices.

Although ERP implementation can be difficult, many efforts have been successful. It is not only large Fortune 1000 companies that are successful in implementing ERP. Even small companies can achieve real business benefits from their ERP efforts. Take the case of Bedford Industries in Adelaide, Australia. This non-profit coordinates employment for 800 people with disabilities who work in one of three divisions: Bedford Furniture, which manufactures ready-to-assemble furniture; Bedford Packaging Services, which provides packaging services for other firms; and Adelaide Property and Gardens, which provides a range of horticultural services from lawn mowing to rubbish collection. The company's legacy systems could not provide consolidated information for planning and scheduling, production, purchasing, financials, and customer relationship management. The desire to improve these core activities led Bedford to evaluate various solutions to meet their needs. They appointed a full-time project manager from the business to lead the effort to select an ERP system. Epicor Vantage was chosen because of its reputation for keeping information system costs at an absolute minimum and because the software is designed for rapid installation, low training costs, and simple operation. Bedford decided to use experienced resources from Vantage distributor Cogita to help implement the system. Another key decision was to follow the business processes as they were implemented in the ERP system, which were based on industry 'best practices', rather than customize the software to conform to existing Bedford business practices. Only one month after implementation, the company's financial managers were able to produce accurate, end-of-financial-year reports. The ERP database provides a valuable source of data to enable more timely decision making and significant improvement in the efficiency and flexibility of the company's operations. Bedford expects to recover the cost of the system within five years, with most savings coming from the company's leaner and more accurate operations.[8]

The following sections will outline how an ERP system can support the various major business processes.

7.4.3 Production and Supply Chain Management

ERP systems follow a systematic process for developing a production plan that draws on the information available in the ERP system database.

The process starts with sales forecasting to develop an estimate of future customer demand. This initial forecast is at a fairly high level with estimates made by product group rather than by each individual product item. The sales forecast extends for months into the future. The sales forecast might be developed using an ERP software module or it might be produced by other means using specialized software and techniques. Many organizations are moving to a collaborative process with major customers to plan future inventory levels and production rather than relying on an internally generated sales forecast. The sales and operations plan takes demand and current inventory levels into account and determines the specific product items that need to be produced and when to meet the forecast future demand. Production capacity and any seasonal variability in demand must also be considered. The result is a high-level production plan that balances market demand to production capacity. Panasonic and other companies have outsourced the development of a sales and operation plan to i2 Technologies in India. Best Buy, a major Panasonic customer, collects information on sales of Panasonic items at its shops' checkout stations and sends the data to i2. i2 processes the data and sends manufacturing recommendations to Panasonic, which become the basis for factory schedules.[9]

Demand management refines the production plan by determining the amount of weekly or daily production needed to meet the demand for individual products. The output of the demand management process is the master production schedule, which is a production plan for all finished goods.

Detailed scheduling uses the production plan defined by the demand management process to develop a detailed production schedule specifying production scheduling details, such as which item to produce first and when production should be switched from one item to another. A key decision is how long to make the production runs for each product. Longer production runs reduce the number of machine setups required, thus reducing production costs. Shorter production runs generate less finished product inventory and reduce inventory holding costs.

Materials requirement planning determines the amount and timing for placing raw material orders with suppliers. The types and amounts of raw materials required to support the planned production schedule are determined based on the existing raw material inventory and the bill of materials or BOM, a sort of 'recipe' of ingredients needed to make each product item. The quantity of raw materials to order also depends on the lead time and lot sizing. Lead time is the time it takes from the time a purchase order is placed until the raw materials arrive at the production facility. Lot size has to do with discrete quantities that the supplier will ship and the amount that is economical for the producer to receive and/or store. For example, a supplier might ship a certain raw material in batches of 80 000 units. The producer might need 95 000 units. A decision must be made to order one or two batches.

Purchasing uses the information from materials requirement planning to place purchase orders for raw materials and transmit them to qualified suppliers. Typically, the release of these purchase orders is timed so that raw materials arrive just in time to be used in production and minimize warehouse and storage costs. Often, producers will allow suppliers to tap into data via an extranet that enables them to determine what raw materials the supplier needs, thus minimizing the effort and lead time to place and fill purchase orders.

Production uses the detailed schedule to plan the details of running and staffing the production operation.

ERP systems do not interface directly with production machines so some means must be provided to capture information about what was produced. This data must be passed onto the ERP accounting modules to keep an accurate count of finished product inventory. Many companies have personal computers on the production floor that count the number of cases of each product item produced by scanning a UPC code on the packing material. Other approaches for capturing production quantities include the use of RFID chips and manually entering the data via a PDA.

Separately, production-quality data can be added based on the results of quality tests run on a sample of the product for each batch of product produced. Typically, this data includes the batch identification number, which identifies this production run versus any other production run and the results of various product quality tests.

7.4.4 Customer Relationship Management and Sales Ordering

Customer Relationship Management

A **customer relationship management (CRM)** system helps a company manage all aspects of customer encounters, including marketing and advertising, sales, customer service after the sale, and programs to keep and retain

customer relationship management (CRM) system
A system that helps a company manage all aspects of customer encounters, including marketing and advertising, sales, customer service after the sale, and programs to retain loyal customers.

loyal customers (see Figure 7.12). The goal of CRM is to understand and anticipate the needs of current and potential customers to increase customer retention and loyalty while optimizing the way that products and services are sold. Businesses implementing CRM systems report business benefits such as improved customer satisfaction, increased customer retention, reduced operating costs, and the ability to meet customer demand.

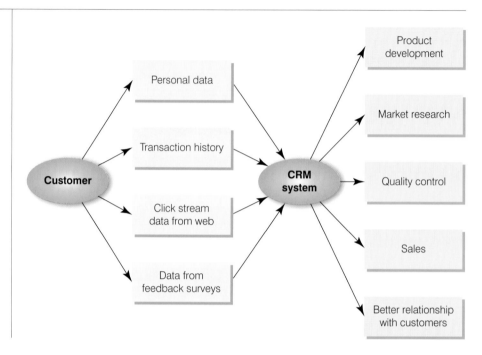

Figure 7.12 Customer Relationship Management System

CRM software automates and integrates the functions of sales, marketing, and service in an organization. The objective is to capture data about every contact a company has with a customer through every channel and store it in the CRM system so the company can truly understand customer actions. CRM software helps an organization build a database about its customers that describes relationships in sufficient detail so that management, salespeople, customer service providers – and even customers – can access information to match customer needs with product plans and offerings, remind them of service requirements, and know what other products they have purchased. Figure 7.13 shows contact manager software from SAP that fills this CRM role.

The focus of CRM involves much more than installing new software. Moving from a culture of simply selling products to placing the customer first is essential to a successful CRM deployment. Before any software is loaded onto a computer, a company must retrain employees. Who handles customer issues and when must be clearly defined, and computer systems need to be integrated so that all pertinent information is available immediately, whether a customer calls a sales representative or customer service representative. In addition to using stationary computers, most CRM systems can now be accessed via wireless devices.

Sales Ordering

Sales ordering is the set of activities that must be performed to capture a customer sales order. A few of the essential steps include recording the items to be purchased, setting the sales price, recording the order quantity, determining the total cost of the order including delivery costs, and confirming the customer's available credit. The determination of the sales prices can become quite complicated and include quantity discounts, promotions, and incentives. After the total

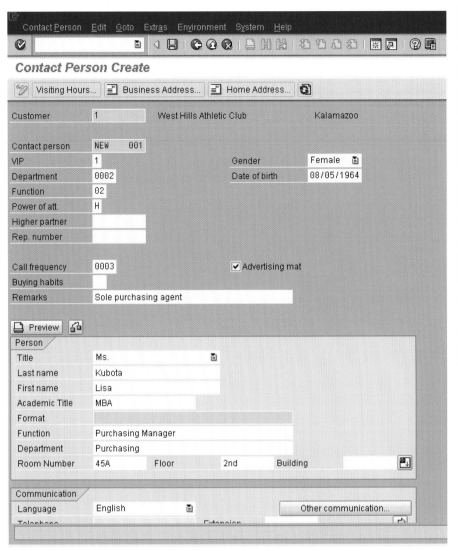

Figure 7.13 SAP
Contact Manager

cost of the order is determined, it is necessary to check the customer's available credit to see if this order puts the customer over his or her credit limit. Figure 7.14 shows a sales order entry window in SAP business software.

Many small-to-medium-sized businesses are turning to ERP software to make it easier for their large customers to place orders with them. Vetco International Inc. is a small supplier of safety equipment to major oil firms such as ExxonMobile and British Petroleum. The firm uses SAP's Business One suite, which has modules that automate purchasing, sales, and distribution; sales management; and other business functions. It cost Vetco about €110 000 to implement the software because it is compatible with the SAP software used by many of its customers. The software enables Vetco to connect its product catalogues via easy web access to the purchasing systems of its much larger customers. The goal is to capture more business by ensuring that its offerings are just a click away from the oil companies' purchasing departments.[10]

Figure 7.14 Sales
Order Entry Window

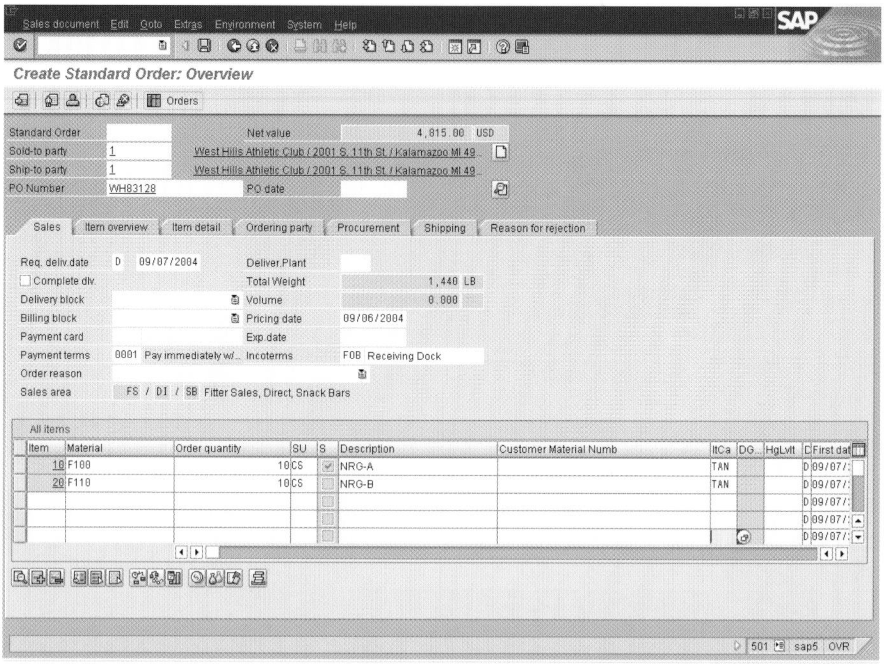

SOURCE: Copyright © by SAP AG.

7.4.5 Financial and Managerial Accounting

The general ledger is the main accounting record of a business. It is often divided into different categories, including assets, liabilities, revenue, expenses, and equity. These categories, in turn, are subdivided into sub-ledgers to capture details such as cash, accounts payable, accounts receivable, and so on. In an ERP system, input to the general ledger occurs simultaneously with the input of a business transaction to a specific module. Here are several examples of how this occurs:

■ An order administrator records a sale and the ERP system automatically creates an accounts receivable entry indicating that a customer owes money for goods received.

■ A buyer enters a purchase order and the ERP system automatically creates an accounts payable entry in the general ledger registering that the company has an obligation to pay for goods that will be received at some time in the future.

■ A dock worker enters a receipt of purchased materials from a supplier and the ERP system automatically creates a general ledger entry to increase the value of inventory on hand.

■ A production worker withdraws raw materials from inventory to support production and the ERP system generates a record to reduce the value of inventory on hand.

Thus, the ERP system captures transactions entered by workers in all functional areas of the business. The ERP system then creates the associated general ledger record to track the financial impact of the transaction. This set of records is an extremely valuable resource that companies can use to support financial accounting and managerial accounting.

Financial accounting consists of capturing and recording all the transactions that affect a company's financial state and then using these documented transactions to prepare financial statements to external decision makers, such as stockholders, suppliers, banks, and government agencies. These financial statements include the profit and loss statement, balance sheet, and cash flow statement. They must be prepared in strict accordance to rules and guidelines of the governing agencies.

All transactions that affect the financial state of the firm are captured and recorded in the database of the ERP system. This data is used in the financial accounting module of the ERP system to prepare the statements required by various constituencies. The data can also be used in the managerial accounting module of the ERP system along with various assumptions and forecasts to perform various analyses such as generating a forecasted profit and loss statement to assess the firm's future profitability.

7.4.6 Hosted Software Model for Enterprise Software

Business application software vendors are experimenting with the hosted software model to see if the approach meets customer needs and is likely to generate significant revenue. This pay-as-you-go approach is appealing to small businesses because they can then experiment with powerful software capabilities without making a major financial investment. Also, using the hosted software model means the small business firm does not need to employ a full-time IT person to maintain key business applications. The small business firm can expect additional savings from reduced hardware costs and costs associated with maintaining an appropriate computer environment (such as air conditioning, power, and an uninterruptible power supply).

Not only is the hosted software model attractive to small- and medium-sized firms, even some large companies are experimenting with it. DuPont, the large, multinational chemical company, is one of the early adopters of the hosted software model. The firm is retooling its sales force by leveraging best practices and focusing its e-business and marketing capabilities into 16 high-powered global centres. As part of the change, DuPont plans to use the hosted SAP Sales on Demand software across the enterprise to provide a common systems platform and a common set of business processes for DuPont's entire sales force. It hopes to integrate the hosted system with its SAP ERP software and retire some of its legacy CRM applications. The business goal is to make sure that the firm presents itself as one DuPont to customers who buy from different DuPont businesses. Its largest customers are served as 'corporate accounts' with a point of contact who can manage all their interactions with DuPont to ensure the maximum benefit to the customer.[11]

7.5 International Issues Associated with Operational Systems

Operational systems must support businesses that interoperate with customers, suppliers, business partners, shareholders, and government agencies in multiple countries. Different languages and cultures, disparities in IS infrastructure, varying laws and customs rules, and multiple currencies are among the challenges that must be met by an operational system of a multinational company. The following sections highlight these issues.

7.5.1 Different Languages and Cultures

Teams composed of people from several countries speaking different languages and familiar with different cultures might not agree on a single work process. In some cultures, people do not routinely work in teams in a networked environment. Despite these complications, many multinational companies can establish close connections with their business partners and roll out standard IS applications for all to use. However, sometimes they require extensive and costly customization. For example, even though English has become a standard business language among executives and senior managers, many people within organizations do not speak English. As a result, software might need to be designed with local language interfaces to ensure the successful implementation of a new system. Other customizations will also be needed; date fields for example: the European format is day/month/year, Japan uses year/month/day, and the U.S. date format is month/day/year. Sometimes, users might also have to implement manual processes to override established formatting to enable systems to function correctly.

7.5.2 Disparities in Information System Infrastructure

The lack of a robust or a common information infrastructure can also create problems. For example, much of Latin America lags behind the rest of the world in Internet usage, and online marketplaces are almost non-existent there. This gap makes it difficult for multinational companies to get online with their Latin American business partners. Even something as mundane as the fact that the power plug on a piece of equipment built in one country might not fit into the power socket of another country can affect the infrastructure.

7.5.3 Varying Laws and Customs Rules

Numerous laws can affect the collection and dissemination of data. For example, labour laws in some countries prohibit the recording of worker performance data. Also, some countries have passed laws limiting the transborder flow of data linked to individuals. Specifically, European Community Directive 95/96/EC of 1998 requires that any company doing business within the borders of the 25 European Union member nations protect the privacy of customers and employees. It bars the export of data to countries that do not have data-protection standards comparable to the European Union's.

Trade custom rules between nations are international laws that set practices for two or more nations' commercial transactions. They cover imports and exports and the systems and procedures dealing with quotas, visas, entry documents, commercial invoices, foreign trade zones, payment of duty and taxes, and many other related issues. For example, the North American Free Trade Agreement (NAFTA) of 1994 created trade custom rules to address the flow of goods throughout the North American continent. Most of these custom rules and their changes over time create headaches for people who must keep systems consistent with the rules.

7.5.4 Multiple Currencies

The enterprise system of multinational companies must conduct transactions in multiple currencies. To do so, a set of exchange rates is defined, and the information systems apply these rates to translate from one currency to another. The systems must be current with foreign currency exchange rates, handle reporting and other transactions such as cash receipts, issue vendor payments and customer statements, record retail store payments, and generate financial reports in the currency of choice.

Summary

An organization must have information systems that support the routine, day-to-day activities that occur in the normal course of business and help a company add value to its products and services. Transaction processing systems (TPS) are at the heart of most information systems in businesses today. A TPS is an organized collection of people, procedures, software, databases, and devices used to capture fundamental data about events that affect the organization (transactions). All TPS perform the following basic activities: data collection, which involves the capture of source data to complete a set of transactions; data editing, which checks for data validity and completeness; data correction, which involves providing feedback of a potential problem and enabling users to change the data; data manipulation, which is the performance of calculations, sorting, categorizing, summarizing, and storing data for further processing; data storage, which involves placing transaction data into one or more databases; and document production, which involves outputting records and reports.

The methods of transaction processing systems include batch and online. Batch processing involves the collection of transactions into batches, which are entered into the system at regular intervals as a group. Online transaction processing (OLTP) allows transactions to be entered as they occur.

Organizations expect TPS to accomplish a number of specific objectives, including processing data generated by and about transactions, maintaining a high degree of accuracy and information integrity, compiling accurate and timely reports and documents, increasing labour efficiency, helping provide increased and enhanced service, and building and maintaining customer loyalty. In some situations, an effective TPS can help an organization gain a competitive advantage.

Traditional TPS support the various business functions of organizations that have not yet implemented enterprise resource planning systems. Many organizations conduct ongoing TPS audits to prevent accounting irregularities or loss of data privacy. The audit can be performed by the firm's internal audit group or by an outside auditor for greater objectivity.

The traditional TPS systems that support the order processing business functions include order entry, sales configuration, shipment planning, shipment execution, inventory control, and accounts receivable.

The traditional TPS that support the purchasing function include inventory control, purchase order processing, accounts payable, and receiving.

The traditional TPS that support the accounting business function include the budget, accounts receivable, payroll, asset management, and general ledger.

Electronic and mobile commerce allow transactions to be made by the customer, with less need for sales staff, and open up new opportunities for conducting business. E-commerce is the conducting of business activities electronically over networks. Business-to-business (B2B) e-commerce allows manufacturers to buy at a low cost worldwide, and it offers enterprises the chance to sell to a global market. Business-to-consumer (B2C) e-commerce enables organizations to sell directly to consumers, eliminating intermediaries. In many cases, this squeezes costs and inefficiencies out of the supply chain and can lead to higher profits and lower prices for consumers. Consumer-to-consumer (C2C) e-commerce involves consumers selling directly to other consumers. Online auctions are the chief method by which C2C e-commerce is currently conducted.

Mobile commerce is the use of wireless devices such as PDAs, mobile phones, and smartphones to facilitate the sale of goods or services – anytime, anywhere. The market for m-commerce in North America is expected to mature much later than in Western Europe and Japan. Although some industry experts predict great growth in this arena, several hurdles must be overcome, including improving the ease of use of wireless devices, addressing the security of wireless transactions, and improving network speed. M-commerce provides a unique opportunity to establish one-on-one marketing relationships and support communications anytime and anywhere.

A company that implements an enterprise resource planning system is creating a highly integrated set of systems, which can lead to many business benefits. Enterprise resource planning (ERP) software supports the efficient operation of business processes by integrating activities throughout a business, including sales, marketing, manufacturing, logistics, accounting, and staffing. Implementation of an ERP system can provide many advantages, including providing access to data for operational decision making; elimination of costly, inflexible legacy systems; providing improved work processes; and creating the opportunity to upgrade technology infrastructure. Some of the disadvantages associated with an ERP system are that they are time consuming, difficult, and expensive to implement.

Although the scope of ERP implementation can vary from firm to firm, most firms use ERP systems to support production and supply chain management, customer relationship management and sales ordering, and financial and managerial accounting.

The production and supply chain management process starts with sales forecasting to develop an estimate of future customer demand. This initial forecast is at a fairly high level with estimates made by product group rather than by each individual product item. The sales and operations plan takes demand and current inventory levels into account and determines the specific product items that need to be produced and when to meet the forecast future demand. Demand management refines the production plan by determining the amount of weekly or daily production needed to meet the demand for individual products. Detailed scheduling uses the production plan defined by the demand management process to develop a detailed production schedule specifying production scheduling details such as which item to produce first and when production should be switched from one item to another. Materials requirement planning determines the amount and timing for placing raw material orders with suppliers. Purchasing uses the information from materials requirement planning to place purchase orders for raw materials and transmit them to qualified suppliers. Production uses the detailed schedule to plan the details of running and staffing the production operation.

Numerous complications arise that multinational corporations must address in planning, building, and operating their TPS. These challenges include dealing with different languages and cultures, disparities in IS infrastructure, varying laws and customs rules, and multiple currencies.

Self-Assessment Test

7

1   Identify the missing TPS basic activity: data collection, data editing, data _____, data manipulation, data storage, and document production.

2   The primary objective of any TPS is to capture, process, and store transactions and to produce a variety of documents related to routine business activities. True or false?

3   Which of the following are not one of the basic components of a TPS?
   a. databases
   b. networks
   c. procedures
   d. analytical models

4   Data should be captured at its source and recorded accurately in a timely fashion, with minimal manual effort, and in an electronic or digital form that can be directly entered into the computer are the principles behind _____.

5   Inventory control, purchase order processing, receiving, and accounts payable systems make up a set of systems that support the _____ business function.

6   eBay is an example of which of the following forms of e-commerce?
   a. G2G
   b. B2B
   c. B2C
   d. C2C

7   Amazon is an example of which of the following forms of e-commerce?
   a. G2G
   b. B2B
   c. B2C
   d. C2C

8   E-commerce websites should be rewritten for mobile devices, to allow for mobile commerce. True or false?

9   Which of the following is a primary benefit of implementing an ERP system?
   a. elimination of inefficient systems
   b. easing adoption of improved work processes
   c. improving access to data for operational decision making
   d. all of the above

10 Only large, multinational companies can justify the implementation of ERP systems. True or false?

Review Questions

1 List several characteristics that distinguish a TPS from an MIS.

2 What basic transaction processing activities are performed by all transaction processing systems?

3 Define e-commerce.

4 List and explain four different types of e-commerce.

5 Identify and briefly describe three limitations that complicate the use of handheld devices used for m-commerce.

6 What is source data automation? Give an example.

7 Identify four complications that multinational corporations must address in planning, building, and operating their ERP systems.

8 How does materials requirement planning support the purchasing process? What are some of the issues and complications that arise in materials requirement planning?

9 What systems are included in the traditional TPS systems that support the accounting business function?

10 List and briefly describe the set of activities that must be performed by the sales ordering module of an ERP system to capture a customer sales order.

Discussion Questions

1 Explain the difference between B2C and B2Me e-commerce. Give examples of each.

2 What do you think are the biggest barriers to wide-scale adoption of m-commerce by consumers? Who do you think is working on solutions to these problems and what might the solutions entail?

3 If a customer prints an order form downloaded from a website, completes it using a black pen, and faxes it off to a company, does this constitute e-commerce? Why or why not?

4 What are the advantages of implementing ERP as an integrated solution to link multiple business processes versus a series of non-integrated TPS systems? Can you identify any disadvantages?

5 What sort of benefits should the suppliers and customers of a firm that has successfully implemented an ERP system see? What sort of issues might arise for suppliers and customers during an ERP implementation?

Web Exercises

1 Visit eBay or another online auction website and choose an item on which to bid. Before entering the bid process, research the site for information about any rules associated with bidding and how to bid effectively. Follow the suggested processes and record your results. Write a brief memo to your instructor summarizing your experience.

2 Do research on the web and identify the most popular ERP system solution for small- and medium-sized businesses. Why is this solution the most popular? Develop a one-page report or send an e-mail message to your instructor about what you found.

Case One

Nike Empowers Customers with Online Customization

Shopping and selling online provide sellers and buyers with an intimate environment in which to do business. Through the use of dynamic websites that are designed to uniquely appeal to each visitor, electronic retailers, or e-tailers, can provide customers with exactly what they desire. Unlike bricks-and-mortar retail shops with promotions designed to appeal to the lowest common denominator, e-tailers can provide visitors with an environment customized to their tastes and interests. For example, frequent Amazon shoppers are not surprised when they are greeted at Amazon's website by name and shown only items that are likely to appeal to them.

Customization, or B2Me, is a powerful tool for online businesses selling to individual consumers and to other businesses. Customization eliminates the frustration consumers feel when they must navigate through massive amounts of unrelated information to find items of interest. Consider, for example, searching the Sunday newspaper for advertisements and coupons of interest, or the percentage of commercials on network TV that are for products that actually appeal to you.

Realising the power of customization and providing shoppers with exactly what they are looking for has inspired Nike and other companies to take advantage of the concept. Going beyond customizing the online shopping experience, Nike is empowering shoppers to custom-design the products themselves. Visitors to the recently upgraded Nikeid.com website can design their own footwear, sports apparel, sports bags, balls, and wristwatches. For example, you can select colours from an extensive palette for the nine elements of a Nike athletic shoe, including a base colour and colours for the tip and heel, lining, tongue, and even the famous Nike swoosh. Furthermore, you can emboss the shoe with your name or slogan, and add a national symbol or flag to the heel tab.

Market analysts believe that the appeal of product customization will increase over time, especially to young shoppers. 'It is really a democratic desire,'

said Sharon Lee, co-founder of a Los Angeles-based consumer research and trend consulting company called Look-Look, Inc. 'Every person wants to say this is much more me and I'm not part of this kind of mass culture.' Customization also connects shoppers more closely with a brand and helps companies attract fickle but lucrative young shoppers by giving them the power to put their personal stamp on what they purchase.

The level of customization provided by Nike is only made possible through e-commerce technologies and supply chain management. E-commerce systems stream the order information from Nike's website to Nike's order processing system and from there to Nike's suppliers and manufacturers, all within seconds of the moment the order is placed. Nike's manufacturing process has been adjusted to accommodate individual products in addition to mass production of its stock items. The result is a wider and happier customer base that is getting exactly what it wants.

Questions

1 Is Nike, by allowing their customers to customize their footwear, really doing B2Me? Are they not customizing the product, rather than the website? Is this distinction important?

2 Is B2Me a tactic only suitable in certain industries? If so, what are some of them?

3 What are some of the privacy issues associated with B2Me?

4 It is often said that one of the main advantages small businesses have is that they know their customers more intimately than larger businesses do. Is B2Me eroding this advantage? Explain your answer.

SOURCES: Kahn, Michael, 'Nike Says Just Do It Yourself', *Reuters*, www.reuters.com, May 30, 2005; Hallett, Vicky, 'Satisfied Customizers', *U.S. News & World Report*, November 21, 2005; *DIVERSIONS*, Vol. 139, No. 19; p. D2, D4, or www.lexis-nexis.com. Nike Customization (website), http://nikeid.nike.com/nikeid/, May 04, 2006.

Case Two

Japanese Mobile Music Service Provides Peek Into M-Commerce Future

Today's most popular m-commerce products are digital media goods such as ring tones, music, games, mobile phone wallpaper graphics, and video clips. Many analysts foresee that digital music will be the product that skyrockets in popularity over the next few years. 'Certain things just naturally go together and satellite radio, and music in general, and cell phones together are a perfect combination for certain customer groups,' observes telecom analyst Jeff Kagan.

A number of mobile phone delivery models for music are being explored by various carriers with no clear indication as to which will find the most success. The following three methods are being explored:

- ▪ *Streaming music*. These services allow you to listen to a song without storing it on your handset; rather like on-demand radio.

- ▪ *Direct-to-handset downloads*. This method allows you to download a music file direct to your handset, where the file becomes your property to listen to repeatedly.

- ▪ *Transfer from PC*. Personal computer-based music services such as iTunes allow you to transfer music files from your computer collection to your handset.

Part of the challenge of translating music e-commerce models to m-commerce are the limitations of the interface. It is tedious and frustrating to search for music from huge online catalogues through the tiny display of the mobile phone. A new music service launched by Japan's second-largest mobile carrier, KDDI, provides an intriguing solution that might provide a model for m-commerce applications of all sorts.

If you are in Japan and subscribe to KDDI's 'Listen and Search' service, acquiring music that you hear and like anywhere anytime involves a few button pushes on your handset. For example, suppose you're in a club and the DJ plays a song you've never heard before but want to add to your private collection. Using your mobile phone, you select 'Listen and Search' on your menu, hold your phone in the air while the song is playing, and then press the Select button on your phone. The KDDI service analyzes the sound bite you provided, identifies the song, and provides a list of vendors from which you can purchase the song. Selecting the vendor with the best deal, you download the song and import it into your private collection to listen to whenever you like.

Three technologies are combined to create KDDI's instant-access music service. California-based Gracenote's Mobile MusicID technology uses a database of six million popular song 'fingerprints' and successfully matches song clips as short as three seconds to a song in the database to provide song title and artist. The Mobile MusicID technology then delivers the name of the song and artist to the handset. Another Gracenote product, known as Link, executes commerce applications that enable the transaction. Software designed by California-based Media Socket is used to transfer the music file to the handset.

Since its introduction in mid-2005, the 'Listen and Search' service has been tremendously successful in Japan. 'We've found that offering instant access to music and purchases is very compelling,' Makoto Takahashi, vice president and general manager of the Content Division at KDDI, said. 'For the first time, our customers will be able to identify songs they're hearing on the television, on the radio or other sources, and buy related content, such as ring songs, full songs or albums, at exactly the moment they're listening to that song.' After releasing the new service, KDDI sold over two million handsets that double as MP3 players, exceeding Apple iPod sales in Japan for the month. KDDI reported 1.8 million full-song downloads in the first month.

New cutting-edge mobile phone technologies are often launched in countries such as Japan and Korea, where mobile phone networks are further evolved and support high-speed network services. Similar services from Japan are becoming available throughout Europe and the rest of the world.

7

Questions

1 Would you subscribe to a music service like the one offered by KDDI? Why or why not?

2 How do you think KDDI profits from its music service?

3 KDDI's 'Listen and Search' service most likely lets customers find music in ways other than holding the handset up to a music source. What alternative methods of finding music would you build into this system?

4 KDDI's music service involves several steps: (1) Identify the desired product, (2) provide a list of vendors for the product, (3) enable commerce between consumer and vendor, and (4) deliver the product. Apply this process to another m-commerce product besides music. Describe what takes place in each step.

SOURCES: Regan, Keith, 'Japanese Mobile Song-ID Feature Hints at M-Commerce Future', *E-Commerce Times*, www.ecommercetimes.com, June 14, 2005; 'Gracenote Acquires Cutting Edge Audio Fingerprinting Technology from Philips Electronics and Announces Long-Term Research Agreement with Philips Research', *PRNewswire*, www.prnewswire.com, August 30, 2005.

Case Three

Pico Electronics Develops TPS to Support Rapid-Fire Transactions

Malaysian electronic components distributor Pico Electronics had a problem that many mid-sized businesses would like to have: orders were coming in too quickly; they had to process an order every few minutes. Pico didn't mind its order volume, but it was having difficulty keeping an accurate picture of current inventory. The company wanted to avoid a scenario in which three salespeople are accepting orders for the same item with only enough inventory to support two of the orders. In 2006, Pico Electronics went shopping for a new order processing system that would provide real-time visibility to avoid such problems.

Pico's procurement division needed to see what was being ordered as soon as it was ordered. The division could then purchase the required materials as necessary to fulfil customers' orders on time. The company wanted to be more nimble in its ability to stay ahead of the competition.

The project evaluation team, headed by finance manager Sharyne Tee, set several primary goals for the new system. The new system should:

■ Go beyond order processing to include all relevant business process-related data.

■ Generate reports to give the management an accurate snapshot of the company's performance in real time.

■ Accurately track inventory and costs in real time so that they could anticipate demand and have reasonable inventory reserves.

■ Allow for fast access to both overseas customer and vendor histories.

■ Provide a stable and fast connection to link their overseas offices in China, Hong Kong, Malaysia, and Thailand.

Pico decided on SAP Business One software as a platform for the new TPS and ERP system. Since the implementation, SAP Business One has allowed Pico management to view current inventory in the warehouse. The software also lets them analyze the performance of the separate divisions in the company. Because this software automates accounting-related data collection, Pico can better handle its accounts receivable, which improves cash flow.

Pico purchased a Jobshop add-on module designed by Sabre that allows the company to add more functionality as it grows. The module manages the entire production environment, from bill of material to shop floor control. With the Jobshop module, Pico can monitor all planning and production control activities and integrate sales, purchasing, inventory, and financial activities.

7

This system development project at Pico Electronics illustrates how improvements to one system often involve changes to many systems. It would be unwise to examine changes to one system, such as a TPS or CRM, without evaluating their effect on related systems, such as ERP.

1   Explain the problem that Pico wanted to address, and why Pico considered it a problem.

2   What is meant by 'real-time visibility'? How does it relate to the pace at which products are sold?

3   Why do changes to one type of system, such as a TPS, affect other systems in an enterprise?

4   What additional challenges do you think Pico faced in extending real-time visibility to its overseas offices?

SOURCES: Liew, Kenneth, 'Pico Electronics Gains Real-Time Visibility', *Computerworld Malaysia*, www.computerworld.com.my, March 23, 2006.

Notes

1   Marlin, Steven, 'Bank Deploys Anti-Money Laundering System', *Information Week*, October 11, 2005.

2   Sullivan, Laurie, 'Bad Online Shopping Experiences Are Bad for Business', *Information Week*, January 24, 2005.

3   Perez, Juan Carlos, 'Amazon Turns 10, Helped by Strong Tech, Service', *Computerworld*, July 15, 2005.

4   Javed, Naseem, 'Move Over B2B, B2C – It's M2E Time,' *E-Commerce Times*, August 17, 2005.

5   'Investor Relations', eBay website, http://investor.ebay.com/fundamentals.cfm, accessed May 4, 2006.

6   Mello, John P. Jr., 'New .mobi Domain Approved but Challenges Remain', *TechNewsWorld*, May 11, 2006.

7   Ibid.

8   Braue, David, 'ERP Boosts Reporting, ROI for Manufacturer', *Computerworld*, April 12, 2006.

9   Anthes, Gary, 'Sidebar: It's All Global Now', *Computerworld*, February 20, 2006.

10 McDougall, Paul, 'Closing the Last Supply Gap', *Information Week*, November 8, 2005.

11 Songini, Marc, 'SAP Launches First Piece of Hosted CRM Service', *Computerworld*, February 16, 2006.

7

08

Management Information and Decision Support Systems

Principles

Good decision-making and problem-solving skills are the key to developing effective information and decision support systems.

A management information system (MIS) must provide the right information to the right person in the right format at the right time.

Decision support systems (DSS) support decision-making effectiveness when faced with unstructured or semi-structured business problems.

Specialized support systems, such as group support systems (GSS) and executive support systems (ESS), use the overall approach of a DSS in situations such as group and executive decision making.

Learning Objectives

- Define the stages of decision making.
- Discuss the importance of implementation and monitoring in problem solving.

- Explain the uses of MIS and describe their inputs and outputs.
- Discuss information systems in the functional areas of business organizations.

- List and discuss important characteristics of DSS that give them the potential to be effective management support tools.
- Identify and describe the basic components of a DSS.

- State the goals of a GSS and identify the characteristics that distinguish it from a DSS.
- Identify the fundamental uses of an ESS and list the characteristics of such a system.

Why Learn About Management Information Systems and Decision Support Systems?

The previous chapter looked at systems at the operational level of a firm (see also Figure 1.5 and Figure 8.14). This chapter considers systems higher up, at the tactical and strategic levels. The true potential of information systems in organizations is in helping employees make more informed decisions, something that is supported by both management information and decision support systems. Transportation coordinators can use management information reports to find the least expensive way to ship products to market and to solve bottlenecks. A bank or credit union can use a group support system to help it determine who should receive a loan. Shop managers can use decision support systems to help them decide what and how much inventory to order to meet customer needs and increase profits. An entrepreneur who owns and operates a temporary storage company can use vacancy reports to help determine what price to charge for new storage units. Everyone wants to be a better problem solver and decision maker. This chapter shows you how information systems can help. It begins with an overview of decision making and problem solving.

8.1 Decision Making and Problem Solving

Organizations need to make good decisions. In most cases, strategic planning and the overall goals of the organization set the course for decision making, helping employees and business units achieve their objectives and goals. Often, information systems also assist with strategic planning, helping top management make better decisions.

In business, one of the highest compliments you can receive is to be recognized by your colleagues and peers as a 'real problem solver'. Problem solving is a critical activity for any business organization. After identifying a problem, you begin the problem-solving process with decision making. A well-known model developed by Herbert Simon divides the **decision-making phase** of the problem-solving process into three stages: intelligence, design, and choice. This model was later incorporated by George Huber into an expanded model of the entire problem-solving process (see Figure 8.1).

decision-making phase The first part of problem solving, including three stages: intelligence, design, and choice.

Figure 8.1 How Decision Making Relates to Problem Solving

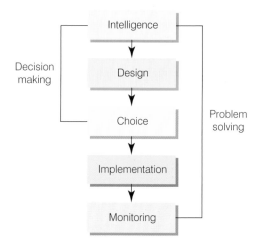

The three stages of decision making – intelligence, design, and choice – are augmented by implementation and monitoring to result in problem solving.

The first stage in the problem-solving process is the **intelligence stage**. During this stage, you identify and define potential problems or opportunities. For example, you might learn about the need for an intervention or change in an unsatisfactory situation. During the intelligence stage, you also investigate resource and environmental constraints. For example, if you were a French farmer, during the intelligence stage you might explore the possibilities of shipping apples from your farm to shops in Ireland. The perishability of the fruit and the maximum price that consumers in Ireland are willing to pay for the fruit are problem constraints. Aspects of the problem environment that you must consider include import/export laws regarding the shipment of food products.

> **intelligence stage** The first stage of decision making, in which potential problems or opportunities are identified and defined.

In the **design stage**, you develop alternative solutions to the problem. In addition, you evaluate the feasibility of these alternatives. In the fruit shipping example, you would consider the alternative methods of shipment, including the transportation times and costs associated with each.

> **design stage** The second stage of decision making, in which alternative solutions to the problem are developed.

The last stage of the decision-making phase, the **choice stage**, requires selecting a course of action. Here you might select the method of shipping fruit by air from you as the solution. The choice stage would then conclude with selection of an air carrier. As you will see later, various factors influence choice; the act of choosing is not as simple as it might first appear.

> **choice stage** The third stage of decision making, which requires selecting a course of action.

Problem solving includes and goes beyond decision making. It also includes the **implementation stage**, when the solution is put into effect. For example, if your decision is to ship fruit to Ireland as air freight using a specific air freight company, implementation involves informing your farming staff of the new activity, getting the fruit to the airport, and actually shipping the product.

> **problem solving** A process that goes beyond decision making to include the implementation and monitoring stages.

> **implementation stage** A stage of problem solving in which a solution is put into effect.

The final stage of the problem-solving process is the **monitoring stage**. In this stage, decision makers evaluate the implementation to determine whether the anticipated results were achieved and to modify the process in light of new information. Monitoring can involve feedback and adjustment. For example, you might need to change your air carrier if they regularly have shipping delays.

> **monitoring stage** The final stage of the problem-solving process, in which decision makers evaluate the implementation.

8.1.1 Programmed versus Non-Programmed Decisions

In the choice stage, various factors influence the decision maker's selection of a solution. One such factor is whether the decision can be programmed. **Programmed decisions** are made using a rule, procedure, or quantitative method. For example, to say that inventory should be ordered when inventory levels drop to 100 units is a programmed decision because it adheres to a rule. Programmed decisions are easy to computerize using traditional information systems. The relationships between system elements are fixed by rules, procedures, or numerical relationships. In other words, they are structured and deal with routine, well-defined decisions.

> **programmed decision** A decision made using a rule, procedure, or quantitative method.

Non-programmed decisions, however, deal with unusual or exceptional situations. In many cases, these decisions are difficult to quantify. Determining the appropriate training program for a new employee, deciding whether to start a new type of product line, and weighing the benefits and drawbacks of installing a new pollution control system are examples. Each of these decisions contains unique characteristics, and standard rules or procedures might not apply to them. Today, decision support systems help solve many non-programmed decisions, in which the problem is not routine and rules and relationships are not well defined (unstructured or ill-structured problems).

> **non-programmed decision** A decision that deals with unusual or exceptional situations that can be difficult to quantify.

8.1.2 Optimization, Satisficing, and Heuristic Approaches

In general, computerized decision support systems can either optimize or satisfice. An optimization model finds the best solution, usually the one that will best help the organization meet its goals. For example, an optimization model can find the appropriate number of products that an organization should produce to meet a profit goal, given certain conditions and assumptions. Optimization models use problem constraints. A limit on the number of available work hours in a manufacturing facility is an example of a problem constraint. Some spreadsheet programs, such as Microsoft Excel, have optimizing features (see Figure 8.2). A business such as an appliance manufacturer can use an optimization program to reduce the time and cost of manufacturing appliances and increase profits. Optimization software also allows decision makers to explore various alternatives.

Figure 8.2
Optimization Software
MS Excel5 Solver, which can find an optimal solution, given certain constraints.

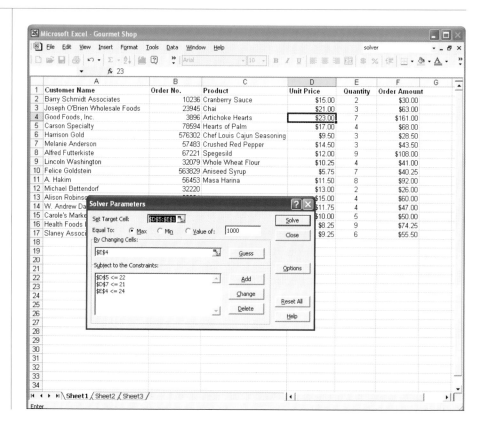

Consider a few examples of how you can use optimization to achieve huge savings. Bombardier Flexjet, a company that sells fractional ownership of jets, used an optimization program to save almost €22 million annually to better schedule its aircraft and crews.[1] Hutchinson Port Holdings, the world's largest container terminal, saved even more – over €37 million annually.[2] The company processes a staggering 10 000 trucks and 15 ships every day, and used optimization to maximize the use of its trucks. Deere & Company, a manufacturer of commercial vehicles and equipment, increased shareholder value by over €75 million annually by using optimization to minimize inventory levels and by enhancing customer satisfaction.[3]

A **satisficing model** is one that finds a good – but not necessarily the best – problem solution. Satisficing is usually used because modelling the problem properly to get an optimal decision would be too difficult, complex, or costly. Satisficing normally does not look at all possible solutions but only at those likely to give good results. Consider a decision to select a location for a

satisficing model A model that will find a good – but not necessarily the best – problem solution.

new manufacturing plant. To find the optimal (best) location, you must consider all cities in Europe. A satisficing approach is to consider only five or ten cities that might satisfy the company's requirements. Limiting the options might not result in the best decision, but it will likely result in a good decision, without spending the time and effort to investigate all cities. Satisficing is a good alternative modelling method because it is sometimes too expensive to analyze every alternative to find the best solution.

Heuristics, often referred to as 'rules of thumb' – commonly accepted guidelines or procedures that usually find a good solution – are often used in decision making. An example of a heuristic is to order four months' supply of inventory for a particular item when the inventory level drops to 20 units or less; although this heuristic might not minimize total inventory costs, it can serve as a good rule of thumb to avoid running out of stock without maintaining excess inventory. Trend Micro, a provider of antivirus software, has developed an antispam product that is based on heuristics. The software examines e-mails to find those most likely to be spam. It doesn't examine all e-mails.

> **heuristics** Commonly accepted guidelines or procedures that usually find a good solution.

8.1.3 Sense and Respond

Sense and Respond (SaR) involves determining problems or opportunities (sense) and developing systems to solve the problems or take advantage of the opportunities (respond).[4] SaR often requires nimble organizations that replace traditional lines of authority with those that are flexible and dynamic. IBM, for example, used SaR with its microelectronics division to help with inventory control. They used mathematical models and optimization routines to control inventory levels. The models sensed when a shortage of inventory for customers was likely and responded by backlogging and storing extra inventory to avoid the shortages. In this application, SaR identified potential problems and solved them before they became a reality. SaR can also identify opportunities, such as new products or marketing approaches, and then respond by building the new products or starting new marketing campaigns. One way to implement the SaR approach is through management information and decision support systems, discussed next.

8.2 An Overview of Management Information Systems

A management information system (MIS) is an integrated collection of people, procedures, databases, hardware, and software that provides managers and decision makers with information to help achieve organizational goals. The primary purpose of an MIS is to help an organization achieve its goals by providing managers with insight into the regular operations of the organization so that they can control, organize, and plan more effectively. One important role of the MIS is to provide the right information to the right person in the right format at the right time. In short, an MIS provides managers with information, typically in reports, that supports effective decision making and provides feedback on daily operations. For example, a manager might request a report of weekly sales, broken down by area. On the basis of this information, she might decide to redistribute her mobile sales staff to have greater coverage in one place, less in another.

Figure 8.3 shows the role of MIS within the flow of an organization's information. Note that business transactions can enter the organization through traditional methods or via the Internet or an extranet connecting customers and suppliers to the firm's ERP or transaction processing systems. The use of MIS spans all levels of management. That is, they provide support to and are used by employees throughout the organization.

Figure 8.3 Sources of Managerial Information
The MIS is just one of many sources of managerial information. Decision support systems, executive support systems, and expert systems also assist in decision making.

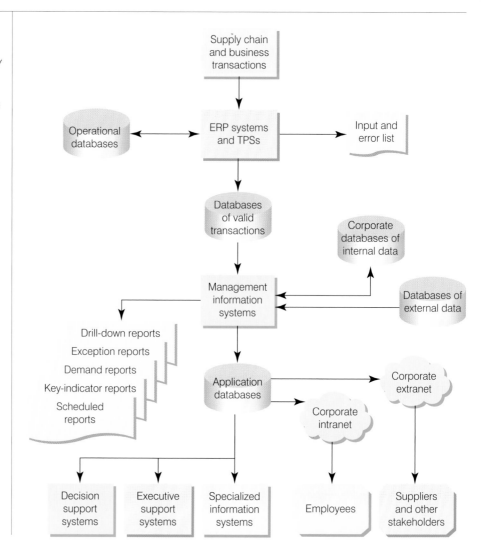

8.2.1 Inputs to a Management Information System

As shown in Figure 8.3, data that enters an MIS originates from both internal and external sources, including the company's supply chain, first discussed in Chapter 2. The most significant internal data sources for an MIS are the organization's various TPS and ERP systems. As discussed in Chapter 5, companies also use data warehouses and data marts to store valuable business information. Other internal data comes from specific functional areas throughout the firm.

External sources of data can include customers, suppliers, competitors, and stockholders whose data is not already captured by the TPS, as well as other sources, such as the Internet. In addition, many companies have implemented extranets to link with selected suppliers and other business partners to exchange data and information.

The MIS uses the data obtained from these sources and processes it into information more usable by managers, primarily in the form of predetermined reports. For example, rather than simply obtaining a chronological list of sales activity over the past week, a national sales manager might obtain his or her organization's weekly sales data in a format that allows him or her to see sales activity by region, by local sales representative, by product, and even in comparison with last year's sales.

8.2.2 Outputs of a Management Information System

The output of most management information systems is a collection of reports that are distributed to managers. These can include tabulations, summaries, charts, and graphs (Figure 8.4). Management reports can come from various company databases, data warehouses, and other sources. These reports include scheduled reports, key-indicator reports, demand reports, exception reports, and drill-down reports (see Figure 8.5).

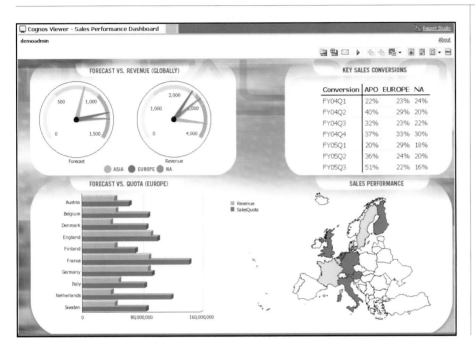

Figure 8.4 An **Executive Dashboard** *This MIS reporting system puts many kinds of real-time information at managers' fingertips to aid in decision making.*

Scheduled Reports

Scheduled reports are produced periodically, or on a schedule, such as daily, weekly, or monthly. For example, a production manager could use a weekly summary report that lists total payroll costs to monitor and control labour and job costs. A manufacturing report generated once per day to monitor the production of a new item is another example of a scheduled report. Other scheduled reports can help managers control customer credit, performance of sales representatives, inventory levels, and more.

> **scheduled report** A report produced periodically, or on a schedule, such as daily, weekly, or monthly.

A **key-indicator report** summarizes the previous day's critical activities and is typically available at the beginning of each workday. These reports can summarize inventory levels, production activity, sales volume, and the like. Key-indicator reports are used by managers and executives to take quick, corrective action on significant aspects of the business.

> **key-indicator report** A summary of the previous day's critical activities; typically available at the beginning of each workday.

Demand Reports

Demand reports are developed to give certain information upon request. In other words, these reports are produced on demand. Like other reports discussed in this section, they often come from an organization's database system. For example, an executive might want to know the production status of a particular item – a demand report can be generated to provide the requested information by querying the company's database. Suppliers and customers can also use demand reports. FedEx, for example, provides demand reports on its website to allow its customers to track

> **demand report** A report developed to give certain information at someone's request.

Figure 8.5 Reports Generated by an MIS *The types of reports are (a) scheduled, (b) key indicator, (c) demand, (d) exception, and (e–h) drill down.*

(a) Scheduled Report

Daily Sales Detail Report

Prepared: 08/10/08

Order #	Customer ID	Salesperson ID	Planned Ship Date	Quantity	Item #	Amount
P12453	C89321	CAR	08/12/08	144	P1234	€3,214
P12453	C89321	CAR	08/12/08	288	P3214	€5,660
P12454	C03214	GWA	08/13/08	12	P4902	€1,224
P12455	C52313	SAK	08/12/08	24	P4012	€2,448
P12456	C34123	JMW	08/13/08	144	P3214	€720
....	....	....	....	....	....	....

(b) Key-Indicator Report

Daily Sales Key-Indicator Report

	This Month	Last Month	Last Year
Total Orders Month to Date	€1,808	€1,694	€1,914
Forecasted Sales for the Month	€2,406	€2,224	€2,608

(c) Demand Report

Daily Sales by Salesperson Summary Report

Prepared: 08/10/08

Salesperson ID	Amount
CAR	€42,345
GWA	€38,950
SAK	€22,100
JWN	€12,350
....	....

(d) Exception Report

Daily Sales Exception Report—Orders Over €10,000

Prepared: 08/10/08

Order #	Customer ID	Salesperson ID	Planned Ship Date	Quantity	Item #	Amount
P12345	C89321	GWA	08/12/08	576	P1234	€12,856
P22153	C00453	CAR	08/12/08	288	P2314	€28,800
P23023	C32832	JMN	08/11/08	144	P2323	€14,400
....	....	....	....	....	....	....
....	....	....	....	....	....	....

8

packages from their source to their final destination. Other examples of demand reports include reports requested by executives to show the hours worked by a particular employee, total sales to date for a product, and so on.

exception report A report automatically produced when a situation is unusual or requires management action.

Exception Reports

Exception reports are reports that are automatically produced when a situation is unusual or requires management action. For example, a manager

Figure 8.5 *Continued*

(e) First-Level Drill-Down Report

Earnings by Quarter (Millions)

		Actual	Forecast	Variance
2nd Qtr.	2008	€12.6	€11.8	6.8%
1st Qtr.	2008	€10.8	€10.7	0.9%
4th Qtr.	2008	€14.3	€14.5	−1.4%
3rd Qtr.	2008	€12.8	€13.3	−3.8%

(f) Second-Level Drill-Down Report

Sales and Expenses (Millions)

Qtr: 2nd Qtr. 2008	Actual	Forecast	Variance
Gross Sales	€110.9	€108.3	2.4%
Expenses	€ 98.3	€ 96.5	1.9%
Profit	12.6	€ 11.8	6.8%

(g) Third-Level Drill-Down Report

Sales by Division (Millions)

Qtr: 2nd Qtr. 2008	Actual	Forecast	Variance
Beauty Care	€ 34.5	€ 33.9	1.8%
Health Care	€ 30.0	€ 28.0	7.1%
Soap	€ 22.8	€ 23.0	−0.9%
Snacks	€ 12.1	€ 12.5	−3.2%
Electronics	€ 11.5	€ 10.9	5.5%
Total	€110.9	€108.3	2.4%

(h) Fourth-Level Drill-Down Report

Sales by Product Category (Millions)

Qtr: 2nd Qtr. 2008 Division: Health Care	Actual	Forecast	Variance
Toothpaste	€12.4	€10.5	18.1%
Mouthwash	€ 8.6	€ 8.8	−2.3%
Over-the-Counter Drugs	€ 5.8	€ 5.3	9.4%
Skin Care Products	€ 3.2	€ 3.4	−5.9%
Total	€30.0	€28.0	7.1%

SOURCE: George W. Reynolds, *Information Systems for Managers* (3rd ed.), St. Paul, MN: West Publishing Co., 1995.

8

might set a parameter that generates a report of all items which have been purchased and then returned by more than five customers. Such items may need to be looked at to identify any production problem, for instance. As with key-indicator reports, exception reports are most often used to monitor aspects important to an organization's success. In general, when an exception report is produced, a manager or executive takes action. Parameters, or trigger points, for an exception report should be set carefully. Trigger points that are set too low might result in too many exception reports; trigger points that are too high could mean that problems requiring action are overlooked. For example, if a manager wants a report that contains all projects over budget by €1000 or more, the system might retrieve almost every company project. The €1000 trigger point is probably too low. A trigger point of €10 000 might be more appropriate.

Drill-Down Reports

Drill-down reports provide increasingly detailed data about a situation. Through the use of drill-down reports, analysts can see data at a high level first (such as sales for the entire company), then at a more detailed level (such as the sales for one department of the company), and then a very detailed level (such as sales for one sales representative). Managers can drill down into more levels of detail to individual transactions if they want.

drill-down report A report providing increasingly detailed data about a situation.

Developing Effective Reports

Management information system reports can help managers develop better plans, make better decisions, and obtain greater control over the operations of the firm, but in practice, the types of reports can overlap. For example, a manager can demand an exception report or set trigger points for items contained in a key-indicator report. In addition, some software packages can be used to produce, gather, and distribute reports from different computer systems. Certain guidelines should be followed in designing and developing reports to yield the best results. Table 8.1 explains some of these guidelines.

Table 8.1 Guidelines for Developing MIS Reports

Guidelines	Reason
Tailor each report to user needs	The unique needs of the manager or executive should be considered, requiring user involvement and input
Spend time and effort producing only reports that are useful	After being instituted, many reports continue to be generated even if no one uses them anymore
Pay attention to report content and layout	Prominently display the information that is most desired. Do not clutter the report with unnecessary data. Use commonly accepted words and phrases. Managers can work more efficiently if they can easily find desired information
Use management-by-exception reporting	Some reports should be produced only when a problem needs to be solved or an action should be taken
Set parameters carefully	Low parameters might result in too many reports; high parameters mean valuable information could be overlooked
Produce all reports in a timely fashion	Outdated reports are of little or no value
Periodically review reports	Review reports at least once per year to make sure they are still needed. Review report content and layout. Determine whether additional reports are needed

8.2.3 Characteristics of a Management Information System

In general, MIS perform the following functions:

- *Provide reports with fixed and standard formats.* For example, scheduled reports for inventory control can contain the same types of information placed in the same locations on the reports. Different managers can use the same report for different purposes.

- *Produce hard-copy and soft-copy reports.* Some MIS reports are printed on paper, which are hard-copy reports. Most output soft copy, using visual displays on computer screens. Soft-copy output is typically formatted in a report format. In other words, a manager might display an MIS report directly on the computer screen, but the report would still appear in the standard hard-copy format.

- *Use internal data stored in the computer system.* MIS reports use primarily internal sources of data that are contained in computerized databases. Some MIS also use external sources of data about competitors, the marketplace, and so on. The web is a frequently used source for external data.

- *Allow users to develop their own custom reports.* Although analysts and programmers might be involved in developing and implementing complex MIS reports that require data from many sources, users are increasingly developing their own simple programs to query databases and produce basic reports. This capability, however, can result in several users developing the same or similar reports, which can increase the total time expended and require more storage, compared with having an analyst develop one report for all users.

- *Require users to submit formal requests for reports to systems personnel.* When IS personnel develop and implement MIS reports, they typically require others to submit a formal request to the IS department. If a manager, for example, wants a production report to be used by several people in his or her department, a formal request for the report is often required. User-developed reports require much less formality.

8.3 Functional MIS

Most organizations are structured along functional lines or areas. This functional structure is usually apparent from an organization chart. Some traditional functional areas are finance, manufacturing, marketing, and human resources, among others. The MIS can also be divided along those functional lines to produce reports tailored to individual functions (see Figure 8.6).

8.3.1 Financial Management Information Systems

A **financial MIS** provides financial information not only for executives but also for a broader set of people who need to make better decisions on a daily basis. Financial MIS are used to streamline reports of transactions. Most financial MIS perform the following functions:

financial MIS A management information system that provides financial information not only for executives but also for a broader set of people who need to make better decisions on a daily basis.

- Integrate financial and operational information from multiple sources, including the Internet, into a single system.

- Provide easy access to data for both financial and non-financial users, often through the use of a corporate intranet to access corporate web pages of financial data and information.

Figure 8.6 An Organization's MIS *The MIS is an integrated collection of functional information systems, each supporting particular functional areas.*

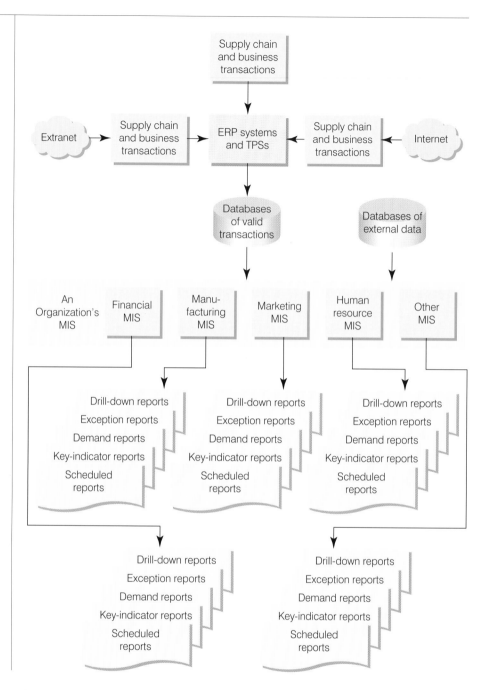

- Make financial data immediately available to shorten analysis turnaround time.
- Enable analysis of financial data along multiple dimensions – time, geography, product, plant, customer.
- Analyze historical and current financial activity.
- Monitor and control the use of funds over time.

auditing Analyzing the financial condition of an organization and determining whether financial statements and reports produced by the financial MIS are accurate.

Figure 8.7 shows typical inputs, function-specific subsystems, and outputs of a financial MIS, including profit and loss, auditing, and uses and management of funds.

Financial MIS are used to compute revenues, costs, profits and for **auditing**. Auditing involves analyzing the financial condition of an organization and

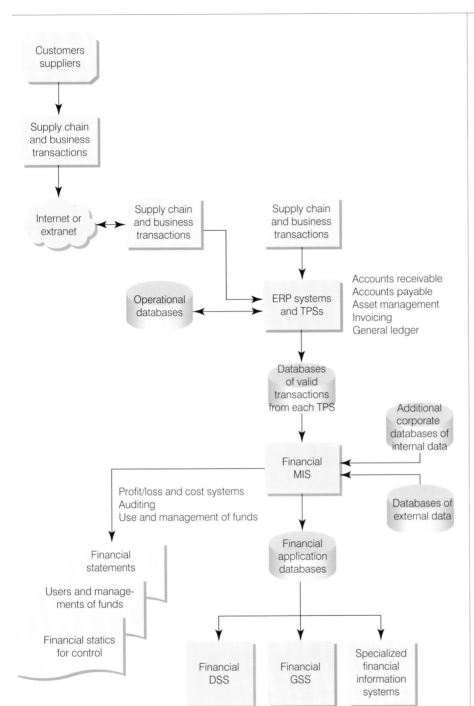

Figure 8.7 Overview of a Financial MIS

determining whether financial statements and reports produced by the financial MIS are accurate. Financial MIS are also used to manage funds. Internal uses of funds include purchasing additional inventory, updating plants and equipment, hiring new employees, acquiring other companies, buying new computer systems, increasing marketing and advertising, purchasing raw materials or land, investing in new products, and increasing research and development. External uses of funds are typically investment related. Companies often invest excess funds in such external revenue generators as bank accounts, stocks, bonds, bills, notes, futures, options, and foreign currency using financial MIS.

8.3.2 Manufacturing Management Information Systems

More than any other functional area, advances in information systems have revolutionized manufacturing. As a result, many manufacturing operations have been dramatically improved over the last decade. Also, with the emphasis on greater quality and productivity, having an effective manufacturing process is becoming even more critical. The use of computerized systems is emphasized at all levels of manufacturing – from the shop floor to the executive suite. People and small businesses, for example, can benefit from manufacturing MIS that once were only available to large corporations. Personal fabrication systems, for example, can make circuit boards, precision parts, radio tags, and more.[5] Personal fabrication systems include precise machine tools, such as milling machines and cutting tools and sophisticated software. The total system can cost €15 000. For example, in a remote area of Norway, Maakon Karlson uses a personal fabrication system that makes radio tags to track sheep and other animals. The use of the Internet has also streamlined all aspects of manufacturing. Figure 8.8 gives an overview of some of the manufacturing MIS inputs, subsystems, and outputs.

Figure 8.8 Overview of a Manufacturing MIS

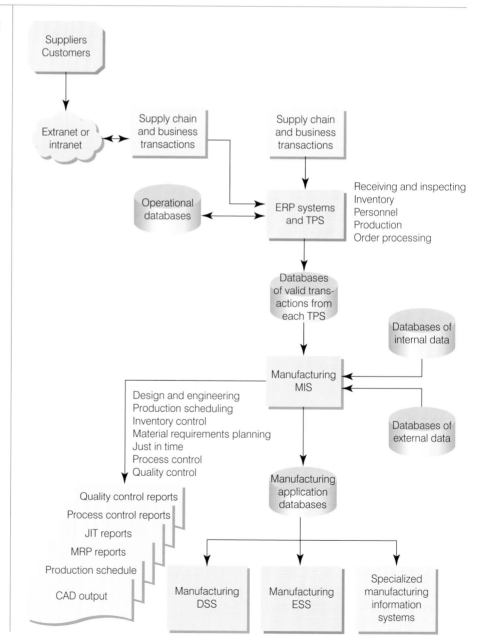

The manufacturing MIS subsystems and outputs monitor and control the flow of materials, products, and services through the organization. As raw materials are converted to finished goods, the manufacturing MIS monitors the process at almost every stage. New technology could make this process easier. Using specialized computer chips and tiny radio transmitters, companies can monitor materials and products through the entire manufacturing process. Car manufacturers, who convert raw steel, plastic, and other materials into a finished automobile, also monitor their manufacturing processes. Auto manufacturers add thousands of dollars of value to the raw materials they use in assembling a car. If the manufacturing MIS also lets them provide additional services, such as customized paint colours, on any of their models, it has added further value for customers. In doing so, the MIS helps provide the company the edge that can differentiate it from competitors. The success of an organization can depend on the manufacturing function. Some common information subsystems and outputs used in manufacturing are discussed next.

■ *Design and engineering.* Manufacturing companies often use computer-aided design (CAD) with new or existing products (Figure 8.9). For example, Boeing uses a CAD system to develop a complete digital blueprint of an aircraft before it ever begins its manufacturing process. As mock-ups are built and tested, the digital blueprint is constantly revised to reflect the most current design. Using such technology helps Boeing reduce its manufacturing costs and the time to design a new aircraft.

■ *Master production scheduling and inventory control.* Scheduling production and controlling inventory are critical for any manufacturing company. The overall objective of master

Figure 8.9 CAD Software

8

production scheduling is to provide detailed plans for both short-term and long-range scheduling of manufacturing facilities. Many techniques are used to minimize inventory costs. Most determine how much and when to order inventory. One method of determining how much inventory to order is called the **economic order quantity (EOQ)**. This quantity is calculated to minimize the total inventory costs. The when-to-order question is based on inventory usage over time. Typically, the question is answered in terms of a **reorder point (ROP)**, which is a critical inventory quantity level. When the inventory level for a particular item falls to the reorder point, or critical level, the system generates a report so that an order is immediately placed for the EOQ of the product. Another inventory technique used when the demand for one item depends on the demand for another is called **material requirements planning (MRP)**. The basic goal of MRP is to determine when finished products, such as automobiles or airplanes, are needed and then to work backward to determine deadlines and resources needed, such as engines and tires, to complete the final product on schedule. **Just-in-time (JIT)** inventory and manufacturing is an approach that maintains inventory at the lowest levels without sacrificing the availability of finished products. With this approach, inventory and materials are delivered just before they are used in a product. A JIT inventory system would arrange for a car windscreen to be delivered to the assembly line just before it is secured to the automobile, rather than storing it in the manufacturing facility while the car's other components are being assembled. JIT, however, can result in some organizations running out of inventory when demand exceeds expectations.[6]

economic order quantity (EOQ) The quantity that should be reordered to minimize total inventory costs.

reorder point (ROP) A critical inventory quantity level.

material requirements planning (MRP) A set of inventory-control techniques that help coordinate thousands of inventory items when the demand of one item is dependent on the demand for another.

just-in-time (JIT) inventory A philosophy of inventory management in which inventory and materials are delivered just before they are used in manufacturing a product.

■ *Process control.* Managers can use a number of technologies to control and streamline the manufacturing process. For example, computers can directly control manufacturing equipment, using systems called **computer-aided manufacturing (CAM)**. CAM systems can control drilling machines, assembly lines, and more. **Computer-integrated manufacturing (CIM)** uses computers to link the components of the production process into an effective system. CIM's goal is to tie together all aspects of production, including order processing, product design, manufacturing, inspection and quality control, and shipping. A **flexible manufacturing system (FMS)** is an approach that allows manufacturing facilities to rapidly and efficiently change from making one product to another. In the middle of a production run, for example, the production process can be changed to make a different product or to switch manufacturing materials. By using an FMS, the time and cost to change manufacturing jobs can be substantially reduced, and companies can react quickly to market needs and competition.

computer-aided manufacturing (CAM) A system that directly controls manufacturing equipment.

computer-integrated manufacturing (CIM) Using computers to link the components of the production process into an effective system.

flexible manufacturing system (FMS) An approach that allows manufacturing facilities to rapidly and efficiently change from making one product to making another.

quality control A process that ensures that the finished product meets the customers' needs.

■ *Quality control and testing.* With increased pressure from consumers and a general concern for productivity and high quality, today's manufacturing organizations are placing more emphasis on **quality control**, a process that ensures that the finished product meets the customers' needs. Information systems are used to monitor quality and take corrective steps to eliminate possible quality problems.

8.3.3 Marketing Management Information Systems

marketing MIS An information system that supports managerial activities in product development, distribution, pricing decisions, and promotional effectiveness.

A **marketing MIS** supports managerial activities in product development, distribution, pricing decisions, promotional effectiveness, and sales forecasting. Marketing functions are increasingly being performed on the Internet.

Many companies are developing Internet marketplaces to advertise and sell products. The amount spent on online advertising is worth billions of euros annually. Software can measure how many customers see the advertising. Some companies use software products to analyze customer loyalty. Some marketing departments are actively using blogs to publish company related information and interact with customers.[7]

Customer relationship management (CRM) programs, available from some ERP vendors, help a company manage all aspects of customer encounters. CRM software can help a company collect customer data, contact customers, educate customers on new products, and sell products to customers through a website. An airline, for example, can use a CRM system to notify customers about flight changes. New Zealand's Jade Stadium, for example, uses CRM software from GlobalTech Solutions to give a single entry point to its marketing efforts and customer databases, instead of using about 20 spreadsheets.[8] The CRM software will help Jade Stadium develop effective marketing campaigns, record and track client contacts, and maintain an accurate database of clients. Yet, not all CRM systems and marketing sites on the Internet are successful. Customization and ongoing maintenance of a CRM system can be expensive. Figure 8.10 shows the inputs, subsystems, and outputs of a typical marketing MIS.

Subsystems for the marketing MIS include marketing research, product development, promotion and advertising, and product pricing. These subsystems and their outputs help

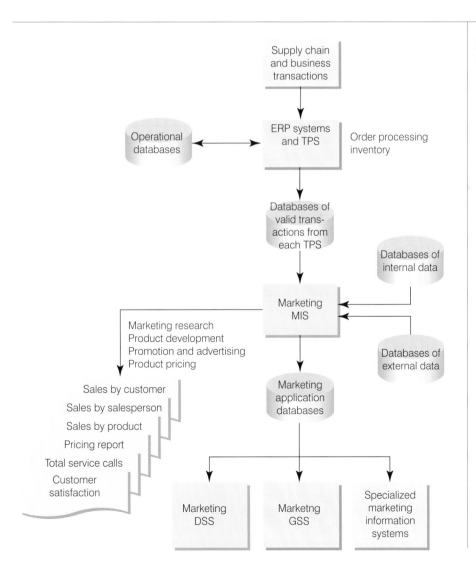

Figure 8.10 Overview of a Marketing MIS

marketing managers and executives increase sales, reduce marketing expenses, and develop plans for future products and services to meet the changing needs of customers.

■ *Marketing research.* The purpose of marketing research is to conduct a formal study of the market and customer preferences. Computer systems are used to help conduct and analyze the results of surveys, questionnaires, pilot studies, and interviews.

■ *Product development.* Product development involves the conversion of raw materials into finished goods and services and focuses primarily on the physical attributes of the product. Many factors, including plant capacity, labour skills, engineering factors, and materials are important in product development decisions. In many cases, a computer program analyzes these various factors and selects the appropriate mix of labour, materials, plant and equipment, and engineering designs. Make-or-buy decisions can also be made with the assistance of computer programs.

■ *Promotion and advertising.* One of the most important functions of any marketing effort is promotion and advertising. Product success is a direct function of the types of advertising and sales promotion done. Increasingly, organizations are using the Internet to advertise and sell products and services.

■ *Product pricing.* Product pricing is another important and complex marketing function. Retail price, wholesale price, and price discounts must be set. Most companies try to develop pricing policies that will maximize total sales revenues. Computers are often used to analyze the relationship between prices and total revenues.

■ *Sales analysis.* Computerized sales analysis is important to identify products, sales personnel, and customers that contribute to profits and those that do not. Several reports can be generated to help marketing managers make good sales decisions (see Figure 8.11). The sales-by-product report lists all major products and their sales for a period of time, such as a month. This report shows which products are doing well and which need improvement or should be discarded altogether. The sales-by-salesperson report lists total sales for each salesperson for each week or month. This report can also be subdivided by product to show which products are being sold by each salesperson. The sales-by-customer report is a tool that can be used to identify high- and low-volume customers.

8.3.4 Human Resource Management Information Systems

A **human resource MIS (HRMIS)**, also called a personnel MIS, is concerned with activities related to previous, current, and potential employees of the organization. Because the personnel function relates to all other functional areas in the business, the human resource (HR) MIS plays a valuable role in ensuring organizational success. Some of the activities performed by this important MIS include workforce analysis and planning, hiring, training, job and task assignment, and many other personnel-related issues. An effective HRMIS allows a company to keep personnel costs at a minimum, while serving the required business processes needed to achieve corporate goals. Although human resource information systems focus on cost reduction, many of today's HR systems concentrate on hiring and managing existing employees to get the total potential of the human talent in the organization. According to the High Performance Workforce Study conducted by Accenture, the most important HR initiatives include improving worker productivity, improving adaptability to new opportunities, and facilitating organizational change. Figure 8.12 shows some of the inputs, subsystems, and outputs of the HRMIS.

Human resource subsystems and outputs range from the determination of human resource needs and hiring through retirement and outplacement. Most medium and large organizations

human resource MIS (HRMIS)
An information system that is concerned with activities related to employees and potential employees of an organization, also called a personnel MIS.

(a) Sales by product

Product	August	September	October	November	December	Total
Product 1	34	32	32	21	33	152
Product 2	156	162	177	163	122	780
Product 3	202	145	122	98	66	633
Product 4	345	365	352	341	288	1691

(b) Sales by salesperson

Salesperson	August	September	October	November	December	Total
Jones	24	42	42	11	43	162
Kline	166	155	156	122	133	732
Lane	166	155	104	99	106	630
Miller	245	225	305	291	301	1367

(c) Sales by customer

Customer	August	September	October	November	December	Total
Ang	234	334	432	411	301	1712
Braswell	56	62	77	61	21	277
Celec	1202	1445	1322	998	667	5634
Jung	45	65	55	34	88	287

Figure 8.11 Reports Generated to Help Marketing Managers Make Good Decisions
(a) This sales-by-product report lists all major products and their sales for the period from August to December. (b) This sales-by-salesperson report lists total sales for each salesperson for the same time period. (c) This sales-by-customer report lists sales for each customer for the period. Like all MIS reports, totals are provided automatically by the system to show managers at a glance the information they need to make good decisions.

have computer systems to assist with human resource planning, hiring, training and skills inventorying, and wage and salary administration. Outputs of the human resource MIS include reports, such as human resource planning reports, job application review profiles, skills inventory reports, and salary surveys.

■ *Human resource planning.* One of the first aspects of any HRMIS is determining personnel and human needs. The overall purpose of this MIS subsystem is to put the right number and kinds of employees in the right jobs when they are needed. Effective human resource planning can require computer programs, such as SPSS and SAS, to forecast the future number of employees needed and anticipating the future supply of people for these jobs. IBM is using an HR pilot program, called Professional Marketplace, to plan for workforce needs, including the supplies and tools the workforce needs to work efficiently.[9] Professional Marketplace helps IBM to catalogue employees into a glossary of skills and abilities. Like many other companies, HR and workforce costs are IBM's biggest expense.

■ *Personnel selection and recruiting.* If the human resource plan reveals that additional personnel are required, the next logical step is recruiting and selecting personnel.

Figure 8.12 Overview of a HRMIS

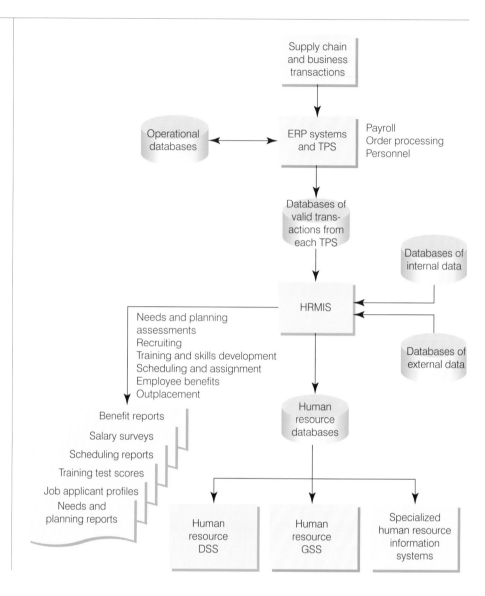

Companies seeking new employees often use computers to schedule recruiting efforts and trips and to test potential employees' skills. Many companies now use the Internet to screen for job applicants. Applicants use a template to load their CVs onto the Internet site. HR managers can then access these CVs and identify applicants they are interested in interviewing.

■ *Training and skills inventory.* Some jobs, such as programming, equipment repair, and tax preparation, require very specific training for new employees. Other jobs may require general training about the organizational culture, orientation, dress standards, and expectations of the organization. When training is complete, employees often take computer-scored tests to evaluate their mastery of skills and new material.

■ *Scheduling and job placement.* Employee schedules are developed for each employee, showing his or her job assignments over the next week or month. Job placements are often determined based on skills inventory reports, which show which employee might be best suited to a particular job. Sophisticated scheduling programs are often used in the airline industry, the military, and many other areas to get the right people assigned to the right jobs at the right time.

▨ *Wage and salary administration.* Another HRMIS subsystem involves determining salaries and benefits, including medical insurance and pension payments. Wage data, such as industry averages for positions, can be taken from the corporate database and manipulated by the HRMIS to provide wage information reports to higher levels of management.

8.3.5 Geographic Information Systems

Although not yet common in organizations, a **geographic information system (GIS)** is a computer system capable of assembling, storing, manipulating, and displaying geographically referenced information, that is, data identified according to its location. A GIS enables users to pair maps or map outlines with tabular data to describe aspects of a particular geographic region. For example, sales managers might want to plot total sales for each region in the countries they serve. Using a GIS, they can specify that each region be shaded to indicate the relative amount of sales – no shading or light shading represents no or little sales, and deeper shading represents more sales. Staples Inc., the large office supply store chain, used a geographic information system to select about 100 new store locations, after considering about 5000 possible sites.[10] Finding the best location is critical. It can cost up to €750 000 for a failed store because of a poor location. Staples uses a GIS tool from Tactician Corporation along with software from SAS. Although many software products have seen declining revenues, the use of GIS software is increasing.

> **geographic information system (GIS)** A computer system capable of assembling, storing, manipulating, and displaying geographic information, that is, data identified according to its location.

8.4 Decision Support Systems

Management information systems provide useful summary reports to help solve structured and semi-structured business problems. Decision support systems (DSS) offer the potential to assist in solving both semi-structured and unstructured problems. A DSS is an organized collection of people, procedures, software, databases, and devices used to help make decisions that solve problems. The focus of a DSS is on decision-making effectiveness when faced with unstructured or semi-structured business problems. As with a TPS and an MIS, a DSS should be designed, developed, and used to help an organization achieve its goals and objectives. Decision support systems offer the potential to generate higher profits, lower costs, and better products and services.

Decision support systems, although skewed somewhat toward the top levels of management, are used at all levels. To some extent, today's managers at all levels are faced with less structured, non-routine problems, but the quantity and magnitude of these decisions increase as a manager rises higher in an organization. Many organizations contain a tangled web of complex rules, procedures, and decisions. DSS are used to bring more structure to these problems to aid the decision-making process. In addition, because of the inherent flexibility of decision support systems, managers at all levels are able to use DSS to assist in some relatively routine, programmable decisions in lieu of more formalized management information systems.

8.4.1 Characteristics of a Decision Support System

Decision support systems have many characteristics that allow them to be effective management support tools, some of which are listed here. Of course, not all DSS work the same.

▨ *Provide rapid access to information.* DSS provide fast and continuous access to information.

▨ *Handle large amounts of data from different sources.* For instance, advanced database management systems and data warehouses have allowed decision makers to search for information with a DSS, even when some data resides in different databases on different computer systems or networks. Other sources of data can be accessed via the Internet or over a corporate intranet. Using the Internet, an oil giant can use a decision support system to save hundreds of millions of euros annually by coordinating a large amount of drilling and exploration data from around the globe.

- *Provide report and presentation flexibility.* Managers can get the information they want, presented in a format that suits their needs. Furthermore, output can be displayed on computer screens or printed, depending on the needs and desires of the problem solvers.

- *Offer both textual and graphical orientation.* DSS can produce text, tables, line drawings, pie charts, trend lines, and more. By using their preferred orientation, managers can use a DSS to get a better understanding of a situation and to convey this understanding to others.

- *Support drill-down analysis.* A manager can get more levels of detail when needed by drilling down through data. For example, a manager can get more detailed information for a project – viewing the overall project cost, then drilling down and seeing the cost for each phase, activity, and task.

- *Perform complex, sophisticated analysis and comparisons using advanced software packages.* Marketing research surveys, for example, can be analyzed in a variety of ways using programs that are part of a DSS. Many of the analytical programs associated with a DSS are actually stand-alone programs, and the DSS brings them together.

- *Support optimization, satisficing, and heuristic approaches.* By supporting all types of decision-making approaches, a DSS gives the decision maker a great deal of flexibility in computer support for decision making. For example, **what-if analysis**, the process of making hypothetical changes to problem data and observing the impact on the results, can be used to control inventory. Given the demand for products, such as automobiles, the computer can determine the necessary parts and components, including engines, transmissions, windows, and so on. With what-if analysis, a manager can make changes to problem data, say the number of cars needed for next month, and immediately see the impact on the parts requirements.

what-if analysis The process of making hypothetical changes to problem data and observing the impact on the results.

- *Perform goal-seeking analysis.* **Goal-seeking analysis** is the process of determining the problem data required for a given result. For example, a financial manager might be considering an investment with a certain monthly net income, and the manager might have a goal to earn a return of 9 percent on the investment. Goal seeking allows the manager to determine what monthly net income (problem data) is needed to yield a return of 9 percent (problem result). Some spreadsheets can be used to perform goal-seeking analysis (see Figure 8.13).

goal-seeking analysis The process of determining the problem data required for a given result.

- *Perform simulation.* **Simulation** is the ability of the DSS to duplicate the features of a real system. In most cases, probability or uncertainty is involved. For example, the number of repairs and the time to repair key components of a manufacturing line can be calculated to determine the impact on the number of products that can be produced each day. Engineers can use this data to determine which components need to be reengineered to increase the mean time between failures and which components need to have an ample supply of spare parts to reduce the mean time to repair. Drug companies are using simulated trials to reduce the need for human participants and reduce the time and costs of bringing a new drug to market. Drug companies are hoping that this use of simulation will help them identify successful drugs earlier in development. Corporate executives and military commanders often use computer simulations to allow them to try different strategies in

simulation The ability of the DSS to duplicate the features of a real system.

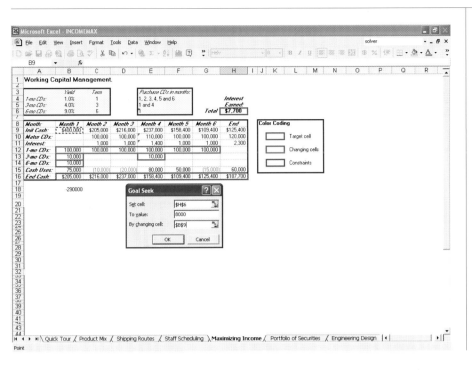

Figure 8.13
Spreadsheet *With a spreadsheet program, a manager can enter a goal, and the spreadsheet will determine the input needed to achieve the goal.*

different situations. Corporate executives, for example, can try different marketing decisions under various market conditions. Military commanders often use computer war games to fine-tune their military strategies in different warfare conditions. The Turkish army, for example, uses simulation to help coordinate its fuel-supply system.[11]

8.4.2 Capabilities of a Decision Support System

Developers of decision support systems strive to make them more flexible than management information systems and to give them the potential to assist decision makers in a variety of situations. DSS can assist with all or most problem-solving phases, decision frequencies, and different degrees of problem structure. DSS approaches can also help at all levels of the decision-making process. A single DSS might provide only a few of these capabilities, depending on its uses and scope.

■ *Support for problem-solving phases.* The objective of most decision support systems is to assist decision makers with the phases of problem solving. As previously discussed, these phases include intelligence, design, choice, implementation, and monitoring. A specific DSS might support only one or a few phases. By supporting all types of decision-making approaches, a DSS gives the decision maker a great deal of flexibility in getting computer support for decision-making activities.

■ *Support for different decision frequencies.* Decisions can range on a continuum from one-of-a-kind to repetitive decisions. One-of-a-kind decisions are typically handled by an ad hoc DSS. An **ad hoc DSS** is concerned with situations or decisions that come up only a few times during the life of the organization; in small businesses, they might happen only once. For example, a company might need to change the layout of its open plan offices. Repetitive decisions are addressed by an institutional DSS. An **institutional DSS** handles situations or decisions that occur more than once, usually several times per year or more. An

ad hoc DSS A DSS concerned with situations or decisions that come up only a few times during the life of the organization.

institutional DSS A DSS that handles situations or decisions that occur more than once, usually several times per year or more. An institutional DSS is used repeatedly and refined over the years.

institutional DSS is used repeatedly and refined over the years. For example, a DSS used to assist help desk staff solve employees' computer problems and queries.

highly structured problems
Problems that are straightforward and require known facts and relationships.

semi-structured or unstructured problems More complex problems in which the relationships among the pieces of data are not always clear, the data might be in a variety of formats, and the data is often difficult to manipulate or obtain.

■ *Support for different problem structures.* As discussed previously, decisions can range from highly structured and programmed to unstructured and non-programmed. **Highly structured problems** are straightforward, requiring known facts and relationships. **Semi-structured or unstructured problems**, on the other hand, are more complex. The relationships among the pieces of data are not always clear, the data might be in a variety of formats, and it is often difficult to manipulate or obtain. In addition, the decision maker might not know the information requirements of the decision in advance.

■ *Support for various decision-making levels.* Decision support systems can provide help for managers at different levels within the organization. Operational managers can get assistance with daily and routine decision making. Tactical decision makers can use analysis tools to ensure proper planning and control. At the strategic level, DSS can help managers by providing analysis for long-term decisions requiring both internal and external information (see Figure 8.14).

Figure 8.14 Decision-Making Level *Strategic managers are involved with long-term decisions, which are often made infrequently. Operational managers are involved with decisions that are made more frequently.*

8.4.3 A Comparison of DSS and MIS

A DSS differs from an MIS in numerous ways, including the type of problems solved, the support given to users, the decision emphasis and approach, and the type, speed, output, and development of the system used. Table 8.2 lists brief descriptions of these differences. You should note that entity resource planning systems include both MIS and DSS (and, as discussed in the previous chapter, TPS).

8.4.4 Components of a Decision Support System

dialogue manager A user interface that allows decision makers to easily access and manipulate the DSS and to use common business terms and phrases.

At the core of a DSS are a database and a model base. In addition, a typical DSS contains a user interface, also called **dialogue manager**, that allows decision makers to easily access and manipulate the DSS and to use common business terms and phrases. Finally, access to the Internet, networks, and other computer-based systems permits the DSS to tie into other powerful systems, including the TPS or function-specific subsystems. Internet

Table 8.2 Comparison of DSS and MIS

Factor	DSS	MIS
Problem Type	A DSS can handle unstructured problems that cannot be easily programmed	An MIS is normally used only with structured problems
Users	A DSS supports individuals, small groups, and the entire organization. In the short run, users typically have more control over a DSS	An MIS supports primarily the organization. In the short run, users have less control over an MIS
Support	A DSS supports all aspects and phases of decision making; it does not replace the decision maker – people still make the decisions	This is not true of all MIS systems – some make automatic decisions and replace the decision maker
Emphasis Approach	A DSS emphasizes actual decisions and decision-making styles. A DSS is a direct support system that provides interactive reports on computer screens	An MIS usually emphasizes information only. An MIS is typically an indirect support system that uses regularly produced reports
Speed	Because a DSS is flexible and can be implemented by users, it usually takes less time to develop and is better able to respond to user requests	An MIS's response time is usually longer
Output	DSS reports are usually screen oriented, with the ability to generate reports on a printer	An MIS, however, typically is oriented towards printed reports and documents
Development	DSS users are usually more directly involved in its development. User involvement usually means better systems that provide superior support. For all systems, user involvement is the most important factor for the development of a successful system	An MIS is frequently several years old and often was developed for people who are no longer performing the work supported by the MIS

Information Systems @ Work

Decision Support Systems in Retail Outlets

MicroStrategy is in the business of management information. They help clients transform data collected in their transaction processing systems, into valuable information, the role of management information systems. Their mission is to empower every business user to make more informed decisions by providing timely, relevant, and accurate answers to their questions. Their software allows for advanced analysis and querying (decision support system operations), and the creation of useful reports. Retailers are now making use of this software to give non-technical users access to powerful decision support information.

(continued)

High street chains such as B&Q, a hardware shop, and home shopping company Littlewoods Shop Direct Group use decision support software from MicroStrategy to analyze their data. The output is shared with thousands of their employees through a form of 'push technology' called DSS Broadcaster. (Push technology means that information is given to the employee without them having to ask for it, rather than it being given in response to a request by the employee.) DSS Broadcaster is designed to send highly personalized short messages to many recipients. These can be sent in a variety of formats – SMS texts, e-mails, faxes, voicemail or by pager. Darren MacManus, project manager at B&Q, the first UK beta test site for Broadcaster, said it would be 'a fundamental tool for the coming twelve months'. He added that B&Q would be offering employees 'targeted reporting, with information based on exception. That way, they don't need to trawl through large paper-based reports.' Information on sales and stock is shared, with employees being notified when key measures move outside pre-defined limits, for example when stock falls below a certain level.

MicroStrategy decision support tools can extract data from TPS, apply models and heuristics to these data in order to make decisions, then DSS Broadcaster can send out these decisions to employees. The system enables users to specify the type of information they want to see, how often they want it and in which format.

Questions

1 What sorts of information might the people who work in the hardware B&Q retail outlets want? What sort of decisions would they need answers on?

2 Why is this technology suitable for use in the retail industry?

3 If employees are unable to query the DSS directly, are they truly 'using' the system?

4 Other than retail, what other industries might benefit from this technology?

SOURCES: 'Retailers to push data out to staff DSS Broadcaster gives the help the high street needs', *Computing*, http://www.microstrategy.com, accessed 14/06/07, http://www.tdwi.org/research/display.aspx?ID=5486, December 4, 1998.

software agents, for example, can be used in creating powerful decision support systems. Figure 8.15 shows a conceptual model of a DSS although specific DSS might not have all these components.

The Database

The database management system allows managers and decision makers to perform qualitative analysis on the company's vast stores of data in databases, data warehouses, and data marts (discussed in Chapter 5). DSS tap into vast stores of information contained in the corporate

Figure 8.15

Conceptual Model of a DSS *DSS components include a model base; database; external database access; and access to the Internet and corporate intranet, networks, and other computer systems.*

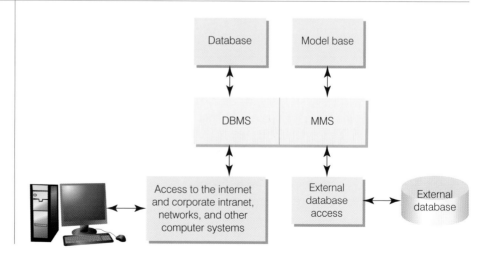

database, retrieving information on inventory, sales, personnel, production, finance, accounting, and other areas.[12] Data mining and business intelligence, introduced in Chapter 5, are often used in DSS. Airline companies, for example, use a DSS to help it identify customers for round-trip flights between major cities. The DSS can be used to search a data warehouse to contact thousands of customers who might be interested in an inexpensive flight. A casino can use a DSS to search large databases to get detailed information on patrons. It can tell how much each patron spends per day on gambling, and more. Opportunity International uses a DSS to help it make loans and provide services to tsunami victims and others in need around the world.[13] According to the information services manager of Opportunity International, 'We need to pull all the data . . . to one central database that we can analyze, and we need a way to get that information back out to people in the field.' DSS can also be used in emergency medical situations to make split-second, life-or-death treatment decisions.[14]

A database management system can also connect to external databases to give managers and decision makers even more information and decision support. External databases can include the Internet, libraries, government databases, and more. The combination of internal and external database access can give key decision makers a better understanding of the company and its environment.

The Model Base

In addition to the data, a DSS needs a model of how elements of the data are related, in order to help make decisions. The **model base** allows managers and decision makers to perform quantitative analysis on both internal and external data.[15] The model base gives decision makers access to a variety of models so that they can explore different scenarios and see their effects. Ultimately, it assists them in the decision-making process. Procter & Gamble, maker of Pringles potato chips, Pampers nappies, and hundreds of other consumer products, use DSS to streamline how raw materials and products flow from its suppliers to its customers, saving millions of euros.[16] Scientists and mathematicians also use DSS.[17] DSS can be excellent at predicting customer behaviours.[18] Most banks, for example, use models to help forecast which customers will be late with payments or might default on their loans.

model base Part of a DSS that provides decision makers access to a variety of models and assists them in decision making.

The models and algorithms used in a DSS are often reviewed and revised over time.[19] As a result of Hurricane Katrina in the U.S., for example, American insurance companies plan to revise their models about storm damage and insurance requirements.[20]

Model management software (MMS) is often used to coordinate the use of models in a DSS, including financial, statistical analysis, graphical, and project-management models. Depending on the needs of the decision maker, one or more of these models can be used (see Table 8.3).

model management software Software that coordinates the use of models in a DSS.

The User Interface or Dialogue Manager

The user interface or dialogue manager allows users to interact with the DSS to obtain information. It assists with all aspects of communications between the user and the hardware and software that constitute the DSS. In a practical sense, to most DSS users, the user interface is the DSS. Upper-level decision makers are often less interested in where the information came from or how it was gathered than that the information is both understandable and accessible.

8.5 Group Support Systems

The DSS approach has resulted in better decision making for all levels of individual users. However, many DSS approaches and techniques are not suitable for a group decision-making environment. Although not all workers and managers are involved in committee meetings and group decision-making sessions, some tactical and strategic-level managers can spend more than

Table 8.3 Model Management Software

DSS often use financial, statistical, graphical, and project-management models

Model Type	Description	Software
Financial	Provides cash flow, internal rate of return, and other investment analysis	Spreadsheet, such as Microsoft Excel
Statistical	Provides summary statistics, trend projections, hypothesis testing, and more	Statistical program, such as SPSS or SAS
Graphical	Assists decision makers in designing, developing, and using graphic displays of data and information	Graphics programs, such as Microsoft PowerPoint
Project Management	Handles and coordinates large projects; also used to identify critical activities and tasks that could delay or jeopardize an entire project if they are not completed in a timely and cost-effective fashion	Project management software, such as Microsoft Project

group support system (GSS)
Software application that consists of most elements in a DSS, plus software to provide effective support in group decision making; also called 'group decision support system'.

half their decision-making time in a group setting. Such managers need assistance with group decision making. A **group support system (GSS)**, also called a group decision support system, consists of most of the elements in a DSS, plus software to provide effective support in group decision-making settings (see Figure 8.16).[21]

Group support systems are used in most industries. Architects are increasingly using GSS to help them collaborate with other architects and builders to develop the best plans and to compete for contracts. Manufacturing companies use GSS to link raw material suppliers to their own company systems.

Figure 8.16
Configuration of a GSS *A GSS contains most of the elements found in a DSS, plus software to facilitate group member communications.*

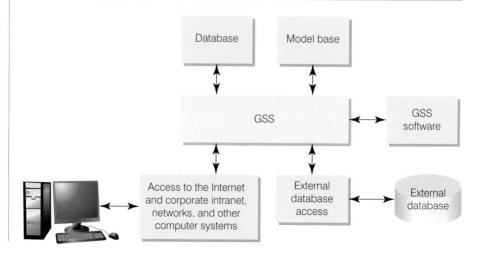

Ethical and Societal Issues

SOCA and Decision Support

The Serious Organized Crime Agency (SOCA) is charged with acting against organized crime in the U.K. Organized crime is a wide-ranging term, including drug trafficking, counterfeiting, serious robbery, organized vehicle and property crime, high tech or computer crime, and tax fraud.

Before 2004, the main threat to the tax credit system was from individuals making false or exaggerated claims. However, according to SOCA, in 2004 and 2005 there was an increase in organized attacks. Identity theft enabled criminal organizations to make multiple fraudulent online claims, often using Internet banking to receive the funds. These identities were often obtained in bulk from stolen payroll data. The losses from fraud and from errors were estimated by the National Audit Office to be over £450 million. In November 2005, the online tax credit claims system was shut down, to counteract abuse by organized fraudsters.

In 2006, 21 instances of tax credit fraud were identified by SOCA. These were uncovered by using data mining and decision support techniques. Data from different government departments were collated and matched against intelligence held by SOCA. This approach identifies patterns of activity rather than specific incidents. As an example, someone claiming unemployment benefit should not also be filing a tax return. Such a person may be the victim of identify theft. The technique of gathering information from different departments was enabled in 2005 by the Serious Organized Crime

and Police Act. 'We need to look at the broader issue of crime,' SOCA director general Bill Hughes told a House of Lords committee. 'If we do not have knowledge we go at it in rifle shots.'

However, critics say that extending police data mining powers raises privacy questions, and that the combination of cheap computing power and data warehouses make it an attractive option for law enforcement agencies with limited budgets.

A Home Office White paper outlines plans for data mining techniques and data-matching practices to be used more frequently in fraud detection. Law enforcement agencies will be able to mine data, not because of specific suspicions, but simply on the basis of data anomalies. Sources of data will be tax records, private company databases and almost all public or private information sources except for health records.

Questions

1 Do you think this approach will benefit society?

2 How might DSS technology be used to identify fraud?

3 Why do you think critics of these methods have 'privacy fears'? Do you share these fears?

4 What safeguards should be put in place to prevent abuse by SOCA officers and others who have access to this information?

SOURCE: Tom Young, 'Soca drills down on crime data', Computing, http://www.soca.gov.uk, 31 May 2007.

8.5.1 Characteristics of a GSS that Enhance Decision Making

It is often said that two heads are better than one. When it comes to decision making, a GSS unique characteristics have the potential to result in better decisions. Developers of these systems try to build on the advantages of individual support systems while adding new approaches, unique to group decision making. For example, some GSS can allow the exchange of information and expertise among people without direct face-to-face interaction. The following sections describe some characteristics that can improve and enhance decision making.

■ *Design for groups.* The GSS approach acknowledges that special procedures, devices, and approaches are needed in group decision-making settings. These procedures must foster creative thinking, effective communications, and good group decision-making techniques.

■ *Ease of use.* Like an individual DSS, a GSS must be easy to learn and use. Systems that are complex and hard to operate will seldom be used. Many groups have less tolerance than do individual decision makers for poorly developed systems.

■ *Flexibility.* Two or more decision makers working on the same problem might have different decision-making styles and preferences. Each manager makes decisions in a unique way, in part because of different experiences and cognitive styles. An effective GSS not only has to support the different approaches that managers use to make decisions, but also must find a means to integrate their different perspectives into a common view of the task at hand.

brainstorming A decision-making approach that often consists of members offering ideas 'off the top of their heads'.

group consensus approach A decision-making approach that forces members in the group to reach a unanimous decision.

nominal group technique A decision-making approach that encourages feedback from individual group members, and the final decision is made by voting, similar to the way public officials are elected.

■ *Decision-making support.* A GSS can support different decision-making approaches such as **brainstorming**, the **group consensus approach** or the **nominal group technique**.

■ *Anonymous input.* Many GSS allow anonymous input, where group members do not know which of them is giving the input. For example, some organizations use a GSS to help rank the performance of managers. Anonymous input allows the group decision makers to concentrate on the merits of the input without considering who gave it. In other words, input given by a top-level manager is given the same consideration as input from employees or other members of the group. Some studies have shown that groups using anonymous input can make better decisions and have superior results compared with groups that do not use anonymous input. Anonymous input, however, can result in flaming, where an unknown team member posts insults or even obscenities on the GSS.

■ *Reduction of negative group behaviour.* One key characteristic of any GSS is the ability to suppress or eliminate group behaviour that is counterproductive or harmful to effective decision making. In some group settings, dominant individuals can take over the discussion, which can prevent other members of the group from presenting creative alternatives. In other cases, one or two group members can sidetrack or subvert the group into areas that are non-productive and do not help solve the problem at hand. Other times, members of a group might assume they have made the right decision without examining alternatives – a phenomenon called 'groupthink'. If group sessions are poorly planned and executed, the result can be a tremendous waste of time. GSS designers are developing software and hardware systems to reduce these types of problems. Procedures for effectively planning and managing group meetings can be incorporated into the GSS approach. A trained meeting facilitator is often employed to help lead the group decision-making process and to avoid groupthink.

■ *Parallel communication.* With traditional group meetings, people must take turns addressing various issues. One person normally talks at a time. With a GSS, every group member can address issues or make comments at the same time by entering them into a PC or workstation. These comments and issues are displayed on every group member's PC or workstation immediately. Parallel communication can speed meeting times and result in better decisions.

■ *Automated recordkeeping.* Most GSS can keep detailed records of a meeting automatically. Each comment that is entered into a group member's PC or workstation can be recorded. In some cases, literally hundreds of comments can be stored for future review and analysis. In addition, most GSS packages have automatic voting and ranking features. After group members vote, the GSS records each vote and makes the appropriate rankings.

A picture showing a meeting using GSS is shown in Figure 8.17.

Figure 8.17 GSS
A group using a GSS.

© Image State/Alamy

8

8.6 Executive Support Systems

Because top-level executives often require specialised support when making strategic decisions, many companies have developed systems to assist executive decision making. This type of system, called an **executive support system (ESS)**, is a specialized DSS that includes all hardware, software, data, procedures, and people used to assist senior-level executives within the organization. In some cases, an ESS, also called an executive information system (EIS), supports decision making of members of the board of directors, who are responsible to stockholders.

executive support system (ESS)
Specialized DSS that includes all hardware, software, data, procedures, and people used to assist senior-level executives within the organization.

An ESS is a special type of DSS, and, like a DSS, an ESS is designed to support higher-level decision making in the organization. The two systems are, however, different in important ways. DSS provide a variety of modelling and analysis tools to enable users to thoroughly analyze problems – that is, they allow users to answer questions. ESS present structured information about aspects of the organization that executives consider important. In other words, they allow executives to ask the right questions.

The following are general characteristics of ESS:

- *Are tailored to individual executives.* ESS are typically tailored to individual executives; DSS are not tailored to particular users. They present information in the preferred format of that executive.

- *Are easy to use.* A top-level executive's most critical resource can be his or her time. Thus, an ESS must be easy to learn and use and not overly complex.

- *Have drill-down abilities.* An ESS allows executives to drill down into the company to determine how certain data was produced. Drilling down allows an executive to get more detailed information if needed.

- *Support the need for external data.* The data needed to make effective top-level decisions is often external – information from competitors, the federal government, trade associations and journals, consultants, and so on. An effective ESS can extract data useful to the decision maker from a wide variety of sources, including the Internet and other electronic publishing sources.

- *Can help with situations that have a high degree of uncertainty.* Most executive decisions involve a high degree of uncertainty. Handling these unknown situations using modelling and other ESS procedures helps top-level managers measure the amount of risk in a decision.

- *Have a future orientation.* Executive decisions are future oriented, meaning that decisions will have a broad impact for years or decades. The information sources to support future-oriented decision making are usually informal – from organizing golf partners to tying together members of social clubs or civic organizations.

- *Are linked with value-added business processes.* Like other information systems, executive support systems are linked with executive decision making about value-added business processes.

8.6.1   Capabilities of Executive Support Systems

The responsibility given to top-level executives and decision makers brings unique problems and pressures to their jobs. The following is a discussion of some of the characteristics of executive decision making that are supported through the ESS approach. ESS take full advantage of data mining, the Internet, blogs, podcasts, executive dashboards, and many other technological innovations. As you will note, most of these decisions are related to an organization's overall profitability and direction. An effective ESS should have the capability to support executive decisions with components such as strategic planning and organizing, crisis management, and more.

- *Support for defining an overall vision.* One of the key roles of senior executives is to provide a broad vision for the entire organization. This vision includes the organization's major product lines and services, the types of businesses it supports today and in the future, and its overriding goals.

strategic planning Determining long-term objectives by analyzing the strengths and weaknesses of the organization, predicting future trends, and projecting the development of new product lines.

- *Support for strategic planning.* ESS also support **strategic planning**. Strategic planning involves determining long-term objectives by analyzing the strengths and weaknesses of the organization, predicting future trends, and projecting the development of new product lines. It also involves planning the acquisition of new equipment, analyzing merger possibilities, and making difficult decisions concerning downsizing and the sale of assets if required by unfavourable economic conditions.

- *Support for strategic organizing and staffing.* Top-level executives are concerned with organizational structure. For example, decisions concerning the creation of new departments or downsizing the labour force are made by top-level managers. Overall direction for staffing decisions and effective communication with labour unions are also major decision areas for top-level executives. ESS can be employed to help analyze the impact of staffing decisions, potential pay raises, changes in employee benefits, and new work rules.

- *Support for strategic control.* Another type of executive decision relates to strategic control, which involves monitoring and managing the overall operation of the organization. Goal seeking can be done for each major area to determine what performance these areas need to achieve to reach corporate expectations. Effective ESS approaches can help top-level managers make the most of their existing resources and control all aspects of the organization.

- *Support for crisis management.* Even with careful strategic planning, a crisis can occur. Major disasters, including hurricanes, tornadoes, floods, earthquakes, fires, and terrorist activities, can totally shut down major parts of the organization. Handling these emergencies is another responsibility for top-level executives. In many cases, strategic emergency plans can be put into place with the help of an ESS. These contingency plans help organizations recover quickly if an emergency or crisis occurs.

Decision making is a vital part of managing businesses strategically. IS systems such as information and decision support, group support, and executive support systems help employees by tapping existing databases and providing them with current, accurate information. The increasing integration of all business information systems – from TPS to MIS to DSS to ESS – can help organizations monitor their competitive environment and make better-informed decisions. Organizations can also use specialized business information systems, discussed in the next two chapters, to achieve their goals.

Summary

Good decision-making and problem-solving skills are the key to developing effective information and decision support systems. Every organization needs effective decision making and problem solving to reach its objectives and goals. Problem solving begins with decision making. A well-known model developed by Herbert Simon divides the decision-making phase of the problem-solving process into three stages: intelligence, design, and choice. During the intelligence stage, potential problems or opportunities are identified and defined. Information is gathered that relates to the cause and scope of the problem. Constraints on the possible solution and the problem environment are investigated. In the design stage, alternative solutions to the problem are developed and explored. In addition, the feasibility and implications of these alternatives are evaluated. Finally, the choice stage involves selecting the best course of action. In this stage, the decision makers evaluate the implementation of the solution to determine whether the anticipated results were achieved and to modify the process in light of new information learned during the implementation stage.

Decision making is a component of problem solving. In addition to the intelligence, design, and choice steps of decision making, problem solving also includes implementation and monitoring. Implementation places the solution into effect. After a decision has been implemented, it is monitored and modified if needed.

Decisions can be programmed or non-programmed. Programmed decisions are made using a rule, procedure, or quantitative method. Ordering more inventory when the level drops to 100 units or fewer is an example of a programmed decision. A non-programmed decision deals with unusual or exceptional situations. Determining the best training program for a new employee is an example of a non-programmed decision.

Decisions can use optimization, satisficing, or heuristic approaches. Optimization finds the best solution. Optimization problems often have an objective such as maximizing profits given production and material constraints. When a problem is too complex for optimization, satisficing is often used. Satisficing finds a good, but not necessarily the best, decision. Finally, a heuristic is a 'rule of thumb' or commonly used guideline or procedure used to find a good decision.

A management information system (MIS) must provide the right information to the right person in the right format at the right time. A management information system is an integrated collection of people, procedures, databases, and devices that provides managers and decision makers with information to help achieve organizational goals. An MIS can help an organization achieve its goals by providing managers with insight into the regular operations of the organization so that they can control, organize, and plan more effectively and efficiently. The primary difference between the reports generated by the TPS and those generated by the MIS is that MIS reports support managerial decision making at the higher levels of management.

Data that enters the MIS originates from both internal and external sources. The most significant internal sources of data for the MIS are the organization's various TPSs and ERP systems. Data warehouses and data marts also provide important input data for the MIS. External sources of data for the MIS include extranets, customers, suppliers, competitors, and stockholders.

The output of most MIS is a collection of reports that are distributed to managers. Management information systems have a number of common characteristics, including producing scheduled, demand, exception, and drill-down reports; producing reports with fixed and standard formats; producing hard-copy and soft-copy reports; using internal data stored in organizational computerized databases; and having reports developed and implemented by IS personnel or end users.

Most MISs are organized along the functional lines of an organization. Typical functional management information systems include financial, manufacturing, marketing, human resources, and other specialized systems. Each system is composed of inputs, processing subsystems, and outputs.

Decision support systems (DSS) support decision-making effectiveness when faced with unstructured or semi-structured business problems. DSS characteristics include the ability to handle large amounts of data; obtain and process data from different sources; provide report and presentation flexibility; support drill-down analysis; perform complex statistical analysis; offer textual and graphical orientations; support optimization, satisficing, and heuristic approaches; and perform what-if, simulation, and goal-seeking analysis.

DSS provide support assistance through all phases of the problem-solving process. Different decision frequencies also require DSS support. An ad hoc DSS addresses unique, infrequent decision situations; an institutional DSS handles routine decisions. Highly structured problems, semi-structured problems, and unstructured problems can be supported by a DSS. A DSS can also support different managerial levels, including strategic, tactical, and operational managers. A common database is often the link that ties together a company's TPS, MIS, and DSS.

The components of a DSS are the database, model base, user interface or dialogue manager, and a link to external databases, the Internet, the corporate intranet, extranets, networks, and other systems. The database can use data warehouses and data marts. Access to other computer-based systems permits the DSS to tie into other powerful systems, including the TPS or function-specific subsystems.

Specialized support systems, such as group support systems (GSS) and executive support systems (ESS), use the overall approach of a DSS in situations such as group and executive decision making. A group support system (GSS) consists of most of the elements in a DSS, plus software to provide effective support in group decision-making settings. GSS are typically easy to learn and use and can offer specific or general decision-making support.

GSS software, also called 'groupware', is specially designed to help generate lists of decision alternatives and perform data analysis. These packages let people work on joint documents and files over a network.

The frequency of GSS use and the location of the decision makers will influence the GSS alternative chosen. The decision room alternative supports users in a single location who meet infrequently. Local area networks can be used when group members are located in the same geographic area and users meet regularly. Teleconferencing is used when decision frequency is low and the location of group members is distant. A wide area network is used when the decision frequency is high and the location of group members is distant.

Executive support systems (ESS) are specialized decision support systems designed to meet the needs of senior management. They serve to indicate issues of importance to the organization, indicate new directions the company might take, and help executives monitor the company's progress. ESS are typically easy to use, offer a wide range of computer resources, and handle a variety of internal and external data. In addition, the ESS performs sophisticated data analysis, offers a high degree of specialization, and provides flexibility and comprehensive communications abilities. An ESS also supports individual decision-making styles. Some of the major decision-making areas that can be supported through an ESS are providing an overall vision, strategic planning and organizing, strategic control, and crisis management.

Self-Assessment Test

1 The last stage of the decision making process is the _____.
   a. initiation stage
   b. intelligence stage
   c. design stage
   d. choice stage

2 Problem solving is one of the stages of decision making. True or false?

3 A decision that inventory should be ordered when inventory levels drop to 500 units is an example of a(n) _____.
   a. synchronous decision
   b. asynchronous decision
   c. non-programmed decision
   d. programmed decision

4 A(n) _____ model will find the best solution, usually the one that will best help the organization meet its goals.

5 A satisficing model is one that will find a good problem solution, but not necessarily the best problem solution. True or false?

6 The focus of a decision support system is on decision-making effectiveness when faced with unstructured or semi-structured business problems. True or false?

7 What component of a decision support system allows decision makers to easily access and manipulate the DSS and to use common business terms and phrases?
   a. the knowledge base
   b. the model base
   c. the user interface or dialogue manager
   d. the expert system

8 What allows a person to give his or her input without his or her identity being known to other group members?
   a. groupthink
   b. anonymous input
   c. nominal group technique
   d. delphi

9 The local area decision network is the ideal GSS alternative for situations in which decision makers are located in the same building or geographic area and the decision makers are occasional users of the GSS approach. True or false?

10 A(n) _____ supports the actions of members of the board of directors, who are responsible to stockholders.

8

Review Questions

1 What is a 'satisficing model'? Describe a situation when it should be used.

2 What is the difference between a programmed decision and a non-programmed decision? Give several examples of each.

3 What are the basic kinds of reports produced by an MIS?

4 What are the functions performed by a financial MIS?

5 Describe the functions of a marketing MIS.

6 What is the difference between decision making and problem solving?

7 What is a geographic information system?

8 Describe the difference between a structured and an unstructured problem and give an example of each.

9 What is the difference between what-if analysis and goal-seeking analysis?

10 What is an executive support system? Identify three fundamental uses for such a system.

Discussion Questions

1 How can management information systems be used to support the objectives of the business organization?

2 How can a strong financial MIS provide strategic benefits to a firm?

3 You have been hired to develop a management information system and a decision support system for a manufacturing company. Describe what information you would include in printed reports and what information you would provide using a screen-based decision support system.

4 You have been hired to develop group support software. Describe the features you would include in your new GSS software.

5 The use of ESS should not be limited to the executives of the company. Do you agree or disagree? Why?

Web Exercises

1 Use a search engine, such as Yahoo! or Google, to explore two or more companies that produce and sell MIS or DSS software. Describe what you found and any problems you had in using search engines on the Internet to find information. You might be asked to develop a report or send an e-mail message to your instructor about what you found.

2 Use the Internet to explore two or more software packages that can be used to make group decisions easier. Summarize your findings in a report.

Case One

French Perfume Company Relies on Management Information Systems to Unify Employees

Beauté Prestige International (BPI) is a French company best known for its three brands of perfume: Issey Miyake, Jean Paul Gaultier, and Narciso Rodriguez. BPI is a small- to mid-sized enterprise (SME) with an international presence through ten subsidiaries located around the world. BPI employs 1300 people who sell its perfumes in 112 countries.

Recently, BPI found itself in need of a centralized system from which managers could produce meaningful business reports to guide decision making. 'Everyone was producing spreadsheets in their own little corner of the company, which of course brought IT maintenance problems with it, especially in terms of consistency for company figures,' BPI's CIO Christophe Davy explained. The company needed to shepherd its managers away from individual spreadsheets towards more centralized decision making based on reports generated by a management information system (MIS). Christophe Davy set off to develop a new system that would include standardized decision support tools, a user-friendly interface, easy implementation, and access to facts most important to decision making, from a single portal.

Christophe found his solution in the ReportNet system from the Cognos Corporation. Cognos worked with the IS staff at BPI to import corporate data into a data warehouse, which could then be manipulated by the MIS to develop useful reports. One year later, the company placed its first batch of financial indicators online for use by the sales force and management control. Six months later, they rolled out merchandising data reports that were used to conduct analysis on the position of its products compared with the contracts negotiated with its customers, and to compare the companies positioning in relation to its competitors.

Importing the corporate data from the many individual spreadsheets was the largest hurdle for developers – but well worth the effort. 'The work to clean up and amalgamate data was exactly what was needed to implement our strategy of having a single unified portal where employees could find reliable information that was shared throughout the entire company,' explained Christophe Davy.

The resulting system has vastly improved business processes and decision making in the organization. Processes that used to take hours in Microsoft Excel are now done virtually in real time. Also BPI no longer requires external companies to provide annual reports on product positioning. Such reports are generated anytime they are needed by the new system. The biggest benefit of the new MIS is the ability to access reliable important corporate information anytime it is needed for any use within the company. Additional benefits include enhanced business monitoring, more effective queries, lower costs, shorter lead times, and enhanced interactivity. BPI is working to extend the power of the portal beyond finance and merchandising to other business areas.

Istock

Questions

1   What are the problems with staff maintaining their own information systems in Microsoft Excel? Are there any advantages?

2   Why do you think , that 'importing the corporate data from the many individual spreadsheets' was the largest hurdle for developers'?

3   What do you think are some of the advantages and disadvantages of a centralized system?

4   Do you have any concerns about data warehouses? Would you feel comfortable if information about you from different sources was being assembled in a 'warehouse'?

SOURCES: Staff, 'Companies Worldwide Choose Cognos 8 Business Intelligence', Press Release, CNW Group, February 14, 2006, www.newswire.ca/en/releases/archive/February2006/14/c2182.html. Beauté Prestige International Case Study, Cognos Web site, accessed June 6, 2006, www.cognos.com/products/cognos8businessintelligence/success-stories.html. Cognos ReportNet Web site, accessed June 6, 2006, www.cognos.com/products/cognos8businessintelligence/reporting.html.

Case Two

Transit New Zealand Reroutes Information to Avoid Traffic Jams

New Zealand's state highway network takes drivers through 11 000 kilometres of some of the most beautiful scenery in the world. Transit New Zealand (TNZ) manages those highways, which carry half the country's traffic, to make sure that drivers have smooth and efficient routes to their destinations. Unfortunately, until recently, the flow of information within TNZ was anything but smooth and efficient. TNZ was in dire need of an upgrade to its management information systems.

The public face of TNZ provides drivers with information about the condition and safety of its roads. Its main mission, however, is to work with external contractors and government bodies that decide on highway building and maintenance projects. TNZ needed to freely exchange information with all these constituencies but lacked the integrated information systems to do so.

'Our content was stored in several siloed systems,' says Geoff Yeats, TNZ's chief information officer. 'This made it difficult for our employees to find the information they needed to do their jobs. For example, to initiate a road repair project using the same contractor that had worked on the road previously, we had to consult a number of disparate systems to find contractor information, spec sheets for the old job and the new repairs, and the government road construction standards that were current at the time. It took a lot of time.'

A siloed system is one that stands alone, disconnected from surrounding systems. Such systems typically stand in the way of establishing one true integrated enterprise information system. TNZ realized that what they needed was an enterprise-wide information management solution so they could centrally manage information from all departments and save it economically for easy and timely retrieval. Because the information would be viewed by different groups of users for different purposes, the system would need to present information in multiple ways.

If TNZ accessed organization-wide data from one central interface, the walls dividing its siloed systems would have to come down. TNZ worked with an information system provider to develop a document, records, and content management system within one repository. The new system provided a consistent and customizable framework that let users access information through scheduled, demand, and drill-down reports. The new MIS could also provide an interface to the corporate applications and services that TNZ developed over time as needed.

The first phase of the system provides access to documents of all types as well as contact data from its customer relationship management and information held in its road asset maintenance management database. This database is one of TNZ's largest repositories of information, containing millions of items of data relating to everything from the technical condition of various stretches of roads and maintenance records to details on traffic lights and signage. 'You can go into this database and find out what sort of gravel has been used to build a road and even what the road surface characteristics are like,' says Yeats.

The new system also provides many other benefits. TNZ is better able to control costs and manage the growth of its information while ensuring the currency and accuracy of that information. Searches made across multiple systems are completed with sub-second response times. Because the new system uses commonly recognized standards, TNZ road information can be published through third parties simply by giving the vendor access to the information system.

The new system provides solid business value by integrating, analyzing, and optimizing heterogeneous types and sources of information throughout its lifecycle to manage risk and create new business insights. It is designed to get the right information to the right people or process at the right time to take advantage of opportunities. 'By responding to opportunities and threats with information on demand, we can lower our costs, optimize our infrastructure, gain control of our master data and manage information complexity,' says Yeats.

Future initiatives include electronic collaboration, browser-based content creation, and a link with TNZ's geographical information system. Because the system is designed to comply with Java Specification Request (JSR) 170, an emerging standard for accessing content repositories, it will be easy for TNZ to continue to realize benefits from the system.

Questions

1 How were 'siloed systems' affecting the flow of information throughout TNZ?

2 What business value does the new system provide for TNZ?

3 Provide two reasons that TNZ wanted to use commonly recognized standards such as JSP 170 in the design of its new system.

4 Why does TNZ find it beneficial to allow third parties to publish information stored in its systems?

SOURCES: Staff, 'Transit New Zealand Drives Business Transformation with IBM Enterprise Content Management Solution', *IBM Case Study*, www-306.ibm.com/software/success/cssdb.nsf/CS/HSAZ-6J728L?OpenDocument&Site=cmportal, January 13, 2006; 'Transit NZ Picks IBM for Enterprise Content Management', *iStart*, www.istart.co.nz, September 2005; Transit New Zealand (website), www.transit.govt.nz.

Case Three

Water Management in Africa

The International Water Management Institute (IWMI) is a non-profit scientific organization funded by the Consultative Group on International Agricultural Research (CGIAR). Its aim is to improve the management of land and water resources for food, livelihood and nature. The Institute concentrates on water and related land management challenges faced by poor rural communities. They are currently experimenting with decision support technology for planning dams in South Africa and indeed throughout all of Africa.

In the past, dams were planned using a fairly simple cost–benefit approach: if the benefit the dam was expected to bring outweighed the cost of the project, the dam was built. This analysis was based on narrow technical data, which failed to take into account the significant social problems caused by dam building, mostly stemming from resettling people living on the land about to be flooded. Some specific problems faced by the people living near a new dam include a loss of grazing resources, degradation of soils, a decrease in population (as people move away from the area), a decline in households involved in agriculture and changes in fish species due to larger areas of dry season open water. The variables leading to these outcomes are complex. Nevertheless, today, dams should be planned with greater emphasis on meeting local needs and with full consideration of hydrological, ecological, and socio-economic factors. The decision of whether or not, and where, to build a dam is a highly unstructured problem, the kind the decision support system were designed to assist with.

The decisions such a system should help with include not only the location of the dam, but also the timing and magnitude of water releases and optimum storage size. The DSS being tested use models based on experimental success from actual operational performance and simulations. They enable the integration of physical variables (the strength of materials for instance) and socio-economic variables (population demographics for example) into one model. Expert and local knowledge can also be included. Results can be presented in a vairety of formats of varying complexity, so that people from a wide variety of backgrounds can understand the output and contribute to discussions. The IWMI is currently experimenting with a range of DSS to determine which is best for planning dams. It is hoped that this technology can bring significant benefits to this difficult and often controversial area of water management.

Questions

1 Why might DSS technology be suitable for this problem domain?

2 What might be some of the benefits of using DSS in this area?

3 Identify some stakeholders of a DSS for dam planning. Describe some of the relevant outputs from the system for each. What format should the outputs take?

4 Can you think of any other technologies that might help with the decision to build a dam, and then managing the impact of the new construction?

SOURCES: McCartney, M.P, et al., 'Decision support Systems for Dam Planning and Operation in Africa', WIMI publications, http://www.iwmi.cgiar.org/.

Notes

1 Lacroix, Yvan, et al., 'Bombardier Flexjet Significantly Improves Its Fractional Aircraft Ownership Operations', *Interfaces,* January–February, 2005, p. 49.

2 Murty, Katta, et al., 'Hongkong International Terminals Gains Elastic Capacity', *Interfaces,* January–February, 2005, p. 61.

3 Troyer, Loren, et al., 'Improving Asset Management and Order Fulfillment at Deere', *Interfaces,* January–February, 2005, p. 76.

4 Kapoor, S., et al., 'A Technical Framework for Sense-and-Respond Business Management', *IBM Systems Journal,* Vol. 44, 2005, p. 5.

5 Port, Otis, 'Desktop Factories', *Business Week,* May 2, 2005, p. 22.

6 Wysocki, Bernard, et al., 'Just-In-Time Inventories Make U.S. Vulnerable in a Pandemic', *Wall Street Journal,* January 12, 2006, p. A1.

7 Richmond, Rita, 'Blogs Keep Internet Customers Coming Back', *Wall Street Journal,* March 1, 2005, p. B8.

8 Peart, Mark, 'Service Excellence & CRM', *New Zealand Management,* May 2005, p. 68.

9 Forelle, Charles, 'IBM Tool Deploys Employees Efficiently', *Wall Street Journal,* July 14, 2005, p. B3.

10 Anthes, Gary, 'Beyond Zip Codes', *Computerworld,* September 19, 2005, p. 56.

11 Sabuncuoglu, Ihsan, et al., 'The Turkish Army Uses Simulation to Model and Optimize Its Fuel-Supply System', *Interfaces,* November–December, 2005, p. 474.

12 Havenstein, Heather, 'Celtics Turn to Data Analytics Tools for Help Pricing Tickets', *Computerworld,* January 9, 2006, p. 43.

13 Havenstein, Heather, 'Business Intelligence Tools Help Nonprofit Group Make Loans to Tsunami Victims', *Computerworld,* March 14, 2005, p. 19.

14 Rubenstein, Sarah, 'Next Step Toward Digitized Health Records', *Wall Street Journal,* May 9, 2005, p. B1.

15 Bhattacharya, K., et al., 'A Model-Driven Approach to Industrializing Discovery Processes in Pharmaceutical Research', *IBM Systems Journal,* Vol. 44, No. 1, 2005, p. 145.

16 Anthes, Gary, 'Modelling Magic', *Computerworld,* February 7, 2005, p. 26.

17 Port, Otis, 'Simple Solutions', *Business Week,* October 3, 2005, p. 24.

18 Mitchell, Robert, 'Anticipation Game', *Computerworld,* June 13, 2005, p. 23.

19 Aston, Adam, 'The Worst Isn't Over', *Business Week,* January 16, 2006, p. 29.

20 Babcock, Charles, 'A New Model for Disasters', *Information Week,* October 10, 2005, p. 47.

21 Majchrak, Ann, et al., 'Perceived Individual Collaboration Know-How Development Through Information Technology-Enabled Contextualization', *Information Systems Research,* March 2005, p. 9.

09

Knowledge Management and Specialized Information Systems

Principles

Knowledge management systems allow organizations to share knowledge and experience among their managers and employees.

Artificial intelligence systems form a broad and diverse set of systems that can replicate human decision making for certain types of well-defined problems.

Expert systems can enable a novice to perform at the level of an expert but must be developed and maintained very carefully.

Virtual reality systems can reshape the interface between people and information technology by offering new ways to communicate information, visualize processes, and express ideas creatively.

Learning Objectives

- Describe the role of the chief knowledge officer (CKO).
- List some of the tools and techniques used in knowledge management.

- Define the term 'artificial intelligence' and state the objective of developing artificial intelligence systems.
- List the characteristics of intelligent behaviour and compare the performance of natural and artificial intelligence systems for each of these characteristics.
- Identify the major components of the artificial intelligence field and provide one example of each type of system.

- List the characteristics and basic components of expert systems.
- Identify at least three factors to consider in evaluating the development of an expert system.
- Outline and briefly explain the steps for developing an expert system.
- Identify the benefits associated with the use of expert systems.

- Define the term 'virtual reality' and provide three examples of virtual reality applications.
- Discuss examples of specialized systems for organizational and individual use.

Why Learn About Knowledge Management and Specialized Information Systems?

Knowledge management systems are used in almost every industry. If you are a manager, you might use a knowledge management system to support decisive action to help you correct a problem. If you are a production manager at a car company, you might oversee robots, a specialized information system, that attach windscreens to cars or paint body panels. As a young stock trader, you might use a system called a neural network to uncover patterns and make money trading stocks and stock options. As a marketing manager for a PC manufacturer, you might use virtual reality on a website to show customers your latest laptop and desktop computers. If you are in the military, you might use computer simulation as a training tool to prepare you for combat. In a petroleum company, you might use an expert system to determine where to drill for oil and gas. You will see many additional examples of using these information systems throughout this chapter. Learning about these systems will help you discover new ways to use information systems in your day-to-day work.

9.1 Knowledge Management Systems

Defining knowledge is difficult. One definition is that knowledge is the awareness and understanding of a set of information and the ways that information can be made useful to support a specific task or reach a decision. Knowing the procedures for ordering more inventory to avoid running out is an example of knowledge. In a sense, information tells you what has to be done (low inventory levels for some items), while knowledge tells you how to do it (make two important phone calls to the right people to get the needed inventory shipped overnight). A knowledge management system (KMS) is an organized collection of people, procedures, software, databases, and devices used to create, store, share, and use the organization's knowledge and experience.[1]

9.1.1 Overview of Knowledge Management Systems

Like the other systems discussed throughout this book, knowledge management systems attempt to help organizations achieve their goals. For businesses, this usually means increasing profits or reducing costs. For non-profit organizations, it can mean providing better customer service or providing special needs to people and groups. Many types of firms use KMS to increase profits or reduce costs. According to a survey of CEOs, firms that use KMS are more likely to innovate and perform better.[2]

A KMS stores and processes knowledge. This can involve different types of knowledge. Explicit knowledge is objective and can be measured and documented in reports, papers, and rules. For example, knowing the best road to take to minimize drive time from home to the office when a major motorway is closed due to an accident is explicit knowledge. It can be documented in a report or a rule, as in 'If the A453 is closed, take the M1 to junction 25 and from there to the office'. Tacit knowledge, on the other hand, is hard to measure and document and typically is not objective or formalized. Knowing the best way to negotiate with a foreign government about nuclear disarmament or deal with a volatile hostage situation often requires a lifetime of experience and a high level of skill. These are examples of tacit knowledge. It is difficult to write a detailed report or a set of rules that would always work in every hostage situation. Many organizations actively attempt to convert tacit knowledge to explicit knowledge to make the knowledge easier to measure, document, and share with others.

In a well-known *Harvard Business Review* paper called 'The Knowledge Creating Company' (from the November–December 1991 issue), Ikujiro Nonaka describes four ways in which knowledge can be created.

1 When an individual learns directly from another individual, in an apprentice type relationship, tacit knowledge is created from tacit knowledge.

2 When two pieces of explicit knowledge are combined. For example, a website mash-up could be considered an example of this type of new knowledge. (Mash-ups were described in Chapter 6 as the combining of information from two or more web pages onto one web page.)

3 When an expert writes a book teaching others, explicit knowledge is being created from tacit knowledge.

4 When someone reads that book, and (eventually) becomes an expert themselves, tacit knowledge has been created by explicit knowledge.

A diverse set of technologies can help capture, create and share knowledge. Expert systems (this chapter) can be used to share explicit knowledge. Blogs (Chapter 10) can be used to share tacit knowledge. Data mining algorithms (Chapter 5) can be used to discover new knowledge.

9.1.2 Obtaining, Storing, Sharing, and Using Knowledge

Knowledge workers are people who create, use, and disseminate knowledge. They are usually professionals in science, engineering, or business, and belong to professional organizations. Other examples of knowledge workers include writers, researchers, educators, and corporate designers. The **chief knowledge officer (CKO)** is a top-level executive who helps the organization work with a KMS to create, store, and use knowledge to achieve organizational goals. The CKO is responsible for the organization's KMS, and typically works with other executives and directors, including the managing director, finance director, and others. Obtaining, storing, sharing, and using knowledge is the key to any KMS.[3] Using a KMS often leads to additional knowledge creation, storage, sharing, and usage. A meteorologist, for example, might develop sophisticated mathematical models to predict the path and intensity of hurricanes. Business professors often conduct research in marketing strategies, management practices, corporate and individual investments and finance, effective accounting and auditing practices, and much more. Drug companies and medical researchers invest billions of pounds in creating knowledge on cures for diseases. Although knowledge workers can act alone, they often work in teams to create or obtain knowledge.

chief knowledge officer (CKO)
A top-level executive who helps the organization use a KMS to create, store, and use knowledge to achieve organizational goals.

After knowledge is created, it is often stored in a 'knowledge repository'. The knowledge repository can be located both inside and outside the organization. Some types of software can store and share knowledge contained in documents and reports. Adobe Acrobat PDF files, for example, allow you to store corporate reports, tax returns, and other documents and send them to others over the Internet. You can use hardware devices and software to store and share audio and video material.[4] Traditional databases and data warehouses, discussed in Chapter 5, are often used to store the organization's knowledge. Specialized knowledge bases in expert systems, discussed later in the chapter, can also be used.

Because knowledge workers often work in groups or teams, they can use collaborative work software and group support systems to share knowledge. Intranets and password-protected Internet sites also provide ways to share knowledge. The social services department of Surrey Council in the U.K., for example, use an intranet to help it create and manipulate knowledge.[5] Because knowledge can be critical in maintaining a competitive advantage, businesses should be careful in how they share it. Although they want important decision makers inside and outside the organization to have complete and easy access to knowledge, they also need to protect knowledge from competitors and others who shouldn't see it. As a result, many businesses use patents, copyrights, trade secrets, Internet firewalls, and other measures to keep prying eyes from seeing important knowledge that is often expensive and hard to create.

In addition to using information systems and collaborative software tools to share knowledge, some organizations use non-technical approaches. These include corporate retreats and gatherings, sporting events, informal knowledge worker lounges or meeting places, kitchen facilities, day-care centres, and comfortable workout centres.

Using a knowledge management system begins with locating the organization's knowledge. This is often done using a knowledge map or directory that points the knowledge worker to the needed knowledge. Drug companies have sophisticated knowledge maps that include database and file systems to allow scientists and drug researchers to locate previous medical studies. Lawyers can use powerful online knowledge maps, such as the legal section of Lexis-Nexis to research legal opinions and the outcomes of previous cases. Medical researchers, university professors, and even textbook authors use Lexis-Nexis to locate important knowledge. Organizations often use the Internet or corporate web portals to help their knowledge workers find knowledge stored in documents and reports. The following are examples of profit and non-profit organizations that use knowledge and knowledge management systems.

China Netcom Corporation uses KM software from Autonomy Corporation to search the records of up to 100 million telecommunications customers and create knowledge about its customers and marketing operations.[6]

Feilden, Clegg, Bradley, and Aedas, an architectural firm, uses KM to share best practices among its architects.[7] According to one designer, 'Knowledge management was one of those ideas that sprang up in the 1990s, along with fads such as total quality management and the concept of the learning organization. But knowledge management (KM) appears to have had staying power, and it is still firmly on the business agenda.'

Munich Re Group, a German insurance organization, uses KM to share best practices and knowledge.[8] 'It was always important to us that knowledge management isn't just an IT platform,' said Karen Edwards, knowledge management consultant in Munich Re's Knowledge Management Center of Competence in Munich, Germany. 'The Munich Re people, they really were the assets. They're the things you try to bring together.'

9.1.3 Technology to Support Knowledge Management

KMS use a number of tools discussed throughout this book. In Chapter 2, for example, we explored the importance of organizational learning and organizational change. An effective KMS is based on learning new knowledge and changing procedures and approaches as a result.[9] A manufacturing company, for example, might learn new ways to program robots on the factory floor to improve accuracy and reduce defective parts. The new knowledge will likely cause the manufacturing company to change how it programs and uses its robots. In Chapter 5 on database systems, we investigated the use of data mining and business intelligence. These powerful tools can be important in capturing and using knowledge. Enterprise resource planning tools, such as SAP, include knowledge management features.[10] We have also seen how groupware could improve group decision making and collaboration. Groupware can also be used to help capture, store, and use knowledge. In the next chapter, we will examine more technology that could be used to share knowledge. Lastly, of course, hardware, software, databases, telecommunications, and the Internet discussed in Part 2 are important technologies used to support knowledge management systems.

Hundreds of companies provide specific KM products and services.[11] In addition, researchers at colleges and universities have developed tools and technologies to support knowledge management[12] (see Figure 9.1). Companies such as IBM have many knowledge management tools in a variety of products, including Lotus Notes and Domino.[13] Lotus Notes is a collection of software products that help people work together to create, share, and store important knowledge and business documents. Its knowledge management features include domain search, content mapping, and Lotus Sametime shown in Figure 9.1. Domain search allows people to perform sophisticated searches for knowledge in Domino databases using a single simple query. Content mapping organizes knowledge by categories, like a table of contents for a book. Lotus Sametime

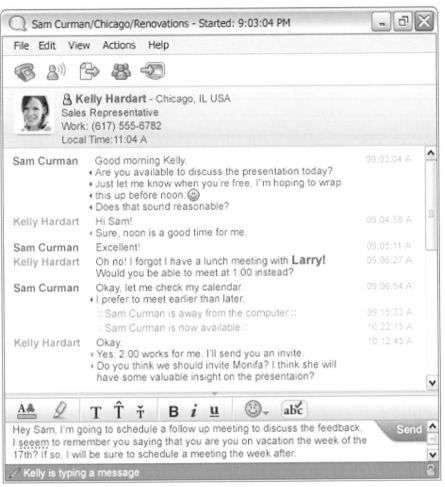

Figure 9.1 Knowledge Management Technology

Lotus Sametime helps people communicate, collaborate, and share ideas in real time.

SOURCE: Courtesy of IBM Corporation.

helps people communicate, collaborate, and share ideas in real time. Lotus Domino Document Manager, formerly called Lotus Domino, helps people and organizations store, organize, and retrieve documents.[14] The software can be used to write, review, archive, and publish documents throughout the organization. Morphy Richards, a leading supplier of small home appliances in the U.K., uses Domino for e-mail, collaboration, and document management.[15] According to one executive, 'Rather than relying on groups of employees emailing each other, we are putting in place a business application through which documents will formally flow – to improve the efficiency of the supply chain and create more transparent working practices.'

Microsoft offers a number of knowledge management tools, including Digital Dashboard, based on the Microsoft Office suite.[16] Digital Dashboard integrates information from different sources, including personal, group, enterprise, and external information and documents. 'Microsoft has revolutionized the way that people use technology to create and share information. The company is the clear winner in the knowledge management business,' according to Rory Chase, managing director of Teleos, an independent knowledge management research company based in the U.K. Other tools from Microsoft include Web Store Technology, which uses wireless technology to deliver knowledge to any location at any time; Access Workflow Designer, which helps database developers create effective systems to process transactions and keep work flowing through the organization; and related products.

In addition to these tools, several artificial intelligence, discussed next, can be used in a KMS.

9.2 Artificial Intelligence

At a Dartmouth College conference in 1956, John McCarthy proposed the use of the term artificial intelligence (AI) to describe computers with the ability to mimic or duplicate the functions of the human brain. Advances in AI have since led to systems to recognize complex patterns.[17] Many AI pioneers attended this first conference; a few predicted that computers would be as 'smart' as people by the 1960s. This prediction has not yet been realized and there is a debate about whether it actually ever could be, however, the benefits of artificial intelligence in business and research can be seen today, and the research continues.

artificial intelligence systems People, procedures, hardware, software, data, and knowledge needed to develop computer systems and machines that demonstrate characteristics of intelligence.

Artificial intelligence systems include the people, procedures, hardware, software, data, and knowledge needed to develop computer systems and machines that demonstrate characteristics of intelligence. Researchers, scientists, and experts on how human beings think are often involved in developing these systems.

9.2.1 The Nature of Intelligence

intelligent behaviour The ability to learn from experiences and apply knowledge acquired from experience, handle complex situations, solve problems when important information is missing, determine what is important, react quickly and correctly to a new situation, understand visual images, process and manipulate symbols, be creative and imaginative, and use heuristics.

From the early AI pioneering stage, the research emphasis has been on developing machines with **intelligent behaviour**. Machine intelligence, however, is hard to achieve. Some of the specific characteristics of intelligent behaviour include the ability to do the following:

- *Learn from experience and apply the knowledge acquired from experience.* Learning from past situations and events is a key component of intelligent behaviour and is a natural ability of humans, who learn by trial and error. This ability, however, must be carefully programmed into a computer system. Today, researchers are developing systems that can learn from experience. For instance, computerized AI chess software can learn to improve while playing human competitors. In one match, Garry Kasparov competed against a personal computer with AI software developed in Israel, called Deep Junior. This match was a 3–3 tie, but Kasparov picked up something the machine would have no interest in – €500 000. The 20 questions (20Q) website, www.20q.net, is another example of a system that learns.[18] The website is an artificial intelligence game that learns as people play (see Figure 9.2).

- *Handle complex situations.* People are often involved in complex situations. World leaders face difficult political decisions regarding terrorism, conflict, global economic conditions, hunger, and poverty. In a business setting, top-level managers and executives must handle a complex market, challenging competitors, intricate government regulations, and a demanding workforce. Even human experts make mistakes in dealing with these situations. Developing computer systems that can handle perplexing situations requires careful planning and elaborate computer programming.

- *Solve problems when important information is missing.* The essence of decision making is dealing with uncertainty. Often, decisions must be made with too little information or inaccurate information because obtaining complete information is too costly or even impossible. Today, AI systems can make important calculations, comparisons, and decisions even when information is missing.

- *Determine what is important.* Knowing what is truly important is the mark of a good decision maker. Developing programs and approaches to allow computer systems and machines to identify important information is not a simple task.

- *React quickly and correctly to a new situation.* A small child, for example, can look over a ledge or a drop-off and know not to venture too close. The child reacts quickly and

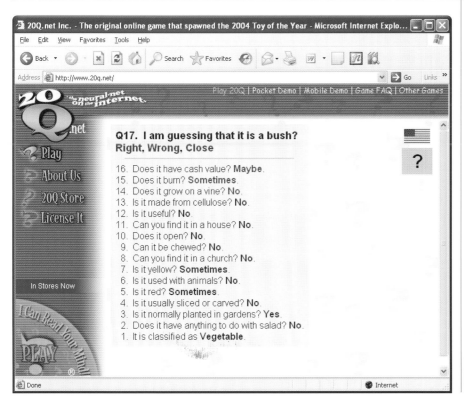

Figure 9.2 **20Q** *20Q is an online game where users play the popular game, Twenty Questions, against an artificial intelligence foe.*

SOURCE: www.20q.net.

correctly to a new situation. Computers, on the other hand, do not have this ability without complex programming.

■ *Understand visual images.* Interpreting visual images can be extremely difficult, even for sophisticated computers. Moving through a room of chairs, tables, and other objects can be trivial for people but extremely complex for machines, robots, and computers. Such machines require an extension of understanding visual images, called a **perceptive system**. Having a perceptive system allows a machine to approximate the way a person sees, hears, and feels objects. Military robots, for example, use cameras and perceptive systems to conduct reconnaissance missions to detect enemy weapons and soldiers. Detecting and destroying them can save lives.

perceptive system A system that approximates the way a person sees, hears, and feels objects.

■ *Process and manipulate symbols.* People see, manipulate, and process symbols every day. Visual images provide a constant stream of information to our brains. By contrast, computers have difficulty handling symbolic processing and reasoning. Although computers excel at numerical calculations, they aren't as good at dealing with symbols and three-dimensional objects. Recent developments in machine-vision hardware and software, however, allow some computers to process and manipulate symbols on a limited basis.

■ *Be creative and imaginative.* Throughout history, people have turned difficult situations into advantages by being creative and imaginative. For instance, when defective mints with holes in the middle were shipped, an enterprising entrepreneur decided to market these new mints as 'LifeSavers' instead of returning them to the manufacturer. Ice cream cones were invented at the St. Louis World's Fair when an imaginative store owner decided to wrap ice cream with a waffle from his grill for portability. Developing new and exciting products and services from an existing (perhaps negative) situation is a human characteristic. Computers cannot be imaginative or creative in this way, although software has been developed to enable a computer to write short stories.

■ *Use heuristics.* For some decisions, people use heuristics (rules of thumb arising from experience) or even guesses. In searching for a job, you might rank the companies you are considering according to profits per employee. Today, some computer systems, given the right programs, obtain good solutions that use approximations instead of trying to search for an optimal solution, which would be technically difficult or too time consuming.

This list of traits only partially defines intelligence. Unlike the terminology used in virtually every other field of IS research, in which the objectives can be clearly defined, the term 'intelligence' is a formidable stumbling block. One of the problems in AI is arriving at a working definition of real intelligence against which to compare the performance of an AI system.

9.2.2 The Difference Between Natural and Artificial Intelligence

Since the term 'artificial intelligence' was defined in the 1950s, experts have disagreed about the difference between natural and artificial intelligence. Can computers be programmed to have common sense? Profound differences separate natural from artificial intelligence, but they are declining in number (see Table 9.1). One of the driving forces behind AI research is an attempt to understand how people actually reason and think. Creating machines that can reason is possible only when we truly understand our own processes for doing so.

Table 9.1 A Comparison of Natural and Artificial Intelligence

Ability to	Natural Intelligence (Human) Low	High	Artificial Intelligence (Machine) Low	High
Use sensors (see hear, touch, smell)		√	√	
Be creative and imaginative		√	√	
Learn from experience		√	√	
Adapt to new situations		√	√	
Afford the cost of acquiring intelligence		√	√	
Acquire a large amount of external information		√		√
Use a variety of information sources		√		√
Make complex calculations	√			√
Transfer information	√			√
Make a series of calculations rapidly and accurately	√			√

Information Systems @ Work

Call Centres Use Artificial Intelligence to Improve Service to Customers

Call centres, sometimes referred to as 'contact centres,' are emerging as an important tactical weapon for corporations in the battle for customers' money. A call centre is a unit within an organization or an outside firm that handles remote customer communications. Internet-based technologies, such as e-mail, discussion boards, and chat, are increasing the duties and boundaries of call centres. Research shows that about 70 percent of real-time customer interactions are handled by call centres. Business executives are picking up on these statistics and investing heavily in new technology to empower call centre operators and provide convenience to customers. Artificial intelligence technology plays a key role.

'Contact centres are entering a new phase and becoming more intelligent,' analyst Catriona Wallace says. 'New technologies will allow them to take an even more central role in organizations.' Wallace, whose research company Callcenters.net tracks growth in the sector, says increasing use of the Internet by consumers, and technologies such as VoIP and speech recognition are driving change.

Increasingly, the software used by call centres is being integrated with powerful CRM systems. This integration provides a solid foundation on which a range of new applications and agent techniques can be built. With ready access to everything from a customer's purchasing history to personal details and demographics, selling can take on a new dimension.

For example, the outbound calling function of call centres has been hampered by consumer resistance to unsolicited calls and the rise of do-not-call lists. Companies need to be smarter about when and why they contact the public. New tools enable companies to optimize the lists they are using, and customize them for specific campaigns. Previous histories and details can be automatically checked to increase the chance of finding a receptive customer, rather than randomly dialling people.

Intelligent software tools can examine demographic profiles to decide the best time to reach customers and whether to call their work, home, or mobile number. Users of the software claim a 40 to 50 percent improvement in speaking to the right person at the right time and the right place.

Intelligent software is also being used to accurately match the number of outgoing calls being made to the number of agents in a call centre. New versions of automatic diallers can predict how often agents will become available and have a caller waiting on the line as soon as they are free, increasing agent utilization.

New intelligent software also helps companies respond smarter when customers or prospective customers call them. James Brooks, senior vice president at call centre specialist Genesys, says leading companies are examining a technique called 'psychographic routing'. This involves routing incoming calls to the agent that the system deems is the best match for the caller. Based on caller line ID, a psychographic system can instantly assess known details such as the age, gender, and previous history of a caller, and automatically route them to the appropriate agent. For example, a 55-year-old shopping for life insurance would be routed to an operator of a similar age who is more likely to understand the concerns of the caller.

Such systems can also provide important customer information relevant to targeted sales. For example, the software can alert an agent that a customer is qualified for an increase in their credit limit, which can then be offered during the call. The success of such targeted sales pitches is high.

More complicated information could be calculated and provided. For example, bank call centre agents can be provided with real-time credit scoring for customers seeking loans. 'You can also undertake things like predictive claims,' says Tim Macdermid, Australia manager for analytical software specialist SPSS. 'An insurance company call centre agent can collect information from a customer and the system will predict whether that claim is fraudulent.'

From the customer's perspective, this call centre evolution will lead to big changes in the way they interact with large organizations. Increasing numbers of transactions and business communications will be conducted through call centres. Call centre agents will be more empowered as their tools become more intelligent and customers will have better experiences when they call companies.

Questions

1   How is intelligent software helping call centre agents be more effective?

2   Why are call centres becoming the primary conduit for communication between a business and its customers?

3   What is psychographic routing, and how might some interpret it as an infringement on their privacy, whereas others consider it a valuable service?

4   List communications technologies that a customer might use to communicate with a call centre agent, along with the pros and cons of each method. How might intelligent systems assist with the cons?

SOURCES: Grayson, Ian, 'Digging Deeper into Data', *Australian IT,* http://australianit.news.com.au, April 25, 2006; Genesys Corporation (website), www.genesyslab.com; SPSS (website), www.spss.com.

9.2.3 The Major Branches of Artificial Intelligence

AI is a broad field that includes several specialty areas, such as expert systems, robotics, vision systems, natural language processing, learning systems, and neural networks. Many of these areas are related; advances in one can occur simultaneously with or result in advances in others.

Expert Systems

expert system Hardware and software that stores knowledge and makes inferences, similar to a human expert.

An **expert system** consists of hardware and software that stores knowledge and makes inferences, similar to those of a human expert. Because of their many business applications, expert systems are discussed in more detail in their own section later in this chapter.

Robotics

robotics Mechanical or computer devices that perform tasks requiring a high degree of precision or that are tedious or hazardous for humans.

Robotics involves developing mechanical or computer devices that can paint cars, make precision welds, and perform other tasks that require a high degree of precision or are tedious or hazardous for human beings. Some robots are mechanical devices that don't use the AI features discussed in this chapter. Others are sophisticated systems that use one or more AI features or characteristics, such as the vision systems, learning systems, or neural networks discussed later in the chapter. For many businesses, robots are used to do the 'three Ds' – dull, dirty, and dangerous jobs.[19] Manufacturers use robots to assemble and paint products. The NASA shuttle crash of the early 2000s, for example, has led some people to recommend using robots instead of people to explore space and perform scientific research (see Figure 9.3). Some robots, such as Sony's Aibo, can be used for companionship (Figure 9.4). Contemporary robotics combine both high-precision machine capabilities and sophisticated controlling software. The controlling software in robots is what is most important in terms of AI.

The field of robotics has many applications, and research into these unique devices continues. The following are a few examples:

■ IRobot is a company that builds a number of robots, including the Roomba Floorvac for cleaning floors and the PackBot, an unmanned vehicle used to assist and protect soldiers.[20] Manufacturers use robots to assemble and paint products.

■ The Porter Adventist Hospital in Denver, Colorado, uses a $90 000 Da Vinci Surgical System to perform surgery on prostate cancer patients.[21] The robot has multiple arms that hold surgical tools. According to one doctor at Porter, 'The biggest advantage is it improves recovery time. Instead of having an eight-inch incision, the patient has a "band-aid" incision. It's much quicker.'

Figure 9.3 Robots in Space *Robots can be used in situations that are hazardous or inaccessible to humans. The ExoMars Rover – the European Space Agency's first field biologist on Mars.*

SOURCE: ESA.

- DARPA (The Defence Advanced Research Project Agency) sponsors the DARPA Grand Challenge, a 212 km (132 mile) race over rugged terrain for computer-controlled cars.[22]

- Because of an age limit on camel jockeys, the state of Qatar decided to use robots in its camel races.[23] Developed in Switzerland, the robots have a human shape and only weigh 27 kg (59 lb). The robots use global positioning systems (GPS), a microphone to deliver voice commands to the camel, and cameras. A camel trainer uses a joystick to control the robot's movements on the camel. Camel racing is very popular in Qatar.

- In military applications, robots are becoming real weapons. The U.S. Air Force is developing a smart robotic jet fighter. Often called 'unmanned combat air vehicles' (UCAVs), these robotic war machines, such as the X-45A, will be able to identify and destroy targets without human pilots. UCAVs send pictures and information to a central command centre and can be directed to strike military targets. These new machines extend the current Predator and Global Hawk technologies the military used in Afghanistan after the September 11th, 2001 terrorist attacks.

Although robots are essential components of today's automated manufacturing and military systems, future robots will find wider applications in banks, restaurants, homes, doctors' offices,

Figure 9.4 Aibo

Unfortunately, Sony have stopped making this robot puppy.

SOURCE: Chris Willson/Alamy.

and hazardous working environments such as nuclear stations. The Repliee Q1 and Q2 robots from Japan are ultra-humanlike robots or androids that can blink, gesture, speak, and even appear to breathe (Figure 9.5).[24] Microrobotics is a developing area. Also called micro-electro-mechanical systems (MEMS), microrobots are the size of a grain of salt and can be used in a person's blood to monitor the body, and for other purposes in air bags, cell phones, refrigerators, and more.

If you would like to try to make a robot, Lego Mindstorms is a good place to start (Figure 9.6).

Vision Systems

vision systems The hardware and software that permit computers to capture, store, and manipulate visual images.

Another area of AI involves **vision systems**. Vision systems include hardware and software that permit computers to capture, store, and manipulate visual images.

For example, vision systems can be used with robots to give these machines 'sight'. Factory robots typically perform mechanical tasks no visual

Figure 9.5 The Repliee Q2 Robot from Japan

SOURCE: Karl F. MacDorman. A student in the Intelligent Robotics Laboratory at Osaka University, Japan, shaking hands with Repliee Q2, an android robot developed by the Intelligent Robotics Laboratory and Kokoro Co., Ltd.

stimuli. Robotic vision extends the capability of these systems, allowing the robot to make decisions based on visual input. Generally, robots with vision systems can recognize black and white and some grey shades but do not have good colour or three-dimensional vision. Other systems concentrate on only a few key features in an image, ignoring the rest. Another potential application of a vision system is fingerprint analysis.

Even with recent breakthroughs in vision systems, computers cannot see and understand visual images the way people can.

Natural Language Processing and Voice Recognition

As discussed in Chapter 4, **natural language processing** allows a computer to understand and react to statements and commands made in a 'natural' language, such as English. In some cases, voice recognition is used with natural language processing. Voice recognition involves converting sound waves into words. Dragon Systems' Naturally Speaking uses continuous voice recognition, or natural speech, allowing the user to input data into the computer by speaking at a normal pace without pausing between words. The spoken words are transcribed immediately onto the computer screen (Figure 9.7). After converting sounds into words, natural language processing systems can be used to react to the words or commands by performing a variety of tasks. Brokerage services are a perfect fit for voice-recognition and natural language processing technology to replace the existing 'press 1 to buy or sell shares' touchpad telephone menu system. People buying and selling use a vocabulary too varied for easy access through menus and touchpads, but still small enough for software to process in real time. Several brokerages – including Charles Schwab & Company, Fidelity Investments, DLJdirect, and TD Waterhouse Group – offer these services. These systems use voice recognition and natural language processing to let customers access retirement accounts, check balances, and find stock quotes. Eventually, the technology may allow people

natural language processing Processing that allows the computer to understand and react to statements and commands made in a 'natural' language, such as English.

Figure 9.6 Lego
Mindstorms *The kit
contains a programmable
brick, Lego bricks, motors
and sensors to build
robots. The robot can be
programmed in a range of
languages, including Java
and Visual Basic, as well as
Lego's own easy to master
RCX Code.*

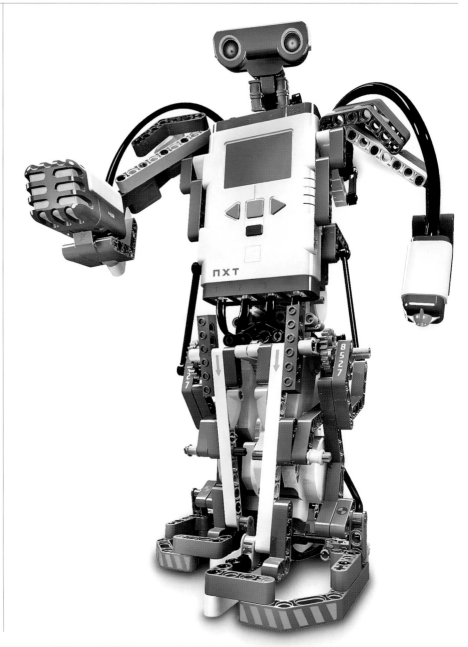

to make transactions using voice commands over the phone and to use search engines to have
their questions answered through the brokerage firm's call centre. One of the big advantages
is that the number of calls routed to the customer service department drops considerably after
new voice features are added. That is desirable to brokerages because it helps them staff their
call centres correctly – even in volatile markets. Whereas a typical person uses a vocabulary of
about 20 000 words or less, voice-recognition software can have a built-in vocabulary of 85 000
words. Some companies claim that voice-recognition and natural language processing software
is so good that customers forget they are talking to a computer and start discussing the weather
or sports results.

SOURCE: Courtesy of Nuance Communications, Inc.

Figure 9.7 Dragon Systems' Naturally Speaking

Learning Systems

Another part of AI deals with **learning systems**, a combination of software and hardware that allows a computer to change how it functions or reacts to situations based on feedback it receives. For example, some computerized games have learning abilities. If the computer does not win a game, it remembers not to make the same moves under the same conditions again. Tom Mitchell, director of the Center for Automated Learning and Discovery at Carnegie Mellon University, is experimenting with two learning software packages that help each other learn.[25] He believes that two learning software packages that cooperate are better than separate learning packages. Mitchell's learning software helps Internet search engines do a better job in finding information. Learning systems software requires feedback on the results of actions or decisions. At a minimum, the feedback needs to indicate whether the results are desirable (winning a game) or undesirable (losing a game). The feedback is then used to alter what the system will do in the future.

learning systems A combination of software and hardware that allows the computer to change how it functions or reacts to situations based on feedback it receives.

Neural Networks

An increasingly important aspect of AI involves **neural networks**, also called 'neural nets'. A neural network is a computer system that can act like or simulate the functioning of a human brain. The systems use massively parallel processors in an architecture that is based on the human brain's own mesh-like structure. In addition, neural network software simulates a neural network using standard computers. Neural networks can process many pieces of data at the same time and learn to recognize patterns. Some of the specific abilities of neural networks include discovering relationships and trends in large databases, and solving complex problems for which all the information is not present.

neural network A computer system that attempts to simulate the functioning of a human brain.

A particular skill of neural nets is analyzing detailed trends. Large amusement parks and banks use neural networks to determine staffing needs based on customer traffic – a task that requires precise analysis, down to the half-hour. Increasingly, businesses are using neural nets to help them navigate ever-thicker forests of data and make sense of a myriad of customer traits and buying habits. One application for example, would be to track the habits of insurance customers and predict which ones will not renew a policy. Staff could then suggest to an insurance agent what changes to make in the policy to persuade the consumer to renew it. Some pattern-recognition software uses neural networks to analyze hundreds of millions of bank, brokerage, and insurance accounts involving a trillion dollars to uncover money laundering and other suspicious money transfers.

Other Artificial Intelligence Applications

A few other artificial intelligence applications exist in addition to those just discussed. A **genetic algorithm**, also called a genetic program, is an approach to solving large, complex problems in which many repeated operations or models change and evolve until the best one emerges. The first step is to change or vary competing solutions to the problem. This can be done by changing the parts of a program or by combining different program segments into a new program. The second step is to select only the best models or algorithms, which continue to evolve. Programs or program segments that are not as good as others are discarded, similar to natural selection or 'survival of the fittest', in which only the best species survive. This process of variation and natural selection continues until the genetic algorithm yields the best possible solution to the original problem. For example, some investment firms use genetic algorithms to help select the best stocks or bonds. Genetic algorithms are also used in computer science and mathematics. Genetic algorithms can help companies determine which orders to accept for maximum profit. This approach helps companies select the orders that will increase profits and take full advantage of the company's production facilities. Genetic algorithms are also being used to make better decisions in developing inputs to neural networks.

genetic algorithm An approach to solving large, complex problems in which a number of related operations or models change and evolve until the best one emerges.

intelligent agent Programs and a knowledge base used to perform a specific task for a person, a process, or another program; also called intelligent robot or bot.

An **intelligent agent** (also called an 'intelligent robot' or 'bot') consists of programs and a knowledge base used to perform a specific task for a person, a process, or another program. Like a sports agent who searches for the best sponsorship deals for a top athlete, an intelligent agent often searches to find the best price, schedule, or solution to a problem. The programs used by an intelligent agent can search large amounts of data as the knowledge base refines the search or accommodates user preferences. Often used to search the vast resources of the Internet, intelligent agents can help people find information on an important topic or the best price for a new digital camera. Intelligent agents can also be used to make travel arrangements, monitor incoming e-mail for viruses or junk mail, and coordinate meetings and schedules of busy executives. In the human resources field, intelligent agents help with online training. The software can look ahead in training materials and know what to start next.

Ethical and Societal Issues

Online Matchmaker eHarmony

The eHarmony Compatibility Matching System is an expert system that has been programmed with Dr. Neil Clark Warren's knowledge about what makes a good relationship. Its goal is to match partners for successful relationships using 29 key dimensions that help predict compatibility and the potential for relationship success. The 29 key dimensions are organized into two general categories: 'core traits' that include emotional temperament, social style, cognitive mode, and physicality; and 'vital attributes' that include relationship skills, values and beliefs, and key experiences.

An eHarmony applicant fills out a 436-item relationship questionnaire that allows the expert system to categorize that person's personality and build a compatibility profile. Heuristics are used to search the eHarmony database for compatible partners whose personality attributes make a good match according to Dr. Warren's studies. An ordered list of potential partners is produced with the best candidates listed first. The service then provides methods to get in touch with prospective mates.

Is the system successful? eHarmony has more than 11 million registered users and, according to an independent poll, more than 90 eHarmony members on average marry every day as a result of being matched through the service.

eHarmony uses artificial intelligence throughout its organization. Technology from SPSS, Inc., is used in various areas of the eHarmony business, including scientific research, brand development, product research, compatibility models, customer satisfaction and retention, and projective analysis. Predictive analytics is a form of data mining that employs artificial intelligence techniques to make assumptions about the future based on historical data and to predict outcomes of events. You can imagine how such technology can be applied to matchmaking as well as traditional business activities.

eHarmony's senior director of research and product development is Steve Carter, a strong believer in AI for business. The numerous analytic and data management tools provided by the SPSS systems enables eHarmony to understand important information in more novel, forward-thinking ways. eHarmony is a prime example of how artificial intelligence and expert system tools are taking a lot of the guesswork out of life.

Questions

1   What role does artificial intelligence play in the matchmaking process at eHarmony?

2   How does eHarmony use predictive analytics in all of its business units?

3   Do you think the scientific methods provided by eHarmony are superior or inferior to traditional random chance encounters for finding a mate? Why?

4   What dangers to privacy and safety, if any, are involved in using a service like eHarmony?

SOURCES: DM Review Editorial Staff, 'eHarmony Expands SPSS Deployment Company-Wide for Research and Development', *DM Direct Newsletter,* www.dmreview.com/article_sub.cfm?articleID=1055723, June 9, 2006; eHarmony (website), www.eharmony.com.

9.3 Expert Systems

An expert system outputs a recommendation based on answers given to it by users (who are not experts in the field). The intention of the system is to capture the expert's knowledge and make it available to those who lack this knowledge. Expert systems have been developed to diagnose medical conditions, resolve engineering problems, and solve energy problems. They have also been used to design new products and systems, develop innovative insurance products, determine the best use of timber, and increase the quality of healthcare (see Figure 9.8). Like human experts, expert systems use heuristics, or rules of thumb, to arrive at conclusions or make suggestions.

Figure 9.8 Using a
Credit Card *Credit card
companies often use expert
systems to determine credit
limits for credit cards.*

SOURCE: David Young-Wolff/Alamy.

The research conducted in AI during the past two decades is resulting in expert systems that explore new business possibilities, increase overall profitability, reduce costs, and provide superior service to customers and clients.

9.3.1 When to Use Expert Systems

Sophisticated expert systems can be difficult, expensive, and time consuming to develop. The following is a list of factors that normally make expert systems worth the expenditure of time and money. Develop an expert system if it can do any of the following:

- Provide a high potential payoff or significantly reduce downside risk.
- Capture and preserve irreplaceable human expertise.
- Solve a problem that is not easily solved using traditional programming techniques.
- Develop a system which is more consistent than human experts.
- Provide expertise needed at a number of locations at the same time or in a hostile environment that is dangerous to human health.
- Provide expertise that is expensive or rare.
- Develop a solution faster than human experts can.
- Provide expertise needed for training and development to share the wisdom and experience of human experts with many people.

9.3.2 Components of Expert Systems

An expert system consists of a collection of integrated and related components, including a knowledge base, an inference engine, an explanation facility, a knowledge base acquisition facility, and a user interface. A diagram of a typical expert system is shown in Figure 9.9.

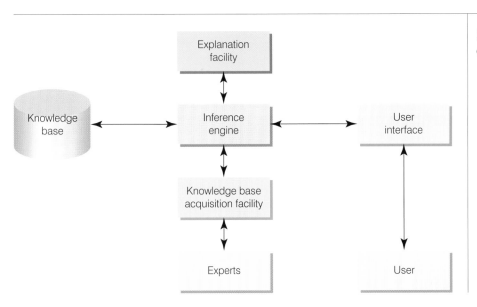

Figure 9.9 Components of an Expert System

The Knowledge Base

The **knowledge base** stores all relevant information, data, rules, cases, and relationships that the expert system uses. A knowledge base is a natural extension of a database (presented in Chapter 5) and an information and decision support system (presented in Chapter 8). A knowledge base must be developed for each unique application. For example, a medical expert system contains facts about diseases and symptoms. The following are some tools and techniques that can be used to create a knowledge base.

knowledge base A component of an expert system that stores all relevant information, data, rules, cases, and relationships used by the expert system.

- *Assembling human experts.* One challenge in developing a knowledge base is to assemble the knowledge of multiple human experts. Typically, the objective in building a knowledge base is to integrate the knowledge of people with similar expertise (for example, many doctors might contribute to a medical diagnostics knowledge base).

■ *Fuzzy logic.* Another challenge for expert system designers and developers is capturing knowledge and relationships that are not precise or exact. Instead of the yes/no, or true/false conditions of typical computer decisions, fuzzy logic allows shades of grey, or what is known as 'fuzzy sets'. Fuzzy logic rules help computers evaluate the imperfect or imprecise conditions they encounter and make educated guesses based on the probability of correctness of the decision.

■ *Rules.* A rule is a conditional statement that links conditions to actions or outcomes. In many instances, these rules are stored as **IF-THEN statements**, such as 'IF a certain set of network conditions exists, THEN a certain network problem diagnosis is appropriate'. In an expert system for a weather forecasting operation, for example, the rules could state that if certain temperature patterns exist with a given barometric pressure and certain previous weather patterns over the last 24 hours, then a specific forecast will be made, including temperatures, cloud coverage, and wind-chill factor. Figure 9.10 shows how to use expert system rules in determining whether a person should receive a mortgage loan from a bank. These rules can be placed in almost any standard program language discussed in Chapter 4 using 'IF-THEN' statements or into special expert systems shells, discussed later in the chapter. In general, as the number of rules that an expert system knows increases, the precision of the expert system also increases.

IF-THEN statements Rules that suggest certain conclusions

Figure 9.10 Rules for a Credit Application

Mortgage application for loans from €100,000 to €200,000

If there are no previous credit problems and

If monthly net income is greater than 4 times monthly loan payment and

If down payment is 15% of the total value of the property and

If net assets of borrower are greater than €25,000 and

If employment is greater than three years at the same company

Then accept loan application

Else check other credit rules

■ *Cases.* An expert system can use cases in developing a solution to a current problem or situation. This process involves (1) finding cases stored in the knowledge base that are similar to the problem or situation at hand and (2) modifying the solutions to the cases to fit or accommodate the current problem or situation.

inference engine Part of the expert system that seeks information and relationships from the knowledge base and provides answers, predictions, and suggestions the way a human expert would.

The Inference Engine

The overall purpose of an **inference engine** is to seek information and relationships from the knowledge base and to provide answers, predictions, and

suggestions the way a human expert would. In other words, the inference engine is the component that delivers the expert advice. To provide answers and give advice, expert systems can use
backward and forward chaining. **Backward chaining** is the process of starting with conclusions and working backward to the supporting facts. If the
facts do not support the conclusion, another conclusion is selected and
tested. This process is continued until the correct conclusion is identified.
Forward chaining starts with the facts and works forward to the conclusions.
Consider the expert system that forecasts future sales for a product. Forward
chaining starts with a fact such as 'The demand for the product last month
was 20 000 units'. With the forward-chaining approach, the expert system searches for rules that
contain a reference to product demand. For example, 'IF product demand is over 15 000 units,
THEN check the demand for competing products'. As a result of this process, the expert system
might use information on the demand for competitive products. Next, after searching additional
rules, the expert system might use information on personal income or national inflation rates.
This process continues until the expert system can reach a conclusion using the data supplied
by the user and the rules that apply in the knowledge base.

> **backward chaining** The process of starting with conclusions and working backward to the supporting facts.
>
> **forward chaining** The process of starting with the facts and working forward to the conclusions.

The Explanation Facility

An important part of an expert system is the **explanation facility**, which
allows a user or decision maker to understand how the expert system arrived
at certain conclusions or results. A medical expert system, for example, might
reach the conclusion that a patient has a defective heart valve given certain
symptoms and the results of tests on the patient. The explanation facility
allows a doctor to find out the logic or rationale of the diagnosis made by the
expert system. The expert system, using the explanation facility, can indicate all the facts and
rules that were used in reaching the conclusion. This facility allows doctors to determine whether
the expert system is processing the data and information correctly and logically.

> **explanation facility** Component of an expert system that allows a user or decision maker to understand how the expert system arrived at certain conclusions or results.

The Knowledge Acquisition Facility

A difficult task in developing an expert system is the process of creating and updating the knowledge base. In the past, when more traditional programming languages were used, developing
a knowledge base was tedious and time consuming. Each fact, relationship, and rule had to be
programmed into the knowledge base. In most cases, an experienced programmer had to create and update the knowledge base.

Today, specialized software allows users and decision makers to create and
modify their own knowledge bases through the **knowledge acquisition facility**. The purpose of the knowledge acquisition facility is to provide a convenient
and efficient means for capturing and storing all components of the knowledge
base. Knowledge acquisition software can present users and decision makers
with easy-to-use menus. After entering the appropriate attributes, the knowledge acquisition facility correctly stores information and relationships in the knowledge base, making the knowledge base easier and less expensive to set up and maintain. Knowledge acquisition
can be a manual process or a mixture of manual and automated procedures. Regardless of how
the knowledge is acquired, the knowledge base must be validated and updated frequently to
make sure that it is still accurate.

> **knowledge acquisition facility** Part of the expert system that provides convenient and efficient means of capturing and storing all the components of the knowledge base.

The User Interface

Specialized user interface software is employed for designing, creating, updating, and using expert
systems. The main purpose of the user interface is to make an expert system easier for users and
decision makers to develop and use. At one time, skilled computer personnel created and operated
most expert systems; today, the user interface permits decision makers to develop and use their
own expert systems. Because expert systems place more emphasis on directing user activities
than do other types of systems, text-oriented user interfaces (using menus, forms, and scripts)

might be more common in expert systems than the graphical interfaces often used with DSS. A typical user interface between a user and the expert system for a credit application.

> **EXPERT SYSTEM:** Are there any previous credit problems?
> **USER:** No.
> **EXPERT SYSTEM:** Is the applicant's net income greater than four times the monthly loan payment?
> **USER:** Yes.
> **EXPERT SYSTEM:** Is the down payment greater than 15 percent of the property value?
> **USER**: Yes.
> **EXPERT SYSTEM:** Are the net assets of the borrower greater than €25 000?
> **USER:** Yes.
> **EXPERT SYSTEM:** Has the borrower worked more than three years at the same company?
> **USER:** Yes.
> **EXPERT SYSTEM:** Accept the loan application.

Expert Systems Development

Like other computer systems, expert systems require a systematic development approach for best results. This approach includes determining the requirements for the expert system, identifying one or more experts in the area or discipline under investigation, constructing the components of the expert system, implementing the results, and maintaining and reviewing the complete system.

Participants in Developing and Using Expert Systems

domain The area of knowledge addressed by the expert system.

domain expert The individual or group who has the expertise or knowledge one is trying to capture in the expert system.

Because of the time and effort involved in the task, an expert system is developed to address only a specific area of knowledge. This area of knowledge is called the **domain**. The **domain expert** is the person or group with the expertise or knowledge the expert system is trying to capture. The domain expert (individual or group) usually can do the following:

- Recognize the real problem.
- Develop a general framework for problem solving.
- Formulate theories about the situation.
- Develop and use general rules to solve a problem.
- Know when to break the rules or general principles.
- Solve problems quickly and efficiently.
- Learn from experience.
- Know what is and is not important in solving a problem.
- Explain the situation and solutions of problems to others.

knowledge engineer A person who has training or experience in the design, development, implementation, and maintenance of an expert system.

knowledge user The person or group who uses and benefits from the expert system.

A **knowledge engineer** is a person who has training or experience in the design, development, implementation, and maintenance of an expert system, including training or experience with expert system shells. The **knowledge user** is the person or group who uses and benefits from the expert system. Knowledge users do not need any previous training in computers or expert systems.

Expert Systems Development Tools and Techniques

Theoretically, expert systems can be developed from any programming language. Since the introduction of computer systems, programming languages have become easier to use, more powerful, and increasingly able to handle specialized requirements. In the early days of expert systems development, traditional high-level languages, including Pascal, FORTRAN, and COBOL, were used (see Figure 9.11). LISP was one of the first special languages developed and used for expert system applications. PROLOG was also developed to build expert systems. Since the 1990s, however, other expert system products (such as shells) have become available that remove the burden of programming, allowing non-programmers to develop and benefit from the use of expert systems.

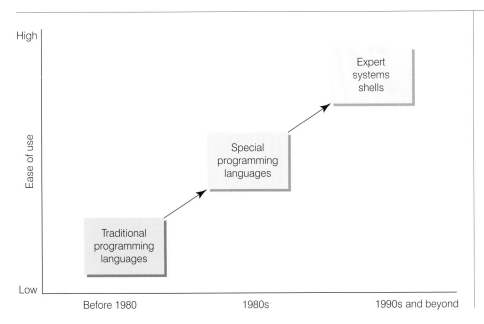

Figure 9.11 Expert Systems Development

An expert system shell is a collection of software packages and tools used to design, develop, implement, and maintain expert systems. Expert system shells are available for both personal computers and mainframe systems. Some shells are inexpensive, costing less than €400. In addition, off-the-shelf expert system shells are complete and ready to run. The user enters the appropriate data or parameters, and the expert system provides output to the problem or situation.

Some expert system products can analyze LAN networks, monitor air quality in commercial buildings, and evaluate oil and drilling operations. Table 9.2 lists a few expert system products.

Table 9.2 Popular Expert System Products

Name of Product	Application and Capabilities
Financial Adviser	Analyzes financial investments in new equipment, facilities, and the like; requests the appropriate data and performs a complete financial analysis
G2	Assists in oil and gas operations. Transco, a British company, uses it to help in the transport of gas to more than 20 million commercial and domestic customers
HazMat Loader	Analyzes hazardous materials in truck shipments
LSI Indicator	Helps determine property values; developed by one of the largest residential title and closing companies
MindWizard	Enables development of compact expert systems ranging from simple models that incorporate business decision rules to highly sophisticated models; PC-based and inexpensive
RAMPART	Analyzes risk. The U.S. General Services Administration uses it to analyze risk to the approximately 8 000 federal buildings it manages

Applications of Expert Systems and Artificial Intelligence

Expert systems and artificial intelligence have wide applications in business and government. A list of applications, some of which have already been mentioned, is given next.

- *Credit granting and loan analysis.* Many banks employ expert systems to review a customer's credit application and credit history data from credit bureaus to make a decision on whether to grant a loan or approve a transaction. KPMG Peat Marwick uses an expert system called Loan Probe to review its reserves to determine whether sufficient funds have been set aside to cover the risk of some uncollectible loans.

- *Stock picking.* Some expert systems help investment professionals pick stocks and other investments.

- *Catching cheats and terrorists.* Some gambling casinos use expert system software to catch cheats. The CIA is testing the software to see whether it can detect possible terrorists when they make hotel or airline reservations.

- *Budgeting.* Car companies can use expert systems to help budget, plan, and coordinate prototype testing programs to save hundreds of millions of euros.

- *Games.* Some expert systems are used for entertainment. For example, 20Q (www.20Q.net).

- *Information management and retrieval.* The explosive growth of information available to decision makers has created a demand for devices to help manage the information. Bots can aid this process. Businesses might use a bot to retrieve information from large distributed databases or a vast network like the Internet.

- *AI and expert systems embedded in products.* The antilock braking system on today's cars is an example of a rudimentary expert system. A processor senses when the tyres are beginning to skid and releases the brakes for a fraction of a second to prevent the skid. AI researchers are also finding ways to use neural networks and robotics in everyday devices, such as toasters, alarm clocks, and televisions.

- *Plant layout and manufacturing.* FLEXPERT is an expert system that uses fuzzy logic to perform plant layout. The software helps companies determine the best placement for equipment and manufacturing facilities. Expert systems can also spot defective welds during the manufacturing process. The expert system analyzes radiographic images and suggests which welds could be flawed.

- *Hospitals and medical facilities.* Some hospitals use expert systems to determine a patient's likelihood of contracting cancer or other diseases. Hospitals, pharmacies, and other healthcare providers can use CaseAlert by MEDecision to determine possible high-risk or high-cost patients. MYCIN is an early expert system developed at Stanford University to analyze blood infections. UpToDate is another expert system used to diagnose patients. To help doctors in the diagnosis of thoracic pain, MatheMEDics has developed THORASK, a straightforward, easy-to-use program, requiring only the input of carefully obtained clinical information. The program helps the less experienced to distinguish the three principal categories of chest pain from each other. It does what a true medical expert system should do without the need for complicated user input. The user answers basic questions about the patient's history and directed physical findings, and the program immediately displays a list of diagnoses. The diagnoses are presented in decreasing order of likelihood, together with their estimated probabilities. The program also provides concise descriptions of relevant clinical conditions and their presentations, as well as brief suggestions for diagnostic approaches.

- *Help desk and assistance.* Customer service help desks use expert systems to provide timely and accurate assistance. The automated help desk frees up staff to handle more complex needs while still providing more timely assistance for routine calls.

- *Employee performance evaluation.* An expert system developed by Austin-Hayne, called Employee Appraiser, provides managers with expert advice for use in employee performance reviews and career development.

- *Virus detection.* IBM is using neural network technology to help create more advanced software for eradicating computer viruses, a major problem in businesses. IBM's neural network software deals with 'boot sector' viruses, the most prevalent type, using a form of artificial intelligence that generalizes by looking at examples. It requires a vast number of training samples, which in the case of antivirus software are fragments of virus code.

- *Repair and maintenance.* ACE is an expert system used by AT&T to analyze the maintenance of telephone networks. IET-Intelligent Electronics uses an expert system to diagnose maintenance problems related to aerospace equipment. General Electric Aircraft Engine Group uses an expert system to enhance maintenance performance levels at all sites and improve diagnostic accuracy.

- *Shipping.* CARGEX cargo expert system is used by Lufthansa, a German airline, to help determine the best shipping routes.

- *Marketing.* CoverStory is an expert system that extracts marketing information from a database and automatically writes marketing reports.

- *Warehouse optimization.* United Distillers uses an expert system to determine the best combinations of liquor stocks to produce its blends of Scotch whiskey. This information is then supplemented with information about the location of the casks for each blend. The system optimizes the selection of required casks, keeping to a minimum the number of 'doors' (warehouse sections) from which the casks must be taken and the number of casks that need to be moved to clear the way. Other constraints must be satisfied, such as the current working capacity of each warehouse and the maintenance and restocking work that may be in progress.

9.4 Virtual Reality

The term 'virtual reality' was initially coined by Jaron Lanier, founder of VPL Research, in 1989. Originally, the term referred to immersive virtual reality in which the user becomes fully immersed in an artificial, three-dimensional world that is completely generated by a computer. Immersive virtual reality can represent any three-dimensional setting, real or abstract, such as a building, an archaeological excavation site, human anatomy, a sculpture, or a crime scene reconstruction. Through immersion, the user can gain a deeper understanding of the virtual world's behaviour and functionality.

A virtual reality system enables one or more users to move and react in a computer-simulated environment. Virtual reality simulations require special interface devices that transmit the sights, sounds, and sensations of the simulated world to the user. These devices can also record and send the speech and movements of the participants to the simulation program, enabling users to sense and manipulate virtual objects much as they would real objects. This natural style of interaction gives the participants the feeling that they are immersed in the simulated world. For example, an car manufacturer can use virtual reality to help it simulate and design factories.

A related term is 'augmented reality', which refers to the combination of computer generated data (images, sounds, etc.) with stimuli from the real world. For example, an augmented reality system might project instructions onto the user's eye, on top of the real world images they are seeing, so they could look at both at the same time.

9.4.1 Interface Devices

To see in a virtual world, often the user wears a head-mounted display (HMD) with screens directed at each eye. The HMD also contains a position tracker to monitor the location of the user's head and the direction in which the user is looking. Using this information, a computer generates images of the virtual world – a slightly different view for each eye – to match the direction that the user is looking and displays these images on the HMD. Many companies sell or rent virtual-reality interface devices, including Virtual Realities (www.vrealities.com), Amusitronix (www.amusitronix.com), I-O Display Systems (www.i-glassesstore.com), and others. With current technology, virtual-world scenes must be kept relatively simple so that the computer can update the visual imagery quickly enough (at least ten times per second) to prevent the user's view from appearing jerky and from lagging behind the user's movements.

The Electronic Visualization Laboratory at the University of Illinois at Chicago introduced a room constructed of large screens on three walls and the floor on which the graphics are projected. The CAVE®, as this room is called, provides the illusion of immersion by projecting stereo images on the walls and floor of a room-sized cube. Several persons wearing lightweight stereo glasses can enter and walk freely inside the CAVE®. A head-tracking system continuously adjusts the stereo projection to the current position of the leading viewer. (See Figure 9.12)

Figure 9.12 *Military personnel design systems in an immersive CAVE® environment.*

SOURCE: Courtesy of Fakespace Systems, Inc.

Users hear sounds in the virtual world through speakers mounted above or behind the screens. Spatial audio is possible, allowing for position tracking. When a sound source in virtual space is not directly in front of or behind the user, the computer transmits sounds to arrive at one ear a little earlier or later than at the other and to be a little louder or softer and slightly different in pitch.

The haptic interface, which relays the sense of touch and other physical sensations in the virtual world, is the least developed and perhaps the most challenging to create. Currently, with the use of a glove and position tracker, the computer locates the user's hand and measures finger movements. The user can reach into the virtual world and handle objects; however, it is difficult to realize sensations of a person tapping a hard surface, picking up an object, or running a finger across a textured surface. Touch sensations also have to be synchronized with the sights and sounds of the user's experience.

9.4.2 Forms of Virtual Reality

Aside from immersive virtual reality, which we just discussed, virtual reality can also refer to applications that are not fully immersive, such as mouse-controlled navigation through a three-dimensional environment on a graphics monitor, stereo viewing from the monitor via stereo glasses, stereo projection systems, and others (see Figure 9.13).

Figure 9.13 The PowerWall

SOURCE: Courtesy of Fakespace Systems, Inc.

Some virtual reality applications allow views of real environments with superimposed virtual objects. Motion trackers monitor the movements of dancers or athletes for subsequent studies in immersive virtual reality. Telepresence systems (such as telemedicine and telerobotics) immerse a viewer in a real world that is captured by video cameras at a distant location and allow for the remote manipulation of real objects via robot arms and manipulators. Many believe that virtual reality will reshape the interface between people and information technology by offering new ways to communicate information, visualize processes, and express ideas creatively.

9.4.3 Virtual Reality Applications

You can find hundreds of applications of virtual reality, with more being developed as the cost of hardware and software declines and people's imaginations are opened to the potential of virtual reality. Having been inspired by the 2002 movie *Minority Report*, Pamela Barry of Raytheon is experimenting with a virtual reality system that uses 'gesture technology'.[26] and several commercial systems are now available from companies such as Solaris Labs. For example, by pointing an index finger towards a picture on a screen, the computer zooms in on the picture. Moving a hand in one direction causes the computer to scroll down through a video clip, and moving a hand in another direction clears the screen. Raytheon hopes 'gesture technology' will have applications in the military and space exploration. There are many other applications for virtual reality, including in the domains of medicine, education, and entertainment.

Summary

Knowledge management systems allow organizations to share knowledge and experience among their managers and employees. Knowledge is an awareness and understanding of a set of information and the ways that information can be made useful to support a specific task or reach a decision. A knowledge management system (KMS) is an organized collection of people, procedures, software, databases, and devices used to create, store, share, and use the organization's knowledge and experience. Explicit knowledge is objective and can be measured and documented in reports, papers, and rules. Tacit knowledge is hard to measure and document and is typically not objective or formalized.

Knowledge workers are people who create, use, and disseminate knowledge. They are usually professionals in science, engineering, business, and other areas. The chief knowledge officer (CKO) is a top-level executive who helps the organization use a KMS to create, store, and use knowledge to achieve organizational goals. Obtaining, storing, sharing, and using knowledge is the key to any KMS. The use of a KMS often leads to additional knowledge creation, storage, sharing, and usage. Many tools and techniques can be used to create, store, and use knowledge. These tools and techniques are available from IBM, Microsoft, and other companies and organizations.

Artificial intelligence systems form a broad and diverse set of systems that can replicate human decision making for certain types of well-defined problems. The term artificial intelligence is used to describe computers with the ability to mimic or duplicate the functions of the human brain. The objective of building AI systems is not to replace human decision making completely but to replicate it for certain types of well-defined problems.

Intelligent behaviour encompasses several characteristics, including the abilities to learn from experience and apply this knowledge to new experiences; handle complex situations and solve problems for which pieces of information might be missing; determine relevant information in a given situation, think in a logical and rational manner, and give a quick and correct response; and understand visual images and process symbols. Computers are better than people at transferring information, making a series of calculations rapidly and accurately, and making complex calculations, but human beings are better than computers at all other attributes of intelligence.

Artificial intelligence is a broad field that includes several key components, such as expert systems, robotics, vision systems, natural language processing, learning systems, and neural networks. An expert system consists of the hardware and software used to produce systems that behave as a human expert would in a specialized field or area (e.g., credit analysis). Robotics uses mechanical or computer devices to perform tasks that require a high degree of precision or are tedious or hazardous for humans (e.g., stacking cartons on a pallet). Vision systems include hardware and software that permit computers to capture, store, and manipulate images and pictures (e.g., face-recognition software). Natural language processing allows the computer to understand and react to statements and commands made in a 'natural' language, such as English. Learning systems use a combination of software and hardware to allow a computer to change how it functions or reacts to situations based on feedback it receives (e.g., a computerized chess game). A neural network is a computer system that can simulate the functioning of a human brain (e.g., disease diagnostics system). A genetic algorithm is an approach to solving large, complex problems in which a number of related operations or models change until the best one emerges.

Expert systems can enable a novice to perform at the level of an expert but must be developed and maintained very carefully. An expert system consists of a collection of integrated and related components, including a knowledge base, an inference engine, an explanation facility, a knowledge acquisition facility, and a user interface. The knowledge base is an extension of a database, discussed in Chapter 5, and an information and decision support system, discussed in Chapter 8. It contains all the relevant data, rules, and relationships used in the expert system. The rules are often composed of IF-THEN statements, which are used for drawing conclusions. Fuzzy logic allows expert systems to incorporate facts and relationships into expert system knowledge bases that might be imprecise or unknown.

The inference engine processes the rules, data, and relationships stored in the knowledge base to provide answers, predictions, and suggestions the way a human expert would. Two common methods for processing include backward and forward chaining. Backward chaining starts with a conclusion, then searches for facts to support it; forward chaining starts with a fact, then searches for a conclusion to support it.

The explanation facility of an expert system allows the user to understand what rules were used in arriving at a decision. The knowledge acquisition facility helps the user add or update knowledge in the knowledge base. The user interface makes it easier to develop and use the expert system.

The people involved in the development of an expert system include the domain expert, the knowledge engineer, and the knowledge users. The domain expert is the person or group who has the expertise or knowledge being captured for the system. The knowledge engineer is the developer whose job is to extract the expertise from the domain expert. The knowledge user is the person who benefits from the use of the developed system.

The steps involved in the development of an expert system include: determining requirements, identifying experts, constructing expert system components, implementing results, and maintaining and reviewing the system.

Expert systems can be implemented in several ways. A fast way to acquire an expert system is to purchase an expert system shell or existing package. The shell program is a collection of software packages and tools used to design, develop, implement, and maintain expert systems.

The benefits of using an expert system go beyond the typical reasons for using a computerized processing solution. Expert systems display 'intelligent' behaviour, manipulate symbolic information and draw conclusions, provide portable knowledge, and can deal with uncertainty. Expert systems can be used to solve problems in many fields or disciplines and can assist in all stages of the problem-solving process.

Virtual reality systems can reshape the interface between people and information technology by offering new ways to communicate information, visualize processes, and express ideas creatively. A virtual reality system enables one or more users to move and react in a computer-simulated environment. Virtual reality simulations require special interface devices that transmit the sights, sounds, and sensations of the simulated world to the user. These devices can also record and send the speech and movements of the participants to the simulation program. Thus, users can sense and manipulate virtual objects much as they would real objects. This natural style of interaction gives the participants the feeling that they are immersed in the simulated world.

Virtual reality can also refer to applications that are not fully immersive, such as mouse-controlled navigation through a three-dimensional environment on a graphics monitor, stereo viewing from the monitor via stereo glasses, stereo projection systems, and others. Some virtual reality applications allow views of real environments with superimposed virtual objects. Virtual reality applications are found in medicine, education and training, and entertainment.

Self-Assessment Test

1 What type of knowledge is objective and can be measured and documented in reports, papers, and rules?

   a. tacit   c. prescriptive

   b. descriptive   d. explicit

2 _____ are rules of thumb arising from experience or even guesses.

3 What is an important attribute for artificial intelligence?

   a. the ability to use sensors

   b. the ability to learn from experience

   c. the ability to be creative

   d. the ability to make complex calculations

4 _____ involves mechanical or computer devices that can paint cars, make precision welds, and perform other tasks that require a high degree of precision or are tedious or hazardous for human beings.

5 What is a disadvantage of an expert system?

a. the inability to solve complex problems

b. the inability to deal with uncertainty

c. limitations to relatively narrow problems

d. the inability to draw conclusions from complex relationships

6 A(n) _____ is a collection of software packages and tools used to develop expert systems that can be implemented on most popular PC platforms to reduce development time and costs.

7 What stores all relevant information, data, rules, cases, and relationships used by the expert system?

a. the knowledge base

b. the data interface

c. the database

d. the acquisition facility

8 What allows a user or decision maker to understand how the expert system arrived at a certain conclusion or result?

a. domain expert

b. inference engine

c. knowledge base

d. explanation facility

9 A(n) _____ enables one or more users to move and react in a computer-simulated environment.

10 What type of virtual reality is used to make human beings feel as though they are in a three-dimensional setting, such as a building, an archaeological excavation site, the human anatomy, a sculpture, or a crime scene reconstruction?

a. chaining

b. relative

c. immersive

d. visual

Review Questions

1 Define the term 'artificial intelligence'.

2 What is a vision system? Discuss two applications of such a system.

3 What is natural language processing? What are the three levels of voice recognition?

4 Describe three examples of the use of robotics. How can a microrobot be used?

5 What is an expert system shell?

6 Under what conditions is the development of an expert system likely to be worth the effort?

7 Identify the basic components of an expert system and describe the role of each.

8 What is virtual reality? Give several examples of its use.

9 Describe the roles of the domain expert, the knowledge engineer, and the knowledge user in expert systems.

10 Describe three applications of expert systems or artificial intelligence.

Discussion Questions

1 What are the requirements for a computer to exhibit human-level intelligence? How long will it be before we have the technology to design such computers? Do you think we should push to try to accelerate such a development? Why or why not?

2 Describe how you might encourage your employees to share their knowledge with one another. What technologies might you use and why?

3 Describe how natural language processing could be used in a university setting.

4 What is the purpose of a knowledge base? How is one developed?

5 Imagine that you are developing the rules for an expert system to select the strongest candidates for a medical school. What rules or heuristics would you include?

Web Exercises

1 Use the Internet to find information about the use of robotics. Describe three examples of how this technology is used.

2 This chapter discussed several examples of expert systems. Search the Internet for two examples of the use of expert systems. Which one has the greatest potential to increase profits? Explain your choice.

Case One

Global Building Supply Leader Gets the Recipe Right Every Time with Artificial Intelligence

Lafarge is a world leader in building-supply products. It is the third largest global supplier of gypsum (a mineral used in the construction industry), the second largest global supplier of aggregates and concrete, and the largest global supplier of cement and roofing. Lafarge has a presence in 76 countries and a workforce of 80 000. If any company knows the most efficient way of turning rocks into building materials, it is Lafarge. The company has built its dominant market position in part by implementing cutting-edge automated systems controlled by intelligent software systems.

Creating high-quality cement is similar to baking a cake. Ingredients are mixed in a specific and precise manner in the plant's raw feed mill, and then heated at exact temperatures in preheaters and a rotary kiln. After heating, baking gypsum and other ingredients are added to the mix to produce the finished dry concrete solution. If ingredients are mixed too little or too long, or if the temperature in the heaters or kiln is too high or too low, imperfections are introduced to the batch, which can cause engineering and construction problems later.

Lafarge engineers know the value of producing a consistent, high-quality product. To achieve that consistency, Lafarge depends on intelligent computer systems to monitor and control every step of cement production. The automated system produces the perfect recipe for production each time by reducing the variability in the process and optimizing production.

An intelligent system named LUCIE automates processes for controlling kilns, grate coolers, and mills at over 40 Lafarge cement plants worldwide. A neural network – computer software that functions like the human brain – and rules-based reasoning are used to judge the process conditions in the plant's raw feed mill, preheaters, rotary kiln, and cement mill. If conditions are not optimum, LUCIE applies short-term and long-term actions to make sure that the cement mixture is always produced in perfect fashion.

Lafarge engineers continue to add valuable functionality to LUCIE. Recently, LUCIE was upgraded to include more statistical and graphical ways to diagnose and optimize key parameters. A built-in fuel manager now improves stability and performance by managing the secondary fuels used in kilns.

9

Questions

1 What advantages does LUCIE have over a decision support system? Are there any disadvantages? List the similarities and differences between the two types of systems.

2 How does LUCIE benefit Lafarge?

3 Why is LUCIE suitable for the task it is given? Consider both the characteristics of the task and of the system.

4 In what others areas could Lafarge use artificial intelligence?

SOURCES: 'Lafarge, Gensym Success Story', www.gensym.com/?p= success_stories&id=15; Lafarge (website), www.lafarge.com.

Case Two

BMW Drives Virtual Prototypes

Today's cars consist of about 20 000 parts, and through virtual reality, BMW assembles the parts and examines how they interact in a variety of simulations in virtual space. The analysis takes place in BMW's virtual reality studio, nicknamed 'the Cave', which features a 175-square-foot PowerWall display and some serious computing power.

Among the many uses of the VR system, the most valuable is simulating test crashes. After an automobile is designed, and prior to building a prototype, technicians wearing 3D glasses can observe how a crash affects a vehicle down to the smallest details. With this information, they recommend changes to the design to improve driver and passenger safety.

Before a new model is assembled, it has been crashed in a hundred different ways in BMW's Cave. Smashing the virtual car into a virtual wall takes two to four days of computing time. The computer works around the clock, breaking down the moment of impact into stages of milliseconds. The resulting 3D film is viewed by technicians in super-slow motion. At any point in the crash, the vehicle can be dissected to examine the effect of the crash on particular automobile areas and components.

Prior to virtual reality, BMW tested actual prototypes of new models. Such prototypes can cost up to a million euros to manufacture. Each virtual 3D simulation costs under €400. After a vehicle's design has been improved based on VR crash tests, actual prototypes are manufactured and also crashed. BMW must prove in real life the theories derived from the virtual reality simulations. Computer simulations are only valid to the extent that they reflect reality. At one time, BMW might have test-crashed six prototypes. Today, they crash only a couple and have the additional benefit of results from the study of over 100 VR crashes. In this way, they can produce safer vehicles for less money.

Safety is only one of several uses of BMW's VR system. Designers use the system to experiment with alternative interior and exterior designs. Surfaces of metal, artificial material, and leather are realistically represented in virtual space to have real textures and properties such as reflection. Designers can examine a vehicle inside and out in a variety of lighting scenarios, changing colours, and materials as desired to find the perfect combinations.

Another department tests add-ons and pays particular attention to ease of operation. For example, how much energy does it take to close the top of a convertible? What happens when you slam the trunk lid? A technician can repeatedly close a virtual trunk lid, using varying degrees of force, carefully analyzing how the metal reacts each time. How difficult is it to open a door? Recently, BMW engineers tried out the door of a new virtual model and heard a subdued, high-pitched metallic ping when the door was shut. They thought that the sound seemed cheap and tinny. Realizing that a customer's opinion of a car is often shaped when they open and close the door, they set out to find the source of the ping. In a matter of days, they had redesigned the latch in the virtual model to eliminate the ping. Before VR, such an alteration would have taken months of work at a test bench.

BMW is also providing training to its technicians and mechanics using virtual reality. A new VR training facility for BMW technicians in Unterschleis-sheim, Germany, dramatically increases the number of technicians who can be trained at the same time. Instead of each trainee working one at a time, teams of technicians can now slip on high-tech goggles and gloves to work on a virtual image of a car or car part that's projected onto the inside of the goggles.

Questions

1 Explain three ways in which BMW uses VR in the design of new models of vehicles.

2 How does VR save BMW money over the long run?

3 How might BMW combine this system with artificial intelligence?

4 When might the results of a simulation in virtual space be considered valid and usable without running the same test in real space?

SOURCES: Staff, 'SGI Case Study: Virtual Reality: Crashes Without Dents', www.cgi.com; 'BMW Virtual Reality Room', www.carpages.co.uk/bmw/bmw_virtual_reality_room_04_09_04.asp; BMW Group (website), www.bmwgroup.com.

Case Three

Neural Network Predicts Movie Success

Consider the neural network developed by Ramesh Sharda and Dursun Delen to determine whether a new movie will be successful or not. The network accepts seven values as input, including the film's category (comedy, science fiction), whether the film is a sequel, the level of special effects in the film and how big a star the main actor is. The output is an estimate of the box-office gross revenues.

Neural networks consist of a number of layers, each layer made up of a number of nodes (see figure below). Each node performs a mathematical calculation on whatever input is given to it, then

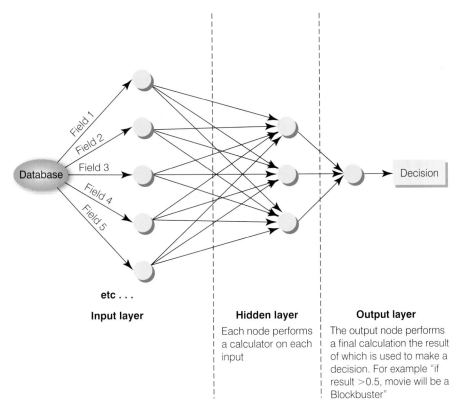

Input layer

etc . . .

Hidden layer

Each node performs a calculator on each input

Output layer

The output node performs a final calculation the result of which is used to make a decision. For example "if result >0.5, movie will be a Blockbuster" passes the results to a node in the next layer. This continues until the output layer, which outputs the result, typically some sort of classification. In this case the output is one of seven classes from 'flop' to 'blockbuster'. But how does each node know what calculation to perform to arrive at the correct output? This is determined during a process known as training.

To train the network, the computer scientists showed it data about over 800 films for which the gross revenue was known. The network then adjusted the calculations performed by each node so that the output for each film in the training set, was as close as possible to the the film's known class. So with a film that was known to be a flop, the nodes were adjusted so that the output was 'flop'. This was repeated with all the films. Then the entire process was repeated again and again, constantly refining the values at each node, until a relatively stable network structure emerged.

To use the network, the user presents it with the seven input variables for a new movie (where the revenue is not known) and it makes its prediction. Sharda and Delen report that their output is accurate 37 percent of the time, and reasonably accurate 75 percent of the time.

Questions

1 Who might be interested in this neural network?

2 A neural network attempts to mimic human thought. Given the above description, do you think it does? Explain your answer.

3 Can you think of any decisions that you make that could benefit from a neural network?

4 Would you trust a neural network with your life? For instance, would you get in a plane about to be flown by a neural network? Do a web search and you will find this is not a theoretical possibility.

SOURCES: Sharda, R. and Delen, D., 'Predicting Box Office Success of Motion Pictures with Neural Networks', *Expert Systems with Applications*, Vol. 30, 2006, pp. 243–254.

© Travel and Places/Alamy

Notes

1 Kimble, Chris, et al., 'Dualities, Distributed Communities of Practice and Knowledge Management', *Journal of Knowledge Management,* Vol. 9, 2005, p. 102.

2 Darroch, Jenny, 'Knowledge Management, Innovation, and Firm Performance', *Journal of Knowledge Management,* Vol. 9, 2005, p. 101.

3 Thurm, Scott, 'Companies Struggle to Pass on Knowledge that Workers Acquire', *Wall Street Journal,* January 23, 2006, p. B1.

4 Woods, Ginny Parker, 'Sony Sets Its Sights on Digital Books', *Wall Street Journal,* February 16, 2006, p. B3.

5 Skok, Walter, et al., 'Evaluating the Role and Effectiveness of an Intranet in Facilitating Knowledge Management: A Case Study at Surrey County Council', *Information and Management,* July 2005, p. 731.

6 Staff, 'Autonomy Links with Blinkx to Offer Search Facilities in China', *ComputerWire,* Issue 5228, July 19, 2005.

7 Staff, 'eArchitect: Share and Enjoy', *Building Design,* June 17, 2005, p. 24.

8 Zolkos, Rodd, 'Sharing the Intellectual Wealth', *BI Industry Focus,* March 1, 2005, p. 12.

9 Hsiu-Fen, Lin, et al., 'Impact of Organizational Learning and Knowledge Management Factors on E-Business Adoption', *Management Decision,* Vol. 43, 2005, p. 171.

10 Pelz-Sharpe, Alan, 'Document Management and Content Management Tucked Away in Several SAP Products', *Computer Weekly,* August 2, 2005, p. 26.

11 McKellar, Hugh, '100 Companies That Matter in Knowledge Management', *KM World,* March 2005, p. 18.

12 Sambamurthy, V., et al., 'Special Issue of Information Technologies and Knowledge Management', *MIS Quarterly,* June 2005, p. 193.

13 Kajmo, David, 'Knowledge Management in R5', www-128.ibm.com/developerworks/lotus/library/ ls-Knowledge_Management/index.html.

14 Staff, 'IBM Lotus Domino Document Manager', www.lotus.com/lotus/offering4.nsf/wdocs/ domdochome.

15 Staff, 'Morphy Richards Integrates Its Global Supply Chain with Lotus Domino', www-306.ibm.com/ software/success/cssdb.nsf/cs/DNSD-6EUNJ7? OpenDocument&Site=lotus.

16 Staff, 'Survey Rates Microsoft Number One in Knowledge Management Efforts', www.microsoft.com/presspass/features/1999/ 11-22award.mspx.

17 Quain, John, 'Thinking Machines, Take Two', *PC Magazine,* May 24, 2005, p. 23.

18 20Q (website),www.20q.net.

19 Staff, 'Send in the Robots', *Fortune,* January 24, 2005, p. 140.

20 iRobot (website), www.irobot.com.

21 Freeman, Diane, 'RobotDoc', *Rocky Mountain News,* June 27, 2005, p. 1B.

22 DARPA Grand Challenge', http://en.wikipedia.org/ wiki/Darpa_grand_challenge.

23 El-Rashidi, Yasime, 'Ride'em Robot', *Wall Street Journal,* October 3, 2005, p. A1.

24 Chamberlain, Ted, 'Ultra-Lifelike Robot Debuts in Japan', *National Geographic News,* June 10, 2005.

25 Anthes, Gary, '*Self Taught*', *Computerworld,* February 6, 2006, p. 28.

26 Karp, Jonathan, 'Minority Report Inspires Technology Aimed at Military', *Wall Street Journal,* April 12, 2005, p. B1.

10

Pervasive Computing

Principles

The term 'computing' no longer refers to a PC on a desktop. Mobile devices are letting employees access information from wherever they happen to be. In addition, these same technologies are allowing customers to interact with businesses in new ways.

Teams made up of people living in different geographical regions are able to work together efficiently and effectively, without ever having to meet. This work is facilitated by a range of technologies.

E-commerce and m-commerce can be used in many innovative ways to improve the operation of an organization.

Learning Objectives

▪ Identify the range of devices that now incorporate computing power.

▪ Describe the business benefits of mobile devices.

▪ Discuss and evaluate the technologies that can be used to support teamwork, when team members are separated by time and/or space.

▪ Describe how to select mobile systems to support business objectives.

> ## Why Learn About Pervasive Computing?
>
> The move of information systems from the office desktop into every aspect of our lives is well underway. Many businesses are exploiting this to their advantage, as are their customers. A mobile sales force can stay in touch with head office easily, and submit orders faster than before. Employees can take work with them on the plane or train, and remain in full contact, using text, audio, and video, or all three at once. Potential customers are starting to expect to be able to communicate with companies in a number of ways, and if a business fails to recognize this fact, it could lose customers to competitors who offer these communication channels. In addition, customers who have experienced poor service from a company are willing and able to communicate those experiences to other potential customers.
>
> This chapter examines some of the technologies that are enabling all of this to happen. New ones are being introduced almost every month. It is important that businesses understand the potential benefits they can bring.

10.1 Introduction

Information systems are no longer tied to a desk in an office. As we saw in the chapter on hardware, mobile devices are allowing computing power to be taken on the move. Increasingly, computers look less and less like the familiar picture shown in Figure 10.1, of a tower unit, keyboard, monitor, and mouse. This change is moving in two directions. New devices are being developed that people are happy to carry with them – tiny devices such as the iPod or a mobile phone. Such devices do not have the functionality of a PC, but they are more convenient and can be taken anywhere. The other diections is that, rather than a new device, computing power is being incorporated into existing devices and objects that are already well known to us, such as a jacket, a pair of glasses, or a car. This move away from the desktop is known as **pervasive computing**, or

pervasive computing A term meaning the move of the computer away from the desktop and towards something that is all around us, all the time.

Figure 10.1 The Conventional View of a Computer

SOURCE: Istock.

ubiquitous computing: ubiquitous because computers are all around us, even if we don't always realize it. Perhaps from where you are sitting you can see a laptop PC, a pocket PC, and a mobile phone. On any one of these devices you could read or post a blog entry, access the Web, and pay for goods and services. People are using these devices to do all sorts of things on the move – buy cinema tickets to avoid queuing for them, check in for a flight, pay for a taxi journey. In this chapter we will look at some of these technologies and examine their business potential. We will also meet a particular class of system use, called **computer supported cooperative work**, which is allowing teams to work together on projects, regardless of where they happen to be.

> **computer supported cooperative work** A term that refers to technologies which allow groups to work together to achieve goals.

10.2 Wi-Fi Hotspots

Central to being able to access information 'on the move', is wireless Internet access. Wireless communication protocols were described in Chapter 6. A wi-fi **hotspot** is an area where wireless access is available (see Figure 10.2). Many bars and cafés provide their customers with wi-fi, often charging by the half-hour, although sometimes access is free. T-Mobile have set up wi-fi hotspots in many airports, coffee houses such as Starbucks, and bookshops such as Borders.[1] Users can buy a pass for one hour, one day or one month costing around €7, €14, and €60 respectively, or can choose to take out a longer terms plan costing around €30 each month. This is useful for employees who are away from the office a lot. A wireless service is now expected by customers in major hotels. Many city centres have free wi-fi access. In the U.K., both Norwich and Bristol have free wi-fi, as do other cities throughout Europe, such as Oulu in Finland.[2] In Norwich, over 200 antennae are used to provide a hotspot blanket over the city.[3] As a user walks out of range of one antenna and into range of another, the system seamlessly hands over access between the two, in the same way that the mobile phone network does. Wi-fi access speeds are slightly slower than broadband, although this is perhaps made up for in convenience. The first entire nation to be given free wireless Internet access was the tiny Polynesian island of Niue with a population of just 2000.[4] The local authorities in the town of Knysna in South Africa have installed wi-fi to allow access to residents who have historically been cut off from Internet access because

> **hotspot** An area where wi-fi wireless Internet access is available.

Figure 10.2 Enjoying Wi-Fi Hotspots

10

the town is so remote. Computers have been installed in the local library to give access to those who can't afford wi-fi enabled devices.

The business benefits of wi-fi are clear – mobile access to information; employees away on business can easily send and receive e-mail, using any one of a number of devices, some of which are discussed next. They can access information on company websites or read about local conditions on news services. They could also access sensitive information on company extranets.

10.3 Mobile Devices

The list of devices that can make use of wi-fi hotspots is growing. It now includes desktop computers (useful if you happen to live within a hotspot), laptops, tablet PCs, mobile phones, mobile game consoles such as the Nintendo DS, pocket PCs and VoIP phones. As we will see, other mobile devices are stand alone and do not require Internet access to make them useful.

10.3.1 Pocket PC

Far from being nothing more than a glorified electronic diary, pocket PCs are a viable alternative to laptops. Shown in Figure 10.3, these tiny devices are cheaper and more robust than laptops and can be combined with a range of accessories to increase their functionality.

Possibly the most useful accessory is a keyboard that can be attached to the pocket PC so that data can be entered into it, as it could into a laptop or PC. Both fold up and roll up versions are available, as shown in Figure 10.4. These keyboards can be attached by a cable or wirelessly

Figure 10.3 Pocket PC

SOURCE: Istock.

10

using the Bluetooth protocol described in Chapter 6. Attaching a keyboard to a pocket PC provides an extremely portable word processor. Many workers in the western world would not be satisfied with such a tiny screen, however, such miniature devices are common in the far east. It is true that you are unlikely to want to type at a pocket PC for as long as you would a laptop, however many people do prefer the light weight of a pocket PC and keyboard to that of a laptop. If a pocket PC and keyboard is combined with wi-fi access, the pocket PC becomes a powerful tool to access all Internet services. Without the keyboard, a pocket PC can be cumbersome to use.

Another useful accessory is a cable to enable the pocket PC to be attached to a projector, as shown in Figure 10.5. Margi Presenter-to-Go[5] can be used to project Microsoft PowerPoint slides

Figure 10.4 Keyboard for a Pocket PC

SOURCE: Ilian studio/Alamy.

Figure 10.5 Using a Pocket PC as a Presentation Device

10

SOURCE: John Crum/Alamy.

from a pocket PC. The system even comes with a remote control so that the speaker can progress from one slide to the next without having to be beside the device – functionality that few PCs provide. This is an extremely convenient way for a business person to take a presentation with them. For example, a salesperson could present to clients all over the world, and only have to carry a pocket PC with accessories and, unless one was available at each location, a data projector.

One drawback to using a pocket PC to give presentations is that it is difficult to create or edit PowerPoint slides on them. Therefore they only become an alternative to carrying a laptop if the presentation is not going to change. If it is known that the presentation will not change, and it is known that there is the appropriate hardware at the presentation location, it becomes more convenient to simply carry the presentation files on a flash drive, or even simply upload them to the Web, where they can be downloaded for the presentation.

global positioning system (GPS)
A navigation system that enables a receiver to determine its precise location.

By connecting a **global positioning system (GPS)** receiver such as that shown in Figure 10.6, and installing map software such as TomTom,[6] a pocket PC can be used as a powerful navigational aid, either in a car or, if the GPS receiver is wireless (again using the Bluetooth protocol), on foot. A picture of what the map would look like to the user is shown in Figure 10.7. Fleet operators use GPS for vehicle tracking, safety and performance monitoring. GPS is also used by breakdown agencies such as the RAC and AA – the location of a broken down vehicle is fed into an information system which uses GPS information on the whereabouts of the fleet to make the decision on which patrol to send to the rescue.

A pocket PC can also be used to play audio and video files. Many people use one instead of a dedicated music device such as an MP3 player or an iPod. Some people download news clips each night from a provider such as the BBC, and watch them on the train on the way to work the next morning. The BBC has just launched a service called 'iPlayer', onto which almost all of their programmes can be downloaded and watched at any time within 30 days.[7]

Watching news programmes in this way could replace the traditional activity of reading the morning newspaper, plus it takes up less space on crowded public transport than a newspaper, is cleaner, and arguably easier to digest and more interesting.

When the functionality of a pocket PC is combined with the functionality of a mobile phone, that is, when you can make phone calls on it, it is known as a 'smartphone'. A smartphone is shown in Figure 10.8.

10.3.2 Wearable Technology

Miniaturizing pocket PC technology further allows it to become part of the clothes we wear, for example, a jacket or belt. Coupled with other things we are comfortable wearing, for instance, glasses with which to receive visual information, or earphones for audio information, computing power can become a something we routinely take with us and use everywhere. The term 'wearable technology' usually refers to computers that are worn on the body, although it could also be used to encompass non-computing technology such as mechanical watches and glasses. The term **wearable computing** is used to distinguish between the two (Figure 10.9).

wearable computing A term that refers to computers and computing technology that are worn on the body.

When a pocket PC is clipped to a user's belt (using the clip that is usually shipped with it), it is, in one sense, being 'worn'. However, wearable computing refers to something more than this. The term really means the use of largely invisible computing technology, to seamlessly augment a human's task. So far, there are few everyday applications for wearable computing, and many of the commercial examples available have more novelty value than business value. However, one application, which is often mentioned, is navigation, where the clothes you wear somehow tell you where to go. For example, a GPS receiver could be built into a special jacket, which could apply pressure on one side of the body to guide the wearer in that direction. The interface for telling the jacket where you want to go could be a pocket PC with a Bluetooth link between it and the jacket.

Figure 10.6 Global Positioning System

SOURCE: John James/Alamy.

A research group at The Massachusetts Institute of Technology (MIT) has developed a platform which can be used to experiment with potential applications. MIThril has a number of ways of interacting with the body.

Suggested uses for MIThril include navigation and accessing the Internet on the move. However, neither of these take the unique nature of wearable computing into account and using it like this, gives little advantage over a pocket PC. The Kitty Project shown in Figure 10.9 allows its wearer to type without a keyboard and see what they are doing on an eye-tap display.

Some other potential applications for wearable computing are recording what the wearer sees and hears and how they move, and transmitting personal information between people, rather like

Figure 10.7 A Global
Positioning System Map

SOURCE: Iain Masterton/Alamy.

Figure 10.8
A Smartphone
*The power of a pocket PC
coupled with the
communication capability of
a mobile phone.*

SOURCE: Courtesy of HTC.

an electronic business card. Indeed another device from MIT, the UberBadge, does exactly that. It can be worn as a name badge and used to transmit personal information. For instance, the system could be used at a business conference to collect information about all the people a delegate has spoken to throughout the day. The same device can collect information useful to conference organizers about where people spent the most time throughout the day. A business

Figure 10.9 Wearable Technology from The Kitty Project (Courtesy of KittyTech.com)

could adapt this to be able to locate its employees within its building, so that phone calls could be routed to the nearest phone. Perhaps wearable technology could be used to help judge a fencing or martial arts competition, or for recording dance moves, something that has been difficult in the past. There could also be applications for teaching – gloves that help teach someone how to play the piano. Another technology to come out of MIT, called Kameraflage, allows digital cameras to photograph colours in fabrics that the human eye cannot see. One possible use of this technology is to replace staff cards with invisible markers – a security guard could easily identify people who do not have authority to be in a certain area, by looking at his or her video monitor, which would pick up the marks on their clothes. Another wearable application is shown in Figure 10.10.

It should be noted that many people would resist wearable technology, for a variety of reasons, some of which are mentioned in the Ethical and Societal issues box, page 352.

Figure 10.10 The
Mermaid ID *When onboard
a boat, passengers put the
Mermaid ID in their pocket. If
anyone falls overboard, the
Captain is alerted.*

SOURCE: http://firstlightsolutions.co.uk

Ethical and Societal Issues

Sousveillance

One of the main players in the world of wearable technology is Steve Mann, another product of the Massachusetts Institute of Technology, now working at the University of Toronto in Canada. Often inventing the technology he wears, Mann has devices that let him look both forward and backward at the same time (something he says takes the human brain about four days to get used to), will remove material from his vision that he deems offensive (such as adverts for cigarettes), and will record everything he sees and hears. Steve Mann essentially has all the information available on the Internet readily accessible wherever he goes, which he can look up while you are speaking to him. This has led some who have met him to call him a genius because he appears to know everything about any topic, or 'brain-damaged', presumably because he has left that

person waiting for a response while he was reading a web page.

Steve Mann is a big believer in something he calls 'sousveillance', the recording of an activity from the perspective of a participant in the activity. In other words, he thinks we should all record our own experiences, thereby taking the power of surveillance away from the authorities and putting it in the hands of individuals. For example, the U.K. has more CCTV cameras in its city centres per head than any other city in Europe. These cameras record activities and are used, among other things, to police crime. Steve Mann believes that everyone has the right to do the same – record everything they see and hear. However, Steve Mann has demonstrated that businesses do not like being recorded. Whenever you go into a shop, there is often a sign saying something like: 'video cameras are being used for your protection'. However when Mann went into these shops wearing his sousveillance equipment, he was often told to stop recording or asked to leave. It seems some businesses like to have the right to video people, but don't like the people videoing them. Steve Mann is taking a stand against this attitude.

Questions

1 Use Google or similar to find some pictures of Steve Mann – would you wear any of this technology? Other than sousveillance, what are some other applications for this technology?

2 What are some of the advantages in recording all of your experiences? Critically evaluate the disadvantages.

3 What is your opinion of the attitude of the shops who like to video you, but don't like you to video them? Why do you think this is? How would you combat this attitude?

4 Does having more CCTV cameras in city centres make the U.K. safer? Explain your answer.

Information Systems @ Work

Logging's Legacy

At 16.8 million acres, Tongass National Forest is the largest national forest in the U.S. Located in the south east corner of Alaska, the area is made up of more than a thousand islands and is home to thousands of people who depend on the forest for their livelihood. Having been given incentives by the government in the middle of the twentieth century, big logging businesses moved in. Their activities in the area have been controversial, with half a million acres having already been logged and plans to increase this to 650 000 acres. In such a vast area, this might seem like a small amount, but less than 4 percent of the land is woodland and, with some of the trees being over a hundred years old, the forest will not grow back within our lifetimes. Naturalists such as Richard Carstensen and Bob Christensen are now examining how plant and animal communities are being changed by the logging. And they are using mobile technology to help.

In their hats, in transparent pouches, are sewn GPS receivers. (The pouches are transparent because the receiver needs a line of sight to at least four satellites.) These are not used to navigate. Instead, their current location is sent wirelessly by Bluetooth to pocket PCs worn in waterproof cases on their belts. The pocket PCs are used to output data on what the area is expected to be like (plant communities, wildlife habitat quality, geology, and land topography), which is compared by the naturalists with what they are seeing – what the area is actually like. Wherever they go they can call up this information without having to find their location manually on a map – the use of GPS is simply a time saver. They both carry digital cameras to photograph what they see and to record voice input describing what they see, for analysis later. Their mission is to evaluate forest resources, especially the sites that are due to be logged.

Questions

1 Using the Web, investigate why the GPS receiver needs a line of sight to four satellites.

2 Are the naturalists using wearable technology? Explain your answer.

3 What other technology could the naturalists use, and how would it be useful to them?

4 What might cause the naturalists' equipment to fail? Outline a possible backup procedure for the naturalists, should that happen.

SOURCE: 'The Truth about Tongass', *National Geographic*, July 2007.

10

10.3.3 E-Money

E-money refers to the transfer of funds happening electronically rather than by handing over physical coins and notes. It can be implemented in a number of ways. The most common is paying for goods and services over the Internet, however it does take other forms. Mobile phones are now also being used to pay for goods and services.

e-money The transfer of funds electronically rather than by handing over physical coins and notes.

LUUP[8] is a payment system (the developers call it a 'digital wallet') that works using the text feature on mobile phones to transfer funds from buyer to seller (see Figure 10.11). The buyer sends LUUP a text with the format 'PAY USERNAME AMOUNT'. LUUP then transfers the specified amount from the buyer's account to the seller's account. For example a buyer might text 'PAY 10943933 EUR10'. This would cause a transfer of €10 to be transferred to account 10943933. Both buyer and seller then receive a text message when payment has been made.

LUUP and systems like it have the potential to negate the need for exact change when paying for things like taxi journeys. In Norway, where the system was developed, users can pay for food, public transport, and shopping bills.

Figure 10.11 LUUP in Action

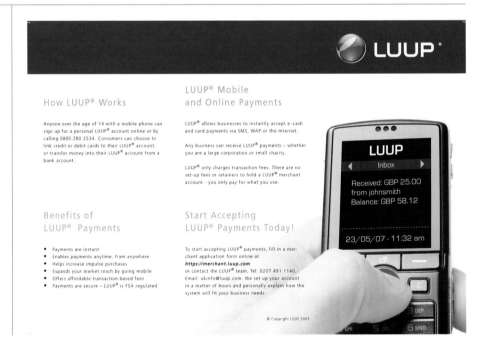

A similar system is being used in developing countries to provide financial services to the least well off. While the physical infrastructure in Kenya (road and rail) is in a poor state, in contrast the country has excellent mobile phone coverage, provided by two companies, Celtel and Safricom. Safricom, part owned by Vodafone, provides a service called M-Pesa. M-Pesa lets customers borrow, withdraw, and pay money using text messaging. In a culture where many people are unable to open bank accounts and must therefore carry cash, it has the potential to revolutionize lives.[9] The system gives security, and allows easily and safe transfer of cash from relatives in the first world. According to the World Bank, this happens a lot – over 200 million migrants worldwide sent €120 billion to their families in 2005, a figure which is more than double the volume of official aid.[10]

Another system to implement a form of e-money, now used in locations throughout the world, relies on RFID technology (described in Chapter 3). An example is Hong Kong's Octopus card, originally intended to be used to pay for public transport, but now used throughout Hong Kong in a range of shops. When used on the city's train service, a passenger 'swipes' their card, shown in Figure 10.12, when they enter the train station and they 'swipe' it again when they leave. The correct fare is then debited from their prepaid account. 'Swiping' the card merely involves waving it near a reader – direct contact is not required. In fact the card doesn't even have to be removed from the passenger's wallet! Octopus gadgets are now available such as the Octopus watch or Octopus ornaments. Whether using the card or a gadget, a chip in the device

Figure 10.12 The Octopus Card

Figure 10.13 Octopus Cards in Action

SOURCE: Ulana Switucha/Alamy.

stores the amount that has been paid into the account. Similar systems have now been implemented throughout Europe and elsewhere. Systems such as these which implement the concept of e-money, make paying for goods fast and convenient.

E-money has two implications for businesses. Firstly there is the convenience of employees using it themselves when on business trips. Perhaps more importantly, depending on the type of business, it may be that customers will come to expect to be able to pay for goods and services using e-money in the future. When this happens, the retailer needs to be ready for it.

10.3.4 Tangible Media

A new and interesting way to represent information stored on a computer is through the use of physical objects. Since this is a new area, very few applications are currently commercially available. However, imagine that you have a bowl of plastic pebbles in your living room and each represents one of your favourite films. To view the film, you pick up one of the pebbles and wave it at your television screen. A moment later the film starts. This is more an artistic application than something most people would want, however a 'killer application' is perhaps just around the corner which will make this technology take off. Perhaps you could think of one yourself and capitalize on your idea.

Most people are comfortable with the concept of icons. An icon on your computer screen represents a file. The icon isn't the same thing as the file, it's more like a pointer to it. Double clicking on the icon, such as that shown in Figure 10.14, opens up the file, in this case an Excel spreadsheet.

Figure 10.14 An Icon Representing an Excel Spreadsheet

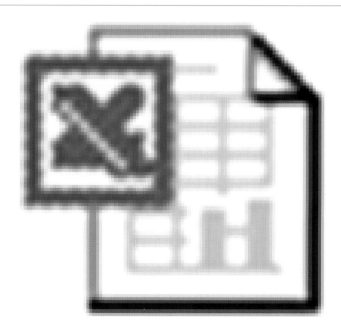

The plastic pebble representing the film is the same idea, only the pebble is a physical icon, or **phicon** (pronounced fi-con). Research is in its infancy, but we can imagine a situation in the future where a business card opens a personal home page automatically whenever it is held near a computer. Or a brouchure, marketing literature for instance, that also contains additional electronic information within it. In the future your lecture handouts could also contain electronic resources built into them! This research area is known as tangible media.

phicon Phicon stands for 'physical icon', and is a physical representation of digital data, in the same way that an icon on a computer screen represents a file.

Figure 10.15 shows a breakfast table with salt and pepper shaker phions. Where the phions are placed on the table, will determine what the computer screen displays.

Figure 10.15 Using Phicons to Read the Morning News

Some companies are experimenting with sending touch over long distances. Such devices currently only have novelty value, but perhaps someone will soon come up with a useful business application. The Kiss Communicator (Figure 10.16) and the Hug shirt (Figure 10.17) are two such devices. The Kiss Communicator allows you to blow a kiss to someone wherever they are. The Hug Shirt allows you to send them a hug. To do this requires two hug shirts. You put on one of them and hug yourself. Sensors in the shirt detect what you have done and send the information needed to recreate this feeling via Bluetooth, to your mobile phone. Your phone then transmits the information as a text message to the receiver of the hug. They get a text asking if they want to accept the hug. If they do, the signal gets passed to their hug shirt, again via Bluetooth, which squeezes them in the same way that you hugged your own shirt. These devices both represent new ways of connecting people.

10

Figure 10.16 The Kiss Communicator

SOURCE: Kiss Communicator Concept – IDEO.

10.3.5 Personal Robotics

Robotics has been mentioned before in this text, mostly in the context of assembly plants and manufacturing. In this section, we will look at some of the robots that are used, and could be used, in our everyday lives.

The Roomba (Figure 10.18) is a robotic vacuum cleaner costing around €250. It can be released into a home where it spends its time continuously cleaning. When it needs a battery recharge, it can go to a base station and recharge itself. It cannot yet, however, empty itself, although it can navigate around furniture and other obstacles. A potential business application of this technology is in cleaning offices – an army of Roombas could be let loose overnight. However, at present, the technology is not really good enough for this. Those interesting is studying robotics should consider that the Roomba gives a cheap platform to experiment with – the makers of the Roomba, who are products of MIT's Artificial Intelligence Lab, have made it so that you can install your own software on it, and modify its behaviour.

Quite a few attempts have been made to develop robots that have personality, to give them a more natural interface to interact with people. Minerva was a talking robot designed to accommodate people in public spaces. She was active in 1998 offering people at the Smithsonian's National Museum of American History tours and leading them from exhibit to exhibit. Minerva had moods – she could be happy and sing or get frustrated and blare her horn.

personal robotics A term which refers to robotic companions that people socialize with.

Minerva was a personal robot. One of the world's leading centres in **personal robotics** is the Robotic Life Group (also known as the Personal Robotics Group) at MIT, led by Cynthia Breazeal. This team builds robots to study our socialization with them. The term personal robotics refers to robots that become part of our everday lives. While currently of little relevance to most businesses, we shall see in the next section that this might change, when we examine among other things, one of the most loved personal robots, Sony's Aibo.

Figure 10.17 The Hug
Shirt

SOURCE: Courtesy of CuteCircuit.

Figure 10.18 The
Roomba Vacuum Cleaner

SOURCE: © 2007 iRobot Corporation.

10.3.6 Virtual Pets

Aibo is a robotic puppy. Intended as a replacement for a real puppy, Aibo will explore its environment, get tried, hungry, grumpy, and sleepy. It sometimes craves attention and can get over excited. Sony sadly no longer manufacture Aibo, but many cheaper versions inspired by it remain on the market. Aibo is an example of a virtual pet.

virtual pet An artificial companion. Could be screen based, i.e., the pet is animated on a computer monitor, or a robot.

Virtual pets started to gain worldwide popularity in the late 1990s when Japanese toy manufacturer Bandai released the Tamagotchi (Figure 10.19). About the size of a key ring, a typical Tamagotchi had a small black and white screen, three buttons, a speaker, a motion sensor and a microphone. Users could feed, clean, and play with their Tamagotchi, call it via the microphone and chase away predators by shaking the unit. The pet would evolve over time and would eventually either die or fly away. Many users became emotionally attached to their pet, which was the ultimate goal of the software designers.

Virtual pets are perhaps unique among information systems in that their goal is to get users to feel a sense of responsibility towards the system and become attached in some way to it. Virtual

Figure 10.19 The **Tamagotchi** *gained worldwide popularity and notoriety in the 1990s.*

SOURCE: Mark Boulton/Alamy.

pets are very popular at the moment. One of the most popular games for the Nintendo DS mobile games console is Nintendogs (Figure 10.20), which is essentially a more sophisticated version of the Tamagotchi.

So why might businesses be interested in virtual pets? Some business tools (or at least software that could be used by businesses) have 'virtual-pet-like' personality built into them. 'Clippy' or 'Clipit', the Microsoft help agent, was one of the first. Shown in Figure 10.21, Clippy would cheerfully offer to help users with their tasks. It was almost universally hated, but it is clear that Microsoft have not yet given up on software with personality – 'Ms Dewey' is the new human interface to their Windows Live Search (Figure 10.22). Other attempts have been made to infuse

Figure 10.20 **Nintendogs** *A virtual pet for the Nintendo DS*

Figure 10.21 The
Microsoft Help Agent
'Clippy'

personality into everyday software. PostPet by Sony was an e-mail application where an on-screen puppy would fetch your mail, just as some real dogs do for their owners, but only if you were nice to it. The Nabaztag Rabbit is a personal companion that sits beside you and reads you the news and tells you when you have a new e-mail.

It is clear that some software developers are interested in giving their products personality. It is also clear that today's teenagers are perfectly comfortable interacting with devices that have personality. It may be that, in the future when they become employees, they will expect their business software to come with personality built in.

10.4 Computer Supported Cooperative Work

Computer supported cooperative work (CSCW) refers to technologies that allow groups to work together to achieve goals. Individuals in the groups can be co-located (in the same place) or geographically separated. The work can happen synchronously (individuals at work at the same time) or asynchronously (they work at different times). Different CSCW technologies exist to support these different modes of work. In global companies, CSCW technology is powerful tool enabling a company to make the best of its human resources no matter where they are located. In this section, we will look at some CSCW tools.

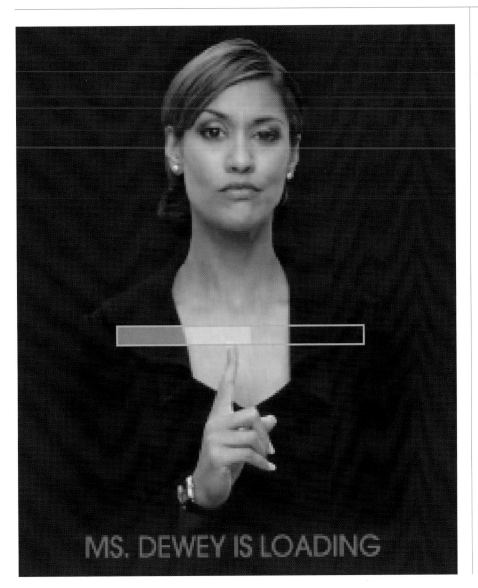

Figure 10.22 Windows Live Search 'Ms Dewey'
Ms Dewey will guide you through searches at 'her' website, www.msdewey.com.

MS. DEWEY IS LOADING

10.4.1 Videoconferencing

For a long time in science fiction, the public has seen the future of the telephone call where both audio and video is transmitted. The technology now exists to achieve this easily and cheaply, and yet it hasn't taken off to any great extent, at least in the home environment. A **videoconference** is a simultaneous communication between two or more parties where they both see and hear each other. A videoconference can be set up using instant messenging software, as shown in Figure 10.23. For businesses, videoconferences are useful to hold global meetings. Visual cues are available to help everyone understand what other people are really feeling – a yawn, a nod of the head, a smile, etc. None of these can be transmitted down a telephone line. However, running a videoconference does take discipline as it is easy for more than one person to talk at once and even a slight delay in transmission time can cause chaos. TKO Video Communications has video conferencing facilities all over the world which can be rented out by businesses who do not want to

videoconference A videoconference is a simultaneous communication between two or more parties where they both see and hear each other.

set up their own. A business in South Africa can hold a meeting with partners in Egypt and the United Arab Emirates by travelling to TKO offices in Cape Town, while their partners go to Cairo and Dubai. This is a shorter and cheaper journey than for them all having to physically meet.

Figure 10.23 A
Videoconference Using
Instant Messenging

SOURCE: Andy Hockridge/Alamy.

10.4.2 Messaging

Messaging technology includes e-mail, instant messaging, and web chat rooms. E-mail has been discussed before. It is useful for asynchronous text-based communication. Instant messaging is used for synchronous communication – two (or more) people are communicating at the same time, usually typing short sentences to build up a conversation. Instant messaging is extremely useful and can be used by employees to work on a problem together. Instant messaging versus a telephone call is largely a matter of personal preference. One advantage messaging has is that the text can be easily saved and re-read at a later date. A chat room is a facility that enables two or more people to engage in interactive 'conversations' over the Web. When you participate in a chat room, dozens of people might be participating from around the world. Multi-person chats are usually organized around specific topics, and participants often adopt nicknames to maintain anonymity.

Instant messaging technology is now being used by a diverse range of companies including Zurich Insurance and Ikea, as an alternative to making customers telephone a call centre. Customers often prefer clicking on the chat icon on a company website and waiting for the 'operator' to respond, than having to phone and wait in a queue. When phoning a call centre you often have to hold the phone to your ear, so at least one hand is tied up, and listen to (usually awful) music until someone answers. With messaging technology you can continue working at your computer until someone answers. You know when this happens as the task bar on your computer screen will start flashing.

10.4.3 Interactive Whiteboards

Essentially, an **interactive whiteboard** is a combination of a whiteboard and a PC. It can be used in a number of ways. Users can write on the whiteboard and then save what has been written as an image on their computer. This negates the need to take notes about what has been written after a meeting has finished. What is saved on the PC needn't be a static image – it could be an animation of everything that was written, including things that were rubbed out. Alternatively, two whiteboards at different locations could be used by people at these different locations to see what each other is writing. Combined with videoconferencing, this can be a powerful way of running meetings when not everyone is present. An interactive whiteboard is shown in Figure 10.24.

interactive whiteboard This term can be used to mean slightly different technologies, but essentially it is a combination of a whiteboard and a desktop computer.

Figure 10.24
Interactive Whiteboard

SOURCE: Patrick Eden/Alamy.

10.4.4 Wikis

A **wiki** is a web page that can be edited by anyone with the proper authority. The most famous example is Wikipedia, which can be edited by any web user – very few restrictions are put in place. To see the usefulness of wikis, have a look at Wikipedia. Its content is breathtaking, considering that all of it was created by volunteers. You might try editing an article you know something about, however, consider this: there is no way to know if the information has been edited by an expert or by a joker, so think twice before you rely on anything you read there.

wiki A web page that can be edited by anyone with the proper authority.

Wikis are clearly a good way of sharing knowledge and are being used by a large number of research groups and businesses, to allow employees to share their thoughts and ideas, and post up good practice. Read the first case at the end of the chapter (page 375) for more information.

10.4.5 MMOGs

Look for information about MMOGs using a search engine and you may be hit with a confusing array of acronyms including MMORTS, MMOFPS and MMOGs. MMORPG. MMOG stands for

virtual world A computer-based environment where users' avatars can interact.

'massively multiplayer online game'. They have a long history, but today they exist as three-dimensional **virtual worlds**. A screen shot from one is shown in Figure 10.25. Users are represented in the world by an avatar, which interacts with other avatars typically by text, but voice is starting to be used. From a business point of view, we are not primarily interested in virtual worlds as games, but as a platform for holding meetings and for their marketing potential. Probably the best virtual world for these activities is Second Life.

Figure 10.25 Second Life

Owned by San Francisco–based Linden Lab, Second Life is a huge virtual world where residents meet socially and commercially. It has its own currency, the Linden dollar, which has a floating exchange rate with the U.S. dollar. This means you can make (and spend) real money in Second Life. Several people are making a good living there (mostly by land speculation and by creating and selling animations) and big businesses are starting to get involved. IBM and Dell have already held global meetings in Second Life, and you can test drive Toyota cars there.[11] (Note, however, that IBM and Dell were researching the usefulness of using this platform to hold meetings – they were not actually holding a board meeting there; that has yet to happen.) Some commentators are saying that 3D interfaces such as this will become the main way we access information over the Internet in the future. As an example of the direction Linden Lab may be planning for their technology, Jeff Bezos, the founder of Amazon, is one of the financial backers of Second Life, and Philip Rosedale, CEO of Linden Lab, has pointed out that whenever someone visits Amazon, there are thousands of other shoppers on the site with them. He has expressed the opinion that it would be a good thing if all those shoppers could both see and interact with each other.

10.4.6 Blogs and Podcasts

blog An online diary, a combination of the words 'web' and 'log'.

While not strictly (optional if it causes text to spill to next page) a CSCW technology, blogs still allow for the sharing of information from one to many people. A **blog**, short for 'weblog', is a website that people create and use to write about their observations, experiences, and feelings on a wide range of topics.

10

Technically it is identical to any other web page, although the content of a blog is updated much more frequently, typically every day. The community of blogs and bloggers is often called the 'blogosphere'. A 'blogger' is a person who creates a blog, while 'blogging' refers to the process of placing entries or 'posts' on a blog site. A blog is like a diary. When people post information to a blog, it is placed at the top of the blog. Blogs can contain links to other material, and people can usually comment on posts. Blogs are easy to post to, but they can cause problems when people tell or share too much.[12] People have been fired for blogging about work, and the daughter of a politician embarrassed her father when she made personal confessions on her blog.

Blog sites, such as www.blogger.com, include information and tools to help people create and use weblogs. The way blogs are structured, with the most recent post appearing at the top, can make it extremely difficult to read and understand what it is all about – imagine you visit a blog, which you know (from an Internet search) talks about a product you are having problems with. Let's say the first post you come to starts: 'Today's fresh hell – ABC company rep John replied and said it would work. I tried it and ended up breaking the stupid thing. Just my luck.' The blogger is presumably making reference to something written about yesterday or before. It may take you a while to track down what they did to break the product, something you probably want to know about to avoid doing it yourself. Go to blogger.com, select a blog at random (there is a feature to do this) and you will see the problem – it can be difficult to start reading a blog. If you keep a blog, you might want to think about this and how you can keep new and irregular readers interested.

A **podcast** is an audio broadcast over the Internet. The term 'podcast' comes from the word iPod, Apple's portable music player, and the word 'broadcast'. A podcast is essentially an audio blog, like a personal radio station on the Internet, and extends blogging by adding audio messages. Using a computer and microphone, you can record audio messages and place them on the Internet. You can then listen to the podcasts on your computer or download the audio material to a music player, such as Apple's iPod. You can also use podcasting to listen to TV programmes, your favourite radio personalities, music, and messages from your friends and family at any time and place. Finding good podcasts, however, can be challenging. Apple's new version of iTunes allows you to download free software to search for podcasts by keyword.

podcast An audio broadcast over the Internet.

People and corporations can use podcasts to listen to audio material, increase revenues, or advertise products and services.[13] Colleges and universities often use blogs and podcasts to deliver course material to students.

Many blogs and podcasts offer automatic updates to a computer using a technology called Really Simple Syndication (RSS). RSS is a collection of web formats to help provide web content or summaries of web content. With RSS, you can get a blog update without actually visiting the blog website. RSS can also be used to get other updates on the Internet from news websites and podcasts.

10.5 More Applications of Electronic and Mobile Commerce

Lastly in this chapter we will examine how e-commerce and m-commerce are being used in innovative and exciting ways. This section examines a few of the many B2B, B2C, C2C, and m-commerce applications in the retail and wholesale, manufacturing, marketing, investment and finance, and auction arenas.

10.5.1 Retail and Wholesale

E-commerce is being used extensively in retailing and wholesaling. **Electronic retailing**, sometimes called e-tailing, is the direct sale of products or services by businesses to consumers through electronic shops, which are typically

electronic retailing (e-tailing) The direct sale from business to consumer through electronic storefronts, typically designed around an electronic catalogue and shopping cart model.

designed around the familiar electronic catalogue and shopping cart model. Tens of thousands of electronic retail websites sell a wide range. In addition, cyber shopping centres, or 'cyber-malls', are another means to support retail shopping. A cybermall is a single website that offers many products and services at one Internet location. An Internet cybermall pulls multiple buyers and sellers into one virtual place, easily reachable through a web browser. For example, Cyber-mall New Zealand (www.cybermall.co.nz) is a virtual shopping mall that offers retail shopping, travel, and infotainment products and services.

A key sector of wholesale e-commerce is spending on manufacturing, repair, and opera-tions (MRO) of goods and services – from simple office supplies to mission-critical equipment, such as the motors, pumps, compressors, and instruments that keep manufacturing facilities running smoothly. MRO purchases often approach 40 percent of a manufacturing company's total revenues, but the purchasing system can be haphazard, without automated controls. In addition to these external purchase costs, companies face significant internal costs resulting from outdated and cumbersome MRO management processes. For example, studies show that a high percentage of manufacturing downtime is often caused by not having the right part at the right time in the right place. The result is lost productivity and capacity. E-commerce software for plant operations provides powerful comparative searching capabilities to enable managers to identify functionally equivalent items, helping them spot opportunities to com-bine purchases for cost savings. Comparing various suppliers, coupled with consolidating more spending with fewer suppliers, leads to decreased costs. In addition, automated work-flows are typically based on industry best practices, which can streamline processes.

10.5.2 Manufacturing

One approach taken by many manufacturers to raise profitability and improve customer service is to move their supply chain operations onto the Internet. Here they can form an **electronic exchange** to join with competitors and suppliers alike, using computers and websites to buy and sell goods, trade market information, and run back-office operations, such as inventory control, as shown in Figure 10.26. With such an exchange, the business centre is not a physical building but a network-based location where business interactions occur. This approach has greatly speeded up the movement of raw materials and finished products among all members of the business community, thus reducing the amount of inventory that must be main-tained. It has also led to a much more competitive marketplace and lower prices. Private exchanges are owned and operated by a single company. The owner uses the exchange to trade exclusively with established business partners. Public exchanges are owned and operated by industry groups. They provide services and a common technology platform to their members and are open, usually for a fee, to any company that wants to use them.

electronic exchange An electronic forum where manufacturers, suppliers, and competitors buy and sell goods, trade market information, and run back-office operations.

Several strategic and competitive issues are associated with the use of exchanges. Many companies distrust their corporate rivals and fear they might lose trade secrets through partici-pation in such exchanges. Suppliers worry that the online marketplaces and their auctions will drive down the prices of goods and favour buyers. Suppliers also can spend a great deal of money in the setup to participate in multiple exchanges. For example, more than a dozen new exchanges have appeared in the oil industry, and the printing industry has up to more than 20 online marketplaces. Until a clear winner emerges in particular industries, suppliers are more or less forced to sign on to several or all of them. Yet another issue is potential government scrutiny of exchange participants – when competitors get together to share information, it raises ques-tions of collusion or antitrust behaviour.

Many companies that already use the Internet for their private exchanges have no desire to share their expertise with competitors. At the U.S. shopping giant Wal-Mart, the world's number-one retail chain, executives turned down several invitations to join exchanges in the retail and

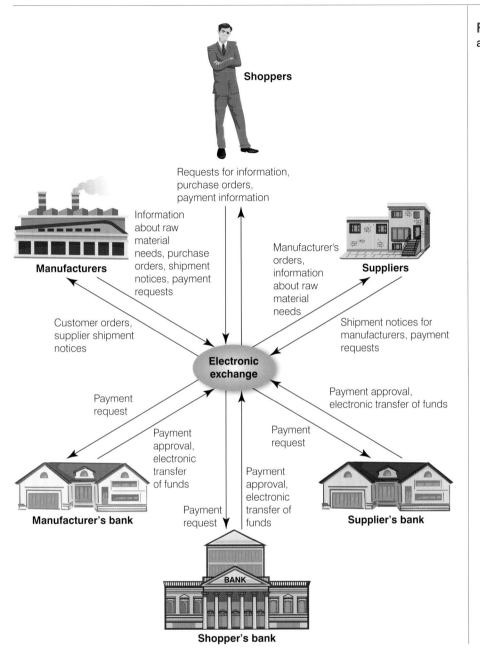

Figure 10.26 Model of an Electronic Exchange

Shoppers

Requests for information, purchase orders, payment information

Information about raw material needs, purchase orders, shipment notices, payment requests

Manufacturers

Manufacturer's orders, information about raw material needs

Suppliers

Customer orders, supplier shipment notices

Shipment notices for manufacturers, payment requests

Electronic exchange

Payment request

Payment approval, electronic transfer of funds

Payment approval, electronic transfer of funds

Payment request

Manufacturer's bank

Payment approval, electronic transfer of funds

Payment request

Supplier's bank

BANK

Shopper's bank

10

consumer goods industries. Wal-Mart is pleased with its in-house exchange, Retail Link, which connects the company to 7000 worldwide suppliers that sell everything from toothpaste to furniture.

10.5.3 Marketing

The nature of the web allows firms to gather much more information about customer behaviour and preferences than they could using other marketing approaches. Marketing organizations can measure many online activities as customers and potential customers gather information and make their purchase decisions. Analysis of this data is complicated because of the web's interactivity and because each visitor voluntarily provides or refuses to provide personal data such as name, address, e-mail address, telephone number, and demographic

market segmentation The identification of specific markets to target them with advertising messages.

technology-enabled relationship management Occurs when a firm obtains detailed information about a customer's behaviour, preferences, needs, and buying patterns and uses that information to set prices, negotiate terms, tailor promotions, add product features, and otherwise customize its entire relationship with that customer.

data. Internet advertisers use the data they gather to identify specific portions of their markets and target them with tailored advertising messages. This practice, called **market segmentation**, divides the pool of potential customers into subgroups, which are usually defined in terms of demographic characteristics, such as age, gender, marital status, income level, and geographic location.

Technology-enabled relationship management is a new twist on establishing direct customer relationships made possible when firms promote and sell on the web. Technology-enabled relationship management occurs when a firm obtains detailed information about a customer's behaviour, preferences, needs, and buying patterns and uses that information to set prices, negotiate terms, tailor promotions, add product features, and otherwise customize its entire relationship with that customer.

DoubleClick is a leading global Internet advertising company that leverages technology and media expertise to help advertisers use the power of the web to build relationships with customers. The DoubleClick Network is its flagship product, a collection of high-traffic and well-recognized sites on the web, including MSN, *Sports Illustrated,* Continental Airlines, the *Washington Post,* CBS, and more than 1500 others. This network of sites is coupled with DoubleClick's proprietary DART targeting technology, which allows advertisers to target their best prospects based on the most precise profiling criteria available. DoubleClick then places a company's ad in front of those best prospects. DART powers over 60 billion ads per month and is trusted by top advertising agencies. Comprehensive online reporting lets advertisers know how their campaign is performing and what type of users are seeing and clicking on their ads. This high-level targeting and real-time reporting provide speed and efficiency not available in any other medium. The system is also designed to track advertising transactions, such as impressions and clicks, to summarize these transactions in the form of reports and to compute DoubleClick Network member compensation.

10.5.4 Investment and Finance

The Internet has revolutionized the world of investment and finance. Perhaps the changes have been so great because this industry had so many built-in inefficiencies and so much opportunity for improvement.

The brokerage business adapted to the Internet faster than any other arm of finance. The allure of online trading that enables investors to do quick, thorough research and then buy shares in any company in a few seconds and at a fraction of the cost of a full-commission firm has brought many investors to the web. In spite of the wealth of information available online, the average consumer buys stocks based on a tip or a recommendation rather than as the result of research and analysis. It is the more sophisticated investor that really takes advantage of the data and tools available on the Internet.[14]

Online banking customers can check balances of their savings, chequing, and loan accounts; transfer money among accounts; and pay their bills. These customers enjoy the convenience of not writing cheques by hand, tracking their current balances, and reducing expenditures on envelopes and stamps.

All of the country's major banks and many of the smaller banks enable their customers to pay bills online; many support bill payment via a mobile phone or other wireless device. Banks are eager to gain more customers who pay bills online because such customers tend to stay with the bank longer, have higher cash balances, and use more of the bank's products.

electronic bill presentment A method of billing whereby a vendor posts an image of your statement on the Internet and alerts you by e-mail that your bill has arrived.

The next advance in online bill paying is **electronic bill presentment**, which eliminates all paper, right down to the bill itself. With this process, the vendor posts an image of your statement on the Internet and alerts you by e-mail that your bill has arrived. You then direct your bank to pay it.

10.5.5 Auctions

eBay has become synonymous with online auctions for both private sellers and small companies. However, hundreds of online auction sites cater to newcomers to online auctions and to unhappy eBay customers. The most frequent complaints are increases in fees and problems with unscrupulous buyers. As a result, eBay is constantly trying to expand and improve its services. eBay spent €1.8 billion to acquire Skype, a pioneer in voice over IP (VoIP) services with the goal of improving communications between sellers and potential buyers for 'high-involvement' items such as automobiles, business equipment, and high-end collectibles. eBay might also provide a pay-for-call service to provide a lead generation service for sellers based on the Skype technology. eBay purchased the payment gateway system of security company VeriSign to provide a payment solution to tens of thousands of new small and midsized businesses. Under the deal, eBay will also receive two million VeriSign security tokens, physical devices like keychain-sized USB plug-ins that are used to create two-factor security where users must provide both a security password and the physical token.[15]

10.5.6 Anywhere, Anytime Applications of Mobile Commerce

Because m-commerce devices usually have a single user, they are ideal for accessing personal information and receiving targeted messages for a particular consumer. Through m-commerce, companies can reach individual consumers to establish one-to-one marketing relationships and communicate whenever it is convenient – in short, anytime and anywhere. Following are just a few examples of potential m-commerce applications:

- Banking customers can use their wireless handheld devices to access their accounts and pay their bills.
- Clients of brokerage firms can view stock prices and company research as well as conduct trades to fit their schedules.
- Information services such as financial news, sports information, and traffic updates can be delivered to people whenever they want.
- On-the-move retail consumers can place and pay for orders instantaneously.
- Telecommunications service users can view service changes, pay bills, and customize their services.
- Retailers and service providers can send potential customers advertising, promotions, or coupons to entice them to try their services as they move past their place of business.

The most successful m-commerce applications suit local conditions and people's habits and preferences. Most people do their research online and then buy offline at a local retailer. As a result, a growing market for local search engines is designed to answer the question, 'where do I buy product x at a brick-and-mortar retailer near me?' Consumers provide their post code and begin by asking a basic question – 'What local stores carry a particular category of items' (e.g., flat-panel televisions). Consumers typically don't start searching knowing that they want a specific model of Panasonic flat-panel TV. The local search engine then provides a list of local stores, including those with a website and those without, which sell this item.

As with any new technology, m-commerce will only succeed if it provides users with real benefits. Companies involved in m-commerce must think through their strategies carefully and ensure that they provide services that truly meet customers' needs.

10.5.7 Advantages of Electronic and Mobile Commerce

According to the Council of Supply Chain Management Professionals, 'Supply Chain Management encompasses the planning and management of all activities involved in sourcing and procurement, conversion, and all logistics management activities. Importantly, it also includes coordination and collaboration with channel partners, which can be suppliers, intermediaries, third-party service providers, and customers'.[16] Conversion to an e-commerce – driven supply chain provides businesses with an opportunity to achieve operational excellence by enabling consumers and companies to gain a global reach to worldwide markets, reduce the cost of doing business, speed the flow of goods and information, increase the accuracy of order processing and order fulfilment, and improve the level of customer service.

- *Global reach.* E-commerce offers enormous opportunities. It allows manufacturers to buy at a low cost worldwide, and it offers enterprises the chance to sell to a global market right from the very start-up of their business. Moreover, e-commerce offers great promise for developing countries, helping them to enter the prosperous global marketplace, and hence helping reduce the gap between rich and poor countries.

- *Reduce costs.* By eliminating or reducing time-consuming and labour-intensive steps throughout the order and delivery process, more sales can be completed in the same period and with increased accuracy. With increased speed and accuracy of customer order information, companies can reduce the need for inventory – from raw materials, to safety stocks, to finished goods – at all the intermediate manufacturing, storage, and transportation points.

- *Speed the flow of goods and information.* When organizations are connected via e-commerce, the flow of information is accelerated because of the already established electronic connections and communications processes. As a result, information can flow easily, directly, and rapidly from buyer to seller.

- *Increased accuracy.* By enabling buyers to enter their own product specifications and order information directly, human data-entry error on the part of the supplier is eliminated.

- *Improve customer service.* Increased and more detailed information about delivery dates and current status can increase customer loyalty. In addition, the ability to consistently meet customers' desired delivery dates with high-quality goods and services eliminates any incentive for customers to seek other sources of supply.

10

Summary

The term 'computing' no longer refers to a PC on a desktop. Mobile devices are letting employees access information from wherever they happen to be. In addition, the same technologies are allowing customers to interact with businesses in new ways. A computer no longer has to look like a huge box with wires attached to a keyboard, monitor and mouse. Maybe people carry around several computer devices with them everyday – a smartphone and iPod are just two examples. Others include laptops and pocket PCs. Fewer people are using wearable technology, where computing power is built into, for example, the clothes that we wear. However, several research groups are interested in this area and if and when a company produces a 'killer application' for wearable technology, the market will grow substantially.

Central to any mobile computing is wireless networking, with wi-fi hotspots being an area where wireless access is available. Many bars and cafés provide their customers with wi-fi, often charging by the half-hour, although sometimes access is free. Tangible media takes concepts from the computer screen and embodies them. Phicons, or physical icons, are one early example. Phicons are used to represent something in the same way that icons on a computer screen represent a computer file. One example of phicons is using them to represent landmarks that can be used to interact with an electronic map.

Personal robotics attempts to make social robots that people want to interact with, as opposed to manufacturing robots which are used to assemble products. Again, several research groups have an interest in this area, but it has not yet really taken off. The robot puppy Aibo is an example of a personal robot. It is also an example of a virtual pet. Virtual pets are perhaps unique among information systems in that their goal is to get users to feel a sense of responsibility towards their pet and become attached in some way to them. Virtual pets are very popular at the moment. They are of interest to businesses as already we are seeing software tools that have been given personality by their developers. In the futures employees will be comfortable interacting with devices that have personality.

Teams made up of people living in different geographical regions are able to work together efficiently and effectively, without ever having to meet. This work is facilitated by a range of technologies. Computer supported cooperative work (CSCW) refers to technologies that allow groups to work together to achieve goals. Individuals in the groups can be co-located (in the same place) or geographically separated. The work can happen synchronously (individuals work at the same time) or asynchronously (they work at different times). Different CSCW technologies exist to support these different modes of work. In global companies, CSCW technology is powerful tool enabling the company to make the best of its human resources no matter where they are located.

A videoconference is a simultaneous communication between two or more parties where they both see and hear each other. A video conference can be set up using easily and cheaply using instant messenging. Videoconferencing is a powerful application, especially when combined with other CSCW tools, allowing people to hold useful meetings when they are geographically distant. Messaging technology includes e-mail, instant messaging and web chat rooms. Each of these are used to communicate via text.

An interactive whiteboard is a combination of a whiteboard and a computer. Users can write on the whiteboard and then save what has been written as an image on their computer. This negates the need to take a note of what has been written after a meeting has finished. Two interactive whiteboards can be used to let people who are separated see what the others have written, and add to it. A wiki is a web page that can be edited by anyone with the proper authority. The most famous example is Wikipedia, which can be edited by any web user – very few restrictions are put in place. Wikis are clearly a good way of knowledge sharing. Virtual worlds are 3D environments populated by avatars. Second Life is a good example. Second Life has been used to host global business meetings, and some large firms are now marketing their products there. Blogs and podcasts are another useful way of sharing knowledge. A blog is an online diary. A podcast is an audio broadcast over the Internet.

E-commerce and m-commerce can be used in many innovative ways to improve the operations of an organization. Electronic retailing (e-tailing) is the direct sale from a business to consumers through electronic storefronts designed around an electronic catalogue and shopping cart model.

A cybermall is a single website that offers many products and services at one Internet location.

Manufacturers are joining electronic exchanges, where they can work with competitors and suppliers to use computers and websites to buy and sell goods, trade market information, and run back-office operations such as inventory control. They are also using e-commerce to improve the efficiency of the selling process by moving customer queries about product availability and prices online.

The web allows firms to gather much more information about customer behaviour and preferences than they could using other marketing approaches. This new technology has greatly enhanced the practice of market segmentation and enabled companies to establish closer relationships with their customers. Detailed information about a customer's behaviour, preferences, needs, and buying patterns allow companies to set prices, negotiate terms, tailor promotions, add product features, and otherwise customize a relationship with a customer.

The Internet has also revolutionized the world of investment and finance, especially online stock trading and online banking. The Internet has also created many options for electronic auctions, where geographically dispersed buyers and sellers can come together.

M-commerce transactions can be used in all these application arenas. M-commerce provides a unique opportunity to establish one-on-one marketing relationships and support communications anytime and anywhere.

Self-Assessment Test

1 A wi-fi _____ is an area where wireless access is available.

2 Keyboards can be wirelessly attached to a pocket PC using the _____ protocol.

3 _____ refers to the transfer of funds that happens electronically rather than by handing over physical coins and notes.

4 The Tamagotchi was an early example of a _____.

5 People only CSCW tools if they geographically distant. True or false?

6 A _____ is a web page that a group of users can easily edit.

7 The term 'blog' is an abbreviation of _____.

8 Buyers and sellers alike can use an electronic exchange to _____.
a. buy and sell goods
b. trade market information
c. run back-office operations
d. all of the above

9 The practice of _____ divides the pool of potential customers into subgroups, which are usually defined in terms of demographic characteristics.

10 An advancement in online bill payment that uses e-mail for the company to post an image of your statement on the Internet so you can direct your bank to pay it is called _____.

Review Questions

1 What is wi-fi?

2 Explain the difference between a pocket PC and a smartphone. Is the distinction blurred?

3 List three ways of implementing e-money.

4 Suggest an application for wearable technology.

5 Define CSCW.

6 What is a videoconference?

7 What is the difference between a wiki and a blog?

8 What is e-tailing?

9 What is technology-enabled relationship management?

10 List some advantages of mobile commerce.

Discussion Questions

1 Explain some of the advantages of e-money. Are there any disadvantages? Which would you rather carry – notes and coins or e-money? Explain your answer.

2 Why do you think videoconferencing has not taken off in the home? Do you use videoconferencing to keep in touch with friends? Why or why not?

3 Do you keep a blog? If so, explain why and who you think you readers are. Outline an approach you could use to increase your readship.

4 Critically evaluate wiki software to determine whether it is a good way to share knowledge. Explain your answer.

5 What are some of the disadvantages of mobile technology? Is there anywhere you would not use a pocket PC, for instance? Why?

Web Exercises

1 Go to blogger.com and search for a blog by an information systems tutor (there are many!). Read the most recent posts and write a short summary of the experience.

2 Have a look at Wikipedia and read some of the articles about the technology discussed in this chapter. Can you spot any mistakes? E-mail a list of the articles you have read to your tutor.

Case One

Volunteers Create Vast Encyclopaedia

Formally launched in 2001 by Jimmy Wales, Wikipedia is an free, online encyclopaedia, which is written entirely by volunteers. In fact, in line with the philosophy of wiki software, anyone with Internet access can add to or change any of the articles, anonymously if they wish. Its main servers are located in Florida and it is maintained by voluntary donations from its readers. Launched in 2001, it is run by the non-profit Wikimedia Foundation. Disputes between authors over content are frequent. These are settled essentially by a process of voting where the authors involved and any other interested parties can discuss the problem between themselves until the truth emerges and is published. Wikipedia claims that none of its articles are ever complete or finished. They also admit that vandalism is a constant problem with people publishing 'with an agenda'. This can be seen on the pages of controversial topics.

Wikipedia's popularity has never been questioned, although its authority has. The website gets around 60 million visitors each day, and the English language version currently has over 1.5 million articles, a figure which is growing daily, on an incredible range of subjects. This alone is testament to the power of wiki software.

However, the ability of anyone to edit articles has been a source of criticism of Wikipedia. Factual errors in content are a constant problem, something Wikipedia is happy to admit. The idea behind Wikipedia's openness is that, with so many volunteers contributing, over time any errors will be edited out and the truth will emerge. Even those who criticize it cannot fail to be impressed by its size.

In a move inspired by Wikipedia's success, the *Los Angeles Times* started a wiki on its website for their readers to write about the Iraq war. One of the paper's former editors criticized this, saying the

content could not be claimed to be reasoned and informed, and that the paper should be checking all the claims made by the wiki's authors which, like Wikipedia, it was not. Someone, he said, needs to be guardian and trustee of the information that is published. Proponents of Wikipedia have hit back by pointing out that the site does not claim to be authoritative or reliable. Several attempts have been made to assess Wikipedia's credibility. One method, frowned upon by Wikipedia, is to deliberately introduce errors into it, and measure if and how long it takes, for them to be corrected. In two studies of this kind, 13 errors were inserted and all were quickly fixed, although because of the way the errors had been inserted, as soon as one had been found, all the others could be easily reverted. In the second, five errors were added, none of which were corrected within a week.

Questions

1 Would you cite a Wikipedia article in a coursework? Why or why not?

2 Why do you think people contribute to Wikipedia? Have you ever edited an article? If you have, why? In an organizational setting, how could employees be encouraged to share their knowledge in a wiki?

3 Compare and contrast sharing knowledge via a wiki and via a blog. What are the strengths and weaknesses of the two approaches?

4 Do you think the Wikipedia model of knowledge sharing would be suitable for a company wanting its employees to share their knowledge? Why or why not?

SOURCE: Chesney, T., 'An Empirical Examination of Wikipedia's Credibility'. *First Monday*, 11(11), 2006.

Case Two

Businesses Go In-World

What do pop group Duran Duran, singer Suzanne Vega, car maker Nissan, Coca-Cola, IBM, Toyota, Sweden, and the Harvard Business School all have in common? Answer: they all have a presence in the virtual world Second Life.

Second Life (http://secondlife.com) is a virtual world that exists only on servers owned by its makers, Linden Lab, where residents, or citizens, interact with each other. Common interactions include chat, role play, cybersex, and building, buying and selling objects such as clothes. According to Linden Lab CEO Phillip Rosedale, Second Life is in direct competition with 'real' life, also known as 'First Life'. With this in mind, a resident can do just about anything in world that can be imagined: fishing, skydiving, jet skiing, shopping, getting married, and even raising children are all common activities.

In appearance, Second Life looks as many computer games do – a three-dimensional world where each resident is represented by an avatar. It is also popular. At the time of writing, there are over eight million residents, a figure that is growing at 20 percent each month, leading some to claim it is the fastest growing economy on the planet.

Earlier this year, a helicopter crashed into Nissan's in-world building, starting a fire that left dead bodies scattered around. The cause of this crash? So called 'griefers', pranksters who enjoy disrupting the world. Many residents feel that big businesses are muscling in on their world, using it as a platform to advertise their goods and putting locals out of business. That is why they are out to cause 'grief'. ('Locals' here is referring to individuals who have come in to Second Life and started a business,

such as designing custom cars to sell to other residents to drive around in.) Others welcome these businesses because they realize that their world is now becoming more popular.

Some marketers are disappointed at the small number of sales their Second Life presence has given them. American Apparel is often hailed as one of the first to open a shop there, but has all but closed it again, having being the constant victim of more griefers who shot at their customers with virtual guns.

Experiences such as these, and the helicopter crash, are making some businesses think twice. The bank Wells Fargo left Second Life only four months after setting up a virtual island claiming that 'going into Second Life now is the equivalent of running a field marketing program in Iraq'.

Questions

1 How could a virtual world be used to market real products?

2 Would some products be easier to sell in a virtual world than others? If so, what are some of them and what about them makes them easier to sell?

3 Describe what your 'Second Life' would be like. What do you think you would get out of living it?

4 Do you think virtual worlds will become viable places to sell goods in the future? Explain your answer.

SOURCES: Rushe, D., 'Life in the Unreal World'. *Sunday Times Magazine*, December 10, 2006; 'Living a Second Life', The Economist, July 30, 2006; Fass, A., 'Sex Pranks and Reality', *Forbes*, February 7, 2007.

10

Case Three

Google Continues to Strive to Manage the Earth's Information

You probably know Google well as a search engine. The company, based in California, has more in mind than being the world's best search resource. It's aim is to 'organize the world's information and make it universally accessible and useful', which

seems a very challenging goal. Bringing this one step nearer is Google Docs.

The last time you wrote a piece of coursework you probably saved it on your PC's hard drive. You maybe copied it to your university's network as a backup in case something happened your computer. The university will keep another backup of your network drive, again in case something should happen to the main server. Google are taking this concept one step further, and trying to be the 'network drive' of the entire planet. Google Docs allows you to create a word processing document, a spreadsheet, or a presentation via a web browser, and save it on their servers where it is accessible from anywhere in the world. Google market the tool as a powerful CSCW technology, allowing more than one person to contribute to a file at the same time. The data is held securely and backed-up. You can also upload your existing files for Google to store them for you, and download files to your computer if you want to work on them when you are not connected to the Internet. At the moment, there is a limit to the amount that can be stored.

Businesses are keen to use this technology. Some are using Google Docs to share press releases so they can be proofread quickly by employees in different offices. Others are entering payroll data from employees based in different buildings onto a Google Doc spreadsheet to be used by headquarters to organize paycheques.

Other people are using Google Docs to collaborate on a wide range of projects – help parents who live in another city with word processing, plan holidays with old college friends, or have family members contribute to the weekly shopping list. Have a look at the Google Docs website to see many more.

Questions

1   By using Google Docs and nothing else you are putting all your valuable information into Google's hands. Is this a good idea? Would you recommend a business do this? Describe an approach to using Google Docs that would minimize your fears.

2   Explain some of the benefits Google Docs brings.

3   Describe how you could use Google Docs to complete a group assignment.

4   Who are some of Google's competitors? What do you think their response to Google Docs will be? What should Google do about this?

SOURCE: Google Docs (website), https://www.google.com/accounts/ServiceLogin?service=writely.

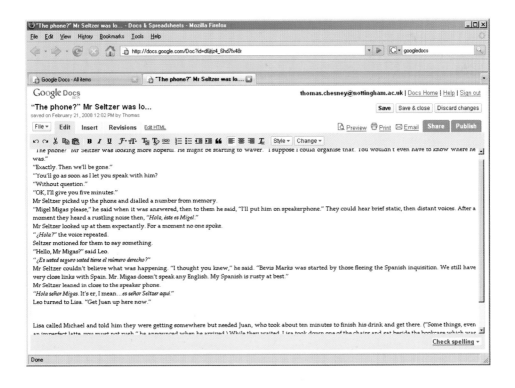

Notes

1 T-Mobile (website), http://www.t-mobile.co.uk.

2 Head, W., 'Nokia Trials Wi-Fi Phones in Finland', *ITNews,* http://www.itnews.com.au/News/ 35423, nokia-trials-wifi-phones-in-finland.aspx.

3 BBC Staff, bbc.co.uk, 'Norwich Pioneers Free City Wi-Fi', http://news.bbc.co.uk/1/hi/technology/ 5297884.stm.

4 BBC Staff, bbc.co.uk, 'Polynesians Get Free Wireless Web', http://news.bbc.co.uk/ 1/hi/technology/ 3020158.stm.

5 Margi (website), http://www.margi.com.

6 Tom Tom (website), http://www.tomtom.com.

7 BBC iPlayer beta (website), http://www.bbc.co.uk/iplayerbeta/.

8 LUUP (website), http://www.luup.com.

9 Staff, bbc.co.uk, 'From Matatu to the Masai via Mobile', http://news.bbc.co.uk/1/hi/technology/ 6241603.stm.

10 World Bank (website), http://web.worldbank.org/ WBSITE/EXTERNAL/EXTABOUTUS/EXTANNREP/ EXTANNREP2K6/0,,contentMDK:21046759~menu PK:2915617~pagePK:64168445~piPK:64168309 ~theSitePK:2838572,00.html.

11 Rushe, D., 'Life in the Unreal World'. *Sunday Times Magazine,* December 10, 2007.

12 Staff, 'Bloggers Learn the Price of Telling Too Much', CNN Online, July 11, 2005.

13 McBride, Sarah; Wingfield, Nick, 'As Podcasts Boom, Big Media Rushes to Stake a Claim', *Wall Street Journal,* October 10, 2005, p. A1.

14 Rosencrance, Linda, 'Survey: User Satisfaction with E-Commerce Sites Rises Slightly', *Computerworld,* February 21, 2006.

15 Regan, Keith, 'Eyeing Expansion of PayPal, eBay Buys VeriSign Payment Gateway', *E-Commerce Times,* October 11, 2005.

16 Council of Supply Chain Management Professionals (website), www.cscmp.org/Website/ AboutCSCMP/Definitions/Definitions.asp.

World Views Case

Kulula.com: The Trials and Tribulations of a South African Online Airline

Anesh Maniraj Singh
University of Durban

Kulula.com was launched in August 2001 as the first online airline in South Africa. Kulula is one of two airlines that are operated by Comair Ltd. British Airways (BA), the other airline that Comair runs, is a full-service franchise operation that serves the South African domestic market. Kulula, unlike BA, is a limited-service operation aimed at providing low fares to a wider domestic market using five aircraft. Since its inception, Kulula has reinvented air travel in South Africa, making it possible for more people to fly than ever before.

Kulula is a true South African e-commerce success. The company boasts as one of its successes the fact that it has been profitable from day one. It is recognized internationally among the top low-cost airlines and participated in a conference attended by other such internationally known low-cost carriers as Virgin Blue, Ryanair, and easyJet. Kulula also received an award from the South African Department of Trade and Industry for being a Technology Top 100 company.

Kulula's success is based on its clearly defined strategy of being the lowest-cost provider in the South African domestic air travel industry. To this end, Kulula has adopted a no-frills approach. Staff and cabin crew wear simple uniforms, and the company has no airport lounges. There are no business class seats and no frequent-flyer programmes. Customers pay for their food and drinks. In addition, Kulula does not issue paper tickets, and very few travel agents book its flights—90 percent of tickets are sold directly to customers. Furthermore, customers have to pay for ticket changes, and the company has a policy of 'no fly, no refund.' Yet, in its drive to keep costs down, Kulula does not compromise on maintenance and safety, and it employs the best pilots and meets the highest safety standards. Like all B2C companies, Kulula aims to create customer value by reducing overhead costs, including salaries, commissions, rent, and consumables such as paper and paper-based documents. Furthermore,

Linda & Colin McKie/Istock

by cutting out the middleman such as travel agents, Kulula is able to keep prices low and save customers the time and inconvenience of having to pick up tickets from travel agents. Instead, customers control the entire shopping experience.

Kulula was the sole provider of low-cost flights in South Africa until early 2004, when One Time launched a no-frills service to compete head-on with Kulula. Due to the high price elasticity of demand within the industry, any lowering of price stimulates a higher demand for flights. The increase in competition in the low-price end of the market has seen Kulula decrease fares by up to 20 percent while increasing passengers by over 40 percent. There, however, has been no brand switching. Kulula has grown in the market at the expense of others.

Apart from its low-cost strategy, Kulula is successful because of its strong B2C business model. As previously mentioned, 90 percent of its revenue is generated from direct sales. However, Kulula has recently ventured into the B2B market by collaborating with Computicket and a few travel agents, who can log on to the Kulula site from their company intranets. Kulula offers fares at substantial reductions to businesses that use it regularly. Furthermore, Kulula bases its success on three simple principles: Any decision taken must bring in additional revenue, save on costs, and/or enhance customer service. Technology contributes substantially to these three principles.

In its first year, Kulula used a locally developed reservation system, which soon ran out of functionality. The second-generation system was AirKiosk, which was developed in Boston for Kulula. The system change resulted in an improvement of functionality for passengers. For example, in 2003, Kulula ran a promotion during which tickets were sold at ridiculously low prices, and the system was overwhelmed. Furthermore, Kulula experienced a system crash that lasted a day and a half, which severely hampered sales and customer service. As a result, year two saw a revamp in all technology: All the hardware was replaced, bandwidth was increased, new servers and database servers were installed, and web hosting was changed. In short, the entire system was replaced. According to IT Director Carl Scholtz, 'Our success depends on infrastructural stability; our current system has an output that is four times better than the best our systems could ever produce.' Kulula staff members are conscious of the security needs of customers and have invested in 128-bit encryption, giving customers peace of mind that their transactions and information are safe.

The success behind Kulula's systems lies in its branding – its strong identity in the marketplace, which includes its name and visual appeal. The term kulula means 'easy', and Kulula's web site has been designed with a simple, no-fuss, user-friendly interface. When visiting the Kulula site, you are immediately aware that an airline ticket can be purchased in three easy steps. The first step allows customers to choose destinations and dates. The second step allows customers to choose the most convenient or cheapest flight based on their need. Kulula also allows customers to book cars and accommodations in step two. Step three is the transaction stage, which allows customers to choose the most suitable payment method. The confirmation and ticket can be printed after payment has been settled. Kulula has not embraced mobile commerce yet, because the technology does not support the ability to allow customers to purchase a ticket in three easy steps. Unlike other e-commerce sites, Kulula is uncluttered and simple to understand, enhancing customer service. Kulula is a fun brand – with offbeat advertising campaigns and bright green and blue corporate and aircraft colours – but behind the fun exterior is a group of people who are serious about business.

Kulula's future is extremely promising. Technology changes continually, and Kulula strives to have the best technology in place at all times. B2B e-commerce will continue to be a major focus of the company to develop additional distribution channels with little or no cost. In conjunction with bank partners, Kulula is developing additional methods of payment to replace credit card payments, allowing more people the opportunity to fly. These transactions will be free. Kulula is also involving customers in its marketing efforts by obtaining their permission to promote special offers by e-mail and short message service to customers' cell phones. The Kulula web site will soon serve as a ticketing portal, where customers can also purchase British Airways tickets, in three easy steps. The company has many other developments in the pipeline that will enhance customer service. According to Scholtz, 'We are not an online airline, just an e-tailer that sells airline tickets.'

Questions

1 This case does not mention any backup systems, either electronic or paper-based. What would you recommend to ensure that the business runs 24/7/365?

2 It is clear from this case that Kulula is a low-cost provider. What else could Kulula do with its technology to bring in additional revenue, save on cost, and enhance customer service?

3 Does the approach taken by Kulula in terms of its strategy, its business model, and the three principles of success lend itself to other businesses wanting to engage in e-commerce?

4 Kulula flights are almost always full. Do you think that by partnering with a company such as Lastminute.com the airline could fly to capacity at all times? What are the risks related to such a collaboration?

5 Kulula initially developed its systems in-house, which it later outsourced to AirKiosk in Boston. Do you think it is wise for an e-business to outsource its systems development? Is it strategically sound to outsource systems development to a company in a different country?

6 With the current trends in mobile commerce, could Kulula offer its services on mobile devices such as cellular phones? Would the company have to alter its strategic thinking to accommodate such a shift? Is it possible to develop a text-based interface that could facilitate a purchase in three easy steps?

World Views Case

How to do Business in Second Life

Alan Hogarth, Glasgow Caledonian University

Virtual worlds such as Second Life are increasingly becoming popular mediums for companies to advertise their products, but can an organization look to a virtual world to generate serious profits in real life? Many organizations are aiming not to miss out by building a virtual presence now.

A major event in the history of software development occurred when Sun Microsystems announced that it would take its Java programming language open source. However, the main interest in this event was that the developer discussions were held at the 'Sun pavilion' in Second Life. Although, this was viewed by many as a publicity stunt and was plagued by technical problems, many observers believe that Second Life could become a serious enterprise tool for performing a range of business functions, from communication and collaboration. Second Life was launched by Linden Labs in 2003, and has since grown to include more than three million 'residents'. Second Life has its own economy that generates an estimated £32m per year, and a currency – Linden dollars – that can be used to buy virtual tools, clothes, land and property, and can be exchanged between real-world currencies. The difference from other popular online worlds is that it is a 3D virtual space where users can interact using instant messaging, network, or create content, objects, tools and applications and not a 'game' as such. Steve Prentice, senior analyst at Gartner says:

'Second Life is a new phenomenon that represents a completely different approach to business, just as the internet did at the beginning. We are now seeing all sorts of commercial businesses taking a serious look at Second Life.'

Prentice further argues that all organizations should be at least experimenting with the new phenomenon and that as a communications and collaboration tool, Second Life could be 'as important as the internet and e-business'. Prentice states that,

'Second Life is unique in that it has created a blank canvas for individuals and organizations to create content and services, and to experiment with them in a virtual world. Whether it will be Second Life or another virtual world, the concept is here to stay, and in the longer term 3D virtual worlds will become important business tools for testing new ideas and models.'

Any user or organization can join Second Life by going to the website and downloading a 25Mbyte software client free of charge for a basic account. Users will then be asked to create their own avatar from a comprehensive list of customisable characteristics.

'Businesses should be experimenting. People in your organization may already be using Second Life, so there is an opportunity to develop home-grown expertise, and to understand what it is all about before your competitors,' says Prentice.

Large IT companies have already seen its potential as a communication tool, and are using Second Life to reach the global community of IT directors, programmers and developers. Cisco, Sun, Dell and IBM have all made significant investments in Second Life, purchasing 'virtual land', which equates to space on Linden Labs' Linux-based servers. PC manufacturer Dell has also created 'Dell Island', which features a 'virtual factory' where visitors can customise computers that will be delivered to their real-life doorstep. Some 'islands' are open to the public and some are private. Ian Hughes, at IBM, says the inherent 'presence' aspect of Second Life makes it ideal for collaboration, meetings, conferences and other networking events. He states that,

'Meetings in Second Life have a more human, memorable and productive element to them. Think of a teleconference, where 30 people dial in, remain silent on the line until the event starts, take part and then dial off. In the virtual world you would enter the conference room to see social groups huddled together chatting just as they would at a real-world conference. Once the event is over, some people hang back to chat, network and maintain old business relationships or to create new ones.'

Various non-IT organizations are also keen to experiment, from hotel chains and automotive companies, to market research houses and architects. For example hotel chain Starwood Hotels recently launched 'Aloft', a virtual concept hotel that will allow the company to observe consumers' response to an 'experimental' style of hotel. Brian McGuinness, Starwood vice-president states that,

'The company saves money by not having to build a physical mock-up of a new hotel. The virtual hotel serves as a "laboratory" that can be reconfigured easily to change or add elements according to consumer feedback.'

Linda Zimmer, CEO of Marcom Interactive, which advises companies on how new media technologies can be applied to their business, describes how Toyota has recently created and released virtual models of its Scion cars into Second Life. Toyota will observe how consumers customise the cars and use any insights gained to feed back into real-world strategy. Zimmer says that,

'This is a testing environment that everyone is watching closely. It might not help sales of Scion cars, but it will help Toyota get into the minds of consumers in the real world.'

Second Life has a number of low-cost business applications too. The use of virtual focus groups, for example, is providing insight for organizations looking to target the young consumers using Second Life. As a result, there is a small, but growing number of market research houses offering consumer research services. Market Truths and Repres are two such research houses using Second Life.

'The biggest advantage for market research is that companies can observe consumers using and interacting with their product,' says Zimmer.

Just visiting Second Life may spark some ideas, says Zimmer. However, there are some important issues that all organizations should take into account before stepping into the virtual world.

'Organizations should provide guidelines for employees' avatar profiles, and a policy about revealing "first life" information. Consider what information may be sensitive and advise your employees about what a positive profile should include when operating in Second Life under your brand name,' she says.

Using avatars can give employees the perception that they are less accountable, although they are still representatives of the brand reputation. The cultural aspects are seen as important and should also be taken seriously, if organizations are not to risk annoying or alienating potential customers. As such, Second Life should be considered as a sensitive and unfamiliar environment and treated in the same way as a business entering a new real-world market, such as the Far East.

Rob Enderle, head of research firm Enderle Group, urges businesses to focus on the importance of privacy and security awareness in Second Life. Unless organizations have invested in creating secure areas for internal communications or collaboration with invited guests, instant messaging conversations are open to anyone in the virtual vicinity.

'There is a risk with any new channel, and there has been [intellectual] theft in Second Life. The security aspects of virtual reality are not fully understood yet, let alone mitigated,' he says.

However, the overall view of Second Life is to try it. No initial investment is required and it could just turn out to be as ubiquitous as the Internet

Questions

1 What do you perceive to be the main advantages or disadvantages for business organizations of a 'virtual world' such as 2nd Life?

2 What type of organization would benefit most from 2nd Life?

3 As a Project Manager of a systems development team how could you envisage utilizing the facilities of 2nd Life?

4 What ethical and privacy issues could you perceive organizations encountering in 2nd Life?

SOURCE: Eastwood, Gary, Feb 2007, Computer weekly.com.

PART 4

Systems Development

11

Systems Analysis

Principles

Effective systems development requires a team effort from stakeholders, users, managers, systems development specialists, and various support personnel, and it starts with careful planning.

Systems development often uses tools to select, implement, and monitor projects, including, prototyping, rapid application development, CASE tools, and object-oriented development.

Systems development starts with investigation and analysis of existing systems.

Learning Objectives

■ Identify the key participants in the systems development process and discuss their roles.

■ Define the term 'information systems' and 'planning' and list several reasons for initiating a systems project.

■ Discuss three trends that illustrate the impact of enterprise resource planning software packages on systems development.

■ Discuss the key features, advantages, and disadvantages of the traditional, prototyping, rapid application development, and end-user systems development lifecycles.

■ Identify several factors that influence the success or failure of a systems development project.

■ Discuss the use of CASE tools and the object-oriented approach to systems development.

■ State the purpose of systems investigation.

■ Discuss the importance of performance and cost objectives.

■ State the purpose of systems analysis and discuss some of the tools and techniques used in this phase of systems development.

| Why Learn About Systems Analysis? | Throughout this book, you have seen many examples of the use of information systems. But where do these systems come from? How can you work with IS personnel, such as systems analysts and computer programmers, to get what you need to succeed on |

the job? This chapter, the first of two chapters on systems development, gives you the answer. You will see how managers can initiate the systems development process and analyze end users' needs with the help of IS personnel. Systems investigation and systems analysis are the first two steps of the systems development process. This chapter provides specific examples of how new or modified systems are initiated and analyzed in a number of industries. In this chapter, you will learn how your project can be planned, aligned with corporate goals, rapidly developed, and much more. The main thrust of this chapter and the next is about a company building their own information system from scratch. However, in the next chapter we will look at alternatives to this – buying in a system that someone else has already built.

We start with an overview of the systems development process.

11.1 An Overview of Systems Development

In today's businesses, managers and employees in all functional areas work together and use business information systems. Because they are central to project success, users are helping with development and, in many cases, leading the way. Users might request that a systems development team determine whether they should purchase a few PCs, update an existing order processing system, develop a new medical diagnostic, or design and implement a new website. In other cases, systems development might involve purchasing or leasing a systems such as an enterprise resource planning (ERP) package discussed in Chapter 7.

This chapter and the next provide you with a deeper appreciation of the systems development process and show how businesses can avoid costly failures. Calculating the cost of an IT project is difficult and a number of high profile mistakes have been made. Most of these are from the public sector (as any mistakes from the private sector are quickly covered up!). In the U.K. there have been IT problems and soaring costs with the system for issuing passports, the system managing payments to children from absent parents, and the system managing patient data in the National Health Service. This last system, the National Programme for IT, which aims to connect every hospital and general practitioner in England and Wales with electronic patient information, was originally to cost €9 billion, although the final cost could rise to €46 billion.[1] Participants in systems development, in this case, government health ministers, hospital managers, doctors and patient groups, are critical to systems development success.

11.1.1 Participants in Systems Development

Effective systems development requires a team effort. The team usually consists of users, managers, systems development specialists, various support personnel and other stakeholders. This team, called the development team, is responsible for determining the objectives of the new information system and delivering a system that meets these objectives. Many development teams use a project manager to head the systems development effort and to help coordinate the systems development process. A project is a planned collection of activities that achieves a goal, such as constructing a new manufacturing plant or developing a new decision support system.[2] All projects should have a defined starting point and ending point, normally expressed as dates such as 2nd March. Most have a set budget, such as €150 000. The project manager is responsible for coordinating all people and resources needed to complete the project on time. In systems development, the project manager can be an IS person inside the organization or an external consultant hired to see the project to completion. Project managers need technical, business, and people skills. In addition to completing the project on time and within the specified budget, the project manager is usually responsible for controlling project quality, training personnel, facilitating communication, managing risks, and acquiring any necessary equipment, including office supplies and sophisticated computer systems. One study reported that almost 80 percent of responding IS managers believe that it is critical to keep project planning skills in-house instead of outsourcing them.[3] Research studies have shown that project management success factors include good leadership from executives and project managers, a high level of trust in the project and its potential benefits, and the commitment of the project team and organization to successfully complete the project and implement its results.

In the context of systems development, stakeholders are people who, either themselves or through the area of the organization they represent, ultimately benefit from the systems development project. Users are people who will interact with the system regularly. They can be employees, managers, or suppliers. For large-scale systems development projects, where the investment in, and value of, a system can be high, it is common for senior-level managers, including the heads of functional areas (finance, marketing, and so on), to be part of the development team.

Depending on the nature of the systems project, the development team might include systems analysts and programmers, among others. A systems analyst is a professional who specializes in analyzing and designing business systems. Systems analysts play various roles while interacting with the users, management, vendors and suppliers, external companies, programmers, and other IS support personnel (see Figure 11.1). Like an architect developing blueprints for a new building, a systems analyst develops detailed plans for the new or modified system. The programmer is responsible for modifying or developing programs to satisfy user requirements. Like a contractor constructing a new building or renovating an existing one, the programmer takes the plans from the systems analyst and builds or modifies the necessary software.

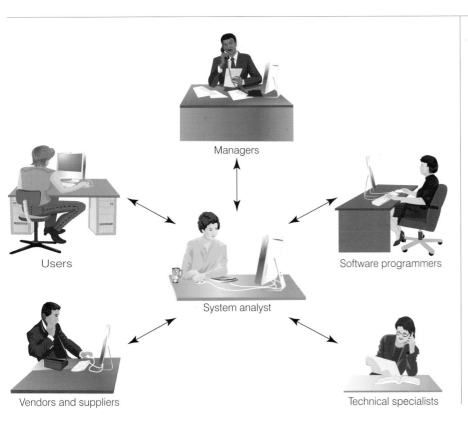

Managers

Users

System analyst

Software programmers

Vendors and suppliers

Technical specialists

Figure 11.1 Role of the Systems Analyst *The systems analyst plays an important role in the development team and is often the only person who sees the system in its totality. The systems analyst is often called on to be a facilitator, moderator, negotiator, and interpreter for development activities.*

11

The other support personnel on the development team are mostly technical specialists, including database and telecommunications experts, hardware engineers, and supplier representatives. One or more of these roles might be outsourced to outside experts. Depending on the magnitude of the systems development project and the number of IS systems development specialists on the team, one or more IS managers might also belong to the team. The composition of a development team can vary over time and from project to project. For small businesses, the development team might consist of a systems analyst and the business owner as the primary stakeholder. For larger organizations, IS staff can include hundreds of people involved in a variety of activities, including systems development. Every development team should have a team leader. This person can be from the IS department, a manager from the company, or a consultant from outside the company. The team leader needs both technical and people skills.

Regardless of the specific nature of a project, systems development creates or modifies systems, which ultimately means change. Managing this change effectively requires development team members to communicate well. Because you probably will participate in systems development during your career, you must learn communication skills. You might even be the individual who initiates systems development. Typical reasons for initiating IS projects are given in Table 11.1.

11.1.2 Information Systems Planning and Aligning Organization and IS Goals

The term information systems planning refers to translating strategic and organizational goals into systems development initiatives. The chief information officer (CIO) of the Marriott hotel chain, for example, attends board meetings and other top-level management meetings so that the he is familiar with, and can contribute to, the firm's strategic plan. According to Doug Lewis, former CIO for many Fortune 100 companies, 'Strategic goals must be finite, measurable, and tangible.' Proper IS planning ensures that specific systems development objectives support organizational goals.

Aligning organizational goals and IS goals is critical for any successful systems development effort.[4] Because information systems support other business activities, IS staff and people in other departments need to understand each other's responsibilities and tasks. Determining whether organizational and IS goals are aligned can be difficult.

Table 11.1 Typical Reasons to Initiate a Systems Development Project

Reason	Example
Problems with existing system	Not processing orders fast enough
Desire to exploit new opportunities	M-commerce
Increasing competition	New competitor enters industry
Desire to make more effective use of information	Wanting to set up a customer relationship management system to expand and exploit information stored on customers
Organizational growth	Expanding customer base
Merger or acquisition	Buying out a competitor
Change in the environment	New regulations imposed by government

11

One of the primary benefits of IS planning and alignment of business goals is a long-range view of information systems use in the organization. The IS plan should guide the development of the IS infrastructure over time. IS planning should ensure better use of IS resources – including funds, personnel, and time for scheduling specific projects. The steps of IS planning are shown in Figure 11.2.

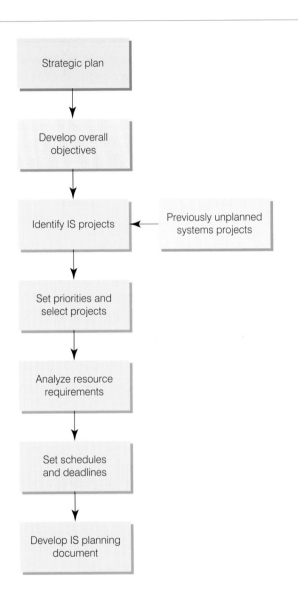

Figure 11.2 The Steps of IS Planning *Some projects are identified through overall IS objectives, whereas additional projects, called 'unplanned projects', are identified from other sources. All identified projects are then evaluated in terms of their organizational priority.*

In today's business environment, many companies seek systems development projects that will provide them with a competitive advantage. Thinking competitively usually requires creative and critical analysis. For example, a company might want to achieve a competitive advantage by improving its customer–supplier relationship. Linking customers and suppliers electronically can result in more efficient communication and ultimately, superior products and services. By looking at problems in new or different ways and by introducing innovative methods to solve them, many organizations have gained significant advantages. In some cases, these new solutions are inspired by people and things not directly related to the problem.

creative analysis The investigation of new approaches to existing problems.

critical analysis The unbiased and careful questioning of whether system elements are related in the most effective ways.

Creative analysis involves investigating new approaches to existing problems. Typically, new solutions are inspired by people and events not directly related to the problem. **Critical analysis** requires unbiased and careful questioning of whether system elements are related in the most effective ways. It involves considering the establishment of new or different relationships among system elements and perhaps introducing new elements into the system. Critical analysis in systems development involves the following actions:

- *Questioning statements and assumptions*. Questioning users about their needs and clarifying their initial responses can result in better systems and more accurate predictions. Too often, stakeholders and users specify certain system requirements because they assume that their needs can only be met that way. Often, an alternative approach would be better. For example, a stakeholder might be concerned because there is always too much of some items in stock and not enough of other items. So, the stakeholder might request a new and improved inventory control system. An alternative approach is to identify the root cause for poor inventory management. This latter approach might determine that sales forecasting is inaccurate and needs improvement or that production cannot meet the set production schedule. All too often, solutions are selected before understanding the complete nature of the problem.

- *Identifying and resolving objectives and orientations that conflict*. Each department in an organization can have different objectives and orientations. The buying department might want to minimize the cost of spare parts by always buying from the lowest-cost supplier, but engineering might want to buy more expensive, higher quality spare parts to reduce the frequency of replacement. These differences must be identified and resolved before a new purchasing system is developed or an existing one modified.

11.1.3 Establishing Objectives for Systems Development

The overall objective of systems development is to achieve business goals, not technical goals, by delivering the right information to the right person at the right time. The impact a particular system has on an organization's ability to meet its goals determines the true value of that system to the organization. Although all systems should support business goals, some systems are more pivotal in continued operations and goal attainment than others. These systems are called 'key operational'. An order processing system, for example, is key operational. Without it, few organizations could continue daily activities, and they clearly would not meet set goals.

The goals defined for an organization also define the objectives that are set for a system. A manufacturing plant, for example, might determine that minimizing the total cost of owning and operating its equipment is critical to meet production and profit goals. Critical success factors (CSFs) are factors that are essential to the success of certain functional areas of an organization. The CSF for manufacturing – minimizing equipment maintenance and operating costs – would be converted into specific objectives for a proposed system. One specific objective might be to alert maintenance planners when a piece of equipment is due for routine preventative maintenance (e.g., cleaning and lubrication). Another objective might be to alert the maintenance planners when the necessary cleaning materials, lubrication oils, or spare parts inventory levels are below specified limits. These objectives could be accomplished either through automatic stock replenishment or through the use of exception reports.

Regardless of the particular systems development effort, the development process should define a system with specific performance and cost objectives. The success or failure of the systems development effort will be measured against these objectives.

11

Performance Objectives

The extent to which a system performs as desired can be measured through its performance objectives. System performance is usually determined by factors such as the following:

■ *The quality or usefulness of the output*. Is the system generating the right information for a value-added business process or by a goal-oriented decision maker?

■ *The accuracy of the output*. Is the output accurate and does it reflect the true situation? As a result of the Enron accounting scandal in the U.S., and similar instances, when some companies overstated revenues or understated expenses, accuracy is becoming more important, and business leaders throughout the world are being held responsible for the accuracy of all corporate reports.

■ *The quality or usefulness of the format of the output*. Is the output generated in a form that is usable and easily understood? For example, objectives often concern the legibility of screen displays, the appearance of documents, and the adherence to certain naming conventions.

■ *The speed at which output is generated*. Is the system generating output in time to meet organizational goals and operational objectives? Objectives such as customer response time, the time to determine product availability, and throughput time are examples.

■ *The scalability of the resulting system*. Scalability allows an information system to handle business growth and increased business volume. For example, if a mid-sized business realizes an annual 10 percent growth in sales for several years, an information system that is scalable will be able to efficiently handle the increase by adding processing, storage, software, database, telecommunications, and other information systems resources to handle the growth.

■ *The risk of the system*. One important objective of many systems development projects is to reduce risk.[5] The BRE Bank in Poland, for example, used systems development to create a model-based decision support system to analyze and reduce loan risk and a variety of related risks associated with bank transactions. The new project uses a mathematical algorithm, called FIRST (financial institutions risk scenario trends), to reduce risk.

In some cases, the achievement of performance objectives can be easily measured (e.g., by tracking the time it takes to determine product availability). In other cases, it is sometimes more difficult to ascertain in the short term. For example, it might be difficult to determine how many customers are lost because of slow responses to customer inquiries regarding product availability. These outcomes, however, are often closely associated with business goals and are vital to the long-term success of the organization. Senior management usually dictates their attainment.

Cost Objectives

Organizations can spend more than is necessary during a systems development project. The benefits of achieving performance goals should be balanced with all costs associated with the system, including the following:

■ *Development costs*. All costs required to get the system up and running should be included. Some computer vendors give cash rewards to companies using their systems to reduce costs and as an incentive.[6]

■ *Costs related to the uniqueness of the system application*. A system's uniqueness has a profound effect on its cost. An expensive but reusable system might be preferable to a less costly system with limited use.

■ *Fixed investments in hardware and related equipment*. Developers should consider costs of such items as computers, network-related equipment, and environmentally controlled data centres in which to operate the equipment.

■ *Ongoing operating costs of the system*. Operating costs include costs for personnel, software, supplies, and resources such as the electricity required to run the system.

11

Balancing performance and cost objectives within the overall framework of organizational goals can be challenging. Setting objectives are important, however, because they allow an organization to allocate resources effectively and measure the success of a systems development effort.

11.2 Systems Development Lifecycles

The systems development process is also called the 'systems development lifecycle' (SDLC) because the activities associated with it are ongoing. As each system is built, the project has timelines and deadlines, until the system is installed and accepted. The life of the system then continues as it is maintained and reviewed. If the system needs significant improvement beyond the scope of maintenance, if it needs to be replaced because of a new generation of technology, or if the IS needs of the organization change significantly, a new project will be initiated and the cycle will start over.

A key fact of systems development is that the later in the SDLC an error is detected, the more expensive it is to correct (see Figure 11.3). One reason for the mounting costs is that if an error which occurred in a early stage of the SDLC isn't found until a later phase, the previous phases must be reworked to some extent. Another reason is that the errors found late in the SDLC affect more people. For example, an error found after a system is installed might require retraining users when a 'work-around' to the problem has been found. Thus, experienced systems developers prefer an approach that will catch errors early in the project lifecycle.

Figure 11.3
Relationship Between Timing of Errors and Costs *The later that system changes are made in the SDLC, the more expensive these changes become.*

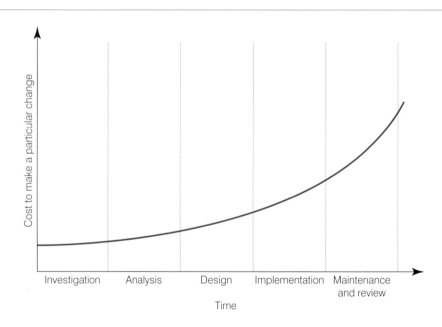

Several common systems development lifecycles exist: the traditional, or waterfall approach, prototyping, rapid application development (RAD), and end-user development. In addition, companies can outsource the systems development process. With many companies, and most public sector organizations, these approaches are formalized and documented so that systems developers have a well-defined process to follow; in other companies, less formalized approaches are used. Keep Figure 11.3 in mind as you are introduced to alternative SDLCs in the next section.

11.2.1 The Traditional Systems Development Lifecycle

Traditional systems development efforts, can range from a small project, such as purchasing an inexpensive computer program, to a major undertaking. The steps of traditional systems development might vary from one company to the next, but most approaches have five common phases: investigation, analysis, design, implementation, and maintenance and review (see Figure 11.4). Traditional systems development is also known as the waterfall approach.

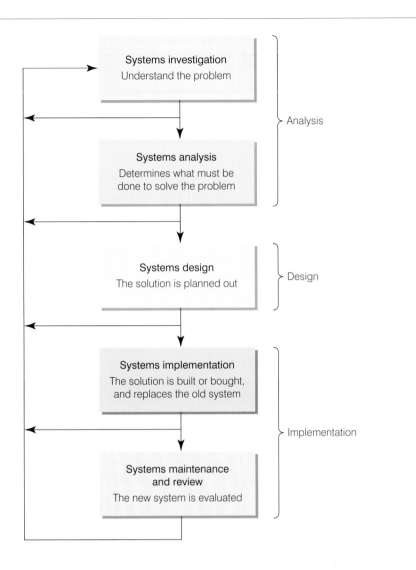

Figure 11.4 The Traditional Systems Development Lifecycle
Sometimes information learned in a particular phase requires cycling back to a previous phase.

In the systems investigation phase, potential problems and opportunities are identified and considered in light of the goals of the business. Systems investigation attempts to answer the questions 'what is the problem, and is it worth solving?'. The primary result of this phase is a defined development project for which business problems or opportunity statements have been created, to which some organizational resources have been committed, and for which systems analysis is recommended. Systems analysis attempts to answer the question 'what must the information system do to solve the problem?'. This phase involves studying existing systems and work processes to identify strengths, weaknesses, and opportunities for improvement. The major outcome of systems analysis is a list of requirements and priorities. Systems design seeks to answer the question 'how will the information system do what it must do to obtain the problem solution?'. The primary result of this phase is a technical design that either describes the new system or describes how existing systems will be modified. The system design details system outputs, inputs, and user interfaces; specifies hardware, software, database, telecommunications, personnel, and procedure components; and shows how these components are related. Systems implementation involves creating or buying the various system components detailed in the systems design, assembling them, and placing the new or modified system into operation. An important task during this phase is to train the users. Systems implementation results in an installed, operational information system that meets the business needs for which it was developed. The purpose of systems maintenance and review is to ensure that the system operates as intended and to modify the system so that it continues to meet changing business needs. As shown in Figure 11.4, a system under development moves from one phase of the traditional SDLC to the next.

The traditional SDLC allows for a large degree of management control. However, a major problem is that the user does not use the solution until the system is nearly complete. Table 11.2 lists advantages and disadvantages of the traditional SDLC.

11.2.2 Prototyping

Prototyping, also known as the evolutionary lifecycle, takes an iterative approach to the systems development process. During each iteration, requirements and alternative solutions to the problem are identified and analyzed, new solutions are designed, and a portion of the system is implemented. Users are then encouraged to try the prototype and provide feedback (see Figure 11.5). Prototyping begins with creating a preliminary model of a major subsystem or a scaled-down version of the entire system. For example, a prototype might show sample report formats and input screens. After they are developed and refined, the prototypical reports and input screens are used as models for the actual system, which can be developed using an end-user programming language such as Visual Basic. The first preliminary model is refined to form the second- and third-generation models, and so on until the complete system is developed. One potential problem with prototyping is knowing when the system is finished as people can always think of extra refinements they would like.

Prototypes can be classified as operational or non-operational. An operational prototype is a prototype that has functionality – it does something toward solving the problem. It may accept input, partially process it and output the results. Then, perhaps in the second iteration, the processing is refined and expanded. A non-operational prototype is a mock-up, or model. It typically includes output and input specifications and formats. The outputs include mocked up reports to and the inputs include the layout of the user interface either on paper on a computer screen. The primary advantage of a non-operational prototype is that it can be developed much faster than an operational prototype. Non-operational prototypes can be discarded, and a fully operational system can be built based on what was learned from the prototypes. The

Table 11.2 Advantages and Disadvantages of Traditional SDLC

Advantages	Disadvantages
Formal review at the end of each phase allows maximum management control	Users get a system that meets the needs as understood by the developers; this might not be what is really needed
This approach creates considerable system documentation	Documentation is expensive and time consuming to create. It is also difficult to keep current
Formal documentation ensures that system requirements can be traced back to stated business needs	Often, user needs go unstated or are misunderstood
It produces many intermediate products that can be reviewed to see whether they meet the users' needs and conform to standards	Users cannot easily review intermediate products and evaluate whether a particular product (e.g., data flow diagram) meets their business requirements

11

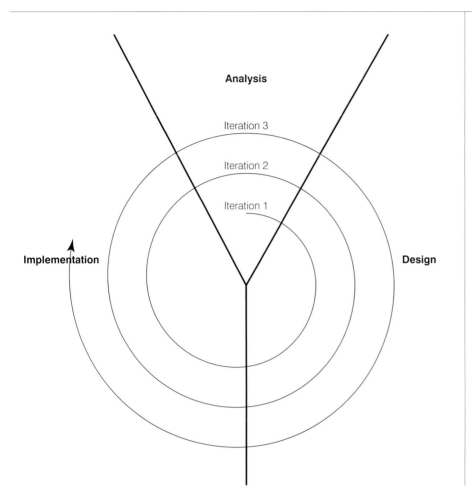

Figure 11.5 Prototyping
Prototyping is an iterative approach to systems development.

advantages and disadvantages of prototyping are summarized in Table 11.3. Prototypes can be useful communication tools – imagine asking a user what they need the new system to do. Many people may find it difficult to verbalize what they want. However, if you show them a prototype, they will soon be able to say what is right and wrong with it.

Table 11.3 Advantages and Disadvantages of Prototyping

Advantages	Disadvantages
Users can try the system and provide constructive feedback during development	Each iteration builds on the previous one. The final solution might be only incrementally better than the initial solution
An operational prototype can be produced in weeks	Formal end-of-phase reviews might not occur. Thus, it is very difficult to contain the scope of the prototype, and the project never seems to end
As solutions emerge, users become more positive about the process and the results	System documentation is often absent or incomplete because the primary focus is on development of the prototype
Prototyping enables early detection of errors and omissions	System backup and recovery, performance, and security issues can be overlooked in the haste to develop a prototype

11

Information Systems @ Work

Australia's Maroochy Shire Council Gains Control Over Information Overload

Maroochy Shire is a region located in Australia's sunshine coast and governed locally by the Maroochy Shire Council. Maroochy Shire is a favourite tourist destination as well as an increasingly popular place to live. With Australians flocking to the Maroochy Shire in pursuit of the beach lifestyle, the past six years has brought unprecedented growth to the region and extraordinarily turbulent times for the Maroochy Shire Council. Over six years, the council has endured six organizational restructures. It is currently working to replace all of its core information systems to meet the information demands of its ever-expanding population. In so doing, it is also working to transform itself from a traditional local government organization to one that is far more focused on customers and results.

The council hopes that new management information systems will help them dig out from under an overload of information. 'We've got information all over the place: There are personal filing systems in hard copy, we have official records file systems, we have e-mails, we have intranet, we have network drives, so there's information all over the place and it's hard to get the complete picture of a particular issue. In a single year between 2003 and 2004, the number of records created rose by 45 percent,' explained Wayne Bunker, the council's business process architect. During the same period, the number of e-mails handled grew by 23 percent, the number of files created grew by 32 percent, and the number of electronic documents and images grew by 26 percent.

Wayne Bunker envisioned a new system that would provide two important benefits: electronic document management – the ability to track documents as they entered and moved through the organization – and the capacity to support solid business processes. 'We needed to have workflow that could move the information around the organization and encapsulate and code

processes, including major exceptions, but we also wanted real-time reporting,' Bunker says.

The council started analyzing all its existing processes, classifying the information sources for those processes, documenting employee roles and security, and designing and modelling new processes for the entire organization. After two years of systems development and piloting, Maroochy recently went live with its first implementation designed for its licensing and compliance area. Bunker says the pilot achieved 'terrific benefits', including doubling the number of documents and records captured.

Even with the evident benefits, stakeholders were somewhat reluctant to buy into the new system. Many in the business conceived of technology as a silver bullet that would solve all their problems. Helping them understand that their activities comprised processes that then flowed through to other parts of the business made a major difference. 'When they understand that we are all part of the one corporate process, then we start to get some change in behaviour and some buying, some understanding,' explained Bunker.

'The other point is that the whole business case for doing this was to increase our productivity so that we can manage our growth into the future without having to necessarily put on too many additional bodies. That's why, when they came and said: "You want to get rid of our jobs", we said: "No, we want to be able to do more with less."'

The council is anticipating significant gains from the new systems, particularly in time saved searching the organization for information. Previous studies indicated that on average, people were spending two hours a week searching for information but not always coming up with the result that they wanted. The new system allows the council to accomplish more in its day-to-day business with less effort. As Maroochy Shire's population grows, the council's staff can remain at the same size and accomplish more in less time, with less frustration.

Questions

1 The pilot system was a success. What developmet approach would you suggest Maroochy Shire now use to continue the project. Explain your answer.

2 Explain some of the ways in which 'electronic document management' might help Maroochy Shire.

3 How is the degree of change caused by the new system's pilot being handled by Maroochy

Shire employees and managed by the business process architect Wayne Bunker?

4 Suggest and critically evaluate some performance objectives for Maroochy Shire's new system.

SOURCES: Bushell, Sue, 'Processes Undergo a Sea Change', *CIO Australia*, March 2, 2006, www.cio.com.au; Maroochy Shire Council (website), www.maroochy.qld.gov.au.

11.2.3 Rapid Application Development, Agile Development, Joint Application Development, and Other Systems Development Approaches

Rapid application development (RAD) employs tools, techniques, and methodologies designed to speed up application development. Some people consider it to be the same as prototyping. Vendors, such as Computer Associates International, IBM, and Oracle, market products targeting the RAD market. Rational Software, a division of IBM, has a RAD tool, called Rational Rapid Developer, to make developing large Java programs and applications easier and faster. Locus Systems, a program developer, used a RAD tool called OptimalJ to generate more than 60 percent of the computer code for three applications it developed. Advantage Gen is a RAD tool from Computer Associates International. It can be used to rapidly generate computer code from business models and specifications.

> **rapid application development (RAD)** A systems development approach that employs tools, techniques, and methodologies designed to speed application development.

RAD reduces paper-based documentation, automatically generates program source code, and facilitates user participation in design and development activities. It makes adapting to changing system requirements easier.

Other approaches to rapid development, such as agile development, allow the systems to change as they are being developed. Agile development requires frequent face-to-face meetings with the systems developers and users as they modify, refine, and test how the system meets users' needs and what its capabilities are. Extreme programming (XP), a form of agile development, uses pairs of programmers who work together to design, test, and code parts of the systems they develop. The iterative nature of XP helps companies develop robust systems, with fewer errors.

RAD makes extensive use of the joint application development (JAD) process for data collection and requirements analysis. Originally developed by IBM Canada in the 1970s, JAD involves group meetings in which users, stakeholders, and IS professionals work together to analyze existing systems, propose possible solutions, and define the requirements of a new or modified system. JAD groups consist of both problem holders and solution providers. A group normally requires one or more top-level executives who initiate the JAD process, a group leader for the meetings, potential users, and one or more individuals who act as secretaries and clerks to record what is accomplished and to provide general support for the sessions. Many companies have found that groups can develop better requirements than individuals working independently and have assessed JAD as a very successful development technique. Today, JAD often uses group support systems (GSS) software to foster positive group interactions, while suppressing negative group behaviour.

RAD should not be used on every software development project. In general, it is best suited for DSS and MIS and less well suited for TPS. During a RAD project, the level of participation of stakeholders and users is much higher than in other approaches. Table 11.4 lists advantages and disadvantages of RAD.

11.2.4 The End-User Systems Development Lifecycle

The term end-user systems development describes any systems development project in which business managers and users assume the primary effort. Rather than ignoring these initiatives, astute IS professionals encourage them by offering guidance and support. Providing technical assistance, communicating standards, and sharing 'best practices' throughout the organization are some ways IS professionals work with motivated managers and employees undertaking their own systems development. In this way, end-user-developed systems can be structured as complementary to, rather than in conflict with, existing and emerging information systems. In addition, this open communication among IS professionals, managers of the affected business area, and users allows the IS professionals to identify specific initiatives so that additional organizational resources, beyond those available to business managers or users, are provided for its development.

User-developed systems range from the very small (such as a software routine to merge data from Microsoft Excel into Microsoft Word to produce a personalized letter for customers) to those of significant organizational value (such as a customer contact database). Initially, IS professionals discounted the value of these projects. As the number and magnitude of these projects increased, however, IS professionals began to realize that, for the good of the entire organization, their involvement with these projects needed to increase.

End-user systems development does have some disadvantages. Some end users don't have the training to effectively develop and test a system. Expensive mistakes can be made using faulty spreadsheets, for example, that have never been tested. Most end-user systems are also poorly documented and therefore difficult to maintain. When these systems are updated, problems can be introduced that make the systems error-prone. In addition, some end users spend time and corporate resources developing systems that are already available.

A survey of South African employers found that the IS skills they want in their new employees are the ability to type, create documents, and a basic working knowledge of computer applications.

Table 11.4 Advantages and Disadvantages of RAD

Advantages	Disadvantages
For appropriate projects, this approach puts an application into production sooner than any other approach	This intense SDLC can burn out systems developers and other project participants
Documentation is produced as a by-product of completing project tasks	This approach requires systems analysts and users to be skilled in RAD systems development tools and RAD techniques
RAD forces teamwork and lots of interaction between users and stakeholders	RAD requires a larger percentage of stakeholders' and users' time than other approaches

11.2.5 Outsourcing and On-Demand Computing

Many companies hire an outside consulting firm or computer company that specializes in systems development to take over some or all of its development and operations activities.[7] Some companies, such as General Electric, have their own outsourcing subunits or have spun off their outsourcing subunits as separate companies.[8] Outsourcing can be a good idea under the following circumstances:

- When a company believes it can cut costs.
- When a firm has limited opportunity to distinguish itself competitively through a particular IS operation or application.
- When uninterrupted IS service is not crucial.
- When outsourcing does not strip the company of technical know-how required for future IS innovation.
- When the firm's existing IS capabilities are limited, ineffective, or technically inferior.
- When a firm is downsizing.

The decision to outsource systems development is often a response to downsizing, which reduces the number of employees or managers, equipment and systems, and even functions and departments. Outsourcing allows companies to downsize their IS department and alleviate difficult financial situations by reducing payroll and other expenses.

Organizations can outsource any aspect of their information system, including hardware maintenance and management, software development, database systems, networks and telecommunications, Internet and intranet operations, hiring and staffing, and the development of procedures and rules regarding the information system.[9] Eurostar, for example, hired the outsourcing company Occam to develop a new website and back-end database to give its travel customers greater travel information.[10] According to Scott Logie, managing director of Occam, 'The quality and volume of data that Eurostar possesses is extremely valuable. By working together we will allow the firm to develop real insight into its customers. This can be used to drive a strong customer acquisitions strategy, which will enhance its business and customer relationships.'

Reducing costs, obtaining state-of-the-art technology, eliminating staffing and personnel problems, and increasing technological flexibility are reasons that companies have used the outsourcing and on-demand computing approaches.[11] A number of companies offer outsourcing and on-demand computing services – from general systems development to specialized services. IBM's Global Services, for example, is one of the largest full-service outsourcing and consulting services.[12] IBM has consultants located in offices around the world. Electronic Data Systems (EDS) is another large company that specialises in consulting and outsourcing.[13] EDS has approximately 140 000 employees in almost 60 countries and more than 9000 clients worldwide. Accenture is another company that specializes in consulting and outsourcing.[14] The company has more than 75 000 employees in 47 countries.

Organizations can use a number of guidelines to make outsourcing a success, including the following:[15]

- Keep tight controls on the outsourcing project.
- Treat outsourcing companies as partners.
- Start with smaller outsourcing jobs.
- Create effective communications channels between the organization and the outsourcing company.
- Carefully review legal outsourcing contracts, including rights and remedies clauses.[16]

Old Mutual South Africa have outsourced their IS infrastructure to CSC, who are a global company and have a data centre in Cape Town, to control their costs and access CSC's expertise.

Outsourcing has some disadvantages, however. Internal expertise can be lost and loyalty can suffer under an outsourcing arrangement. When a company outsources, key IS personnel with expertise in technical and business functions are no longer needed. When these IS employees leave, their experience with the organization and expertise in information systems is lost. For some companies, it can be difficult to achieve a competitive advantage when competitors are using the same computer or consulting company. When the outsourcing or on-demand computing is done offshore or in a foreign country, some people have raised security concerns. How will important data and trade secrets be guarded?

11.3 Factors Affecting System Development Success

Successful systems development means delivering a system that meets user and organizational needs – on time and within budget. There is no formula for achieving this, but the following factors are known to have an impact on success.

11.3.1 Involvement

Getting users and other stakeholders involved in systems development is critical for most systems development projects. Having the support of top-level managers is also important. The involvement of users throughout the development will mean they are less likely to resist the software when it is delivered. Historically, communication between people on the domain side (users, managers, and other stakeholders) and on the systems side (systems analysts, programmers, and other technical people) has been problematic, with there being little common ground between them. Each group has its own set of terminology and its own culture. Getting users and managers involved in systems development is one way of building bridges between the two and kick-starting dialogue. This may be done simply by inviting them to development meetings, organizing social gatherings, producing a questionnaire to survey user views, running interviews, etc., or by using joint application development (see page 399). If users have been involved throughout development they will be less likely to resist the changes the new system brings when it is implemented.

11.3.2 Degree of Change

A major factor that affects the quality of systems development is the degree of change associated with the project. The scope can vary from implementing minor enhancements to an existing system, up to major reengineering. The project team needs to recognize where they are on this spectrum of change.

As discussed in Chapter 2, continuous improvement projects do not require significant business process or IS changes, or retraining of people; thus, they have a high degree of success. Typically, because continuous improvement involves minor improvements, these projects also have relatively modest benefits. On the other hand, reengineering involves fundamental changes in how the organization conducts business and completes tasks. The factors associated with successful reengineering are similar to those of any development effort, including top management support, clearly defined corporate goals and systems development objectives, and careful management of change. Major reengineering projects tend to have a high degree of risk but also a high potential for major business benefits (see Figure 11.6).

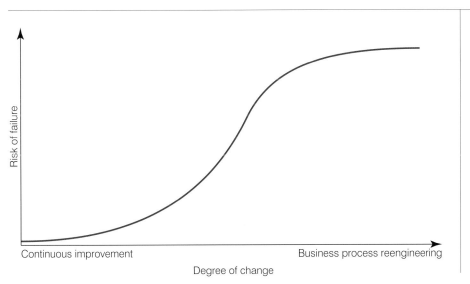

Figure 11.6 Degree of Change *The degree of change can greatly affect the probability of a project's success.*

11.3.3 Managing Change

The ability to manage change is critical to the success of systems development. New systems inevitably cause change. For example, the work environment and habits of users are invariably affected by the development of a new information system. Unfortunately, not everyone adapts easily, and the increasing complexity of systems can multiply the problems. Managing change requires the ability to recognize existing or potential problems (particularly the concerns of users) and deal with them before they become a serious threat to the success of the new or modified system. Here are several of the most common problems:

- Fear that the employee will lose his or her job, power, or influence within the organization.
- Belief that the proposed system will create more work than it eliminates.
- Reluctance to work with 'computer people'.
- Anxiety that the proposed system will negatively alter the structure of the organization.
- Belief that other problems are more pressing than those solved by the proposed system or that the system is being developed by people unfamiliar with 'the way things need to get done'.
- Unwillingness to learn new procedures or approaches.

Preventing or dealing with these types of problems requires a coordinated effort from stakeholders and users, managers, and IS personnel. One remedy is simply to talk with all people concerned and learn what their biggest concerns are. Management can then deal with those concerns and try to eliminate them. After immediate concerns are addressed, people can become part of the project team.

11.3.4 Quality and Standards

Another key success factor is the quality of project planning. The bigger the project, the more likely that poor planning will lead to significant problems. Many companies find that large systems projects fall behind schedule, go over budget, and do not meet expectations. A systems development project for the U.K. Child Support Agency, for example, fell behind schedule and over £250 million over budget.[17] When it was delivered, two years late, there were interference problems – screens took too long to refresh and there was no delete key to undo accidental typing

11

mistakes, staff training was also ineffective and inappropriate. The delayed project may have hurt the agency's ability to deliver important services to children. Although proper planning cannot guarantee that these types of problems will be avoided, it can minimize the likelihood of their occurrence. Good systems development is not automatic. Certain factors contribute to the failure of systems development projects. These factors and countermeasures to eliminate or alleviate the problem are summarized in Table 11.5.

The development of information systems requires a constant trade-off of schedule and cost versus quality. Historically, the development of application software has overemphasized schedule and cost to the detriment of quality. Techniques, such as use of the ISO 9001 standards, have been developed to improve the quality of information systems. ISO 9001 is a set of international quality standards originally developed in Europe in 1987. These standards address customer satisfaction and are the only standards in the ISO 9000 family where third-party certification can be achieved. Adherence to ISO 9001 is a requirement in many international markets[18] (see Figure 11.7).

Organizational experience with the systems development process is also a key factor for systems development success.[19] The capability maturity model (CMM) is one way to measure this experience.[20] It is based on research done at Carnegie Mellon University and work by the Software Engineering Institute (SEI).[21] CMM is a measure of the maturity of the software development process in an organization. CMM grades an organization's systems development maturity using five levels: initial, repeatable, defined, managed, and optimized.

Table 11.5 Project Planning Issues Frequently Contributing to Project Failure

Factor	Countermeasure
Solving the wrong problem	Establish a clear connection between the project and organizational goals
Poor problem definition and analysis	Follow a standard systems development approach
Poor communication	There is no easy answer to this common problem
Project is too ambitious	Narrow the project focus to address only the most important business opportunities
Lack of top management support	Identify the senior manager who has the most to gain from the success of the project, and recruit this person to champion the project
Lack of management and user involvement	Identify and recruit key stakeholders to be active participants in the project
Inadequate or improper system design	Follow a standard systems development approach
Lack of standards	Implement a standards system, such as ISO 9001
Poor testing and implementation	Plan sufficient time for this activity
Users cannot use the system effectively	Develop a rigorous user-training program and budget sufficient time in the schedule to execute it
Lack of concern for maintenance	Include an estimate of employee effort and costs for maintenance in the original project justification

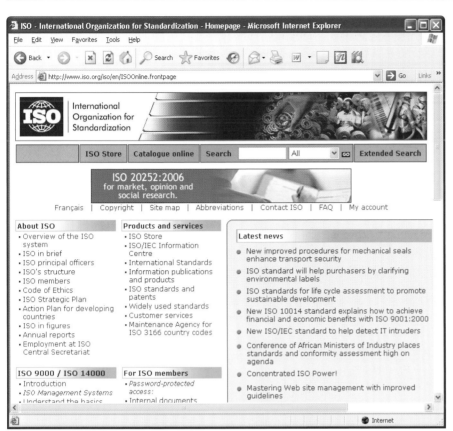

Figure 11.7 ISO Home **Page** *ISO 9000 is a set of international quality standards used by IS and other organizations to ensure the quality of products and services.*

SOURCE: www.iso.org.

11.3.5 Use of Project Management Tools

Project management involves planning, scheduling, directing, and controlling human, financial, and technological resources for a defined task whose result is achievement of specific goals and objectives. Even small systems development projects must employ some type of project management.[22]

A project schedule is a detailed description of what is to be done. Each project activity, the use of personnel and other resources, and expected completion dates are described. A project milestone is a critical date for the completion of a major part of the project. The completion of program design, coding, testing, and release are examples of milestones for a programming project. The project deadline is the date the entire project is to be completed and operational – when the organization can expect to begin to reap the benefits of the project.

In systems development, each activity has an earliest start time, earliest finish time, and slack time, which is the amount of time an activity can be delayed without delaying the entire project. The critical path consists of all activities that, if delayed, would delay the entire project. These activities have zero slack time. Any problems with critical-path activities will cause problems for the entire project. To ensure that critical-path activities are completed in a timely fashion, formalized project management approaches have been developed. Tools such as Microsoft Project are available to help compute these critical project attributes.

Although the steps of systems development seem straightforward, larger projects can become complex, requiring hundreds or thousands of separate activities. For these systems development efforts, formal project management methods and tools become essential. A formalized approach

program evaluation and review technique (PERT) A formalized approach for developing a project schedule.

Gantt chart A graphical tool used for planning, monitoring, and coordinating projects.

called the **program evaluation and review technique (PERT)** creates three time estimates for an activity: shortest possible time, most likely time, and longest possible time. A formula is then applied to determine a single PERT time estimate. A **Gantt chart** is a graphical tool used for planning, monitoring, and coordinating projects; it is essentially a grid that lists activities and deadlines. Each time a task is completed, a marker such as a darkened line is placed in the proper grid cell to indicate the completion of a task (see Figure 11.8).

Figure 11.8 Sample Gantt Chart *A Gantt chart shows progress through systems development activities by putting a bar through appropriate cells.*

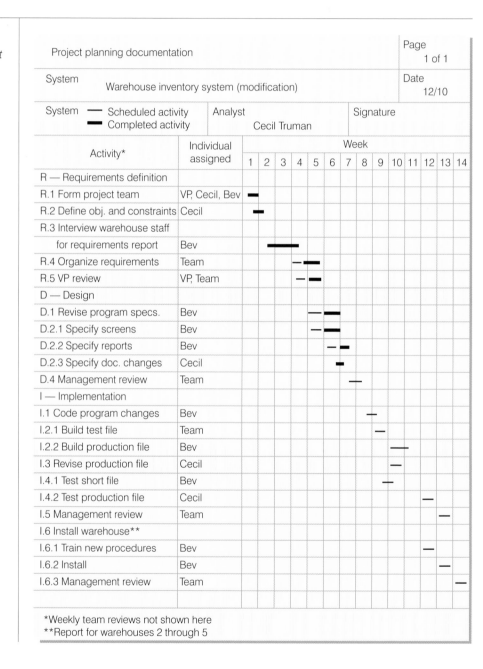

Project planning documentation		Page 1 of 1

System	Warehouse inventory system (modification)	Date 12/10

System	— Scheduled activity	Analyst		Signature	
	▬ Completed activity		Cecil Truman		

Activity*	Individual assigned	Week													
		1	2	3	4	5	6	7	8	9	10	11	12	13	14
R — Requirements definition															
R.1 Form project team	VP, Cecil, Bev	▬													
R.2 Define obj. and constraints	Cecil	▬													
R.3 Interview warehouse staff															
for requirements report	Bev			▬▬											
R.4 Organize requirements	Team				—▬										
R.5 VP review	VP, Team				—▬										
D — Design															
D.1 Revise program specs.	Bev						—▬								
D.2.1 Specify screens	Bev						—▬								
D.2.2 Specify reports	Bev						—▬								
D.2.3 Specify doc. changes	Cecil						▬								
D.4 Management review	Team							—							
I — Implementation															
I.1 Code program changes	Bev								—						
I.2.1 Build test file	Team								—						
I.2.2 Build production file	Bev									—					
I.3 Revise production file	Cecil								—						
I.4.1 Test short file	Bev								—						
I.4.2 Test production file	Cecil										—				
I.5 Management review	Team											—			
I.6 Install warehouse**															
I.6.1 Train new procedures	Bev											—			
I.6.2 Install	Bev												—		
I.6.3 Management review	Team													—	

*Weekly team reviews not shown here
**Report for warehouses 2 through 5

Both PERT and Gantt techniques can be automated using project management software. Several project management software packages are identified in Table 11.6. This software monitors all project activities and determines whether activities and the entire project are on time and within budget. Project management software also has workgroup capabilities to handle multiple projects and to allow a team to interact with the same software. Project management software helps managers determine the best way to reduce project completion time at the least cost. Many project managers, however, fear that the quality of a systems development project will suffer with shortened deadlines and think that slack time should be added back to the schedule as a result.

11.3.6 Use of Computer-Aided Software Engineering (CASE) Tools

Computer-aided software engineering (CASE) tools automate many of the tasks required in a systems development effort and encourage adherence to the SDLC, thus instilling a high degree of rigor and standardization to the entire systems development process. VRCASE, for example, is a CASE tool that a team of developers can use when developing applications in C++ and other languages. Prover Technology has developed a CASE tool that searches for programming bugs. The CASE tool searches for all possible design scenarios to make sure that the program is error free. Other CASE tools include Visible Systems (www .visible.com) and Popkin Software (www.popkin.com). Popkin Software, for example, can generate code in programming languages such as C++, Java, and Visual Basic. Other CASE-related tools include Rational Rose from IBM; and Visio, a charting and graphics program from Microsoft. Other companies that produce CASE tools include Accenture and Oracle. Oracle Designer and Developer CASE tools, for example, can help systems analysts automate and simplify the development process for database systems. See Table 11.7 for a list of CASE tools and

computer-aided software engineering (CASE) Tools that automate many of the tasks required in a systems development effort and encourage adherence to the SDLC.

Table 11.6 Selected Project Management Software Packages

Software	Vendor
AboutTime	NetSQL Partners
Job Order	Management Software
OpenPlan	Welcom
Microsoft Project	Microsoft
Project Scheduler	Scitor
Super Project	Computer Associates

Table 11.7 Typical CASE Tools

CASE Tool	Vendor
Oracle Designer	Oracle Corporation www.oracle.com
Visible Analyst	Visible Systems Corporation www.visible.com
Rational Rose	Rational Software www.ibm.com
Embarcadero Describe	Embarcadero Describe www.embarcadero.com

their providers. The advantages and disadvantages of CASE tools are listed in Table 11.8. CASE tools that focus on activities associated with the early stages of systems development are often called 'upper-CASE tools'. These packages provide automated tools to assist with systems investigation, analysis, and design activities. Other CASE packages, called 'lower-CASE tools', focus on the later implementation stage of systems development, and can automatically generate structured program code.

11.4 Systems Investigation

As discussed earlier in the chapter, systems investigation is the first phase in the traditional SDLC of a new or modified business information system. The purpose is to identify potential problems and opportunities and consider them in light of the goals of the company. In general, systems investigation attempts to uncover answers to the following questions:

- What primary problems is the new system to solve?
- What opportunities might a new or enhanced system provide?
- What new hardware, software, databases, telecommunications, personnel, or procedures will improve an existing system or are required in a new system?
- What are the potential costs (variable and fixed)?
- What are the associated risks?

11.4.1 Initiating Systems Investigation

Because systems development requests can require considerable time and effort to implement, many organizations have adopted a formal procedure for initiating systems development, beginning with systems investigation. The systems request form is a document that is filled out by someone who wants the IS department to initiate systems investigation. This form typically includes the following information:

- Problems in or opportunities for the system.
- Objectives of systems investigation.
- Overview of the proposed system.
- Expected costs and benefits of the proposed system.

The information in the systems request form helps to rationalize and prioritize the activities of the IS department. Based on the overall IS plan, the organization's needs and goals, and the estimated

Table 11.8 Advantages and Disadvantages of CASE Tools

Advantages	Disadvantages
Produce systems with a longer effective operational life	Increase the initial costs of building and maintaining systems
Produce systems that more closely meet user needs and requirements	Require more extensive and accurate definition of user needs and requirements
Produce systems with excellent documentation	Can be difficult to customize
Produce systems that need less systems support	Require more training of maintenance staff
Produce more flexible systems	Can be difficult to use with existing systems

value and priority of the proposed projects, managers make decisions regarding the initiation of each systems investigation for such projects.

11.4.2 Participants in Systems Investigation

After a decision has been made to initiate systems investigation, the first step is to determine what members of the development team should participate in the investigation phase of the project. Members of the development team change from phase to phase (see Figure 11.9).

The investigation team

Managers, users, and stakeholders ⟷ IS personnel

- Undertakes feasibility analysis
- Establishes systems development goals
- Selects systems development methodology
- Prepares systems investigation report

Figure 11.9 The Systems Investigation Team *The team consists of upper- and middle-level managers, a project manager, IS personnel, users, and stakeholders.*

Ideally, functional managers are heavily involved during the investigation phase. Other members could include users or stakeholders outside management, such as an employee who helps initiate systems development. The technical and financial expertise of others participating in investigation help the team determine whether the problem is worth solving. The members of the development team who participate in investigation are then responsible for gathering and analyzing data, preparing a report justifying systems development, and presenting the results to top-level managers.

11.4.3 Feasibility Analysis

A key step of the systems investigation phase is **feasibility analysis**, which assesses technical, economic, legal, operational, and schedule feasibility. **Technical feasibility** is concerned with whether the hardware, software, and other system components can be acquired or developed to solve the problem.

Economic feasibility determines whether the project makes financial sense and whether predicted benefits offset the cost and time needed to obtain them. One securities company, for example, investigated the economic feasibility of sending research reports electronically instead of through the mail. Economic analysis revealed that the new approach could save the company up to €370 000 per year. Economic feasibility can involve cash flow analysis such as that done in net present value or internal rate of return (IRR) calculations.

Net present value is an often-used approach for ranking competing projects and for determining economic feasibility. The net present value represents the net amount by which project savings exceed project expenses, after allowing for the cost of capital and the passage of time. The cost of capital is the average cost of funds used to finance the operations of the business. Net present value takes into account that a euro returned at a later date is not worth as much as one received today because the euro in hand can be invested to earn profits or interest in the interim. Spreadsheet programs, such as Lotus and Microsoft Excel, have built-in functions to compute the net present value and internal rate of return.

feasibility analysis Assessment of the technical, economic, legal, operational, and schedule feasibility of a project.

technical feasibility Assessment of whether the hardware, software, and other system components can be acquired or developed to solve the problem.

economic feasibility The determination of whether the project makes financial sense and whether predicted benefits offset the cost and time needed to obtain them.

net present value The preferred approach for ranking competing projects and determining economic feasibility.

11

legal feasibility The determination of whether laws or regulations may prevent or limit a systems development project.

operational feasibility The measure of whether the project can be put into action or operation.

Legal feasibility determines whether laws or regulations can prevent or limit a systems development project. For example, some music sharing websites have been into trouble for infringement of copyright. If legal feasibility had been conducted, it would have identified this vulnerability during the website development phase. Legal feasibility involves an analysis of existing and future laws to determine the likelihood of legal action against the systems development project and the possible consequences.

Operational feasibility is a measure of whether the project can be put into action or operation. It can include logistical and motivational (acceptance of change) considerations. Motivational considerations are important because new systems affect people and data flows and can have unintended consequences. As a result, power and politics might come into play, and some people might resist the new system. On the other hand, recall that a new system can help avoid major problems. For example, because of deadly hospital errors, a healthcare consortium looks into the operational feasibility of developing a new computerized physician order-entry system to require that all prescriptions and every order a doctor gives to staff are entered into the computer. The computer then checks for drug allergies and interactions between drugs. If operationally feasible, the new system could save lives and help avoid lawsuits.

schedule feasibility The determination of whether the project can be completed in a reasonable amount of time.

Schedule feasibility determines whether the project can be completed in a reasonable amount of time – a process that involves balancing the time and resource requirements of the project with other projects.

11.4.4 The Systems Investigation Report

systems investigation report A summary of the results of the systems investigation and the process of feasibility analysis and recommendation of a course of action.

The primary outcome of systems investigation is a **systems investigation report**, also called a feasibility study. This report summarizes the results of systems investigation and the process of feasibility analysis and recommends a course of action: continue on into systems analysis, modify the project in some manner, or drop it. A typical table of contents for the systems investigation report is shown in Figure 11.10.

Figure 11.10 A Typical Table of Contents for a Systems Investigation Report

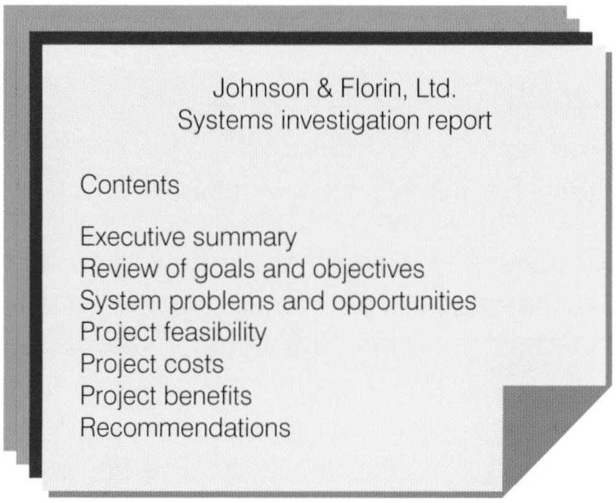

Johnson & Florin, Ltd.
Systems investigation report

Contents

Executive summary
Review of goals and objectives
System problems and opportunities
Project feasibility
Project costs
Project benefits
Recommendations

steering committee An advisory group consisting of senior management and users from the IS department and other functional areas.

The systems investigation report is reviewed by senior management, often organized as an advisory committee, or **steering committee**, consisting of senior management and users from the IS department and other functional areas. These people help IS personnel with their decisions about the use of information systems in the business and give authorization to pursue further

Ethical and Societal Issues

Identity Cards in the U.K.

The U.K. government is currently at the start of the process which will eventually see all its citizens carry identity cards. The scheme is intended to fight identity theft and other fraud, and help combat international terrorism. The design for the card itself is not yet finalized, but it is to carry biometric data about its owner such as fingerprints and an iris scan. Companies have already started bidding to provide the technology to create the cards. However, the cards themselves are only half the story. They will be linked to what is known as the National Identity Register, a huge database that will contain information on all U.K. residents. This information will include name, address, date, and place of birth, driving licence number, passport number and a head photograph. The scheme is expected to cost over £5 billion and it has not yet been decided who will pay this, with one suggestion being that citizens themselves will have to pay for their own card. Computer specialists are nervous at the size of the project, with some claiming that due to its size, the database is fraught with implementation pitfalls.

Despite its cost, the benefits of the system are unclear. One politician has said that '[a] piece of plastic will not stop a suicide bomber and illegal workers have documentation. It would be better spending money on the police rather than on a piece of plastic.'

The act that governs the introduction of identity cards, the Identity Cards Act 2006, allows for the addition of information into the National Identity Register. This means that in the future, the database

may be extended to store information on employment history. In addition, the databases from other government departments could be merged to build up an intimate picture of someone's life. This has led to fears of 'feature creep', where the original purpose of the cards, is not what they end up being used for. The strongest argument against ID cards is perhaps that they will alter the relationship between citizens and their government. The director of the civil rights group Liberty, has said that '[p]rivacy is a societal not an individual right. It is the police that should produce warrant cards not citizens that should be forced to carry ID cards.'

Questions

1   How might identifty cards fight identify theft? How do you think the identity thieves will respond?

2   Why is the development of the database fraught with pitfalls?

3   Why are some people nervous about being required to carry an identity card? Would you be happy to carry one? Explain your answer.

4   How would the merging government databases build up an intimate picture of someone's life? Describe what your 'picture' would look like.

SOURCES: Office of Public Sector Information (website), Identity Cards Act 2006, c.15, http://www.opsi.gov.uk/ACTS/acts2006/60015–b.htm#sch1; Wakefield, Jane, 'Opponents Take On ID Card Plans', BBC News (website), http://news.bbc.co.uk/1/hi/technology/3731465.stm; Arnott, S., 'The Brown Era Begins as Challenges for IT Increase', *Computing,* June 28, 2007.

---

systems development activities. After review, the steering committee might agree with the recommendation of the systems development team or suggest a change in project focus to concentrate more directly on meeting a specific company objective. Another alternative is that everyone might decide that the project is not feasible and cancel the project.

11

11.5 Systems Analysis

After a project has been approved for further study, the next step is to answer the question 'what must the information system do to solve the problem?'. The process needs to go beyond mere computerisation of existing systems. The entire system, and the business process with which it is associated, should be evaluated. Often, a firm can make great gains if it restructures both business activities and the related information system simultaneously. The overall emphasis of analysis is gathering data on the existing system, determining the requirements for the new system, considering alternatives within these constraints, and investigating the feasibility of the solutions. The primary outcome of systems analysis is a prioritized list of systems requirements.

11.5.1 General Considerations

Systems analysis starts by clarifying the overall goals of the organization and determining how the existing or proposed information system helps meet them. A manufacturing company, for example, might want to reduce the number of equipment breakdowns. This goal can be translated into one or more informational needs. One need might be to create and maintain an accurate list of each piece of equipment and a schedule for preventative maintenance. Another need might be a list of equipment failures and their causes.

Analysis of a small company's information system can be fairly straightforward. On the other hand, evaluating an existing information system for a large company can be a long, tedious process. As a result, large organizations evaluating a major information system normally follow a formalized analysis procedure, involving these steps:

1　Assembling the participants for systems analysis.

2　Collecting appropriate data and requirements.

3　Analyzing the data and requirements.

4　Preparing a report on the existing system, new system requirements, and project priorities.

11.5.2 Participants in Systems Analysis

The first step in formal analysis is to assemble a team to study the existing system. This group includes members of the original investigation team – from users and stakeholders to IS personnel and management. Most organizations usually allow key members of the development team not only to analyze the condition of the existing system but also to perform other aspects of systems development, such as design and implementation.

After the participants in systems analysis are assembled, this group develops a list of specific objectives and activities. A schedule for meeting the objectives and completing the specific activities is also devised, along with deadlines for each stage and a statement of the resources required at each stage, such as administrative personnel, supplies, and so forth. Major milestones are normally established to help the team monitor progress and determine whether problems or delays occur in performing systems analysis.

11.5.3 Data Collection and Analysis

direct observation Watching the existing system in action by one or more members of the analysis team.

questionnaires A method of gathering data when the data sources are spread over a wide geographic area.

The purpose of data collection is to seek additional information about the problems or needs identified in the systems investigation report. During this process, the strengths and weaknesses of the existing system are emphasized.

Data collection begins by identifying and locating the various sources of data, including both internal and external sources (see Figure 11.11).

After data sources have been identified, data collection begins. Figure 11.12 shows the steps involved. Data collection might require a number of tools and techniques, such as interviews, **direct observation**, and **questionnaires**.

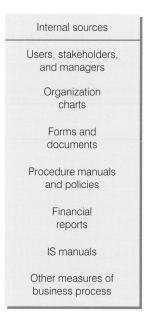

Figure 11.11 Internal and External Sources of Data for Systems Analysis

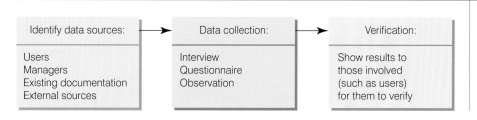

Figure 11.12 The Steps in Data Collection

Interviews can either be structured or unstructured. In a **structured interview**, the questions are written in advance. In an **unstructured interview**, the questions are not written in advance; the interviewer relies on experience in asking the best questions to uncover the inherent problems of the existing system. An advantage of the unstructured interview is that it allows the interviewer to ask follow-up or clarifying questions immediately.

structured interview An interview where the questions are prepared in advance.

unstructured interview An interview where the questions are not prepared in advance.

With direct observation, one or more members of the analysis team directly observe the existing system in action. One of the best ways to understand how the existing system functions is to work with the users to discover how data flows in certain business tasks. Determining the data flow entails direct observation of users' work procedures, their reports, current screens (if automated already), and so on. From this observation, members of the analysis team determine which forms and procedures are adequate and which are inadequate and need improvement. Direct observation requires a certain amount of skill. The observer must be able to see what is really happening and not be influenced by attitudes or feelings. In addition, many people don't like being observed and may change their behaviour when they are. However, observation can reveal important problems and opportunities that would be difficult to obtain using other data collection methods.

When many data sources are spread over a wide geographic area, questionnaires sent to all stakeholders might be the best method. Like interviews, questionnaires can be either structured or unstructured. In most cases, a pilot study is conducted to fine-tune the questionnaire. A follow-up questionnaire can also capture the opinions of those who do not respond to the original questionnaire. Questionnaires can be used to collect data from a large number of users, and make them feel part of systems development. As stated earlier, this feeling of involvement will make users less likely to resist the new system when it is installed.

11

Other data collection techniques can also be employed. In some cases, telephone calls are an excellent method. Activities can also be simulated to see how the existing system reacts. Thus, fake sales orders, stock shortages, customer complaints, and data-flow bottlenecks can be recreated to see how the existing system responds to these situations. **Statistical sampling**, which involves taking a random sample of data, is another technique. For example, suppose that you want to collect data that describes 10 000 sales orders received over the last few years. Because it is too time consuming to analyze each of the 10 000 sales orders, you could collect a random sample of around 200 sales orders from the entire batch. You can assume that the characteristics of this sample apply to all 10 000 orders.

statistical sampling Selecting a random sample of data and applying the characteristics of the sample to the whole group.

Data Analysis

The data collected in its raw form is usually not adequate to determine the effectiveness of the existing system or the requirements for the new system. The next step is to manipulate the collected data so that the development team members who are participating in systems analysis can use the data. This manipulation is called **data analysis**. Data and activity modelling and using data-flow diagrams and entity-relationship diagrams are useful during data analysis to show data flows and the relationships among various objects, associations, and activities. Other common tools and techniques for data analysis include application flowcharts, grid charts, CASE tools, and the object-oriented approach. Often two versions of the models are created – a version showing how things happen currently in the organization, and another showing how they will happen after the new system has been installed.

data analysis The manipulation of collected data so that the development team members who are participating in systems analysis can use the data.

Data Modelling

Data modelling was explained in Chapter 5, along with a technique you can use to create a data model. The purpose of this model is to visualize and structure the data that the organization stores. An example data model is shown in Figure 11.13a.

Activity (or Process) Modelling

To fully describe a business problem or solution, the related objects, associations, and activities must be described. Activities in this sense are events or items that are necessary to fulfil the business relationship or that can be associated with the business relationship in a meaningful way.

Activity modelling is sometimes accomplished through the use of data-flow diagrams or use case models. A **data-flow diagram (DFD)** models objects, associations, and activities by describing how data can flow between and around various objects. DFDs work on the premise that every activity involves some communication, transference, or flow that can be described as a data element. DFDs describe the activities that fulfil a business relationship or accomplish a business task, not how these activities are to be performed. That is, DFDs show the logical sequence of associations and activities, not the physical processes. A system modelled with a DFD could operate manually or could be computer based; if computer based, the system could operate with a variety of technologies.

data-flow diagram (DFD) A model of objects, associations, and activities that describes how data can flow between and around various objects.

A use case model consists of two parts – a diagram showing each process and the 'actors' who use the them. An actor is someone who gets something out of the process. Typical actors are customers and suppliers. 'Buy a product' is a typical process, or 'Reorder stock'. The second part of the model is a text description of each process broken down into numbered steps.

Comparing entity-relationship diagrams with data-flow diagrams provides insight into the concept of top-down design. Figures 11.13a and b show a data model and a data-flow diagram for the same business relationship – namely, a member of a golf club playing golf. Figure 11.13c provides a brief description of the business relationship for clarification.

11

(a)

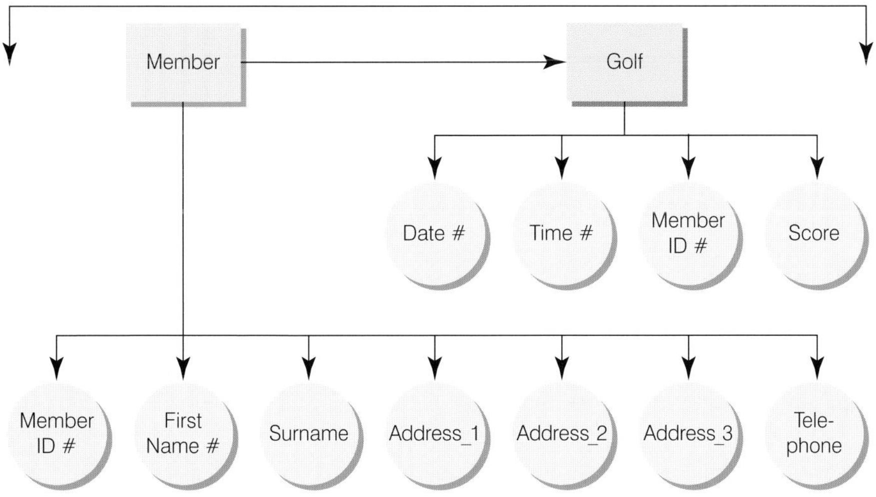

Figure 11.13 Sample Data Model, Data-Flow Diagram, and Description
This model shows a data model, data-flow diagram, and brief description of the business relationship for a member of a golf club playing golf.

(b)

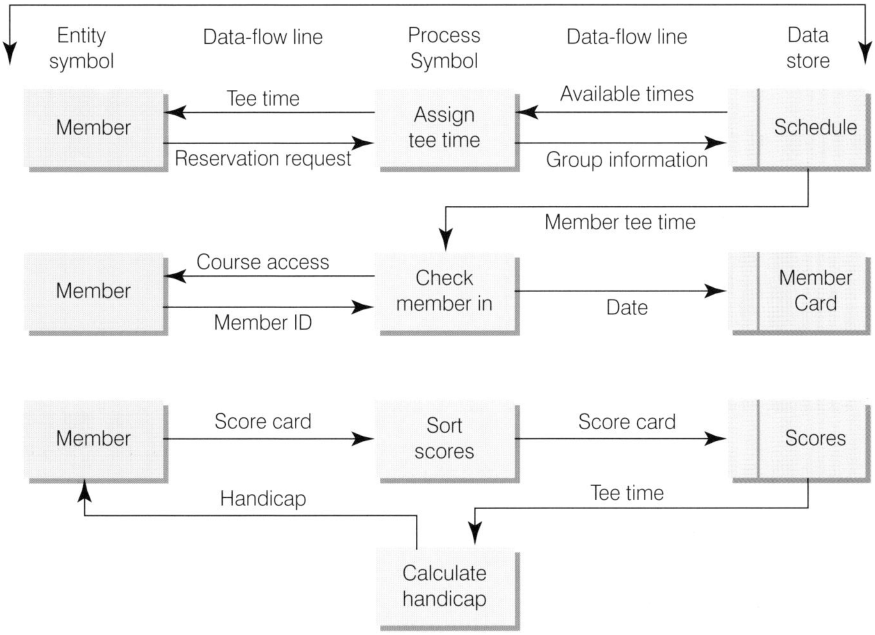

(c)

To play golf at the course, you must first pay a fee to become a member of the golf club. Members are issued member cards and are assigned member ID numbers. To reserve a tee time (a time to play golf), a member calls the club house at the golf course and arranges an available time slot with the reception clerk. The reception clerk reserves the tee time by writing the member's name and number of players in the group on the course schedule. When a member arrives at the course, he or she checks in at the reception desk where the reception clerk checks the course schedule and notes the date on the member's card. After a round of golf has been completed, the members leave their score card with the reception clerk. Member scores are tracked and member handicaps are updated on a monthly basis.

11

Figure 11.14 A Telephone Order Process Application Flowchart

The flowchart shows the relationships among various processes.

Telephone order processing

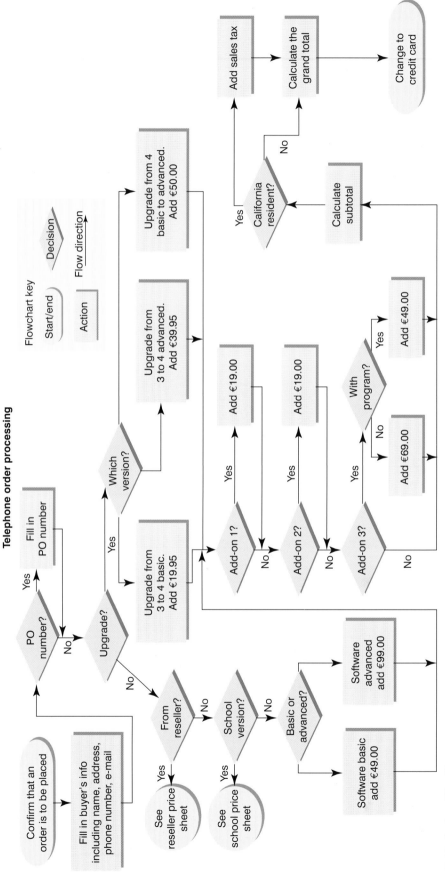

SOURCE: Courtesy of SmartDraw.com.

Application Flowcharts

Application flowcharts show the relationships among applications or systems. Let's say that a small business has collected data about its order processing, inventory control, invoicing, and marketing analysis applications. Management is thinking of modifying the inventory control application. The raw facts collected, however, do not help in determining how the applications are related to each other and the databases required for each. These relationships are established through data analysis with an application flowchart (see Figure 11.14). Using this tool for data analysis makes clear the relationships among the order processing functions.

In the simplified application flowchart in Figure 11.14, you can see that the telephone order administrator provides important data to the system about items such as versions, quantities, and prices. The system calculates sales tax and order totals. Any changes made to this order processing system could affect the company's other systems, such as inventory control and marketing.

Grid Charts

A grid chart is a table that shows relationships among various aspects of a systems development effort. For example, a grid chart can reveal the databases used by the various applications (see Figure 11.15).

Databases → Applications ↓	Customer database	Inventory database	Supplier database	Accounts receivable database
Order processing application	X	X		
Inventory control application		X	X	
Marketing analysis application	X	X		
Invoicing application	X			X

Figure 11.15 A Grid Chart *The chart shows the relationships among applications and databases.*

The simplified grid chart in Figure 11.15 shows that the customer database is used by the order processing, marketing analysis, and invoicing applications. The inventory database is used by the order processing, inventory control, and marketing analysis applications. The supplier database is used by the inventory control application, and the accounts receivable database is used by the invoicing application. This grid chart shows which applications use common databases and reveals that, for example, any changes to the inventory control application must investigate the inventory and supplier databases.

CASE Tools

As discussed earlier, many systems development projects use CASE tools to complete analysis tasks. Most computer-aided software engineering tools have generalized graphics programs that can generate a variety of diagrams and figures. Entity-relationship diagrams, data-flow diagrams, application flowcharts, and other diagrams can be developed using CASE graphics programs to help describe the existing system. During the analysis phase, a CASE repository – a database of system descriptions, parameters, and objectives – will be developed.

11.5.4 Requirements Analysis

The overall purpose of requirements analysis is to determine user, stakeholder, and organizational needs. For an accounts payable application, the stakeholders could include suppliers and members of the purchasing department. An accounts payable manager might want a better procedure for tracking the amount owed by customers. Specifically, the manager wants a weekly report that shows all customers who owe more than €1000 and are more than 90 days past due on their account. A financial manager might need a report that summarizes total amount owed by customers to consider whether to loosen or tighten credit limits. A sales manager might want to review the amount owed by a key customer relative to sales to that same customer. The purpose of requirements analysis is to capture these requests in detail. Questions that should be asked during requirements analysis include the following:

■ Are these stakeholders satisfied with the current accounts payable application?

■ What improvements could be made to satisfy suppliers and help the purchasing department?

One of the most difficult procedures in systems analysis is confirming user or systems requirements. In some cases, communications problems can interfere with determining these requirements. Numerous tools and techniques can be used to capture systems requirements. In addition to the data collection techniques already discussed (interview, questionnaire, etc.), others can be used in the context of a JAD session to determine system requirements.

11.5.5 Critical Success Factors

Managers and decision makers are asked to list only the factors that are critical to the success of their area of the organization. A critical success factor (CSF) for a production manager might be adequate raw materials from suppliers; a CSF for a sales representative could be a list of customers currently buying a certain type of product. Starting from these CSFs, the system inputs, outputs, performance, and other specific requirements can be determined.

11.5.6 The IS Plan

As we have seen, the IS plan translates strategic and organizational goals into systems development initiatives. The IS planning process often generates strategic planning documents that can be used to define system requirements. Working from these documents ensures that requirements analysis will address the goals set by top-level managers and decision makers (see Figure 11.16). There are unique benefits to applying the IS plan to define systems requirements. Because the IS plan takes a long-range approach to using information technology within the organization, the requirements for a system analyzed in terms of the IS plan are more likely to be compatible with future systems development initiatives.

Figure 11.16
Converting Organizational
Goals into Systems
Requirements

11.5.7 Screen and Report Layout

Developing formats for printed reports and screens to capture data and display information are some of the common tasks associated with developing systems. Screens and reports relating to systems output are specified first to verify that the desired solution is being delivered. Manual or computerized screen and report layout facilities are used to capture both input and output requirements.

Using a screen layout, a designer can quickly and efficiently design the features, layout, and format of a display screen. In general, users who interact with the screen frequently can be presented with more data and less descriptive information; infrequent users should have more descriptive information presented to explain the data that they are viewing (see Figure 11.17).

Report layout allows designers to diagram and format printed reports. Reports can contain data, graphs, or both. Graphic presentations allow managers and executives to quickly view trends and take appropriate action, if necessary.

Figure 11.17 Screen Layouts *(a) A screen layout chart for frequent users who require little descriptive information. (b) A screen layout chart for infrequent users who require more descriptive information.*

Screen layout diagrams can document the screens users desire for the new or modified application. Report layout charts reveal the format and content of various reports that the application will prepare. Other diagrams and charts can be developed to reveal the relationship between the application and outputs from the application.

11.5.8 Requirements Analysis Tools

A number of tools can be used to document requirements analysis, including CASE tools. As requirements are developed and agreed on, entity-relationship diagrams, data-flow diagrams, screen and report layout forms, and other types of documentation are stored in the CASE repository. These requirements might also be used later as a reference during the rest of systems development or for a different systems development project.

11.5.9 Object-Oriented Systems Analysis

An alternative to analyzing the existing system using data-flow diagrams and flowcharts is the object-oriented approach to systems analysis. Like traditional analysis, problems or potential opportunities are identified during object-oriented analysis. Identifying key participants and collecting data is still performed.

With the object-oriented approach, systems analysts are looking for classes – things within the system that have data and action – rather than entities (see Chapter 5). These classes are then modelled with the messages and data that flow between them, and this model is used to capture the requirements of the new system. An order processing administrator might be a class – they have data (the order) and action (they input the data into the computer). The term 'object' refers to an instance of a class; in this case, the class is order processing administrator, whereas 'Bill Jones', who happens to be an order processing administrator, is an object.

In object-oriented systems, analysis all the classes in the system are identified and how they work together to solve a problem is documented. A class could be a piece of software or a human.

11.5.10 The Systems Analysis Report

Systems analysis concludes with a formal systems analysis report. It should cover the following elements:

- The strengths and weaknesses of the existing system from a stakeholder's perspective.
- The user/stakeholder requirements for the new system (also called the functional requirements).
- The organizational requirements for the new system.

A description of what the new information system should do to solve the problem Suppose analysis reveals that a marketing manager thinks a weakness of the existing system is its inability to provide accurate reports on product availability. These requirements and a preliminary list of the corporate objectives for the new system will be in the systems analysis report. Particular attention is placed on areas of the existing system that could be improved to meet user requirements. The table of contents for a typical report is shown in Figure 11.18.

Figure 11.18 A Typical Table of Contents for a Report on an Existing System

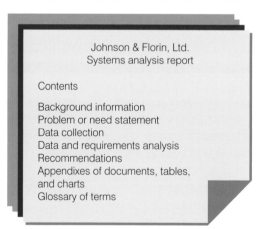

Johnson & Florin, Ltd.
Systems analysis report

Contents

Background information
Problem or need statement
Data collection
Data and requirements analysis
Recommendations
Appendixes of documents, tables, and charts
Glossary of terms

11

The systems analysis report gives managers a good understanding of the problems and strengths of the existing system. If the existing system is operating better than expected or the necessary changes are too expensive relative to the benefits of a new or modified system, the systems development process can be stopped at this stage. If the report shows that changes to another part of the system might be the best solution, the development process might start over, beginning again with systems investigation. Or, if the systems analysis report shows that it will be beneficial to develop one or more new systems or to make changes to existing ones, systems design, which is discussed in the next chapter, begins.

Summary

Effective systems development requires a team effort from stakeholders, users, managers, systems development specialists, and various support personnel, and it starts with careful planning. The systems development team consists of stakeholders: users, managers, systems development specialists, and various support personnel. The development team determines the objectives of the information system and delivers to the organization a system that meets its objectives.

A systems analyst is a professional who specializes in analyzing and designing business systems. The programmer is responsible for modifying or developing programs to satisfy user requirements. Other support personnel on the development team include technical specialists, either IS department employees or outside consultants. Depending on the magnitude of the systems development project and the number of IS development specialists on the team, the team might also include one or more IS managers. At some point in your career, you will likely be a participant in systems development. You could be involved in a systems development team – as a user, as a manager of a business area or project team, as a member of the IS department, or maybe even as a CIO.

Systems development projects are initiated for many reasons, including the need to solve problems with an existing system, to exploit opportunities to gain competitive advantage, to increase competition, to make use of effective information, to create organizational growth, to settle a merger or corporate acquisition, or to address a change in the market or external environment. External pressures, such as potential lawsuits or terrorist attacks, can also prompt an organization to initiate systems development.

Information systems planning refers to the translation of strategic and organizational goals into systems development initiatives. Benefits of IS planning include a long-range view of information technology use and better use of IS resources. Planning requires developing overall IS objectives; identifying IS projects; setting priorities and selecting projects; analyzing resource requirements; setting schedules, milestones, and deadlines; and developing the IS planning document. IS planning can result in a competitive advantage through creative and critical analysis.

Establishing objectives for systems development is a key aspect of any successful development project. Critical success factors (CSFs) can identify important objectives. Systems development objectives can include performance goals (quality and usefulness of the output and the speed at which output is generated) and cost objectives (development costs, fixed costs, and ongoing investment costs).

Systems development often uses tools to select, implement, and monitor projects, including prototyping, rapid application development, CASE tools, and object-oriented development. The five phases of the traditional SDLC are investigation, analysis, design, implementation, and maintenance and review. Systems investigation identifies potential problems and opportunities and considers them in light of organizational goals. Systems analysis seeks a general understanding of the solution required to solve the problem; the existing system is studied in detail and weaknesses are identified. Systems design creates new or modifies existing system requirements. Systems implementation encompasses programming, testing, training, conversion, and operation of the system. Systems maintenance and review entails monitoring the system and performing enhancements or repairs.

Advantages of the traditional SDLC include the following: It provides for maximum management control, creates considerable system documentation, ensures that system requirements can be traced back to stated business needs, and produces many intermediate products for review. Its disadvantages include the following: Users may get a system that meets the needs as understood by the developers, the documentation is expensive and difficult to maintain, users' needs go unstated or might not be met, and users cannot easily review the many intermediate products produced.

Prototyping is an iterative approach that involves defining the problem, building the initial version, having users work with and evaluate the initial version, providing feedback, and incorporating suggestions into the second version. Prototypes can be fully operational or non-operational, depending on how critical the system under development is and how much time

11

and money the organization has to spend on prototyping.

Rapid application development (RAD) uses tools and techniques designed to speed application development. Its use reduces paper-based documentation, automates program source code generation, and facilitates user participation in development activities. RAD can use newer programming techniques, such as agile development or extreme programming. RAD makes extensive use of the joint application development (JAD) process to gather data and perform requirements analysis. JAD involves group meetings in which users, stakeholders, and IS professionals work together to analyze existing systems, propose possible solutions, and define the requirements for a new or modified system.

The term 'end-user systems development' describes any systems development project in which the primary effort is undertaken by a combination of business managers and users.

Many companies hire an outside consulting firm that specializes in systems development to take over some or all of its systems development activities. This approach is called 'outsourcing'. Reasons for outsourcing include companies' belief that they can cut costs, achieve a competitive advantage without having the necessary IS personnel in-house, obtain state-of-the-art technology, increase their technological flexibility, and proceed with development despite downsizing. Many companies offer outsourcing services, including computer vendors and specialized consulting companies.

A number of factors affect systems development success. The degree of change introduced by the project, continuous improvement and reengineering, the use of quality programs and standards, organizational experience with systems development, the use of project management tools, and the use of CASE tools and the object-oriented approach are all factors that affect the success of a project. The greater the amount of change a system will endure, the greater the degree of risk and often the amount of reward. Continuous improvement projects do not require significant business process or IS changes, while reengineering involves fundamental changes in how the organization conducts business and completes tasks. Successful systems development projects often involve such factors as support from top management, strong user involvement, use of a proven methodology, clear project goals and objectives, concentration on key problems and straightforward designs, staying on schedule and within budget,

good user training, and solid review and maintenance programs. Quality standards, such as ISO 9001, can also be used during the systems development process.

The use of automated project management tools enables detailed development, tracking, and control of the project schedule. Effective use of a quality assurance process enables the project manager to deliver a high-quality system and to make intelligent trade-offs among cost, schedule, and quality. CASE tools automate many of the systems development tasks, thus reducing an analyst's time and effort while ensuring good documentation. Object-oriented systems development can also be an important success factor. With the object-oriented systems development (OOSD) approach, a project can be broken down into a group of objects that interact. Instead of requiring thousands or millions of lines of detailed computer instructions or code, the systems development project might require a few dozen or maybe a hundred objects.

Systems development starts with investigation and analysis of existing systems. In most organizations, a systems request form initiates the investigation process. The systems investigation is designed to assess the feasibility of implementing solutions for business problems, including technical, economic, legal, operations, and schedule feasibility. Net present value analysis is often used to help determine a project's economic feasibility. An investigation team follows up on the request and performs a feasibility analysis that addresses technical, economic, legal, operational, and schedule feasibility.

If the project under investigation is feasible, major goals are set for the system's development, including performance, cost, managerial goals, and procedural goals. Many companies choose a popular methodology so that new IS employees, outside specialists, and vendors will be familiar with the systems development tasks set forth in the approach. A systems development methodology must be selected. Object-oriented systems investigation is being used to a greater extent today.

Systems analysis is the examination of existing systems, which begins after a team receives approval for further study from management. Additional study of a selected system allows those involved to further understand the system's weaknesses and potential areas for improvement. An analysis team is assembled to collect and analyze data on the existing system.

11

Data collection methods include observation, interviews, questionnaires, and statistical sampling. Data analysis manipulates the collected data to provide information. The analysis includes grid charts, application flowcharts, and CASE tools. The overall purpose of requirements analysis is to determine user and organizational needs.

Data analysis and modelling is used to model organizational objects and associations using text and graphical diagrams. It is most often accomplished through the use of entity-relationship (ER) diagrams. Activity modelling is often accomplished through the use of data-flow diagrams (DFD), which model objects, associations, and activities by describing how data can flow between and around various objects. DFD use symbols for data flows, processing, entities, and data stores. Application flowcharts, grid charts, and CASE tools are also used during systems analysis.

Requirements analysis determines the needs of users, stakeholders, and the organization in general. Asking directly, using critical success factors, and determining requirements from the IS plan can be used. Often, screen and report layout charts are used to document requirements during systems analysis.

Like traditional analysis, problems or potential opportunities are identified during object-oriented analysis.

Self-Assessment Test

1 _____ is the activity of creating or modifying existing business systems. It refers to all aspects of the process – from identifying problems to be solved or opportunities to be exploited to the implementation and refinement of the chosen solution.

2 Which of the following people ultimately benefit from a systems development project?

a. computer programmers

b. systems analysts

c. stakeholders

d. senior-level manager

3 What factors are essential to the success of certain functional areas of an organization?

a. critical success factors

b. systems analysis factors

c. creative goal factors

d. systems development factors

4 What employs tools, techniques, and methodologies designed to speed application development?

a. rapid application development

b. joint optimization

c. prototyping

d. extended application development

5 System performance is usually determined by factors such as fixed investments in hardware and related equipment. True or false?

6 _____ takes an iterative approach to the systems development process. During each iteration, requirements and alternative solutions to the problem are identified and analyzed, new solutions are designed, and a portion of the system is implemented.

7 Joint application development involves group meetings in which users, stakeholders, and IS professionals work together to analyze existing systems, propose possible solutions, and define the requirements for a new or modified system. True or false?

8 Feasibility analysis is typically done during which systems development stage?

a. investigation

b. analysis

c. design

d. implementation

9 Data modelling is most often accomplished through the use of _____, whereas activity modelling is often accomplished through the use of _____.

10 The overall purpose of requirements analysis is to determine user, stakeholder, and organizational needs. True or false?

11

Review Questions

1 What is an IS stakeholder?

2 What is the goal of IS planning? What steps are involved in IS planning?

3 What are the typical reasons to initiate systems development?

4 What is the difference between a programmer and a systems analyst?

5 Why is it important to identify and remove errors early in the systems development lifecycle?

6 Identify four reasons that a systems development project might be initiated.

7 List factors that have a strong influence on project success.

8 What is the difference between systems investigation and systems analysis?

9 How does the JAD technique support the RAD systems development lifecycle?

10 Describe some of the models that are used to document systems analysis.

Discussion Questions

1 Why is it important for business managers to have a basic understanding of the systems development process?

2 Briefly describe the role of a system user in the systems investigation and systems analysis stages of a project.

3 For what types of systems development projects might prototyping be especially useful? What are the characteristics of a system developed with a prototyping technique?

4 How important are communications skills to IS personnel? Consider this statement: 'IS personnel need a combination of skills – one-third technical skills, one-third business skills, and one-third communications skills'. Do you think this is true? How would this affect the training of IS personnel?

5 Discuss three reasons why aligning overall business goals with IS goals is important.

Web Exercises

1 A number of tools can be used to develop a new web-based application. Describe the Web development tools you would use and the steps you would complete to implement a website to rent movies and games over the Internet. You might be asked to develop a report or send an e-mail message to your instructor about what you have found.

2 Using the Internet, locate an organization that is currently involved in a systems development project. Describe how they are using project management tools. Is project management software being used?

11

Case One

Applebee's Simplifies Life for Managers while Improving Service to Customers

U.S.-based restaurant chain Applebee's is the largest casual dining chain in the world and currently has 89 locations in 17 countries including Italy, Greece, and Saudi Arabia. Like many of the large restaurant chains, Applebee's maintains specific performance criteria for its restaurants. These include metrics for the speed of getting customers in and out of a restaurant, quality of food, and levels of customer satisfaction. Five hundred of the 1850 restaurants are company owned, and the rest are franchises. Communication between all Applebee's restaurants is critical for maintaining consistent standards across all restaurants.

To provide the most current corporate information to each Applebee's restaurant, the company provides portal software from BEA Systems Inc. The portal software provides a browser interface to different enterprise applications. Restaurant managers have access to daily performance records through dashboards in the portal.

Upper-level management at Applebee's in Overland Park, Kansas, recently became concerned over some restaurant manager's complaints about difficulties in keeping up with constantly evolving menus and corporate policies. Managers felt that they were required to spend too much time monitoring performance using the corporate portal software. Applebee's launched a systems investigation to learn more about the complaints and to determine the feasibility of providing a fix.

Systems analysts found that the complexity of using the dashboard systems was too much for most managers. To access performance statistics and metrics, managers were faced with 'a sea of information these managers are supposed to weed through every day', explained Patty Cutter, Applebee's IT project manager. What's more, when metrics for performance standards indicated that a restaurant was substandard, the manager would have to phone Applebee's headquarters to learn strategies for improvement – a process that was time consuming for both manager and supervisor. With a full understanding of the problem, Patty Cutter and fellow systems analysts set out to perform the analysis to define how the problem could be addressed through the development of a new system. They determined that an ideal system should:

- Provide managers with the latest menu specifications along with instructions on how to execute any changes.
- Provide managers with alerts whenever the restaurant's performance in a specific area falls below the corporate threshold, eliminating the need for managers to dig through a 'sea of information'.
- Provide suggested action plans with each alert that provides steps the manager should take to rise to corporate standards, eliminating the need to phone headquarters.
- Provide flexibility within the system so that software in all restaurants can be changed and updated from headquarters to reflect changes within the organization.

With a clear view of what the new system should do, Patty Cutter consulted with BEA Systems to see if the company that provided the original portal software could provide a solution that would meet the new organizational needs and general corporate goals. Developers at BEA Systems recommended their AquaLogic HiPer Workspace for Retail software as an ideal solution. The AquaLogic software uses a Service Oriented Architecture (SOA) that would provide the flexibility that Applebee's wanted. The software is a composite application that can use web services to quickly notify store managers when a restaurant isn't meeting certain performance criteria, and provide possible solutions to the problem. An added advantage is that the AquaLogic software is designed to work with the portal software already installed in all Applebee's.

Applebee's is rolling out a production version of the new application for its portal to its 500 company-owned restaurants. After being fully tested in those restaurants, the software will be recommended to each of the company's 1350 franchise restaurants. The company views the software

11

as a big time-saver for its managers. 'It is extremely important to us that we minimize the amount of time our managers are spending behind a computer,' said Frank Ybarra, associate director of communications at Applebee's. What makes this an ideal solution is that it saves manager's time, while actually improving their ability to maintain Applebee's high standards.

Questions

1 Suggest some ways in which end users could be involved in this project from Day One. Why is it important that end users are involved?

2 Should change menagement be an important part of Applebee's implementation strategy? Explain your answer.

3 What advantage does a SOA provide for Applebee's? Why do you think SOA and web services have become so popular in new systems?

4 What benefit(s) did Applebee's gain by choosing BEA Systems to design the new system?

SOURCES: Havenstein, Heather, 'Applebee's Taps BEA Tool to Boost Operations', *Computerworld*, June 19, 2006, www.computerworld.com; Applebee's International (website), www.applebees.com; BEA Systems (website), www.bea.com.

Case Two

German Dairy Products Manufacturer Upgrades Systems to Meet Organizational Goals

Nordmilch produces dairy products such as cheese, cream, long-life milk, dried powdered milk, and yogurt. Based in Bremen, Germany, ownership of the business is in the hands of the region's milk producers. It is a successful global business with annual sales of more than €2.1 billion, and around 3800 employees. Nordmilch has earned its success by constantly evaluating its market position and organizational goals, and then taking action to achieve those goals. New information systems are continuously developed to support changing organizational strategies.

Recently, Nordmilch reached a decisive turning point. Company leaders realized that Nordmilch needed radical strategic and organizational changes to compete with recent entrants into the market. Management set new goals that would allow the company to become more nimble as it responded to changes in the market. The company needed to reduce costs, increase flexibility, and introduce enhanced production quality control. Chairman Stephan Tomat put it this way: 'In addition to restructuring our production plants, a company-wide efficiency program is aimed at bringing about a sustained increase in Nordmilch's ability to perform.' To accomplish its goals, the company needed to develop new information systems to speed valued information to its decision makers.

Nordmilch was using SAP software as its core suite of business management solutions and was pleased with the software's capabilities and SAP's support of the product. Nordmilch management wanted to implement additional SAP solutions and upgrade their existing SAP applications to provide more detailed production data. By closely monitoring production, Nordmilch could react more quickly to market demands and also provide assurances to customers and government agencies concerned about health and safety issues.

Further systems investigation showed that Nordmilch had yet another reason to upgrade its systems. Its Sun and EMC2 servers and storage hardware were nearing the end of their life and could no longer support the needs of the growing organization. A full analysis of Nordmilch systems uncovered that this systems development project would involve implementing new SAP applications, new servers on which those applications would run, new storage hardware for corporate data, and a new database system to manage that data because the current database was not compatible with the SAP applications – in other words, Nordmilch needed a total system overhaul. Karl-Heinz Mansholt, chief information officer at Nordmilch, describes the strategy: 'To meet our business objectives, we selected SAP software. To run new SAP applications successfully, we needed a new approach to our IT infrastructure. We did not want to over-invest in servers that would be over-sized in the beginning, and invited several vendors to propose possible solutions.'

Nordmilch compared offers for new servers and storage hardware from IBM partners, FSC, and Sun. It also evaluated offers for database systems from IBM and Oracle. Karl-Heinz Mansholt and his team analyzed factors such as ease of administration, maintenance, database performance, scalability, and reliability.

In the end, Nordmilch implemented new SAP applications for the materials management, sales and distribution, financials/controlling, human resources, and production planning departments. The SAP applications were installed on two IBM p5 model 570 servers running the IBM AIX 5L operating system. The IBM system was chosen because it was scalable, allowing Nordmilch to pay for only the computing power it currently needed with support for growth for at least five years.

Nordmilch chose an IBM TotalStorage DS8100 storage server, providing high performance storage resources for both p5-570 servers. For a database system, Nordmilch chose IBM's DB2. The inter-operability between the SAS applications, and the IBM servers, storage system, and database ideally suited Nordmilch's needs. 'The improved technical performance is down to the combination of hardware, AIX operating system, database and storage – it's very hard to split the benefits between these components. In summary, the IBM and SAP solution gives Nordmilch the flexible IT infrastructure and applications required to meet our business goals,' concludes Karl-Heinz Mansholt.

Questions

1 Describe what more 'detailed production data' might look like? Who would be viewing this data and what format would they want it in? Should it be up to the user to decide what format any output should take?

2 What were Nordmilch's performance objectives?

3 How might Nordmilch have analyzed the requirements for the new system?

4 What other situations can arise within a business to trigger new systems development initiatives?

SOURCES: 'NORDMILCH Refreshes Five-Year IT Strategy with Flexible SAP and IBM Solutions', IBM Case Study, February 15, 2006, www.ibm.com; Nordmilch (website), www.nordmilch.de/nm/web/en/home.html; SAP (website), www.sap.com.

Case Three

Waeco Pacific Employees Work Together to Create New ERP System

Waeco Pacific Pty Ltd. is the Australian branch of Germany-based Waeco International, a worldwide leading supplier of active coolers for all mobile applications – boats and RVs, cars and trucks, buses, and other commercial vehicles. Waeco Pacific's legacy ERP system was frustrating employees throughout the organization from the assemblers in manufacturing plants, to shippers at warehouses, to executives at headquarters. Its antiquated systems were driving Waeco Pacific managers to create separate systems in their departments, limiting interoperability and efficiency.

Problems in the system's warehousing module meant critical operations like stocktaking, stock control, and communication had to be done manually. 'We were unable to create bin locations or look at a stocktaking module in the software,' Waeco Pacific national logistics manager James Stuart said. 'It was all done manually to compensate for having a poor system in place. When staff entered an order they would take the printed order to the old system, type in the docket, and twice a day, an employee would take invoice dockets to the warehouse where staff pick, pack and dispatch the stock.'

When Waeco Pacific finally committed to a system overhaul, its first step was to consult the users of the system to find out what they needed. By involving staff from all departments, requirements, procedures, and expectations for the new ERP system were made clear. Stakeholders were briefed on the plans for the new system. Users provided screenshots and instructions to developers to illustrate how they used the current system and how it could be improved. Through their involvement in its design, each user became a subject expert on how the new system would be utilized in his or her area.

After consultation was complete, the project manager decided the company needed a well-supported, wireless, and unified platform where it could build a system to support growth and improvements. It was hoped that a solution could be developed within three months. With this type of time frame, Waeco Pacific would have to opt for commercially available software; to develop a custom solution would take too much time.

After a bit of research, the company decided to adopt Microsoft's Dynamics NAV software. The primary benefits being its global reach and its ease of integration with Microsoft Word and Excel – software already well established within the organization. Microsoft Dynamics NAV helps growing, mid-sized companies integrate financial, manufacturing, distribution, customer relationship management, and e-commerce data. Integrating Microsoft Dynamics NAV into Waeco Pacific's existing Microsoft environment would be easier than other solutions because it runs on a Microsoft SQL Server back end.

The rollout of the new system began in late 2005 in the Australian cities of Melbourne, Brisbane, and Perth as well as in New Zealand at a cost of $186 000. Waeco Pacific partnered with Tectura to implement a simple, wireless infrastructure, upgrading its administration complex and warehouse systems.

The chosen solution integrated systems from all departments, which promoted efficiency, flexibility, and communication. Waeco Pacific managing director Andreas Bischof said, 'We were starting to run individual solutions for each area of the business but now we have everything under one umbrella. This lets us integrate our business areas such as CRM, warehousing and stock control to make us more productive and efficient in our use of resources.'

Today, when an order is placed, the docket automatically prints in the correct warehouse location at the dispatch supervisor's desk and a consignment note is automatically generated. 'This has drastically improved performance with less room for human error making the entire warehousing system more reliable and efficient,' concludes Waeco Pacific IT manager Mark Maki-Neste.

Questions

1 What drove Waeco Pacific to implement this systems development initiative?

2 Explain some possible advantages and disadvantages of going with a Microsoft solution.

3 Why did users give developers screen shots the current system? How did this help development?

4 Waeco Pacific dedicated a considerable amount of time and effort in consulting with employees. What are the costs and benefits of this approach?

SOURCES: Pauli, Darren, 'Ausie Manufacturer Puts Outdated ERP System on Ice', *Computerworld Australia*, July 5, 2006, www.computerworld.com.au; Waeco Pacific (website), www.waeco.com.au; Microsoft Dynamics NAV (website), www.microsoft.com/dynamics/nav/default.mspx.

Notes

1   Staff, BBC, 'Q&A: NHS Computer System', http://news.bbc.co.uk/1/hi/health/3613516.stm.

2   Brandel, Mary, 'Five Biggest Project Challenges for 2006', *Computerworld,* January 2, 2006, p. 16.

3   Kolbasuk, Marianne, 'Skills That Will Matter', *Information Week,* January 2, 2006, p. 53.

4   Hess, H.M., 'Aligning Technology and Business', *IBM Systems Journal,* Vol. 44, No. 1, 2005, p. 25.

5   Staff, 'BRE Bank Subscribes to Risk Management Database', *Asian Banker,* January 15, 2006.

6   Havenstein, Heather, 'Medical Groups Offered Rewards to IT Use', *Computerworld,* February 6, 2006, p. 14.

7   Engardio, Pete, 'The Future of Outsourcing', *Business Week,* January 30, 2006, p. 50.

8   Kripalani, Manjeet, 'Offshoring: Spreading the Gospel', *Business Week,* March 6, 2006, p. 46.

9   Shellenbarger, Sue, 'Outsourcing Jobs to the Den', *Wall Street Journal,* January 12, 2006, p. D1.

10 Staff, 'Eurostar Briefs Occam to Boost Traveler Insight', *Precision Marketing,* January 6, 2006, p. 6.

11 Arsanjani, A., 'Empowering the Business Analyst for On Demand Computing', *IBM Systems Journal,* Vol. 44, No. 1, 2005, p. 67.

12 IBM (website), www.ibm.com.

13 EDS (website), www.eds.com.

14 Accenture (website), www.accenture.com.

15 Vijayan, Jaikumar, 'Outsourcing Savvy', *Computerworld,* January 3, 2005, p. 16

16 Hoffman, Thomas, 'Prenuptials for Outsourcing', *Computerworld,* January 23, 2006, p. 34.

17 Rohde, Laura, 'Report Details Flaws in UK Case Management IT System', *Computerworld,* April 18, 2005, p. 21.

18 ISO – International Standards Organization (website), www.iso.org.

19 Capability Maturity Model for Software home page (website), www.sei.cmu.edu.

20 Kay, Russell, 'CMMI', *Computerworld,* January 24, 2005, p. 28.

21 Staff, 'Capability Maturity Model for Software', www.sei.cmu.edu/cmm.

22 42 Glen, Paul, 'Detecting Disaster Projects', *Computerworld,* February 6, 2006, p. 39.

12

Systems Design and Implementation

Principles

Designing new systems or modifying existing ones should always help an organization achieve its goals.

The primary emphasis of systems implementation is to make sure that the right information is delivered to the right person in the right format at the right time.

Maintenance and review add to the useful life of a system but can consume large amounts of resources. These activities can benefit from the same rigorous methods and project management techniques applied to systems development.

Learning Objectives

- State the purpose of systems design and discuss the differences between logical and physical systems design.
- Describe some considerations in design modelling and the diagrams used during object-oriented design.
- Outline key considerations in interface design and control and system security and control.
- Define the term 'RFP' and discuss how this document is used to drive the acquisition of hardware and software.
- Describe the techniques used to make systems selection evaluations.

- State the purpose of systems implementation and discuss the activities associated with this phase of systems development.
- List the advantages and disadvantages of purchasing versus developing software.
- Discuss the software development process and some of the tools used in this process, including object-oriented program development tools.

- State the importance of systems and software maintenance and discuss the activities involved.
- Describe the systems review process.

Why Learn About Systems Design and Implementation?

The previous chapter talked about how problems are analyzed. This chapter looks at how this analysis can be used to design and build IT solutions. The chapter mainly looks at developing a new system but also examines solving a problem by buying an existing IS that has already been developed.

Information systems are used in every industry and almost every career. A manager at a hotel chain can use an information system to look up client preferences. An accountant at a manufacturing company can use an information system to analyze the costs of a new plant. A sales representative for a music store can use an information system to determine which CDs to order and which to discount because they are not selling. A computer engineer can use an information system to help determine why a computer system is running slowly. This chapter shows how you can be involved in designing and implementing an information system that will directly benefit you, and the options your company has for acquiring an new IS. It also shows how to avoid errors or recover from disasters. The way an information system is designed, implemented, and maintained profoundly affects the daily functioning of an organization. Like systems investigation and analysis covered in the last chapter; design, implementation, maintenance, and review (all covered in this chapter) strive to achieve organizational goals, such as reducing costs, increasing profits, or improving customer service. The goal is to develop a new or modified system to deliver the right information to the right person at the right time.

12.1 Systems Design

The purpose of **systems design** is to answer the question 'how will the information system solve the problem?'. The primary result of the systems design phase is a technical design that details system inputs and the processing required to produce outputs, user interfaces, hardware, software, databases, telecommunications, personnel, and procedures, and shows how these components are related.[1] The system that is designed should meet all the requirements specified during the analysis phase (explained in the previous chapter), overcome the shortcomings of the existing system and help the organization achieve its goals. Two key aspects of systems design are logical and physical design.

systems design A stage of systems development where a solution to the problem is planned out and documented.

The **logical design** refers to what the system will do. Logical design describes the functional requirements of a system. That is, it conceptualizes what the system will do to solve the problems identified through earlier analysis. Without this step, the technical details of the system (such as which hardware devices should be acquired) often obscure the best solution. Logical design involves planning the purpose of each system element, independent of hardware and software considerations. The logical design specifications that are determined and documented include output, input, process, file and database, telecommunications, procedures, controls and security, and personnel and job requirements.

logical design A description of the functional requirements of a system.

The **physical design** refers to how the tasks are accomplished, including how the components work together and what each component does. Physical design specifies the characteristics of the system components necessary to put the logical design into action. In this phase, the characteristics of the hardware, software, database, telecommunications, personnel, and procedure and control specifications must be detailed.

physical design The specification of the characteristics of the system components necessary to put the logical design into action.

There are a number of notation that can be used to document the design stage. Data flow diagrams and class diagrams (mentioned in the previous chapter) are used, as is the notation shown in Chapter 5 for illustrating a data model. Sequence diagrams are used in object-oriented systems design to illustrate how messages pass between objects and to show the sequence of events in a process. Programmers use various notations to design the code that they will write.

12.1.1 Interface Design and Controls

Some special system characteristics should be considered during both logical and physical design. These characteristics relate to how users access and interact with the system. For example, with a **menu-driven system** (see Figure 12.1), users simply pick what they want to do from a list of alternatives. Most people can easily operate these types of systems and are familiar with them. They select an option or respond to questions (or prompts) from the system, and the system does the rest. An alternative is a command line interface such as that shown in Figure 12.2. **Command line interfaces** involve users typing commands at a prompt. For example, typing the name of a software package, opens it.

> **menu-driven system** A system in which users simply pick what they want to do from a list of alternatives.
>
> **command line interface** An interface where the user types text commands to the computer.

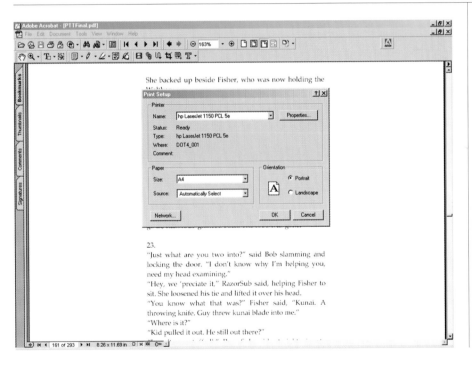

Figure 12.1
Menu-Driven System

Some other interface considerations are whether or not to include interactive help, whether the interface should be two or three dimensional, whether or not to use virtual reality, a touch screen or a keyboard, and whether to include procedures to help with data entry. Such procedures include spell checking and lookup tables. For example, if you are entering a sales order for a company, you can type its abbreviation, such as ABCO. The program will then go to the customer table, normally stored on a disk, and look up all the information pertaining to the company abbreviated ABCO that you need to complete the sales order. Other data entry control include a presence check, which you may have experienced when you've tried to

Figure 12.2 Command
Line Interface

submit an order to an e-commerce website but forgot to enter your e-mail address – the system makes you enter this information before it lets you proceed, and a range check which makes sure the data you enter is within a sensible, perhaps disallowing any year of birth before 1910.

The interface can be documented simply with a drawing of what it is to look like. Designing a good interface is an art that few people seem to possess. It's easy to find numerous examples of bad (annoying, frustrating, non-intuitive) interface design. Table 12.1 lists some characteristics that many interfaces should have. This list however, does not apply to all systems. For example, in Chapter 10 we looked at virtual pets – to keep the user interested a virtual pet should not consistently have the same response time or respect for the user.

12.1.2 Design of System Security and Controls

In addition to considering the system's interface and user interactions, designers must also develop system security and controls for all aspects of the system, including hardware, software, database systems, telecommunications, and Internet operations.[2] These key considerations involve error prevention, detection, and correction; disaster planning and recovery; and systems controls.[3]

Disaster Planning and Recovery

Disaster planning is the process of anticipating and providing for disasters. A disaster can be an act of nature (a flood, fire, or earthquake) or a human act (terrorism, error, deliberate sabotage by a disgruntled employee). Disaster planning often focuses primarily on two issues: maintaining the integrity of corporate information and keeping the information system running until normal operations can be resumed. **Disaster recovery** is the implementation of the disaster plan.[4] When Hurricane Katrina hit New Orleans in the U.S., investment and trading company Howard Weil Inc. had a plan to keep the firm operating[5] – they would move its employees to Houston, Texas. But when Houston also had to be evacuated, the company had to move its employees to another location – Stamford, Connecticut – according to its disaster plan. The company was able to rapidly re-create its trading desk and IS infrastructure to continue trading. According to Jefferson Parker, president of Howard Weil, 'You don't normally develop a backup plan for the backup plan.'

Although companies have known about the importance of disaster planning and recovery for decades, many do not adequately prepare. The primary tools used in disaster planning and recovery are backups. Hardware, software and data can all be 'backed up'.

For example, hot and cold sites can be used to back up hardware and software. A **hot site** is a space, usually some distance away from the main operation, where spare computers with the appropriate telecommunication links set up, and software installed wait, along with any associated pereriphals such as printers, in case some problem occurs to disrupt the technology in the main location. The hot site is physically separate in case the problem is something like a flood, which would damage a wide area. If a disaster occurs, all that is needed is transportation to take staff to the hot site, along with the latest data backup. As soon as the data is uploaded, operations can continue. Another approach is to use a **cold site**, also called a shell, which is a

disaster planning The process of anticipating and providing for disasters.

disaster recovery The implementation of the disaster plan.

hot site A duplicate, operational hardware system or immediate access to one through a specialized vendor.

cold site A computer environment that includes rooms, electrical service, telecommunications links, data storage devices, and the like; also called a 'shell'.

Table 12.1 The Elements of Good Interactive Dialogue

Element	Description
Clarity	The computer system should ask for information using easily understood language. Whenever possible, the users themselves should help select the words and phrases used for dialogue with the computer system
Response time	Ideally, responses from the computer system should approximate a normal response time from a human being carrying on the same sort of dialogue
Consistency	The system should use the same commands, phrases, words, and function keys for all applications. After a user learns one application, all others will then be easier to use
Format	The system should use an attractive format and layout for all screens. The use of colour, highlighting, and the position of information on the screen should be considered carefully and applied consistently
Jargon	All dialogue should be written in easy-to-understand terms. Avoid jargon known only to IS specialists
Respect	All dialogue should be developed professionally and with respect. Dialogue should not talk down to or insult the user. Avoid statements such as 'You have made a fatal error'

12

computer environment that includes rooms, electrical service, telecommunication links, but no hardware. If a primary computer has a problem, backup computer hardware is brought into the cold site, and the complete system is made operational. A warm site sits somewhere between the two (see Figures 12.3 and 12.4).

Figure 12.3 A Hot Site
A hot site waits, ready for action, in case it is needed.

© Lourens Smak/Alamy.

Figure 12.4 *A disaster that caused staff to need to move to a hot site*

SOURCE: Simon Vine/Alamy.

Databases can be backed up by making a copy of all files and databases changed during the last few days or the last week, a technique called **incremental backup**. One approach to backup uses a transaction log, which is a separate file that contains only changes to the database and is backed up more frequently than the database itself (which is much bigger). If a problem occurs with a current database, the transaction log, and the last backup of the database, can be used to re-create the current database.

incremental backup Making a backup copy of all files changed during the last few days or the last week.

Systems Controls

Security lapses, fraud, and the invasion of privacy can present disastrous problems. For example, because of an inadequate security and control system, a futures and options trader for a British bank lost almost £1 billion. A simple systems control might have prevented a problem that caused the 200-year-old Bearings bank to collapse. In addition, from time to time, tax officials have been caught looking at the returns of celebrities and others. Preventing and detecting these problems is an important part of systems design. Prevention includes the following:

- ▓ Determining potential problems.
- ▓ Ranking the importance of these problems.
- ▓ Planning the best place and approach to prevent problems.
- ▓ Deciding the best way to handle problems if they occur.

Every effort should be made to prevent problems, but companies must establish procedures to handle problems if they occur, including **system controls**.

systems controls Rules and procedures to maintain data security.

Most IS departments establish tight systems controls to maintain data security. Systems controls can help prevent computer misuse, crime, and fraud by managers, employees, and others. The accounting scandals in the early 2000s caused many IS departments to develop systems controls to make it more difficult for executives to mislead investors and employees. Some of these scandals involved billions of euros.

Most IS departments have a set of general operating rules that helps protect the system (see Figure 12.5). Some of these are listed below.

- ▓ *Input controls:* Maintain input integrity and security. Their purpose is to reduce errors while protecting the computer system against improper or fraudulent input. Input controls range from using standardized input forms to eliminating data-entry errors and using tight password and identification controls.
- ▓ *Processing controls:* Deal with all aspects of processing and storage. The use of passwords and identification numbers, backup copies of data, and storage rooms that have tight security systems are examples of processing and storage controls.
- ▓ *Output controls:* Ensure that output is handled correctly. In many cases, output generated from the computer system is recorded in a file that indicates the reports and documents that were generated, the time they were generated, and their final destinations.
- ▓ *Database controls:* Deal with ensuring an efficient and effective database system. These controls include the use of identification numbers and passwords, without which a user is denied access to certain data and information. Many of these controls are provided by database management systems.
- ▓ *Telecommunications controls:* Provide accurate and reliable data and information transfer among systems. Telecommunications controls include firewalls and encryption to ensure correct communication while eliminating the potential for fraud and crime.

12

Figure 12.5 Building
Access *Only authorised
personnel can enter using
their swipe card.*

© Image Source Pink/Alamy.

■ *Personnel controls:* Make sure that only authorized personnel have access to certain
systems to help prevent computer-related mistakes and crime. Personnel controls can
involve the use of identification numbers and passwords that allow only certain people
access to particular data and information. ID badges and other security devices (such as
smart cards) can prevent unauthorized people from entering strategic areas in the information systems facility.

12.1.3 Generating Systems Design Alternatives

The development team will want to generate different designs. One approach is to come up with
a basic, cheaper solution; a top-of-the-range solution at the edge of what can be afforded; and
a mix solution sitting somewhere between the two. If the new system is complex, it might want

to involve personnel from inside and outside the firm in generating alternative designs. If new hardware and software are to be acquired from an outside vendor, a formal request for proposal (RFP) can be made.

Request for Proposals

The **request for proposal (RFP)** is an important document for many organizations involved with large, complex systems development efforts. Smaller, less complex systems often do not require an RFP. A company that is purchasing an inexpensive piece of software that will run on existing hardware, for example, might not need to go through a formal RFP process.

request for proposal (RFP) A document that specifies in detail required resources such as hardware and software.

When an RFP is used, it often results in a formal bid that is used to determine who gets a contract for new or modified systems. The RFP specifies in detail the required resources such as hardware and software.[6] Although it can take time and money to develop a high-quality RFP, it can save a company in the long run. Companies that frequently generate RFPs can automate the process. Software such as The RFP Machine from Pragmatech Software can be used to improve the quality of RFPs and reduce the time it takes to produce them. The RFP Machine stores important data needed to generate RFPs and automates the process of producing RFP documents.

In some cases, separate RFPs are developed for different needs. For example, a company might develop separate RFPs for hardware, software, and database systems. The RFP also communicates these needs to one or more vendors, and it provides a way to evaluate whether the vendor has delivered what was expected. In some cases, the RFP is part of the vendor contract. The table of contents for a typical RFP is shown in Figure 12.6.

Figure 12.6 A Typical Table of Contents for a Request for Proposal

```
                    Johnson & Florin
                 Systems investigation report

        Contents

            Cover page (with company name and contact person)
            Brief description of the company
            Overview of the existing computer system
            Summary of computer-related needs and/or problems
            Objectives of the project
            Description of what is needed
            Hardware requirements
            Personnel requirements
            Communications requirements
            Procedures to be developed
            Training requirements
            Maintenance requirements
            Evaluation procedures (how vendors will be judged)
            Proposal format (how vendors should respond)
            Important dates (when tasks are to be completed)
            Summary
```

Financial Options

When acquiring computer systems, several choices are available, including purchase, lease, or rent. Cost objectives and constraints set for the system play a significant role in the choice, as do the advantages and disadvantages of each. In addition, traditional financial tools, including net present value and internal rate of return, can be used. Table 12.2 summarizes the advantages and disadvantages of these financial options.

Determining which option is best for a particular company in a given situation can be difficult. Financial considerations, tax laws, the organization's policies, its sales and transaction growth, marketplace dynamics, and the organization's financial resources are all important factors. In some cases, lease or rental fees can amount to more than the original purchase price after a few years. As a result, some companies prefer to purchase their equipment.

On the other hand, constant advances in technology can make purchasing risky. A company would not want to purchase a new multimillion-dollar computer only to have newer and more powerful computers available a few months later at a lower price, unless the computer can be easily and inexpensively upgraded. Some servers, for example, are designed to be scalable to allow processors to be added or swapped, memory to be upgraded, and peripheral devices to be installed. Companies often employ several people to determine the best option based on all the factors. This staff can also help negotiate purchase, lease, or rental contracts.

Evaluating and Selecting a Systems Design

The final step in systems design is to evaluate the various alternatives and select the one that will offer the best solution for organizational goals. Depending on their weight, any one of these objectives might result in the selection of one design over another. For example, financial concerns might make a company choose rental over equipment purchase. Specific performance objectives – for example, that the new system must perform online data processing – might result in a complex network design for which control procedures must be established. Evaluating and selecting

Table 12.2 Advantages and Disadvantages of Acquisition Options

Renting (Short-Term Option)	
Advantages	**Disadvantages**
No risk of obsolescence	No ownership of equipment
No long-term financial investment	High monthly costs
No initial investment of funds	Restrictive rental agreements
Maintenance usually included	

Leasing (Longer-Term Option)	
Advantages	**Disadvantages**
No risk of obsolescence	High cost of cancelling lease
No long-term financial investment	Longer time commitment than renting
No initial investment of funds	No ownership of equipment
Less expensive than renting	

Purchasing	
Advantages	**Disadvantages**
Total control over equipment	High initial investment
Can sell equipment at any time	Additional cost of maintenance
Can depreciate equipment	Possibility of obsolescence
Low cost if owned for a number of years	Other expenses, including taxes and insurance

the best design involves achieving a balance of system objectives that will best support organizational goals. Normally, evaluation and selection involves both a preliminary and a final evaluation before a design is selected.

The Preliminary Evaluation

A **preliminary evaluation** begins after all design proposals have been submitted. The purpose of this evaluation is to dismiss unwanted proposals. If external vendors have submitted proposals, some of them can usually be eliminated by investigating their proposals and comparing them with the original criteria. Those that compare favourably are often asked to make a formal presentation to the analysis team. The vendors should also be asked to supply a list of companies that use their equipment for a similar purpose. The organization then contacts these references and asks them to evaluate their hardware, their software, and the vendor.

> **preliminary evaluation** An initial assessment whose purpose is to dismiss the unwanted proposals; begins after all proposals have been submitted.

The Final Evaluation

The **final evaluation** begins with a detailed investigation of the proposals offered by the remaining vendors. The vendors should be asked to make a final presentation and to fully demonstrate the system. The demonstration should be as close to actual operating conditions as possible. Applications such as payroll, inventory control, and billing should be conducted using a large amount of test data.

> **final evaluation** A detailed investigation of the proposals offered by the vendors remaining after the preliminary evaluation.

After the final presentations and demonstrations have been given, the organization makes the final evaluation and selection. Cost comparisons, hardware performance, delivery dates, price, flexibility, backup facilities, availability of software training, and maintenance factors are considered. In addition to comparing computer speeds, storage capacities, and other similar characteristics, companies should also carefully analyze whether the characteristics of the proposed systems meet the company's objectives. In most cases, the RFP captures these objectives and goals.

Group Consensus Evaluation

In **group consensus**, a decision-making group is appointed and given the responsibility of making the final evaluation and selection. Usually, this group includes the members of the development team who participated in either systems analysis or systems design. This approach might be used to evaluate which of several screen layouts or report formats is best.

> **group consensus** Decision making by a group that is appointed and given the responsibility of making the final evaluation and selection.

Cost–Benefit Analysis Evaluation

Cost–benefit analysis is an approach that lists the costs and benefits of each proposed system. After they are expressed in monetary terms, all the costs are compared with all the benefits. Table 12.3 lists some of the typical costs and benefits associated with the evaluation and selection procedure. This approach is used to evaluate options whose costs can be quantified, such as which hardware or software vendor to select.

> **cost–benefit analysis** An approach that lists the costs and benefits of each proposed system. After they are expressed in monetary terms, all the costs are compared with all the benefits.

Benchmark Test Evaluation

A **benchmark test** is an examination that compares computer systems operating under the same conditions. Most computer companies publish their own benchmark tests, but some forbid disclosure of benchmark tests without prior written approval. Thus, one of the best approaches is for an organization to develop its own tests, and then use them to compare the equipment it is considering. This approach might be used to compare the end-user system response time on two similar systems. Several independent companies also rate computer systems. *Computerworld, PC Week,* and many other publications, for example, not only summarize various systems, but also evaluate and compare computer systems and manufacturers according to a number of criteria.

> **benchmark test** An examination that compares computer systems operating under the same conditions.

12

Point Evaluation

One of the disadvantages of cost–benefit analysis is the difficulty of determining the monetary values for all the benefits. An approach that does not employ monetary values is a **point evaluation system**. Each evaluation factor is assigned a weight, in percentage points, based on importance. Then each proposed information system is evaluated in terms of this factor and given a score, such as one ranging from 0 to 100, where 0 means that the alternative does not address the feature at all and 100 means that the alternative addresses that feature perfectly. The scores are totalled, and the system with the greatest total score is selected. When using point evaluation, an organization can list and evaluate literally hundreds of factors. Figure 12.7 shows a simplified version of this process. This approach is used when there are many options to be evaluated, such as which software best matches a particular business's needs.

point evaluation system An evaluation process in which each evaluation factor is assigned a weight, in percentage points, based on importance. Then each proposed system is evaluated in terms of this factor and given a score ranging from 0 to 100. The scores are totalled, and the system with the greatest total score is selected.

Table 12.3 Cost–Benefit Analysis Table

Costs	Benefits
Development costs	Reduced costs
Personnel	Fewer personnel
Computer resources	Reduced manufacturing costs
	Reduced inventory costs
	More efficient use of equipment
	Faster response time
	Reduced downtime or crash time
	Less spoilage
Fixed costs	**Increased Revenues**
Computer equipment	New products and services
Software	New customers
One-time licence fees for software and maintenance	More business from existing customers
	Higher price as a result of better products and services
Operating costs	**Intangible benefits**
Equipment lease and/or rental fees	Better public image for the organization
Computer personnel (including salaries, benefits, etc.)	Higher employee morale
	Better service for new and existing customers
Electric and other utilities	The ability to recruit better employees
Computer paper, tape, and disks	Position as a leader in the industry
Other computer supplies	System easier for programmers and users
Maintenance costs	
Insurance	

		System A		System B	
Factor's importance		Evaluation	Weighted evaluation	Evaluation	Weighted evaluation
Hardware	35%	95 35%	33.25	75 35%	26.25
Software	40%	70 40%	28.00	95 40%	38.00
Vendor support	25%	85 25%	21.25	90 25%	22.50
Totals	100%		82.5		86.75

Figure 12.7 An Illustration of the Point Evaluation System *In this example, software has been given the most weight (40 percent), compared with hardware (35 percent) and vendor support (25 percent). When system A is evaluated, the total of the three factors amounts to 82.5 percent. System B's rating, on the other hand, totals 86.75 percent, which is closer to 100 percent. Therefore, the firm chooses system B.*

12.1.4 Freezing Design Specifications

Near the end of the design stage, some organizations prohibit further changes in the design of the system. Freezing systems design specifications means that the user agrees in writing that the design is acceptable. Other organizations, however, allow or even encourage design changes. These organizations often use the rapid systems development approaches, introduced in Chapter 11.

12.1.5 The Contract

One of the most important steps in systems design, if new computer facilities are being acquired, is to develop a good contract. Finding the best terms where everyone makes a profit can be difficult. Most computer vendors provide standard contracts; however, such contracts are designed to protect the vendor, not necessarily the organization buying the computer equipment.

Organizations often use outside consultants and legal firms to help them develop their contracts. Such contracts stipulate exactly what they expect from the system vendor and what interaction will occur between the vendor and the organization. All equipment specifications, software, training, installation, maintenance, and so on are clearly stated. Also, the contract stipulates deadlines for the various stages or milestones of installation and implementation, as well as actions that the vendor will take in case of delays or problems. Some organizations include penalty clauses in the contract, in case the vendor does not meet its obligation by the specified date. Typically, the request for proposal becomes part of the contract. This saves a considerable amount of time in developing the contract, because the RFP specifies in detail what is expected from the vendors.

12.1.6 The Design Report

System specifications are the final results of systems design. They include a technical description that details system outputs, inputs, and user interfaces, as well as all hardware, software, databases, telecommunications, personnel, and procedure components and the way these components are related. The specifications are contained in a **design report**, which is the primary result of systems design. The design report reflects the decisions made for systems design and prepares the way for systems implementation.

design report The primary result of systems design, reflecting the decisions made and preparing the way for systems implementation.

12

Information Systems @ Work

Open-Source Development Requires Non-Traditional Methods

According to economists, open-source software should not exist – extremely talented programmers are spending hours on developing professional quality software and then giving it away for free. The programmers involved are often spread out geographically and have full-time jobs that compete for their time. So how do open-source projects get started and how are they managed?

Apache is one of the world's most popular web servers. Started in 1995, Apache is open-source software used by many commercial organizations to run their websites. The project was started by a small team of software developers to work on an existing program developed by Rob McCool, who was one of the main contributors. The teams of people who worked on Apache grew, all of them volunteers, spread throughout the world and without any traditional organizational structure within which to make decisions. The programmers would work independently of each other and at different times, meaning that the team needed a decentralized, asynchronous communication medium. The team used, and continues to use, e-mail lists and a quorum voting system to resolve conflicts. (So when a minimum number of the team agree on something, then the decision is made.) When new functionality in the software is suggested by a user (or a member of the development team) the team must somehow do the following:

◼ Determine whether they will implement the changes.

◼ Identify a solution or solutions and choose one.

◼ Write the changes.

◼ Test the new software.

◼ Commit the code and document the changes.

The initial suggestion is made via the public mailing lists. The team discusses amongst itself via the developers' mailing lists whether they will implement the suggestion. To identify a solution, certain members of the team are recognized by the others as the expert in a certain area. Generally, if the change concerns their area of expertise, the team defers the solution to them, which is sent to the team again for feedback. If the feedback is positive, the developer makes the changes and tests the code locally on their computer. No additional testing is performed before committing the change. Committing the change involves making the new software available as either a patch users can install on their current version of Apache, or as an a new version of Apache. A release manager volunteers to identify and resolve any problems with the committed software. This entire procedure happens iteratively and constantly.

Questions

1 Compare and contrast the above process with the traditional software development approach.

2 Do you think the test procedure is rigorous enough? Explain your answer.

3 Why do you think talented programmers do this? Suggest ways the team could encourage more programmers to join them. What role do end users play in the development, if any. Explain your answer.

4 Why do you think Apache is so popular? Explain your answer.

SOURCES: Mockus, A., Fielding, R., Herbsleb, J., 'Two Case Studies of Open Source Software Development: Apache and Mozilla', *ACM Transactions on Software Engineering and Methodology*, Vol. 11, No. 3, July 2002, pp. 309–346.

12.2 Systems Implementation

After the information system has been designed, **systems implementation** involves a number of tasks which lead to the system being installed and ready to operate.[7] These include hardware acquisition, software acquisition or development (programming), user preparation, documentation preparation, hiring and training of personnel, site and data preparation, installation, testing, start-up, and user acceptance. Spending on systems implementation is on the rise.[8]

The typical sequence of systems implementation activities is shown in Figure 12.8.

systems implementation A stage of systems development that includes hardware acquisition, software acquisition or development, user preparation, hiring and training of personnel, site and data preparation, installation, testing, start-up, and user acceptance.

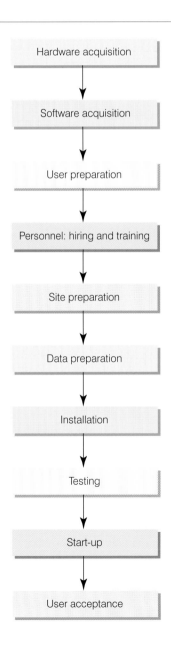

Figure 12.8 Typical Steps in Systems Implementation

12.2.1 Acquiring Hardware from an IS Vendor

To obtain the components for an information system, organizations can purchase, lease, or rent computer hardware and other resources from an IS vendor.[9] An IS vendor is a company that offers hardware, software, telecommunications systems, databases, IS personnel, or other computer-related resources. Types of IS vendors include general computer manufacturers (such as IBM and Hewlett-Packard), small computer manufacturers (such as Dell and Gateway), peripheral equipment manufacturers (such as Epson and Cannon), computer dealers and distributors (such as PC World), and leasing companies (such as Hamilton Rentals and Hire Intelligence).

In addition to buying, leasing, or renting computer hardware, companies can pay only for the computing services that it uses. Called 'pay-as-you-go', 'on-demand', or 'utility' computing, this approach requires an organization to pay only for the computer power it uses, as it would pay for a utility such as electricity. Hewlett-Packard offers its clients a 'capacity-on-demand' approach, in which organizations pay according to the computer resources actually used, including processors, storage devices, and network facilities.

Companies can also purchase used computer equipment. This option is especially attractive to firms that are experiencing an economic slowdown. Companies often use traditional Internet auctions to locate used or refurbished equipment. Popular Internet auction sites sometimes sell more than millions of euros of computer-related equipment annually. However, buyers need to be-ware: prices are not always low, and equipment selection can be limited on Internet auction sites.

In addition, companies are increasingly turning to service providers to implement some or all of the systems they need. As discussed in Chapter 4, an application service provider (ASP) can help companies implement software and other systems. The ASP can provide both user support and the computers on which to run the software. ASPs often focus on high-end applications, such as database systems and enterprise resource planning packages. As mentioned in Chapter 6, an Internet service provider (ISP) assists a company in gaining access to the Internet. ISPs can also help a company in setting up an Internet site. Some service providers specialize in specific systems or areas, such as marketing, finance, or manufacturing.

12.2.2 Acquiring Software: Make or Buy?

As with hardware, application software can be acquired in several ways. As previously mentioned, it can be purchased from external developers or developed in-house.[10] This decision is often called the **make-or-buy decision**. A comparison of the two approaches is shown in Table 12.4. Today, most software is purchased 'off the shelf'. SAP, the large international software company headquartered in Germany, produces modular software it sells to a variety of companies.

make-or-buy decision The decision regarding whether to obtain the necessary software from internal or external sources.

Table 12.4 Comparison of Off the Shelf and Developed Software

Factor	Off the Shelf (Buy)	Bespoke (Make)
Cost	Lower cost	Higher cost
Needs	Might not exactly match needs	Software should exactly match needs
Quality	Usually high quality	Quality can vary depending on the programming team
Speed	Can acquire it now	Can take years to develop
Competitive advantage	Other organizations can have the same software and same advantage	Can develop a competitive advantage with good software

12

The approach gives its customers using the software more flexibility in what they use and what they pay for SAP's modules.[11] The key is how the purchased systems are integrated into an effective system.

Off the shelf software shold be of higher quality that developed, or 'bespoke' software, as it will have been tested 'in the field' by other users. Often those users form an online community, which can be of help to new users. New users often go to online discussion groups to ask questions about the software, rather than calling the developer's own hotline. The audio software Cakewalk, for example, used by amateur and professional musicians, has a thriving forum where beginers and experienced users can post questions, and answer other peoples' questions. Off the shelf software will likely be better documented than bespoke software.

In some cases, companies use a blend of external and internal software development. That is, in-house personnel modify or customize off the shelf or proprietary software programs. Software can also be rented. Salesforce.com, for example, rents software online that helps organizations manage their sales force and internal staff. Increasingly, software is being viewed as a utility or service, not a product you purchase.

System software, such as operating systems or utilities, is typically purchased from a software company. Increasingly, however, companies are obtaining open-source systems software, such as the Linux operating system, which can be obtained free or for a low cost.

Externally Acquired Software

A company planning to purchase or lease software from an outside company has many options. Commercial off the shelf development is often used. The commercial off the shelf (COTS) development process involves the use of commonly available products from software vendors. It combines software from various vendors into a finished system. In many cases, it is necessary to write some original software from scratch and combine it with purchased or leased software. For example, a company can purchase or lease software from several software vendors and combine it into a finished software program. COTS can be less expensive than developing an application from scratch. It can streamline and shorten the time needed to develop software. The other steps of the systems development lifecycle, such as requirements analysis, testing, and implementation, must still be carefully done. A major challenge with COTS development is integrating all the off the shelf components into a unified software package. Other potential problems of the COTS development approach can include no access to the source code, the inability to make changes or updates, and the possibility of quality and security problems concerning the COTS software or components.

Developing Software

Another option is to develop software internally or hire a software house to develop it. Some advantages inherent with developing software include meeting user and organizational requirements and having more features and increased flexibility in terms of customization and changes. Such software programs also have greater potential for providing a competitive advantage because competitors cannot easily duplicate them in the short term.

If software is to be developed, there should be a **chief programmer team**. The chief programmer team is a group of skilled IS professionals with the task of designing and implementing a set of programs. This team has total responsibility for building the best software possible. Individuals on a chief programmer team often have excellent programming skills.

The following tools and techniques may also be used:

- *CASE and object-oriented approaches* (mentioned in Chapter 11).

- *Cross-platform development:* One software development technique, called **cross-platform development**, allows programmers to develop programs that can run on computer systems that have different

chief programmer team A group of skilled IS professionals who design and implement a set of programs.

cross-platform development A development technique that allows programmers to develop programs that can run on computer systems having different hardware and operating systems, or platforms.

12

hardware and operating systems, or platforms. Web service tools, such as .NET by Microsoft are examples. With cross-platform development, for example, the same program can run on both a personal computer and a mainframe or on two different types of PCs.

integrated development environments (IDEs) A development approach that combines the tools needed for programming with a programming language into one integrated package.

■ *Integrated development environment:* **Integrated development environments (IDEs)** combine the tools needed for programming with a programming language in one integrated package. An IDE allows programmers to use simple screens, customized pull-down menus, and graphical user interfaces. Visual Studio 2005 from Microsoft is an example of an IDE. Oracle Designer, which is used with Oracle's database system, is another example of an IDE.

structured walkthrough A planned and pre-announced review of the progress of a program module.

■ *Structured walkthroughs:* As shown in Figure 12.9, a **structured walkthrough** is a planned and pre-announced review of the progress of a program or program module. The walkthrough helps team members review and evaluate the progress of components of a project. The structured walkthrough approach is also useful for programming projects that do not use the structured design approach.

Figure 12.9 Structured **Walkthrough** *A structured walkthrough is a planned, pre-announced review of the progress of a particular project objective.*

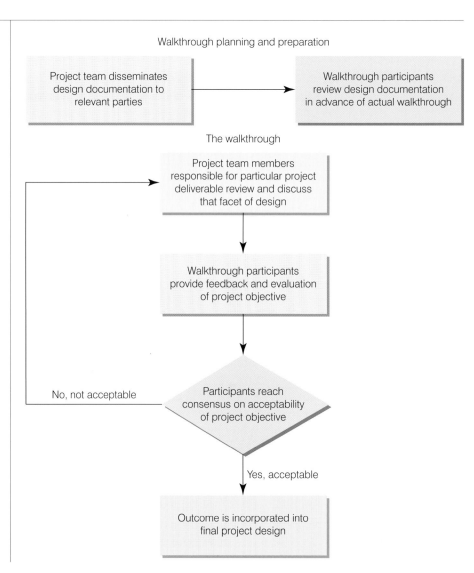

■ *Documentation:* With developed software, documentation is always important. **Technical documentation** is used by computer operators to execute the program and by analysts and programmers to solve problems or modify the program. In technical documentation, the purpose of every major piece of computer code is written out and explained. Key variables are also described. User documentation might be developed for the people who use the program. This type of documentation shows users, in easy-to-understand terms, how the program can and should be used, although an alternative such as a demonstration video may be created instead.

technical documentation Written details used by computer operators to execute the program and by analysts and programmers to solve problems or modify the program.

12.2.3 Acquiring Database and Telecommunications Systems

Because databases are a blend of hardware and software, many of the approaches discussed earlier for acquiring hardware and software also apply to database systems. For example, an upgraded inventory control system might require database capabilities, including more hard disk storage or a new DBMS. If so, additional storage hardware will have to be acquired from an IS vendor. New or upgraded software might also be purchased or developed in house. With the increased use of e-commerce, the Internet, intranets, and extranets, telecommunications is one of the fastest-growing applications for today's businesses and people. Over 200 e-commerce websites have implemented a new payment system.[12] Like database systems, telecommunications systems require a blend of hardware and software. Again, the earlier discussion on acquiring hardware and software also applies to the acquisition of telecommunications hardware and software.

12.2.4 User Preparation

User preparation is the process of readying managers, decision makers, employees, other users, and stakeholders for the new systems. This activity is an important but often ignored area of systems implementation. For example, if a small airline does not adequately train employees with a new software package, the result could be a grounding of most of its flights and the need to find hotel rooms to accommodate unhappy travellers who are stranded.

user preparation The process of readying managers, decision makers, employees, other users, and stakeholders for new systems.

Without question, training users is an essential part of user preparation, whether they are trained by internal personnel or by external training firms. In some cases, companies that provide software also train users at no charge or at a reasonable price. The cost of training can be negotiated during the selection of new software. Other companies conduct user training throughout the systems development process. Concerns and apprehensions about the new system must be eliminated through these training programs. Employees should be acquainted with the system's capabilities and limitations by the time they are ready to use it.

12.2.5 IS Personnel: Hiring and Training

Depending on the size of the new system, an organization might have to hire and, in some cases, train new IS personnel. An IS manager, systems analysts, computer programmers, data-entry operators, and similar personnel might be needed for the new system.

As with users, the eventual success of any system depends on how it is used by the IS personnel within the organization. Training programs should be conducted for the IS personnel who will be looking after the new computer system. These programs are similar to those for the users, although they can be more detailed in the technical aspects of the systems. Effective training will help IS personnel use the new system to perform their jobs and support other users in the organization.

12

12.2.6 Site Preparation

The location of the new system needs to be prepared, a process called **site preparation**. For a small system, site preparation can be as simple as rearranging the furniture in an office to make room for a computer. With a larger system, this process is not so easy because it can require special wiring and air conditioning. One or two rooms might have to be completely renovated, and additional furniture might have to be purchased. A special floor might have to be built, under which the cables connecting the various computer components are placed, and a new security system might be needed to protect the equipment. For larger systems, additional power circuits might also be required.

site preparation Preparation of the location of a new system.

12.2.7 Data Preparation

Data preparation, or data conversion, involves making sure that all files and databases are ready to be used with the new computer software and systems. If an organization is installing a new payroll program for instance, the old employee-payroll data might have to be converted into a format that can be used by the new computer software or system. After the data has been prepared or converted, the computerized database system or other software will then be used to maintain and update the computer files.

data preparation (data conversion) Ensuring all files and databases are ready to be used with new computer software and systems.

12.2.8 Installation

Installation is the process of physically placing the computer equipment on the site and making it operational. Although normally the hardware manufacturer is responsible for installing computer equipment, someone from the organization (usually the IS manager) should oversee the process, making sure that all equipment specified in the contract is installed at the proper location. After the system is installed, the manufacturer performs several tests to ensure that the equipment is operating as it should. After this, the acquired software can be installed on the new hardware and the system is again tested.

installation The process of physically placing the computer equipment on the site and making it operational.

12.2.9 Testing

Good testing procedures are essential to make sure that the new or modified information system operates as intended. Inadequate testing can result in mistakes and problems. A popular tax preparation company in the U.S., for example, implemented a web-based tax preparation system, but people could see one another's tax returns. The president of the tax preparation company called it 'our worst-case scenario'. Better testing can prevent these types of problems.

Several forms of testing should be used, including testing each program (**unit testing**), testing the entire system of programs (**system testing**), testing the application with a large amount of data (**volume testing**), and testing all related systems together (**integration testing**), as well as conducting any tests required by the user (**acceptance testing**).

Alpha testing involves testing an incomplete or early version of the system, while **beta testing** involves testing a complete and stable system by end users. Alpha-unit testing, for example, is testing an individual program before it is completely finished. Beta-unit testing, on the other hand, is performed after alpha testing, when the individual program is complete and ready for use by end users.

Unit testing is accomplished by developing test data that will force the computer to execute every statement in the program. In addition, each program is tested with abnormal data to determine how it will handle problems.

unit testing Testing of individual programs.

system testing Testing the entire system of programs.

volume testing Testing the application with a large amount of data.

integration testing Testing all related systems together.

acceptance testing Conducting any tests required by the user.

alpha testing Testing an incomplete or early version of the system.

beta testing Testing a complete and stable system by end users.

12

System testing requires the testing of all the programs together. It is not uncommon for the output from one program to become the input for another. So, system testing ensures that the output from one program can be used as input for another program within the system. Volume testing ensures that the entire system can handle a large amount of data under normal operating conditions. Integration testing ensures that the new programs can interact with other major applications. It also ensures that data flows efficiently and without error to other applications. For example, a new inventory control application might require data input from an older order processing application. Integration testing would be done to ensure smooth data flow between the new and existing applications. Integration testing is typically done after unit and system testing. Metaserver, a software company for the insurance industry, has developed a tool called iConnect to perform integration testing for different insurance applications and databases.

Ethical and Societal Issues

E-Voting in the U.K.

The term 'e-voting' encompasses several concepts including electronic counting of votes and voting 'from a distance', where voters cast their vote, which is transferred electronically to the relevant authorities.

The Open Rights Group in the U.K. aims to raise awareness of digital rights abuses. One of its recent reports concerns e-voting, trialed in May 2007 in Scotland and England. The government is keen to push e-voting as an alternative to casting paper votes, in order to get more of the population involved in politics – in the past voter apathy has seen low turnouts on election day. E-voting is seen to be more convenient that the traditional system and therefore the government thinks more people will vote. However, according to the Open Rights Group, the systems that were piloted need substantial

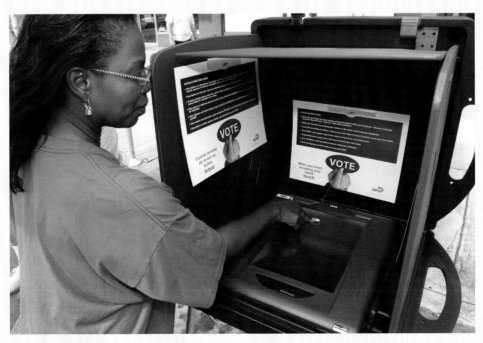

© Jeff Greenberg/Alamy.

(continued)

12

improvement. They found that the PCs used in the polling stations often lacked basic security measures – it would have been very easy for someone to install a program onto the system to alter the results without detection.

In a Scottish region, an Excel spreadsheet was used to calculate the result. The problem was, there were more parties than could fit on the screen at the same time, meaning that the votes for one of the most popular parties in Scotland were almost ignored by the officer about the announce the results. The candidate himself had to point this out to the officer. In another incident, on the web page, there was a mix up with the logo of one party appearing beside the candidate for another party.

Questions

1 In order to be used, an e-voting system must be trusted by citizens. After incidents such as these, will the public ever be able to trust e-voting?

2 What would the government have to do to ensure public trust?

3 Do you think e-voting will overcome voter apathy? Explain your answer.

4 What technologies could be used to encourage people to vote? Is a technology answer appropriate?

SOURCES: Evans, D. 'E-voting Trial Fails to Answer Technology Questions', *Computing*, July 26, 2007, http://www.computing.co.uk/computing/ analysis/2194955/voting-trial-fails-answer; Open Rights Group (website), http://www.openrightsgroup.org/e-voting-main/.

Finally, acceptance testing makes sure that the new or modified system is operating as intended. Run times, the amount of memory required, disk access methods, and more can be tested during this phase. Acceptance testing ensures that all performance objectives defined for the system or application are satisfied. Involving users in acceptance testing can help them understand and effectively interact with the new system. Acceptance testing is the final check of the system before start-up.

12.2.10 Start-Up

Start-up, also called cutover, begins with the final tested information system. When start-up is finished, the system is fully operational. Start-up can be critical to the success of the organization. If not done properly, the results can be disastrous. One of the authors is aware of a small manufacturing company that decided to stop an accounting service used to send out bills on the same day they were going to start their own program to send out bills to customers. The manufacturing company wanted to save money by using their own billing program developed by an employee of the company. The new program didn't work, the accounting service wouldn't help because they were upset about being terminated, and the manufacturing company wasn't able to send out any bills to customers for more than three months. The company almost went bankrupt.

start-up The process of making the final tested information system fully operational.

Various start-up approaches are available (see Figure 12.10). **Direct conversion** (also called plunge, big bang, or direct cutover) involves stopping the old system and starting the new system on a given date. Direct conversion is usually the least desirable approach because of the potential for problems and errors when the old system is shut off and the new system is turned on at the same instant.

direct conversion Stopping the old system and starting the new system on a given date.

phase-in approach Slowly replacing components of the old system with those of the new one. This process is repeated for each application until the new system is running every application and performing as expected; also called a piecemeal approach.

The **phase-in approach** is a popular technique preferred by many organizations. In this approach, sometimes called a piecemeal approach, components of the new system are slowly phased in while components of the old one are slowly phased out. When everyone is confident that the new system is performing as expected, the old system is completely phased out. This gradual replacement is repeated for each application until the new system is running every application. In some cases, the phase-in approach can take months or years.

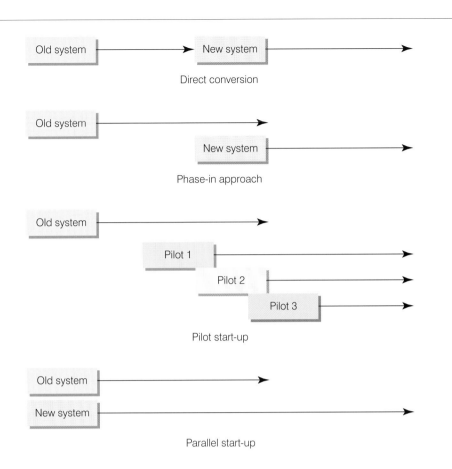

Figure 12.10 Start-Up Approaches

Pilot running involves introducing the new system with direct conversion for one group of users rather than all users. For example, a manufacturing company with many retail outlets throughout the country could use the pilot start-up approach and install a new inventory control system at one of the retail outlets. When this pilot retail outlet runs without problems, the new inventory control system can be implemented at other retail outlets. The National Health Service Cancer Registry in England, for example, used a pilot start-up approach to implement and test a new system to manage and integrate hundreds of cancer-related data sources.[13]

pilot running Introducing the new system by direct conversion for one group of users rather than all users.

Parallel running involves running both the old and new systems for a period of time. The output of the new system is compared closely with the output of the old system, and any differences are reconciled. When users are comfortable that the new system is working correctly, the old system is eliminated.

Parallel running running both the old and the new systems for a period of time.

12.2.11 User Acceptance

Most mainframe computer manufacturers use a formal **user acceptance document** – a formal agreement the user signs stating that a phase of the installation or the complete system is approved. This is a legal document that usually removes or reduces the IS vendor's liability for problems that occur after the user acceptance document has been signed. Because this document is so important, many companies get legal assistance before they sign it. Stakeholders can also be involved in acceptance testing to make sure that the benefits to them are indeed realized.

user acceptance document A formal agreement signed by the user that states that a phase of the installation or the complete system is approved.

12

12.3 Systems Operation and Maintenance

Systems operation involves all aspects of using the new or modified system in all kinds of operating conditions. Getting the most out of a new or modified system during its operation is the

systems operation Use of a new or modified system.

most important aspect of systems operations for many organizations. Throughout this book, we have seen many examples of information systems operating in a variety of settings and industries. Thus, we will not cover the operation of an information system in detail in this section. The operation of any information system, however, does require adequate training and support before the system is used and continual support while the system is being operated. This training and support is required for all stakeholders, including employees, customers, and others. Companies typically provide training through seminars, manuals, and online documentation. To provide adequate support, many companies use a formal help desk. A help desk consists of people with technical expertise, computer systems, manuals, and other resources needed to solve problems and give accurate answers to questions. With today's advances in telecommunications, help desks can be located around the world. If you are having trouble with your PC and call a toll-free number for assistance, you might reach a help desk in India or China. For most organizations, operations costs over the life of a system are much greater than the development costs.

systems maintenance and review The systems development phase that ensures the system operates as intended and modifies the system so that it continues to meet changing business needs.

Systems maintenance involves checking, changing, and enhancing the system to make it more useful in achieving user and organizational goals.[14] Maintenance is important for individuals, groups, and organizations.[15] Organizations often have personnel dedicated to maintenance.

The maintenance process can be especially difficult for older software. A legacy system is an old system that might have been patched or modified repeatedly over time. An old payroll program written in COBOL decades ago and frequently changed is an example of a legacy system. Legacy systems can be very expensive to maintain. At some point, it becomes less expensive to switch to new programs and applications than to repair and maintain the legacy system. Maintenance costs for older legacy systems can be 50 percent of total operating costs in some cases.

Software maintenance is a major concern for organizations. In some cases, organizations encounter major problems that require recycling the entire systems development process. In other situations, minor modifications are sufficient to remedy problems. Hardware maintenance is also important. Companies such as IBM are investigating autonomic computing, in which computers will be able to manage and maintain themselves.[16] The goal is for computers to be self-configuring, self-protecting, self-healing, and self-optimizing. Being self-configuring allows a computer to handle new hardware, software, or other changes to its operating environment. Being self-protecting means a computer can identify potential attacks, prevent them when possible, and recover from attacks if they occur. Attacks can include viruses, worms, identity theft, and industrial espionage. Being 'self-healing' means a computer can fix problems when they occur, and being 'self-optimizing' allows a computer to run faster and get more done in less time. Getting rid of old equipment is an important part of maintenance. The options include selling it on web auction sites such as eBay, recycling the equipment at a computer recycling centre, and donating it to a charitable organization, such as a school, library, or religious organization. When discarding old computer systems, it is always a good idea to permanently remove sensitive files and programs. Companies, including McAfee, have software to help people remove data and programs from old computers and transfer them to new ones.[17]

12.3.1 Reasons for Maintenance

After a program is written, it will need ongoing maintenance. To some extent, a program is similar to a car that needs oil changes, tune-ups, and repairs at certain times. Experience shows that frequent, minor maintenance to a program, if properly done, can prevent major system failures later. Some of the reasons for program maintenance are the following:

- Changes in business processes.
- New requests from stakeholders, users, and managers.
- Bugs or errors in the program.
- Technical and hardware problems.
- Corporate mergers and acquisitions.
- Government regulations.
- Change in the operating system or hardware on which the application runs.
- Unexpected events, such as severe weather or terrorist attacks.

Most companies modify their existing programs instead of developing new ones because existing software performs many important functions, and companies can have millions of dollars invested in their old legacy systems. So, as new systems needs are identified, the burden of fulfilling the needs most often falls on the existing system. Old programs are repeatedly modified to meet ever-changing needs. Yet, over time, repeated modifications tend to interfere with the system's overall structure, reducing its efficiency and making further modifications more burdensome.

12.3.2 Types of Maintenance

Software companies and many other organizations use four generally accepted categories to signify the amount of change involved in maintenance. A **slipstream upgrade** is a minor upgrade – typically a code adjustment or minor bug fix. Many companies don't announce to users that a slipstream upgrade has been made. A slipstream upgrade usually requires recompiling all the code, so it can create entirely new bugs. This maintenance practice can explain why the same computers sometimes work differently with what is supposedly the same software. A **patch** is a minor change to correct a problem or make a small enhancement. It is usually an addition to an existing program. That is, the programming code representing the system enhancement is usually 'patched into', or added to, the existing code. Although slipstream upgrades and patches are minor changes, they can cause users and support personnel big problems if the programs do not run as before. A new **release** is a significant program change that often requires changes in the documentation of the software. Finally, a new **version** is a major program change, typically encompassing many new features.

slipstream upgrade A minor upgrade – typically a code adjustment or minor bug fix – not worth announcing. It usually requires recompiling all the code and, in so doing, it can create entirely new bugs.

patch A minor change to correct a problem or make a small enhancement. It is usually an addition to an existing program.

release A significant program change that often requires changes in the documentation of the software.

version A major program change, typically encompassing many new features.

12.3.3 The Request for Maintenance Form

Because of the amount of effort that can be spent on maintenance, many organizations require a **request for maintenance form** to authorize modification of programs. This form is usually signed by a business manager, who documents the need for the change and identifies the priority of the change relative to other work that has been requested. The IS group reviews the form and identifies the programs to be changed, determines the programmer who will be assigned to the project, estimates the expected completion date, and develops a technical description of the change. A cost–benefit analysis might be required if the change requires substantial resources.

request for maintenance form A form authorizing modification of programs.

12

12.3.4 Performing Maintenance

Depending on organizational policies, the people who perform systems maintenance vary. In some cases, the team who designs and builds the system also performs maintenance. This on-going responsibility gives the designers and programmers an incentive to build systems well from the outset: If there are problems, they will have to fix them. In other cases, organizations have a separate **maintenance team**. This team is responsible for modifying, fixing, and updating existing software.

maintenance team A special IS team responsible for modifying, fixing, and updating existing software.

In the past, companies had to maintain each computer system or server separately. With hundreds or thousands of computers scattered throughout an organization, this task could be very costly and time consuming. Today, the maintenance function is becoming more automated. Some companies, for example, use maintenance tools and software that will allow them to maintain and upgrade software centrally.

A number of vendors have developed tools to ease the software maintenance burden. Relativity Technologies has developed RescueWare, a product that converts third-generation code such as COBOL to highly maintainable C++, Java, or Visual Basic object-oriented code. Using RescueWare, maintenance personnel download mainframe code to Windows NT or Windows 2000 workstations. They then use the product's graphical tools to analyze the original system's inner workings. RescueWare lets a programmer see the original system as a set of object views, which visually illustrate module functioning and program structures. IS personnel can choose one of three levels of transformation: revamping the user interface, converting the database access, and transforming procedure logic (Figure 12.11).

Figure 12.11 Relativity Technologies' Modernization Workbench *Relativity Technologies' Modernization Workbench is a PC-based software solution that enables companies to consolidate legacy or redundant systems into one, more maintainable and modern application.*

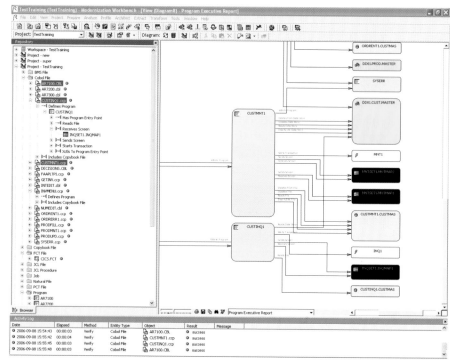

SOURCE: Courtesy of Relativity Technologies.

12.3.5 The Financial Implications of Maintenance

The cost of maintenance is staggering. For older programs, the total cost of maintenance can be up to five times greater than the total cost of development. In other words, a program that originally cost €25 000 to develop might cost €125 000 to maintain over its lifetime. The average programmers can spend more than half their time on maintaining existing programs instead of developing new ones. In addition, as programs get older, total maintenance expenditures in time and money increase. With the use of newer programming languages and approaches, including object-oriented programming, maintenance costs are expected to decline. Even so, many organizations have literally millions of dollars invested in applications written in older languages (such as COBOL), which are both expensive and time consuming to maintain. The financial implications of maintenance mean companies must keep track of why systems are maintained, instead of simply keeping cost figures. This is another reason that documentation of maintenance tasks is so crucial. A determining factor in the decision to replace a system is the point at which it is costing more to fix it than to replace it.

12.3.6 The Relationship Between Maintenance and Design

Programs are expensive to develop, but they are even more expensive to maintain. Programs that are well designed and documented to be efficient, structured, and flexible are less expensive to maintain in later years. Thus, there is a direct relationship between design and maintenance. More time spent on design up front can mean less time spent on maintenance later.

In most cases, it is worth the extra time and expense to design a good system. Consider a system that costs €250 000 to develop. Spending ten percent more on design would cost an additional €25 000, bringing the total design cost to €275 000. Maintenance costs over the life of the program could be €1 000 000. If this additional design expense can reduce maintenance costs by ten percent, the savings in maintenance costs would be €100 000. Over the life of the program, the net savings would be €75 000 (€100 000–€25 000).

The need for good design goes beyond mere costs. Companies risk ignoring small system problems when they arise, but these small problems can become large in the future. As mentioned earlier, because maintenance programmers spend an estimated 50 percent or more of their time deciphering poorly written, undocumented program code, they have little time to spend on developing new, more effective systems. If put to good use, the tools and techniques discussed in this chapter will allow organizations to build longer-lasting, more reliable systems.

12.4 Systems Review

Systems review, the final step of systems development, is the process of analyzing systems to make sure that they are operating as intended. This process often compares the performance and benefits of the system as it was designed with the actual performance and benefits of the system in operation.[18] A payroll application being developed for the Irish Health Service, for example, was almost €120 million over budget.[19] As a result, work on the application that serves about 37 000 workers was halted so the entire project could be reviewed in detail. The purpose of the systems review is to make sure that any additional work will result in a program that will work as intended.

systems review The final step of systems development, involving the analysis of systems to make sure that they are operating as intended.

Problems and opportunities uncovered during systems review trigger systems development and begin the process anew. For example, as the number of users of an interactive system increases, it is not unusual for system response time to increase. If the increase in response time is too great, it might be necessary to redesign some of the system, modify databases, or increase the power of the computer hardware. When faced with a possible patent infringement problem, RIM, the maker of the popular BlackBerry phone and e-mail service, developed backup software that could be used in case the courts ruled against the company.[20] Even though RIM was able to settle the suit out of court, BlackBerry users were happy that the company had a backup plan.

12

Internal employees, external consultants, or both can perform systems review. When the problems or opportunities are industry-wide, people from several firms can get together. In some cases, they collaborate at an IS conference or in a private meeting involving several firms.

12.4.1 Types of Review Procedures

There are two types of review procedures: event driven and time driven (see Table 12.5). An **event-driven review** is triggered by a problem or opportunity such as an error, a corporate merger, or a new market for products.[21] Natural disasters often revealed flaws in older systems, causing many companies and organizations to review their existing systems. Recent floods in the U.K., for example, caused insurance companies to introduce flood maps to their quotation systems.

event-driven review A review triggered by a problem or opportunity such as an error, a corporate merger, or a new market for products.

In contrast, some companies use a continuous improvement approach to systems development. With this approach, an organization makes changes to a system even when small problems or opportunities occur. Although continuous improvement can keep the system current and responsive, repeatedly designing and implementing changes can be both time consuming and expensive.

A **time-driven review** is performed after a specified amount of time. Many application programs are reviewed every six months to one year. With this approach, an existing system is monitored on a schedule. If problems or opportunities are uncovered, a new systems development cycle can be initiated. A payroll application, for example, can be reviewed once a year to make sure that it is still operating as expected. If it is not, changes are made.

time-driven review Review performed after a specified amount of time.

Most companies use both approaches. A billing application, for example, might be reviewed once a year for errors, inefficiencies, and opportunities to reduce operating costs. This is a time-driven approach. In addition, the billing application might be redone after a corporate merger, if one or more new managers require different information or reports, or if federal laws on bill collecting and privacy change. This is an event-driven approach.

12.4.2 Factors to Consider During Systems Review

Systems review should investigate a number of important factors, such as the following:

- *Mission:* Is the computer system helping the organization achieve its overall mission? Are stakeholder needs and desires satisfied or exceeded with the new or modified system?
- *Organizational goals:* Does the computer system support the specific goals of the various areas and departments of the organization?
- *Hardware and software:* Are hardware and software up to date and adequate to handle current and future processing needs?

Table 12.5 Examples of Review Types

Event Driven	Time Driven
Problem with an existing system	Monthly review
Merger	Yearly review
New accounting system	Review every few years
Executive decision that an upgraded Internet site is needed to stay competitive	Five-year review

■ *Database:* Is the current database up to date and accurate? Is database storage space adequate to handle current and future needs?

■ *Telecommunications:* Is the current telecommunications system fast enough, and does it allow managers and workers to send and receive timely messages? Does it allow for fast order processing and effective customer service?

■ *Information systems personnel:* Are there sufficient IS personnel to perform current and projected processing tasks?

■ *Control:* Are rules and procedures for system use and access acceptable? Are the existing control procedures adequate to protect against errors, invasion of privacy, fraud, and other potential problems?

■ *Training:* Are there adequate training programs and provisions for both users and IS personnel?

■ *Costs:* Are development and operating costs in line with what is expected? Is there an adequate IS budget to support the organization?

■ *Complexity:* Is the system overly complex and difficult to operate and maintain?

■ *Reliability:* Is the system reliable? What is the mean time between failures (MTBF)?

■ *Efficiency:* Is the computer system efficient? Are system outputs generated by the right amount of inputs, including personnel, hardware, software, budget, and others?

■ *Response time:* How long does it take the system to respond to users during peak processing times?

■ *Documentation:* Is the documentation still valid? Are changes in documentation needed to reflect the current situation?

12.4.3 System Performance Measurement

Systems review often involves monitoring the system, called **system performance measurement**. The number of errors encountered, the amount of memory required, the amount of processing or CPU time needed, and other problems should be closely observed.[22] If a particular system is not performing as expected, it should be modified, or a new system should be developed or acquired.

Setting up benchmarks for performance measurement can be critical. **System performance products** have been developed to measure all components of the information system, including hardware, software, database, telecommunications, and network systems. When properly used, system performance products can quickly and efficiently locate actual or potential problems.

system performance measurement Monitoring the system – the number of errors encountered, the amount of memory required, the amount of processing or CPU time needed, and other problems.

system performance products Software that measures all components of the computer-based information system, including hardware, software, database, telecommunications, and network systems.

A number of products have been developed to assist in assessing system performance. OMEGAMON from IBM can monitor system performance in real time. Precise Software Solutions has system performance products that provide around-the-clock performance monitoring for Oracle database applications. Mercury Interactive offers a software tool called Diagnostic to help companies analyze the performance of their computer systems, diagnose potential problems, and take corrective action if needed.[23]

Measuring a system is, in effect, the final task of systems development. The results of this process can bring the development team back to the beginning of the development lifecycle, where the process begins again.

12

Summary

Designing new systems or modifying existing ones should always help an organization achieve its goals. The purpose of systems design is to prepare the detailed design needs for a new system or modifications to the existing system. Logical systems design refers to the way that the various components of an information system will work together. The logical design includes data requirements for output and input, processing, files and databases, telecommunications, procedures, personnel and job design, and controls and security design. Physical systems design refers to the specification of the actual physical components. The physical design must specify characteristics for hardware and software design, database and telecommunications, and personnel and procedures design.

Logical and physical design can be accomplished using the traditional systems development lifecycle or the object-oriented approach. Using the object-oriented approach, analysts design key objects and classes of objects in the new or updated system. The sequence of events that a new or modified system requires is often called a scenario, which can be diagrammed in a sequence diagram.

A number of special design considerations should be taken into account during both logical and physical system design. Interface design and control relates to how users access and interact with the system. A sign-on procedure consists of identification numbers, passwords, and other safeguards needed for individuals to gain access to computer resources. If the system under development is interactive, the design must consider menus, help facilities, table lookup facilities, and restart procedures. A good interactive dialogue will ask for information in a clear manner, respond rapidly, be consistent among applications, and use an attractive format. Also, it will avoid use of computer jargon and treat the user with respect.

System security and control involves many aspects. Error prevention, detection, and correction should be part of the system design process. Causes of errors include human activities, natural phenomena, and technical problems. Designers should be alert to prevention of fraud and invasion of privacy.

Disaster recovery is an important aspect of systems design. Disaster planning is the process of anticipating and providing for disasters. A disaster can be an act of nature (a flood, fire, or earthquake) or a human act (terrorism, error, labour unrest, or erasure of an important file). The primary tools used in disaster planning and recovery are hardware, software, database, telecommunications, and personnel backup.

Security, fraud, and the invasion of privacy are also important design considerations. Most IS departments establish tight systems controls to maintain data security. Systems controls can help prevent computer misuse, crime, and fraud by employees and others. Systems controls include input, output, processing, database, telecommunications, and personnel controls.

Whether an individual is purchasing a personal computer or an experienced company is acquiring an expensive mainframe computer, the system could be obtained from one or more vendors. Some of the factors to consider in selecting a vendor are the vendor's reliability and financial stability, the type of service offered after the sale, the goods and services the vendor offers and keeps in stock, the vendor's willingness to demonstrate its products, the vendor's ability to repair hardware, the vendor's ability to modify its software, the availability of vendor-offered training of IS personnel and system users, and evaluations of the vendor by independent organizations.

If new hardware or software will be purchased from a vendor, a formal request for proposal (RFP) is needed. The RFP outlines the company's needs; in response, the vendor provides a written reply. Financial options to consider include purchase, lease, and rent.

RFPs from various vendors are reviewed and narrowed down to the few most likely candidates. In the final evaluation, a variety of techniques – including group consensus, cost–benefit analysis, point evaluation, and benchmark tests – can be used. In group consensus, a decision-making group is appointed and given responsibility for making the final evaluation and selection. With cost–benefit analysis, all costs and benefits of the alternatives are expressed in monetary terms. Benchmarking involves comparing computer systems operating under the same condition. Point evaluation assigns weights to evaluation factors, and each alternative is evaluated in terms of each factor and given a score from 0 to 100. After the vendor is chosen, contract negotiations can begin.

One of the most important steps in systems design is to develop a good contract if new computer facilities are being acquired. A final design report is developed at the end of the systems design phase.

The primary emphasis of systems implementation is to make sure that the right information is delivered to the right person in the right format at the right time. The purpose of systems implementation is to install the system and make everything, including users, ready for its operation. Systems implementation includes hardware acquisition, software acquisition or development, user preparation, hiring and training of personnel, site and data preparation, installation, testing, start-up, and user acceptance. Hardware acquisition requires purchasing, leasing, or renting computer resources from an IS vendor. Hardware is typically obtained from a computer hardware vendor.

Software can be purchased from vendors or developed in-house – a decision termed the make-or-buy decision. A purchased software package usually has a lower cost, less risk regarding the features and performance, and easy installation. The amount of development effort is also less when software is purchased. Developing software can result in a system that more closely meets the business needs and has increased flexibility in terms of customization and changes. Developing software also has greater potential for providing a competitive advantage. Increasingly, companies are using service providers to acquire software, Internet access, and other IS resources. Software development is often performed by a chief programmer team – a group of IS professionals who design, develop, and implement a software program. Structured design is a philosophy of designing and developing application software. Other tools, such as cross-platform development and integrated development environments (IDEs), make software development easier and more thorough. CASE tools are often used to automate some of these techniques.

Database and telecommunications software development involves acquiring the necessary databases, networks, telecommunications, and Internet facilities. Companies have a wide array of choices, including newer object-oriented database systems.

Implementation must address personnel requirements. User preparation involves readying managers, employees, and other users for the new system. New IS personnel might need to be hired, and users must be well trained in the system's functions. Preparation of the physical site of the system must be done, and any existing data to be used in the new system will require conversion to the new format. Hardware installation is done during the implementation step, as is testing. Testing includes program (unit) testing, systems testing, volume testing, integration testing, and acceptance testing.

Start-up begins with the final tested information system. When start-up is finished, the system is fully operational. There are a number of different start-up approaches. Direct conversion involves stopping the old system and starting the new system on a given date. With the phase-in approach, sometimes called a piecemeal approach, components of the new system are slowly phased in while components of the old one are slowly phased out. When everyone is confident that the new system is performing as expected, the old system is completely phased out. Pilot start-up involves running the new system for one group of users rather than all users. Parallel start-up involves running both the old and new systems for a period of time. The output of the new system is compared closely with the output of the old system, and any differences are reconciled. When users are comfortable that the new system is working correctly, the old system is eliminated. Many IS vendors ask the user to sign a formal user acceptance document that releases the IS vendor from liability for problems that occur after the document is signed.

Maintenance and review add to the useful life of a system but can consume large amounts of resources. These activities can benefit from the same rigorous methods and project management techniques applied to systems development. Systems operation is the use of a new or modified system. Systems maintenance involves checking, changing, and enhancing the system to make it more useful in obtaining user and organizational goals. Maintenance is critical for the continued smooth operation of the system. The costs of performing maintenance can well exceed the original cost of acquiring the system. Some major causes of maintenance are new requests from stakeholders and managers, enhancement requests from users, bugs or errors, technical or hardware problems, newly added equipment, changes in organizational structure, and government regulations.

Maintenance can be as simple as a program patch to correct a small problem to the more complex upgrading of software with a new release from a vendor. For older programs, the total cost of maintenance can be greater than the total cost of development. Increased emphasis on design can often reduce maintenance costs. Requests for maintenance should be documented with a request for maintenance form, a document that formally authorizes modification of programs. The development team or a specialized maintenance team can then make approved changes. Maintenance can be greatly simplified with the object-oriented approach.

Systems review is the process of analyzing and monitoring systems to make sure that they are operating as intended. The two types of review procedures are the event-driven review and the time-driven review. An event-driven review is triggered by a problem or opportunity. A time-driven review is started after a specified amount of time.

Systems review involves measuring how well the system is supporting the mission and goals of the organization. System performance measurement monitors the system for number of errors, amount of memory and processing time required, and so on.

Self-Assessment Test

1 Determining the needed hardware and software for a new system is an example of _____.
   a. logical design
   b. physical design
   c. interactive design
   d. object-oriented design

2 Disaster planning is an important part of designing security and control systems. True or false?

3 The _____ often results in a formal bid that is used to determine who gets a contract for designing new or modifying existing systems. It specifies in detail the required resources such as hardware and software.

4 Near the end of the design stage, an organization prohibits further changes in the design of the system. This is called _____.

5 Software can be purchased from external developers or developed in house. This decision is often called the _____ decision.

6 What type of documentation is used by computer operators to execute a program and by analysts and programmers?
   a. unit documentation
   b. integrated documentation
   c. technical documentation
   d. user documentation

7 _____ testing involves testing the entire system of programs.

8 The phase-in approach to conversion involves running both the old system and the new system for three months or longer. True or false?

9 A(n) _____ is a minor change to correct a problem or make a small enhancement to a program or system.

10 Corporate mergers and acquisitions can be a reason for systems maintenance. True or false?

Review Questions

1 What is the purpose of systems design?

2 What is interactive processing? What design factors should be taken into account for this type of processing?

3 What is the difference between logical and physical design?

4 What are the different types of software and database backup? Describe the procedure you use to back up your homework files.

5 Identify specific controls that are used to maintain input integrity and security.

6 What is an RFP? What is typically included in one? How is it used?

7 What are the major steps of systems implementation?

8 What are some tools and techniques for software development?

9 Describe how you back up the files you use on your PC.

10 What are the steps involved in testing the information system?

Discussion Questions

1 Describe the participants in the systems design stage. How do these participants compare with the participants of systems investigation?

2 Assume that you want to start a new DVD rental business for students at your college or university. Go through logical design for a new information system to help you keep track of the videos in your inventory.

3 Assume that you are the owner of an online stock-trading company. Describe how you could design the trading system to recover from a disaster.

4 Identify some of the advantages and disadvantages of purchasing versus developing software.

5 Is it equally important for all systems to have a disaster recovery plan? Why or why not?

Web Exercises

1 Use the Internet to find two different systems development projects that failed to meet cost or performance objectives. Summarize the problems and what should have been done. You might be asked to develop a report or send an e-mail message to your instructor about what you found.

2 Using the Web, search for information on structured design and programming. Also search the web for information about the object-oriented approach to systems design and implementation. Write a report on what you found. Under what conditions would you use these approaches to systems development and implementation?

Case One

Technology Development at Harrods

Since it first opened its doors in 1849, Harrods has placed a great emphasis on selling high quality merchandise and has become one of the world's most famous shops. Most of Harrods' technology is managed by an in-house IT department. David Llamas, IT director at Harrods, has spent the past three years refreshing the luxury retailer's IT infrastructure. 'It has been a huge challenge,' he says. 'But my view is that we now have the most proficient IT department of any company I have worked for.' Such progress means the business can now start reaping the benefits of consolidation and standardization – and Llamas, meanwhile, can start innovating, rather than renovating. 'We had a very old IT infrastructure that had become unreliable,' says Llamas, who joined Harrods in 2003 after 12 years working as a consultant and ERP manager. 'It meant we would have a critical systems failure on

an almost weekly basis.' Change at Harrods was inevitable. And Llamas' first step was to reduce staff numbers, with the IT team more than halved from 165 to 80 during the past four years. 'It is not because we run fewer projects – we actually run more,' he says. 'It is because the profile of the IT department has changed. Technology is not about numbers,' he says. 'It is about the quality of people you have.'

Going forward, Llamas says his key focus is on business growth because the opportunity for cost savings is reduced. Key areas of concentration will include business intelligence and attempts to improve efficiency through analytics. Llamas says revenue generation projects could cover a range of areas, including online purchasing, smarter planning, and consumer shopping behaviour. 'We are now looking for the business to come up with models about how they want to save money and this decision-making process is the real focus for Harrods,' he says. 'It is about how we can become smarter with regards to our pricing strategy and replenishment models.' In an attempt to provide increased intelligence, the firm will roll out an integrated online infrastructure next month. Till-based retail sales have already been converted to an electronic point of sale (Epos) platform – and the e-commerce system will deal with direct purchases from the company's website and call centre.

As part of the retailer's service-oriented architecture – and regardless of which channel the customer decides to purchase from, such as store, airport, shop, website or phone – information from the online and Epos system will be fed into an SAP enterprise resource planning database. Llamas says the approach will make data management more straightforward. Before, the systems were not talking to each other and not sharing information, he says. 'We had quite a fragmented applications landscape, so you would have a legacy system that was only used by food and beverage and another that was only used by the furniture department. Now we still have a flexible infrastructure and everything is web services-enabled, but from a data management perspective you do not have all these different systems that hold information. What we have got is one version of the truth – a single platform.'

Llamas says that users are now used to working with data and unless you have a flexible and online architecture, you cannot run at the correct pace. 'Four years ago we would not have instant reporting on sales and now you can see how the store is performing by the minute,' he says. 'Sales are reporting to BlackBerrys by the hour – and if it fails, it is a massive disaster.'

The IT director is keen to implement other systems that can help improve efficiency. He is investigating how virtualization can provide more benefits to the business, especially with regards to vendors that provide industry-standard applications on a pay-as-you-go basis. He is also analyzing the possibility of using Citrix's thin client technology for desktop systems and is keen to expand the company's use of service-oriented architecture. 'It is all about closing the loop when it comes to analysis,' says Llamas. 'Now you have all that information in your hands and you can rely on the quality of data that you have, the business is in a very good position to analyze and understand what is happening.' 'Clientelling', meanwhile, is one innovative project that attempts to improve business knowledge. Llamas describes clientelling – a process that stores the knowledge that sales assistants traditionally keep about clients in black books – as a strategic project for the business. 'Harrods has a relationship and loyalty with the customer,' says Llamas. 'Any retailer will agree that black book information belongs to the business.' Successful clienteling would allow Harrods to build successful after-sales schemes for its high-end customers, he says. Such pioneering projects help Llamas define the luxury retailer as a dynamic business. With sound financial backing and a concentration on service orientation, it would be sensible to expect more pioneering changes from Llamas and his team in the next few years.

Questions

1 What was the problem with Harrods' existing systems?

2 IT projects have been known to make people redundant. How should systems analysts and management respond to this fact? Should more than expected profits be used to assess projects?

3 What sort of people would you advise Llamas to hire and why? What technical and personal skills would they need? Can you outline a typical job advert for his IT department?

4 What are likley to be the big IT challenges for Harrods in the future?

SOURCES: Samuels, M, 'Making It Big', *Computing,* July 26, 2007, http://www.computing.co.uk/computing/analysis/2194855/making-big.

Case Two

Port of Brisbane Develops System to Tighten Security

Since the World Trade Center terrorist attacks of September 11, 2001, security has become a major concern for countries around the world, especially security at borders, airports, and seaports. In 2005, the Australian government passed a law that mandates Australian airports and ports allow the government to run background security checks on all employees. After they are cleared, airport and seaport employees should be issued security ID cards: Aviation Security Identification Cards (ASICs) and Maritime Security Identification Cards (MSICs).

The Australian government established a new department called AusCheck that should work with the Australian Security Intelligence Organization (ASIO) and the Australian Federal Police (AFP) to perform the background checks and issue ID cards. It is left to the seaports to provide security training for employees, make sure employees fill out the application forms for ID cards, submit applications to AusCheck, distribute ID cards to cleared employees, and work with government officials to deal with employees who don't clear the security check.

The government-owned Port of Brisbane Corporation is responsible for the operation and management of Australia's third busiest container port and the first to develop a system to process their 250 employees through the security check process. Believing strongly in the power of computer-based information systems, the administrators at the Port of Brisbane provided the requirements of the system to their system analysts as the basis for developing a system to automate the process.

Systems analysts first considered alternatives to training Port employees. They decided that the ideal method of delivery for the required 15-page security awareness course was over the web. Rather than creating the training system themselves, they turned to TodayCorp, the Asia-Pacific's largest online learning, development, and recruitment company, and one of the top ten eLearning solutions companies globally.

TodayCorp worked with Port of Brisbane systems experts to design an all-in-one solution that includes a web-based eLearning program and ID card registration system. Providing the training online saves the Port of Brisbane from having to hire trainers to provide face-to-face classes. An online system allows employees to work through the training at times convenient for them rather than attending a class at a required time. It also saves the Port the expense and inconvenience of taking employees off duty for training.

TodayCorp developed a training system that provided an enjoyable and thorough method of training. Quizzes are provided throughout the training to make sure employees are obtaining and retaining the necessary information. At the conclusion of the lesson, employees fill out an electronic registration form for a security ID card. When submitted, the system collects the employee information gathered from the online form and transfers it directly to the AusCheck database over a secure VPN connection.

After AusCheck has completed the security check, data is returned to the Port, which then notifies the employee. Employees report to the Port office where a photo is taken and the ID card is issued.

It took two months for systems developers at the Port of Brisbane and TodayCorp to develop and deliver the system. The system was reviewed and tested by Port administrators and given approval for use in February 2006.

TodayCorp developed the training and registration system using Macromedia Flash and XML. The system was developed in a manner that will allow TodayCorp to custom fit the system for other Australian ports with only a few minor changes.

Questions

1 What motivated the Port of Brisbane to develop its new system? What were the requirements of the system?

2 Are there any differences in developing a system for a government system and a system for a commercial organization? Explain your answer.

3 What were the benefits and costs of the new system to the Port of Brisbane Corporation, its employees, the Australian government, and Australian citizens?

4 What benefits were obtained by developing this system using commonly accepted standards such as Flash and XML in a manner that allow for customization?

SOURCES: Crawford, Michael, 'Aussie Ports Float Online Training to Meet Security Mandate', *Computerworld*, April 10, 2006, www.computerworld.com; Ferguson, Iain, 'Government Turns to IT for Airport, Port Security', *ZDNet Australia*, www.zdnet.com.au; TodayCorp (website), www.todaycorp.com; Port of Brisbane (website), www.portbris.com.au; Australian Government (website), www.tisn.gov.au/agd/WWW/agdHome.nsf/Page/RWP5C5D02388E1D3F35CA25719300234577.

Case Three

New Systems Allow Timex to Innovate Faster and with Less Risk

For nearly all of the 150 years that Timex has been manufacturing watches, the watch industry has been more about style than engineering. That trend has changed recently as technology is playing a more active role in all stages of product development, as well as being embedded in products themselves. In the past ten years, 'innovation' has become the industry buzzword as consumers demand new features in their watches. For example, consider watches that include wireless heart rate monitors or can use Earth satellites to compute the wearer's speed and distance.

Timex has 7500 employees in the U.S., South America, Europe, and Asia and sells 30 million watches annually. For years, Timex relied on an active project system to manage its products through their stages of development. The system was limited because it used individual files scattered in various locations that made it difficult for project participants to access information. The inefficient active project system created a 'disconnect between R&D and brand managers', as Bernd Becker, vice president of product development, puts it. Becker explains that this is 'a typical problem in many companies because engineers and brand managers talk in different languages'.

After executing a systems investigation and analysis, Timex systems analysts had a solid understanding of what they needed in a new system. The new system should improve communication and information access for all involved in product development, and help them innovate, speeding new products to market that were sure to sell. The company issued a request for proposals to three software vendors who specialize in product lifecycle management: Sopheon, Centric, and Oracle. Each vendor was invited to present solutions for review. Timex management and systems specialists were most impressed by Sopheon's Accolade software. Accolade employs a stage-gate approach, which uses milestones, or gates, at each step of innovation. It also allows everyone from designers and engineers to product marketing staffers to analyze discussions, reviews, planning, and decisions.

Sopheon software engineers worked with systems specialists at Timex to custom design the software to meet Timex's needs. After creating a detailed design of the system, Sopheon delivered the software to Timex. After a two-month implementation and testing phase, Timex began using the system in early 2006 in its daily operations to support actual projects. The package cost about €180 000 to deploy, including the first year of maintenance and user licenses. The new system is under scrutiny as it is being used to manage 45 projects, including new watch designs and feature innovations. It will take between six and ten months for the first Timex watch project to be completed and sent to market using Accolade.

So far, Timex is impressed with the results of the new system. By using Accolade, Timex expects to shave up to 30 percent off the time needed to develop a watch and get it to market. Furthermore, because Accolade runs on Microsoft Windows and integrates with Microsoft Office applications, with a familiar Windows-style and web-based interface, it has been easy for employees to learn. Investment in employee training has been minimal.

For the first time, Accolade allows Timex to bring all of its product development data into one place, making it easier and more efficient for Timex employees to offer suggestions in real time. The new system provides decision makers with key information regarding products, market demand, production requirements, and other variables that assist with risk management. New products are introduced to market faster and with less risk, providing Timex with a competitive advantage.

Questions

1 What led Timex to investigate a new system?

2 Did Timex make or buy? Explain your answer.

3 Describe the sort of activities that should have taken place during the testing phase. Who should have been involved and what should have been their role?

4 What grounds might Timex use to be 'impressed' with their new system? How could they measure if it is actually providing any benefits?

SOURCES: Weiss, Todd, 'Timex Ticking with New Product Innovation Software', *Computerworld,* June 30, 2006, www.computerworld.com; Timex (website), www.timex.com; Sopheon (website), www.sopheon.com.

Notes

[1] Arnott, David, 'Cognitive Biases and Decision Support Systems Development: A Design Science Approach', *Information Systems Journal,* January, 2006, p. 55.

[2] Greenemeier, Larry, 'Wanted: Up-Front Security', *Information Week,* January 2, 2006, p. 35.

[3] Cavusoglu, Huseyin, et al., 'The Value of Intrusion Detection Systems in Information Technology Security Architecture', *Information Systems Research,* March 2005, p. 28.

[4] Mearian, Lucas, 'CNL Financial Updates Disaster Recovery Plan', *Computerworld,* January 9, 2006, p. 8.

[5] Hadi, Mohammed, 'New Orleans Firm Fled Houston for Stamford', *Wall Street Journal,* September 27, 2005, p. C3.

[6] Brandel, Mary, 'Getting to Know You', *Computerworld,* February 21, 2005, p. 36.

[7] Zha, Xuan, 'Knowledge-Intensive Collaborative Design Modeling and Support: System Implementation and Application', *Computers in Industry,* January 2006, p. 56.

[8] McGee, Marianne, 'Outlook 2006', *Information Week,* January 2, 2006, p. 28.

[9] Thibodeau, Patrick, 'HP Gives Reprieve on Support to e300 Users', *Computerworld,* January 2, 2006, p. 8.

[10] Hoffman, Thomas, 'Return on Software', *Computerworld,* January 31, 2005, p. 39.

[11] Reinhardt, Andy, 'SAP: A Sea of Change in Software', *Business Week,* July 11, 2005, p. 46.

[12] Burrows, Peter, 'Bill Me Later', *Business Week,* January 16, 2006, p. 38.

[13] Havenstein, Heather, 'Pilot Project Aims to Improve Analysis and Delivery of Cancer Treatment', *Computerworld,* January 30, 2006, p. 24.

[14] Koten, C., Gray, A.R., 'An Application of Bayesian Network for Predicting Object-Oriented Software Maintainability', *Information and Software Technology,* January 2006, p. 59.

[15] Pratt, Mark, 'Shining a Light on Maintenance', *Computerworld,* February 13, 2006, p. 41.

[16] Thibodeau, Patrick, 'IBM Adds Autonomic Tools to Speed Up Error Detection', *Computerworld,* July 4, 2005, p. 7.

[17] Nuzu, Christine M., 'Before You Throw It Out', *Wall Street Journal,* September 12, 2005, p. R9.

[18] Songini, Marc, 'Buggy App Causes Tax Problems in Wisconsin', *Computerworld,* January 9, 2006, p. 12.

[19] Songini, Marc, 'Irish Agency Halts Work on Two SAP Application Projects', *Computerworld,* October 17, 2005, p. 12.

[20] Malykhina, Elena, 'BlackBerry Backup Plan', *Information Week,* February 13, 2006, p. 28.

[21] Hayashi, Yuka, 'Tokyo Exchange to Retool Trading System', *Wall Street Journal,* January 21, 2006, p. B1.

[22] Yang, Ching-Chien, et al., 'A Study of the Factors Impacting ERP System Performance – From the User's Perspective', *Journal of American Academy of Business,* March 2006, p. 161.

[23] Havenstein, Heather, 'Tools Bridge IT, Operations', *Computerworld,* April 4, 2005, p. 12.

World Views Case

Brandon Trust Develops MIS Capability for Improved Operations and Services

Andy Igonor

University of the West of England

Organizations typically exist to make money and to save money. But what about those organizations registered as charities, whose goals are something other than profit making? Brandon Trust, a major player in the healthcare sector, with an annual turnover exceeding £20 million, is a registered charity in England. It does not exist to make money; rather, in the words of its chief executive officer, Steve Bennett, Brandon Trust is a 'people supporting people' organization. As a visionary, Brandon Trust's CEO believes that making a difference is essential to sustaining the organization's aim and purpose.

In the quest to improve service operations, Steve Bennett met with Charles Harvey, a business strategist and expert in leadership and management practices, who also currently serves as dean of the U.K.'s Bristol Business School. The decision to invest in information systems followed from this preliminary study of the Brandon Trust's strategy and business systems. The study revealed a lack of consistency and some redundancy in existing processes stemming from a lack of integration. Brandon Trust's situation is similar to other enterprises and was of both theoretical and practical interest to researchers at the Bristol Business School who were studying business systems and innovation. The outcome of this consultation led to a partnership agreement to help in the strategic streamlining of service operations and delivery. Sponsored by the Knowledge Transfer Partnership (KTP) – a government-funded program – the project involves the automation, rationalization, and reengineering of part of Brandon Trust's activities and procedures, with the goal of eliminating bottlenecks in information production, distribution, and use.

Brandon Trust operates community teams, employment and training units, and daycare centers spread across various areas of Bristol and the South West region of England (of which Bristol is a part). Brandon Trust also provides intensive support and supported living so that people with disabilities can live in a place of their preference. In meeting its obligations, the Trust runs a coordinated operational network, where people, both office and field staff, have to effectively communicate in meeting clients' needs. Apart from its full-time employees, the Trust also recruits part-time, hourly workers to facilitate the efficient flow of services. Brandon Trust exists in a large market for learning disability care in which purchasers demand greater efficiency and effectiveness. Brandon Trust is a market leader in providing learning disability services, and it has grown by taking over contracts. Its service area is mainly confined to Bristol, South Gloucestershire, Bath, Northeast Somerset, and North Somerset. Its competitive

Brandon Trust — People supporting people

UNIQUE FUTURES

By kind permission of Brandon Trust

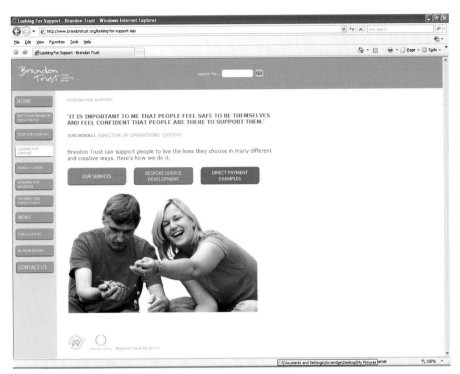

By kind permission of Brandon Trust

advantage lies in service innovation, user-centred provision, and quality management. Its main competitors are local authorities and other charitable trusts, which are typically quite small and less developed in terms of management and systems. The Trust is now trying to improve the quality of its own management systems by using innovative approaches to maximize its effectiveness.

Brandon Trust's finance and business systems director, Hilary Pearce, believes that information systems can, if efficiently applied and deployed, be used to improve facets of the organization's business. In her words, 'I believe that by working with our academic partner and our KTP Associate that the Brandon Trust will derive real benefit from the project. The pooling of ideas and expertise will be vital as we analyze our information needs and data sources and identify key result areas that we need to focus on to improve the management of the Trust. I envisage an innovative and integrated business system solution that will continue to evolve and grow along with the Trust's operational needs.' The role of information systems in strengthening the Trust's service level cannot be overemphasized. Its chief executive officer, Steve Bennett, had this to say: 'As an organization that has grown 500 percent in the ten years of its existence, it is important [for Brandon Trust] to take stock and look for continual improvements in our performance. Information and the systems that provide it are fundamental to performance management, and the importance of having systems that utilize available technology in a pragmatic and useable way cannot be overstated. I therefore am excited to address this with our academic partners and KTP associates in a two-year project, the outcome of which will be an integrated business system solution that will continue to evolve and grow with the continuing development of Brandon Trust.'

The Trust's services are distributed via 50 sites, and it is essential to improve information flows for efficiency and the management of risk. This development project was, therefore, focused on implementing new management systems and integrating them with other core business systems, including finance, following a detailed analysis of information requirements. Lack of systems integration currently makes provision of sound information for management controls, budgeting, and costing of contract proposals difficult to achieve. Improving information and business systems across the Trust will enhance its capacity for further growth by ensuring the best possible quality and design in its services. It is anticipated that the program will significantly reduce costs through business process reengineering, resulting in savings in the region of £250 000 per annum.

One KTP associate, Abid Mohammed, was recruited to serve as industrial manager and to work with Andy Igonor (academic advisor and project manager) and Hilary Pearce (director of finance and business systems). Abid's initial task included a review and evaluation of all existing business systems, particularly computer systems at the Trust. Although a number of systems existed in the Trust, the systems did not talk to one another; notably, the crucial financial system needed to manage all finance-related issues from payroll to payment for contract services. The hoped-for result of the development project is a system with the following capabilities:

An effective system capable of delivering relevant information when needed

An integrated system with simplified information presentation and elimination of redundancy

The development of an IS/IT audit report indicating current operating resources, which also serves as a guide for future work, including identification of appropriate software and hardware for improved operations, improved access to information, improved management information systems reporting, and improved performance.

Questions

1 What are the key issues to be looked into during systems investigation? How might they affect the overall success of the project?

2 Brandon Trust does not exist to make money. How relevant will this systems development project be to the organization?

3 Why is it necessary for Brandon Trust's systems to be integrated? Of what benefit would this be to the organization?

4 In what ways can a management information system benefit an organization?

5 How often should reports be generated within such systems to fulfill managerial needs?

Note: All information provided in this case is courtesy of the Brandon Trust. Used with permission.

World Views Case

Strategic Enterprise Management at International Manufacturing Corporation (IMC)

Bernd Heesen

University of Applied Sciences Furtwangen, Germany

The International Manufacturing Corporation (IMC), with 3000 employees worldwide, is a supplier of automotive parts and is headquartered in the U.S. Given the increasing market pressure and the need to operate internationally, IMC has recently made three acquisitions. The acquisition of one company in the U.K. and two companies in Germany is expected to leverage the companies' complementary manufacturing and sales capabilities to gain a stronger market presence in North America and Europe. The subsidiaries are still managed by their former management teams, who are now reporting to the U.S. headquarters. Each of the subsidiaries still operates its own management information system because the system fulfilled the requirements in the past and at the time of the acquisition there was no visible benefit to change what was working. A couple of interfaces were created to facilitate the monthly financial reporting to the headquarters.

Recently, the CEO of IMC realized some disadvantages of the diversity of hardware and software platforms. When one IT expert from one German subsidiary terminated her employment, no other IT expert within IMC had detailed knowledge of the local system, which threatened regular operations in that plant. The company needed to seek external consulting support to maintain the system until a new IT expert could be hired. This dependency on individual experts in each location was expensive and caused problems during periods when the experts were on leave. In addition, the interfaces between the subsidiaries' systems and the headquarters' system that were created right after the acquisition had to be modified whenever a change or upgrade was made to one of the subsidiary systems. Even minor changes, such as the reorganization of product codes or sales organizations, required reprogramming, maintenance of conversion tables, and subsequent testing of the related business processes in the system. The IT departments worked overtime and still did not find the time to invest in new initiatives such as enabling mobile computing for the sales force and developing a strategic enterprise management system that would allow consolidated planning and monitoring of all key performance indicators for the organization, a project long requested by the CEO. The two German subsidiaries had recently upgraded their systems, and problems identified during the testing of the interfaces could not be corrected in time for the submission of the monthly reports to headquarters. The data was finally corrected, but the monthly reporting was several days late. This was not the first time that the monthly financial reporting had been delayed or that the data needed to be corrected because of system-related problems, which caused other problems at headquarters.

The CEO finally requested consolidation of the systems in the coming year to allow for an integrated strategic enterprise management system that would provide current information from all legal entities and support a consolidated budgeting and planning process. He compared the company's current system with the cockpit of an airplane and stated that 'no one would expect a pilot to fly an airplane with malfunctioning instruments; hence nobody can expect management to run a company based on incomplete or incorrect information'. The CIO was asked to develop a business case for the implementation of such a system, considering the savings from personnel, hardware, and software, as well as process improvements.

After IMC's board approved the business case to implement enterprise resource planning (ERP) software from SAP, the CIO established a project in January 1999. The project schedule called for completion of the financial, human resource, supply chain management, and customer relationship

Istock

management functions for the complete organization – called the Big Bang – in January 2000. A prototype of the application was planned to be ready by July 1999 so that the departments could test all functionality with a set of converted data extracted from the current systems. The plan also called for complete conversion of live data by the end of November 1999 so that in December both the current system and the new system could be used in parallel before making the decision to switch systems. Consultants from SAP were hired to support the implementation – for project management and configuration of the system – and an independent training organization was charged with planning the end-user training and developing computer-based training (CBT) programs for ongoing use. The project plan allowed for hiring temporary staff to help with the cutover and redundant data entry in December 1999.

The project started with a kickoff meeting in February, after which nearly all team members began their project work. The complete prototype of the application could only be made available in September because some of the team members had to fulfill their regular jobs while providing their expertise to the project. Some of the early project decisions had to be revised to accommodate the best-practice business model from IMC, after the IMC team members better understood how the SAP system worked and the consultants had gained a better understanding of how IMC wanted to operate. The CIO still wanted to maintain the timeline and called weekly meetings of the project's team leaders for finance, human resources, supply chain management, and customer relationship management. Those meetings led to the decision to delay rollout of some of the functionality and to reduce the functionality to what was really needed (eliminating nice-to- have functionality). The prototype testing produced additional feedback from the departments that needed to be incorporated in the design of the final solution prior to the conversion. Many of the department heads, who had not been part of the core project team, only then became aware of the changes and started to talk about the new software, saying that it was not working properly yet and some of the team members were scared they would not make the deadline. In November, the data conversion revealed some additional problems (e.g., with data-entry errors made by the temporary staff who were keying data into the new system in instances in which an automated conversion was not cost-effective). As a result, the parallel use of the current and new system, which depended on all data being available, was delayed. To add to the pressure, the CIO believed that delaying the project's completion could be perceived as his failure. The CIO and steering committee of the project needed to make a decision on how to move forward: (1) Continue with the project's completion in January 2000 as planned or (2) delay conversion to the new system until a proper parallel test could be completed.

Questions

1 How would you develop a business case to justify an investment in an integrated strategic enterprise management system?

2 What are the essential requirements for a strategic management system?

3 Which tasks would you consider when developing the original project plan for the implementation?

4 Given IMC's current situation, what would you decide if you were the CIO?

Note: The name International Manufacturing Corporation was selected to protect the identity of the real company featured in the case.

PART 5

Information Systems in Business and Society

13

Security, Privacy, and Ethical Issues in Information Systems

Principles

Policies and procedures must be established to avoid computer waste and mistakes.

Computer crime is a serious and rapidly growing area of concern requiring management attention.

Jobs, equipment, and working conditions must be designed to avoid negative health effects.

Learning Objectives

- Describe some examples of waste and mistakes in an IS environment, their causes, and possible solutions.
- Identify policies and procedures useful in eliminating waste and mistakes.
- Discuss the principles and limits of an individual's right to privacy.

- Explain the types and effects of computer crime.
- Identify specific measures to prevent computer crime.

- List the important effects of computers on the work environment.
- Identify specific actions that must be taken to ensure the health and safety of employees.
- Outline criteria for the ethical use of information systems.

Why Learn About Security, Privacy, and Ethical Issues in Information Systems?

Our last chapter will look at security, privacy, and ethical issues, something that has been in the background right throughout this book. A wide range of non-technical issues associated with the use of information systems provide both opportunities and threats to modern organizations. The issues span the full spectrum – from preventing computer waste and mistakes, to avoiding violations of privacy, to complying with laws on collecting data about customers, to monitoring employees. If you become a member of a human resources, information systems, or legal department within an organization, you will likely be charged with leading the rest of the organization in dealing with these and other issues covered in this chapter. As a user of information systems, especially the Internet, it is in your own self-interest to become well versed on these issues. You need to know about the topics in this chapter to help avoid or recover from crime, fraud, privacy invasion, or other potential problems.

13.1 Computer Waste and Mistakes

Computer-related waste and mistakes are major causes of computer problems, contributing as they do to unnecessarily high costs and lost profits. Computer waste involves the inappropriate use of computer technology and resources. It includes employees wasting computer resources and time by playing games and surfing the web, sending unnecessary e-mail, printing documents and other material that is then not read, developing systems that are not used to their full extent, and discarding old hardware when it could be recycled or given to charity. U.K.-based Computers for Charities for instance, will collect old technology, wipe clean any data stored on them and deliver them to charities where they are still useful. Junk e-mail, also called spam, and junk faxes also cause waste. People receive hundreds of e-mail messages and faxes advertising products and services not wanted or requested. Not only does this waste time, but it also wastes paper and computer resources. Worse yet, spam messages often carry attached files with embedded viruses that can cause networks and computers to crash or allow hackers to gain unauthorized access to systems and data.[1] Image-based spam is a new tactic spammers use to circumvent spam-filtering software that rejects e-mail based on the content of messages and the use of keywords. The message is presented in a graphic form that can be read by people but not computers. This form of spam can be quite offensive and can contain pornographic photos and extremely graphic language.[2] When waste is identified, it typically points to one common cause: the improper management of information systems and resources.

Computer-related mistakes refer to errors, failures, and other computer problems that make computer output incorrect or not useful, caused mostly by human error. Despite many people's distrust, computers themselves rarely make mistakes. Even the most sophisticated hardware cannot produce meaningful output if users do not follow proper procedures. Mistakes can be caused by unclear expectations and a lack of feedback. Or a programmer might develop a program that contains errors. In other cases, a data-entry administrator might enter the wrong data. Unless errors are caught early and prevented, the speed of computers can intensify mistakes. As information technology becomes faster, more complex, and more powerful, organizations and computer users face increased risks of experiencing the results of computer-related mistakes.

13.1.1 Preventing Computer-Related Waste and Mistakes

To remain profitable in a competitive environment, organizations must use all resources wisely. Preventing computer-related waste and mistakes like those just described should therefore be a goal. To achieve it involves (1) establishing, (2) implementing, (3) monitoring, and (4) reviewing effective policies and procedures.

Establishing Policies and Procedures

The first step to prevent computer-related waste is to establish policies and procedures regarding efficient acquisition, use, and disposal of systems and devices. Most companies have implemented stringent policies on the acquisition of computer systems and equipment, including requiring a formal justification statement before computer equipment is purchased, definition of standard computing platforms (operating system, type of computer chip, minimum amount of RAM, etc.), and the use of preferred vendors for all acquisitions.

Prevention of computer-related mistakes begins by identifying the most common types of errors, of which there are surprisingly few. Types of computer-related mistakes include the following:

- Data-entry or data-capture errors.
- Errors in computer programs.
- Errors in handling files, including formatting a disk by mistake, copying an old file over a newer one, and deleting a file by mistake.
- Mishandling of computer output.
- Inadequate planning for and control of equipment malfunctions.
- Inadequate planning for and control of environmental difficulties (electrical problems, humidity problems, etc.).
- Installing computing capacity inadequate for the level of activity on corporate websites.
- Failure to provide access to the most current information by not adding new and not deleting old URL links.

Training programs for individuals and workgroups, and manuals and documents on how computer systems are to be maintained and used can help prevent problems. Other preventative measures include needing approval of certain systems and applications before they are implemented and used to ensure compatibility and cost-effectiveness, and a requirement that documentation and descriptions of certain applications be submitted to a central office, including all cell formulas for spreadsheets and a description of all data elements and relationships in a database system (which, as we saw in Chapter 5, is already recorded in the data dictionary). After companies have planned and developed policies and procedures, they must consider how best to implement them.

Sometimes, computer error combines with human procedural errors to lead to the loss of human life. In March 2003, a Patriot missile battery on the Kuwait border accidentally shot down a British Royal Air Force Tornado GR-4 aircraft that was returning from a mission over Iraq. Two British pilots were killed in the incident. Many defence industry experts think the accident was caused by problems with the Patriot's radar combined with human error.

Implementing Policies and Procedures

Implementing policies and procedures to minimize waste and mistakes varies according to the type of business. Most companies develop such policies and procedures with advice from the firm's internal auditing group or its external auditing firm. The policies often focus on the implementation of source data automation and the use of data editing to ensure data accuracy and completeness, and the assignment of responsibility for data accuracy within each information system. Some useful policies to minimize waste and mistakes include the following:

- Changes to critical tables, HTML, and URLs should be tightly controlled, with all changes authorized by responsible owners and documented.
- A user manual should be available that covers operating procedures and documents the management and control of the application.

- Each system report should indicate its general content in its title and specify the time period it covers.
- The system should have controls to prevent invalid and unreasonable data entry.
- Controls should exist to ensure that data input, HTML, and URLs are valid, applicable, and posted in the right time frame.
- Users should implement proper procedures to ensure correct input data.

Training is another key aspect of implementation. Many users are not properly trained in using applications, and their mistakes can be very costly. One home in the small town of Valparaiso, in the U.S., fairly valued at $88 550, was incorrectly recorded in the county's computer system as being worth over $290 million. The erroneous figure was used to forecast future income from property taxes. When the error was uncovered, the local school district and government agencies were forced to slash their budgets by $2 million when they found they wouldn't be getting the tax money after all.[3]

Monitoring Policies and Procedures

To ensure that users throughout an organization are following established procedures, the next step is to monitor routine practices and take corrective action if necessary. By understanding what is happening in day-to-day activities, organizations can make adjustments or develop new procedures. Many organizations implement internal audits to measure actual results against established goals, such as percentage of end-user reports produced on time, percentage of data-input errors detected, number of input transactions entered per eight-hour shift, and so on.

Reviewing Policies and Procedures

The final step is to review existing policies and procedures and determine whether they are adequate. During review, people should ask the following questions:

- Do current policies cover existing practices adequately? Were any problems or opportunities uncovered during monitoring?
- Is the organization planning any new activities in the future? If so, does it need new policies or procedures on who will handle them and what must be done?
- Are contingencies and disasters covered?

This review and planning allows companies to take a proactive approach to problem solving, which can enhance a company's performance, such as by increasing productivity and improving customer service. Information systems professionals and users still need to be aware of the misuse of resources throughout an organization. Preventing errors and mistakes is one way to do so. Another is implementing in-house security measures and legal protections to detect and prevent a dangerous type of misuse: computer crime.

Information Systems @ Work

Scotch Spam

This is less 'Information Systems @ Work' and more 'Information Law @ Work'.

Tired of receiving spam e-mails, Gordon Dick decided to do something about it. After successfully prosecuting one company for sending him just one unsolicited message, he set up a website to help others do the same. ScotchSpam .org.uk advises citizens of the European Union to use two laws to make legal claims against spammers: the Data Protection Act 1998 and the

Privacy and Electronic Communications Regulations 2003.

Basically the relevant part of the Data Protection Act says that your e-mail address cannot be stored by a business unless they have a reason to store it (for example, if you have done business with them in the past). In addition, the Privacy and Electronic Communications Regulations 2003 says that no company can send you an electronic marketing communication unless you have previously notified them that you consent to receiving such communications (although there are some exceptions to this). Companies throughout Europe and beyond have similar laws. In South Africa, the Electronic Communications and Transactions Act governs electronic messages.

In 2006, after receiving an unsolicited e-mail, Gordon Dick contacted the company involved asking them to explain how they were not in breach of information law. The company wrote back telling him that all e-mail addresses they used had been legally obtained and that they would defend their position in court, which Mr. Dick eventually made them do. He filed a complaint in the Sheriff Court and submitted a Small Claim Summons.

Mr. Dick was asking for:

1 An undertaking from them never to send unsolicited commercial e-mail again

2 An apology for sending the original message

3 Settlement in full of his claim of about €1000.

After the legal process had run its course, Mr. Dick was awarded the money but the company explicitly refused to give an undertaking to not send unsolicited commercial e-mail again or to apologize.

Questions

1 In your opinion, was Mr. Dick right to take this action? Was it just a lot of fuss about nothing, or was there a legitimate principle to defend?

2 Had you been on the company's board, what would your approach to Mr. Dick's initial contact have been?

3 Whose responsibility is it to deal with spam and what can they do? Is it down to the IS department or individual users? What about responsibility to stop employees, possibly unintentionally, sending out spam? What steps should a company take to avoid this?

4 Investigate on the Web any other legal actions against spammers. Discuss your findings.

SOURCE: Scotch Spam! (website), http://scotchspam.org.uk.

13.2 Computer Crime

According to the British Home Office, in 2004, debit and credit card fraud over the Internet cost the U.K. £117 million. During the same period, 77 percent of medium to large businesses reported virus attacks costing £27.8 million while 17 percent suffered financial fraud costing £133 million. The term computer crime covers a wide variety of activities, including these. Some more examples are listed next and then some types of computer crime are discussed.

■ The largest consumer fraud in the U.S. was committed by the Gambino crime family involving two different computer-related ploys and resulted in a loss to the public of over $265 million. One of the schemes offered 'free' tours of adult Internet sites but required the victim to provide a credit card supposedly for age-verification purposes. Victims took the free tours and then their credit cards were hit for charges over and over again. The second prong to this scheme involved the use of a third-party billing provider to add charges on peoples' telephone bills for services not provided.[4]

■ A 20-year-old man was sentenced to 57 months in prison for hijacking more than 400 000 PCs over the Internet and turning them into a 'botnet' or 'zombie network', a network of personal computers used to perform a task without the owner's knowledge. He then would rent the zombie network out to spyware distributors, hackers, and spammers to use in performing work.[5]

13

■ Russian organized crime extorted untold thousands of dollars from firms doing business on the Internet by demanding €7000 or more for protection from being hit by a denial-of-service attack on their website. Some firms bought the 'protection'; some of those that did not were attacked.[6]

■ A British information systems expert accessed a series of computer networks used by the U.S. Army, Navy, Air Force, and Department of Defence, searching for what he called 'suppressed technology'. U.S. authorities claimed he caused more than $700 000 of damage.[7]

■ The U.K. government's tax credit website, which allowed qualifying citizens to claim tax benefits, was shut down in 2005 because it was being targeted by organized gangs claiming many millions of pounds from the government.[8]

Identify Theft

Identity theft is one of the fastest growing crimes. It is a crime where an imposter obtains key pieces of personal identification information, such as date of birth, address, national insurance number, and mother's maiden name, and uses them to open bank accounts, get credit cards, loans, benefits, and documents such as passports and driving licences in the victim's name. In other cases, the identity thief uses personal information to gain access to the person's existing accounts. Typically, the thief changes the mailing address on an account and runs up a huge bill before the person whose identity has been stolen realizes there is a problem. The Internet has made it easier for an identity thief to use the stolen information because transactions can be made without any personal interaction. The U.K. Home Office has a website, http://www.identitytheft.org.uk/, to advise its citizens and help victims. A wide range of methods are used by the perpetrators of these crimes that it makes investigating them difficult. Frequently, a critical computer password has been talked out of a person, or guessed based on a knowledge of the person, a practice called **social engineering**. For example, many people use the name of their pet as their password. Many teenagers use the name of their favourite pop artist. Alternatively, the attackers might simply go through the person's rubbish, looking for a disgarded utility bill or bank statement. In addition, over 2000 websites offer the digital tools – for free – that will let people snoop, crash computers, hijack control of a machine, or retrieve a copy of every keystroke.

social engineering Using one's social skills to get computer users to provide you with information to access an information system or its data.

Another popular method to get information is 'shoulder surfing' – the identity thief simply stands next to someone at a public office, such as the passport office, or even when filling in a form to join a video rental shop such as Blockbuster, and watches as the person fills out personal information on a form. The same thing can happen at a bank ATM where the attacker simply watches the person enter their PIN, or at a shop when the victim is using their credit card to make a purchase (see Figure 13.1).

Consumers can help protect themselves by regularly checking their credit reports, following up with creditors if their bills do not arrive on time, not revealing any personal information in response to unsolicited e-mail or phone calls, and shredding bills and other documents that contain sensitive information.[9]

Cyberterrorism

cyberterrorist Someone who intimidates or coerces a government or organization to advance his or her political or social objectives by launching computer-based attacks against computers, networks, and the information stored on them.

Government officials and IS security specialists have documented a significant increase in Internet probes and server scans since early 2001. A growing concern among authorities is that such intrusions are part of an organized effort by cyberterrorists to map potential security holes in critical systems. A **cyberterrorist** is someone who intimidates or coerces a government or organization to advance their political or social objectives by launching computer-based attacks against computers, networks, and the information

Figure 13.1 Shoulder Surfing *Always take care when using an ATM that no one can see you enter your PIN.*

SOURCE: Ferruccio/Alamy.

stored on them. Attacks would likely be aimed at critical infrastructure, which includes telecommunications, energy, banking and finance, water systems, government operations, and emergency services. Successful cyberattacks against the facilities that provide these services could cause widespread and massive disruptions to the normal function of a society.

A similar term, 'cyberwar', is arguably not a crime but involves a country or state attacking another using the same techniques as a cyberterrorist.

cracker A person who enjoys computer technology and spends time learning and using computer systems.

script kiddie A cracker with little technical savvy who downloads programs called scripts, which automate the job of breaking into computers.

insider An employee, disgruntled or otherwise, working solo or in concert with outsiders to compromise corporate systems.

Illegal Access and Use

Crimes involving illegal system access and use of computer services are a concern to both government and business. Since the outset of information technology, computers have been plagued by criminal crackers. A **cracker**, often called a hacker, although this term has a range of meanings, is a computer-savvy person who attempts to gain unauthorized or illegal access to computer systems. Often they are 'just looking' but could also be trying to corrupt files, steal data, or even transfer money. In many cases, crackers are people who are looking for fun and excitement – the challenge of beating the system. **Script kiddies** admire crackers, but have little technical savvy. They are crackers who download programs called 'scripts' that automate the job of breaking into computers. **Insiders** are employees, disgruntled or otherwise, working solo or in concert with outsiders to compromise corporate systems.

Catching and convicting criminal hackers remains a difficult task. The method behind these crimes is often hard to determine. Even if the method behind the crime is known, tracking down the criminals can take a lot of time.

Data and information are valuable corporate assets. The intentional use of illegal and destructive programs to alter or destroy data is as much a crime as destroying tangible goods. The most common of these programs are viruses and worms, which are software programs that, when loaded into a computer system, will destroy, interrupt, or cause errors in processing. Such programs are also called 'malware'. Internet security firm McAfee released virus threat definition number 200 000 in July 2006 and predicts that there will be twice that many viruses within two years.[10] McAfee also predicts the increased connectivity of smartphones will lead to serious and widespread attacks on these devices. '…a mobile threat targeting several (smartphone) operating systems could infect up to 200 million connected smartphones simultaneously because the majority of these devices do not currently have mobile security protection installed'.[11]

virus A computer program file capable of attaching to disks or other files and replicating itself repeatedly, typically without the user's knowledge or permission.

A **virus** is a computer program file capable of attaching to disks or other files and replicating itself repeatedly, typically without the user's knowledge or permission. Some viruses attach to files, so when the infected file executes, the virus also executes. Other viruses sit in a computer's memory and infect files as the computer opens, modifies, or creates the files. They are often disguised as games or images with clever or attention-grabbing titles such as 'Boss, naked'. Some viruses display symptoms, and some viruses damage files and computer systems. The m00p virus gang, for example, conspired to infect computers with a virus that would turn each infected machine into a zombie machine under their control. The zombie network could then be used to spread viruses and other malware across the Internet, without the owners of the compromised computers even being aware.[12] Hoax viruses can also be a problem. A hoax virus is a message, usually distributed by e-mail, warning recipients to carry out a procedure on their computer to protect themselves from a 'virus threat', when the procedure itself is actually doing the damage. Typically a hoax virus encourages people to delete an important systems file. The message will encourage people to forward it on to all their contacts.

worm A parasitic computer program that can create copies of itself on the infected computer or send copies to other computers via a network.

Worms are computer programs that replicate but, unlike viruses, do not infect other computer program files. Worms can create copies on the same computer or can send the copies to other computers via a network. Worms often spread via Internet Relay Chat (IRC). For example, the MyDoom worm, also known as Shimgapi and Novarg, started spreading in January 2004 and quickly became the most virulent e-mail worm ever. The worm arrived as an e-mail with an attachment with various names and extensions, including .exe, .scr, .zip, and .pif. When the attachment executed, the worm sent copies of itself to other e-mail addresses stored in the infected computer. The first version of the virus, MyDoom.A, was designed to attack The SCO Group Inc.'s website. A later variant, dubbed MyDoom.B, was designed to enable similar denial-of-service attacks against the Microsoft website. The B variant also included a particularly nasty feature in that it blocked infected computers from accessing sites belonging to vendors of antivirus products. Infected e-mail messages carrying the MyDoom worm have been intercepted from over 142 countries and at one time accounted for 1 in every 12 e-mail messages.

A **Trojan horse** program is a malicious program that disguises itself as a useful application and purposefully does something the user does not expect. Trojans are not viruses because they do not replicate, but they can be just as destructive. Many people use the term to refer only to non-replicating malicious programs, thus making a distinction between Trojans and viruses. A German language e-mail, for example, was used to spread a Trojan horse that steals passwords and logon details of customers' online bank accounts and then relays them back to a remote server. The malware tried to get users to install the Trojan horse by disguising itself as a software patch for a new flaw in Microsoft software.[13] Spyware is often spread using the Trojan hourse method. Spyware is software which record all manner of personal information about users and forwards it to the spyware's owner, all without the user's consent. Name, address, credit card numbers, and passwords can all be collected by spyware, as can information on web browsing behaviour, which would be valuable useful for marketing.

> **Trojan horse** A malicious program that disguises itself as a useful application and purposefully does something the user does not expect.

A logic bomb is a type of Trojan horse that executes when specific conditions occur. Triggers for logic bombs can include a change in a file by a particular series of keystrokes or at a specific time or date.

A variant is a modified version of a virus that is produced by the virus's author or another person who amends the original virus code. If changes are small, most antivirus products will also detect variants. However, if the changes are significant, the variant might go undetected by antivirus software.

In some cases, a virus or a worm can completely halt the operation of a computer system or network for days or longer until the problem is found and repaired. In other cases, a virus or a worm can destroy important data and programs. If backups are inadequate, the data and programs might never be fully functional again. The costs include the effort required to identify and neutralize the virus or worm and to restore computer files and data, as well as the value of business lost because of unscheduled computer downtime.

As a result of the increasing threat of viruses and worms, most computer users and organizations have installed **antivirus programs** on their computers. Such software runs in the background to protect your computer from dangers lurking on the Internet and other possible sources of infected files. Some antivirus software is even capable of repairing common virus infections automatically, without interrupting your work. The latest virus definitions are downloaded automatically when you connect to the Internet, ensuring that your PC's protection is current. To safeguard your PC and prevent it from spreading viruses to your friends and coworkers, some antivirus software scans and cleans both incoming and outgoing e-mail messages. Table 13.1 lists some of the most popular antivirus software.

> **antivirus program** Software that runs in the background to protect your computer from dangers lurking on the Internet and other possible sources of infected files.

Table 13.1 Antivirus Software

Antivirus Software	Software Manufacturer	Website
Symantec's Norton AntiVirus 2005	Symantec	www.symantec.com
McAfee Virus Scan	McAfee	www.mcafee.com
Panda Antivirus Platinum	Panda Software	www.pandasoftware.com
Vexira Antivirus	Central Command	www.centralcommand.com
Sophos Antivirus	Sophos	www.sophos.com
PC-cillin	Trend Micro	www.trendmicro.com

Proper use of antivirus software requires the following steps:

1 Install antivirus software. These programs should automatically check for viruses each time you boot up your computer or insert a disk or CD, and some even monitor all e-mail and file transmissions and copying operations.

2 Ensure the antivirus software updates often. New viruses are created all the time, and antivirus software suppliers are constantly updating their software to detect and take action against these new viruses. The software should itself check for updates regularly, without the need for an instruction from the user.

3 Scan all removable media, including CDs, before copying or running programs from them. Hiding on disks or CDs, viruses often move between systems. If you carry document or program files on removable media between computers at school or work and your home system, always scan them.

4 Install software only from a sealed package or secure website of a known software company. Even software publishers can unknowingly distribute viruses on their program disks or software downloads. Most scan their own systems, but viruses might still remain.

5 Follow careful downloading practices. If you download software from the Internet or a bulletin board, check your computer for viruses immediately after completing the transmission.

6 If you detect a virus, take immediate action. Early detection often allows you to remove a virus before it does any serious damage.

Despite careful precautions, viruses can still cause problems. They can elude virus-scanning software by lurking almost anywhere in a system. Future antivirus programs might incorporate 'nature-based models' that check for unusual or unfamiliar computer code. The advantage of this type of virus program is the ability to detect new viruses that are not part of an antivirus database.

Hoax, or false, viruses are another problem. Crackers sometimes warn the public of a new and devastating virus that doesn't actually exist just to create fear. Companies sometimes spend hundreds of hours warning employees and taking preventative action against a non-existent virus. Security specialists recommend that IS personnel establish a formal paranoia policy to thwart virus panic among gullible end users. Such policies should stress that before users forward an e-mail alert to colleagues, they should send it to the help desk or the security team. The corporate intranet can be used to explain the difference between real viruses and fakes, and it can provide links to websites to set the record straight.

Be aware that virus writers also use known hoaxes to their advantage. For example, AOL4FREE began as a hoax virus warning. Then, a hacker distributed a destructive Trojan attached to the original hoax virus warning. Always remain vigilant and never open a suspicious attachment.[14]

Equipment Theft

During illegal access to computer systems, data can be stolen. In addition to theft of data and software, all types of computer systems and equipment have been stolen from offices. Mobile computers such as laptops and smartphones are especially easy for thieves to take. Very often the data stored on these devices is more valuable than the device itself. Pop star Natasha Bedingfield had her laptop, which contained music and lyrics to some of her new material, stolen. An MI5 agent's laptop containing sensitive government information was stolen at Paddington train station in London, and a senior British Army official's laptop was taken at Heathrow Airport.[15] To fight computer crime, many companies use devices that disable the disk drive and/or lock the computer to the desk (see Figure 13.2).

Figure 13.2 Locking a Laptop to a Desk

SOURCE: Istock.

Software and Internet Software Piracy

Like books and movies – other intellectual properties – software is protected by copyright laws. Often, people who would never think of plagiarizing another author's written work have no qualms about using and copying software programs they have not paid for. Such illegal duplicators are called 'pirates'; the act of illegally duplicating software is called **software piracy**.

software piracy The act of illegally duplicating software.

Technically, software purchasers are granted the right only to use the software under certain conditions; they don't really own the software. Licences vary from program to program and can authorize as few as one computer or one person to use the software or as many as several hundred network users to share the application across the system. Making additional copies, or loading the software onto more than one machine, might violate copyright law and be considered piracy.

The Business Software Alliance estimates that the software industry loses over €8 billion per year in revenue to software piracy annually. Half the loss comes from Asia, where China and Indonesia are the biggest offenders. In Western Europe, annual piracy losses range between 1.5 and 2 billion euros. Although the rate of software piracy is quite high in Latin America and Central Europe, those software markets are so small that the monetary losses are considerably lower. Overall, it is estimated that 35 percent of the world's software is pirated.[16]

Internet-based software piracy occurs when software is illegally downloaded from the Internet. It is the most rapidly expanding type of software piracy and the most difficult form to combat. The same purchasing rules apply to online software purchases as for traditional purchases. Internet piracy can take several forms, including the following:

■ Pirate websites that make software available for free or in exchange for uploaded programs.

■ Internet auction sites that offer counterfeit software, which infringes copyrights.

■ Peer-to-peer networks, which enable unauthorized transfer of copyrighted programs.

Computer-Related Scams

People have lost hundreds of thousands of euros on property, travel, stock, and other business scams. Now, many of these scams are being perpetrated with computers. Using the Internet, scam artists offer get-rich-quick schemes involving bogus property deals, tout 'free' holidays with huge hidden costs, commit bank fraud, offer fake telephone lotteries, sell worthless penny stocks, and promote illegal tax-avoidance schemes.

Over the past few years, credit card customers of various banks have been targeted by scam artists trying to get personal information needed to use their credit cards. The scam typically works by sending an e-mail to many thousands of people, asking them to click on a link that seems to direct users to a bank's website, to fill in essential security information. Some of the recipients will probably be customers of the bank. At the site, they are asked for their full debit and credit card numbers and expiration dates, their name, address, and other personal information. The problem is that the website customers are directed to is a fake site operated by someone trying to gain access to that information. As discussed previously, this form of scam is called 'phishing'. The website used is often extremely similar to the bank's real website and may contain links to the real site. During November 2005, the Anti-Phishing Working Group received 16 882 unique reports of phishing attacks aimed at the consumers of 93 different brands – this was double the number of reports received the previous November.[17]

In the weeks following Hurricane Katrina in the U.S., the FBI warned that over half the Hurricane Katrina aid sites it checked were registered to people outside the U.S. and likely to be fraudulent. A 20-year-old man was charged with setting up websites designed to look like those of the American Red Cross and other organizations accepting donations to help the victims. He then sold these to 'would-be scammers' for about $140 each. For his trouble, this person is facing 50 years in prison and a fine of $1 million.[18]

The following is a list of tips to help you avoid becoming a scam victim:

■ Don't agree to anything in a high-pressure meeting or seminar. Insist on having time to think it over and to discuss things with your spouse, your partner, or even your solicitor. If a company won't give you the time you need to check it out and think things over, you don't want to do business with it. A good deal now will be a good deal tomorrow; the only reason for rushing you is if the company has something to hide.

■ Don't judge a company based on appearances. Professional-looking websites can be created and published in a matter of days. After a few weeks of taking money, a site can vanish without a trace in just a few minutes. You might find that the perfect money-making opportunity offered on a website was a money-maker for the crook and a money-loser for you.

■ Avoid any plan that pays commissions simply for recruiting additional distributors. Your primary source of income should be your own product sales. If the earnings are not made primarily by sales of goods or services to consumers or sales by distributors under you, you might be dealing with an illegal pyramid.

■ Beware of 'shills', people paid by a company to lie about how much they've earned and how easy the plan was to operate. Check with an independent source to make sure that you aren't having the wool pulled over your eyes.

■ Beware of a company's claim that it can set you up in a profitable home-based business but that you must first pay up front to attend a seminar and buy expensive materials. Frequently, seminars are high-pressure sales pitches, and the material is so general that it is worthless.

■ If you are interested in starting a home-based business, get a complete description of the work involved before you send any money. You might find that what you are asked to do after you pay is far different from what was stated in the ad. You should never have to pay for a job description or for needed materials.

■ Get in writing the refund, buy-back, and cancellation policies of any company you deal with. Do not depend on oral promises.

■ If you need advice about an online solicitation, or if you want to report a possible scam, contact your country's computer crime unit. In the U.K., you can find more information at www.direct.gov.uk or www.met.police.uk/computercrime.

13.3 Preventing Computer-Related Crime

Because of increased computer use, greater emphasis is placed on the prevention and detection of computer crime. Many countries have passed data laws governing how data can be stored, processed, and transferred, and laws on computer crime. Some believe that these laws are not effective because companies do not always actively detect and pursue computer crime, security is inadequate, and convicted criminals are not severely punished. However, all over the world, private users, companies, employees, and public officials are making individual and group efforts to curb computer crime, and recent efforts have met with some success.

13.3.1 Crime Prevention by the State

In the U.K., the Computer Misuse Act of 1990, which criminalizes unauthorized access to computer systems, and the Data Protection Act of 1984 (expanded in 1998), which governs when and how data about individuals can be stored and processed, have been passed. Many countries have passed similar laws.

In the U.K., the Home Office is charged with tackling computer crime with some police forces having a 'cyber crime' unit. The Information Commissioner's Office is in charge of the U.K.'s independent authority set up to protect personal information (and as we shall see later in this chapter, to promote access to official information). The U.K. also has an organization dedicated to fighting specific types of computer crime. The Child Exploitation and Online Protection Centre (CEOP) tackles child sex abuse, especially where it has been facilitated in some way by the Internet.

13.3.2 Crime Prevention by Organizations

Companies are also taking crime-fighting efforts seriously. Many businesses have designed procedures and specialized hardware and software to protect their corporate data and systems. Specialized hardware and software, such as encryption devices, can be used to encode data and information to help prevent unauthorized use. Encryption is the process of converting an original electronic message into a form that can be understood only by the intended recipients. A key is a variable value that is applied using an algorithm to a string or block of unencrypted text to produce encrypted text or to decrypt encrypted text. Encryption methods rely on the limitations of computing power for their effectiveness – if breaking a code requires too much computing power, even the most determined code crackers will not be successful. The length of the key used to encode and decode messages determines the strength of the encryption algorithm.

Public-key infrastructure (PKI) enables users of an unsecured public network such as the Internet to securely and privately exchange data through the use of a public and a private cryptographic key pair that is obtained and shared through a trusted authority. PKI is the most common method on the Internet for authenticating a message sender or encrypting a message. PKI uses two keys to encode and decode messages. One key of the pair, the message receiver's public key, is readily available to the public and is used by anyone to send that individual encrypted messages. The second key, the message receiver's private key, is kept secret and is known only by the message receiver. Its owner uses the private key to decrypt messages – convert encoded messages back into the original message. Knowing a person's public key does not enable you to decrypt an encoded message to that person.

> **public-key infrastructure (PKI)** A means to enable users of an unsecured public network such as the Internet to securely and privately exchange data through the use of a public and a private cryptographic key pair that is obtained and shared through a trusted authority.

Using **biometrics** is another way to protect important data and information systems. Biometrics involves the measurement of one of a person's traits, whether physical or behavioral. Biometric techniques compare a person's unique characteristics against a stored set to detect differences between

> **biometrics** The measurement of one of a person's traits, whether physical or behavioural.

13

them. Biometric systems can scan fingerprints, faces, handprints, irises, and retinal images to prevent unauthorized access to important data and computer resources. Most of the interest among corporate users is in fingerprint technology, followed by face recognition. Fingerprint scans hit the middle ground between price and effectiveness (see Figure 13.3). Iris and retina scans are more accurate, but they are more expensive and involve more equipment.

Figure 13.3 Fingerprint **Authentication** *Fingerprint authentication devices provide security in the PC environment by using fingerprint information instead of passwords.*

SOURCE: Jochen Tack/Alamy.

Co-op Mid Counties is the first U.K. retailer to implement a payment by biometrics system with fingerprint readers supplied by the U.S. company Pay By Touch. The system is installed in just three of its stores in Oxford, but if successful, the system will be expanded to all of its 150 stores. To use the system, customers must register with Co-op Mid Counties by providing a photo ID and submit to fingerprinting. In addition to providing improved security, the system takes less time to process a payment – three seconds compared with seven seconds for traditional payment approval methods.[19]

As employees move from one position to another at a company, they can build up access to multiple systems if inadequate security procedures fail to revoke access privileges. It is clearly not appropriate for people who have changed positions and responsibilities to still have access to systems they no longer use. To avoid this problem, many organizations create role-based system access lists so that only people filling a particular role (e.g. line manager) can access a specific system.

Crime-fighting procedures usually require additional controls on the information system. Before designing and implementing controls, organizations must consider the types of computer-related crime that might occur, the consequences of these crimes, and the cost and complexity of needed controls. In most cases, organizations conclude that the trade-off between crime and the additional cost and complexity weighs in favour of better system controls. Having knowledge of some of the methods used to commit crime is also helpful in preventing, detecting, and developing systems resistant to computer crime (see Table 13.2). Some companies actually hire former criminals to thwart other criminals.

Although the number of potential computer crimes appears to be limitless, the actual methods used to commit crime are limited. The following list provides a set of useful guidelines to protect your computer from criminal hackers.

■ Install strong user authentication and encryption capabilities on your firewall.

■ Install the latest security patches, which are often available at the vendor's Internet site.

■ Disable guest accounts and null user accounts that let intruders access the network without a password.

■ Do not provide overfriendly logon procedures for remote users (e.g., an organization that used the word 'welcome' on their initial logon screen found they had difficulty prosecuting a criminal hacker).

■ Restrict physical access to the server and configure it so that breaking into one server won't compromise the whole network.

■ Give each application (e-mail, FTP, and domain name server) its own dedicated server.

■ Turn audit trails on.

■ Consider using caller ID.

■ Install a corporate firewall between your corporate network and the Internet.

■ Install antivirus software on all computers and regularly download vendor updates.

■ Conduct regular IS security audits.

■ Verify and exercise frequent data backups for critical data.

Companies are also joining together to fight crime. The Software and Information Industry Alliance (SIIA) was the original antipiracy organization, formed and financed by many of the large software publishers. Microsoft financed the formation of a second antipiracy organization, the Business Software Alliance (BSA). The BSA, through intense publicity, has become the more

Table 13.2 Common Methods Used to Commit Computer Crimes

Methods	Examples
Add, delete, or change inputs to the computer system	Delete records of absences from class in a student's school records
Modify or develop computer programs that commit the crime	Change a bank's program for calculating interest to make it deposit rounded amounts in the criminal's account
Alter or modify the data files used by the computer system	Change a student's grade from C to A
Operate the computer system in such a way as to commit computer crime	Access a restricted government computer system
Divert or misuse valid output from the computer system	Steal discarded printouts of customer records from a company trash bin
Steal computer resources, including hardware, software, and time on computer equipment	Make illegal copies of a software program without paying for its use
Offer worthless products for sale over the Internet	Send e-mail requesting money for worthless hair growth product
Blackmail executives to prevent release of harmful information	Eavesdrop on organization's wireless network to capture competitive data or scandalous information
Blackmail company to prevent loss of computer-based information	Plant logic bomb and send letter threatening to set it off unless paid considerable sum

13

prominent organization. Other software companies, including Apple, Adobe, Hewlett-Packard, and IBM, now contribute to the BSA.

13.3.3 Crime Prevention by Individuals

A number of individuals – victims, former criminals, concerned parents – have set up websites offering support for those worried about computer crime, and advice on how to fight it. One of these, Scotch Spam, is discussed in the Information Systems @ Work box section on page 480.

13.3.4 Using Intrusion Detection Software

An **intrusion detection system (IDS)** monitors system and network resources and notifies network security personnel when it senses a possible intrusion. Examples of suspicious activities include repeated failed logon attempts, attempts to download a program to a server, and access to a system at unusual hours. Such activities generate alarms that are captured on log files. Intrusion detection systems send an alarm, often by e-mail or pager, to network security personnel when they detect an apparent attack. Unfortunately, many IDSs frequently provide false alarms that result in wasted effort. If the attack is real, network security personnel must make a decision about what to do to resist the attack. Any delay in response increases the probability of damage from a criminal hacker attack. Use of an IDS provides another layer of protection in the event that an intruder gets past the outer security layers – passwords, security procedures, and corporate firewall.

intrusion detection system (IDS) Software that monitors system and network resources and notifies network security personnel when it senses a possible intrusion.

The following story is true, but the company's name has been changed to protect its identity. The ABC company employs more than 25 IDS sensors across its worldwide network, enabling it to monitor 90 percent of the company's internal network traffic. The remaining 10 percent comes from its engineering labs and remote sales offices, which are not monitored because of a lack of resources. The company's IDS worked very well in providing an early warning of an impending SQL Slammer attack. The Slammer worm had entered the network via a server in one of the engineering labs. The person monitoring the IDS noticed outbound traffic consistent with SQL Slammer at about 7:30 a.m. He contacted the network operations group by e-mail and followed up with a phone call and a voice mail message. Unfortunately, the operations group gets so many e-mails that if a message is not highlighted as URGENT, the message might be missed. That is exactly what happened – the e-mail alert wasn't read, and the voice message wasn't retrieved in time to block the attack. A few hours later, the ABC company found itself dealing with a massive number of reports of network and server problems.

13.3.5 Using Managed Security Service Providers (MSSPs)

Keeping up with computer criminals – and with new regulations – can be daunting for organizations. Criminal hackers are constantly poking and prodding, trying to breach the security defences of companies. For most small and mid-sized organizations, the level of in-house network security expertise needed to protect their business operations can be quite costly to acquire and maintain. As a result, many are outsourcing their network security operations to managed security service providers (MSSPs) such as Counterpane, Guardent, Internet Security Services, Riptech, and Symantec. MSSPs monitor, manage, and maintain network security for both hardware and software. These companies provide a valuable service for IS departments drowning in reams of alerts and false alarms coming from virtual private networks (VPNs); antivirus, firewall, and intrusion detection systems; and other security monitoring systems. In addition, some provide vulnerability scanning and web blocking/filtering capabilities.

13.3.6 Preventing Crime on the Internet

As mentioned in Chapter 6, Internet security can include firewalls and many methods to secure financial transactions. A firewall can include both hardware and software that act as a barrier between an organization's information system and the outside world. Some systems have been developed to safeguard financial transactions on the Internet.

To help prevent crime on the Internet, the following steps can be taken:

1 Develop effective Internet usage and security policies for all employees.

2 Use a stand-alone firewall (hardware and software) with network monitoring capabilities.

3 Deploy intrusion detection systems, monitor them, and follow up on their alarms.

4 Monitor managers and employees to make sure that they are using the Internet for business purposes.

5 Use Internet security specialists to perform audits of all Internet and network activities.

Even with these precautions, computers and networks can never be completely protected against crime. One of the biggest threats is from employees. Although firewalls provide good perimeter control to prevent crime from the outside, procedures and protection measures are needed to protect against computer crime by employees. Passwords, identification numbers, and tighter control of employees and managers also help prevent Internet-related crime.

13.4 Privacy

Privacy is a big issue for many people. When information is computerized and can be porcessed and transferred easily, augmented and collated, summarized and reported, privacy concerns mushroom. The European Union has a data-protection directive that requires firms transporting data across national boundaries to have certain privacy procedures in place. This directive affects virtually any company doing business in Europe, and it is driving much of the attention being given to privacy in the U.S.

13.4.1 Privacy and the Government

Many people are suspicious of the government when it comes to information that is stored about them. In the U.K., the government is currently introducing an identity card scheme which, it is claimed, will help fight international terrorism and identify theft and other fraud. The card would be linked to a database, which would hold names, addresses, and biometric information on all citzens. Expected to cost many billions of euros, some people have pledged never to carry them, claiming that the scheme would create a 'big brother' society. Many of these fears are unfounded, although the debate does highlight a lack of trust in the state.

Many governments are in fact quite open about the information that they store. Numerous countries have implemented some sort of freedom of information legistration. In South Africa, it is the Promotion of Access to Information Act. In the U.K. it is the Freedom of Information Act. Similar laws have been passed throughout Europe.

The U.K. Freedom of Information Act governs all data that is not about an individual, in any public organization including government, local councils, schools, universities and hospitals. The Act basically states that all such organizations must give out whatever information is requested of them, as long as it is not about an individual (which is protected under the Data Protection Act) or some other sensitive information. So for example, you would be able to ask your university how many people achieved A grades in one of your modules last year (this information is probably published on the students' portal anyway). However, you couldn't request information about a professor's salary. You could, though, ask for information about lecturers' pay scales (which again is already freely available form the relevant union's website).

13.4.2 Privacy at Work

The right to privacy at work is an important issue. Currently, the rights of workers who want their privacy and the interests of companies that demand to know more about their employees are in conflict. Recently, companies that have been monitoring their workers have raised concerns. For example, workers might find that they are being closely monitored via computer technology. These computer-monitoring systems tie directly into workstations; specialized computer programs can track every keystroke made by a user. This type of system can determine what workers are doing while at the keyboard. The system also knows when the worker is not using the keyboard or computer system. These systems can estimate what people are doing and how many breaks they are taking. Needless to say, many workers consider this close supervision very dehumanizing.

13.4.3 E-mail Privacy

E-mail also raises some interesting issues about work privacy. A company has the right to look at any data stored on its servers, which includes its e-mail servers and therefore all messages sent by or to its employees. Many companies routinely store all e-mails sent or received for several years and many employees have lost their jobs for forwarding inappropriate messages. Others have sent embarassing messages that have been forwarded exponentially by recipients who pass the 'joke' on to their friends. A solicitor at a London firm, for example, sent one message to some friends about his girlfriend's sexual preferences and a week later the message had been distributed to over a million people, through many blue chip firms.[20]

13.4.4 Privacy and the Internet

Some people assume that there is no privacy on the Internet and that you use it at your own risk. Others believe that companies with websites should have strict privacy procedures and be accountable for privacy invasion. Regardless of your view, the potential for privacy invasion on the Internet is huge. People wanting to invade your privacy could be anyone from criminal hackers to marketing companies to corporate bosses. E-mail is a prime target, as discussed previously. When you visit a website, information about you and your computer can be captured. When this information is combined with other information, companies can know what you read, what products you buy, and what your interests are. According to an executive of an Internet software monitoring company, 'It's a marketing person's dream'.

Most people who buy products on the web say it's very important for a site to have a policy explaining how personal information is used, and the policy statement must make people feel comfortable and be extremely clear about what information is collected and what will and will not be done with it. However, many websites still do not prominently display their privacy policy or implement practices completely consistent with that policy. The real issue that Internet users need to be concerned with is 'what do content providers want with their personal information?'. If a site requests that you provide your name and address, you have every right to know why and what will be done with it. If you buy something and provide a shipping address, will it be sold to other retailers? Will your e-mail address be sold on a list of active Internet shoppers? And if so, you should realize that it's no different than the lists compiled from the orders you place with catalogue retailers – you have the right to be taken off any mailing list.

These same questions can be asked of Internet chat rooms that require you to register before you can post messages. It is important for the forum moderators to know who is posting, but users should also have confidence that their information will not be misused.

Platform for Privacy Preferences (P3P) A screening technology that shields users from websites that don't provide the level of privacy protection they desire.

13

A potential solution to some consumer privacy concerns is the screening technology called the **Platform for Privacy Preferences (P3P)** being proposed to shield users from sites that don't provide the level of privacy protection they desire. Instead of forcing users to find and read through the privacy policy for each site they visit, P3P software in a computer's browser will download the privacy policy from each site, scan it, and notify the user if the policy does not match his or her preferences. (Of course, unethical marketers can post a privacy policy that does not accurately reflect the manner in which the data is treated.) The World Wide Web Consortium (W3C), an international industry group whose members include Apple, Commerce One, Ericsson, and Microsoft, is supporting the development of P3P.

A social network service employs the web and software to connect people for whatever purpose. There are thousands of such networks, which have become popular among teenagers. Some of the more popular social networking websites include Bebo, Classmates.com, Facebook, Hi5, Imbee, MySpace, Namesdatabase.com, Tagged, and XuQa. Most of these allow one to easily create a user profile that provides personal details, photos, even videos that can be viewed by other visitors to the website. Some of the websites have age restrictions or require that a parent register their pre-teen by providing a credit card to validate the parent's identity. Teens can provide information about where they live, go to school, their favourite music, and interests in hopes of meeting new friends. Unfortunately, they can also meet ill-intentioned strangers at these sites. Many documented encounters involve adults masquerading as teens attempting to meet young people for illicit purposes. Parents are advised to discuss potential dangers, check their children's profiles, and monitor their activities at such websites.

Whenever someone registers a domain name such as www.mydomain.co.uk, the name and address given during registration becomes public information and can be seen by simply running a 'whois' query, which can be easily done on many websites. Parents should be aware of this before they let their children have their own web page.

13.4.5 Fairness in Information Use

Selling information to other companies can be so lucrative that many companies will continue to store and sell the data they collect on customers, employees, and others. When is this information storage and use fair and reasonable to the people whose data is stored and sold? Do people have a right to know about data stored about them and to decide what data is stored and used? As shown in Table 13.3, these questions can be broken down into four issues that should be addressed: knowledge, control, notice, and consent.

Table 13.3 The Right to Know and the Ability to Decide

Fairness Issues	Database Storage	Database Usage
The right to know	Knowledge	Notice
The ability to decide	Control	Consent

Knowledge. Should people know what data is stored about them? In some cases, people are informed that information about them is stored in a corporate database. In others, they do not know that their personal information is stored in corporate databases

Control. Should people be able to correct errors in corporate database systems? This is possible with most organizations, although it can be difficult in some cases

Notice. Should an organization that uses personal data for a purpose other than the original purpose notify individuals in advance? Most companies don't do this

Consent. If information on people is to be used for other purposes, should these people be asked to give their consent before data on them is used? Many companies do not give people the ability to decide if information on them will be sold or used for other purposes

In the U.K., the Data Protection Act governs the answers to these questions. The act relates to data about individuals and states that:

1 Personal data shall be processed fairly and lawfully.
2 Companies must have a reason for collecting and storing the data – they can't arbitrarily start hoarding it, and they cannot process it in any manner incompatible with that reason.
3 The data collected shall be adequate, relevant, and not excessive in relation to the reason for collecting it.
4 Companies must make an effort to ensure the data is accurate and, where necessary, up to date.
5 The data will not be stored for longer than necessary.
6 All of the above applies to processing the data, not just collecting and storing it.
7 Companies must take steps to ensure that the data is secure.
8 The data must not be transferred to somewhere that does not have a similar law on processing it.

The act allows individuals to access information stored about them and, if necessary, have the data updated or deleted. Similar laws have been implemented throughout Europe.

Even though privacy laws for private organizations are not very restrictive, most organizations are very sensitive to privacy issues and fairness. They realize that invasions of privacy can hurt their business, turn away customers, and dramatically reduce revenues and profits. Consider a major international credit card company. If the company sold confidential financial information on millions of customers to other companies, the results could be disastrous. In a matter of days, the firm's business and revenues could be reduced dramatically. Therefore, most organizations maintain privacy policies, even though they are not required by law. Corporate privacy policies should address a customer's knowledge, control, notice, and consent over the storage and use of information. They can also cover who has access to private data and when it can be used.

Multinational companies face an extremely difficult challenge in implementing data-collection and dissemination processes and policies because of the multitude of differing country or regional statutes. A good database design practice is to assign a single unique identifier to each customer – so that each has a single record describing all relationships with the company across all its business units. That way, the organization can apply customer privacy preferences consistently throughout all databases. Failure to do so can expose the organization to legal risks – aside from upsetting customers who opted out of some collection practices.

13.4.6 Individual Efforts to Protect Privacy

Many people are taking steps to increase their own privacy protection. Some of the steps that you can take to protect personal privacy include the following:

■ If you are concerned about what information a company is holding on you, use the Data Protection Act (or your country's equivalent) to find out what is stored about you in existing databases.

■ Be careful when you share information about yourself. Don't share information unless it is absolutely necessary.

■ Be vigilant in insisting that your doctor, bank, or financial institution not share information about you with others without your written consent.

■ Be proactive to protect your privacy. For instance, you could get an unlisted phone number and think twice about registering for a service if it means you must supply a postal address. Consider registering for the telephone preference and mail preference services in your country (which stops commercial calls and post). In the U.K. the address is www.tpsonline.org.uk.

■ When purchasing anything from a website, make sure that you safeguard your credit card numbers, passwords, and personal information. Do not do business with a site unless you know that it handles credit card information securely (look for https:// in the address bar). Do not provide personal information without reviewing the site's data privacy policy.

When some people give over personal information, they change it slightly somehow, maybe changing their name from John T. Smith to John R. Smith. Then in the future, if they get contacted as John R. Smith from an unknown source, they know which company the information must have come from, and can take the appropriate steps.

13.5 The Work Environment

The use of computer-based information systems has changed the makeup of the workforce. Jobs that require IS literacy have increased, and many less-skilled positions have been eliminated. Corporate programs, such as reengineering and continuous improvement, bring with them the concern that, as business processes are restructured and information systems are integrated within them, the people involved in these processes will be removed.

However, the growing field of computer technology and information systems has opened up numerous avenues to professionals and nonprofessionals of all backgrounds. Enhanced telecommunications has been the impetus for new types of business and has created global markets in industries once limited to domestic markets. Even the simplest tasks have been aided by computers, making cash registers faster, smoothing order processing, and allowing people with disabilities to participate more actively in the workforce. As computers and other IS components drop in cost and become easier to use, more workers will benefit from the increased productivity and efficiency provided by computers. However, information systems can raise other concerns.

13.5.1 Health Concerns

Organizations can increase employee effectiveness by paying attention to the health concerns in today's work environment. For some people, working with computers can cause occupational stress. Anxieties about job insecurity, loss of control, incompetence, and demotion are just a few of the fears workers might experience. In some cases, the stress can become so severe that workers might sabotage computer systems and equipment. Monitoring employee stress can alert companies to potential problems. Training and counselling can often help the employee and deter problems.

Computer use can affect physical health as well. Strains, sprains, tendonitis, tennis elbow, the inability to hold objects, and sharp pain in the fingers can result. Also common is repetitive strain injuries (RSI), including carpal tunnel syndrome (CTS), which is the aggravation of the pathway for nerves that travel through the wrist (the carpal tunnel). CTS involves wrist pain, a feeling of tingling and numbness, and difficulty grasping and holding objects. It can be caused by many factors, such as stress, lack of exercise, and the repetitive motion of typing on a computer keyboard. Decisions on workers' compensation related to repetitive stress injuries have been made both for and against employees.

Other work-related health hazards involve emissions from improperly maintained and used equipment. Some studies show that poorly maintained laser printers can release ozone into the air; others dispute the claim. Numerous studies on the impact of emissions from display screens have also resulted in conflicting theories. Although some medical authorities believe that long-term exposure can cause cancer, studies are not conclusive at this time. In any case, many organizations are developing conservative and cautious policies.

Most computer manufacturers publish technical information on radiation emissions from their CRT monitors, and many companies pay close attention to this information. In addition, adjustable chairs and workstations should be supplied if employees request them.

13.5.2 Avoiding Health and Environmental Problems

Many computer-related health problems are caused by a poorly designed work environment. The computer screen can be hard to read, with glare and poor contrast. Desks and chairs can also be uncomfortable. Keyboards and computer screens might be fixed in place or difficult to move. The hazardous activities associated with these unfavourable conditions are collectively referred to as 'work stressors'. Although these problems might not be of major concern to casual users of computer systems, continued stressors such as repetitive motion, awkward posture, and eyestrain can cause more serious and long-term injuries. If nothing else, these problems can severely limit productivity and performance (see Figure 13.4).

Figure 13.4 **Repetitive Strain Injury** *Research has shown that developing certain ergonomically correct habits can reduce the risk of RSI when using a computer.*

SOURCE: Istock.

ergonomics The science of designing machines, products, and systems to maximize the safety, comfort, and efficiency of the people who use them.

The science of designing machines, products, and systems to maximize the safety, comfort, and efficiency of the people who use them, called **ergonomics**, has suggested some approaches to reducing these health problems. The slope of the keyboard, the positioning and design of display screens, and the placement and design of computer tables and chairs have been carefully studied. Flexibility is a major component of ergonomics and an important feature of computer devices. People come in many sizes, have differing preferences, and require different positioning of equipment for best results. Some people, for example, want to place the keyboard in their laps; others prefer it on a solid table. Because of these individual differences, computer designers are attempting to develop systems that provide a great deal of flexibility. In fact, the revolutionary design of Apple's iMac computer came about through concerns for users' comfort, and after using basically the same keyboard design for over a decade, Microsoft introduced a new split keyboard called the Natural Ergonomic Keyboard 4000. The keyboard provides improved ergonomic features such as improved angles that reduce motion and how much you must stretch your fingers when you type. The design of the keyboard also provides more convenient wrist and arm postures, which make typing more convenient for users.[21]

Computer users who work at their machines for more than an hour per day should consider using LCD screens, which are much easier on your eyes than CRT screens. If you stare at a CRT screen all day long, your eye muscles can get fatigued from all the screen flicker and bright backlighting of the monitor. LCD screens provide a much better viewing experience for your eyes by virtually eliminating flicker and while still being bright without harsh incandescence.[22]

In addition to steps taken by hardware manufacturing companies, computer users must also take action to reduce strain injury and develop a better work environment. For example, when working at a workstation, the top of the monitor should be at or just below eye level. Your wrists and hands should be in line with your forearms, with your elbows close to your body and supported. Your lower back needs to be well supported. Your feet should be flat on the floor. Take an occasional break to get away from the keyboard and screen. Stand up and stretch while at your workplace. Do not ignore pain or discomfort. Many workers ignore early signs of strain injury, and as a result, the problem becomes much worse and more difficult to treat.

Ethical and Societal Issues

Microsoft versus the EU

The European Union's anti-trust case against Microsoft goes back to the early 1990s, when software developer Novel complained about Microsoft's licensing agreements with PC manufacturers, which required payment of royalties based on the number of computers shipped, regardless of whether they actually had Windows installed on them. In the late 1990s, Sun Microsystems had also complained that Microsoft would not disclose technical information about Windows, which Sun needed if they were to write compatible software. Then the EU expanded the investigation to look at how Windows Media had been incorporated into Windows. The issue here was that Windows Media was essentially being given away for free with Windows, which meant that those software developers who had their own software for playing audio and video were being disadvantaged. Eventually Microsoft did release a version of Windows (called Windows XP N) available without Media Player installed, but it has been almost universally ignored by customers. In addition, Microsoft was given a record fine and ordered to disclose technical information about its operating system. In response, Microsoft did release some information but, as yet, the EU claims it has not achieved full disclosure of what is required. The EU is currently fining Microsoft €1.5 million a day, until it complies with the court's decision. Microsoft recently lost its appeal against this.

Questions

1 Why have PC buyers ignored Windows XP N?

2 Does anyone really care who has written the software they are using, as long as it does what they want it to? Do only certain groups of users care? Who are they? Carefully explain your answers.

3 Why would Microsoft not want to release technical details of Windows to other software developers?

4 Some people have strong feelings for and against Microsoft. What is your opinion and explain why.

SOURCES: Abu-Haidar, L., 'Microsoft Investigated in Europe, CNET News.com, 16 October 1997; McCullagh, D., 'EU Looks to Wrap Up Microsoft Probe', CNET News.com, 1 July 2002; Marson, I., 'Still "No Demand" for Media-Player-Free Windows', CNET News.com, 18 November 2005.

13.6 Ethical Issues in Information Systems

As you've seen throughout the book in our Ethical and Societal Issues boxes, ethical issues deal with what is generally considered right or wrong. As we have seen, laws do not provide a complete guide to ethical behaviour. Just because an activity is defined as legal does not mean that it is ethical. As a result, practitioners in many professions subscribe to a **code of ethics** that states the principles and core values that are essential to their work and, therefore, govern their behaviour. The code can become a reference point for weighing what is legal and what is ethical. For example, doctors adhere to varying versions of the 2000-year-old Hippocratic Oath, which medical schools offer as an affirmation to their graduating classes.

code of ethics A code that states the principles and core values that are essential to a set of people and, therefore, govern their behaviour.

Some IS professionals believe that their field offers many opportunities for unethical behaviour. They also believe that unethical behaviour can be reduced by top-level managers developing, discussing, and enforcing codes of ethics. Various IS-related organizations and associations promote ethically responsible use of information systems and have developed useful codes of ethics. The British Computer Society has a code of ethics and professional conduct that can be used to help guide the actions of IS professionals. These guidelines can also be used for those who employ or hire IS professionals to monitor and guide their work and can be seen at www.bcs.org.

The mishandling of the social issues discussed in this chapter – including waste and mistakes, crime, privacy, health, and ethics – can devastate an organization. The prevention of these problems and recovery from them are important aspects of managing information and information systems as critical corporate assets. Increasingly, organizations are recognizing that people are the most important component of a computer-based information system and that long-term competitive advantage can be found in a well-trained, motivated, and knowledgeable workforce.

Summary

Policies and procedures must be established to avoid computer waste and mistakes. Computer waste is the inappropriate use of computer technology and resources in both the public and private sectors. Computer mistakes relate to errors, failures, and other problems that result in output that is incorrect and without value. Waste and mistakes occur in government agencies as well as corporations. At the corporate level, computer waste and mistakes impose unnecessarily high costs for an information system and drag down profits. Waste often results from poor integration of IS components, leading to duplication of efforts and overcapacity. Inefficient procedures also waste IS resources, as do thoughtless disposal of useful resources and misuse of computer time for games and personal processing jobs. Inappropriate processing instructions, inaccurate data entry, mishandling of IS output, and poor systems design all cause computer mistakes.

A less dramatic, yet still relevant, example of waste is the amount of company time and money employees can waste playing computer games, sending unimportant e-mail, or accessing the Internet. Junk e-mail, also called spam, and junk faxes also cause waste.

Preventing waste and mistakes involves establishing, implementing, monitoring, and reviewing effective policies and procedures. Careful programming practices, thorough testing, flexible network interconnections, and rigorous backup procedures can help an information system prevent and recover from many kinds of mistakes. Companies should develop manuals and training programs to avoid waste and mistakes. Company policies should specify criteria for new resource purchases and user-developed processing tools to help guard against waste and mistakes.

Computer crime is a serious and rapidly growing area of concern requiring management attention. Some crimes use computers as tools (e.g., to manipulate records, counterfeit money and documents, commit fraud via telecommunications links, and make unauthorized electronic transfers of money). Identity theft is a crime in which an imposter obtains key pieces of personal identification information to impersonate someone else. The information is then used to obtain credit, merchandise, and services in the name of the victim, or to provide the thief with false credentials.

A cyberterrorist is someone who intimidates or coerces a government or organization to advance his or her political or social objectives by launching computer-based attacks against computers, networks, and the information stored on them. A cracker, or criminal hacker, is a computer-savvy person who attempts to gain unauthorized access to computer systems to steal passwords, corrupt files and programs, and even transfer money. Script kiddies are crackers with little technical savvy. Insiders are employees, disgruntled or otherwise, working solo or in concert with outsiders to compromise corporate systems.

Computer crimes target computer systems and include illegal access to computer systems, alteration and destruction of data and programs by viruses (system, application, and document), and simple theft of computer resources. A virus is a program that attaches itself to other programs. A worm functions as an independent program, replicating its own program files until it destroys other systems and programs or interrupts the operation of computer systems and networks. Malware is a general term for software that is harmful or destructive. A Trojan horse program is a malicious program that disguises itself as a useful application and purposefully does something the user does not expect. A logic bomb is designed to 'explode' or execute at a specified time and date.

Because of increased computer use, greater emphasis is placed on the prevention and detection of computer crime. Antivirus software is used to detect the presence of viruses, worms, and logic bombs. Use of an intrusion detection system (IDS) provides another layer of protection in the event that an intruder gets past the outer security layers – passwords, security procedures, and corporate firewall. It monitors system and network resources and notifies network security personnel when it senses a possible intrusion.

Many small and mid-sized organizations are outsourcing their network security operations to managed security service providers (MSSPs), which monitor, manage, and maintain network security hardware and software.

Software and Internet piracy might represent the most common computer crime. Computer scams have cost people and companies thousands of dollars. Computer crime is also an international issue.

Many organizations and people help prevent computer crime. Security measures, such as using passwords, identification numbers, and data encryption, help to guard against illegal computer access, especially when supported by effective control procedures. Public-key infrastructure (PKI) enables users of an unsecured public network such as the Internet to securely and privately exchange data through the use of a public and a private cryptographic key pair that is obtained and shared through a trusted authority. The use of biometrics, involving the measurement of a person's unique characteristics, such as the iris, retina, or voice pattern, is another way to protect important data and information systems. Virus-scanning software identifies and removes damaging computer programs. Although most companies use data files for legitimate, justifiable purposes, opportunities for invasion of privacy abound. Privacy issues are a concern with government agencies, e-mail use, corporations, and the Internet. A business should develop a clear and thorough policy about privacy rights for customers, including database access. That policy should also address the rights of employees, including electronic monitoring systems and e-mail. Fairness in information use for privacy rights emphasizes knowledge, control, notice, and consent for people profiled in databases. People should know about the data that is stored about them and be able to correct errors in corporate database systems. If information on people is to be used for other purposes, they should be asked to give their consent beforehand. Each person has the right to know and the ability to decide. Platform for Privacy Preferences (P3P) is a screening technology that shields users from websites that don't provide the level of privacy protection they desire.

Jobs, equipment, and working conditions must be designed to avoid negative health effects. Computers have changed the makeup of the workforce and even eliminated some jobs, but they have also expanded and enriched employment opportunities in many ways. Computers and related devices can affect employees' emotional and physical health. Some critics blame computer systems for emissions of ozone and electromagnetic radiation.

The study of designing and positioning computer equipment, called ergonomics, has suggested some approaches to reducing these health problems. Ergonomic design principles help to reduce harmful effects and increase the efficiency of an information system. The slope of the keyboard, the positioning and design of display screens, and the placement and design of computer tables and chairs are essential for good health. Good practice includes keeping good posture, not ignoring pain or problems, performing stretching and strengthening exercises, and

seeking proper treatment. Although they can cause negative health consequences, information systems can also be used to provide a wealth of information on health topics through the Internet and other sources.

Ethics determine generally accepted and discouraged activities within a company and society at large. Ethical computer users define acceptable practices more strictly than just refraining from committing crimes; they also consider the effects of their IS activities, including Internet usage, on other people and organizations. Many IS professionals join computer-related associations and agree to abide by detailed ethical codes.

Self-Assessment Test

1 It is solely up to IS professionals to implement and follow proper IS usages policies to ensure effective use of company resources. True or false?

2 Preventing waste and mistakes involves establishing, implementing, _____, and reviewing effective policies and procedures.

3 Computer crime is frequently easily detected and the amount of money involved is often quite small. True or false?

4 _____ is a crime in which an imposter obtains key pieces of personal identification information, such as National Insurance or driving licence numbers, to impersonate someone else.

5 Someone who intimidates or coerces a government to advance his or her political objectives by launching computer-based attacks against computers, networks, and the information stored on them is called a _____.
   a. cyberterrorist
   b. hacker
   c. criminal hacker or cracker
   d. social engineer

6 A logic bomb is a type of Trojan horse that executes when specific conditions occur. True or false?

7 Malware capable of spreading itself from one computer to another is called a _____.
   a. logic bomb
   b. Trojan horse
   c. virus
   d. worm

8 Phishing is a computer scam that seems to direct users to a bank's website but actually captures key personal information about its victims. True or false?

9 CTS, or _____, is the aggravation of the pathway of nerves that travel through the wrist.

10 The study of designing and positioning computer equipment to improve worker productivity and minimize worker injuries is called _____.

Review Questions

1 What special issues are associated with the prevention of image-based spam?

2 Identify three types of common computer-related mistakes.

3 What is a variant? What dangers are associated with such malware?

4 What is phishing? What actions can you take to reduce the likelihood that you will be a victim of this crime?

5 What is a virus? What is a worm? How are they different?

6 Outline measures you should take to protect yourself against viruses and worms.

7 Identify at least five tips to follow to avoid becoming a victim of a computer scam.

8 What is biometrics, and how can it be used to protect sensitive data?

9 What is the difference between antivirus software and an intrusion detection system?

10 What is a code of ethics? Give an example.

Discussion Questions

1 Outline an approach, including specific techniques that you could employ to gain personal data about the members of your class. Explain how they could protect themselves from what you have suggested.

2 Your 12-year-old niece shows you a profile of her male maths teacher posted on Facebook that includes a list of dozens of students as the instructor's friends and a quote: 'I hope to make lots of new friends and, who knows, maybe find Miss Right'. What would you do?

3 Imagine that you are a hacker and have developed a Trojan horse program. What tactics might you use to get unsuspecting victims to load the program onto their computer?

4 Briefly discuss the potential for cyberterrorism to cause a major disruption in your daily life. What are some likely targets of a cyberterrorist? What sort of action could a cyberterrorist take against these targets?

5 You travel a lot in your role as vice president of sales and carry a laptop containing customer data, budget information, product development plans, and promotion information. What measures should you take to ensure against potential theft of your laptop and its critical data?

Web Exercises

1 Search the Web for a site that provides software to detect and remove spyware. Write a short report for your instructor summarizing your findings.

2 Do research on the Web to find evidence of an increase or decrease in the number of viruses being developed and released. To what is the change attributed? Write a brief memo to your instructor identifying your sources and summarizing your findings.

Case One

Checking for Fraud in Online Gambling

Betfair is one of the largest online gaming companies in the world, with more than a million registered users. It provides online sports betting, casino, poker and exchange-based games and it depends on its customers handing over legitimate credit card details. Sandra Barton-Nicol, head of risk investigations at Betfair, says minimizing credit card fraud is extremely high on the company's agenda. 'The risk associated with gambling is that you don't have a product, and so you can't hold an order while you deal with the financials,' she says. 'Therefore we tend to be extra cautious, which reduces the risk to the business so that it isn't significantly higher than most other types of online retailing.'

Minimizing fraudulent transactions is a process that has been built in and embedded as part of the whole proposition of the Betfair online site, with risk rules put in place during the site design and traffic flow optimization stages. 'In addition to software that analyzes transactions it is important to have dedicated staff that look at the trades that are going through the business,' says Barton-Nicol. 'A large part of fraud detection is in identifying traffic and transactions that fall outside the norm – Internet protocol (IP) addresses that don't match the registered company, credit cards details that differ from the given particulars and so on.'

For Betfair, building up a picture of trust with its customers from the scant facts with which it is provided is an important part of business. 'If a customer says they live in England, we can check from their IP address if their Internet service provider mail server is in the U.K., whether their e-mail address is real, and if their landline telephone number exists and corresponds with other details,' says Barton-Nicol. 'We also create a profile of an average punter's activity and see if the behaviour tallies. Are they acting out of the ordinary and if so, why?'

Betfair uses a number of different technologies to identify the exceptions within its business. Some provide weighted rules, while others employ artificial intelligence to identify unusual patterns of behaviour. Betfair has seen a significant reduction in 'card not present fraud' as it has added more tools to its fraud detection investigation. Good people, robust processes and investment in technology are the three key components of the equation. Although schemes such as Verified by Visa are part of the solution, Betfair believes that the responsibility to control the level of fraud going through any business rests firmly with the business itself. 'We want to protect our clients and we don't want people coming to our site and using other people's credit cards,' says Barton-Nicol. 'Good fraud detection and prevention builds trust, and the more confidence people have in our site the more they will use it.'

Questions

1 What steps does Betfair take to check for fraud? Why is Betfair extra cautious when it comes to processing credit card transactions?

2 What other aspects of trust come into play in online gambling? How can Betfair ensure this trust exists?

3 Why aren't these techniques being used by all Internet traders?

4 In your opinion, should an IS professional work for a gambling organization? Explain your answer.

SOURCES: More, L., 'Case Study: Betfair', *Computing*, 26 July 2007, http://www.computing.co.uk/computing/analysis/2194860/case-study-betfair.

Case Two

Johnson & Johnson Maintain Secure Global Connections

Johnson & Johnson (J&J) is a healthcare industry giant with more than 200 separate companies operating in 54 countries. Many J&J companies and their partners conduct e-commerce business with J&J through extranet connections to the corporate network. This presented a problem to J&J network security specialists because partners' networks sometimes introduced worms and viruses into J&J's network. Not only was security an issue, but also the process of reviewing business requests for J&J network access had become burdensome, often delaying e-commerce transactions.

To remedy the problem, the J&J systems group set out to define policies and processes to streamline the process of connecting to the J&J intranet in a secure manner. J&J information system and security professionals worked with the legal department to design standard procedures for requests and evaluations. They also designed a contract or memo of understanding regarding the network connection to be established.

Under the new system, when a business manager at J&J wants to provide counterparts in outside firms with access to internal applications for e-commerce, the IT department is summoned to assess risk. First, the J&J unit and the outside firm complete a detailed questionnaire about the nature of the connection request, says Denise Medd, information security senior analyst. In addition, J&J expects the intended e-commerce partner to submit to a security assessment and evaluation. A neutral third party typically carries out the vulnerability assessment. The goal is to ensure that doing business via the network connection, which is typically opened up through the J&J firewall, presents no unnecessary risks. The outside firm must maintain systems free of viruses and worms, protected with a firewall, with up-to-date security patches. The J&J operating company, officially known as 'the sponsor', is held to the same standards.

Occasionally, a request for network access is turned down, especially if the servers lack proper patch-update mechanisms or have other shortcomings. Patches are released by software vendors to fix bugs in software that often leave the system vulnerable to hackers.

After they are connected, the partner company's system is subject to an inspection process every six months to ascertain the security of the network connection. The risk management procedure has resulted in a dramatic drop in virus and worm outbreaks. Sometimes, business project managers grumble about the assessment process, but J&J management's solid backing of it has made it a uniformly enforced process that is in effect with hundreds of outside firms, says Thomas Bunt, director of worldwide information security at J&J. Also, companies are typically more willing to undergo the security assessment after J&J explains why they need to do it and how they will benefit.

Questions

1 What are some of J&J's concerns regarding security?

2 What is an extranet? Explain some of the advantages and disadvantages of an extranet. Outline some of the privacy concerns extranets raise.

3 Why use a neutral third party to carry out the assessments?

4 How might it affect partnerships, if a request for access is turned down? What could J&J do to minimize any negative impact?

SOURCES: Messmer, Ellen, 'Johnson & Johnson Tackles Security Pain', *Network World*, March 30, 2005, www.networkworld.com; Johnson & Johnson (website), www.jnj.com.

Case Three

Disgruntled Employee Plants Time Bomb in Get-Rich-Quick Scheme

Recently in the U.S., another hacker went to trial to determine if he will be spending the next several years in jail or as a free man. Unlike many hacker trials, the defendant in this case is not an adolescent, but a 63-year-old systems administrator earning over $160 000 per year with a big-name financial company. After working for the company for many years, the systems administrator came to expect a $25 000 bonus at the end of each year. One year, the company suffered financial losses and the employee received only a $10 000 bonus. The employee had been counting on $25 000 for his son's college tuition. Feeling cheated, the employee began building the code that would punish his employer while creating a windfall for him and his family.

According to the prosecution, the systems administrator developed a malicious code to delete files and cause a major disruption on his company's network. The time bomb was ingenious in design. Working remotely on the corporate system from his home, the employee allegedly built four separate components of the time bomb:

- Component 1, the Payload: This destructive portion of the code told the servers to delete files.

- Component 2, Distribution: This code pushed the bomb from the central server in the company's data centre out to the 370 branch offices scattered across the country.

- Component 3, Persistence: This code kept the bomb running despite reboots and any loss of power.

- Component 4, Triggers: To avoid mistakes, he built not one, but two triggers for the bomb. If one trigger was accidentally discovered and deleted off the system, another one would be silently waiting to go off, setting a destructive chain of events into motion.

With the bomb in place, the employee went to his supervisor and demanded the bonus that he felt he was due, and threatened to quit if he didn't get it. Then, he packed his things and left. Prosecutors said that 'within an hour or so' of walking out the door, he was at a securities office buying 'put' options against his company. 'Put' options are a high-risk, high-payoff type of share trade where the buyer profits if the company stock goes down. Over the three weeks that followed, the employee spent nearly $25 000 to purchase a total of 330 'puts', almost all of them against his company. He had not bought one before that month, and he never bought another one afterward. He purchased more than 'half of the 'puts' the day before the disaster struck.

The damage caused by the malicious code impaired trading at the firm that day, hampering more than 1000 servers and 17 000 individual workstations. The attack cost the company about $3 million to assess and repair. The prosecution claimed: 'It took hundreds of people, thousands of man hours and millions of dollars to correct.'

The unusual purchase of 'puts' is the primary incriminating evidence against the employee. Investigators also determined that the bomb was planted by someone logged on with the employee's username and password. The employee's primary defence was that other company users could have accessed the system using his password and that the systems were vulnerable to outside attackers. He was jailed for eight years.

Questions

1 Why were the four components of this time bomb considered ingenious?

2 Name the two pieces of evidence you think are most damaging to this employee. Explain why.

3 Based on the information presented here, do you think the employee is guilty beyond a reasonable doubt? Why or why not? Is guilt more difficult to prove in cases of cybercrime as opposed to ordinary crimes?

4 What steps could the company have taken to avoid this type of destruction?

SOURCES: Solheim, Shelley, 'UBS Employee Stands Trial for Detonating "Computer Bomb"', *IDG News Service,* June 8, 2006, www.infoworld.com; Gaudin, Sharon, 'Prosecutors: UBS Sysadmin Believed "He Had Created The Perfect Crime"', *Information Week,* July 10, 2006; 'Disgruntled UBS PaineWebber Employee Charge with Allegedly Unleashing "Logic Bomb" on Company Computers', U.S. Department of Justice (website), www.usdoj.gov/criminal/cybercrime/duronioIndict.

Notes

[1] McGillicuddy, Shamus, 'Thwarting Spam from the Inside and the Outside', ComputerWeekly.com, July 11, 2006.

[2] McGillicuddy, Shamus, 'Image-Based Spam on the Rise', ComputerWeekly.com, August 3, 2006.

[3] Whiting, Rick, 'Hamstrung by Defective Data', *Information Week,* May 8, 2006.

[4] Mitchell, Robert, 'Q&A: Making A Federal Case – How the FBI Collars Cybercriminals', *Computerworld,* July 28, 2006.

[5] Koprowski, Gene J., 'Study: Nearly a Quarter Million PCs Turned into "Zombies" Daily', *E-commerce Times,* January 14, 2006.

[6] McMillian, Robert, 'Internet Sieges Can Cost Businesses a Bundle', *Computerworld,* August 25, 2005.

[7] BBC News (website), 'U.K. hacker "should be extradited"', May 10, 2006, http://news.bbc.co.uk/1/hi/technology/4757375.stm.

[8] BBC News (website), 'Tax Credit Errors "Waste £1.4bn"', May 8, 2007, http://news.bbc.co.uk/1/hi/business/6634843.stm.

[9] Keizer, Gregg, 'U.S. Consumers Taking Steps to Stymie ID Theft', *Information Week,* May 19, 2006.

[10] Savaas, Antony, 'McAfee: 400 000 Virus Definitions on Users' Machines by 2008', ComputerWeekly.com, July 6, 2006.

[11] Lyman, Jay, 'Study: Mobile Malware Threat to Grow in '06', *E-commerce Times,* December 10, 2005.

[12] Savvas, Antony, 'Police Arrest m00p Gang Suspects', ComputerWeekly.com, June 28, 2006.

[13] Savvas, Antony, 'Trojan Steals Bank Details After Pretending to Be Microsoft Patch', ComputerWeekly.com, May 31, 2006.

[14] McAfee (website), 'Virus Hoaxes', August 24, 2006, http://vil.mcafee.com/hoax.asp.

[15] BBC News (website), 'Defence Consultant's Laptop Stolen', April 16, 2001, http://news.bbc.co.uk/1/hi/uk/1279584.stm.

[16] Business Software Alliance (website home page), www.bsa.org/usa.

[17] Garretson, Cara, 'Stats Show Phishing Attacks Doubled', *Computerworld,* January 13, 2006.

[18] McMillan, Robert, 'Man Charged in Hurricane Katrina Phishing Scams', *Computerworld,* August 18, 2006.

[19] Hadfield, Will, 'Co-op Goes Live with First Payment by Biometrics System', ComputerWeekly.com, March 10, 2006.

[20] Wakefield, J., 'E-mail Embarrassment for City Lawyer', ZDNet U.K., December 14, 2000, http://news.zdnet.co.uk/internet/0,1000000097,2083185,00.htm.

[21] Shah, Agam, 'Microsoft Revamps Keyboards and Mice', *Computerworld,* September 6, 2005.

[22] Merrin, John, 'Review: Six 19-inch LCD Monitors', *Information Week,* June 8, 2005.

World Views Case

Coping with a Major IT Security Breach

Alan Hogarth
Glasgow Caledonian University

'Legal pressures, not to mention your moral obligation to assist unwitting victims, means that you should never delay when disclosing IT security incidents,' says Martin Allen of Pointsec.

Computer security breaches are becoming increasingly common. One need look no further than the recent misplacing of the UK Government's Revenue disks containing personal information on approximately 25M people. However this was by no means the first example of such a breach.

Another high profile example was in November 2005 when a laptop belonging to an employee of the Boeing Corporation was stolen. The information held on this machine was essentially personal finance details on about 161 000 current and former employees. As none of the confidential information was encrypted the thieves would have had easy access to the information to exploit as they saw fit. This serves to highlight Boeing's IT security failings, but furthermore to compound the situation they did not own up to the incident. Boeing still will not explain the precise timings but has admitted that it was 'several days' after the theft before the 161 000 'victims' were officially informed that their personal details were now in the public domain. Boeing is not alone, companies across the world, have always preferred to keep silent on any security breaches that have affected them. Because he problem is so bad the UK Metropolitan Police guaranteed anonymity if a company were to report a breach of their system. Basically, without such a scheme, police were unable to prosecute the hackers because officers were unaware that the incidents had taken place. The dilemma of the targeted organization is understandable. A simple breach of security could cost a typical bank £250 000 in terms of lost productivity, replacement hardware, or system downtime. However, if the attack is reported to the police and the perpetrators are subsequently tried the whole episode could then become public knowledge, which results in customers losing trust in the bank concerned.

José Luis Gutiérrez/Istock

There are many and varied types of issues, ranging from loss of key information, adverse publicity, loss of trust, legal action by customers, and official censure by regulators. All of which can be avoided with a little forethought and a professional attitude to the use of data encryption. Where once key data was held on a few PCs, now the information is far more portable and prone to all manner of mishaps intentional or otherwise. Laptops, which we have seen, are particularly easy to lose or steal.

Furthermore, unscrupulous staff or dishonest visitors can easily download information from a bank's main systems to a multitude of external storage devices. These include USB flash drives, digital cameras, MP3 players even mobile phones. All of which then become vulnerable if subsequently lost, stolen, or re-copied. Although Windows provides some encryption with its Encrypting File System, EFS is difficult to manage and impossible to enforce. Importantly, if files are copied from a Windows PC to these devices they invariably lose their encryption, often without the user being aware that this has happened. As such, an effective encryption policy needs to encompass every device onto which employees might wish to copy files. It also needs to be transparent to users, so that it can be centrally controlled without any user action being required. And it should be impossible to disable, except by authorized administrators.

Ideally it should also have the selective ability to block files from being copied to external devices at all, or if the target device doesn't support the same level of encryption as that which protects the source data. If you choose a proprietary encryption system and, if anyone discovers the secret mathematical formula behind it, all of the files that you have every encrypted instantly become public knowledge. Therefore, use a known international standard such as the Advanced Encryption System, or AES, with a key length of at least 256 bits.

Another situation relevant to the above discussion is one where a director of a company attended a conference last week, during which his briefcase was stolen. This case held his laptop and on the laptop were a list of the top 10 000 accounts by revenue. The information was not encrypted. This happened on a Friday afternoon, but the loss was not reported until Monday morning. This is an obviously unacceptable situation for any company.

The trust of one's customers and investors is among the greatest assets that your organization owns. Lose it, and you're well on your way to being out of business. But failing to protect key information and data, or to introduce unnecessary delays in making losses public, could make such a situation a reality. Therefore a full disk encryption should be mandatory to all organizations.

Questions

1 What IT security measures should have been implemented to prevent an occurrence like the Boeing incident referred to in the case study?

2 How important is it to an organization that the measures discussed in Question 1 should form part of an IT Security Policy? Who should be responsible for this policy and who should have access to it?

3 If you were a Director of a company whose 10 000 client accounts went missing during a laptop theft, how would you ensure that those clients are discreetly informed as soon as possible?

4 What action should the marketing department take to help regain the trust of new customers who have decided to take their accounts elsewhere?

SOURCE: electronicsweekly.com, Martin Allen, February 2006.

World Views Case

Preparing IT Systems in the Public Sector for a Pandemic

Frightening though it may be, but the Avian influenza, commonly known as the 'bird flu', is a real danger and has the potential to change the way we live and work. The World Health Organization (WHO) advises that everyone be prepared for an influenza pandemic that could strike at any moment. Now is the time for organizations, particularly public bodies, to plan and prepare for the worst so that they can continue to execute their mission regardless of the external environment. As such employees must be able to work from geographically dispersed areas because a pandemic will not only lead to mass telecommuting, it will also make the public more dependent upon government agencies than ever. You also need to find a reliable backup solution for all data, including email, to help ensure that your vital information remains available, The first wave of the pandemic, could cause outbreaks to occur simultaneously in many locations throughout a country, possibly hampering national emergency service undertaking their task. This in turn would leave the local populace reliant on local resources to respond. Despite this the national governments will be expected to be available and operating. How effective government agencies are at this stage will depend on the contingency plans that are made in advance. For example, in his November 2005 'national Strategy fore Pandemic Influenza', President Bush stated one of the governments responsibilities was to ensure, *'that federal departments and agencies have developed and exercised preparedness and response plans that take into account the potential impact of a pandemic on the federal workforce, and are configured to support state, local and private sector efforts as appropriate.'*

Jennifer Nuzzo, an analyst with the Centre for Biosecurity, further states that *'organizations should be thinking about who could potentially work from home, how much technology would be required to keep operations running, who would need to be in the office, and how antiviral medicines and vaccine could be distributed to protect them.'*

© WHO/P. Virot

© WHO/P. Virot

If a pandemic should strike it is highly likely that employees will be unable to go into the office. As such it will be necessary to prepare for the worst by ensuring that key employees can perform their duties from home. Therefore, conducting an actual dry run in which all employees try to perform their work using the programs and communications they can access from home all at the same time, can help identify potential problem areas or weaknesses if a pandemic should strike. Such are the demands on complex data centres that they are becoming virtually unmanageable. Therefore standardizing the IT environment on a consistent software platform will give your IT staff the control they need to continue to perform their duties remotely.

If critical public records are to be maintained, you can't run the risk that files will be lost or accidentally deleted in a crisis situation. A disk-based backup solution will help keep data protected and available regardless of geographical location. The solution should make it easy for IT and users to perform tasks from any location, likely through a web-based interface. Investing in a backup environment for email traffic is also important. Backing up email locally, as well as on the agency's archival server, will keep emails safe.

According to Richard Nesbit, WHO's acting regional director for the Western Pacific, the public should not be despondent despite the fact that the threat for a pandemic 'bird flu' has faded somewhat from the public eye. He argues that, *'Scientists are telling us that the risk is just as present as ever… After three years now, I'm sure that many journalists and the public are starting to get tired of the same message that there's a potential global pandemic around the corner, but we have a responsibility to continue to give this message.'*

Essentially it is necessary to prepare IT systems well in advance of a possible pandemic. The pandemic threat must be taken seriously and implement solutions and strategies that will help keep systems running, regardless of where employees are working. It's also important to consider accessibility for the citizens who will need the most help from public agencies. Importantly, find a reliable backup solution for all data, including email, to help ensure that your vital information remains available during a pandemic. While no one wants to think about planning for any kind of crisis situation, taking proactive steps now will lead to less chaos should we be faced with a very real influenza outbreak.

Questions

1 Discuss the contingency measures that a business organization should undertake in order to lesson the effects of a pandemic on their IT processes and ensure business continuity?

2 Given that a major element in a contingency plan should be a backup system, how should this backup be protected from the disaster that may affect the main system?

3 As a manager of a government department responsible for getting emergency services to the population in the event of a major disaster what would you do in order that your IT services keep functioning?

4 Discuss the importance staff training for prevention and recovery in the event of a major disaster that could affect an organization's systems? What elements would you include in such a training course?

SOURCE: Online at: http://www.symantec.com/business/library/article.jsp

Answers to Self-Assessment Tests

Chapter 1

1 information system

2 system

3 a

4 False

5 computer-based information system (CBIS)

6 c

7 d

8 Mobile commerce (m-commerce)

9 d

10 Information systems

Chapter 2

1 True

2 organization

3 True

4 a

5 Outsourcing

6 False

7 process redesign

8 c

9 Return on investment

10 d

11 True

12 chief information officer (CIO)

Chapter 3

1 True

2 the goals of the organization

3 terabyte

4 c

5 execution

6 Source data automation

7 c

8 b

9 Heat is generated that can corrupt data and instructions and cause the computer to behave erratically.

10 a

Chapter 4

1 Paging

2 False

3 True

4 a

5 proprietary software

6 c

7 a

8 workgroup application software

9 syntax

10 False

Chapter 5

1 c

2 entity

3 enterprise rules

4 primary key

5 cardinality

6 b

7 a

8 data warehouse

9 b

10 Online analytical processing (OLAP)

Chapter 6

1 False

2 a

3 broadband over power lines

4 d

5 multiplexer

6 personal area network

7 Internet service provider (ISP)

8 extranet

9 True

Chapter 7

1 correction

2 True

3 d

4 source data automation

5 purchasing

6 d

7 c

8 True

9 d

10 False

Chapter 8

1 d

2 False

3 d

4 optimization

5 True

6 True

7 c

8 b

9 False

10 executive information system (EIS)

Chapter 9

1 d

2 Heuristics

3 d

4 Robotics

5 c

6 expert system shell

7 a

8 d

9 virtual reality system

10 c

Chapter 10

1 hotspot

2 Bluetooth

3 E-money

4 virtual pet

5 False

6 wiki

7 weblog

8 d

9 market segmentation

10 electronic bill presentment

Chapter 11

1 Systems development

2 c

3 a

4 a

5 False

6 Prototyping

7 True

8 a

9 entity-relationship (ER) diagrams; data-flow diagrams

10 True

Chapter 12

1	b	**6**	c
2	True	**7**	System
3	request for proposal (RFP)	**8**	False
4	freezing design specifications	**9**	patch
5	make-or-buy	**10**	True

Chapter 13

1	False	**6**	True
2	monitoring	**7**	d
3	False	**8**	True
4	Identity theft	**9**	carpal tunnel syndrome
5	a	**10**	ergonomics

Glossary

acceptance testing Conducting any tests required by the user.

accounting systems Systems that include budget, accounts receivable, payroll, asset management, and general ledger.

ad hoc DSS A DSS concerned with situations or decisions that come up only a few times during the life of the organization.

alignment When the output from an information system is exactly what is needed to help a company achieve its strategic goals, the two are said to be in alignment.

alpha testing Testing an incomplete or early version of the system.

analogue signal A variable signal continuous in both time and amplitude so that any small fluctuations in the signal are meaningful.

antivirus program Software that runs in the background to protect your computer from dangers lurking on the Internet and other possible sources of infected files.

applet A small program embedded in web pages.

application flowcharts Diagrams that show relationships among applications or systems.

application program interface (API) An interface that allows applications to make use of the operating system.

application service provider (ASP) A company that provides software, support, and the computer hardware on which to run the software from the user's facilities.

applications portfolio A scheme for classifying information systems according to the contribution they make to the organization.

arithmetic/logic unit (ALU) The part of the CPU that performs mathematical calculations and makes logical comparisons.

ARPANET A project started by the U.S. Department of Defense (DoD) in 1969 as both an experiment in reliable networking and a means to link DoD and military research contractors, including many universities doing military-funded research.

artificial intelligence (AI) The ability of computer systems to mimic or duplicate the functions or characteristics of the human brain or intelligence.

artificial intelligence systems People, procedures, hardware, software, data, and knowledge needed to develop computer systems and machines that demonstrate characteristics of intelligence.

asking directly An approach to gather data that asks users, stakeholders, and other managers about what they want and expect from the new or modified system.

asynchronous communication A form of communications where there is a measurable delay between the sending and receiving of the message, sometimes hours or even days.

auditing Analyzing the financial condition of an organization and determining whether financial statements and reports produced by the financial MIS are accurate.

B2Me A form of e-commerce where the business treats each customer as a separate market segment. Typical B2Me features include customizing a website for each customer, perhaps based on their previous purchases and personalized (electronic) marketing literature.

backbone One of the Internet's high-speed, long-distance communications links.

backward chaining The process of starting with conclusions and working backward to the supporting facts.

batch processing system A form of data processing where business transactions are accumulated over a period of time and prepared for processing as a single unit or batch.

benchmark test An examination that compares computer systems operating under the same conditions.

best practices The most efficient and effective ways to complete a business process.

beta testing Testing a complete and stable system by end users.

biometrics The measurement of one of a person's traits, whether physical or behavioural.

blade server A server that houses many individual computer motherboards that include one or more processors, computer memory, computer storage, and computer network connections.

blog An online diary, a combination of the words 'web' and 'log'.

brainstorming A decision-making approach that often consists of members offering ideas 'off the top of their heads'.

bridge A telecommunications device that connects one LAN to another LAN that uses the same telecommunications protocol.

broadband communications A telecommunications system in which a very high rate of data exchange is possible.

business intelligence The process of gathering enough of the right information in a timely manner and usable form and analyzing it to have a positive impact on business strategy, tactics, or operations.

business-to-business (B2B) e-commerce A subset of e-commerce where all the participants are organizations.

business-to-consumer (B2C) e-commerce A form of e-commerce in which customers deal directly with an organization and avoid intermediaries.

byte (B) Eight bits that together represent a single character of data.

cache memory A type of high-speed memory that a processor can access more rapidly than main memory.

cardinality In a relationship, cardinality is the number of one entity that can be related to another entity.

CASE repository A database of system descriptions, parameters, and objectives.

central processing unit (CPU) The part of the computer that consists of three associated elements: the arithmetic/logic unit, the control unit, and the register areas.

centralized processing Processing alternative in which all processing occurs at a single location or facility.

certification A process for testing skills and knowledge, which results in a statement by the certifying authority that states an individual is capable of performing a particular kind of job.

channel bandwidth The rate at which data is exchanged over a communications channel, usually measured in bits per second (bps).

chief knowledge officer (CKO) A top-level executive who helps the organization use a KMS to create, store, and use knowledge to achieve organizational goals.

chief programmer team A group of skilled IS professionals who design and implement a set of programs.

choice stage The third stage of decision making, which requires selecting a course of action.

client/server An architecture in which multiple computer platforms are dedicated to special functions such as database management, printing, communications, and program execution.

clock speed A series of electronic pulses produced at a predetermined rate that affects machine cycle time.

code of ethics A code that states the principles and core values that are essential to a set of people and, therefore, govern their behaviour.

cold site A computer environment that includes rooms, electrical service, telecommunications links, data storage devices, and the like; also called a 'shell'.

command line interface An interface where the user types text commands to the computer.

command-based user interface A user interface that requires you to give text commands to the computer to perform basic activities.

communications protocol A set of rules that governs the exchange of information over a communications channel.

compact disk read-only memory (CD-ROM) A common form of optical disk on which data, once it has been recorded, cannot be modified.

competitive advantage The ability of a firm to outperform its industry, that is, to earn a higher rate of profit than the industry norm.

competitive intelligence One aspect of business intelligence limited to information about competitors and the ways that knowledge affects strategy, tactics, and operations.

compiler A special software program that converts the programmer's source code into the machine-language instructions consisting of binary digits.

computer literacy Knowledge of computer systems and equipment and the ways they function; it stresses equipment and devices (hardware), programs and instructions (software), databases, and telecommunications.

computer network The communications media, devices, and software needed to connect two or more computer systems and/or devices.

computer program A sequence of instructions for the computer.

computer supported cooperative work A term that refers to technologies which allow groups to work together to achieve goals.

computer-aided manufacturing (CAM) A system that directly controls manufacturing equipment.

computer-aided software engineering (CASE) Tools that automate many of the tasks required in a systems development effort and encourage adherence to the SDLC.

computer-based information system (CBIS) A single set of hardware, software, databases, telecommunications, people, and procedures that are configured to collect, manipulate, store, and process data into information.

computer-integrated manufacturing (CIM) Using computers to link the components of the production process into an effective system.

concurrency control A method of dealing with a situation in which two or more people need to access the same record in a database at the same time.

consumer-to-consumer (C2C) e-commerce A subset of e-commerce that involves consumers selling directly to other consumers.

continuous improvement Constantly seeking ways to improve business processes to add value to products and services.

control unit The part of the CPU that sequentially accesses program instructions, decodes them, and coordinates the flow of data in and out of the ALU, registers, primary storage, and even secondary storage and various output devices.

coprocessor The part of the computer that speeds processing by executing specific types of instructions while the CPU works on another processing activity.

cost–benefit analysis An approach that lists the costs and benefits of each proposed system. After they are expressed in monetary terms, all the costs are compared with all the benefits.

counterintelligence The steps an organization takes to protect information sought by 'hostile' intelligence gatherers.

cracker A person who enjoys computer technology and spends time learning and using computer systems.

creative analysis The investigation of new approaches to existing problems.

criminal hacker (cracker) A computer-savvy person who attempts to gain unauthorized or illegal access to computer systems to steal passwords, corrupt files and programs, or even transfer money.

critical analysis The unbiased and careful questioning of whether system elements are related in the most effective ways.

critical path Activities that, if delayed, would delay the entire project.

critical success factors (CSFs) Factors that are essential to the success of a functional area of an organization.

cross-platform development A development technique that allows programmers to develop programs that can run on computer systems having different hardware and operating systems, or platforms.

customer relationship management (CRM) system A system that helps a company manage all aspects of customer encounters, including marketing and advertising, sales, customer service after the sale, and programs to retain loyal customers.

cyberterrorist Someone who intimidates or coerces a government or organization to advance his or her political or social objectives by launching computer-based attacks against computers, networks, and the information stored on them.

data administrator A non-technical position responsible for defining and implementing consistent principles for a variety of data issues.

data analysis The manipulation of collected data so that the development team members who are participating in systems analysis can use the data.

database An organized collection of information.

database administrator (DBA) The role of the database administrator is to plan, design, create, operate, secure, monitor, and maintain databases.

data collection Capturing and gathering all data necessary to complete the processing of transactions.

data correction The process of re-entering data that was not typed or scanned properly.

data definition language (DDL) A collection of instructions and commands used to define and describe data and relationships in a specific database.

data dictionary A detailed description of all the data used in the database.

data editing The process of checking data for validity and completeness.

data entry Converting human-readable data into a machine-readable form.

data-flow diagram (DFD) A model of objects, associations, and activities that describes how data can flow between and around various objects.

data-flow line Arrows that show the direction of data element movement.

data input Transferring machine-readable data into the system.

data manipulation The process of performing calculations and other data transformations related to business transactions.

data manipulation language (DML) The commands that are used to manipulate the data in a database.

data mining The process of analyzing data to try to discover patterns and relationships within the data.

data preparation (data conversion) Ensuring all files and databases are ready to be used with new computer software and systems.

data storage The process of updating one or more databases with new transactions.

data store Representation of a storage location for data.

data warehouse A database or collection of databases that collects business information from many sources in the enterprise, covering all aspects of the company's processes, products, and customers.

decentralized processing Processing alternative in which processing devices are placed at various remote locations.

decision-making phase The first part of problem solving, including three stages: intelligence, design, and choice.

decision support system (DSS) An organized collection of people, procedures, software, databases, and devices used to support problem-specific decision making.

degree The number of entities involved in a relationship.

demand report A report developed to give certain information at someone's request.

design report The primary result of systems design, reflecting the decisions made and preparing the way for systems implementation.

design stage The second stage of decision making, in which alternative solutions to the problem are developed.

desktop computer A relatively small, inexpensive, single-user computer that is highly versatile.

dialogue manager A user interface that allows decision makers to easily access and manipulate the DSS and to use common business terms and phrases.

digital audio player A device that can store, organize, and play digital music files.

digital camera An input device used with a PC to record and store images and video in digital form.

digital signal A signal that represents bits.

digital versatile disk (DVD) A storage medium used to store digital video or computer data.

direct access A retrieval method in which data can be retrieved without the need to read and discard other data.

direct access storage device (DASD) A device used for direct access of secondary storage data.

direct conversion Stopping the old system and starting the new system on a given date.

direct observation Watching the existing system in action by one or more members of the analysis team.

disaster planning The process of anticipating and providing for disasters.

disaster recovery The implementation of the disaster plan.

disk mirroring A process of storing data that provides an exact copy that protects users fully in the event of data loss.

distributed database A database in which the data is spread across several smaller databases connected via telecommunications devices.

distributed processing Processing alternative in which computers are placed at remote locations but are connected to each other via a network.

document production The process of generating output records and reports.

documentation The text that describes the program functions to help the user operate the computer system.

domain The area of knowledge addressed by the expert system.

domain expert The individual or group who has the expertise or knowledge one is trying to capture in the expert system.

downsizing Reducing the number of employees to cut costs.

drill-down report A report providing increasingly detailed data about a situation.

e-commerce Any business transaction executed electronically between companies (business-to-business), companies and consumers (business-to-consumer), consumers and other consumers (consumer-to-consumer), business and the public sector, and consumers and the public sector.

economic feasibility The determination of whether the project makes financial sense and whether predicted benefits offset the cost and time needed to obtain them.

economic order quantity (EOQ) The quantity that should be reordered to minimize total inventory costs.

effectiveness A measure of the extent to which a system achieves its goals; it can be computed by dividing the goals actually achieved by the total of the stated goals.

efficiency A measure of what is produced divided by what is consumed.

e-government The use of information and communications technology to simplify the sharing of information, speed formerly paper-based processes, and improve the relationship between citizen and government.

electronic bill presentment A method of billing whereby a vendor posts an image of your statement on the Internet and alerts you by e-mail that your bill has arrived.

electronic business (e-business) Using information systems and the Internet to perform all business-related tasks and functions.

electronic commerce Conducting business transactions (e.g., distribution, buying, selling, and servicing) electronically over computer networks such as the Internet, extranets, and corporate networks.

electronic exchange An electronic forum where manufacturers, suppliers, and competitors buy and sell goods, trade market information, and run back-office operations.

electronic retailing (e-tailing) The direct sale from business to consumer through electronic storefronts, typically designed around an electronic catalogue and shopping cart model.

e-money The transfer of funds electronically rather than by handing over physical coins and notes.

empowerment Giving employees and their managers more responsibility and authority to make decisions, take certain actions, and have more control over their jobs.

end-user systems development Any systems development project in which the primary effort is undertaken by a combination of business managers and users.

enterprise resource planning (ERP) system A set of integrated programs capable of managing a company's vital business operations for an entire multi-site, global organization.

enterprise rules The rules governing relationships between entities.

entity A person, place or thing about whom or about which an organization wants to store data.

entity symbol Representation of either a source or destination of a data element.

ergonomics The science of designing machines, products, and systems to maximize the safety, comfort, and efficiency of the people who use them.

event-driven review A review triggered by a problem or opportunity such as an error, a corporate merger, or a new market for products.

exception report A report automatically produced when a situation is unusual or requires management action.

execution time (e-time) The time it takes to execute an instruction and store the results.

executive support system (ESS) Specialized DSS that includes all hardware, software, data, procedures, and people used to assist senior-level executives within the organization.

expert system Hardware and software that stores knowledge and makes inferences, similar to a human expert.

explanation facility Component of an expert system that allows a user or decision maker to understand how the expert system arrived at certain conclusions or results.

Extensible Markup Language (XML) The markup language for web documents containing structured information, including words, pictures, and other elements.

extranet A network based on web technologies that allows selected outsiders, such as business partners, suppliers, or customers, to access authorized resources of a company's intranet.

feasibility analysis Assessment of the technical, economic, legal, operational, and schedule feasibility of a project.

feedback Output that is used to make changes to input or processing activities.

field A characteristic or attribute of an entity that is stored in the database

File Transfer Protocol (FTP) A protocol that describes a file transfer process between a host and a remote computer and allows users to copy files from one computer to another.

final evaluation A detailed investigation of the proposals offered by the vendors remaining after the preliminary evaluation.

financial MIS A management information system that provides financial information not only for executives but also for a broader set of people who need to make better decisions on a daily basis.

five-forces model A widely accepted model that identifies five key factors that can lead to attainment of competitive advantage, including (1) the rivalry among existing competitors, (2) the threat of new entrants, (3) the threat of substitute products and services, (4) the bargaining power of buyers, and (5) the bargaining power of suppliers.

flash memory A silicon computer chip that, unlike RAM, is non-volatile and keeps its memory when the power is shut off.

flat organizational structure An organizational structure with a reduced number of management layers.

flexible manufacturing system (FMS) An approach that allows manufacturing facilities to rapidly and efficiently change from making one product to making another.

forecasting Predicting future events.

foreign key When a primary key is posted into another table to create a relationship between the two, it is known as a foreign key.

forward chaining The process of starting with the facts and working forward to the conclusions.

front-end processor A special-purpose computer that manages communications to and from a computer system serving hundreds or even thousands of users.

future strategic application Future strategic applications are ideas for systems which, if fully developed and deployed, might one day become strategic applications.

Gantt chart A graphical tool used for planning, monitoring, and coordinating projects.

gateway A telecommunications device that serves as an entrance to another network.

genetic algorithm An approach to solving large, complex problems in which a number of related operations or models change and evolve until the best one emerges.

geographic information system (GIS) A computer system capable of assembling, storing, manipulating, and displaying geographic information, that is, data identified according to its location.

gigahertz (GHz) Billions of cycles per second.

global positioning system (GPS) A navigation system that enables a receiver to determine its precise location.

goal-seeking analysis The process of determining the problem data required for a given result.

graphical user interface (GUI) An interface that allows users to manipulate icons and menus displayed on screen to send commands to the computer system.

grid chart A table that shows relationships among the various aspects of a systems development effort.

grid computing The use of a collection of computers, often owned by multiple individuals or organizations, to work in a coordinated manner to solve a common problem.

group consensus Decision making by a group that is appointed and given the responsibility of making the final evaluation and selection.

group consensus approach A decision-making approach that forces members in the group to reach a unanimous decision.

group support system (GSS) Software application that consists of most elements in a DSS, plus software to provide effective support in group decision making; also called 'group decision support system'.

handheld computer A single-user computer that provides ease of portability because of its small size.

hardware Any machinery (most of which uses digital circuits) that assists in the input, processing, storage, and output activities of an information system.

heuristics Commonly accepted guidelines or procedures that usually find a good solution.

highly structured problems Problems that are straightforward and require known facts and relationships.

home page A cover page for a website that has graphics, titles, and text.

hot site A duplicate, operational hardware system or immediate access to one through a specialized vendor.

hotspot An area where wi-fi wireless Internet access is available.

HTML tags Codes that let the web browser know how to format text – as a heading, as a list, or as body text – and whether images, sound, or other elements should be inserted.

human resource MIS (HRMIS) An information system that is concerned with activities related to employees and potential employees of an organization, also called a personnel MIS.

hypermedia An extension of hypertext where the data, including text, images, video and other media, on web pages is connected allowing users to access information in whatever order they wish.

hyptertext Text used to connect web pages, allowing users to access information in whatever order they wish.

Hypertext Markup Language (HTML) The standard page description language for web pages.

IF-THEN statements Rules that suggest certain conclusions

implementation stage A stage of problem solving in which a solution is put into effect.

incremental backup Making a backup copy of all files changed during the last few days or the last week.

inference engine Part of the expert system that seeks information and relationships from the knowledge base and provides answers, predictions, and suggestions the way a human expert would.

information system (IS) A set of interrelated components that collect, manipulate, store, and disseminate information and provide a feedback mechanism to meet an objective.

information systems literacy Knowledge of how data and information are used by individuals, groups, and organizations.

information systems planning Translating strategic and organizational goals into systems development initiatives.

input The activity of gathering and capturing data.

insider An employee, disgruntled or otherwise, working solo or in concert with outsiders to compromise corporate systems.

installation The process of physically placing the computer equipment on the site and making it operational.

institutional DSS A DSS that handles situations or decisions that occur more than once, usually several times per year or more. An institutional DSS is used repeatedly and refined over the years.

instruction time (I-time) The time it takes to perform the fetch-instruction and decode-instruction steps of the instruction phase.

integrated development environments (IDEs) A development approach that combines the tools needed for programming with a programming language into one integrated package.

integration testing Testing all related systems together.

intelligence stage The first stage of decision making, in which potential problems or opportunities are identified and defined.

intelligent agent Programs and a knowledge base used to perform a specific task for a person, a process, or another program; also called intelligent robot or bot.

intelligent behaviour The ability to learn from experiences and apply knowledge acquired from experience, handle complex situations, solve problems when important information is missing, determine what is important, react quickly and correctly to a new situation, understand visual images, process and manipulate symbols, be creative and imaginative, and use heuristics.

interactive whiteboard This term can be used to mean slightly different technologies, but essentially it is a combination of a whiteboard and a desktop computer.

international network A network that links users and systems in more than one country.

Internet The world's largest computer network, actually consisting of thousands of interconnected networks, all freely exchanging information.

Internet Protocol (IP) A communication standard that enables traffic to be routed from one network to another as needed.

Internet service provider (ISP) Any company that provides people or organizations with access to the Internet.

intranet An internal company network built using Internet and World Wide Web standards and products that allows people within an organization to exchange information and work on projects.

intrusion detection system (IDS) Software that monitors system and network resources and notifies network security personnel when it senses a possible intrusion.

Java An object-oriented programming language from Sun Microsystems based on C++ that allows small programs (applets) to be embedded within an HTML document.

joint application development (JAD) A process for data collection and requirements analysis in which users, stakeholders, and IS professionals work together to analyze existing systems, propose possible solutions, and define the requirements of a new or modified system.

just-in-time (JIT) inventory A philosophy of inventory management in which inventory and materials are delivered just before they are used in manufacturing a product.

kernel The heart of the operating system, which controls the most critical processes.

key-indicator report A summary of the previous day's critical activities; typically available at the beginning of each workday.

key operational application Key operational applications are essential. Without them the organization could not conduct business.

key-operational systems Systems that play a pivotal role in an organization's continued operations and goal attainment.

knowledge acquisition facility Part of the expert system that provides convenient and efficient means of capturing and storing all the components of the knowledge base.

knowledge base A component of an expert system that stores all relevant information, data, rules, cases, and relationships used by the expert system.

knowledge engineer A person who has training or experience in the design, development, implementation, and maintenance of an expert system.

knowledge user The person or group who uses and benefits from the expert system.

LCD display Flat display that uses liquid crystals – organic, oil-like material placed between two polarizers – to form characters and graphic images on a backlit screen.

learning systems A combination of software and hardware that allows the computer to change how it functions or reacts to situations based on feedback it receives.

legal feasibility The determination of whether laws or regulations may prevent or limit a systems development project.

local area network (LAN) A computer network that connects computer systems and devices within a small area, such as an office, home, or several floors in a building.

logical design A description of the functional requirements of a system.

machine cycle The instruction phase followed by the execution phase.

magnetic disk A common secondary storage medium, with bits represented by magnetized areas.

magnetic stripe card A type of card that stores limited amounts of data by modifying the magnetism of tiny iron-based particles contained in a band on the card.

magnetic tape A secondary storage medium; Mylar film coated with iron oxide with portions of the tape magnetized to represent bits.

mainframe computer A large, powerful computer often shared by hundreds of concurrent users connected to the machine via terminals.

maintenance team A special IS team responsible for modifying, fixing, and updating existing software.

make-or-buy decision The decision regarding whether to obtain the necessary software from internal or external sources.

management information system (MIS) An organized collection of people, procedures, software, databases, and devices that provides routine information to managers and decision makers.

market segmentation The identification of specific markets to target them with advertising messages.

marketing MIS An information system that supports managerial activities in product development, distribution, pricing decisions, and promotional effectiveness.

massively parallel processing systems A form of multiprocessing that speeds processing by linking hundreds or thousands of processors to operate at the same time, or in parallel, with each processor having its own bus, memory, disks, copy of the operating system, and applications.

material requirements planning (MRP) A set of inventory-control techniques that help coordinate thousands of inventory items when the demand of one item is dependent on the demand for another.

megahertz (MHz) Millions of cycles per second.

menu-driven system A system in which users simply pick what they want to do from a list of alternatives.

mesh networking A way to route communications between network nodes (computers or other device) by allowing for continuous connections and reconfiguration around blocked paths by 'hopping' from node to node until a connection can be established.

metropolitan area network (MAN) A telecommunications network that connects users and their devices in a geographical area that spans a campus or city.

microcode Predefined, elementary circuits and logical operations that the processor performs when it executes an instruction.

middleware Software that allows different systems to communicate and exchange data.

MIPS Millions of instructions per second.

mobile commerce (m-commerce) Conducting business transactions electronically using mobile devices such as smartphones.

model base Part of a DSS that provides decision makers access to a variety of models and assists them in decision making.

model management software Software that coordinates the use of models in a DSS.

modem A telecommunications hardware device that converts (modulates and demodulates) communications signals so they can be transmitted over the communication media.

monitoring stage The final stage of the problem-solving process, in which decision makers evaluate the implementation.

Moore's Law A hypothesis that states that transistor densities on a single chip double every 18 months.

MP3 A standard format for compressing a sound sequence into a small file.

multicore microprocessor A microprocessor that combines two or more independent processors into a single computer so they can share the workload and deliver a big boost in processing capacity.

multiple instruction/multiple data (MIMD) A form of parallel computing in which the processors all execute different instructions.

multiplexer A device that encodes data from two or more data sources onto a single communications channel, thus reducing the number of communications channels needed and therefore, lowering telecommunications costs.

multiprocessing The simultaneous execution of two or more instructions at the same time.

narrowband communications A telecommunications system that supports a much lower rate of data exchange than broadband.

natural language processing Processing that allows the computer to understand and react to statements and commands made in a 'natural' language, such as English.

net present value The preferred approach for ranking competing projects and determining economic feasibility.

network Computers and equipment that are connected in a building, around the country, or around the world to enable electronic communications.

network-attached storage (NAS) Storage devices that attach to a network instead of to a single computer.

network-management software Software that enables a manager on a networked desktop to monitor the use of individual computers and shared hardware (such as printers), scan for viruses, and ensure compliance with software licences.

network operating system (NOS) Systems software that controls the computer systems and devices on a network and allows them to communicate with each other.

neural network A computer system that attempts to simulate the functioning of a human brain.

nominal group technique A decision-making approach that encourages feedback from individual group members, and the final decision is made by voting, similar to the way public officials are elected.

non-operational prototype A mock-up, or model, that includes output and input specifications and formats.

non-programmed decision A decision that deals with unusual or exceptional situations that can be difficult to quantify.

object-oriented database A database that stores both data and its processing instructions.

object-oriented database management system (OODBMS) A group of programs that manipulate an object-oriented database and provide a user interface and connections to other application programs.

object-relational database management system (ORDBMS) A DBMS capable of manipulating audio, video, and graphical data.

on-demand computing Contracting for computer resources to rapidly respond to an organization's varying workflow. Also called 'on-demand business' and 'utility computing'.

online analytical processing (OLAP) Software that allows users to explore data from a number of perspectives.

online transaction processing (OLTP) A form of data processing where each transaction is processed immediately, without the delay of accumulating transactions into a batch.

operating system (OS) A set of computer programs that controls the computer hardware and acts as an interface with application programs.

operational feasibility The measure of whether the project can be put into action or operation.

operational prototype A functioning prototype that accesses real data files, edits input data, makes necessary computations and comparisons, and produces real output.

optical disk A rigid disk of plastic onto which data is recorded by special lasers that physically burn pits in the disk.

optimization model A process to find the best solution, usually the one that will best help the organization meet its goals.

optionality If a binary relationship is optional for an entity, that entity doesn't have to be related to the other.

organization A formal collection of people and other resources established to accomplish a set of goals.

organizational change The responses that are necessary so that for-profit and non-profit organizations can plan for, implement, and handle change.

organizational learning The adaptations to new conditions or alterations of organizational practices over time.

organizational structure Organizational subunits and the way they relate to the overall organization.

output Production of useful information, often in the form of documents and reports.

outsourcing Contracting with outside professional services to meet specific business needs.

parallel computing The simultaneous execution of the same task on multiple processors to obtain results faster.

Parallel running Running both the old and the new systems for a period of time.

parallel start-up Running both the old and new systems for a period of time and comparing the output of the new system closely with the output of the old system; any differences are reconciled. When users are comfortable that the new system is working correctly, the old system is eliminated.

patch A minor change to correct a problem or make a small enhancement. It is usually an addition to an existing program.

perceptive system A system that approximates the way a person sees, hears, and feels objects.

personal area network (PAN) A network that supports the interconnection of information technology within a range of three metres or so.

personal robotics A term which refers to robotic companions that people socialize with.

pervasive computing A term meaning the move of the computer away from the desktop and towards something that is all around us, all the time.

phase-in approach Slowly replacing components of the old system with those of the new one. This process is repeated for each application until the new system is running every application and performing as expected; also called a piecemeal approach.

phicon Phicon stands for 'physical icon', and is a physical representation of digital data, in the same way that an icon on a computer screen represents a file.

physical design The specification of the characteristics of the system components necessary to put the logical design into action.

pilot running Introducing the new system by direct conversion for one group of users rather than all users.

pipelining A form of CPU operation in which multiple execution phases are performed in a single machine cycle.

pixel A dot of colour on a photo image or a point of light on a display screen.

Platform for Privacy Preferences (P3P) A screening technology that shields users from websites that don't provide the level of privacy protection they desire.

podcast An audio broadcast over the Internet.

point evaluation system An evaluation process in which each evaluation factor is assigned a weight, in percentage points, based on importance. Then each proposed system is evaluated in terms of this factor and given a score ranging from 0 to 100. The scores are totalled, and the system with the greatest total score is selected.

point-of-sale (POS) device A terminal used in retail operations to enter sales information into the computer system.

policy-based storage management Automation of storage using previously defined policies.

portable computer A computer small enough to be carried easily.

predictive analysis A form of data mining that combines historical data with assumptions about future conditions to predict outcomes of events such as future product sales or the probability that a customer will default on a loan.

preliminary evaluation An initial assessment whose purpose is to dismiss the unwanted proposals; begins after all proposals have been submitted.

primary key A field in a table that is unique – each record in that table has a different value in the primary key field. The primary key is used to uniquely identify each record, and to create relationships between tables.

primary storage (main memory; memory) The part of the computer that holds program instructions and data. Primary storage, also called main memory or memory, is closely associated with the CPU. Memory holds program instructions and data immediately before or after the registers.

problem solving A process that goes beyond decision making to include the implementation and monitoring stages.

procedures The strategies, policies, methods, and rules for using a CBIS.

process symbol Representation of a function that is performed.

processing Converting or transforming input into useful outputs.

productivity A measure of the output achieved divided by the input required. Productivity = (Output / Input) × 100%.

program evaluation and review technique (PERT) A formalized approach for developing a project schedule.

programmed decision A decision made using a rule, procedure, or quantitative method.

programmer A specialist responsible for modifying or developing programs to satisfy user requirements.

programming language Sets of keywords, symbols, and a system of rules for constructing statements by which humans can communicate instructions to be executed by a computer.

project deadline The date the entire project is to be completed and operational.

project milestone A critical date for the completion of a major part of the project.

project organizational structure A structure centred on major products or services.

project schedule A detailed description of what is to be done.

public-key infrastructure (PKI) A means to enable users of an unsecured public network such as the Internet to securely and privately exchange data through the use of a public and a private cryptographic key pair that is obtained and shared through a trusted authority.

quality control A process that ensures that the finished product meets the customers' needs.

questionnaires A method of gathering data when the data sources are spread over a wide geographic area.

radio frequency identification (RFID) A technology that employs a microchip with an antenna that broadcasts its unique identifier and location to receivers.

random access memory (RAM) A form of memory in which instructions or data can be temporarily stored.

rapid application development (RAD) A systems development approach that employs tools, techniques, and methodologies designed to speed application development.

read-only memory (ROM) A non-volatile form of memory.

record A row in a table; all the data pertaining to one instance of an entity

redundant array of independent/inexpensive disks (RAID) A method of storing data that generates extra bits of data from existing data, allowing the system to create a 'reconstruction map' so that if a hard drive fails, the system can rebuild lost data.

reengineering Also known as 'process redesign' and 'business process reengineering' (BPR). The radical re-design of business processes, organizational structures, information systems, and values of the organization to achieve a breakthrough in business results.

register A high-speed storage area in the CPU used to temporarily hold small units of program instructions and data immediately before, during, and after execution by the CPU.

relational database A series of related tables, stored together with a minimum of duplication to achieve consistent and controlled pool of data.

relationship degree The degree of a relationship is the number of entities that are involved.

release A significant program change that often requires changes in the documentation of the software.

reorder point (ROP) A critical inventory quantity level.

replicated database A database that holds a duplicate set of frequently used data.

report layout A technique that allows designers to diagram and format printed reports.

request for maintenance form A form authorizing modification of programs.

request for proposal (RFP) A document that specifies in detail required resources such as hardware and software.

requirements analysis The determination of user, stakeholder, and organizational needs.

requirements engineering Also known as 'requirements analysis' and 'requirements capture'. Identifying what an information systems is needed (required) to do. Once the requirements have been identified, a solution can then be designed.

return on investment (ROI) One measure of IS value that investigates the additional profits or benefits that are generated as a percentage of the investment in IS technology.

robotics Mechanical or computer devices that perform tasks requiring a high degree of precision or that are tedious or hazardous for humans.

router A telecommunications device that forwards data packets across two or more distinct networks towards their destinations, through a process known as routing.

satisficing model A model that will find a good – but not necessarily the best – problem solution.

scalability The ability to increase the capability of a computer system to process more transactions in a given period by adding more, or more powerful, processors.

schedule feasibility The determination of whether the project can be completed in a reasonable amount of time.

scheduled report A report produced periodically, or on a schedule, such as daily, weekly, or monthly.

screen layout A technique that allows a designer to quickly and efficiently design the features, layout, and format of a display screen.

script kiddie A cracker with little technical savvy who downloads programs called scripts, which automate the job of breaking into computers.

search engine A web search tool.

secondary storage (permanent storage) Devices that store larger amounts of data, instructions, and information more permanently than allowed with main memory.

semi-structured or unstructured problems More complex problems in which the relationships among the pieces of data are not always clear, the data might be in a variety of formats, and the data is often difficult to manipulate or obtain.

sequential access A retrieval method in which data must be accessed in the order in which it is stored.

sequential access storage device (SASD) A device used to sequentially access secondary storage data.

server A computer designed for a specific task, such as network or Internet applications.

shareware and freeware Software that is very inexpensive or free, but whose source code cannot be modified.

simulation The ability of the DSS to duplicate the features of a real system.

single instruction/multiple data (SIMD) A form of parallel computing in which the processors all execute the same instruction on many data values simultaneously.

site preparation Preparation of the location of a new system.

slipstream upgrade A minor upgrade – typically a code adjustment or minor bug fix – not worth announcing. It usually requires recompiling all the code and, in so doing, it can create entirely new bugs.

smartphone A phone that combines the functionality of a mobile phone, camera, web browser, e-mail tool, and other devices into a single handheld device.

social engineering Using one's social skills to get computer users to provide you with information to access an information system or its data.

software The computer programs that govern the operation of the computer.

software piracy The act of illegally duplicating software.

software suite A collection of single application programs packaged in a bundle.

source data automation Capturing and editing data where the data is initially created and in a form that can be directly input to a computer, thus ensuring accuracy and timeliness.

speech-recognition technology Input devices that recognize human speech.

stakeholders People who, either themselves or through the organization they represent, ultimately benefit from the systems development project.

start-up The process of making the final tested information system fully operational.

statistical sampling Selecting a random sample of data and applying the characteristics of the sample to the whole group.

steering committee An advisory group consisting of senior management and users from the IS department and other functional areas.

storage area network (SAN) The technology that provides high-speed connections between data-storage devices and computers over a network.

strategic alliance (strategic partnership) An agreement between two or more companies that involves the joint production and distribution of goods and services.

strategic application A strategic application gives a firm a competitive advantage.

strategic planning Determining long-term objectives by analyzing the strengths and weaknesses of the organization, predicting future trends, and projecting the development of new product lines.

structured interview An interview where the questions are prepared in advance.

structured walkthrough A planned and pre-announced review of the progress of a program module.

supercomputers The most powerful computer systems with the fastest processing speeds.

support application Support applications make work more convenient but are not essential.

switch A telecommunications device that uses the physical device address in each incoming message on the network to determine to which output port it should forward the message to reach another device on the same network.

synchronous communication A form of communications where the receiver gets the message instantaneously, when it is sent.

syntax A set of rules associated with a programming language.

system A set of elements or components that interact to accomplish goals.

system performance measurement Monitoring the system – the number of errors encountered, the amount of memory required, the amount of processing or CPU time needed, and other problems.

system performance products Software that measures all components of the computer-based information system, including hardware, software, database, telecommunications, and network systems.

system performance standard A specific objective of the system.

system testing Testing the entire system of programs.

systems analysis The systems development phase involving the study of existing systems and work processes to identify strengths, weaknesses, and opportunities for improvement.

systems analyst A professional who specializes in analyzing and designing business systems.

systems controls Rules and procedures to maintain data security.

systems design A stage of systems development where a solution to the problem is planned out and documented.

systems development The activity of creating or modifying existing business systems.

systems implementation A stage of systems development that includes hardware acquisition, software acquisition or development, user preparation, hiring and training of personnel, site and data preparation, installation, testing, start-up, and user acceptance.

systems investigation The systems development phase during which problems and opportunities are identified and considered in light of the goals of the business.

systems investigation report A summary of the results of the systems investigation and the process of feasibility analysis and recommendation of a course of action.

systems maintenance and review The systems development phase that ensures the system operates as intended and modifies the system so that it continues to meet changing business needs.

systems operation Use of a new or modified system.

systems request form A document filled out by someone who wants the IS department to initiate systems investigation.

systems review The final step of systems development, involving the analysis of systems to make sure that they are operating as intended.

team organizational structure A structure centred on work teams or groups.

technical documentation Written details used by computer operators to execute the program and by analysts and programmers to solve problems or modify the program.

technical feasibility Assessment of whether the hardware, software, and other system components can be acquired or developed to solve the problem.

technology diffusion A measure of how widely technology is spread throughout the organization.

technology-enabled relationship management Occurs when a firm obtains detailed information about a customer's behaviour, preferences, needs, and buying patterns and uses that information to set prices, negotiate terms, tailor promotions, add product features, and otherwise customize its entire relationship with that customer.

technology infrastructure All the hardware, software, databases, telecommunications, people, and procedures that are configured to collect, manipulate, store, and process data into information.

technology infusion The extent to which technology is deeply integrated into an area or department.

telecommunications The electronic transmission of signals for communications; enables organizations to carry out their processes and tasks through effective computer networks.

telecommunications medium Any material substance that carries an electronic signal and serves as an interface between a sending device and a receiving device.

Telnet A terminal emulation protocol that enables users to log on to other computers on the Internet to gain access to public files.

thin client A low-cost, centrally managed computer with essential but limited capabilities and no extra drives, such as a CD or DVD drive, or expansion slots.

time-driven review Review performed after a specified amount of time.

total cost of ownership (TCO) The measurement of the total cost of owning computer equipment, including desktop computers, networks, and large computers.

traditional organizational structure An organizational structure similar to a managerial pyramid, where the hierarchy of decision making and authority flows from strategic management at the top down to operational management and non-management employees. Also called a hierarchical structure.

transaction Any business-related exchange, such as payments to employees, sales to customers, and payments to suppliers.

transaction processing cycle The process of data collection, data editing, data correction, data manipulation, data storage, and document production.

transaction processing system (TPS) An organized collection of people, procedures, software, databases, and devices used to record completed business transactions.

Transmission Control Protocol (TCP) The widely used transport-layer protocol that most Internet applications use with IP.

Trojan horse A malicious program that disguises itself as a useful application and purposefully does something the user does not expect.

tunnelling The process by which VPNs transfer information by encapsulating traffic in IP packets over the Internet.

uniform resource locator (URL) An assigned address on the Internet for each computer.

unit testing Testing of individual programs.

unstructured interview An interview where the questions are not prepared in advance.

user Person who will interact with the system regularly.

user acceptance document A formal agreement signed by the user that states that a phase of the installation or the complete system is approved.

user documentation Written descriptions developed for people who use a program, showing users, in easy-to-understand terms, how the program can and should be used.

user interface The element of the operating system that allows you to access and command the computer system.

user preparation The process of readying managers, decision makers, employees, other users, and stakeholders for new systems.

utility programs Programs that help to perform maintenance or correct problems with a computer system.

value chain A series (chain) of activities that includes inbound logistics, warehouse and storage, production, finished product storage, outbound logistics, marketing and sales, and customer service.

version A major program change, typically encompassing many new features.

videoconference A videoconference is a simultaneous communication between two or more parties where they both see and hear each other.

virtual organizational structure A structure that employs individuals, groups, or complete business units in geographically dispersed areas that can last for a few weeks or years, often requiring telecommunications or the Internet.

virtual pet An artificial companion. Could be screen based, i.e., the pet is animated on a computer monitor, or a robot.

virtual private network (VPN) A secure connection between two points on the Internet.

virtual reality The simulation of a real or imagined environment that can be experienced visually in three dimensions.

virtual reality system A system that enables one or more users to move and react in a computer-simulated environment.

virtual tape A storage device that manages less frequently needed data so that it appears to be stored entirely on tape cartridges, although some parts of it might actually be located on faster hard disks.

virtual world A computer-based environment where users' avatars can interact.

virus A computer program file capable of attaching to disks or other files and replicating itself repeatedly, typically without the user's knowledge or permission.

vision systems The hardware and software that permit computers to capture, store, and manipulate visual images.

volume testing Testing the application with a large amount of data.

wearable computing A term that refers to computers and computing technology that are worn on the body.

web browser Software that creates a unique, hypermedia-based menu on a computer screen, providing a graphical interface to the Web.

web services Standards and tools that streamline and simplify communication among websites for business and personal purposes.

what-if analysis The process of making hypothetical changes to problem data and observing the impact on the results.

wide area network (WAN) A telecommunications network that ties together large geographic regions.

wiki A web page that can be edited by anyone with the proper authority.

workstation A more powerful personal computer that is used for technical computing, such as engineering, but still fits on a desktop.

World Wide Web (WWW or W3) A collection of tens of thousands of independently owned computers that work together as one in an Internet service.

worm A parasitic computer program that can create copies of itself on the infected computer or send copies to other computers via a network.

Index